CORE
READINGS
IN
PSYCHIATRY

CORE
READINGS
IN
PSYCHIATRY

An Annotated Guide to the Literature

edited by

MICHAEL H. SACKS, M.D.

WILLIAM H. SLEDGE, M.D.

PHYLLIS RUBINTON, M.L.S.

Library of Congress Cataloging in Publication Data
Main entry under title:

Core readings in psychiatry.

  Bibliography: p.
  Includes index.
  1. Psychiatry—Abstracts. 2. Psychology, Pathological
—Abstracts. 3. Psychotherapy—Abstracts. 4. Developmental
psychology—Abstracts. I. Sacks, Michael H., 1940–
II. Sledge, William H., 1945–   . III. Rubinton,
Phyllis, 1927–   . [DNLM: 1. Mental disorders—
Abstracts. 2. Psychiatry—Abstracts. ZWM 100 C797]
RC454.C655   1983   016.61689   83-21287
ISBN   0-03-062542-4

For Judith, Betsy, and Noel

Published in 1984 by Praeger Publishers
CBS Educational and Professional Publishing
a Division of CBS Inc.
521 Fifth Avenue, New York, NY 10175 USA
© 1984 by Praeger Publishers

456789   052   98765432

Printed in the United States of America
on acid-free paper

TABLE OF CONTENTS

PART II
PSYCHOPATHOLOGY

PART III
ASSESSMENT

PART IV
TREATMENT

PART V
NORMALITY AND DEVELOPMENT

PART VI
SPECIAL TOPICS

PREFACE

Psychiatric education has a strong tradition of training, that is, of learning by copying, modeling, apprenticeship, and practice. The field is marked by conflicting views about its appropriate boundaries and domain, multiple competing theoretical paradigms, major gaps in data, frequent disagreements about the validity or significance of the data that do exist, and a consequent tendency to fragment into multiple relatively sequestered fragments or minidisciplines. One corollary of this is that many training programs or academic departments of psychiatry have representatives of two or three of these minidisciplines; the largest and the best may have five or six. However, no program can provide strength in all of them. This leads to several possible patterns in psychiatric education. Some programs define the field as those components that interest their own faculty, while ignoring the remainder. The result is a narrowing of perspective, although the theoretical homogeneity that results often leads to a happy complacency. Other programs seek an eclectic synthesis, emphasizing what is compatible and translatable among the various approaches, at the cost of avoiding what is most special, unique, or distinctive. This can lead to an intellectual shallowness, although it often provides a pragmatic framework for the daily tasks of the profession. Finally, a program can strive to provide a pluralistic exposure to the concepts and findings of many different approaches. However, this requires going beyond the limitations of a single teacher, a single textbook, or even a single faculty. Essential in this endeavor is exposure to the broader scientific and professional world, scientific meetings, visiting scholars, and above all a psychiatric library. However, the library without some orientation to how to use it may be more confusing than helpful to a beginning student. What it needs is a guide, or actually a series of guides, each expert in the particular field and each familiar with the special problems involved in teaching it. This book offers just such a series of guides. Edited by two thoughtful and experienced psychiatric educators who have central roles in two of our finest psychiatric residency programs and by a master psychiatric librarian, it provides the student an annotated guide to the literature of each of the major themes of contemporary psychiatry. With its help, the teacher and student can construct a curriculum that goes beyond the limitations of a single faculty, and that introduces the student to the many ongoing dialogues that characterize the science and the profession of today.

ROBERT MICHELS, M.D.
Psychiatrist-in-Chief
The New York Hospital

Barklie McKee Henry Professor and
    Chairman,
Department of Psychiatry
Cornell University Medical College

INTRODUCTION

This book is a collection of annotated core references to the psychiatric literature. It is intended to provide both educators and students with an introduction and guide to primary works that have inspired the profession and influenced its thinking. Unlike a textbook that summarizes and often homogenizes existing knowledge and controversy, these references document the richness, diversity, and originality of the field.

We believe this book is needed for several reasons. Behavioral science and clinical psychiatry have experienced enormous growth during the past 25 years. Different perspectives on human behavior and psychopathology such as biological, psychological, and sociocultural considerations increasingly shape clinical practice. With this literature proliferation it is becoming increasingly difficult to be familiar with major works in different areas without the guidance of an expert.

Furthermore, we believe that traditional teaching methods of psychiatry have subtlely discouraged thorough use of the literature. Education in psychiatry has tended to follow an apprentice model relying heavily on dyadic supervision for development of clinical skills with a neglect of the literature. An unfortunate feature of this neglect is the loss of the vital dialogue between the past work and present strivings of the profession. An intimate knowledge of the literature fosters professional growth and provides a safeguard against idiosyncratic or biased perspectives.

Since the psychiatric field is much too large for any one or two people to master, we approached the task of producing this book by selecting contributors who as clinicians, researchers, or educators have demonstrated expertise on their particular topic. Our assignment to them was to provide a limited number of core references which would be of special value to psychiatric trainees. We loosely defined *core* either as *classic in introducing a new concept, finding, or methodology that influenced the development of the field,* or as *highly relevant to a current understanding of the topic area.* We also asked for citations that were good teaching references.

Since we expected that each contributor would bring a unique perspective to the task, we asked for a brief introduction to the topic that included a definition of the area and the "selection paradigm," or organizing principles used in choosing the references. The result is a series of chapters that will enable beginners to immerse themselves successfully in a new topic and will stimulate more informed readers to reevaluate their own understanding and implicit "selection paradigms."

Although the book is intended primarily for psychiatry residents, medical students and mental health trainees in other professions will find it useful. Another audience for the book includes educators, both program directors and teachers, who may need or wish assistance in identifying the core literature of a particular topic.

ORGANIZATION

The book is organized by different topics or chapters grouped by categories of basic science, psychopathology, assessment, treatment, and special topics. The chapters are introduced by an introductory statement prepared by the individual contributors. In many chapters the contributors have subdivided the readings under subheadings. The citations are listed alphabetically by first author under these subheadings. When there is one annotation for multiple citations, the primary citation is listed first. The annotations were to be brief and to indicate how and why the citation was believed to be core. We also requested our contributors to designate citations that they considered essential; these citations are marked here with an asterisk (*).

Inevitably there is topic overlap and some citations could be easily and logically included in more than one chapter. We have attempted to diminish multiple listings of one citation in different places but not at the expense of the coherence of the contributor's chapter. We decided it was desirable to maintain the contributor's organization of the literature on a particular topic despite the resulting redundancy. Interestingly, in most instances of multiple annotation of the same citation different aspects of the citation are emphasized.

A subject index is included that addresses the issue of topic overlap and cross-referencing of citations. There is an author index that includes all authors cited. Citations are referred to in the indices by the chapter number with a decimal and then the citation number within that chapter (i.e., Chapter 1 reference number 20 would read 1.20).

As editors, we have tried to respect our colleagues' organization, selection, and annotation of the core literature. What suggestions we made were usually accepted so that we assume responsibility for whatever inconsistencies, awkwardness, and inaccuracies are to be found. We hope after looking through this book the reader will share the same pride in the psychiatric literature that we have in presenting this work.

ACKNOWLEDGMENTS

This work was stimulated by the first two authors' work as members of the American Association of Directors of Psychiatric Residency Training (AADPRT). Dr. Sacks, interested in the core literature of psychiatry, had begun to collect reading lists from member programs of the AADPRT. Independently, Dr. Sledge, as Chairman of the Curriculum committee of the AADPRT, was seeking to identify core objectives and to define model curricula for special topics. One of the resources frequently missed in this work was a "core reading list." A joining of goals was desirable. From the materials Dr. Sacks had gathered, it became clear that the development of a core reading list was not only desirable but possible. We wish to acknowledge the generosity of those program directors who responded with their reading lists and curricular materials in the spring of 1980. Phyllis Rubinton, medical librarian, provided the confirmation of the value of such a book and the immense labor of bibliographical checking. Others, of course, have made major silent contributions. Leslie Warner, Maria Arango, and Mary Ruth Goodley have tirelessly and good naturedly typed, retyped, and organized beyond words.

CONTRIBUTORS

Nancy C. Andreasen, M.D., Ph.D.
Professor of Psychiatry
University of Iowa
Iowa City, Iowa

Gordon G. Ball, Ph.D.
Clinical Assistant Professor of
  Psychiatry
Cornell University Medical College
New York, New York

Aaron T. Beck, M.D.
Professor of Psychiatry
University of Pennsylvania
Philadelphia, Pennsylvania

Jonathan F. Borus, M.D.
Associate Professor of Psychiatry
Harvard Medical School
Massachusetts General Hospital
Boston, Massachusetts

Charles L. Bowden, M.D.
Professor of Psychiatry and
  Pharmacology
University of Texas Health Science
  Center at San Antonio
San Antonio, Texas

Eric D. Caine, M.D.
Associate Professor of Psychiatry
  and Neurology
University of Rochester School of
  Medicine and Dentistry
Rochester, New York

Arthur C. Carr, Ph.D.
Professor of Clinical Psychology in
  Psychiatry

Cornell University Medical College
White Plains, New York

Dennis S. Charney, M.D.
Assistant Professor of Psychiatry
Yale University School of Medicine
New Haven, Connecticut

John F. Clarkin, Ph.D.
Associate Professor of Clinical
  Psychology in Psychiatry
Cornell University Medical College
White Plains, New York

John P. Docherty, M.D.
Chief, Psychosocial Treatment
  Branch
National Institute of Mental Health
Rockville, Maryland

Mina K. Dulcan, M.D.
Assistant Professor of Psychiatry
University of Pittsburgh School
  of Medicine
Pittsburgh, Pennsylvania

James S. Eaton, Jr., M.D.
Clinical Professor of Psychiatry
Georgetown University School of
  Medicine
Washington, D.C.

Marshall Edelson, M.D., Ph.D.
Professor of Psychiatry
Yale University School of Medicine
New Haven, Connecticut

Aaron H. Esman, M.D.
Professor of Clinical Psychiatry

Cornell University Medical College
New York, New York

Stephen Fleck, M.D.
Professor of Psychiatry and
  Public Health
Yale University School of Medicine
New Haven, Connecticut

William A. Frosch, M.D.
Professor of Psychiatry
Cornell University Medical College
New York, New York

David R. Gastfriend, M.D.
Clinical Fellow in Psychiatry
Harvard Medical School
Massachusetts General Hospital
Boston, Massachusetts

Ezra E.H. Griffith, M.D.
Associate Professor of Psychiatry
  and Lecturer in Afro-American
  Studies
Yale University School of Medicine
New Haven, Connecticut

John G. Gunderson, M.D.
Associate Professor of Psychiatry
Harvard Medical School
McLean Hospital
Belmont, Massachusetts

Seymour L. Halleck, M.D.
Professor of Psychiatry and
  Adjunct Professor of Law
University of North Carolina
  Medical School
Chapel Hill, North Carolina

Peter B. Henderson, M.D.
Associate Professor of Child
  Psychiatry
University of Pittsburgh School
  of Medicine
Pittsburgh, Pennsylvania

Stanley W. Jackson, M.D.

Professor of Psychiatry and
  History of Medicine
Yale University School of Medicine
New Haven, Connecticut

Selby C. Jacobs, M.D.
Associate Professor of Psychiatry
Yale University School of Medicine
New Haven, Connecticut

David R. Jones, M.D., M.P.H.
  (Col, USAF, MC)
Chief, Neuropsychiatry Branch
United States Air Force School
  of Aerospace Medicine
Brooks Air Force Base, Texas

Martin S. Kesselman, M.D.
Professor of Clinical Psychiatry
Kings County Hospital Center
Brooklyn, New York

Howard D. Kibel, M.D.
Assistant Professor of Psychiatry
Cornell University Medical College
White Plains, New York

James H. Kocsis, M.D.
Assistant Professor of Psychiatry
Cornell University Medical College
New York, New York

Howard B. Levine, M.D.
Associate Professor of Psychiatry
Boston University School of
  Medicine
Brookline, Massachusetts

Victor Lidz, Ph.D.
Assistant Professor of Sociology
University of Pennsylvania
Philadelphia, Pennsylvania

James W. Lomax, II, M.D.
Assistant Professor of Psychiatry
Baylor College of Medicine
Houston, Texas

Armand W. Loranger, Ph.D.
Associate Professor of Psychiatry
  and Clinical Psychology
Cornell University Medical College
White Plains, New York

Alexander R. Lucas, M.D.
Professor of Psychiatry
Mayo Clinic, Mayo Medical School
Rochester, Minnesota

Alan A. McLean, M.D.
Clinical Associate Professor
  of Psychiatry
Cornell University Medical College
New York, New York

Philippa Mathieu-Coughlan, Ph.D.
Associate Clinical Professor of
  Psychology in Psychiatry
Yale University School of Medicine
New Haven, Connecticut

Frank J. Menolascino, M.D.
Professor of Psychiatry
University of Nebraska Medical
  Center
Omaha, Nebraska

Arthur T. Meyerson, M.D.
Associate Professor of Psychiatry
Mount Sinai School of Medicine
New York, New York

Frank T. Miller, M.D.
Assistant Professor of Clinical
  Psychiatry
Cornell University Medical College
New York, New York

Richard L. Munich, M.D.
Associate Professor of Clinical
  Psychiatry
Cornell University Medical College
White Plains, New York

Carol C. Nadelson, M.D.
Professor of Psychiatry

Tufts-New England Medical Center
Boston, Massachusetts

Craig S. Nelson, M.D.
Associate Professor of Psychiatry
Yale University School of Medicine
New Haven, Connecticut

John C. Nemiah, M.D.
Professor of Psychiatry
Harvard University
Beth Israel Hospital
Boston, Massachusetts

Malkah T. Notman, M.D.
Clinical Professor of Psychiatry
Tufts-New England Medical Center
Boston, Massachusetts

Robert A. Novelly, Ph.D.
Assistant Clinical Professor of
  Neurology and Psychiatry
Yale University School of Medicine
New Haven, Connecticut

John M. Oldham, M.D.
Associate Professor of Clinical
  Psychiatry
Cornell University Medical College
White Plains, New York

John T. Patten, M.D.
Assistant Professor of Psychiatry
Cornell University Medical College
New York, New York

Samuel W. Perry, M.D.
Associate Professor of Clinical
  Psychiatry
Cornell University Medical College
New York, New York

James H. Reich, M.D.
Postdoctoral Fellow in Psychosocial
  Epidemiology
Yale University School of Medicine
New Haven, Connectiuct

Barry Reisberg, M.D.
Assistant Professor of Psychiatry
New York University Medical
  Center
New York, New York

Phyllis Rubinton, M.L.S.
Librarian, Payne Whitney Clinic
Cornell University Medical College
New York, New York

F. David Rudnick, M.D.
Assistant Clinical Professor of
  Psychiatry University of
California at
  Los Angeles Neuropsychiatric
  Institute
Los Angeles, California

Michael H. Sacks, M.D.
Associate Professor of Psychiatry
Cornell University Medical College
New York, New York

Philip M. Sarrel, M.D.
Associate Professor of Obstetrics
  and Gynecology, and Psychiatry
Yale University School of Medicine
New Haven, Connecticut

Jeffrey Satinover, M.D.
Postdoctoral Fellow in Psychiatry
Yale University School of Medicine
New Haven, Connecticut

Randolph B. Schiffer, M.D.
Assistant Professor of Psychiatry
  and Neurology
University of Rochester School of
  Medicine and Dentistry
Rochester, New York

Jonathan Schwartz, M.D.
Instructor of Psychiatry
Mount Sinai School of Medicine
New York, New York

Roger C. Sider, M.D.
Associate Professor of
  Psychiatry
University of Rochester School of
  Medicine and Dentistry
Rochester, New York

Bennett Simon, M.D.
Clinical Associate Professor of
  Psychiatry
Harvard University
  School of Medicine
Beth Israel Hospital
Boston, Massachusetts

Jerome L. Singer, Ph.D.
Professor of Psychology
Yale University
New Haven, Connecticut

William H. Sledge, M.D.
Associate Professor of Psychiatry
Yale University School of Medicine
New Haven, Connecticut

Stefan P. Stein, M.D.
Associate Professor of Clinical
  Psychiatry
Cornell University Medical College
White Plains, New York

David E. Sternberg, M.D.
Clinical Director
Falkirk Hospital
Central Valley, New York

Fred D. Strider, Ph.D.
Professor of Medical Psychology
University of Nebraska Medical
  Center
Omaha, Nebraska

John A. Talbott, M.D.
Professor of Psychiatry
Cornell University Medical College
New York, New York

Kenneth Tardiff, M.D., M.P.H.
Associate Professor of Psychiatry
   and Assistant Professor of
   Public Health

Cornell University Medical College
New York, New York

Milton Viederman, M.D.
Professor of Clinical Psychiatry
Cornell University Medical College
New York, New York

Robert J. Waldinger, M.D.
Clinical Instructor in Psychiatry
Harvard University School of
   Medicine McLean Hospital
Belmont, Massachusetts

Marvin D. Wasserman, M.D.
Assistant Clinical Professor of
   Psychiatry
Cornell University Medical College
New York, New York

Myrna M. Weissman, Ph.D.
Professor of Psychiatry and
   Epidemiology
Yale University School of Medicine
New Haven, Connecticut

Harriet L. Wolfe, M.D.
Assistant Professor of Psychiatry
Yale University School of Medicine
New Haven, Connecticut

Joel Yager, M.D.
Associate Professor of Psychiatry
University of California at
   Los Angeles Neuropsychiatric
   Institute Los Angeles, California

Leonard S. Zegans, M.D.
Professor of Psychiatry
University of California at
   San Francisco
San Francisco, California

ABBREVIATIONS

CTP I   Freedman, A.M., and Kaplan, H.I., eds. Comprehensive Textbook of Psychiatry. Baltimore: Williams and Wilkins, 1967.

CTP II   Freedman, A.M., Kaplan, H.I., and Sadock, B.J., eds. Comprehensive Textbook of Psychiatry/II (2nd ed.). 2 vols. Baltimore: Williams and Wilkins, 1975.

CTP III   Kaplan, H.I., Freedman, A.M., and Sadock, B.J., eds. Comprehensive Textbook of Psychiatry/III (3rd ed.). 3 vols. Baltimore: Williams and Wilkins, 1980.

AHP   Arieti, S. ed. American Handbook of Psychiatry (1st ed.). 3 vols. New York: Basic Books, 1959–1966.

AHP   Arieti, S., ed. American Handbook of Psychiatry (2nd ed.). 7 vols. New York: Basic Books, 1974–1981.

S.E.   Strachey, J., ed. The Standard Edition of the Complete Psychological Works of Sigmund Freud. 24 vols. London: Hogarth Press, 1953–1974.

I   Introduction to chapter (used in index)

*   Most essential citations

PART I

BASIC SCIENCES: BIOLOGICAL, PSYCHOLOGICAL, AND SOCIAL

1. NEUROSCIENCE

CHARLES L. BOWDEN, M.D.

These references on the neurosciences need be approached from a different perspective than many other sections in this book. First, there are few "classics." Rather, the modern study of the brain, its ultrastructure, chemistry, and function are essentially a product of the last two decades. This is in large part because the analytical methods needed to study the infinitesimally small concentrations of neurotransmitters and other key substances have only been developed over that period. Second, for many persons entering psychiatry and related fields, the neurosciences are a forbidding, recondite field. In part, this may be related to their prior training, which has not prepared them for the methodologies recently employed in this field. For that reason, several methods papers are included.

Why study such an area if it seems far removed from the professional career objectives of most psychiatrists? The excitement in this field is immense. It is closely tied to a major aim of neuroscience investigation: the description in cellular and molecular terms of the processes that we know as perception, emotion, thought, and memory. Some of the brightest minds in all of science are entering the field and are producing sophisticated and ingenious studies daily. The results of such studies quickly translate into clinical studies and improved patient care.

The readings here are organized under subheadings of: basic texts, structural properties of brain, neurochemistry, and applied methods.

BASIC TEXTS

1. *Cooper, J.R., Bloom, F.E., and Roth, R.H. The Biochemical Basis of Neuropharmacology (4th ed.). New York: Oxford, 1982.

This book is without peer as a single compilation of the key information known about the biochemistry and physiology of the nervous system pertinent to the psychiatrist. The writing is free of jargon and not forbidding to the person with relatively little background in neurochemistry.

2. **Iverson, L.L., Iverson, S.D., and Snyder, S.H.,** eds. Handbook of Psychopharmacology. Biochemial Principles and Techniques in Neuropharmacology, Vol. 1. New York: Plenum, **1975.**

    Most of the key analytical techniques in neuroscience research are summarized in this text. The full series of 13 volumes contains a wealth of information on basic and clinical areas of the neurosciences, and is a good, if somewhat dated, reference for the person wanting a detailed review of an area. Each volume addresses a particular topic area.

3. **Usdin, E., Bunney, W.E., and Davis, J.M.,** eds. Neuroreceptors. Basic and Clinical Aspects. New York: Wiley, **1981.**

    Numerous publications in the neurosciences are of all papers presented at a symposium or conference. Often the result is uneven and unsatisfactory. This is an exception. The reader will get a well-balanced sampling of several key areas of neuroscience research from these papers.

STRUCTURAL PROPERTIES OF BRAIN

4. **Changeux, J-P, Theiry, J., Tung, Y., et al.** On the cooperativity of biological membranes. Proc. Natl. Acad. Sci. USA 57:335–341, **1967.**

    A basic, though highly technical, treatise on the manner in which receptors exist in an active and inactive state, a concept important to the understanding of agonist and antagonist neurotransmitter effects.

5. **Galaburda, A.M., LeMay, M., Kemper, T.L., et al.** Right-left asymmetries in the brain. Science 199: 852–856, **1978.**

    This is an interesting and new area of study, directed at a wide range of issues, including intelligence, language function, sexual dimorphism, and dementias.

6. **Galin, D.** Implications for psychiatry of left and right cerebral specialization. A neurophysiological context for unconscious processes. Arch Gen. Psychiatry 31: 572–583, **1974.**

    These intriguing differences include cognitive modes of processing information, coping responses, and responses to electroconvulsive treatments.

7. **Iverson, L.L.** Role of transmitter uptake mechanisms in synaptic neurotransmission. Br. J. Pharmacol. 41: 571–591, **1971.**

8. **Kupferman, I.** Modulatory actions of neurotransmitters. Annu. Rev. Neurosci. 2: 447–465, **1979**.

There is no single best description of the synapse and its functions, but these are representative, clear treatments. In particular, Iverson's paper, delivered as the Gaddum Memorial Lecture, ties together several interrelated lines of study.

9. **Kandel, E.R.** Psychotherapy and the single synapse. The impact of psychiatric thought on neurobiologic research. N. Engl. J. Med. 301: 1028–1037, **1979**.

Genetic and developmental processes determine the connections between neurons. Learning, habituation, and thought alter the efficacy of these synaptic pathways. As Kandel states, "What we conceive as our mind is an expression of the function of our brain."

10. **Kluver, H. and Bucy, P.C.** Preliminary analysis of functions of the temporal lobes in monkeys. Arch Neurol. Psychiatry 42: 979–1000, **1939**.

This classic work describes the relationship of a structural area of the brain to a specific behavioral syndrome which was later established in humans as well.

11. **MacLean, P.D.** New findings relevant to the evolution of psychosexual functions of the brain. J. Nerv. Ment. Dis. 135: 289–301, **1962**.

MacLean's intriguing concepts about ways in which thought, emotion, and sexuality are tied to the evolutionary development of complex brain areas have had wide heuristic impact.

12. **Papez, J.W.** A proposed mechanism of emotion. Arch. Neurol. Psychiatry 38: 725–743, **1937**.

The classic description of the limbic system of the brain.

13. **Singer, S.J. and Nicolson, G.L.** The fluid mosaic model of the structure of cell membranes. Science 175: 720–731, **1972**.

A workable, even elegant, model of the dynamic characteristics of the membranes. Important in understanding neurohumoral activation of a cell.

14. **Sperry, R.W.** The great cerebral commisure. Sci. Am. 210(1): 42–52, **1964**.

This Nobel prize–winning physician describes his work on patients with separately, rather than integratedly, functioning left and right brain cortices.

NEUROCHEMISTRY

15. **Bloom, F.E.** Cyclic nucleotides in central synaptic function. Fed. Proc. 38: 2203–2207, **1979.**

    Neurotransmitter effects are in part mediated by a cascading series of events. One main pathway involves cyclic nucleotides and the phosphorylation of key proteins.

16. **Bloom, F.E., Segal, D., Ling, N., et al.** Endorphins: Profound behavioral effects in rats suggest new etiological factors in mental illness. Science: 194: 630–632, **1976.**

    Endorphin study has been an exciting area in the scant few years these substances have been known. It is also frustrating, because the rapid developments and the panoply of functions attributed to endorphins mean that the reader should react cautiously to new developments. For example, most recent studies do not support the idea that these compounds account for symptoms of major mental illnesses.

17. **Brodie, B.B., Kurz, H., and Schanker, L.S.** The importance of dissociation-constant and lipid-solubility in influencing the passage of drugs into the cerebrospinal fluid. J. Pharmacol. Exp. Ther. 130: 20–25, **1960.**

    The straightforward conclusions about the critical importance of lipid solubility and degree of ionization as the two key factors determining the degree to which a drug enters the brain are as pertinent today as they were 22 years ago.

18. **Cheung, W.Y.** Calmodulin plays a pivotal role in cellular regulation. Science 207: 19–27, **1980.**

19. **DeLorenzo, R.J.** Role of calmodulin in neurotransmitter release and synaptic function. Ann. N.Y. Acad. Sci. 356: 92–109, **1980.**

    Calcium acts in concert with cyclic AMP to link a stimulus (neurotransmitter or hormone activation of a receptor) to the secretion of a neurotransmitter from the cell. Calmodulin, a protein to which calcium binds, is a key element in the process. This is a rapidly developing area.

20. ***Edelman, A.M., Berger, P.A., and Reson, J.F.** 5-hydroxytryptamine: Basic and clinical perspectives, pp. 177–187. In: Neuroregulators and Psychiatric Disorders. Eds.: E. Usdin, D. Hamburg, and J. Barchas. New York: Oxford, **1977.**

    An overview of the possible involvement of serotonergic systems in affective disorders.

21. ***Enna, S.J.** GABA receptor pharmacology. Functional considerations. Biochem. Pharmacol. 30: 907–913, **1981.**

GABA receptors are important in part because the actions of benzodiazepines involve this system.

22. ***Ettigi, P.G. and Brown, G.M.** Psychoneuroendocrinology of affective disorder: An overview. Am. J. Psychiatry 134: 493–501, **1977.**

Neuroendocrine substances both modulate and are modulated by neurotransmitters. Although a complex area of study because it is difficult to isolate the single variable of interest, several promising leads have developed, especially in the affective disorders.

23. **Hirata, F. and Axelrod, J.** Phospholipid methylation and biological signal transmission. Science 209: 1082–1090, **1980.**

Neurotransmitters may set off the methylation of phospholipids, which in turn are coupled to calcium movement into neurons and the release of arachidonic acid and prostaglandins. This is an important part of the so-called second messenger system, although many details are as yet unclear.

24. **Maas, J.W., Hattox, S.E., Greene, N.M., et al.** 3-methoxy-4-hydroxyphenethyleneglycol production by human brain in vivo. Science 205: 1025–1027, **1979.**

An elegant study on live human subjects utilizing arterial-venous differences in MHPG to estimate the rate of production of MHPG by the brain. Venous specimens were obtained from the internal jugular vein above the site of extracranial inflow.

25. ***Meltzer, H.Y. and Stahl, S.M.** The dopamine hypothesis of schizophrenia: A review. Schiz. Bull. 2: 19–76, **1976.**

Dopaminergic transmission seems tied to some psychotic disturbance and the mechanism of action of neuroleptic drugs.

26. ***Minneman, K.P., Pittman, R.N., and Molinoff, P.B.** Beta adrenergic receptor subtypes: Properties, distribution, and regulation. Annu. Rev. Neurosci. 4: 419–461, **1981.**

A treatise on different adrenergic receptor types. As studies proceed with most transmitters, an increasing number of receptor subtypes are being discovered. It is important to understand the issue, as it is closely tied to an understanding of drug actions.

27. ***Moore, R.Y. and Bloom, F.E.** Central catecholamine neuron systems: Anatomy and physiology of the dopamine systems. Annu. Rev. Neurosci. 1: 129–169, **1978.**

A comprehensive treatment of the subject.

28. ***Nathanson, J.A. and Greengard, P.** "Second messengers" in the brain. Sci. Am. 237(1): 108–119, **1977.**

A succinct review, with nice illustrations, of the several roles of "second messengers," from transient (voluntary muscle contraction) to sustained (long-term memory) events.

29. ***Olds, J.** Self stimulation of the brain. Its use to study local effects of hunger, sex and drugs. Science 127: 315–324, **1958.**

This seminal work has been a major stimulus to subsequent studies of reward systems in the brain and drugs and environmental stimuli related to them.

30. **Preskorn, S.H., Irwin, G.H., Simpson, S., et al.** Medical therapies for mood disorders alter the blood brain barrier. Science 213: 469–471, **1981.**

This interesting work indicates that antidepressant drugs increase cerebral permeability in a manner consistent with their adrenergic effects. It suggests that this effect may be related to their clinical effectiveness.

31. **Routtenberg, A.** The reward system of the brain. Sci. Am. 239(5): 154–164, **1978.**

Dopaminergic transmission in the median forebrain bundle appears to be an important component of reward systems.

32. **Siesjo, B.K.** Brain Energy Metabolism. New York: Wiley, **1978.**

33. **Passonneau, J.V., Hawkins, R.A., Lust, W.D., et al.** eds. Cerebral Metabolism and Neural Function. Baltimore, MD: Williams and Wilkins, **1980.**

The brain utilizes glucose as practically its sole oxidative energy source. The role of these energy systems is important in developing brain and conditions such as seizures.

34. **Wallace, P.** Neurochemistry: Unraveling the mechanism of memory. Science 190: 1076–1078, **1975.**

Despite the title, the mechanisms are far from unravelled, but this does summarize several important areas of study.

35. **Wehr, T.A., Muscettola, G., and Goodwin, F.K.** Urinary 3-methoxy-4-hyroxyphenylglycol circadian rhythm. Arch. Gen. Psychiatry 37: 257–263, **1980.**

Biological rhythms related to a day, a year, or other periods may well influence several illness states. This study, for example, reported that bipolar depressed patients had their daily peak excretion of MHPG approximately 3 hours sooner than healthy controls.

36. **Yamamura, H. and Snyder, S.H.** Choline: High-affinity uptake by rat brain synatosomes. Science 178: 626–628, **1972.**

There are two distinct systems for the uptake of choline into neurons. Only the high affinity system is tied to acetylcholine production.

APPLIED METHODS

37. **Adams, R.N.** Chemistry with electroanalytical techniques. Anal. Chem. 48: 1128A, **1976.**

A novel technique that determines the concentration of substances based on their ability to conduct an electric current. Its application in psychiatric research and even routine biochemical monitoring is expanding rapidly.

38. **Cole, S.** Squid axon membrane: Impedance decrease to voltage clamp. Annu. Rev. Neurosci. 5: 305–323, **1982.**

Please do not be put off by the title. Dr. Cole and his colleague Curtis opened the modern study of the physiology of neurons with their 1938 report of techniques utilizing the giant squid axon. This report summarizes what has evolved in the area from 1938 to 1982.

39. **Creese, I. and Snyder, S.H.** A simple and sensitive radio-receptor assay for antischizophrenic drugs in blood. Nature 270: 180–182, **1977.**

Radioreceptor assays have application not only in measuring functional activity of drugs, but also for studying the density of receptors in an area of brain or other tissue, such as the platelet. Again, an important and expanding technique.

40. **Gunby, P.** The new wave in medicine: Nuclear magnetic resonance. JAMA 247: 151–159, **1982.**

41. **Brownell, G.L., Budinger, T.F., Lauterbur, P.C., et al.** Positron tomography and nuclear magnetic resonance imaging. Science 215: 619–626, **1982.**

A powerful new technique that has the potential for demonstrating changes in regional brain energy metabolism with a higher degree of resolution than positron emission tomography.

42. **Maas, J.W., Koslow, S.H., Davis, J.M., et al.** Biological component of the NIMH Clinical Research Branch Collaborative Program on the psychobiology of depression: I. Background and theoretical considerations. Psychol. Med. 10: 759–776, **1980.**

The story of new neuroscience knowledge is closely tied to the development of interdisciplinary and collaborative investigations. This paper provides an insight into the organization needed for one such study.

43. ***Murphy, D.L., Wright, C., Buchsbaum, M.S., et al.** Platelet and plasma amine oxidase activity in 680 normals: Sex and age differences and stability over time. Biochem. Med. 16: 254–265, **1976.**

Monoamine oxidase measurement is important in studies for so-called biological markers of schizophrenia, affective disorder, and attention deficit disorder. It can also be used to monitor the clinical efficacy of the monoamine oxidase inhibitor phenelzine. In addition, it ties in to an important thrust in neuroscience research, the effort to establish peripheral models that in some way reflect CNS activity. The assay method described here is one frequently used.

44. **Platt, J.R.** Strong inference. Certain systematic methods of scientific thinking may produce much more rapid progress than others. Science 146: 347–353, **1964.**

This article lucidly summarizes one major reason for rapid advances in the neurosciences: today's neuroscientists are increasingly able to frame their hypotheses and conduct their experiments so as to maximize the likelihood that meaningful and clear results will be produced.

45. **Ter-Pogossian, M.M., Raichle, M.E., and Sobel, B.E.** Positron-emission tomography. Sci. Am. 243(4): 170–181, **1980.**

46. **Phelps, M.E., Mazziotta, J.C., and Huang, S.C.** Study of cerebral function with positron computed tomography. J. Cerebral Blood Flow Metab. 2: 113–162, **1982.**

47. **Buschbaum, M.S., Ingvar, D.H., Kessler, R., et al.** Cerebral glucography with positron tomography. Arch Gen. Psychiatry 39: 251–259, **1982.**

This technique allows the expensive but impressive assessment of differences in glucose utilization in brain regions. Early studies suggest characteristic differences in some schizophrenic and affectively ill patients.

2. GENETICS

Armand W. Loranger, Ph.D.

Genetic investigations of human behavior and its abnormalities usually begin with family studies. Because family members share a common environment as well as genes, the findings from such studies must be buttressed by those derived from two other methodological strategies. Comparisons of monozygotic and dizygotic twins provide a means of determining the effect of identical genes on individuals who are exposed to similar environments. Subjects of adoption and foster care, because they have been reared by parents who provided their family environment but not their genes, offer investigators a unique opportunity to test specific hypotheses about the interaction of heredity and environment.

The largest body of twin and adoption data on a mental disorder concerns schizophrenia, and it provides unequivocal evidence that both heredity and environment are major etiological factors. A similar conclusion can be drawn from the literature on affective disorders. However, those findings are often more problematic and difficult to interpret, because the older studies often did not distinguish between the unipolar and bipolar forms of manic-depression, and the genetic implications of the distinction have yet to be completely unraveled. Interpretations of the data are also complicated by the lack of consensus concerning a suitable nosology for unipolar depression, and the divergent views about the relative importance of various syndromal features, the severity of symptoms, the presence or absence of precipitants, and the implications of co-existing conditions such as schizophrenia and the personality disorders.

Genetic investigators have paid less attention to anxiety disorders, phobias, neurosis, alcoholism, and most of the personality disorders. These conditions are likely to become the subject of an increasing number of studies. This is especially true of the personality disorders, because of the new criteria introduced by *DSM-III*. We can also anticipate more inquiries into the role of heredity in the dementias, as a result of the resurgence of interest in those conditions. There is also a thriving area of research on the effect of heredity on personality, temperament, and intelligence, much of which is germane to clinical psychiatry.

The primary criteria for selecting the references on genetics were their methodological sophistication and the impact they have had on the field. Books and reviews were favored because they provide useful summations and interpretations of the work of many investigators and are convenient introductions to the literature in general. In a few instances articles were selected either because of their historical importance or because they herald new lines of inquiry.

GENERAL

1. ***Henderson, N.D.** Human behavior genetics. Annu. Rev. Psychol. 33: 403–440, **1982.**

   A sampler of recent publications in human behavior genetics where the reader can view the exciting new developments in this complex and challenging field. Includes commentary on developments in genetic studies of perception, cognition, intelligence, personality, temperament, and psychopathology.

2. ***Rosenthal, D.** Genetic Theory and Abnormal Behavior. New York: McGraw-Hill, **1970.**

   A textbook distinguished by its careful attention to methodological issues encountered in studies of the inheritance of abnormal behavior. Excellent coverage of the literature prior to 1970 on schizophrenia, manic depression, psychopathy and criminality, psychoneurosis, homosexuality, alcoholism, and chromosome abnormalities.

3. ***Slater, E. and Cowie, V.** The Genetics of Mental Disorders. London: Oxford University Press, **1971.**

   An excellent textbook of psychiatric genetics based on the literature prior to 1970. Provides extensive coverage of mental deficiency, organic brain disease, and chromosome abnormalities.

SCHIZOPHRENIA

4. ***Gottesman, I.I. and Shields, J.** Schizophrenia, the Epigenetic Puzzle. New York: Cambridge University Press, **1982.**

   The best and last word on the genetics of schizophrenia at this time by two pre-eminent investigators and authorities on the subject.

5. ***Gottesman, I.I. and Shields, J.** Schizophrenia and Genetics: A Twin Study Vantage Point. New York: Academic Press, **1972.**

The results of the most methodologically sophisticated major twin study of schizophrenia ever undertaken.

6. ***Heston, L.L.** Psychiatric disorders in foster home–reared children of schizophrenic mothers. Br. J. Psychiatry 112: 819–825, **1966.**

The first study of infants separated from their schizophrenic mothers at birth and reared by foster and adoptive parents. Comparison is made in adulthood with foster children of normal parentage.

7. ***Kety, S.S., Rosenthal, D., Wender, P.H., and Schulsinger, F.** Studies based on a total sample of adopted individuals and their relatives: Why they were necessary, what they demonstrated and failed to demonstrate. Schizophr. Bull. 2: 413–428, **1976.**

The frequently cited and important ongoing Danish adoption studies of schizophrenia described in summary fashion by the investigators themselves.

8. ***Shields, J.** Genetics, pp. 53–87. In: Schizophrenia: Toward a New Synthesis. Ed.: J.K. Wing. London: Academic Press, **1978.**

One of the best reviews of the genetics of schizophrenia.

AFFECTIVE DISORDERS

9. ***Bertelsen, A., Harvald, B., and Hauge, M.** A Danish twin study of manic-depressive disorders. Br. J. Psychiatry 130: 330–351, **1977.**

Results of the latest major twin study on manic depression.

10. ***Maugh, T.H.** Is there a gene for depression? Science 214: 1330–1331, **1981.**

Critical observations on a much publicized human leukocyte antigen (HLA) locus study of depression.

11. ***Weissman, M.M., Kidd, K.K., and Prusoff, B.A.** Variability in rates of affective disorders in relatives of depressed and normal probands. Arch. Gen. Psychiatry 39: 1397–1403, **1982.**

A family study of the first-degree relatives of unipolar depressives and normals. There is approximately a twofold to fivefold increase in the rates of depression in the relatives of the depressed patients.

12. ***Zerbin-Rüdin, E.** Genetics of affective psychoses, pp. 35–58. In: Handbook of Biological Psychiatry. Part III, Basic Mechanisms and Abnormal Behavior. Genetics and Neuroendocrinology. Eds.: H.M. van Praag et al. New York: M. Dekker, **1980.**

A brief survey of recent trends and developments in the genetics of affective disorders by a leading European investigator. It will alert the reader to many of the complexities and ambiguities of the field.

OTHER

13. ***Crowe, R.R.** Genetic models of mental illness, pp. 75–94. In: AHP (2nd ed.), Vol. 7, **1981.**

A lucid account of genetic models of transmission applied to schizophrenia, affective disorders, antisocial personality, hysteria, alcoholism, and panic disorder.

14. ***Goodwin, D.W.** Alcoholism and heredity. A review and hypothesis. Arch. Gen. Psychiatry 36: 57–61, **1979.**

Reviews recent evidence for hereditary factor in alcoholism. Speculates on how heredity combined with conditioning might facilitate or inhibit the development of alcoholism.

15. ***Heston, L.L., Mastri, A.R., Anderson, E., et al.** Dementia of the Alzheimer type: Clinical genetics, natural history, and associated conditions. Arch. Gen. Psychiatry 38: 1085–1090, **1981.**

Exemplifies the resurgence of interest in the dementias. Relatives of Alzheimer patients exhibit an increased risk of dementing illness, Down's syndrome, lymphoma, and immune diathesis.

16. ***Loranger, A.W., Oldham, J.M., and Tulis, E.H.** Familial transmission of DSM-III borderline personality disorder. Arch. Gen. Psychiatry 39: 795–799, **1982.**

The first evidence of familial transmission of the *DSM-III* version of the so-called borderline conditions.

17. ***Zerbin-Rüdin, E.** Genetic factors in neurosis, psychopathy, and alcoholism, pp. 59–80. In: Handbook of Biological Psychiatry. Part III, Basic Mechanisms and Abnormal Behavior. Genetics and Neuroendocrinology. Eds.: H.M. van Praag et al. New York: M. Dekker, **1980.**

A review of genetic studies on neurosis, anxiety states, obsessional neurosis and phobias, depressive neuroses, psychopathy, criminality, suicide, hysteria, and alcoholism.

3. ETHOLOGY AND SOCIOBIOLOGY

LEONARD S. ZEGANS, M.D.

Ethology can roughly be defined as the branch of zoology that studies animal behavior, often in a naturalistic setting, in order to understand the adaptive-survival value of genetically influenced patterns of behavior. Ethologists are bound together primarily by their techniques of animal observation and their concern with three basic questions in the analysis of a unit of behavior: (1) What causes it to be here? (2) What is its function? (3) What is its evolutionary history? Some ethologists believe that man as a higher primate can be studied like any other member of his order and have begun ethological investigations in nurseries, lying-in homes, child care institutions, and mental hospitals. Ethology may make its most important contribution to the study of man by facilitating the accurate and rich description of how people communicate motivational and affective messages to one another in a natural rather than experimental setting. Ethological studies in man examine affiliative behavior, aggression, and sexuality.

Sociobiology is defined as the systematic study of the biological basis of all social behavior, focusing on animal societies with population structures, castes, and communication together with investigations of physiology underlying the social adaptations. It is also concerned with the social behaviors of early man and the adaptive features of organization in the more primitive contemporary human societies.

1. **Alcock, J.** Animal Behavior: An Evolutionary Approach. Sunderland, MA: Sinauer Associates, **1975.**

   This textbook presents in a sophisticated, yet uncomplicated, fashion the physiology, genetics, and evolution of animal behavior. It places special emphasis on understanding ecological considerations in studying and analyzing the behavior. There is an especially good chapter dealing with the altered selection pressures that may be responsible for human evolution. The bibliography is comprehensive, but not exhausting.

2. **Bowlby, J.** An ethological approach to research in child development. Br. J. Med. Psychol. 30: 230–240, **1957**.

One of the classical papers by Dr. Bowlby in which he attempts to discuss ethology's contribution to the behavioral sciences with reference to psychoanalytic theory, learning theory, the cognitive theories of Piaget, and child development research. He traces the origins of ethology through Darwin, Lorenz, and Tinbergen.

3. ***Bowlby, J.** The nature of the child's tie to his mother. Int. J. Psychoan. 39: 350–373, **1958**.

The critical essay by Dr. Bowlby applying ethological postulates to development of human object relations. He develops the concept that attachment behavior in the infant comprises a number of component instinctual responses.

4. ***Grant, E.C.** An ethological description of some schizophrenic patterns of behavior, pp. 99–113. In: Proceedings of the Leeds Symposium on Behavioral Disorders. Ed.: F.A. Jenner, Essex, Engl, **1965**.

Probably the only paper that attempts to take ethological observational methods and apply them to a study of schizophrenic patients in an inpatient ward setting, it illustrates some of the advantages and difficulties in applying the techniques of naturalists to an unstructured clinical situation.

5. **Grant, E.C.** An ethological description of nonverbal behavior during interviews. Br. J. Med. Psychol. 41: 177–184, **1968**.

This is an attempt of an ethologist to apply behavioral techniques mostly worked out with primates to the interpersonal situation of individual human interviews. This technique has research as well as clinical usefulness.

6. ***Lorenz, K.** Evolution and Modification of Behavior. Chicago: University of Chicago Press, **1965**.

Lorenz's major theoretical statement covering concepts such as fixed action patterns, innate releasing mechanisms, social releasers, vacuum activity, appetitive and consumatory behavior. There is also a critique of modern theories of learning.

7. ***McGrew, W.C.** An Ethological Study of Children's Behavior. New York: Academic Press, **1972**.

The author applies the methods of ethological-biological study of animal behavior to research problems that arise from the social development of preschool children.

8.   **Sahlins, M.D.** The Use and Abuse of Biology: An Anthropological Critique of Sociobiology. Ann Arbor: University of Michigan Press, **1976**.

This book challenges some of the recent arguments and theories of sociobiology that have become popular both in the scientific and lay literature. It is the thoughtful analysis by an anthropologist of the interaction between genetic factors and social, environmental, and economic influences in shaping animal and human behavior.

9.   **Scott, J.P.** Early Experience and the Organization of Behavior. Belmont, CA: Brooks-Cole, **1968**.

Important for discussing the applications of ethological animal research in the course of human development. He concentrates on the issue of how early behavioral and social influences on the infant and young child can alter the course of later child and adult development.

10.   **Trivers, R.L.** The evolution of reciprocal altruism. Q. Rev. Biol. 46: 35–57, **1971**.

A critical article that forms the foundation of sociobiology. It discusses how evolutionary factors have influenced the development of altruism in animal species, and traces how specific social behavioral traits are related to genetically coded influences.

11.   ***Wilson, E.O.** Sociobiology: The New Synthesis. Cambridge: Harvard University Press, **1975**.

The classic text defining the hypothesis and controversies of sociobiology. It looks at a number of human traits, particularly altruism and cooperation, from the perspective of evolutionary theory and behavioral zoology.

12.   ***Zegans, L.S.** An appraisal of ethological contributions to psychiatric theory and research. Am. J. Psychiatry 124: 729–739, **1967**.

This article reviews the major conceptual theories of ethology, outlines the possible contributions that ethology can make to the study of human behavior and psychopathology. Emphasis is on ethology both as a tool of observational research for studying humans in actualistic settings, as well as a perspective on developmental theory.

4. PSYCHOANALYSIS

MARSHALL EDELSON, M.D., PH.D.

The major problems facing psychoanalysis as a behavioral science are: systematizing psychoanalytic theory; clarifying the relation of the theory to other bodies of knowledge and other theories in behavioral science; and deciding what kind of empirical evidence will test it and how.

Therefore, the following list of references gives priority to works that: (1) explicate or attempt to systematize psychoanalytic theory; (2) relate psychoanalytic theory to conceptual developments in such behavioral sciences as linguistics, sociology, and learning theory; (3) consider features of the psychoanalytic situation that have bearing upon the kind of evidence obtained in it; or (4) raise questions about, point out where the need exists for, or suggest how to obtain, evidence that is relevant to an evaluation of the scientific credibility of psychoanalytic hypotheses.

In a first introduction to psychoanalysis, one cannot do better than to let Freud speak for himself. He remains his own most able expositor.

Works are organized under the subheadings: (1) introduction to psychoanalysis; (2) the essential Freud; (3) psychoanalytic theory; (4) psychoanalysis and other disciplines; (5) the psychoanalytic situation and method; (6) the scientific status of psychoanalysis.

INTRODUCTION TO PSYCHOANALYSIS

1. **Brenner, C.** An Elementary Textbook of Psychoanalysis (Rev. and exp. ed.). New York: International Universities Press, **1973**.

   For students who want a relatively authoritative, up-to-date exposition of the fundamentals of psychoanalytic theory as it now stands, to serve as an introduction to, and a guide in reading, the primary sources.

2. ***Freud, S.** (1915–1916, 1916–1917) Introductory Lectures on Psychoanalysis. S.E. 15: **1961**, S.E. 16: **1963**.

3. ***Freud, S.** (1933) New introductory lectures on psychoanalysis. S.E. 22: 5–182, **1964**.

The *Introductory Lectures* are the best relatively brief introduction to Freud's work. His anticipation of the reader's questions and objections is a powerful rhetoric. Lecture II ("Parapraxes"), among others, exemplifies his mode of argument about necessary and sufficient causes. Lecture XVII ("The Sense of Symptoms"), among others, exemplifies his use of questions to focus on distinctive problems. (What is the sense of an apparently senseless phenomenon? How can it be discovered?) Lecture XXIII ("The Paths to the Formation of Symptoms") presents a sophisticated causal model for explaining neurotic symptoms; his use of a complemental series (constitutional dispositions/experiences) at different stages of symptom formation is often neglected in reductions of psychoanalytic theory.

If, in an introduction to Freud's thinking, it is desirable to avoid mixing in early and subsequently rejected formulations, then Lectures XXXI ("The Dissection of the Psychical Personality") and XXXII ("Anxiety and Instinctual Life") from the *New Introductory Lectures* can be substituted for the earlier XXIV ("The Common Neurotic State") and XXV ("Anxiety") in a reading of the *Introductory Lectures*. It can also be useful to substitute Freud's *Three Essays on the Theory of Sexuality* as a more complete formulation of a difficult subject for Lectures XX and XXI on sexuality and libido.

4.   ***Freud, S.** (1926) The question of lay analysis: Conversations with an impartial person. S.E. 20: 183–258, **1959**.

The polemic about the relation between medicine and psychoanalysis aside (it certainly has its own interest), this nontechnical presentation of psychoanalysis is one of Freud's most delightful and rhetorically effective expositions—and written after significant theoretical developments had taken place in his work.

5.   **Groddeck, G.** The Book of the It (1923). New York: Vintage, **1961**. (Available from New York: International Universities Press, **1976**.)

Partly incredible but still enjoyable. Lively, witty, didactic letters from "Patrick Troll" to "dearest friend" about the marvelous contents and manifestations of unconscious mental life. Each of us is lived by his It. The It, if rejected, expresses itself, believe it or not, in every kind of bodily illness. Nothing for it, but to give up trying to subdue or master the It. Instead, one must make peace with the It. Besides being fun to read and giving a good feel for the kind of phenomena of central interest for psychoanalysis, this work is an antidote to current overestimation of the activity and strength of "the ego" in relation to "the id," and also to the popular (if not indeed at times, professional) misconception that conflict is the inevitable relation between a good achievement-oriented and reality-oriented "ego" and a bad chaotic and demonic "id" and that therapy is a process of getting rid of the latter in favor of the former.

6. **Jones, E.** The Life and Work of Sigmund Freud. New York: Basic Books, **1953–1957.** 3 vols.

7. **Sulloway, F.** Freud, Biologist of the Mind. Beyond the Psychoanalytic Legend. New York: Basic Books, **1979**.

8. **Clark, R.** Freud: The Man and the Cause. New York: Random House, **1980**.

Jones's is the definitive biography for those interested in a detailed account of the relation between the personal life and the work of Freud, for it scants neither. Sulloway, asserting against Jones that Freud remained in his work and aims a biologist, contributes some interesting material about the intellectual influences on Freud of psychophysics, sexual biology and sexology, and the Darwinian revolution. Clark's focus is on Freud as the charismatic political leader of a movement.

9. **Nemiah, J.C.** Foundations of Psychopathology. New York: Oxford University Press, **1961**. (Available from New York: Aronson, **1973**.)

A presentation of psychopathology, with emphasis on the role of conflict and defense, the unconscious and repression, and the childhood roots of emotional disorder in symptom-formation; and on the relevance of these concepts—which are illustrated by many vivid, detailed clinical examples—to the practice of medicine. Especially appropriate for use as part of an introduction of psychoanalysis to medical students.

THE ESSENTIAL FREUD

10. ***Freud, S.** (1900–1901) The Interpretation of Dreams. S.E. 4 and 5: **1953**.

A classic in behavioral science, which (like Durkheim's *Suicide*) unites formulation of a theory of broad scope and an unexpected body of data. Exemplifies (throughout) the kind of argument Freud used as a scientist. Presents his method of free association (Chapter II); his way of relating hypotheses and evidence (Chapters III–VI); and his model of the mind (Chapter VII). Chapter II should be related to the account of the "theorems" presupposed in using the method of free association given in Chapter VII (part A). Chapter 1, a masterful but neglected review of the literature, locates problems and paradoxical findings, and in Chapter VII (part D) Freud summarizes the way in which his work resolves them. If one were to read only one work by Freud, this should be the one.

11. ***Freud, S.** (1901) The Psychopathology of Everyday Life. S.E. 6: **1960**.

12. ***Freud, S.** (1905) Jokes and Their Relation to the Unconscious. S.E. 8: **1960**.

    Should be read together with *The Interpretation of Dreams*. Freud's three most seminal, innovative, and ground-breaking works, and the core of his extension of his theory to empirical realms other than the neuroses.

13. ***Freud, S.** (1905) Three essays on the theory of sexuality. S.E. 7: 130–243, **1953**.

    Essential for understanding Freud's thinking about infantile sexuality. His use of information about the perversions in explicating infantile sexuality is often overlooked. In general, as readers of this work (including the footnotes) discover, what Freud actually wrote about sexuality differs considerably from the views sometimes attributed to him.

14. ***Freud, S.** (1911) Formulations on the two principles of mental functioning. S.E. 12: 218–226, **1958**.

    An important clarification of the difference between primary and secondary mental processes, one of Freud's major discoveries, in terms of the difference between the principles (pleasure principle and reality principle) regulating these processes, or the aims (maximizing immediate gratification and maximizing accommodation to external reality) governing them. Can profitably be read with *The Interpretation of Dreams* (Chapter VII).

15. ***Freud, S.** (1915) Instincts and their vicissitudes. S.E. 14: 117–140, **1957**.

16. ***Freud, S.** (1915) The unconscious. S.E. 14: 166–215, **1957**.

    Examples of Freud's efforts to clarify central theoretical concepts. Both reveal Freud as scientist thinking about the relation between phenomena and concepts. The first can profitably be read with *Three Essays on Sexuality*, and the second with *The Interpretation of Dreams* (Chapter VII).

17. ***Freud, S.** (1923) The ego and the id. S.E. 19: 12–66, **1961**.

18. ***Freud, S.** (1926) Inhibitions, symptoms and anxiety. S.E. 20: 87–172, **1959**.

    Major revisions of psychoanalytic theory. The psychological system is described in terms of subsystems (ego, id, superego) with different characteristics and aims. Anxiety, rather than a transformation of dammed-up libido, serves the ego as a signal of, first, external and, ultimately, inner or instinctual danger. Both works suggest that, however determined Freud was not to give up the fundamental discoveries of psychoanalysis about mental life, when it came to the theoretical superstructure, he was responsive to data, especially data obtained in the psychoanalytic situation, and that his attempts to incorporate observations and to mitigate conceptual inconsistencies in dealing with observations motivated whatever major revisions of psychoanalytic theory he proposed.

PSYCHOANALYTIC THEORY

19. **Abraham, K.** (1924) A short study of the development of the libido viewed in light of mental disorders, pp. 418–501. In: Selected Papers. By: K. Abraham. London: Hogarth Press, **1949.**

Abraham's hypothesis is that what kind of psychopathology occurs depends upon the stage of libidinal development to which regression has occurred.

20. **Erikson, E.H.** Childhood and Society. (2nd ed., rev. and enl.) New York: Nortoñ, **1963**.

A restatement of the theory of infantile sexuality (Chapter 2) describes stages of development in terms of dominant bodily zones, characteristic modes of action or approach to objects, and typical nuclear conflicts.

21. **Fairbairn, W.** Psychoanalytic Studies of the Personality. London: Tavistock, **1952**.

In "Schizoid Factors in the Personality" (1940), schizoid characterology and symptomatology are determined by a libidinal oral attitude; the themes, preoccupations, attitudes, and object relations found in work with schizoid characters are vividly captured. In "A Revised Psychopathology of the Psychoses and Psychoneuroses" (1941), however, Fairbairn rejects Abraham's hypothesis that regression to different stages of libidinal development determines the form of psychopathology. In fact, he rejects in its entirety the conception of libidinal phases presented by Abraham, and by Freud in *Three Essays on Sexuality*. In an object-relations formulation, Fairbairn proposes that it is the disposition (externalization or internalization) of good and bad objects that determines the variety of symptomatology that may be associated with either a fundamental schizoid or depressive position.

22. **Federn, P.** Ego Psychology and the Psychoses. New York: Basic Books, **1952**.

Focuses on the patient's introspective-subjective experience of ego and nonego. Concludes that schizophrenia arises from a disturbance in the distribution of ego feeling, in what is felt (which may conflict with what is thought) to be part of the ego and what is felt to be outside the ego, in what the ego feels and does not feel is real and significant. Draws conclusions about treatment. The chapters on ego feeling (1, 3), psychoanalysis and psychotherapy of psychoses (6, 7), and the ego aspects of schizophrenia (10, 11, 12) are more accessible than the others.

23.   **Fenichel, O.** The Psychoanalytic Theory of Neurosis. New York: Norton, **1945**.

An encyclopedic summary of and attempt to systematize the psychoanalytic theory of neurosis. So comprehensive that, although clearly written, it is difficult to just read through. An invaluable reference.

24.   **Freud, A.** The Ego and the Mechanisms of Defense (Rev. ed.). New York: International Universities Press, **1966**.

Psychoanalysis shifts in its study of the vicissitudes of intrapsychic conflict from a focus on detecting derivatives of instinctual impulses to a detailed examination of defensive operations. A classic.

25.   **Gill, M.** Topography and systems in psychoanalytic theory. Psychol. Issues 3(Monograph #10): 1–179, **1963**.

26.   **Arlow, J. and Brenner, C.** Psychoanalytic Concepts and the Structural Theory. New York: International Universities Press, **1964.**

27.   **Lewin, B.D.** Phobic symptoms and dream interpretation. Psychoanal. Q. 21: 295–322, **1952**.

What is the relation between the terminology and model of the mind of Freud's *The Interpretation of Dreams* and the terminology and model of the mind of his major works of revision "The ego and the id" and "Inhibitions, symptoms and anxiety"? Gill, in an exemplary scholarly monograph of conceptual clarification, makes important distinctions and documents that the relation between the two terminologies and models is subtle and complex and that significant problems have been left unsolved by the revision. For Arlow and Brenner, everything is settled. The relation between the two is simple and straightforward. They are incompatible, and the former should be rejected in favor of the latter. Lewin argues that the two, each having its own purposes and advantages, may with profit be used interchangeably; he gives an account of phobic symptoms in the language of dream interpretation.

28.   **Hartmann, H.** Ego Psychology and the Problem of Adaptation. New York: International Universities Press, **1958**.

A seminal effort to increase the scope of psychoanalytic theory so that, as a general psychology, it encompasses those structures and processes of personality serving adaptation and achievement, which are neither derived from nor necessarily involved in conflict.

29.   **Hartmann, H., Kris, E., and Loewenstein, R.** The function of theory in psychoanalysis. Psychol. Issues 4 (Monograph #14): 117–143, **1964.**

Addressing psychoanalysts who distrust theory, it identifies the difficulties and misunderstandings leading to that distrust and sources of dissatisfaction with psychoanalytic theory. Comments at length on the interdependence of theory and clinical work and observations in psychoanalysis.

30.   **Isaacs, S.** The nature and function of phantasy, pp. 67-121. In: Developments in Psycho-Analysis. By: M. Klein, P. Heimann, S. Isaacs, et al. London: Hogarth Press, **1952.**

31.   **Schafer, R.** The mechanisms of defence. Int. J. Psychoanal. 49: 49–62, **1968**.

32.   **Segal, H.** Introduction to the Work of Melanie Klein. New York: Basic Books, **1964**. (New and rev. ed. Basic, 1973.)

Freud discovered that psychic reality has causal efficacy: i.e. mere phantasies (as distinct from physical lesions or features of an experienced situation) produce psychopathology. This discovery underlies his theory of instinctual drives, for such phantasies appear to be relatively independent of accidents of experience. Phantasy is central to psychoanalytic thought and practice, and these three works focus on its nature and function. All three question in different ways the sharp conceptual distinction between instinctual impulses and "mechanisms" of defense in conflict, and not only because a defense may serve instinctual gratification. A defense is far from being a contentless mechanism, but itself is in its essence the expression or manifestation of a phantasy.

33.   **Jones, E.** Papers on Psycho-analysis (5th ed.). Baltimore: Williams and Wilkins, **1948**.

The paper on anal-erotic character traits (Chapter 24), in addition to elaborating one of Freud's startling findings (the unexpected correlation of certain traits), illuminates and makes vivid the theoretical paper on the important subject of symbolism (Chapter 8).

34.   **Loewald, H.W.** Internalization, separation, mourning, and the superego. Psychoanal. Q. 31: 483–504, **1962**.

35. **Loewald, H.W.** The superego and the ego-ideal. II. Superego and time. Int. J. Psychoanal. 43: 264–268, **1962**.

Evocative essays on psychic structure, emphasizing its essential temporal nature, and especially a view of the superego in terms of internal representations of, or orientation to, the future.

36. **Rapoport, D.** The Collected Papers of David Rapoport. Ed.: M.M. Gill. New York: Basic Books, **1967**.

Includes papers on the conceptual model of psychoanalysis (1951), and on the psychoanalytic theory of thinking (1950), affects (1953), and motivation (1960); these make a major contribution to the effort to systematize psychoanalytic theory and to integrate and contrast it with other streams of psychological science. The 1960 paper on motivation can profitably be read in conjunction with a reading of Freud's *Three Essays on Sexuality*. Important contributions to ego psychology include two papers on autonomy of the ego (1951, 1957) and one on activity and passivity (1953).

37. **Waelder, R.** The principle of multiple function, observations on over-determination. Psychoanal. Q. 5: 45–62, **1936**.

Every psychic act is an attempt, at one and the same time, with varying degrees of success, to achieve multiple purposes, arising, e.g., from the necessity to meet simultaneously claims of the instinctual drives, of the outer world, and of internalized commands and prohibitions, and to meet them in certain ways (e.g., by means resulting in active mastery of, rather than mere submission to, these claims). Any psychic act responds to different demands, serves or is exploited to achieve different ends, and therefore has multiple meanings or significances. Waelder here points to an ineluctable characteristic of the subject matter of psychoanalysis. Theory in psychoanalysis must take into account the multiple causation of, and the multiple meanings possessed by, phenomena of interest to it.

PSYCHOANALYSIS AND OTHER DISCIPLINES

38. **Edelson, M.** Language and dreams: The interpretation of dreams revisited. Psychoanal. Study Child 27: 203–282, **1972**.

39. **Edelson, M.** Language and Interpretation in Psychoanalysis. New Haven: Yale University Press, **1975**.

"Language and dreams" is a reading of Freud's *The Interpretation of Dreams* in the light of Noam Chomsky's linguistic theory. Freud's interest in language and view of dreams as dependent on language are documented. Continuing the attempt to bring psychoanalysis and linguistics together, in *Language and Interpretation*, Edelson demystifies the psychoanalytic clinical instrument by arguing that "empathy" and "clinical intuition" might in part be the result of the psychoanalyst's unwitting response to complex syntactic, semantic, and phonetic patterns in the analysand's speech.

40.   ***Freud, S.** (1913) Totem and taboo. S.E. 13: xiii–162, **1953**.

41.   ***Freud, S.** (1921) Group psychology and the analysis of the ego. S.E. 18: 67–143, **1955**.

Both of these works have influenced attempts to explain social and group phenomena, especially the relations between a group and its leader.

42.   **Klein, G.S.** Consciousness in psychoanalytic theory: Some implications for current research in perception. J. Am. Psychoanal. Assoc. 7: 5–34, **1959**.

An illustration of the impact of psychoanalytic theory on research in another discipline.

43.   **Mahl, G.** Psychological Conflict and Defense. Ed.: I.L. Janis. New York: Harcourt Brace Jovanovich, **1971**.

Brings the perspective of learning theory to an introduction of the mechanisms of defense. Can be usefully read with A. Freud's book on the same subject.

44.   **Parsons, T.** Social structure and the development of personality: Freud's contribution to the integration of psychology and sociology. Psychiatry 21: 321–340, **1958**.

Read together with Freud's *Three Essays on Sexuality*, this sociological perspective on the same subject will provoke thought and discussion.

45.   **Redl, F.** Group emotion and leadership. Psychiatry 5: 573–596, **1942**.

A development of Freud's ideas on group psychology. Describes 10 types of group formation distinguished by differences in the relation to a central person, who is an object of identification, an object of drives, or an ego support. The assuagement of guilt and fear by the initiatory act of a seducer, and the infection, with respect to expressing a particular drive, of a conflicted personality by a nonconflicted personality, are two mechanisms postulated to operate in processes of group formation around a leader. Examples from and applications to teacher-students relations.

46.   **Reiser, M.F.** Changing theoretical concepts in psychosomatic medicine, pp. 477–500. In: AHP (2nd ed.), Vol. 4, **1975.**

A review of the vicissitudes of psychoanalytic explanation in the realm of psychosomatic medicine.

THE PSYCHOANALYTIC SITUATION AND METHOD

47.   **Fenichel, O.** Problems of Psychoanalytic Technique. New York: Psychoanalytic Quarterly, **1941.**

To evaluate the data obtained in the psychoanalytic situation, one must be clear about the nature of the psychoanalyst's interventions. Fenichel's theory of psychoanalytic therapy is distinguished by its use of meta-psychological concepts to consider the dynamic, economic, and structural aspects of interpretation. He is lucid and pithy. The psychoanalytic task is "reversing displacements, abolishing isolations, or guiding traces of affect to their proper relationships" (pp. 42–43). The patient's childhood "is still actively present . . . in the behavior of the patient today; otherwise it would not interest us at all. If only we put the present in order correctly and understand it, we shall thereby make new impulses possible for the patient, until the childhood material comes of itself" (p.49). A classic.

48.   **Kris, E.** On some vicissitudes of insight in psychoanalysis. Int. J. Psychoanal. 37: 445–455, **1956**.

The acquisition of insight is generally held to be not only a necessary condition for therapeutic success in psychoanalysis, but when insight leads to therapeutic success it is also regarded as evidence justifying provisional acceptance of psychoanalytic hypotheses. Kris's paper makes clear that the conditions leading to insight are very complex indeed. He emphasizes the role of preceding analytic work, preparatory preconscious mental activity, and the integrative capacity and functioning of the ego; questions that the occurrence of negative transference is always an obstacle; distinguishes between compliance with the analyst and compliance with the treatment process; and contrasts the characteristics of insight, partial or pseudo-insight, and the insight used in the service of defense and resistance. Influential individual differences have to do with capacities to control regression; to view the self objectively; and to control the discharge of affects.

49.   **Searl, M.N.** Some queries on principles of technique. Int. J. Psychoanal. 17: 471–493, **1936**.

50. **Kris, A.** Free Association: Method and Process. New Haven: Yale University Press, **1982.**

Both authors approach the psychoanalytic process—with what they consider to be a minimal theoretical apparatus—from the point of view of free association, the unique method of investigation of psychoanalysis. The focus of the psychoanalyst's attention is on the vicissitudes of the analysand's reluctances and resistances, which appear in the course of attempting to report whatever comes to mind. These works are invaluable, from the point of view of interest in psychoanalysis as science, for understanding in what ways a psychoanalyst with a disciplined technique evaluates and does influence the data obtained in the psychoanalytic situation, and in what ways such a psychoanalyst does not influence these data.

51. **Stone, L.** The Psychoanalytic Situation, An Examination of Its Development and Essential Nature. New York: International Universities Press, **1961.**

52. ***Freud, S.** (1911–1915) Papers on technique. S.E. 12: 89–171, **1958.**

The establishment and maintenance of the psychoanalytic situation is essential not only for treatment but for obtaining unique data hard to come by otherwise. Stone responds to Freud's technical recommendations as they are frequently interpreted by characterizing the multiple dilemmas the psychoanalyst traverses in creating and maintaining the psychoanalytic situation.

53. **Strachey, J.** The nature of the therapeutic action of psycho-analysis. Int. J. Psychoanal. 15: 127–159, **1934.**

That the past lives again in the transference is essential to the claim that data obtained in the psychoanalytic situation can serve to support psychoanalytic hypotheses. Strachey characterizes a mutative interpretation as one leading to awareness that a particular impulse is directed to the psychoanalyst, that anxiety and defense are responses to the occurrence of this impulse, that directing the impulse to the psychoanalyst is in some way inexplicable in terms of what is otherwise known about the psychoanalyst, and that the determinants of both impulse and conflict lie in unconscious phantasy and memory from infancy and childhood.

THE SCIENTIFIC STATUS OF PSYCHOANALYSIS

54. ***Breuer, J. and Freud, S.** (1893–1895) Studies on Hysteria. S.E. 2: **1955.**

55. ***Freud, S.** (1937) Constructions in analysis. S.E. 23: 257–269, **1964.**

56. **Kris, E.** The recovery of childhood memories in psychoanalysis. Psychoanal. Study Child 11: 54–88, **1956**.

These works represent the move from the position that the patient suffers from unconscious memories of recent traumatic experiences, and that successful therapeuetic outcome depends on the recovery of these memories, to the position that what is etiologic are unconscious memories of infancy and childhood which often cannot be recovered and must be reconstructed, and that the recovery of childhood memories is not essential to successful therapeutic outcome. The implication of this change for the scientific status of psychoanalysis has been discussed by Edelson (1983) and Grunbaum (1982), who come to different conclusions about it.

57. **Edelson, M.** Hypothesis and Evidence in Psychoanalysis. Chicago: University of Chicago Press, **1983**.

58. **Grunbaum, A.** Can psychoanalytic theory be cogently tested "on the couch"? Parts I and II. Psychoanal. Contemp. Thought 5: 155–255, 311–436, **1982**.

Edelson assesses the scientific status of psychoanalysis in the light of new conceptions in the philosophy of science—e.g., the nonstatement view of theory; the objective-propensity interpretation of probability; and conceptual and methodological developments in single-subject research. That psychoanalytic hypotheses can be empirically confirmed and falsified is, in general, accepted, but that psychoanalytic hypotheses are scientifically credible is not. Edelson rejects and presents a detailed argument to refute the assertion of the philosopher of science Grunbaum that it is impossible to obtain evidence in the psychoanalytic situation warranting provisional acceptance of psychoanalytic hypotheses as scientifically credible.

59. *****Freud, S.** (1909) Notes upon a case of obsessional neurosis. S.E. 10: 155–318, **1955**.

60. **Glymour, C.** Freud, Kepler, and the clinical evidence, pp. 285–304. In: Freud, A Collection of Critical Essays. Ed.: R. Wollheim. New York: Anchor, **1974**.

Freud uses a case study (the Rat Man) to test and revise his theory. Glymour argues that Freud's methods here are essentially those of other scientists. Glymour's discussion of the Rat Man case suggests a way of thinking about testing theoretical hypotheses in a clinical case study.

61. *****Freud, S.** (1937) Analysis terminable and interminable. S.E. 23: 216–253, **1964**.

A dark paper. Because it focuses on factors that unavoidably limit the efficacy of psychoanalysis as therapy, it constrains excessive therapeutic zeal, ambition, and optimism—and implies that the ultimate value of psychoanalysis lies in making, through its method of investigation, contributions to human knowledge.

62.   **Glover, E.** The therapeutic effect of inexact interpretation: A contribution to the theory of suggestion. Int. J. Psychoanal. 12: 397–411, **1931**.

An important contribution to consideration of the problem of suggestion, as it influences what data are obtained in the psychoanalytic situation—a topic also discussed by Edelson (1983) and Grunbaum (1982), who come to different conclusions about the extent to which these data are unavoidably contaminated by suggestion, and therefore about their value for testing psychoanalytic hypotheses.

63.   **Luborsky, L.** Momentary forgetting during psychotherapy and psychoanalysis. In: Motives and Thought. Ed.: R. Holt. Psychol. Issues (Monograph #18/19): 177–217, **1967**.

64.   **Luborsky, L.** Forgetting and remembering (momentary forgetting) during psychotherapy: A new sample. Psychol. Issues (Monograph #30): 29–55, **1973**.

65.   **Luborsky, L. and Mintz, J.** What sets off momentary forgetting during a psychoanalysis? Investigations of symptom-onset conditions. Psychoanal. Contemp. Sci. 3: 233–268, **1975**.

Stages in the invention of the symptom-context method, which uses data obtained from the psychoanalytic situation and is capable of testing, according to canons of scientific reasoning and method, many psychoanalytic hypotheses other than those mentioned in these studies. Luborsky's work decisively demonstrates that data from the psychoanalytic situation can be used as evidence to test psychoanalytic hypotheses.

66.   **Waelder, R.** Basic Theory of Psychoanalysis. New York: International Universities Press, **1960**.

This introduction to psychoanalytic theory is written by an author who knows science. He begins with a section on the validation of psychoanalytic interpretations and theories, and throughout his presentation of the historical development of psychoanalytic thought and his discussion of basic concepts, the author raises questions he believes require further study and research.

5. LEARNING THEORY IN BEHAVIOR THERAPY

GORDON G. BALL, PH.D.

Theories of learning laid the foundations for a viable behavior therapy. The two most influential learning models are the classical conditioning paradigm developed in Russia, especially by Bechterev and Pavlov, and the operant conditioning procedures developed in the United States by Thorndike. At the present time, many behavioral approaches use a combination of these two models as a means of explaining and predicting maladaptive behaviors.

This is well illustrated in Mowrer's two-factor theory of avoidance behavior and Wolpe's reciprocal inhibition theory. Skinner and Miller place more emphasis on operant conditioning while Salter places Pavlov's cortical processes as central to his theory.

Dissatisfaction has been expressed by many behavior therapists about the usefulness of these conditioning theories, based on animal experimentation, to explain all of human behavior. Consequently in the last few years there has been a trend away from the more rigid behavioral approach and toward theories related to cognitive processes and their modification. In general, they are based on expectancy theory. Examples are the Becks' cognitive theory of depression, Seligman's learned-helplessness theory, and Meichenbaum's cognitive approach to behavior modification. However, it is too early to judge their impact on the continuing development of behavior therapy.

The references cover a sample of the learning theories, both behavioral and cognitive, that are presently guiding the direction of behavior therapy. However, theories remain viable in behavior therapy only as long as they prove useful for assessment and treatment. With further experimentation, it is assumed that they will eventually be discarded for more sophisticated theoretical approaches.

GLOBAL THEORETICAL ISSUES

1. **Dollard, J. and Miller, N.E.** Personality and Psychotherapy. New York: McGraw Hill, **1950**.

31

This is one of the earlier attempts to extrapolate from animal behavior the important role of conflict between drives in the development of psychopathology.

2. **Eysenck, H.J.** The Effects of Psychotherapy. New York: International Science Press, **1966**.

This book contains an extension of Eysenck's earlier arguments concerning the ineffectiveness of traditional psychotherapy.

3. **Gray, J.A.** The Neuropsychology of Anxiety. New York: Oxford University Press, **1982**.

This is a scholarly work that combines behavioral, biochemical, and neuroanatomical data in an attempt to integrate present knowledge about anxiety.

4. ***Hilgard, E.R. and Bower, G.H.** Theories of Learning (3rd ed.). New York: Appleton-Century-Crofts, **1966**.

All the fundamental theories of learning are well covered in this text. It is extremely useful for understanding the variations between the different types of conditioning procedures.

5. **Meichenbaum, D.H.** Cognitive Behavior Modification. New York: Plenum Press, **1977**.

Over the last few years, cognitive approaches have made a considerable impact on the practice of behavior therapy, with Meichenbaum being one of the leaders in this area. This book elaborates on the cognitive theory and illustrates the procedures.

6. **Salter, A.** The theory and practice of conditioned reflex therapy. In: The Conditioning Therapies. Eds.: J. Wolpe, A. Salter, and L.J. Reyna. New York: Holt, Rinehart, and Winston, **1964**.

Pavlov's excitation and inhibition model of the cerebral cortex inspired Salter to develop a therapy based on the classically conditioned reflex. This approach has been incorporated into several of the current theories in behavior therapy.

7. ***Skinner, B.F.** Science and Human Behavior. New York: MacMillan Co., **1953**.

In this book, Skinner elaborated his principles of operant conditioning to diverse areas including government, law, religion, and psychotherapy. He emphasized how the reinforcement contingencies of the therapist resulted in changes in the patient.

THEORIES RELATED TO SPECIFIC PROBLEMS

8. **Beck, A.T., Rush, A.S., Shaw, B.F., et al.** Cognitive Therapy of Depression. New York: Guilford Press, **1979**.

   Approaches in behavior therapy for conceptualizing depression place the etiology on either reinforcement or cognitive factors. The underlying assumption is that the depressed patient's acquired maladaptive reaction patterns can be unlearned. The cognitive approach summarized in this book has marshalled impressive support as an effective intervention strategy with the depressed individual.

9. **Hunt, H.F.** Problems in the interpretation of "experimental neurosis." Psychol. Reports 15: 27–35, **1964**.

   Hunt presents a critical review of those laboratory experiments that have produced behavior in animals resembling the neurotic behaviors of humans.

10. **Jacobson, E.** Biology of Emotions. Springfield, IL: Thomas, **1967**.

    The relaxation procedures of Jacobson have had a major impact in behavior therapy. His findings and assumptions are described in this book.

11. ***Mowrer, O.H.** Learning theory and behavior. New York: Wiley, **1960**.

    Mowrer's two-factor theory of avoidance behavior is one of the most widely used models in behavior therapy for explaining phobic behavior. In this book, Mowrer expands his principles of learning, developed with animals, to encompass several of the problems of human pathology.

12. **Seligman, M.E.P.** Helplessness: On Depression, Development, and Death. San Francisco: Freeman, **1975**.

    The learned-helplessness theory, based on animal experiments, attempts to explain some of the behavior characteristics found in depressed individuals. It emphasized the cognitive aspects in the development of the syndrome and has been extended recently to include attribution theory.

6. PSYCHOLOGY

Jerome L. Singer, Ph.D.

In the decade between 1960 and 1970 one can identify what may be termed a "paradigm shift" in psychology with respect to the conceptions of human functions and the organization of psychological processes. From 1910 to about 1960 under the influence of behaviorism and its emphasis on animal research as a basis for understanding human processes of learning, motivation psychology was dominated by stimulus-response and drive-reduction models of behavior. During the decade of the 1960s a confluence of theoretical analysis and research findings led to a shift from the more peripheralist concepts of organ-related drives to a more centralist view of humans as information-seeking and information-processing organisms with a much greater focus upon the close tie between cognition and differentiated emotional system in the person. Theoretical contributions by Ernest Schachtel, Robert W. White, and Silvan S. Tomkins may be cited among many others as anticipating or signaling this shift, while the research on sensory deprivation stimulated by Donald O. Hebb, the studies of the sleep and dream cycles initiated by Kleitman and Dement, and the computer models of human thought developed by Newell and Simon all were influences on the changing perspective.

In effect, the current pervasive orientation of psychology increasingly emphasizes a systems approach and a biopsychosocial integration as a guiding schema. Humans are conceived as reflecting a series of differentiated but interacting systems of biological processes and information-processing as well as affective functions, which are themselves organized to relate to a surrounding milieu of physical objects and persons who themselves reflect a broader culture or social system. Humans are viewed as seeking to organize complex novel stimulation into meaningful informational structures that can then be related to previously acquired knowledge and stored as new schemata "ticketed" for effective retrieval as necessary. The emotions are closely tied to the novelty and complexity of information to be processed and are evoked specifically in relation to the degree of uncertainty or ambiguity in a stimulus-field or to the extent that previous anticipations, "plans," or "scripts" are confirmed or disconfirmed by each new encounter with people or physical settings. The emphasis on information-processing and the extensive research in cognitive psychology has demonstrated that attention and perception are not simply responses to a stimulus but are processes occurring across time (at great but measurable speeds). Such processes have definable sequences and phases usually reflected in flow charts. There are key points along the way where individual variations in how a search of a stimulus configuration is carried out, how it is reflected upon and encoded for storage (i.e., as a word-meaning or as an episode or event, as a visual or auditory image or as an abstract class of events or objects) and how it is mentally rehearsed in the form of daydreams or fantasies after storage, may lead to different cognitive or personality styles or may reflect defensive maneuvers occasioned by threats to beliefs about the self.

A consequence of the cognitive-affective orientation is an increased interest in basic research on processes of mental representation, thinking, imagery, planning, fantasizing. Organized belief systems such as those built around the self or the differentiation of the self from others are increasingly explored. Social psychologists are focusing their attention on how information about situations is stored and retrieved. In the following bibliography we will include references that can provide basic scientific information on the origins of the cognitive-affective paradigm, the nature of cognition, the differentiated affect system, and the problems of storing, retrieving, and communicating information.

THE SHIFT FROM DRIVE TO COGNITIVE-AFFECTIVE THEORIES

The following readings reflect the beginnings of a shift in perspective and the emergence of a view of humans as more than drive-reducing organisms. All reflect a reappraisal of the classical psychoanalytic or drive-reduction learning theory models in the light of new findings on the motivating properties of human curiosity, competence, and the role of positive emotions of joy, excitement, and interest as well as negative emotions such as anxiety or anger.

1. **Schachtel, E.** Metamorphosis. New York: Basic Books, **1959**.

    Examines the psychoanalytic model of motivation and emotion in the form elaborated by David Rapaport as a definitive view of classical theory and shows the necessity for a broader view of emotions and their relation to attention and memory.

2. ***Tomkins, S.S.** Affect, Imagery, Consciousness, Vols. I and II. New York: Springer, **1962** and **1963**.

The most ambitious and original attempt at developing a new conception of personality of the past quarter of a century. This work also reappraises drive theory, argues for the importance of understanding conscious thought, and proposes a revolutionary theory of emotion that has since found considerable empirical support in the careful research of Paul Ekman, Carroll Izard, and Gary Schwartz, among others.

3. ***White, R.W.** Motivation reconsidered: The concept of competence. Psychol. Rev. 66: 297–333, **1959**.

Documents the limitation of drive theories of motivation based on remarkable review of research findings.

MODERN RESEARCH IN COGNITIVE PROCESSES

The following references provide an up-to-date account of the nature of the information-processing sequence from initial attention through encoding and memory.

4. **Kreitler, H. and Kreitler, S.** Cognitive Orientation and Behavior. New York: Springer, **1976**.

Addresses broader aspects of cognition such as the role of meaningfulness and of one's cognitive orientation as a predictor of not only private attitude but of subsequent behavior.

5. ***Lachman, R., Lachman, J., and Butterfield, E.** Cognitive Psychology and Information-Processing: An Introduction. Hillsdale, NJ.: Erlbaum, **1979**.

6. **Lindsay, P.H. and Norman, D.A.** Human Information-Processing, (2nd ed.). New York: Academic Press, **1977**.

7. ***Neisser, U.** Cognition and Reality. San Francisco: Freeman, **1967**.

8. **Neisser, U.** Cognitive Psychology. Princeton, N.J.: Appleton-Century-Crofts, **1967**.

These books are texts that incorporate the recent research studies pointing to the central role of a sequence of information processing in human experience.

9. **Schank, R. and Abelson, R.** Scripts, Plans, Goals and Understanding. New York: Halsted, **1977**.

Recent advances derived from studies of computer modeling and artificial intelligence that have led to a formulation that human thought is organized not just into verbal phrases or fleeting images but into story-like scripts, some shared in common in a culture but many highly personalized because of unique experiences. The notion of personal scripts undoubtedly has important implications not only for research on memory and thought but also for the psychoanalytic concept of transference.

10.   **Witkin, H.A. and Goodenough, D.R.** Cognitive Styles: Essence and Origins. New York: International Universities Press, **1981**.

Extensive research on a major cognitive style, the field-dependence–independence axis.

DIFFERENTIATED EMOTIONS: THEORY AND RESEARCH

Although clinicians have always stressed the special role of emotions in human experience and in clinical intervention, there has been little development of a systematic theory of emotions in any of the psychotherapeutic theories of personality.

11.   **Ekman, P. and Freisen, W.** Unmasking the Face. Englewood Cliffs, NJ: Prentice-Hall, **1975**.

12.   ***Izard, C.** Human Emotions. New York: Plenum, **1977**.

13.   **Tomkins, S.S.** The quest for primary motives: Biography and auto-biography of an idea. J. Pers. Soc. Psychol. 41: 306–329, **1981**.

This paper formulates the concept of emotions as a basic organismic system characterized by: (a) a distinct pattern of physiological representation in the brain and in peripheral autonomic or musculature processes, (b) a distinctive facial expression, and (c) a specific "felt" experience. Tomkins's theory has been supported by an increasing body of research.

IMAGERY, IMAGINATION, AND CONSCIOUSNESS

The increased attention to conscious processes and to how humans represent the external social or physical environment that stems from a cognitive-affective perspective has led also to an increased interest in ongoing thought, to the study of images, fantasies, and day and night dreams. The phenomenon of hypnosis, long linked to neurotic trends, is now also being recognized as a basic human capacity or skill related to the absorption in imagery under conditions of self-attenuated consciousness. The following references document some of the major research findings relating to hypnosis, the stream of consciousness and imagery, the studies of nocturnal dreaming derived from psychophysiological research in the sleep cycle. They point toward some of the clinical applications of the recent advances in understanding imaginative processes.

14.   **Arkin, A., Antrobus, J., and Ellman, S.** The Mind in Sleep. Hillsdale, NJ: Erlbaum, **1979**.

The best single compendium of the current scientific knowledge and research on thought processes during sleep. Basic reading for any modern understanding of dreams.

15.   ***Fromm, E. and Shorr, R.** Hypnosis: Developments in Research and New Perspectives (2nd ed.). New York: Aldine, **1979**.

An exciting group of chapters reviewing practically all that is known scientifically about the phenomenon of hypnosis.

16.   ***Horowitz, M.** Image Formation and Cognition. New York: Appleton-Century-Crofts, **1970**. (2nd ed., **1978**.)

An original and thoughtful study of visual imagery, its role in cognition, and the clinical implications of imagery distortions.

17.   ***Pope, K. and Singer, J.L.** The Stream of Consciousness. New York: Plenum, **1978**.

18.   ***Singer, J.L. and Pope, K.S.** The Power of Human Imagination. New York: Plenum, **1978**.

These companion volumes include chapters reviewing the scientific literature on daydreaming, the stream of conscious, and related phenomena of ongoing thought. The second volume addresses applications of these scientific findings in a variety of approaches to psychodynamic and to behavioral forms of psychotherapy.

19.   ***Schwartz, G. and Shapiro, D.** Consciousness and Self-regulation, Vols. I and II. New York: Plenum, **1976** and **1978**.

A group of papers laying the foundation in studies of self-regulation for the emerging field of health psychology.

7. FAMILY

STEPHEN FLECK, M.D.

There are several reasons why a basic understanding of family functioning is important. Family therapy as a technique should not be undertaken without basic understanding of intra- and interpersonal psychodynamics and the special nature of the family as a small group. No one should undertake family treatment without basic knowledge of family functions, although the examination of the family as a unit itself has therapeutic implications.

In family interviews the complexities are multiplied so that the therapist can quickly experience input overload. Focus is not only on what is said to the therapist, but also on what family members say to each other and simultaneously how others in the family react nonverbally to what is stated by a particular member. Hence it is important that the beginner have some scheme or outline in his or her mind as to what aspects of family behaviors and dynamics need to be observed and thought through before any response or statement is offered by the therapist.

The general systems view of the family is currently considered the most fruitful and effective mode of understanding families and family processes. Such a systems scheme must take into account that the family is not only a small group, but, unlike a stranger therapy group, is not a temporary aggregate where each member has the option to leave once particular needs have been met or if he or she decides that his or her needs are not being and will not be met. Dynamically speaking, the family is not or ought not to be the same group at different stages of the family life cycle. The family must move through its life cycle, which overlaps with the life cycles of the various members. Lastly, it must be appreciated that each parent/child triangle constitutes a particular "family," albeit integrated with the entire group.

No modern psychiatrist ought to be without knowledge of basic family structure, dynamics, and functioning through the life cycle. In particular, psychiatrists must be enabled to make treatment decisions and recommendations based on their formulations of a particular problem and know the uses and usefulness of family therapy. It should be emphasized, however, that families with a hospitalized member always need therapeutic attention because such hospitalization is a significant stress (if not trauma); the family and their capacity and resources to cope with such an event must be evaluated. Moreover, often continued family involvement is indicated, especially in the case of young patients where significant family pathology may have contributed to the condition, which often cannot be resolved or remedied without working with the families. If the patient returns to live with and be cared for by the family, continued family support or treatment may also be indicated.

These latter principles prevail in all chronic illness situations and psychiatrists are often called upon to advise nonpsychiatric colleagues about family problems, if not family pathology. Schooled and skilled in family assessment, psychiatrists can then help and educate colleagues, particularly those in family practice, about the difficulties and recommend treatment, if indicated.

1. *Ackerman, N.W. The Psychodynamics of Family Life. New York: Basic Books, 1958.

    The first comprehensive statement on modern family studies and treatment by the pioneer of family therapy in outpatient settings. Chapters 1 and 4 are essential.

2. Anthony, E.J. Do emotional problems of the child always have their origin in the family? pp. 97–115. In: Psychiatry at the Crossroads. Eds.: J.P. Brady and H.K.H. Brodie. Philadelphia: Saunders, 1980.

    A classic essay by possibly the most illustrious and sensitive child psychiatrist of our day. Without stating so specifically, it represents the most cogent exposé and argument for a general systems approach to family theory and therapy.

3. Berenson, D. Alcohol and the family system, pp. 284–297. In: Family Therapy: Theory and Practice. Ed.: P.J. Guerin. New York: Gardner Press, 1976.

    A good treatise of the particular forms of family system malfunctioning in families with an alcoholic member.

4. *Fleck, S. The family and psychiatry, pp. 513–530. In: CTP III, Vol. 1, 1980.

    An elementary and rather detailed outline of family structure and dynamics and their impact on individual development through the life cycle. A general systems approach is also presented, as is a brief review of the major types of family pathology related to psychiatric entities.

5. *Glick, I.D. and Kessler, D.R. Marital and Family Therapy. New York: Grune & Stratton, 1974. (2nd ed., 1980.)

This concise introduction to clinical work with families is a must for all beginners.

6. **Goldsmith, J.** The post-divorce family system, pp. 297–330. In: Normal Family Processes. Ed.: F. Walsh. New York: Guilford Press, **1982**.

This is a thoughtful treatise based on clinical observations on the continuation of functional family systems despite legal family fracture.

7. **Lewis, J.A., Beavers, W.R., Gossett, J.T., et al.** No Single Thread. Psychological Health in Family Systems. New York: Brunner/Mazel, **1976**.

The best scientifically rigorous as well as sensitive research to assess the function modes of non-clinical families.

8. **Lidz, T.** The Family and Human Adaptation. New York: International Universities Press, **1963**.

Three lectures presenting scientifically based data on the familial aspects of human adaptation, of personality structure, and of language and communication.

9. **Minuchin, S., Montalvo, B., Guerney, B.G., et al.** Families of the Slums. New York: Basic Books, **1967**.

One of the earliest works on family pathology as found in a class V (Hollingshead) population. It illustrates that adequate parenting demands maturity and physical presence.

10. **Napier, A.Y. and Whitaker, C.A.** The Family Crucible. New York: Harper & Row, **1978**.

An absorbing account of one family's course of therapy, illustrating a master at work, but not a guide to family pathology or treatment in general.

11. **Parker, B.** A Mingled Yarn. New Haven: Yale University Press, **1972**.

An account of one family's history and deviances through the life cycle, presented from the vantage point of a schizophrenic patient.

12. **Parsons, T. and Bales, R.F.** Family, Socialization and Interaction Process. Glencoe, IL: Free Press, **1955**.

13. ***Parsons, T.** Social structure and the development of personality: Freud's contribution to the integration of psychology and sociology. Psychiatry 21: 321–340, **1958**.

Parsons was an important pioneer in our current thinking and understanding of family processes. Despite the age, these readings are still a comprehensive exposition of the family's role in the socialization process of children and, even though not easy to read, they are classic and no student of family process, let alone a therapist, can ignore them.

14. ***Rossi, A.S.** Transitions to parenthood—The problem. J. Marriage and Fam. 30: 26–39, **1968.**

The best treatise addressing the issues and dynamics involved in undertaking parenthood in a planned and forethought fashion.

15. ***Skynner, A.C.R.** An open-systems, group-analytic approach to family therapy, pp. 39–84. In: Handbook of Family Therapy. Eds.: A.S. Gurman and D.P. Kniskern. New York: Brunner/ Mazel, **1981.**

This British pioneer in family treatment has elaborated a convincing integration of psychodynamic principles especially as they pertain to groups and family system interactions and dynamics based on therapeutic work with families.

16. ***Spiegel, J.P.** The resolution of role conflict within the family, pp. 445–466. In: Human Life Cycle. Ed.: W.C. Sze. New York: Aronson, **1975.**

Spiegel and Kluckhohn did the original work on family roles, conflict sources and conflict resolution with particular attention to cultural differences between spouses and their families. This is a latter-day summary of this area of family interaction.

17. ***Walsh, F.** Conceptualizations of normal family functioning, pp. 3–42. In: Normal Family Processes. Ed.: F. Walsh. New York: Guilford Press, **1982.**

An up-to-date (1982) overview with a thorough discussion of "normality." Various types of systems approaches to family study and treatment are presented.

18. **Winnicott, D.W.** The Family and Individual Development. London: Tavistock, **1965.**

A psychoanalyst's view of the family's role in personality development; not a treatise on the family per se.

19. **Wynne, L.C.** Family interaction: An alternative starting point for evaluating risk of psychosis, pp. 293–302. In: The Child and His Family: Vulnerable Children, Vol. IV. Eds.: E.G. Anthony, C. Koupernik, and C. Chiland. New York: Wiley, **1978.**

A review and preview regarding family pathology research with a sound basis in the earlier communication studies by Singer and Wynne.

8. GROUP DYNAMICS

RICHARD L. MUNICH, M.D.

Group dynamics refers to processes inherent in the nature of groups: the vicissitudes of member-to-member interactions, the reciprocal relation between those interactions and between individual members and the group itself, and the relationship of these factors to the issues of group development and authority relations, structure, task, and goals. Group dynamics are active to a greater or lesser extent irrespective of the structure or work of any specific group, whether it be therapeutic, clinical-administrative, organizational, or primarily designed to study itself. Insofar as their services are most often delivered in the context of groups, a familiarity with group dynamics is important for mental health professionals. It may be of even greater relevance that, beginning with their families, clients continue to develop and exist within the framework of various group situations.

Selections for this bibliography have been made to emphasize the three most influential intellectual traditions in the development of group dynamics as a basic social science: individual psychology, social psychology, and sociology. Each of these traditions has its own theoretical assumptions and distinctive language. In his effort to understand group life, the psychologist examines the individual, the sociologist focuses on the cultural or structural aspects of the group itself, and the social psychologist studies the boundary between the social and the psychological and between members themselves. The disparity between their languages and the tension between points of view reflects the historical and theoretical roots of the study of group dynamics.

The struggle to formulate models that organize experience in and of group dynamics are mainly aids in conceptualizing group process rather than prescriptions for action or thorough descriptions of what happens in groups. There is no substitute for experience in groups in order to learn about groups. Most of the first four groupings of annotations are considered core readings and refer to processes in small face-to-face groups that coincide with the majority of our work. The last group represents enduring examples of more practical and experiential applications of group dynamics and are recommended as useful supplements to the core.

43

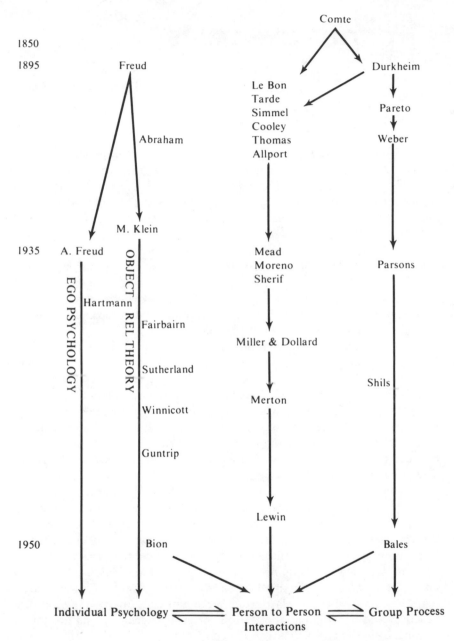

| TIME | PSYCHOANALYSIS | SOCIAL PSYCHOLOGY | SOCIOLOGY |

Figure 8-1. Intellectual and Historical Trends for Group Dynamics Prior to 1950

44

OVERVIEW

1. **Cartwright, D. and Zander, A.,** eds. Group Dynamics. Evanston, IL: Row and Peterson, **1953.** (available in 3rd ed., **1968**).

   An early collection of papers which helps set the stage for many modern developments.

2. ***Munich, R.L. and Astrachan, B.M.** Group dynamics, pp. 15–22. In: Comprehensive Group Psychotherapy. (2nd ed.). Eds.: H.I. Kaplan and B.J. Sadock. Baltimore, MD: Williams and Wilkins, **1983.**

   A comprehensive account of the historical, psychological, sociological, and social-psychological roots and contributions to the study of group dynamics. Although the autonomy of each perspective is respected, an effort is made to integrate them.

INDIVIDUAL PSYCHOLOGY

3. ***Bion, W.** Experience in Groups. New York: Basic Books, **1961.**

   The classic work that shows the development and describes the latent content of group process, labeled and known thereafter as the basic assumptions. The liberal use of the author's personal experiences as a leader of groups serves to intensify the impact as well as the import of the material, especially that relating to authority and leadership.

4. **Freud, S.** Group psychology and the analysis of the ego. In: S.E. 18: 67–133, **1955.**

   One of the earliest and most lucid accounts of the vicissitudes of the individual and his mental activity within the context of a group. Used by Freud to develop his concept of identification.

5. **Rioch, M.J.** The work of Wilfred Bion on groups. Psychiatry 33: 56–66, **1970.**

   A clear and concise exposition of Bion's work, which it takes further, elaborates, and relates more clearly to clinical phenomena. A useful companion to *Experiences in Groups* (Bion above), which it does not replace.

6. ***Slater, P.E.** Microcosm: Structural, Psychological and Religious Evolution in Groups. New York: Wiley, **1966.**

   A detailed analysis of group development with an exposition of boundary formation both of which relate emerging phenomena to primitive and enduring psychological and sociocultural themes. These important issues are abundantly documented with clinical material, especially with respect to the theme of group revolt.

7.   ***Turquet, P.** Threats to identity in the large group, pp. 87–144. In: The Large Group. Ed.: L. Kreeger. Itasca, IL: Peacock, **1975.**

The single most penetrating and illuminating account of the fate of the individual in the large group. Gives specific, concrete notions about the complex machinations of ego boundary transformations vis-à-vis large group membership.

SOCIAL PSYCHOLOGY

8.   ***Bales, R.F. and Slater, P.E.** Role differentiation in small decision-making groups, pp. 259–306. In: Family, Socialization and Interaction Process. Eds.: T. Parsons and R.F. Bales. New York: Free Press, **1955.**

In this critically important study, the authors put a microscope on the step-by-step evolution of roles in a group, with special emphasis on that of the task and emotional leaders and the evolution of a common culture. Also important as a demonstration of basic research strategies in social psychology.

9.   **Gibbard, G.S., Hartmann, J.J., and Mann, R.D.,** eds. Analysis of Groups: Contributions to Theory, Research and Practice. San Francisco: Jossey and Bass, **1973.**

A useful collection of essays, some of which are classics, but which also pulls together various facets of group life derived from group psychotherapy, sensitivity training, and self-analytic classroom traditions. The essays on group development are especially useful.

10.   **Heslin, R. and Dunphy, D.** Three dimensions of member satisfaction in small groups. Hum. Relations 17: 99–112, **1964.**

Outlines how status consensus, progress toward group goals, and freedom to participate generate satisfaction in individuals in the group.

11.   ***Newton, P.M. and Levinson, D.J.** The work group within the organization: A socio-psychological approach. Psychiatry 36: 115–142, 1973.

A brilliant exposition of a social system that becomes the foundation for a useful theoretical framework involving the interrelationship between task, social structure, social processes, and culture. The authors demonstrate how each perspective within the framework interacts with the other and enlarges our understanding of group life.

12. **Tuckman, B.W.** Developmental sequence in small groups. Psychol. Bull. 63: 384–399, **1965.**

Reviews 50 articles to propose a two-dimensional view of group development—temporal and structural—and explains the origin of strains within the group. This view has been validated by subsequent and reliable studies.

SOCIOLOGY

13. ***Durkheim, E.** Suicide: A Study in Sociology. Trans.: J.A. Spaulding and G. Simpson. Glencoe, IL: Free Press, **1951.** (Published originally, **1897.**)

The classic work that uses statistical analysis of social systems to account for anomic, egoistic, and altruistic forms of suicide. A major influence on subsequent sociological thought and group work.

14. **Edelson, M.** Theory of groups, pp. 25–74. In: Sociotherapy and Psychotherapy. Chicago: University of Chicago, **1970.**

A difficult but rewarding effort to conceptualize the lawfulness and regularity of group life. Draws from general systems theory, Tavistock group relations theory, and Parson's theory of action to propose an interactive model of groups based on the framework of values that group members share.

15. **Mills, T.** The Sociology of Small Groups. Englewood Cliffs, NJ: Prentice-Hall, **1967.**

An excellent account and example of model building in group theory from the point of view of the group itself. Gives a clear exposition of the evolution of thinking of the group as a miniature social system.

16. **Parsons, T.** The Structure of Social Action. New York: Free Press, **1937.**

An outstanding, abstract, and complex example of sociological theory building, which is at the foundation of modern sociology. Not for the faint of heart.

PRACTICAL GROUP DYNAMICS

17. **Goffman, E.** Asylums: Essays on the Social Situation of Mental Patients and Other Inmates. Garden City, N.Y.: Doubleday, **1961.**

A biased collection of essays "on the social situation of mental patients and other inmates" that moves from organization to individual.

Although not explicit, the bias is vaguely antipsychiatric and anti-medical, but in this it gathers some of its considerable strength.

18.   **Golding, W.** Lord of the Flies. New York: Putnam, **1964.**

A literary account of powerful group dynamics which at this point is part of the popular culture. That the group is composed of children does not lessen the impact.

19.   **Harrow, M., Astrachan, B.M., Tucker, G.J., et al.** The T-group and study group laboratory experiences. J. Soc. Psychol. 85: 225–237, **1971.**

Description of various experiential group learning situations. Useful as a way of understanding how the theories are validated.

20.   **Jaques, E.** Social systems as a defense against persecutory and depressive anxiety, pp. 478–498. In: New Directions in Psychoanalysis. Eds.: M. Klein, P. Heimann, and R.E. Money-Kyrle. New York: Basic Books, **1955.**

An attempt to illustrate and define how the mechanisms of projective and introjective identification operate in linking individual and social behavior. More specifically, the author hypothesizes that a defense against psychotic anxiety is a crucial element in group cohesion.

21.   **Kernberg, O.** Toward an integrative theory of hospital treatment, pp. 241–275. In: Object Relations Theory and Clinical Psychoanalysis. New York: Aronson, **1976.**

An extension of the author's well-known work on object relations into group and organizational dynamics. The first analyst to make a genuine effort to integrate administrative and clinical concerns in the theory of hospital psychiatry.

22.   **Main, T.F.** The ailment. Br. J. Med. Psychol. 30: 129–145, **1957.**

This paper has probably helped more staff members out of jams with colleagues and patients than any other. The author shows the impact of individual psychopathology on a group's (ward staff) functioning.

23.   **Menzies, I.** A case-study in the functioning of social systems as a defense against anxiety, pp. 281–312. In: Group Relations Reader. Eds.: A.D. Coleman and W.H. Bexton. San Rafael, CA.: Associates Printing and Publishing, **1975.**

Somewhat like Jaques above, but focusing on nursing staff in a general hospital. Considers the functional as well as dysfunctional aspects of the methods used by nursing staffs to alleviate anxiety.

24. **Rice, A.K.** Learning or Leadership. London: Tavistock Publications, **1963.** Also: Selections, pp. 71–158. In: Group Relations Reader. Eds.: A.D. Coleman and W.H. Bexton. San Rafael, CA: Associates Printing and Publishing, **1975.**

A full description of the rationale, method, and process of a group relations conference, established primarily to study authority relations in groups.

9. SOCIAL AND CULTURAL FACTORS IN THE ROLE OF MENTAL ILLNESS

Victor Lidz, Ph.D.

Human life is social life. Human individuals inevitably live in complex social environments, sharing an intricate symbolic culture with communities of others. The social nature of life necessarily affects the totality of the self or personality, even its most intimately interior zones. The very individuality of each human personality can be richly understood only as an outcome of social process, as a unique combination of relational capacities, purposes, standards, and identities. Personality is in key respects an internalization of elements provided by the social and cultural life-world. Disciplined knowledge of culture and society therefore contributes a fundamental and irreducible. dimension to the study of personality and its functioning.

As a topic of research, mental illness fully reflects the heuristic value of this theoretical premise. Social scientific research has by now been able to shed light on quite diverse phenomena of mental illness. Social and cultural factors at a variety of levels of organization—e.g., from general values stressing specific kinds of activities, abilities, and relationships, to the institutions of social class, community, and moral custom, to the interactive patterns of family life—have been implicated in the genesis of mental illness of several types. Moreover, mental illness seems in all societies to be a source of social disturbances sufficient to call out specialized modes of social control. Everywhere there is a role of mental illness, but one that is articulated with roles of normality and other modes of deviance, and with roles of treatment and informal socioemotional support, in highly variable ways. Hence the social and personal consequences of mental illnesses, even of given nosological types, are under institutional variation. Mental illness must itself be viewed as in part normatively organized social process, involving the role-related reactions of many independent actors, as well as being the "breakdown" of an individual person.

50

To convey the foregoing perspective on mental illness, I have assembled readings under several distinct headings. First, I have listed a core group of classic works to represent the general analytic frameworks of sociology and anthropology as they bear on the sociocultural aspects of personality, individuality, and mental illness and its control. These core readings set forth the conceptual schemata within which the remaining works take on sharper significance. A second section presents works that demonstrate, with respect to various societies, how fundamentally human personalities are shaped by the normative standards of particular cultures and social structures—and by the stresses they generate. As well as the cross-cultural variability in human personality, these readings are intended to convey still more fundamentally the cultural and institutional makeup of personality under all circumstances—including the clinical encounter within our own society. The third section consists of leading studies that have explored the variations in types and rates of mental illness in association with such factors as value-pattern, community integration, class structure, and family organization. The fourth section brings together recent studies bearing on the role-relationships through which social control of mental illness is exercised by the society at large. The main focus of the readings, as of current controversies, is the mental hospital. Its historical origins, its legitimacy in terms of broad social values, its social organization, and recent efforts to supplant it are examined sociologically. A final section is directed in a more tentative way toward problems that are less well codified in the literature but which appear to be crucial. Given the widely reported finding that only modest portions of personality disorders are effectively brought into psychiatric treatment, it seems important to have more knowledge of the forms of social control that are active within the broader community, their strengths, vulnerabilities, and relations to normal treatment. I have listed a number of works that seem to give valuable insight into these aspects of the role of mental illness.

In constructing the entire reading list, I have chosen works that seem to develop the implications of fundamental social scientific perspectives for the understanding of phenomena of mental illness. I have tried also to select studies that all provide linkage with the lists covering family, group dynamics, epidemiology, milieu therapy, and community psychiatry without overlapping them unduly. The reader should hold in mind that many works in those areas complement and extend the perspectives incorporated in the following list.

SOCIOCULTURAL THEORY

1.   ***Durkheim, E.** Suicide: A Study in Sociology. Glencoe, IL: Free Press, **1951**. (Original French edition, **1897**.)

Develops the sociological method of treating *rates* of suicide—or by extension other forms of deviant conduct—as "social facts" indicative of basic conditions of society. Discusses anomie, egoism, and altruism as "pathological" conditions that can elevate rates of suicide or other types of deviance, including mental illness.

2. **Evans-Pritchard, E.E.** Witchcraft, Oracles and Magic Among the Azande. London: Oxford University Press, **1965**.

Cultural beliefs and social institutions surrounding the practice and control of witchcraft, divination, and magic in East African tribal society. The kinds of motives and social situations that lead to use of witchcraft and magic. The role of witch-doctor and the grounds of popular faith in it.

3. ***Mead, M.** Sex and Temperament in Three Primitive Societies. New York: Morrow, **1935**.

Socialization and personality development among three New Guinea tribes. Emphasis on variation in male and female roles and in relations between the sexes. The malleability of human personality under variation in cultural patterns.

4. **Merton, R.K.** Continuities in the theory of reference groups and social structure, pp. 281–386. In: Social Theory and Social Structure. Ed.: R.K. Merton. Glencoe, IL: Free Press, **1957**. (Available in **1969** edition.)

The kinds of relationships with social groups through which individuals take on standards for judging their own conduct and the conduct of others. Important for understanding the complexity of group environments affecting personal orientation and conduct.

5. ***Parsons, T.** The Social System. New York: Free Press, **1951**.

Basic concepts for the analysis of social interaction. Emphasizes that personal motivation is integrated through normative institutions. Reciprocal normative expectations are treated as the basis for stabilizing social relationships. Chapter VI on socialization, Chapter VII on the genesis of deviant motivation and its social control, and Chapter X on the doctor-patient role-relationship are key.

6. ***Parsons, T.** Social Structure and Personality. New York: Free Press, **1964**.

Essays that integrate psychoanalysis with sociological theory, focusing on concepts of object-relations and social structure. Applications of theory to family relationships, processes of socialization, stages in the life cycle, oedipal themes in culture, and institutions of social control, including medicine.

7. **Parsons, T. and Bales, R.F., with the collaboration of Olds, J., Zelditch, M., Jr., and Slater, P.E.** Family, Socialization, and Interaction Process. Glencoe, IL: Free Press, **1955.**

Social structure of the nuclear family as a template for the processes of socialization of children. The organization and dynamic mechanisms of the personality treated as motivational entities developed through interpersonal relationships centering in the family. Distortions or breakdowns in family functioning and their possible consequences for personal pathology.

8. **Simmel, G.** On Individuality and Social Forms: Selected Ratings. Ed.: D.N. Levine. Chicago: University of Chicago Press, **1971.**

Exceptionally insightful writings about the qualities of social relationships in modern societies. Exchange, authority, conflict, sociable relations in modern times. Modern individualism and rationalism; the complexity of modern social settings. The stresses engendered by the loss of communal ties and the impersonality of modern urban life.

9. ***Weber, M.** From Max Weber: Essays in Sociology. Ed.: H.H. Gerth and C.W. Mills. New York: Oxford University Press, **1946.**

Parts III and IV present key materials from Weber's studies of religion and social institutions: the ways of life of American Puritans, Prussian Junkers, Indian Brahmans, Confucian Mandarins. Treats variation in religious ethics, as embodied in the life-styles of leading status groups, as the key source of differences among civilizations regarding valued activities, modes of achievement, qualities of social relationships, and personal capacities.

CULTURE, SOCIAL ORDER, AND PERSONALITY IN COMPARATIVE PERSPECTIVE

10. ***Bellah, R.N.** Father and son in Christianity and Confucianism. In: Beyond Belief; Essays on Religion in a Post-Traditional World. R.N. Bellah. New York: Harper and Row, **1970.**

Reconsiders the relation between attention to Confucianism and Chinese family patterns. In its ethic of filiality, Chinese civilization accentuates the motivational complex of the latency period rather than the oedipal period emphasized in the West. The latency symbolism of filial piety is treated as a key to the general motivational patterns of Chinese society.

11. **Carstairs, G.M.** The Twice-Born: A Study of a Community of High-Caste Hindus. Bloomington, IN: Indiana University Press, **1957.**

Psychoanalytic and ethnographic study of members of Brahmin, Rajput, and Bania caste groups in a North India town. Interview and projective test materials as well as selected autobiographies. Early socialization and the life course. Emphasis on general Indian motivational patterns of resignation, self-control, serenity in interpersonal relations, but also their adaptation to the life circumstances of the different castes.

12. *Doi, T. The Anatomy of Dependence. San Francisco: Kodansha International, Ltd., 1973.

The sociopsychological pattern of *amae* (loved dependence or being indulged as a loved or admired person) as a fundament of interpersonal relations in Japan. The elaborations of *amae* in various Japanese institutions, e.g., family, business firm, political agency. The distortions of *amae* as a source of personal pathologies in Japan and as a feature of many Japanese social problems.

13. *Levy, R.I. Tahitians: Mind and Experience in the Society Islands. Chicago: University of Chicago Press, 1973.

Ethonography of psychological experience among Society islanders. Patterns of thinking and feeling, styles of interpersonal relations, and the nature of moral conduct. Socialization, maturation in social roles, and the maintenance of personal integration in Tahitian culture and society.

14. Parsons, T. Certain primary sources and patterns of aggression in the social structure of the Western world. In: Essays in Sociological Theory (rev. ed.). Ed.: T. Parsons. New York: Free Press, 1954.

Argues that the strongly activistic values of Western civilization, when frustrated, generate exceptionally aggressive patterns of reaction. Aggression as deeply seated in Western culture and the patterns of personal motivation that it values.

SOCIAL STRUCTURE AND RATES OF MENTAL DISORDER

15. Carstairs, G.M. and Kapur, R.L. The Great Universe of Kota: Stress, Change and Mental Disorder in an Indian Village. Berkeley: University of California Press, 1976.

Rates of psychiatric symptoms and needs among three caste groups of a village in Southwest India, based on a sample survey using a schedule adapted to Indian culture. Emphasis on the high levels of psychiatric need, the relations between symptomatology and caste institutions, and the pathogenic stress of recent social change.

16. **Hendin, H.** Suicide and Scandinavia. New York: Grune and Stratton, **1964.**

    A sociological as well as clinical psychiatric study. Suicide rates are elevated in Denmark by social patterns establishing strong dependency motives and in Sweden by frustration of institutionalized performance expectations and trouble in gaining emotional comfort from others. Rare suicides in Norway follow more traumatic life histories and guilt over antisocial behavior.

17. ***Hollingshead, A.B. and Redlich, F.C.** Social Class and Mental Illness: A Community Study. New York: Wiley, **1958.**

    Rates and types of mental illness in the population of New Haven as they vary by social class. Uses simple scheme of class analysis, but does show the concentration of mental illness, especially the psychoses, at the bottom of the class structure. The different kinds of psychiatric care and treatment provided to the higher and lower classes.

18. ***Scheper-Hughes, N.** Saints, Scholars and Schizophrenics. Mental Illness in Rural Ireland. Berkeley: University of California Press, **1979.**

    The decline of the rural Irish way of life into dispirited anomie. The culture of community and family relations that engenders an ascetic, affectively constricted personality structure. The passivity, inferiority, and isolation with which males especially must often make stressful life-course decisions. The embedding of an elevated rate of schizophrenic withdrawal and of depression in a general sociocultural pattern.

19. **Srole, L., Langner, T.S., Michael, S.T., et al.** Mental Health in the Metropolis: The Midtown Manhattan Study. New York: McGraw-Hill, **1962.** (Also available from New York University Press, **1978.**)

    Psychiatric profile of the population of midtown Manhattan based on a large-scale interdisciplinary survey. Focus on socioeconomic status, but also on age groups, marital status, religious and national backgrounds, and length of city residence. The large amounts of personal pathology that are not brought into psychiatric treatment.

THE MENTAL HOSPITAL AND MEDICALIZATION OF MENTAL DISORDER

20. ***Estroff, S.E.** Making It Crazy: An Ethnography of Psychiatric Clients in an American Community. Berkeley: University of California Press, **1981.**

    Participant-observer study of an outpatient program for the chronically disturbed. The many discontents of the sociopsychophysiological experience and the role of taking antipsychotic medications. The disorganized and stigmatized life arrangements maintained by most of the patients. The limitations of a program providing little social and emotional support.

21.   **Foucault, M.** Madness and Civilization: A History of Insanity in the Age of Reason. New York: Random House, **1965.**

The transformation of the social role of the insane wrought by the Enlightenment. As European society became more thoroughly devoted to ideals of Reason, madness was perceived as a greater and more unified social threat. Hospitals were established to confine the insane. Professionals were given new moral authority to treat madness totalistically. The new conceptions of and treatments for insanity devised under the cultural presuppositions of Enlightened devotion to Reason.

22.   **Fox, R.C.** The medicalization and demedicalization of American society. In: Essays in Medical Sociology: Journeys into the Field. Ed.: R.C. Fox. New York: Wiley, **1979.**

Current social dilemmas and public controversies about the boundaries of medical institutions and role-relationships in sensitive areas of practice. Emphasis on the ways in which boundary issues have been activating values deeply seated in American culture.

23.   **Murphy, J.M.** Psychiatric labeling in crosscultural perspective. Science 191: 1019–1028, **1976.**

Juxtaposes recent work on invidious "labeling" as a factor in the social genesis of mental illness with cross-cultural research on the social roles of psychologically disturbed persons. Emphasizes that all societies provide special roles for the "mentally ill."

24.   ***Rothman, D.J.** The Discovery of the Asylum: Social Order and Disorder in the New Republic. Boston: Little, Brown, **1971.**

The related social movements in Jacksonian America through which prisons, insane asylums, almshouses, orphanages, and reformatories were founded as public responses to various forms of deviance. The anxiety raised in the public by insanity, crime, and economic dependence when seen as indications that the emerging social order was prone to demoralization, corruption, and breakdown. The humanitarian program of asylum-based moral treatment for the insane and the forces that brought it into decline.

25.   ***Stanton, A.H. and Schwartz, J.S.** The Mental Hospital: A Study of

Institutional Participation in Psychiatric Illness and Treatment. New York: Basic Books, **1954.**

Ethnography of the disturbed ward at Chestnut Lodge. The ongoing structure of role relationships in the hospital and its impact on patients' care and treatment. Events in the social life of the ward that can affect the emotional states of all the patients, even producing epidemiclike waves of symptoms. Ways in which individual psychotherapy may be hindered or advanced by qualities of personal relationships on the ward.

SOCIAL SUPPORT AND SOCIAL CONTROL IN THE COMMUNITY

26.   **Anderson, E.** A Place on the Corner: Identity and Rank Among Black Streetcorner Men. Chicago: University of Chicago Press, **1978.**

The group of lower-class Black men who frequent a bar in Chicago, including subgroups of employed "regular" citizens, street "hoodlums," and "wineheads." The tactics of interaction by which members place on another in the status orders of their group and of metropolitan society generally. The relationships of caring and mutual support through which members assist one another in coping with personal problems and stresses.

27.   ***Erikson, K.T.** Everything in Its Path; Destruction of Community in the Buffalo Creek Flood. New York: Simon and Schuster, **1976.**

The loss of communal relationships and personal capacities to enter into them in the aftermath of a local disaster. The adverse factors in the history of the community that left people vulnerable to feelings of isolation and helplessness after the flood had disrupted their life routines. The personal pathologies suffered for years afterwards.

28.   **Kadushin, C.** Why People Go to Psychiatrists. New York: Atherton, **1969.**

Questionnaire study of outpatients at 10 psychiatric clinics in New York, focusing on how they came to seek treatment as a way of dealing with personal problems. The key role of a large but loosely structured reference group of laymen who favor a psychiatric view of personal difficulties and modes of treatment. Advice to clinics about how to present resources effectively to the mentally disturbed.

29.   **Lemert, E.** Human Deviance, Social Problems, and Social Control (2nd ed.). Englewood Cliffs, NJ: Prentice-Hall, **1972.**

Sociocultural factors in the genesis and stabilization of deviant conduct, emphasizing the reactions of others as confirming individuals in deviant roles. Chapter 15 poignantly discusses the informal group plotting that often arises in response to—and then serves to confirm—the paranoia of a member.

30. ***Wiseman, J.P.** Stations of the Lost: The Treatment of Skid Row Alcoholics. Chicago: University of Chicago Press, **1970.**

The life circumstances of skid row alcoholics in a large West Coast city. The relationships in which skid-rowers become involved with police, courts, jails, social workers, mental hospitals, and home missions. Important analysis of how skid-rowers undermine rehabilitative programs of various kinds, including psychiatric ones.

10. PSYCHIATRIC EPIDEMIOLOGY

JAMES H. REICH, M.D.

MYRNA M. WEISSMAN, PH.D.

Epidemiology is the study of variations in the distribution of specific disorders in populations and the factors that influence that distribution. Epidemiologic studies can generate information on rates (prevalence and incidence); their variations by person, time and place; and risk factors that increase the probability of developing the disorder. Such information can potentially generate new ideas about etiology, pathogenesis, treatment, and prevention, and can provide insights to improve practice and planning for care.

In recent decades the scope of epidemiology has expanded markedly from its origins in the study of infectious disease to include studies of chronic conditions such as heart disease and cancer. More recently, the scope of chronic disease epidemiology also has expanded to include psychiatric disorders. The articles cited here are representative of these developments.

Included are conceptual and methodologic reviews, cross-cultural studies to resolve diagnostic issues, and descriptive epidemiologic studies of children and of adults. Variations in rates associated with risk factors are examined, including genetic familial risk factors, life events, and social class. The implications of epidemiologic findings for public health are also examined.

CONCEPTUAL AND METHODOLOGICAL REVIEWS

1. **Gruenberg, E.M.** Science of human behavior: Quantitative and experimental methods in psychiatry, pp. 531–548. In: Epidemiology. CTP III, Vol. 1, **1980.**

   This is an introduction to the basic concepts of epidemiology—morbidity, incidence, and prevalence.

2. **Robins, L.N.** Psychiatric epidemiology. Arch. Gen. Psychiatry 35: 697–702, **1978.**

Psychiatric epidemiologic techniques can provide guidance for social policy makers. Improvement of diagnostic interview methods, instruments to assess environmental factors, studies examining the relationship between physical and mental disorders, and cross-national psychiatric diagnostic comparisons are required.

3. *Weissman, M.M. and Klerman, G.L. Epidemiology of mental disorders: Emerging trends in the United States. Arch. Gen. Psychiatry 35: 705-712, **1978.**

A historical review of United States psychiatric epidemiology. Advances in psychopathology, genetics, and psychopharmacology have shifted the focus of psychiatric epidemiology from studies of overall psychosocial impairment to epidemiologic studies of rates and risks of discrete psychiatric disorders.

DESCRIPTIVE EPIDEMIOLOGIC STUDIES OF CHILDREN

4. Gould, M.S., Wansch-Hitzig, R., and Dohrenwend, B.P. Estimating the prevalence of childhood psychopathology: A critical review. J. Am. Acad. Child Psychiatry 20: 462-476, **1981.**

A review of the psychiatric epidemiologic studies of children suggests an estimated prevalence of less than 1 percent for psychotic disorders and about 12 percent for "clinical maladjustment" for a United States population. Before puberty male cases outnumber female 2:1. This ratio reverses after puberty.

5. *Rutter, M., Cox, A., Tupling, C., et al. Attainment and adjustment in two geographic areas. I: The prevalence of psychiatric disorders. Br. J. Psychiatry 126: 493-509, **1975.**

This community survey documents that twice as many disturbed 10-year-olds were found in London as compared to the Isle of Wight. The increase in London was greatest for females, and differences were attributed to the particular living conditions of London.

DESCRIPTIVE EPIDEMIOLOGIC STUDIES OF ADULTS

6. Blazer, D. and Williams, C.D. Epidemiology of dysphoria and depression in an elderly population. Am. J. Psychiatry 137: 439-444, **1980.**

A community survey of 997 elderly people yielded a current prevalence of about 15 percent for dysphoric symptoms and 2 percent for *DSM III* Major Depression. Only 1 percent of the population were seeing mental health counselors.

7. **Taylor, M.A. and Abrams, R.** The prevalence of schizophrenia: A reassessment using modern diagnostic criteria. Am. J. Psychiatry 135: 945–948, **1978.**

Based on a review of the literature on schizophrenia, the prevalence of schizophrenia has been stable since Kraepelin (1893). Higher prevalence rates, such as reported in the 1977 United States government statistics are only found when broad diagnostic criteria are used.

8. ***Weissman, M.M. and Klerman, G.L.** Sex differences and the epidemiology of depression. Arch. Gen. Psychiatry 34: 98–111, **1977.**

Substantial evidence is presented that the reported high rate of female depression in clinic and community survey data is a real finding and not an artifact of reporting bias or the help-seeking behavior of women. Possible explanations for the sex ratio differences are discussed.

CROSS-CULTURAL STUDIES TO RESOLVE DIAGNOSTIC ISSUES

9. ***Cooper, J.E., Kendell, R.E., Gurland, B.J., et al.** Psychiatric Diagnosis in New York and London: A Comparative Study of Mental Hospital Admissions. Institute of Psychiatry (Maudsley Monographs No. 20). London: Oxford University Press, **1972.**

Using a standardized diagnostic scheme, no difference in rates of schizophrenia or affective disorders were found in New York and London. Different diagnostic criteria explained previous reports of differences.

10. ***Sartorius, N., Jablensky, A., and Shapiro, R.** Preliminary communication: Two year follow-up of the patients included in the WHO International Pilot Study of Schizophrenia. Psychol. Med. 7: 529–541, **1977.**

This study demonstrated that schizophrenic diagnoses were stable over a two-year interval. Outcomes were highly variable and, in general, better than expected. Outcomes for schizophrenics in developing countries were significantly better than those in developed countries.

11. ***Strauss, J.S., Carpenter, W.T., and Bartko, J.J.** A review of some findings from the International Pilot Study of Schizophrenia, pp. 74–88. In: Annual Review of the Schizophrenic Syndrome, Vol. 4. Ed.: R. Cancro. New York: Brunner/Mazel, **1974–1975.**

Analysis of the results of standardized interviews yielded a core group of schizophrenics whose symptoms were consistent across cultures. Schizophrenic subgroups were not stable across cultures.

VARIATIONS IN RATES ASSOCIATED WITH RISK FACTOR

12. ***Robins, L.N.** Sturdy childhood predictors of adult outcomes: Replications from longitudinal studies, pp. 219–236. In: Stress and Mental Disorders. Ed.: J.E. Barrett, R.M. Rose, and G.L. Klerman. New York: Raven Press, **1979.**

Three longitudinal studies on antisocial behavior in males are compared. Adult antisocial behavior is best predicted by antisocial behavior in childhood and a history of antisocial behavior in the subject's parents. At least 50 percent of child antisocial behavior do not progress to the adult syndrome.

13. **Rounsaville, B.J., Weissman, M.M., Kleber, H., et al.** Heterogeneity of psychiatric diagnosis in treated opiate addicts. Arch. Gen. Psychiatry 39: 161–166, **1982.**

Rates for major and minor depression, chronic mood disorders, alcoholism, and antisocial personality were substantially higher in addicts than in subjects identified in community surveys. Single marital status was a general risk factor for psychopathology.

INCLUDING GENETIC-FAMILIAL RISK FACTORS

14. **Heston, L.L.** Psychiatric disorders in foster home–reared children of schizophrenic mothers. Br. J. Psychiatry 112: 819–825, **1966.**

This report investigates familial versus genetic determinants of schizophrenia. Children of schizophrenics and matched children of normal parents, all adopted at birth and never having known their biological parents, were interviewed. About 16 percent of children of schizophrenics and 0 percent of children of normals developed schizophrenia.

15. **Kety, S.S.** Observations on genetic and environmental influences in the etiology of mental disorders from studies on adoptees and their relatives. In: Genetics of Neurological Psychiatric Disorders. Eds.: S.S. Kety, L.P. Rowland, R.L. Sedman, et al. New York: Raven Press, **in press.**

Genetic contributions to both suicide and schizophrenia were confirmed by studies examining adopted children of schizophrenics raised by nonschizophrenics and their half-siblings raised by schizophrenic parents.

16. **Kidd, K.K. and Matthysse, S.** Research designs for the study of gene-environment interactions in psychiatric disorders. Arch. Gen. Psychiatry 35: 925–932, **1978.**

The authors examine the various ways in which genetic differences can manifest themselves, review mathematical models used for testing genetic hypotheses, and make specific recommendations for future research on gene-environment interactions.

17. **Mendlewicz, J. and Rainer, J.D.** Adoption study supporting genetic transmission in manic-depressive illness. Nature 268: 327–329, **1977.**

Greater psychopathology, especially affective illness, was found in biologic parents of manic-depressive children (when compared to adoptive parents) suggesting that manic-depressive disorder breeds true.

18. ***Wender, P.H., Rosenthal, D., Kety, S.S. et al.** Cross fostering. Arch. Gen. Psychiatry 30: 121–128, **1974.**

This report of a cross-fostering study examines the outcome of 28 Danish adoptees without schizophrenic relatives who were raised by schizophrenic foster parents. No increased incidence of schizophrenia in adoptees raised by schizophrenics was found when compared to a matched control group.

INCLUDING LIFE EVENTS

19. ***Brenner, M.H.** Influence of the social environment on psychopathology: The historic perspective, pp. 161–177. In: Stress and Mental Disorders. Eds.: J.E. Barrett, R.M. Rose, and G.L. Klerman. New York: Raven Press, **1979.**

This study examines the effects of national economic changes on changes in national mental and physical health. Rapid economic growth (a positive factor) and increased unemployment and short-term income losses (negative factors) were significantly related to pathologic indices.

20. ***Dohrenwend, B.S. and Dohrenwend, B.P.** Life stress and illness: Formulation of the issues, pp. 1–27. In: Stressful Life Events and their Contexts. Eds.: B.S. Dohrenwend and B.P. Dohrenwend. New York: Prodist, **1981.**

The literature on life events is reviewed. Although the correlations are small, the relation between life events and psychiatric illness is definite, as is the relation between physical illness and poor emotional health.

21. **Myers, J.K., Lindenthal, J.J., Pepper, M.P., et al.** Life events and mental status: A longitudinal study. J. Health Soc. Behav. 13: 398–406, **1972.**

The relationship between changes in life events and psychiatric symptomatology was prospectively examined in a community sample over two years, and an association was found. Only changes involving entrance of people into the social field (births, adoptions, marriages) did not increase symptomatology.

INCLUDING SOCIAL CLASS

22. *Hollingshead, A.B. and Redlich, F.C.* Class positions and types of mental illness, pp. 220–250. In: Social Class and Mental Illness: A Community Study. New York: Wiley, **1958.**

This chapter examines the relationship between social class and mental illness in New Haven in 1955. More psychotic disorders were found in the lower social classes, and more neurotic illnesses were found in the higher social classes.

23. *Kohn, M.L.* The interaction of social class and other factors in the etiology of schizophrenia. Am. J. Psychiatry 133: 177–180, **1976.**

The author proposes an interaction model of genetics, stress, and adoptiveness for the development of schizophrenia and postulates that living in the lower social classes decreases ability to adapt.

24. **Turner, R.J. and Wagonfeld, M.O.** Occupational mobility and schizophrenia: An assessment of the social causation and social selection hypotheses. Am. Sociol. Rev. 32: 104–113, **1967.**

This study replicates the finding that there are disproportionately more schizophrenics in the lower social classes. Relative contributions of social selection (failure of patients to reach parental social class levels), social drift (downward social movement by the patient after onset of schizophrenic symptoms), and social causation (schizophrenia as a result of low social class) are examined. Social selection, they conclude, accounts for the bulk of phenomena.

IMPLICATIONS OF EPIDEMIOLOGIC
FINDS FOR PUBLIC HEALTH

25. **Leighton, A.H.** Research directions in psychiatric epidemiology. Psychol. Med. 9: 235–247, **1979.**

The high current prevalence rates of mental illness (minimum 20 percent) can no longer be doubted. Priorities in mental health care should be directed to the treatable, chronic, and severely impaired emotionally ill. The empirical use of epidemiologic studies to define discrete syndromes, symptom behavior, and disability can facilitate this process.

26.   ***Regier, D.A., Goldberg, I.D., and Taube, C.A.** The de facto United States mental health services system. Arch. Gen. Psychiatry 35: 685–693, **1978.**

Based on United States population data, only 21 percent of those needing mental health care received it from a mental health professional; the remainder were treated by primary care physicians, general hospitals, or not at all. It was estimated that 15 percent of the United States population were in need of help for mental problems.

11. HISTORY OF PSYCHIATRY

STANLEY W. JACKSON, M.D.

While the last half century has seen a considerable increase in interest in the history of psychiatry and a phenomenal growth in its literature, the field still lacks a sound textbook. As a result, a large proportion of the readings are drawn from the periodical literature, with some admixture of chapters from books. To stay within the limits set for this bibliography, primary sources will be infrequently cited. On the other hand, the secondary sources used will usually serve to lead the interested reader to the important primary sources via the valuable references on which they are based.

For 40 years Zilboorg and Henry's *A History of Medical Psychology* (reprinted more recently in unrevised form, but with Henry's name and contributions deleted) has been a readable and romantically entertaining textbook, but a seriously misleading one; and other authors have drawn heavily on this work to produce texts (not to mention innumerable articles) that were equally misleading without being as entertaining. Zilboorg badly misrepresented the Western Europe witchcraft craze by promulgating the view that persons accused of witchcraft were usually mentally ill and that their persecution and harmful treatment were that era's characteristic ways of dealing with the mentally ill. In considering the late eighteenth century he committed numerous historical inaccuracies in picturing Philippe Pinel as dramatically striking off the chains of the mad in Paris, in contrast to the much less colorful facts that constitute just as impressive an accomplishment. He also frequently committed the "presentistic" error of viewing a theory or a practice as an instance of anticipatory wisdom on the path to the psychoanalytic views and practices of the twentieth century. Zilboorg continues to hold a leading position among the romantic distortionists who tend to picture matters in the history of psychiatry as worse than they probably were, to identify heroes who came along to set things right, and to trace how things got better and better until they reached the glorious present.

Unfortunately, the writing of the history of psychiatry in recent years has been cursed by another group, the conspiracy theorists, who have been just as effective in misleading students of the field. These authors seem to have all the answers before they even start to look for any historical data and are often not above distorting what they do find to suit their pre-existing conclusions. They apparently come from one position or another in some modern polemic, look back and suggest that things were not so bad for the mad after all, and then portray the emergence of a group of professional oppressors or oppressive professionals to persecute the mad, to take away their freedom and lock them up, and to develop the world of the institutionalized mad that has come so to trouble the twentieth century.

1. **Ackerknecht, E.H.** The history of the drug treatment of mental diseases. Trans. Stud. Coll. Physicians Phila. Ser. 5, 1: 161–170, **1979.**

   A leading medical historian brings his encyclopedic knowledge to bear on the history of psychopharmacology.

2. **Braceland, F.J.** Kraepelin, his system and his influence. Am. J. Psychiatry 113: 871–876, **1957.**

   Valuable study, complementary to that by Havens, of the "father of descriptive psychiatry."

3. **Carlson, E.T. and Dain, N.** The psychotherapy that was moral treatment. Am. J. Psychiatry 117: 519–524, **1960.**

   Excellent outline of the orientation and practices that emerged as "moral treatment" at the end of the eighteenth century, were central in early nineteenth century asylums, and bear a significant relationship to twentieth century milieu therapy.

4. **Chamberlain, A.S.** Early mental hospitals in Spain. Am. J. Psychiatry 123: 143–149, **1966.**

   An illuminating study of the founding of seven hospitals for the care and protection of the mentally ill in fifteenth century Spain.

5. **Deutsch, A.** The Mentally Ill in America: A History of their Care and Treatment from Colonial Times (2nd ed.). New York: Columbia University Press, **1949.**

   Still the best coverage of the history of American psychiatry.

6. **Diethelm, O. and Heffernan, T.F.** Felix Platter and psychiatry. J. Hist. Behav. Sci. 1: 10–23, **1965.**

   Valuable study of an important medical author's clinical and theoretical perspectives on mental disorders. In brief form it provides a sense of sixteenth century views and of seventeenth century thought prior to the waning of the humoral theory.

7. **Ducey, C. and Simon, B.** Ancient Greece and Rome, pp. 1–38. In: World History of Psychiatry. Ed.: J.G. Howells. New York: Brunner/Mazel, **1975.**

Surveys classic Greek literature in terms of four models of mind, mental disturbance, and therapy—Homeric (epic), tragic, Platonic (philosophical), and Hippocratic (medical)—and then surveys madness in Roman civilization through legal writings, literary works, and philosophy. While the psychodynamic analysis of Roman society has its questionable features, the authors otherwise provide a very valuable orientation to a complex mass of material and to its relevance for the history of psychiatry.

8.   **Ellenberger, H.F.** The Discovery of the Unconscious: The History and Evolution of Dynamic Psychiatry. New York: Basic Books, **1970.**

A history of psychological healing. Surveys primitive healing, certain Greco-Roman practices, and "the cure of souls." Then, beginning with Gassner, Mesmer, and Puysegur in the eighteenth century, traces "the first dynamic psychiatry" from exorcism through mesmerism and magnetism to the hypnotism of Charcot, Liebeault, and Bernheim in the late nineteenth century. Latter portion devoted to the "new dynamic psychiatry" with emphasis on the work of Janet, Freud, Adler, and Jung.

9.   **Grob, G.N.** Mental Institutions in America: Social Policy to 1875. New York: Free Press, **1973.**

10.   **Grob, G.N.** Mental Illness and American Society: 1875–1940. Princeton: Princeton University Press, **1983.**

In these two companion volumes a gifted social historian makes a superb contribution toward a more faithful perspective on a society's concerns about the mad and its various efforts to care for or otherwise deal with this set of persons. While serving as an admirable corrective for the unfortunate distortions of the conspiracy theorists, these volumes still provide a troubling picture with little basis for a profession to rejoice or feel complacent about its past. They also clearly indicate the extent to which a society at large, its politicians, and its public officials share with the various professionals the responsibility for the situation.

11.   **Guttmacher, M.S.** A historical outline of the criminal law's attitude toward mental disorder. Arch. Crim. Psychodynam. 4: 647–670, **1961.**

Traces this theme from ancient times to modern times.

12.   **Havens, L.L.** Emil Kraepelin. J. Nerv. Ment. Dis. 141: 16–28, **1965.**

Fine study of a psychiatrist who has had a lasting influence on twentieth-century psychiatry.

13.   **Henry, G.W.** Organic mental diseases, general paralysis, pp. 526–551.

In: A History of Medical Psychology. Eds.: G. Zilboorg and G.W. Henry. New York: W.W. Norton, **1941.**

Outlines the history of general paresis of the insane. Admirably illustrates the paradigm for biological psychiatry.

14.   **Hunter, R., and Macalpine, I.** Three Hundred Years of Psychiatry, 1535–1860. London: Oxford University Press, **1963.**

An excellent source book composed of well over 300 English language selections, including translations, drawn from both printed and manuscript sources in the form of medical writings and numerous other relevant literatures. Further enhanced by the editors' invaluable commentaries with each selection.

15.   **Jackson, S.W.** Galen—On mental disorders. J. Hist. Behav. Sci. 5: 365–384, **1969.**

Outlines Galen's (131–201 A.D.) physiology and pathology and then his descriptive, theoretical, and therapeutic views on madness and related disorders. Helpful guide to the medical psychology of the ancient world and valuable for understanding writings on mental disorders for many centuries thereafter, even into the seventeenth century.

16.   **Jackson, S.W.** Unusual mental states in medieval Europe. I. Medical syndromes of mental disorder: 400–1100 A.D. J. Hist Med. Allied Sci. 27:262–297, **1972.**

Outlines the medical views—descriptive, theoretical, and therapeutic— on mental disorders that were significant in early medieval Europe and that were to be influential for over a millenium. Some perspective on the medicine of the era is provided, and then the main influences (Soranus, Galen, Oribasius, Alexander of Tralles, Paul of Aegina) are drawn on to present the three traditional types of madness—phrenitis, melancholia, mania—and a series of other mental disorders of the era. The discussion considers these disturbances in contemporary context, relates them to the thought of subsequent centuries, and provides a sense of their probable connections with modern psychiatric thought.

17.   **Kroll, J.** A reappraisal of psychiatry in the Middle Ages. Arch. Gen. Psychiatry 29: 276–283, **1973.**

Corrects for the omissions and distortions that have tended to characterize the history of the care of the mentally ill in the medieval era. Effectively challenges the notion that the Inquisition was established to persecute witches, hysterics, and the mad and the tendency to focus on medieval insanity in terms of demonology.

18.   **Lidz, T.** Adolf Meyer and the development of American psychiatry. Am. J. Psychiatry 123: 320–332, **1966.**

A penetrating study of a man whose strong influence on American psychiatry often goes unappreciated.

19.   **Menninger, K.A., Mayman, M., and Pruyser, P.** A history of psychiatric classifications, pp. 419–489. In: The Vital Balance: The Life Process in Mental Health and Illness. K. Menninger, M. Mayman, and P. Pruyser. New York: Viking Press, **1963.**

Traces over 2,000 years of nosologies in very useful fashion.

20.   **Mora, G.** Historical and theoretical trends in psychiatry, pp. 4–98. In: CTP III. Vol. 1., **1980.**

While the section on the witchcraft craze is open to serious question, this is a very valuable overview. Especially noteworthy for the wide range of material given useful coverage and for its extensive bibliography.

21.   **Mora, G.** Vincenzo Chiarugi (1759–1820) and his psychiatric reform in Florence in the late eighteenth century. J. Hist. Med. Allied Sci. 14: 424–433, **1959.**

Excellent study of a relatively unsung figure in the late eighteenth-century emergence of moral treatment and specialized institutions for the care of the insane.

22.   **Rosen, G.** Madness in Society. New York: Harper and Row, **1968.**

Ranging from the ancient world to the recent past, this collection of essays provides a sense of the place of the mentally ill in various societies in different historical eras and gives special attention to sociocultural factors that seem to have been involved.

23.   **Schoeneman, T.J.** Criticisms of the psychopathological interpretation of witch hunts: A review. Am. J. Psychiatry 139: 1028–1032, **1982.**

Useful review that speaks for the growing number of historians who have successfully challenged the seriously misleading errors inherent in viewing the witchcraft craze of the fifteenth to seventeenth centuries as indicative of how the Western world conceived of and treated the mentally ill.

24.   **Scull, A.,** ed., Madhouses, Mad-Doctors, and Madmen: The Social History of Psychiatry in the Victorian Era. Philadelphia: University of Pennsylvania Press, **1981.**

Very useful collection of essays, mostly by social historians, dealing with aspects of psychiatric theory and practice in nineteenth-century England

and America. While the main emphases are on the emergence and development of asylums and on social themes of importance for the care of the mentally ill, valuable attention is also given to phrenology, conflicts between neurologists and psychiatrists, "mental hygiene," and forensic psychiatry.

25. **Tourney, G.** History of biological psychiatry in America. Am. J. Psychiatry. 126: 29–42, **1969.**

Traces the philosophy, methods, and theories of biological psychiatry from early nineteenth-century gross brain pathology to twentieth-century neurosciences and somatotherapies. Themes outlined are relevant to more than the American scene.

26. **Tuke, S.** Description of the Retreat. (Reprinted with an intro.) Eds.: R. Hunter and I. Macalpine. London: Dawsons of Pall Mall, **1964.**

A facsimile reprint of the 1813 edition enhanced by the editors' fine introduction, this volume recounts the history of the Retreat at York that was a central force in the emergence of moral treatment and an influence on many other such institutions.

27. **Weiner, D.B.** The apprenticeship of Philippe Pinel: A new document, 'Observations of Citizen Pussin on the insane.' Am. J. Psychiatry. 136: 1128–1134, **1979.**

28. **Weiner, D.B.** Health and mental health in the thought of Philippe Pinel: The emergence of psychiatry during the French Revolution, pp. 59–85. In: Healing and History: Essays for George Rosen. Ed.: C.E. Rosenberg. New York: Science History Publications, **1979.**

Long misrepresented as dramatically "striking the chains off the insane," in recent years Pinel's accomplishments have been shown to have been much less dramatic, but remarkable accomplishments nonetheless. A humane, conscientious physician who systematically studied his patients, he carefully introduced extensive and influential reforms into the care of the mad. As a leading Pinel scholar, Weiner has contributed to this corrective process, as shown by these two valuable works. For further useful information on Pinel, see Mora's "Historical and Theoretical Trends in Psychiatry."

PART II
PSYCHOPATHOLOGY

12. NOSOLOGY, PHENOMENOLOGY, AND DIAGNOSIS

Nancy C. Andreasen, M.D., Ph.D.
Frank T. Miller, M.D.

Systems for diagnosing and classifying people with mental illness have been described since classical times. The Greeks recognized and described disorders such as melancholia, mania, phrenitis, hysteria, and epilepsy. These illnesses were seen as due either to abnormalities in the brain or to imbalances in the body's humors, and most classification systems attempted to describe illnesses in terms of both their symptoms and their etiology. Mental illnesses are described in classical medical texts alongside other types of illnesses, and there appears to have been no stigma attached to them.

The relatively enlightened classical attitudes toward mental illness waned during the Middle Ages. The mentally ill were perceived as spiritually depraved and treated accordingly. Only during the late eighteenth and early nineteenth centuries, with the development of the Enlightenment and the great revolutions in America and France, did interest in mental illness return. Every human being, even one with a deranged mind, was seen as having inherent dignity and value. In France, Pinel freed the mentally ill from their chains, and Esquirol wrote detailed descriptions of the symptoms of patients under his care and attempted to classify them. In the United States, Benjamin Rush, who also signed the Declaration of Independence, wrote the first American textbook on mental illness.

Those seeds planted during the eighteenth century led to a great flowering of knowledge concerning phenomenology and nosology during the late nineteenth and early twentieth centuries. Two great traditions for studying the mentally ill emerged.

The first tradition, that of Emil Kraepelin, is closely allied with approaches used by other medical specialties. Kraepelin assumed that mental illnesses were discrete diseases with specific causes. Kraepelin himself was primarily a clinician interested in defining and describing those diseases on the basis of their symptoms and course. This led him to make the first major breakthrough in the nosology of mental illness since classical times: the separation of manic-depressive illness from dementia praecox, a distinction made primarily because the two disorders differed in onset, course, and outcome. Kraepelin wrote an influential series of textbooks that went through 11 editions. While Kraepelin emphasized phenomenology and classification, other members of his department, such as Brodmann, Alzheimer, and Nissl, searched for underlying causes in the brain.

The second major approach to phenomenology and psychopathology was contributed by Kraepelin's great contemporary, Sigmund Freud. While Freud began within the medical tradition represented by Kraepelin, his work in private practice gradually led him into new directions. As he struggled like any good doctor to cure the patients who came to him, who suffered from peculiar neurological complaints without physical basis and from problems with anxiety, he developed methods for understanding and treating their symptoms that stressed an emphasis on unconscious drives and underlying dynamics. Symptoms and their psychological causes, not diagnoses and their physical causes, became the major emphasis of the psychodynamic approach, described in detail under other headings in this book. For a time, particularly in the United States, the psychodynamic approach prevailed over the Kraepelinian approach, and consequently psychiatrists took very little interest in nosology and diagnosis. When attempts were made to study the diagnostic practices of psychiatrists, most of them led to the conclusion that psychiatric diagnoses tended to be unreliable and therefore not particularly useful.

During the late 1960s and early 1970s, several factors changed this situation, leading to a renaissance of interest in diagnosis that has been called the "neo-Kraepelinian revival." This revival has been led by clinicians at Washington University in St. Louis, a department that has always maintained a strong alliance with Kraepelinian traditions and with empirical British approaches to diagnosis.

The development of specific treatments was one major factor leading to a return of interest in diagnosis. As new drugs were developed during the 1950s and 1960s, for the first time psychiatrists had specific somatic therapies available. Some of these, such as lithium for mania or tricyclics for depression, appeared to be relatively specific. Consequently, it became very important to diagnose patients correctly, since diagnosis had important treatment implications. A second major factor was the development of large cross-national studies of diagnosis, such as the International Pilot Study of Schizophrenia (IPSS) or the US/UK Study. These large international studies indicated that American psychiatrists tended to be aberrant in comparison with their European colleagues. In particular, they tended to overdiagnose schizophrenia. When American diagnostic practices were compared with others throughout the world, only the Russians shared a similar broad conceptualization of schizophrenia. This led many American psychiatrists to re-examine American approaches to diagnosis and classification. A third factor, stimulated in part by the previous two, was the attempt to rethink techniques for describing and defining phenomenology and for making diagnoses. This led to the development of specific rating scales, structured interviews, and diagnostic criteria, many examples of which are described in the following references.

As a consequence of these factors, during the 1970s a fresh perspective emerged, leading to a "paradigm shift" with respect to the importance of diagnosis and classification. Careful empirical study of patients, emphasis on making a correct diagnosis, and interest in developing valid classification systems were not just intellectually respectable again: they were mandatory for doing good clinical work and good research. Further, with the emergence of the neurosciences during the 1970s, many investigators began to believe, like the members of Kraepelin's department, that the causes of major mental illnesses could be discovered through careful study of the neurochemistry and neuroanatomy of the brain. The new rating scales, structured interviews, and diagnostic criteria provide the foundation for this research, since they permit symptoms to be defined reliably and diagnoses to be made reliably. So widespread was the acceptance of this new approach to phenomenology that it led to the introduction of diagnostic criteria into *DSM-III*, thereby making attention to careful diagnosis mandatory for all American psychiatrists.

The following references provide a selection of articles that chronicle the development of the neo-Kraepelinian revival. Other portions of this book will provide information on psychodynamic aspects of phenomenology. The following references provide a selection of classic articles that stress the empirical approach to describing phenomenology and developing systems of classification.

HISTORY

1. ***Bleuler, E.** Dementia Praecox or the Group of Schizophrenias. Trans.: J. Zinkin. New York: International Universities Press, **1950.**

   The classic contribution by E. Bleuler in which he argues that schizophrenia or the splitting of the mental apparatus characterizes the syndrome or group of diseases that Kraepelin called *dementia praecox*.

2. **Jaspers, K.** General Psychopathology. Trans.: J. Hoenig and M.W. Hamilton. Manchester: Manchester University Press, **1963.**

   In this classic text the author attempts to define, clarify, and systematize our knowledge of psychopathology from a phenomenological perspective. The text is most successful when it discusses discrete psychopathological phenomena that can easily be located in this large text with the index and table of contents. The discussion of disease entities is more controversial, but has had a major influence on European psychiatry, principally through Kurt Schneider and Mayer-Gross.

3.   ***Kraepelin, E.** Dementia Praecox and Paraphrenia. Ed. by G.M. Robertson. Huntington, N.Y.: Krieger, **1971.**

This classic contribution has become increasingly important during the past decade; it is Kraepelin's most developed view of his concept of dementia praecox. Of special interest is the precision and liveliness of the clinical phenomenology. No one, with the possible exception of E. Bleuler, has done it better.

4.   ***Kraepelin, E.** Manic-Depressive Insanity and Paranoia. Edinburgh: E. and S. Livingstone, **1921.** (Also available from Arno, **1976.**)

Now available in facsimile, this classic text is best understood as a work in progress that documents Kraepelin's continually evolving views. It is as relevant today as it was in 1920.

5.   **Leonhard, K.** The Classification of Endogenous Psychoses (5th ed.). Ed.: E. Robins. New York: Wiley, **1979.**

The author describes his classification derived from clinical observations and family studies. The book is of interest for its challenge of the historic classifications of Kraepelin and Bleuler. See especially his discussion of cycloid psychoses.

6.   **Schneider, K.** Clinical Psychopathology. Trans.: M.W. Hamilton. New York: Grune and Stratton, **1959.**

A general textbook of psychopathology that contains Schneider's description of first-rank symptoms of schizophrenia. Although not rich with clinical detail, it is interesting reading for its approach to the psychoses and personality disorders.

NOSOLOGY AND CLASSIFICATION

7.   **Andreasen, N.C. and Spitzer, R.L.** Classification of psychiatric disorders, pp. 377–397. In: Handbook of Biological Psychiatry, Vol. 1. Eds.: H.M. van Praag, M.H. Lader, O.J. Rafaelson, et al. New York: M. Dekker, **1979.**

A review of the purpose and principles of classification with discussions of reliability, validity, and dimensional vs. typological classification.

8. **Blashfield, R.K. and Draguns, J.G.** Evaluative criteria for psychiatric classification. J. Abnorm. Psychol. 85: 140–150, **1976.**

Argues that prediction is the ultimate goal of psychiatric classification.

9. **Blashfield, R.K. and Draguns, J.G.** Toward a taxonomy of psycho-pathology: The purpose of psychiatric classification. Br. J. Psychiatry 129: 574–583, **1976.**

The authors argue that any biological classification or diagnostic system must be viewed as a historically determined reconciliation of different and often conflicting perspectives such as clinical, social, political, theoretical, scientific, and statistical. A provocative paper.

10. **Everitt, B.S.** Cluster analysis: A brief discussion of some of the problems. Br. J. Psychiatry 120: 143–145, **1972.**

In this report the author discusses the problems associated with cluster analysis, a widely used multivariate statistical method to develop new empirical classifications.

11. ***Everitt, B.S., Gourlay, A.J., and Kendell, R.E.** An attempt at validation of traditional psychiatric syndromes by cluster analysis. Br. J. Psychiatry 119: 399–412, **1971.**

The authors employed a cluster analysis statistical technique to data from a population of psychiatric patients and found that identifiable clusters could be obtained for mania and paranoid schizophrenia. Some clustering could be obtained for chronic schizophrenia, but no signifi-cant clustering for depression, personality disorder, alcoholism, or neuroses could be found. A well-conceived study.

12. **Garside, R.S. and Roth, M.** Multivariate statistical methods and problems of classification in psychiatry. Br. J. of Psychiatry 133: 53–67, **1978.**

The authors argue that multivariate statistical methods are uniquely valuable in validating psychiatric diagnoses and classifications, but acknowledge that a general agreement as to how best to utilize these techniques has not been achieved.

13. **Pfohl, B. and Andreasen, N.C.** Development of classification systems in psychiatry. Compr. Psychiatry 19: 197–207, **1978.**

The authors provide a rational approach to the development of new classification systems in psychiatry, including statistical and meth-odological options to be considered, selection of patients and variables, division of patients into groups, development of diagnostic criteria, and evaluation of the diagnostic system itself.

14. **Robins, E. and Guze, S.B.** Establishment of diagnostic validity in psychiatric illness: Its application to schizophrenia. Am. J. Psychiatry 126: 983–987, **1970.**

A widely quoted statement on the basic requirements for defining a psychiatric illness by the Washington University group. Notable for its emphasis on family and outcome studies as methods for validating a diagnosis. The principles are illustrated by demonstrating that "good" prognosis schizophrenia and "poor" prognosis schizophrenia may be two different illnesses. This article has provided a strong basis for re-evaluating classification systems during the 1970s and 1980s.

15. **Shepherd, M.** Psychotropic drugs and taxonomic systems. Psychol. Med. 10: 25–33, **1980.**

Shepherd presents a biological and molecular classification. Also opens to question the whole concept of classification and the different purposes classification serves.

16. **Spitzer, R.L., Endicott, J., and Robins, E.** Clinical criteria for psychiatric diagnosis and DSM III. Am. J. Psychiatry 132: 1187–1192, **1975.**

The authors argue that criterion variance (the formal inclusion or exclusion of specific criteria) is the greatest source of unreliability in psychiatric diagnosis. Their view was accepted and is reflected in the structure of the *DSM III.*

17. **Zubin, J.** Classification of the behavior disorders. Ann. Rev. Psychol. 18: 373–406, **1967.**

A general discussion of problems of psychiatric classification by a widely respected senior researcher in the field. Has an excellent discussion of Jaspers and the relationship between psychopathology and personality.

INTERVIEWS AND RATING SCALES

18. **Andreasen, N.C.** Thought, language, and communication disorders: I. Clinical assessment, definition of terms and evaluation of their reliability. Arch. Gen. Psychiatry 36: 1315–1321, **1979.**

19. **Andreasen, N.C.** Thought, language, and communication disorders: II. Diagnostic significance. Arch. Gen. Psychiatry 36: 1325–1330, **1979.**

The author presents a useful and reliable set of definitions for 18 different subtypes of thought disorder. She demonstrates that thought disorder is a broad concept used incorrectly in many instances and not pathognomonic for schizophrenia or any other psychiatric disorder.

20. **Andreasen, N.C.** Affective flattening and the criteria for schizophrenia. Am. J. Psychiatry 136: 944–947, **1979.**

Depressed and schizophrenic patients could not be discriminated on a rating scale designed to assess flattening of affect, raising questions about about the generally accepted belief that flatness of affect is specific to schizophrenia.

21. **Carpenter, W.T., Sacks, M.H., Strauss, J.S., et al.** Evaluating signs and symptoms: Comparison of structured interview and clinical approaches. Br. J. Psychiatry 128: 397–403, **1976.**

A comparison of structured interviews with routine clinical assessment. It was found that the structured interview is generally acceptable in documenting symptoms but was inadequate in documenting signs.

22. **Carroll, B.J., Feinberg, M., Smouse, P.E., et al.** The Carroll Rating Scale for Depression: Development, reliability, and validation. Br. J. Psychiatry 138: 194–200, **1981.**

A self-rating instrument for depression. The authors suggest that this scale be used in conjunction with observer rating such as the Hamilton Scale to yield complementary results.

23. **Chapman, L.J. and Chapman, J.P.** Scales for rating psychotic and psychotic-like experiences as continua. Schizophr. Bull. 6: 476–489, **1980.**

A rating scale that rates psychotic phenomena on a continuum of deviancy rather than as dichotomously deviant or nondeviant. The rating scale and the demonstration of its application challenged a prevailing view that psychotic symptoms are dichotomous events.

24. **Endicott, J., Spitzer, R.L., Fleiss, J.L., et al.** The Global Assessment Scale: A procedure for measuring overall severity of psychiatric disturbance. Arch. Gen. Psychiatry 33: 766–771, **1976.**

A description of the Global Assessment Scale (GAS). A sensitive measure of overall severity of psychiatric illness. The GAS has a wide application in psychiatric research especially for patients in the community.

25. ***Endicott, J. and Spitzer, R.L.** A diagnostic interview: The Schedule for Affective Disorders and Schizophrenia. Arch. Gen. Psychiatry 35: 837–844, **1978.**

The authors describe a structured diagnostic interview designed to obtain detailed information about the current episode of illness and level of functioning during the week prior to evaluation. A lifetime version is also available for epidemiological work. This instrument, called the SADS, is currently one of the most widely used for psychiatric research in the U.S. This interview forms the basis for making RDC diagnoses.

26.   *Hamilton, M. A rating scale for depression. J. Neurol. Neurosci. Psychiatry 23: 56–62, **1960.**

A widely used objective rating scale for depression. Clinicians as well as researchers will find it a useful device to reduce the effects of idiosyncratic clinical assessment. Often used to monitor clinical change in psychopharmacologic research, it is one of the oldest rating scales available, but still widely used.

27.   Hamilton, M. Measurement in psychiatry, pp. 85–106. In: Handbook of Biological Psychiatry, Vol. 1. Eds.: H.M. van Praag, M.H. Lader, O.J. Rafaelson, et al. New York: M. Dekker, **1979.**

A review of principles of measurement in psychiatry including types of scales, methods of constructing scales and their actual application. The importance of addressing the issues of interrater reliability and validity is stressed.

28.   Helzer, J.E., Robins, L.N., Croughan, J.L., et al. Renard Diagnostic Interview: Its reliability and procedural validity with physicians and lay interviewers. Arch. Gen. Psychiatry 38: 393–398, **1981.**

The authors describe a diagnostic interview intended for hospitalized patients. They report that the instrument is reliable even when used by lay interviewers after a brief period of training. This interview forms the basis for making diagnoses using the St. Louis criteria.

29.   *Helzer, J.E., Robins, L.N., Taibleson, M., et al. Reliability of psychiatric diagnosis: I. A methodological review. Arch. Gen. Psychiatry 34: 129–133, **1977.**

30.   *Helzer, J.E., Clayton, P.J., Pambakian, R., et al. Reliability of psychiatric diagnosis: II. The test-retest reliability of psychiatric classification. Arch. Gen. Psychiatry 34: 136–141, **1977.**

The authors present valuable insight on the problems of interrater reliability and recommend as correctives structured interviews, concise diagnostic criteria, and the creation of a residual diagnostic category, *undiagnosed psychiatric illness.* These two papers are essential reading for all those evaluating or designing psychiatric research. These articles provide reliability data for the St. Louis criteria.

31.   Spitzer, R.L., Cohen, J., Fleiss, J.L., et al. Quantification agreement in psychiatric diagnosis. Arch. Gen. Psychiatry 17: 83–87, **1967.**

In this seminal contribution the authors summarized the significant problems in quantifying psychiatric diagnosis and recommended the use of the weighted kappa to measure reliability and computer-assisted diagnosis.

32. **Spitzer, R.L., Endicott, J., Cohen, J., et al.** Constraints on the validity of computer diagnosis. Arch. Gen. Psychiatry 31: 197–203, **1974.**

An interesting contribution that argues that the present limitations encountered in attempts to produce high levels of diagnostic validity with computers are not to be found in the computers' technical limitations but in the limitations inherent in our current diagnostic systems.

DIAGNOSTIC CRITERIA

33. ***Feighner, J.P., Robins, E., Guze, S.B., et al.** Diagnostic criteria for use in psychiatric research. Arch. Gen. Psychiatry 26: 57–63, **1972.**

Stimulating and provocative, this paper is a classic contribution. In an extremely usable form, the authors present 14 psychiatric illnesses with highly specific diagnostic criteria. These "St. Louis criteria" were the first developed and were responsible for popularizing the use of diagnostic criteria.

34. **Kendell, R.E.** The stability of psychiatric diagnoses. Br. J. Psychiatry 124: 352–356, **1974.**

The author found that while depressive illness, schizophrenia, alcoholism, and dementia were relatively stable diagnoses over time, personality disorders and paranoid disorders were not. Paranoid states tended to be rediagnosed as schizophrenia, while personality disorders tended to be rediagnosed as depression.

35. **Kendell, R.E.** Psychiatric diagnoses: A study of how they are made. Br. J. Psychiatry 122: 437–445, **1973.**

Raters trained at the same institution made consensually validated diagnoses with only two or five minutes exposure to video tapes of psychotic patients. This finding suggests that diagnoses of psychotic patients are made in the first few minutes of an interview.

36. **Kendell, R.E., Cooper, J.E., Gourlay, A.J., et al.** Diagnostic criteria of American and British psychiatrists. Arch. Gen. Psychiatry 25: 123–130, **1971.**

This paper presents the differences in diagnostic criteria for schizophrenia and manic depression in England and America as it existed in 1971. This study provided impetus for a critical re-evaluation of American diagnostic practices.

SPECIFIC SYNDROMES

37. **Andreasen, N.C.** Negative symptoms in schizophrenia: Definition and reliability. Arch. Gen. Psychiatry 39: 784–788, **1982.**

38. **Andreasen, N.C. and Olsen, S.** Negative vs. positive schizophrenia: Definition and validation. Arch. Gen. Psychiatry 39: 789–794, **1982.**

The important distinction between deficit or negative symptoms and florid or positive symptoms of schizophrenia is made in these studies. Using the scale for the assessment of negative symptoms, patients with negative symptoms are shown to have poorer premorbid adjustments and less successful hospital courses.

39. **De Koning, A.J., and Jenner, F.A.,** eds. Phenomenology and Psychiatry. New York: Grune and Stratton, **1982.**

The editors have assembled essays from European, American, and Japanese phenomenologists covering a wide spectrum of psychiatric phenomenology including anxiety, hallucinations, and delusions. An excellent guide to a very neglected area.

40. **Fish, F.J.** Clinical Psychopathology. Signs and Symptoms in Psychiatry. Briston, Eng.: J. Wright, **1967.**

Fish presents a coherent overview of the signs and symptoms of psychiatric disorder. The work reflects the mainstream views of British psychiatry in the 1960s. An excellent primer.

41. **Mellor, C.S.** First-rank symptoms of schizophrenia. Br. J. Psychiatry 117: 15–23, **1970.**

The paper provides a clear description of the Schneiderian first-rank symptoms with excellent clinical examples. It was influential in introducing them into American psychiatry.

42. ***Spitzer, R.L., Endicott, J., and Robins, E.** Research Diagnostic Criteria: Rationale and reliability. Arch. Gen. Psychiatry 35: 773–782, **1978.**

The authors describe the initial reliaiblity students for their Research Diagnostic Criteria (RDC). The RDC is widely used in research and along with the St. Louis criteria represents the seminal thinking that culminated in the creation of the *DSM III.*

43.   **World Health Organization.** Schizophrenia: An International Followup Study. New York: Wiley, **1979.**

The description and conclusions of a nine-country study of the diagnosis and outcome of schizophrenia. Includes chapters on prior studies, feasibility of multinational studies, reliability of the interview schedule, the Present State Examination (PSE), comparison among diagnostic groups within and between centers, subgroups of schizophrenia, and predictors of outcome. An immensely rich study because of the multination patient population.

13. SCHIZOPHRENIA

JOHN P. DOCHERTY, M.D.

The *DSM-III* succinctly and clearly states a contemporary view of the group of patients referred to by the term *schizophrenia*. In general, four major approaches have been taken to defining schizophrenia and categorizing patients as schizophrenic: (1) the presence of psychosis for a variable period of time, (2) psychosis in association with progressive deterioration (Kraepelin), (3) the presence of disturbances in certain key psychological processes (Bleuler), (4) the presence of pathognomonic symptoms (Schneider).

In essence the *DSM-III* approach requires the presence of a psychotic state at some point in the patient's history. It is useful to note that this differs from the current Soviet system, which does not require psychosis for the designation "sluggish schizophrenia," or for the Bleulerian system, which is based on the identification of certain "underlying" psychological processes (the so-called 4 "As": loose association, autistic thought, flat affect, ambivalence) and which heavily influenced American diagnostic practice through the early 1970s.

Psychosis is recognized by the presence during an active phase of the illness of certain delusions or hallucinations or marked disturbance of thought in association with delusions, hallucinations, or disorganized behavior. This category is limited by the requirement of an active phase of illness for at least six months, which may include a nonpsychotic prodromal or residual phase, and the requirement for deterioration in work, social relations, and self-care. Finally, the category is also limited by the exclusion of certain other specific categories of disorder such as organic psychosis and affective psychosis.

The books and articles chosen for this bibliography cover the following major areas: reviews, diagnosis, epidemiology, course and prognosis, biology, psychology, family, psychosocial treatment, drug treatment, and community care and aftercare.

Selection of articles was based on several criteria: (1) they are well written, (2) they have advanced or strongly influenced the field, (3) they have been seminal works themselves or are frequently referenced reviews, and (4) they represent a major area of current or past thought. Clearly, in dealing with a clinical problem such as schizophrenia and its voluminous literature, significant omissions will occur in a limited bibliography. This bibliography, however, should acquaint the reader with some of the more important past and present issues and provide a reasonably inclusive framework for understanding contemporary approaches to treatment and research in schizophrenia.

REVIEWS

1.   **Arieti, S.** Interpretation of Schizophrenia (2nd ed.). New York: Basic Books, **1974.**

This book is a fine overview of schizophrenia. It is a remarkably well-written and lucid book that is particularly successful in drawing together key material relevant to a systematic understanding of the psychother-apeutic clinical care and management of the schizophrenic patient.

2.   **Bleuler, E.** Dementia Praecox or the Group of Schizophrenias. New York: International Universities Press, **1950.**

This is the classic text that shaped current thinking about schizophrenia including diagnosis (the 4 As). The richness and thoroughness of clinical description is unsurpassed.

3.   ***Strauss, J.S. and Carpenter, W.T.** Schizophrenia. New York: Plenum Press, **1981.**

This rather thin volume is probably the best available current introduction to schizophrenia. It provides an ideal beginning for the new psychiatrist and an elegant review for the experienced psychiatrist.

DIAGNOSIS

4.   **Astrachan, B.M., Harrow, M., Adler, D., et al.** A checklist for the diagnosis of schizophrenia. Br. J. Psychiatry 121: 529–539, **1972.**

This article presents a novel approach to objectifying and standardizing the diagnosis of schizophrenia. It casts a wider net than most other systems and for this reason has a special clinical and research utility.

5.   **Kendell, R.E., Brockington, I.F., and Leff, J.P.** Prognostic implications of six alternative definitions of schizophrenia. Arch. Gen. Psychiatry 36: 25–31, **1979.**

This article presents the criteria for six major systems for making the diagnosis of schizophrenia and the differences in type of patients defined by these criteria reflected in differential outcome.

6.   **Rutter, M.** Childhood schizophrenia reconsidered. J. Autism Childhood Schizophr. 2: 315–337, **1972.**

This is an excellent review of the issues involved in the classification of the childhood psychosis.

7.   ***Spitzer, R.L., Andreasen, N.C., and Endicott, J.** Schizophrenia and other psychotic disorders in DSM III. Schizophr. Bull. 4: 489–509, **1978.**

This paper reviews the rationale for the criteria used for the diagnosis of schizophrenia in **DSM III.**

8.   **Strauss, J.S. and Gift, T.E.** Choosing an approach for diagnosing schizophrenia. Arch. Gen. Psychiatry 34: 1248–1253, **1977.**

Compares and contrasts the major diagnostic systems for categorizing patients as schizophrenic and demonstrates the varying boundaries and relative restrictiveness of different criteria.

9.   **World Health Organization.** Report of the International Pilot Study of Schizophrenia, Vol. 1. Geneva: WHO Press, **1973.**

This book reports results from the International Pilot Study of Schizophrenia regarding the degree to which international diagnostic consensus could be reached for schizophrenia and presents worldwide preliminary comparative epidemiologic and outcome findings.

EPIDEMIOLOGY

10.   ***Kohn, M.L.** Social class and schizophrenia: A critical review, pp. 155–173. In: Transmission of Schizophrenia. Eds.: D. Rosenthal and S. Kety. London: Pergamon Press, **1968.**

This paper presents an excellent, thoughtful review of the data relating social class to the incidence of schizophrenia and appraisal of the relevance of these data to the competing explanatory hypotheses of "social causation" and "downward drift."

11.   **Mednick, S.A.** Breakdown in individuals at high risk for schizophrenia: Possible predispositional perinatal factors. Ment. Hygiene 54: 50–63, **1970.**

This article reports results of the use of the "high risk strategy" for studying schizophrenia, a research approach that has come to represent a significant advance in research strategy.

COURSE AND PROGNOSIS

12. **Bleuler, M.** The Schizophrenic Disorders: Long-term Patient and Family Studies. New Haven: Yale University Press, **1978.**

    This book reports the intensive and extensive investigation of the family and personal history and course of illness of 200 schizophrenics whom the author not only studied but treated over a period of more than 20 years.

13. **Chapman, J.P.** The early symptoms of schizophrenia. Br. J. Psychiatry 112: 225–251, **1966.**

    This is a landmark study using a semistructured symptom oriented interview that revealed a wealth of previously unappreciated symptomatology during the prodromal phase of the acute psychotic episode.

14. ***Docherty, J.P., Van Kammen, D., Siris, S., et al.** Stages of onset of schizophrenic psychosis. Am. J. Psychiatry 135: 420–426, **1978.**

    This seminal paper proposes and presents preliminary data supporting a descriptive model of the often-mentioned but little-studied process of psychotic decompensation in schizophrenic patients. Five stages are described: (1) equilibrium, (2) over-extension, (3) restricted consciousness, (4) disinhibition, and (5) psychotic disorganization.

15. ***Phillips, L.** Case history data and prognosis in schizophrenia. J. Nerv. Ment. Dis. 117: 515–525, **1953.**

    This modest article introduced the Phillips Prognostic Scale of Pre-Morbid Psychosexual Adjustment, which bases prognosis on premorbid social maturity. This scale has had an enormous influence on the field and is the basis for the good/poor premorbid categorization of schizophrenic patients.

16. ***Strauss, J.S. and Carpenter, W.T.** The prediction of outcome in schizophrenia: I. Characteristics of outcome. Arch. Gen. Psychiatry 27: 739–746, **1972.**

    This is one of a series of papers by these authors that analyzes data for the WHO-sponsored International Pilot Study of Schizophrenia and that has contributed greatly to clarifying understanding of the course of schizophrenia by introducing and empirically investigating the multidimensional structure (symptoms, social function, work function, hospitalization) of course and outcome.

17. **Vaillant, G.E.** Prospective prediction of schizophrenic remission. Arch. Gen. Psychiatry 11: 509–518, **1964.**

On the basis of review of the literature this investigator developed a seven-item scale (acute onset, confusion, depressive heredity, non-schizoid adjustment, depression, precipitating factors, concern with diets) applicable to the admission picture that predicted recovery from psychosis. This scale has become one of the established instruments for evaluation prognosis.

BIOLOGY

18. **Buchsbaum, M.S., Ingvar, D.H., Kessler, R., et al.** Cerebral glucography with positron tomography. Arch. Gen. Psychiatry 39: 251–259, **1981.**

This paper is one of the still early reports of the use of advanced computer-assisted neuroradiologic procedures to search for clinically salient deviance in schizophrenic patients.

19. **Carlson, A. and Lindquist, M.** Effects of chlorpromazine and haloper-idol on formation of 3-methoxytyramine and normetanephrine in mouse brain. Acta. Pharmacol. (Series C. Stockholm) 20: 140–144, **1960.**

This is the first paper to propose the hypothesis that phenothiazines effect their therapeutic action by establishing a blockade of dopa-minergic neuron postsynaptic receptor sites.

20. ***Davis, J.M.** Dopamine theory of schizophrenia: A two-factor theory, pp. 105–115. In: The Nature of Schizophrenia. Eds.: L. Wynne, R. Cromwell, and S. Matthysse. New York: Wiley, **1978.**

This outstanding scholar once again brings his clear thinking and broad knowledge to a brief review of data supporting a dopamine hypothesis of schizophrenia and indicates some of the conceptual problems with the hypothesis.

21. **Holzman, P.S., Levy, D.L., and Proctor, L.R.** Smooth pursuit eye movements, attention and schizophrenia. Arch. Gen. Psychiatry 33: 1415–1420, **1976.**

This article is one of a series of reports beginning in 1973 that documents the presence of a dysfunction of smooth pursuit eye movements. This dysfunction has an unusually high prevalence in schizophrenic patients and their relatives but is not limited to schizophrenia.

22. ***Kety, S.S., Rosenthal, D., Wender, P.H., et al.** Mental illness in the biological and adoptive families of adopted schizophrenics. Am. J. Psychiatry 128: 302–306, **1971.**

This paper reports the results of the highly influential Copenhagen Study of the prevalence of mental illness, particularly schizophrenia and "schizophrenia spectrum" disorders. This work found significantly more schizophrenic illness in the biological relatives of the schizophrenic probands than in the biological relatives of a central group of nonschizophrenic adoptees.

23. ***Kety, S.S.** The syndrome of schizophrenia: Unresolved questions and opportunities for research. Br. J. Psychiatry 136: 421–436, **1980.**

This article is an excellent overview of the biological research findings in schizophrenia presented from the integrative perspective of one of the eminent psychiatric researchers in the field.

24. **Shagass, C.** An electrophysiological view of schizophrenia. Biol. Psychiatry 11: 3–30, **1976.**

This paper reviews the major types of electrophysiological studies in schizophrenia, summarizes the main findings, and indicates the relation of electrophysiology to other areas of neurobiology and the clinical phenomena.

25. **Snyder, S.H., Banerjee, S., Yamamura, H., et al.** Drugs, neurotransmitters, and schizophrenia. Science 184: 1243–1253, **1974.**

A review of the relevant pharmacological and basic neurochemical studies supporting a dopamine hypothesis of schizophrenia.

26. **Stevens, J.R.** An anatomy of schizophrenia? Arch. Gen. Psychiatry 29: 177–189, **1973.**

This is a brilliant article and, although it may not be "true," it is a *tour de force* of neurological detail, reasoning, and understanding, which has properly made it a classic.

27. **Wyatt, R.J., Termini, B.A., and Davis, J.M.** Biochemical and sleep studies of schizophrenics: A review of the literature 1960–1970, Part I. Biochemical studies. Schizophr. Bull. 4: 10–44, **1971.**

A fairly complete and even-handed review of the major competing biochemical hypotheses of schizophrenia—prior to the rise of the dopamine hypothesis.

28. **Wyatt, R.J., Potkin, S.G., and Murphy, D.L.** Platelet monoamine

oxidase activity in schizophrenia: A review of the data. Am. J. Psychiatry 136: 377–385, **1979.**

This article presents a good overview of the work accomplished in trying to understand the still elusive significance of altered MAO activity in schizophrenic patients.

PSYCHOLOGY

29.   *****Chapman, L.J.** Recent advances in the study of schizophrenia cognition. Schizophr. Bull. 5: 568–580, **1979.**

This is a lucid review of the state-of-the-art of the study of cognitive disturbance in schizophrenia patients by one of the field's major investigators.

30.   *****Shakow, D.** Some observations on the psychology (and some fewer on the biology) of schizophrenia. J. Nerv. Ment. Dis. 153: 300–330, **1971.**

This article presents a review of the behavioral theory of "segmental set," which points out that much of the schizophrenic's disturbed behavior derives from the inability to maintain a major set, that is, a state of readiness to respond to an incoming stimulus that facilitates the optimal response called for by a given situation.

31.   **Spring, B., Neuchterlein, K., Sugarman, J., et al.** The "new look" in studies of schizophrenic attention and information processing. Schizophr. Bull. 3: 470–482, **1977.**

This article presents a synthetic overview that highlights the multidisciplinary nature of current research on attention in schizophrenics and need for more sophisticated and detailed theoretical development.

FAMILY

32.   *****Brown, G.W., Birley, J.L.T., and Wing, J.K.** Influence of family life on the course of schizophrenic disorders: A replication. Br. J. Psychiatry 121: 241–258, **1972.**

This paper reports the important study investigating the effects of a high degree of expressed emotion consisting of hostility and overinvolvement by relatives of schizophrenic patients with the propensity to relapse. They found that schizophrenic patients who lived with and were in close contact with relatives expressing such emotions were at significantly increased risk for relapse.

33. *Lidz, T. The Origin and Treatment of Schizophrenic Disorders. New York: Basic Books, 1973.

This work summarizes and integrates the work of Lidz and colleagues in understanding the influence of family life and rearing on the development and expression of schizophrenic psychopathology. It is an invaluable book for psychotherapeutic treatment of these patients.

34. Wynne, L.C., Ryckoff, I.M., Day, J., et al. Pseudo-mutuality in the family relation of schizophrenics. Psychiatry 21: 205–220, 1958.

This article presents one of a series of reports from NIMH during the period of 1954 to 1970. It presents a concept that integrates a great deal of the aberrant social behavior observed in the families of these patients. While the etiological role of these processes has not been demonstrated, they still have impressive relevance for clinical management.

35. Wynne, L.C. Current concepts about schizophrenics and family relationships. J. Nerv. Ment. Dis. 169: 82–89, 1981.

This article presents a clear and concise overview of the two main lines of current family studies in schizophrenic communication deviance and expressed emotion.

PSYCHOSOCIAL TREATMENT

36. Falloon, I.R.H., Boyd, H., McGill, C.W., et al. Family management in the prevention of exacerbations of schizophrenia: A controlled study. N. Engl. J. Med. 306: 1437–1440, 1982.

This paper reports a study that found that problem-solving family therapy in conjunction with antipsychotic drug treatment significantly reduced the relapse rate in schizophrenic outpatients.

37. Fromm-Reichmann, F. Notes on the development of treatment of schizophrenia by psycho-analytic psychotherapy. Psychiatry 11: 263–273, 1948.

This is a lucid article synthesizing a highly sophisticated understanding of the subjective state and interpersonal needs of the schizophrenic patient and conveying in clear, down-to-earth language basic principles for psychotherapeutic treatment.

38. *Hill, L.B. Psychotherapeutic Intervention in Schizophrenia. Chicago: University of Chicago Press, 1955.

This book is a classic description of the life experience of the schizophrenic and of the experience of psychotherapy with such a person. It is an excellent introduction to the undertaking of psychotherapy.

39. **Kellam, S.** Ward atmosphere, continuity of treatment, and the mental health system, pp. 141–158. In: Principles and Practice of Milieu Therapy. Eds.: J. Gunderson, O. Will, and L. Mosher. New York: Aronson, **1983.**

Summarizes five studies by the author carried out in the 1960s that relate aspects of ward atmosphere to symptomatology in schizophrenia. This work has great significance both from a clinical and research methodology perspective and has received too little attention.

40. **Laing, R.D.** The Divided Self, An Existential Study in Sanity and Madness. London: Tavistock Publications, **1959.**

This is a beautifully written book that clearly describes the deep and painful conflict of schizophrenic patients. It is an articulate testimony of the alienation from self and life such patients experience and states the basis for Laing's concerns regarding the structure of the institution in which such patients receive care.

41. ***May, P.R.A.** Treatment of Schizophrenia: A Cooperative Study of Five Treatment Methods. New York: Science House, **1968.**

A report of this critical study comparing five forms of treatment for hospitalized first-admission schizophrenic patients. The five treatment groups are: (1) "control" or basic care alone, (2) individual psychotherapy alone, (3) antipsychotic drug treatment alone, (4) individual psychotherapy plus antipsychotic drug, (5) electroshock. These patients were followed for five years following discharge. Only those patients treated with drugs either with or without psychotherapy showed greater hospital improvement than the control group.

42. **Mosher, L.R. and Keith, S.J.** Psychosocial treatment: Individual, group, family and community support approaches. Schizophr. Bull. 6: 10–41, **1980.**

This article is an excellent and comprehensive review of controlled outcome studies of psychosocial treatment of schizophrenia, critically assessing the specific usefulness of each type of therapy.

43. ***Paul, G.L. and Lentz, R.J.** Psychosocial Treatment of Chronic Mental Patients: Milieu Versus Social Learning Programs. Cambridge: Harvard University Press, **1977.**

This book describes an exquisitely executed and elegantly designed research program that investigated the relative efficacy of milieu and social learning programs in the case of very chronic schizophrenic patients. In the course of this work, sophisticated technology for the behavioral observation and treatment of schizophrenic patients was developed.

44. ***Searles, H.** Collected Papers on Schizophrenia and Related Subjects. New York: International Universities Press, **1965.**

These papers report the careful and exquisitely insightful observations of the personal and interpersonal experience of the schizophrenic, of his or her therapist, and the relevance of these experiences to treatment.

45. **Sullivan, H.S.** Schizophrenia as a Human Process. New York: Norton, **1962.**

This book is a "clinical classic" that provides the reader with a fine sense of how to be with and interact helpfully with a schizophrenic patient.

46. **Wallace, C.J., Nelson, C.J., Liberman, R.P., et al.** A review and critique of social skills training with schizophrenic patients. Schizophr. Bull. 6: 42–64, **1980.**

This article reviews the application of behavioral techniques to the treatment of schizophrenic patients.

DRUG TREATMENT

47. **American Psychiatric Association.** Effects of antipsychotic drugs: Tardive dyskinesia. Summary of a task force report of the American Psychiatric Association. Am. J. Psychiatry 137: 1163–1172, **1980.**

This is a well-written report summarizing the major issues and current knowledge regarding the management of tardive dyskinesia in patients receiving antipsychotic medication.

48. **Baldessarini, R.J. and Davis, J.M.** What is the best maintenance dose of neuroleptics in schizophrenia? Psychiatry Res. 3: 115–122, **1980.**

This article introduced the notion, based on review of the literature, that perhaps the majority of schizophrenic patients could receive appropriate maintenance therapy with very low doses of drug. This suggestion currently finds support in ongoing prospective studies.

49. ***Davis, J.M.** Overview: Maintenance therapy in psychiatry: I. Schizophrenia. Am. J. Psychiatry 132: 1237–1245, **1975.**

This article reviews all available controlled outpatient studies of the efficacy of antipsychotic drugs in prevention of psychotic relapse and rehospitalization in schizophrenics and demonstrates the overwhelming evidence supporting the efficacy of this treatment.

50. ***Davis, J.M., Schaffer, C.B., Killian, G., et al.** Important issues in the drug treatment of schizophrenia. Schizophr. Bull. 6: 70–87, **1980.**

This article identifies the major management issues and decisions that must be made in the pharmacological treatment of schizophrenic patients and recommends guidelines.

51. ***Gardos, G., Cole, J., and La Brie, R.** The assessment of tardive dyskinesia. Arch. Gen. Psychiatry 34: 1206–1212, **1977.**

This paper reviews the major methods and treatments available for assessing the abnormal movements of tardive dyskinesia and discusses the relative advantages and disadvantages of each.

52. **Hogarty, G.E., Goldberg, S.C., Schooler, N., et al.** Drug and sociotherapy in the aftercare of schizophrenic patients: II. Two-year relapse rates. Arch. Gen. Psychiatry 31: 603–608, **1974.**

This is one of a series of reports from an elegant study of the effect on the prevention of relapse in schizophrenic patients of chlorpromazine, sociotherapy, and their combination. This careful study further verifies the efficacy, but also suggests the limits, of maintenance antipsychotic drugs.

COMMUNITY CARE

53. **Fairweather, G.W., Sander, S., Cressler, D.H., et al.** Community Life for the Mentally Ill: An Alternative to Institutional Care. Chicago: Aldine, **1969.**

This book describes the success of placing chronic schizophrenic patients in semi-independent living facilities. It was an early salvo in the community-based care and half-way house movement.

54. **Hammer, M.** Social supports, social networks and schizophrenia. Schizophr. Bull. 7: 45–57, **1981.**

This is a crisp little article that disentangles and clarifies the usage of the term "social network," a construct that is currently gaining increasing attention in schizophrenia studies.

55. **Herz, M., Endicott, J., Spitzer, R.L., et al.** Day versus in-patient

hospitalization: A controlled study. Am. J. Psychiatry 127: 1371–1382, **1971.**

This paper reports the finding that many schizophrenic patients can be treated adequately during exacerbations without the necessity for hospitalization.

56. **Intagliata, J.** Improving the quality of community care for the chronically mentally disabled: The role of cost management. Schizophr. Bull. 8: 655–674, **1982.**

This article presents a detailed review of the cost management literature, identifies its key elements, and illustrates practical implementation.

57. **Pasamanick, B., Scarpitti, F.R., and Dinitz, S.** Schizophrenics in the Community: An Experimental Study in the Prevention of Rehospitalization. New York: Appleton-Century-Crofts, **1967.**

This is one of the most well done of a group of independent studies that demonstrates the feasibility of home or community care for the treatment of acute episodes of disturbance in the schizophrenic patient.

58. ***Turner, J.C. and TenHoor, W.J.** The NIMH community support program: Pilot approach to a needed social reform. Schizophr. Bull. 4: 319–348, **1978.**

This paper discusses the basis and necessity for community support programs and the 10 major elements of such programs.

14. AFFECTIVE DISORDERS

CRAIG S. NELSON, M.D.
DENNIS S. CHARNEY, M.D.

Affective disorder research has been heavily influenced during the last two decades by the introduction of effective pharmacologic agents. The clinical need to identify responders to the tricyclic antidepressants and monoamine oxidase inhibitors renewed interest in description of depressive subtypes. The drugs also provided a "pharmacologic bridge" to study basic biological mechanisms related to the action of the drugs and the biological basis of depression. Recently, "laboratory tests" have been proposed that might be useful for identifying patients having a "biological depression." The introduction of lithium, a drug effective for the treatment of bipolar illness, generated similar research inquiries, but in particular it increased interest in the identification of manic patients who might be diagnosed as schizophrenic. The considerable interest in the description of depression led to extensive changes in classification, which are reflected in *DSM III.* At the same time, findings in biological research were beginning to provide a conceptual framework for explaining some aspects of depressive illness. In this chapter, we have emphasized the descriptive studies and biological studies that have preoccupied the field during the past decades.

We first review important historical works, particularly those that had an important and lasting impact. Next, papers presenting conceptual models of depression are reviewed. A few studies of the relationship of stress and life events with depression are selected to illustrate the methodologic problems inherent in this area, as well as the findings. Studies of diagnosis, classification, and description are presented. Laboratory tests that may have potential for identifying depressed patients are reviewed (under the subheading "biological markers") as well as examples of recent genetic studies of depression. Finally, we review a number of papers dealing with the neurobiology of depression. In selecting references, we have leaned towards primary source articles that describe original findings, but we also include papers that provide useful reviews of an area. This material should be useful for trainees in psychiatry as well as other mental health professionals. Certain areas related to depression such as epidemiology, suicide, bereavement, and pharmacologic treatment are discussed in other sections.

EARLY PAPERS

1. **Freud, S.** (1917) Mourning and melancholia. S.E. 14: 239–258, **1957.**

   Freud's paper is the source of the popularized "anger-turned-inwards" theory of depression. While subsequent empirical studies failed to support this hypothesis, the work nevertheless paved the way for psychological theories of depression.

2. **Gillespie, R.D.** The clinical differentiation of types of depression. Guy's Hosp. Rep. 79: 306–344, **1929.**

   While Gillespie's work is not well known, his work of 1929 seems surprisingly contemporary. While others argued whether depression was the result of stress, Gillespie suggested that it was the nature of the depressive syndrome that was important. His ideas antedated current theories of biological vulnerability.

3. **Kendell, R.E.** The Classification of Depressive Illnesses. London: Oxford University Press, **1968.**

   The first chapter on the history of depressive classification is a very interesting account of diagnostic controversies of the first half of the century. His colorful descriptions of the debates between the differing British "schools" makes very interesting reading.

4. **Kraepelin, E.** Manic-Depressive Insanity and Paranoia. Edinburgh: E & S Livingstone, **1921.**

   Kraepelin's work of 1896 is a cornerstone of descriptive psychiatry of the past century. The distinction he made between manic-depressive disorders (or affective illness) and the nonaffective psychoses remains important to the present. His description of depression as an endogenous illness was consistent with the thinking of that period.

CONCEPTUAL MODELS

5. ***Akiskal, H.S. and McKinney, Jr., W.T.** Overview of recent research in depression: Integration of ten conceptual models into a comprehensive clinical frame. Arch. Gen. Psychiatry 32: 285–305, **1975.**

   This is one of the most comprehensive reviews of conceptual models for depression available. It is a very useful overview for trainees and a valuable reference for researchers.

6. **Beck, A.T.** Depression: Clinical Experimental and Theoretical Aspects. New York: Harper and Row, **1967.**

Negative attitudes and perceptions that distort the patient's experience are emphasized in Beck's theory of depression. These notions may be particularly important for understanding chronic characterologic depressions.

7. ***Bibring, E.** The mechanism of depression, pp. 13–48. In: Affective Disorders. Ed.: P. Greenacre. New York: International Universities Press, **1953.** (Also available in **1961** edition).

This paper is one of the most important current psychodynamic explanations of depression. Bibring emphasizes an ego psychological model in which failure to meet standards and low self-esteem are central.

8. **Seligman, M.E.P.** Learned helplessness and depression. In: The Psychology of Depression: Contemporary Theory and Research. Eds.: R. Friedman and M. Katz. Washington, D.C.: U.S. Government Printing Office. **(to be published).**

Seligman's animal studies add another dimension to behavioral theories about depression. Seligman describes "learned helplessness" as an experimental animal model that may be relevant to understanding depression in human subjects.

9. **Weissman, M.M., Klerman, G.L., and Paykel, E.S.** Clinical evaluation of hostility in depression. Am. J. Psychiatry 128: 261–266, **1971.**

In this study depressed patients frequently displayed irritability or hostility toward others although they may have felt guilty about it. The data challenge the theory of retroflexed anger.

10. ***Whybrow, P. and Parlatore, A.** Melancholia, a model in madness: A discussion of recent psychobiologic research into depressive illness. Int. J. Psychiatry Med. 4: 351–378, **1973.**

The authors describe a model of depression consistent with current notions of biological vulnerability. They distinguish between variations of normal sadness and melancholia.

STRESS AND LIFE EVENTS

11. ***Clayton, P.J.** Bereavement, pp. 403–415. In: Handbook of Affective Disorders. Ed.: E.S. Paykel. Edinburgh: Churchill Livingstone, **1982.**

This chapter is included here since bereavement is one form of "reactive" depression. Bereaved patients frequently experience depressive symptoms in response to a common life event.

12.   **Garmany, G.** Depressive states: Their aetiology and treatment. Br. Med. J. 2: 341–344, **1958.**

This was one of the first empirical studies to examine the presence or absence of stress prior to the onset of depression. In a large patient sample, stress commonly preceded both reactive and endogenous depressions.

13.   **Paykel, E.S., Myers, J.K., Dienelt, M., et al.** Life events and depression: A controlled study. Arch. Gen. Psychiatry 21: 753–760, **1969.**

An interesting study of the relationship of stress and depression that also reviews the methodologic issues in a study of this kind: for example, the effect of depression on the patient's description of prior events.

MAJOR DEPRESSION

14.   ***Kendell, R.E.** The classification of depressions: A review of contemporary confusion. Br. J. Psychiatry 129: 15–28, **1976.**

Kendell reviews a variety of concepts and models which have been generated to explain severe depressive illness. He concludes that endogenous depression is a distinct entity but that nonendogenous depression is a heterogeneous grouping.

15.   ***Klein, D.F.** Endogenomorphic depression: A conceptual and terminological revision. Arch. Gen. Psychiatry 31: 447–454, **1974.**

Klein reiterates the view that endogenous depression is characterized by the nature of the syndrome once developed rather than the presence or absence of precipitating stress. The loss of the ability to experience pleasure is a central feature. He also predicts differences in drug and placebo response for acute situational depressions, endogenous depressions, and chronic dysphorias.

16.   ***Nelson, J.C. and Charney, D.S.** The symptoms of major depressive illness. Am. J. Psychiatry 138: 1–13, **1981.**

The authors review prior studies of the endogenous-nonendogenous distinction and use this review as a basis for deriving symptoms characteristic of endogenous depression.

17.   **Rosenthal, S.H. and Klerman, G.L.** Content and consistency in the endogenous depressive pattern. Br. J. Psychiatry 112: 471–484, **1966.**

The authors contend that endogenous depression indicates not only depression with an absence of precipitating stress, but other distinguishing characteristics as well.

18. **Rosenthal, S.H.** The involutional depressive syndrome. Am. J. Psychiatry 124 (11-suppl.): 21–35, **1968.**

The diagnosis of involutional melancholia has only recently been discarded. This is a comprehensive review of involutional melancholia and the evidence suggesting that it does not constitute a distinct entity.

PSYCHOTIC DEPRESSION

19. **Charney, D.S. and Nelson, J.C.** Delusional and nondelusional unipolar depression: Further evidence for distinct subtypes. Am. J. Psychiatry 138: 328–333, **1981.**

A descriptive study of psychotic depression that supports the view that this syndrome constitutes a distinct entity.

20. **Glassman, A.B., Kantor, J.S., and Shostak, M.** Depressive delusions, and drug response. Am. J. Psychiatry 132: 716–719, **1975.**

This brief paper argues that delusional or psychotic depressed patients respond less well to tricyclic antidepressants than nonpsychotic patients. The paper stimulated considerable research and is in part responsible for the *DSM III* distinction of psychotic depression.

PRIMARY-SECONDARY DEPRESSION

21. **Andreasen, N.C. and Winokur, G.** Secondary depression: Familial, clinical, and research perspectives. Am. J. Psychiatry 136: 62–66, **1979.**

This is a useful review of the concept of secondary depression.

22. **Woodruff, R.A., Murphy, G.E., and Herjanic, M.** The natural history of affective disorders: I. Symptoms of 72 patients at the time of index hospital admission. J. Psychiatr. Res. 5: 255–263, **1967.**

This is one of the earliest papers describing the distinction between primary and secondary depression as a means of separating patients with "primary affective disorder" from patients with depressions associated with other psychiatric syndromes. This distinction has gained considerable acceptance and has been of major importance during the past decade.

chiatric syndromes. This distinction has gained considerable acceptance and has been of major importance during the past decade.

BIPOLAR DISORDER

23. **Bunney, W.E., Murphy, D.L., Goodwin, F.K., et al.** The "switch process" in manic depressive illness. 1. A systematic study of sequential behavioral changes. Arch. Gen. Psychiatry 27: 295–302, **1972.**

   The "switch process" is an important concept that has become part of the psychiatric vocabulary and has stimulated further research.

24. **Carlson, G.A. and Goodwin, F.K.** The stages of mania: A longitudinal analysis of the manic episode. Arch. Gen. Psychiatry 28: 221–228, **1973.**

   This interesting description of the progression of symptoms during an acute manic episode is one of the few reports in the literature that not only details symptom differences between patients but emphasizes how symptoms may differ with respect to the stage of the illness.

25. **Leonhard, K.** Auftelung der endogenen Psychosen (2nd ed.). Berlin: Akademie Verlag, **1959.**

   This work describes the distinction between unipolar and bipolar depressive illness. This distinction has remained important to the present.

26. **Lipkin, K.M., Dyrud, J., and Meyer, G.G.** The many faces of mania: Therapeutic trial of lithium carbonate. Arch. Gen. Psychiatry 22: 262–267, **1970.**

   This article persuasively argues that manic patients may present with paranoid psychotic symptoms that may be mistaken for schizophrenia. Cases are presented.

27. **Perris, C.** A study of bipolar (manic-depressive) and unipolar recurrent depressive psychoses. Acta Psychiatr. Scand. (Suppl. no. 194) 42: **1966.**

   Perris examines a series of variables in unipolar and bipolar patients. The monograph provided support for the unipolar-bipolar distinction.

28. **Taylor, M.A. and Abrams, R.** The phenomenology of mania: A new look at some old patients. Arch. Gen. Psychiatry 29: 520–522, **1973.**

   This study demonstrated that many patients receiving the diagnosis of "schizophrenia" in fact had symptoms and other characteristics suggestive of bipolar illness.

OTHER DEPRESSIVE DISEASES

29. **Akiskal, H.S.** Dysthymic disorder: Psychopathology of proposed chronic depressive subtypes. Am. J. Psychiatry 140: 11–20, **1983.**

The author discusses current concepts of "characterologic depression" and makes the distinction between depressions associated with personality disorder and those associated with affective disorder that has become chronic.

30. ***Davidson, J.R.T., Miller, R.D., Turnbull, C.D., et al.** Atypical depression. Arch. Gen. Psychiatry 39: 527–534, **1982.**

A very helpful review of the literature on atypical depression. It describes different uses of the term and summarizes the current status of this disorder.

31. **Klerman, G.L., Endicott, J., Spitzer, R.L., et al.** Neurotic depressions: A systematic analysis of multiple criteria and meanings. Am. J. Psychiatry 136:: 57–61, **1979.**

This article describes the current status of neurotic depression and systematically reviews the various meanings of the term.

32. **Quitkin, F.M., Rifin, A., and Klein, D.F.** Monoamine oxidase inhibitors: A review of antidepressant effectiveness. Arch. Gen. Psychiatry 36: 749–760, **1979.**

One of the best reviews of the current status of monoamine oxidase inhibitors. It uses response to monoamine oxidase inhibitors to define a group of patients with "hysteroid dysphoria."

33. **West, E.D. and Dally, P.J.** Effects of iproniazid in depressive syndromes. Br. Med. J. 1: 1491–1494, **1959.**

This is one of the earliest papers describing atypical depression and the particular usefulness of MAOI drugs for its treatment.

GENETIC STUDIES

34. ***Gershon, E.S., Hamovit, J., Guroff, J.J., et al.** A family study of schizoaffective bipolar I, bipolar II, unipolar, and normal control probands. Arch. Gen. Psychiatry 39: 1157–1167, **1982.**

35. **Weissman, M.M., Kidd, K., and Prusoff, B.A.** Variability in rates of affective disorders in relatives of depressed and normal probands. Arch. Gen. Psychiatry 39: 1397–1403, **1982.**

In these papers, data from two of the largest, most carefully designed genetic studies are presented. There is clear support for the heritability of affective illness. They propose a continuum of genetic vulnerability, such that bipolar illness is manifested when vulnerability is most severe and unipolar illness manifested when it is less severe.

BIOLOGICAL MARKERS

36.   ***Carroll, B.J.** The dexamethasone suppression tests for melancholia. Br. J. Psychiatry 140: 292–304, **1982.**

37.   ***Carroll, B.J., Feinberg, M., Greden, J.F., et al.** A specific laboratory test for the diagnosis of melancholia. Standardization, validation and clinical utility. Arch. Gen. Psychiatry 38: 15–22, **1981.**

These two excellent reviews describe the use of the Dexamethasone Suppression Test as a useful diagnostic laboratory test for endogenous depression. These papers review the research leading to the standardization of the test and its present uses and limitations.

38.   **Gillin, J.C., Duncan, W., Pettigrew, K.D., et al.** Successful separation of depressed, normal, and insomniac patients by EEG sleep data. Arch. Gen. Psychiatry 36: 85–90, **1979.**

39.   ***Kupfer, D.J., Foster, F.G., Coble, P., et al.** The application of EEG sleep for the differential diagnosis of affective disorders. Am. J. Psychiatry 135: 69–74, **1978.**

40.   **Kupfer, D.J.** REM latency: A psychobiologic marker for primary depressive illness. Biol. Psychiatry 11: 159–174, **1976.**

41.   **Kupfer, D.J., Shaw, D.H., Ulrich, R., et al.** Application of automated REM analysis in depression. Arch. Gen. Psychiatry 39: 569–573, **1982.**

There is abundant evidence supporting the presence of rapid eye movement (REM) sleep abnormalities in depressed patients. In addition, changes in REM sleep by antidepressants may be related to clinical response. These four papers present these findings and suggest the need for further research.

42.   **Langer, S.Z., Zarifian, E., Briley, M., et al.** High-affinity 3H-imipramine binding: A new biological marker in depression. Pharmacopsychiatria 15: 4–10, **1982.**

43.   **Paul, S.M., Rehavi, M., Skolnick, P., et al.** Depressed patients have

decreased binding of tritiated imipramine to platelet serotonin "transporter." Arch. Gen. Psychiatry 38: 1315–1317, **1981.**

44.   **Meltzer, H.Y., Arora, R.C., Baber, R., et al.** Serotonin uptake in blood platelets of psychiatric patients. Arch. Gen. Psychiatry 38: 1322–1326, **1981.**

Investigations by Langer and associates have succeeded in showing that in man imipramine is bound in the brain with a high degree of affinity to sites which are responsible for the uptake of serotonin. It has been suggested that this binding of imipramine in both brain and platelets may be a biological marker and diagnostic aid in depression. This work also supports the contention that serotonin function is abnormal in depression.

45.   ***Loosen, P.T. and Prange, A.J.** Serum thyrotropin response to thyrotropin-releasing hormone in psychiatric patients: A review. Am. J. Psychiatry 139: 405–416, **1982.**

There is extensive evidence that the serum thyrotropin (TSH) response to thyrotropin-releasing hormone (TRH) is blunted in a subgroup of depressed patients. This paper is an excellent review of 41 studies describing 917 depressed patients.

NEUROBIOLOGY

46.   **Asberg, M., Traskman, L., and Thoren, P.** 5-HIAA in the cerebrospinal fluid—a biochemical suicide predictor? Arch. Gen. Psychiatry 33: 1193–1197, **1976.**

47.   **Traskman, L., Asberg, M., Bertilsson, L., et al.** Monoamine metabolite in CSF and suicidal behavior. Arch. Gen. Psychiatry 38: 631–636, **1981.**

These two papers provide evidence for an association between a low concentration of CSF 5-HIAA and suicidal behavior. These data are consistent with the hypothesis that altered brain serotonin function is of etiologic significance in depression.

48.   ***Bunney, W.E., Wehr, T.R., Gillin, J.C., et al.** The switch process in manic depressive psychosis. Ann. Intern. Med. 87: 319–335, **1977.**

A comprehensive paper describing the neurobiology of the rapid shifts from mania to depression and vice versa. An important review paper that set the stage for numerous subsequent investigations.

49.   ***Charney, D.S., Menkes, D.B., and Heninger, G.R.** Receptor sensitivity

and the mechanism of action of antidepressant treatment: Implications for the etiology and therapy of depression. Arch. Gen. Psychiatry 38: 1160–1180, **1981**.

This extensive review evaluates the catecholamine and indolamine hypotheses of depression in light of recent research on the effect of antidepressant treatment on monoamine receptor sensitivity. A revised etiological model of depressive illness is presented and future research direction elaborated.

50. **Charney, D.S., Heninger, G.R., Sternberg, D.E., et al.** Presynaptic adrenergic receptor sensitivity in depression. Arch. Gen. Psychiatry 38: 1334–1340, **1981**.

51. **Charney, D.S., Heninger, G.R., Sternberg, D.E., et al.** Adrenergic receptor sensitivity in depression. Arch. Gen. Psychiatry 39: 290–294, **1982**.

52. **Checkley, S.A., Slade, A.P., and Shur, E.** Growth hormone and other responses to clonidine in patients with endogenous depression. Br. J. Psychiatry 136: 51–55, **1981**.

53. **Garcia-Sevilla, J.A., Zis, A.P., Hollingsworth, P.J., et al.** Platelet 2-adrenergic receptors in major depressive disorder. Arch. Gen. Psychiatry 38: 1327–1333, **1981**.

54. **Matussek, N., Ackenheil, M., Hippius, H., et al.** Effect of clonidine on growth hormone release in psychiatric patients and controls. Psychiatr. Res. 2: 25–36, **1980**.

There is increasing evidence that the sensitivity of adrenergic receptors may be abnormal in depressed patients. These papers provide an update of recent research in this area and examine research strategies designed to evaluate specific receptor systems in brain.

55. ***Checkley, S.A.** Neuroendocrine tests of monamine function in man: A review of basic theory and its application to the study of depressive illness. Psychol. Med. 10: 35–53, **1980**.

An excellent review of the findings of neuroendocrine studies designed to evaluate the monoamine deficiency hypothesis of depressive illness.

56. ***Maas, J.W., Kocsis, J.M., Bowden, C.L., et al.** Pretreatment neurotransmitter metabolites and response to imipramine or amitryptyline treatment. Psychol. Med. 12: 37–43, **1982**.

Previous studies suggested low levels of urinary 3-methoxy-4-hydroxy phenylethyleneglycol (MHPG) are associated with a positive treatment response to imipramine and high MHPG levels a positive response to amitriptyline. However, this large scale collaborative study found that, while low urinary MHPG predicted response to imipramine, there was not a relationship between pretreatment MHPG and response to amitryptyline.

57. ***Murphy, D.L., Campell, I.C., and Costa, J.L.** The brain serotonergic system in the affective disorders. Progr. Neuropsychopharmacol. 2: 1–31, **1978.**

58. ***Praag, H.M. van.** Central monoamines and the pathogenesis of depression, pp. 159–205. In: Handbook of Biological Psychiatry. Part IV. Brain Mechanisms and Abnormal Behavior—Chemistry. Eds.: H.M. van Praag, M.H. Loder, O.J. Rafailsen, et al. New York: Marcel Dekker, **1981.**

59. **Cowdry, R.W. and Goodwin, F.K.** Amine neurotransmitter studies and psychiatric illness: Toward more meaningful diagnostic concepts, pp. 281–304. In: Clinical Issues in Psychiatric Diagnosis. Eds.: R.L. Spikes and D.F. Klein New York: Raven Press, **1978.**

These three papers are informative reviews of the role of abnormal serotonin function in the genesis of depressive illness. In particular, studies comparing the levels of the serotonin metabolite, 5-hydroxy-indolacetic acid (5-HIAA) in the cerebrospinal fluid of depressed patients and healthy subjects are discussed.

60. ***Schildkraut, J.J.** Current status of the catecholamine hypothesis of affective disorders, pp. 1223–1234. In: Psychopharmacology: A Generation of Progress. Eds.: M.A. Lipton, A. DiMascio, and K.F. Killam. New York: Raven Press, **1978.**

A review of the evidence supporting the hypothesis that decreased catecholamine function exists in at least a subgroup of depressed patients. Particular attention is directed toward studies of catecholamine metabolite levels in depressed patients.

61. ***Wehr, T.A., Goodwin, F.K., Wirz-Justice, A., et al.** 48 hours sleep-wake cycles in manic-depressive illness. Naturalistic observations and sleep deprivation experiments. Arch. Gen. Psychiatry 39: 559–565, **1982.**

62. **Kripke, D.F., Mullaney, D.J., Atkinson, M., et al.** Circadian rhythm disorders in manic-depressives. Biol. Psychiatry 13: 335–351, **1978.**

63. **Wehr, T.A., Muscettola, G., and Goodwin, F.K.** Urinary 3-methoxy-4-

hydroxy phenylglycol circadian rhythm. Arch. Gen. Psychiatry 37: 257–263, **1980.**

64. **Wehr, T.A., Wirz-Justice, A., Goodwin, F.K., et al.** Phase advance of the circadian sleep wake cycle as an anti-depressant. Science 206: 710–713, **1979.**

These four papers provide evidence of circadian rhythm disturbances in depressive illness and suggest that alteration in circadian rhythms may relate to the precipitation and duration of depression as well as the mechanism of action of anti-depressant treatments.

15. OTHER PSYCHOSES

MARTIN S. KESSELMAN, M.D.

Besides the main body of literature concerning the psychotic disorders that forms the basis for *DSM III*, an apocrypha has developed describing uncommon or exotic psychoses or those whose nosological status is as yet uncertain. For self-evident reasons, this body of work has a relatively weak claim for representation in a volume devoted to "core" readings. Nevertheless, there are important reasons for residents to become familiar with this area of the literature, and it is these which have served as the criteria for its inclusion.

The psychoses in this group fall into three rather broad categories: a group of culture-bound ("exotic") psychoses mainly drawn from anthropological descriptions, a group of syndromes that, although recognizably relatable to one or another of the major psychoses, are sufficiently infrequent and distinctive as to warrant separate designation, and finally, a group of alternative nosological entities that have been suggested to accommodate otherwise common illnesses that fail to sufficiently conform to standard *DSM III* categories. The *paranoid disorder* group is included with the latter because, although it is codable by *DSM III*, its status as a separate entity is still being vigorously debated; indeed the recent literature appears to support those who have argued the merits of splitting off a subset of these disorders from the schizophrenias.

In many cases, the original authors put forth claims for more than syndromal status for these "illnesses," and these claims have been almost uniformly rejected, in American psychiatry at least. Why should the student concern himself about them at all, then?

First, of course, for their inherent fascination. An interest in the manifestations of psychopathology is a necessary prerequisite for the study of psychiatry, and the classical descriptions summarized in these readings extend one's appreciation of the range and variety of mental disorder. Precisely because we have come to understand these syndromes as variants of our own familiar "culture-bound" psychoses, we can judge the effects of those pathoplastic influences transmitted through sociocultural mechanisms. Indeed, as Langness emphasizes, social responses to the "patient's" behavior may play an important reciprocal role in their being sustained.

Second, the debate concerning this group of illnesses allows the reader to witness the nosological process in active ferment. Trainees are often insufficiently aware that the official diagnostic practices they are taught describe not illness, but how experts think about illness. In considering alternative or rejected nosological categories, they will have an opportunity to observe specific controversies that lie not far under the surface of the seemingly settled waters of the official diagnostic and statistical manuals. It is for this reason that, in the following list, critical reviews rather than original descriptions are emphasized. From these, the reader can trace his way back to original sources if he wishes.

If there is an overarching theme that binds the readings in this section, it is that the search for the foreign and esoteric in psychopathology has largely proven fruitless. The terms of transcultural psychiatry are coming increasingly to resemble those of social psychiatry. More and more, we have come to understand the importance of the similarities between cultures rather than their differences, of the critical importance of acculturation and institutional change in our own society as well as in distant ones, and of the strong impact of socially learned roles and prohibitions in the shaping of mental disorder, if not in their origins.

1. ***Enoch, M.D., Trethowan, W.H., and Barker, J.S.** Some Uncommon Psychiatric Syndromes. Bristol: John Wright, **1976.** (2nd ed. available— Chicago: Year Book Medical Publishers, **1979.**)

   Detailed and critical reviews of several of the classic syndromes discussed in this section and a group of nonpsychotic but uncommon disorders as well. The authors present case illustrations from their own experience. An excellent source for an overview of the area with a fine bibliography.

2. **Hollender, M.H. and Hirsch, S.J.** Hysterical psychosis. Am. J. Psychiatry 20: 1066–1074, **1964.**

   Argues for the utility of a diagnostic category that has seen informal use but has never been officially accepted into our nomenclature. Should be read in conjunction with the Langness article.

3. ***Langness, L.L.** Hysterical psychosis: The cross-cultural evidence. Am. J. Psychiatry 124: 143–152, **1967.**

   A good review of a broad range of culture-bound psychoses. Many appear to correspond to "hysterical psychoses" (for which see Hollender and Hirsch). Stresses sociocultural determinants of presentation and course.

4. **Laseque, C. and Falcet, J.** La folie à deux (ou folie communiquée). (J. Ann. Med. Psychol. 18: 321–355, 1877) Trans. and Biblio.: R. Michaud. Am. J. Psychiatry 121 (4: Suppl.): 1–23, **1964.**

The classic description. *Folie à deux* remains a useful concept because it corresponds to a condition that is still encountered with a fair degree of frequency, but also because the diagnosis must be taken into account in formulating a treatment plan. The state sheds light on the "induction" of psychotic states.

5. ***Leonhard, K.** The Classification of Endogenous Psychoses (5th ed.). Ed.: E. Robins. Trans.: R. Berman New York: Irvington Publishers, **1979.**

    A classic text in European psychiatry by a senior clinician. Perhaps the most extensive discussion available in English of Leonhard's concept of cycloid psychoses.

6. **McCabe, M.S.** Reactive psychosis. A clinical and genetic investigation. Acta Psychiatr. Scand. Suppl. 51: (Suppl. no. 259), **1975.**

    An excellent presentation of a diagnostic category used in Scandanavia. It appears to be distinct from traditional *DSM III* groups and to predict a different clinical course from the latter.

7. ***Magaro, P., ed.** The paranoid as an emerging character. Schizophr. Bull. 7: 586–735, **1981.**

    Taken as a whole, this multiauthor volume represents a comprehensive and current review of paranoid psychoses. Besides noting the differences in presentation and outcome between paranoid and nonparanoid schizophrenics, which have been commented on for almost a century, several of the contributing authors suggest that the paranoid patient adapts a different cognitive strategy from other schizophrenics.

8. **Monroe, R.R.** Episodic behavioral disorders: An unclassified syndrome, pp. 237–254. In: AHP (2nd ed.), Vol. 3, **1974.**

    Perhaps the most extensive American attempt to delineate a group of psychotic (and nonpsychotic) disorders on the basis of the episodic occurrence of behaviors discontinuous with the patient's usual mental state. Foreshadows recent speculations on the role of "kindling" phenomena and periodicity in the major psychoses.

9. **Murphy, H.B.M.** History and the evolution of syndromes: The striking case of Latah and Amok, pp. 33–55. In: Psychopathology: Contributions from the Social Behavioral and Biological Sciences. Eds.: M. Hammer, K. Salzinger, and S. Sutton. New York: Wiley, **1973.**

    In a scholarly and cogent review of the literature on these two exotic syndromes, Murphy argues that they are not static entities, but have evolved as Malayan culture has undergone a series of radical transitions in response to its contact with Western culture.

10.   **Seeman, M.V.** Delusional loving. Arch. Gen. Psychiatry 35: 1265–1267, **1978.**

Reviews features of erotania and proposes two main subcategories: "Fixed delusional lovers" and "recurrent delusional lovers." This is a stimulating attempt to relate a syndrome (De Clerambault's) to diagnosis and psychodynamics.

11.   **Whitlock, F.A.** The Ganser syndrome. Br. J. Psychiatry 113: 19–29, **1967.**

A critical review of a symptom complex usually regarded as closer to the dissociative states but which the author cogently argues is a psychosis.

16. THE NEUROSES: HYSTERIA, OBSESSIVE-COMPULSIVE NEUROSES, PHOBIAS, AND SYMPTOM FORMATION

JOHN C. NEMIAH, M.D.
BENNETT SIMON, M.D.

During the course of the nineteenth century clinicians began explicitly to observe, describe, and define psychoneurotic symptoms as we conceive of them today. Janet's bipartite classification of neurotic disorders into hysteria and psychasthenia (which included anxiety, depression, phobias, and obsessive-compulsive phenomena) provided a first approach to an orderly classification of the clinical observations. It was not, however, till the end of the century that Freud in his early clinical papers imposed the classificatory scheme on the neuroses that is still employed by most Western psychiatrists. The modern division of neurotic disorders into hysteria, phobic neurosis, obsessive-compulsive neurosis, and neurotic depression is based on the recognition that they are the surface manifestations of psychodynamic conflict, the form of each being determined by the specific elements of that conflict.

The recent important discoveries of biological psychiatry and the useful phenomenological approach of *DSM III* (the third edition of the *Diagnostic and Statistic Manual* of the American Psychiatric Association) have posed a challenge to the more traditional classification. At the same time, while helping to clarify and to standardize the definition of neurotic disorders, *DSM III* ignores much that has been learned about the clinical and psychodynamic relationships of neurotic syndromes. For example, the separation in *DSM III* of conversion disorder and dissociative disorder into two distinct and unrelated diagnostic categories overlooks the facts that the symptoms of each frequently appear together in the same patient and are both closely associated with the underlying mechanism of dissociation—facts that suggest that the two disorders are significantly related clinically and etiologically.

In the selected readings that follow we have included a number of historically important papers since, in our view, modern concepts are best understood against the background of their evolution. The majority of the papers we have chosen deal with the psychodynamic aspect of neurotic disorders, since this remains the most useful model for understanding their genesis. We have, however, included several articles and monographs describing more recent behavioral and biological discoveries, which point to the fact that neurotic symptoms are the end result of processes that, conceptually speaking, are both psychological and physiological in nature. To understand the etiology of the neuroses and to treat them properly, one must be intelligently eclectic in outlook and avoid the damaging polarization of thinking exclusively in either biological or psychodynamic terms.

PSYCHOPATHOLOGY AND SYMPTOM FORMATION

1. ***Brenner, C.** An Elementary Textbook of Psychoanalysis (rev. ed.). New York: International Universities Press, **1973.**

   For its combination of accessibility, readability, brevity, low cost, and depth of clinical experience, this is still the best single introduction to psychoanalytic theory and clinical practice. Should be read very early in training and then reread at a more advanced stage.

2. **Brenner, C.** Depressive affect, anxiety and psychic conflict in the phallic-oedipal phase. Psychoanal. Q. 48: 177–197, **1979.**

   An extension of the author's earlier thinking on the variety of painful affects (that is, not only anxiety) that can serve a signal function in symptom formation. Emphasizes the embeddedness of affects in fantasies and their role in symptom formation at the oedipal period.

3. **Fenichel, O.** Outline of Clinical Psychoanalysis. New York: Psycho-analytic Quarterly Press, **1934.**

   Most useful for its concise and readable clinical descriptions and lucid (though somewhat dated) formulations about the classical symptom neuroses, hysteria, phobia ("anxiety hysteria"), and compulsion neuroses. Easier reading than his later (1945) textbook, but more difficult to obtain.

4. ***Fenichel, O.** The Psychoanalytic Theory of the Neuroses. New York: Norton, **1945.**

   The supreme encyclopedia of clinical psychoanalysis as of 1945. Its detailed descriptions of the clinical picture and of the dynamic issues in the classical neuroses are unsurpassed. At times difficult to read, but always immensely rewarding, even when dated or incorrect.

5. **Freud, S.** (1894) Neuro-psychoses of defence. S.E. 3: 45–66, **1962.**

In this early clinical paper, Freud addresses the relation of symptom formation to psychological conflict and suggests that the differing forms of neurotic symptoms are determined by the nature of the defences that are called into operation against unacceptable mental contents (ideas, fantasies, feelings).

6. **Freud, S.** (1895) On the grounds for detaching a particular syndrome from neurasthenia under the description 'anxiety neurosis.' S.E. 3: 90–115, **1962.**

An early clinical paper in which Freud not only gave a clinical definition of anxiety neurosis, but suggested that, unlike hysterical symptoms, anxiety represented the direct somatic transformation of repressed drives without the intervention of higher psychic processes—a concept that was lost to sight in the later formulation of signal anxiety (cf. Freud, S. Inhibitions, Symptoms and Anxiety).

7. ***Freud, S.** (1915–1916, 1916–1917) Introductory Lectures on Psycho-analysis. S.E. 15, **1961**; S.E. 16, **1963.**

Still the best introduction to symptom formation as compromise formation. Examples of parapraxes, dreams, and symptoms are concise, clever, often witty, and memorable.

8. ***Freud, S.** (1962) Inhibitions, symptoms and anxiety. S.E. 20: 87–112, **1959.**

One of Freud's later important theoretical monographs. Against the background of the new structural model of the psyche, anxiety is viewed as a signal of the disruption of the psychic equilibrium (cf. Freud, S. "On the Grounds for Detaching a Particular Syndrome from Neurasthenia under the Description 'Anxiety Neurosis'").

9. ***Freud, S.** (1933) New introductory lectures on psycho-analysis. S.E. 22: 3–182, **1964.**

Contains some important revisions relevant to symptom formation, most notably in the section on anxiety. Freud replaces his earlier "anxiety as undischarged libido" theory with his formulations about anxiety as a signal in the process of "symptom formation."

10. **Galler, F.B.** The two faces of regression: A conceptual review. Psycho-anal. Inquiry 1: 133–154, **1981.**

A useful summary of the changing meanings of regression as used in psychoanalytic thinking, both in relation to psychopathology and to health. Good bibliography. The entire issue, Vol. 1, No. 1, is devoted to the topic of regression.

11. ***Gedo, J.E. and Goldberg, A.** Models of the Mind: A Psychoanalytic Theory. Chicago: University of Chicago Press, **1973.**

    A scheme for conceptualizing the relationships among the neuroses, borderline and narcissistic states, and other primitive personalities. Controversial, but quite useful, especially for advanced trainees.

12. ***Hartmann, H. and Kris, E.** The genetic approach in psychoanalysis. Psychoanal. Study Child 1: 11–30, **1945.**

    An important theoretical paper dealing with the dynamic and genetic aspects of symptom formation and emphasizing the importance of direct observation of infants and children during their sequential phases of growth and development.

13. ***Klein, D.F. and Rabkin, J.G.,** eds. Anxiety. New Research and Changing Concepts. New York: Raven Press, **1980.**

    An excellent collection of papers that summarize recent biological advances in the understanding and treatment of anxiety and attempt to correlate these with established psychological observations and theory.

14. **Levin, K.** Freud's Early Psychology of the Neuroses. A Historical Perspective. Pittsburgh: University of Pittsburgh Press, **1978.**

    An original, provocative, and admirably clear discussion of the historical background and development of Freud's early psychodynamic theories.

15. ***Loewald, H.W.** The waning of the Oedipus Complex. J. Am. Psychoanal. Assoc. 27: 751–775, **1979.**

    An excellent and balanced discussion of the role of the oedipus complex in symptom and character formation, especially the vicissitudes of guilt, and of the "waning," rather than the dissolution in life after the oedipal years. The article also considers the waning of psychoanalytic interest in the oedipus complex and the current emphasis on preoedipal and narcissistic issues, taking up briefly societal correlates of this shift in psychoanalytic concerns.

16. **Miller, M.B.,** ed. Psychoanalysis and Women: Contributions to New Theory and Therapy. New York: Brunner/Mazel, **1973.**

    A useful collection of articles for considering how changing views on masculinity and feminity, both in the society and within the community of psychotherapists, affect the form and content of psychopathology and, concomitantly, the psychotherapeutic treatment.

17.   ***Moore, B.E. and Fine, F.F.,** eds. A Glossary of Psychoanalytic Terms and Concepts (2nd ed.). New York: American Psychoanalytic Association, **1968.**

A short, inexpensive, and concise source of definitions of basic terms relevant to symptom formation and psychopathology. Especially useful at the beginning phase of readings in psychodynamic and psychoanalytic material. A revised edition is in preparation.

18.   ***Nagera, H.** Early Childhood Disturbances, The Infantile Neurosis, and Adult Disturbances. (Monograph Series of the Psychoanalytic Study of the Child, no. 2.) New York: International Universities Press, **1966.**

A concise and thoughtful discussion by a distinguished child analyst of the relationship between childhood disturbance and adult neurosis. Shows that life and the clinical situation are even more complex than the theory.

19.   **Nagera, H., Baker, S., Colonna, A., et al.** Basic Psychoanalytic Concepts on the Libido Theory. (The Hampstead Clinic Psychoanalytic Library, Vol. I.) New York: Basic Books, **1969.**

A series of short articles surveying and summarizing Freud's ideas on various aspects of "libido theory," which here is almost synonymous with the issue of symptom formation. Particularly valuable are the chapters on the oedipus complex of the girl and of the boy, the dissolution of the complex and the castration complex.

20.   **Nagera, H., Colonna, A., Dansky, E., et al.** Basic Psychoanalytic Concepts on Metapsychology, Conflicts, Anxiety and Other Subjects. (The Hampstead Clinic Psychoanalytic Library, Vol. IV.) New York: Basic Books, **1970.**

A series of relatively short, clearly written, scholarly articles summarizing changes in Freud's writings of the major psychoanalytic terms in relation to symptom formation and psychopathology. Chapters 8 ("Conflict"), 9 ("Fixation"), 10 ("Regression") and 11 ("Anxiety") are particularly useful.

21.   ***Nemiah, J.C.** Foundations of Psychopathology. New York: Aronson, **1973.**

Aimed at the student who has not yet had extensive clinical experience, this is an introductory text of psychodynamic psychiatry, which describes the psychological aspects of symptom formation through the extensive use of case material.

22.   **Nemiah, J.C.** Neurotic disorders, pp. 1483–1561. In: CTP III, Vol. 2, **1980.**

The section on anxiety disorder provides a systematic review of the clinical, phenomenological, and psychotherapeutic aspects of anxiety, with special reference to its central role in psychological conflict. Also includes sections on conversion and dissociative disorders, phobic conditions, and obsessive-compulsive neuroses.

23.   **Shapiro, T.** On the quest for the origins of conflict. Psychoanal. Q. 50: 1–21, **1981.**

A fine discussion of one of the main controversies in understanding psychopathology and symptom formation—how far back in development does the relevant conflict go? Questions of evidence of the pertinence of the controversy are succinctly presented with the author's biases made explicit.

24.   **Stone, S. and Stone, A.** The Abnormal Personality Through Literature. Englewood Cliffs, NJ: Prentice-Hall, **1966.**

In an imaginative approach to psychiatric phenomenology, the authors illustrate the wide variety of psychiatric disorders and symptoms by highly apposite selections from famous novels and plays. Combined with the brief didactic commentaries that tie the selections together, this volume provides the reader with an unusually illuminating and enjoyable elementary textbook of psychiatry.

25.   ***Waelder, R.** The principle of multiple function: Observations on overdetermination. Psychoanal. Q. 5: 45–62, **1936.** (Also in: Psychoanalysis: Observation, Theory, Application: Selected Papers of Robert Waelder, pp. 68–83. Ed.: S. Guttman. New York: International Universities Press, **1976.**)

A classic article, indispensable for conceptualizing how the different needs and aims of the psyche, or of the person, are synthesized whether in symptom formation or character traits. Waelder takes us beyond Freud's notion of compromise formation to a conception that is crucial for the conduct of open-ended listening to the patient.

HYSTERIA

26.   **Bornstein, B.** Hysterical twilight states in an eight-year-old child. Psychoanal. Study Child 2: 229–240, **1947.**

One of the few detailed presentations of the symptoms and treatment of hysteria in childhood, particularly valuable for sexual trauma.

27.   ***Breuer, J. and Freud, S.** (1893–1895) Studies on hysteria. S.E. 2: 3–309, **1955.**

A classic monograph from the early days of psychoanalysis, which illuminates the emergence of the concept of psychological conflict from the earlier formulations concerning dissociation. Contains Breuer's famous case history of "Anna O." and the "Preliminary Communication" written jointly by Breuer and Freud.

28.   ***Chodoff, P. and Lyons, H.** Hysteria, the hysterical personality, and "hysterical" conversion. Am. J. Psychiatry 144: 734–740, **1958.**

An important study that demonstrates the lack of a significant correlation between hysterical conversion symptoms and hysterical personality traits.

29.   **Flournoy, T.** Une mystique moderne. (Documents pour la psychologie réligieuse.) Arch. Psychol. (Génève) 15: 1–224, **1915.**

Written in French and buried in the early twentieth-century literature, this moving account of a woman's struggles with hysteria is to the neuroses as Schreber's *Memoirs* is to schizophrenia. Too little known, it should be read by all who are interested in the genesis of hysterical symptoms.

30.   ***Freud, S.** (1893) Some points for a comparative study of organic and hysterical motor paralyses. S.E. 1: 160–172, **1966.**

A masterpiece of a clinical article, summarizing the then current understanding of the differentiation of hysterical paralyses from other conditions and with Freud's additional insights. An eminently readable and still exceptionally usable paper. Good for residents on consultation service and useful for neurology residents as well.

31.   ***Freud, S.** (1905) Fragment of an analysis of a case of hysteria. S.E. 7: 7–22, **1953.**

The famous "Dora" case remains an excellent example of the psychic mechanisms that go into hysterical symptoms, character traits, and the problems and possibilities of treatment. A fine example of the work of dream interpretation and interpretation of the transference.

32.   **Goldberg, A.** Commentary on the analysis of a hysterical personality, pp. 297–361. In: Psychology of the Self: A Casebook. Ed.: A. Goldberg. New York: International Universities Press, **1978.**

A detailed report of psychoanalytic treatment of a woman with hysterical character as conducted from a self-psychological (Kohut) viewpoint. A valuable article, especially when used with the M. Horowitz article detailing an analysis from a more "classical" perspective. For advanced residents.

33. **Hilgard, E.R.** Dissociation revisited, pp. 205–219. In: Historical Conceptions of Psychology. Eds.: M. Henle, J. Jaynes, and J.J. Sullivan. New York: Springer Publishing, **1973.**

A reassessment of dissociation made in the light of modern research on hypnosis. (cf. Janet, P., *L'Automatisme Psychologique.*)

34. **Hollender, M.H. and Hirsch, S.J.** Hysterical psychosis. Am. J. Psychiatry 120: 1066–1074, **1964.**

A classic modern study reviving the nineteenth-century concept of "hysterical psychosis"; the disorder is defined and succinctly described through the presentation of case reports.

35. **Horowitz, M.,** ed. Hysterical Personality. New York: Aronson, **1977.**

An important book presenting a fine collection of articles on historical, cross-cultural, clinical, and psychotherapeutic aspects of hysteria, especially hysterical character.

36. **Horowitz, M.** Structure and the processes of change, pp. 329–399. In: Hysterical Personality. Ed.: M. Horowitz. New York: Aronson, **1977.**

This is a detailed study of psychoanalytic treatment of a young woman with hysterical character and presents an elegant and clinically usable set of schemata for understanding how change takes place in treatment. For advanced residents.

37. **Janet, P.** L'Automatisme Psychologique. Paris: Felix Alcan, **1889.**

Janet's first major work, in which he presented in detail his observations and concepts of dissociation. Although never translated from the French, it provides a valuable historical background for the current revival of interest in dissociative phenomena. (cf. Hilgard, E., "Dissociation Revisited.")

38. ***Janet, P.** The Major Symptoms of Hysteria: Fifteen Lectures given in the Medical School of Harvard University. New York: Macmillan, **1907.**

Written in English and delivered as a series of lectures at Harvard Medical School, this readable monograph presented Janet's synopsis of his clinical observations and theoretical formulations derived from over two decades of study. The final chapter is particularly useful as a summary of his concept of dissociation.

39. **Kiersch, R.A.** Amnesia: A clinical study of ninety-eight cases. Am. J. Psychiatry 119: 57–60, **1962.**

A useful clinical study of a larger series of patients that demonstrates the variety of syndromes that are associated with the presenting symptom of amnesia.

40. ***Krohn, A.** Hysteria: The Elusive Neurosis. Psychol. Issues 12: 1/2 (Mon. no. 45/46), **1978.**

A thoughtful psychodynamic study of the problems of defining, understanding and treating hysteria. Reviews the problem of the relationship between hysteria and conversion, cross-cultural aspects, and the problem of male-female differences in form and in incidence. Good bibliography.

41. **Meissner, W.W.** A study on hysteria: Anna O. rediviva. Annu. Psychoanal. 7: 17–52, **1979.**

The latest study of Breuer's patient "Anna O." with a review of the biography of the patient, who was named Bertha Pappenheim and was the founder of social work in Germany. The dynamics of the case are reconsidered in the light of some modern psychoanalytic formulations, and our understanding of the more primitive underpinnings of some cases of hysteria is thereby furthered.

42. ***Prince, M.** The Dissociation of a Personality. New York: Longmans, Green, **1906.**

A graphic, detailed biography of a patient with dissociative hysteria (multiple personality), this was the subject of a popular play on the Edwardian stage and has become a classic of the clinical literature. It admirably illustrates the complexity of the relations among the personalities resulting from dissociation.

43. **Prince, M.** An introspective analysis of co-conscious life. (My life as a dissociated personality.) By a personality (B) claiming to be co-conscious. J. Abnorm. Psychol. 3: 311–334, **1908, 1909.**

The verbatim diary of a secondary personality of a patient with dissociative hysteria, this demonstrates the poorly-understood phenomenon of "co-consciousness"—the self-aware, autonomous existence of a secondary personality below the threshhold of consciousness.

44. **Purtell, J.G., Robins, E., and Cohen, M.E.** Observations on clinical aspects of hysteria: A quantitative study of 50 hysteria patients and 156 control subjects. JAMA 146: 902–909, **1951.**

One of the first modern clinical studies of hysteria in the tradition of Briquet and Savill, this study helped to lay the groundwork that led eventually to the phenomenological definition of Briquet's syndrome.

45. ***Roy, A.,** ed. Hysteria. New York: Wiley, **1982.**

A collection of papers, many by British and European authors, with a primary focus on the phenomenology of hysteria. The initial chapter by Henri Ey provides a useful discussion of the various meanings and usages of the term "hysteria."

46. **Shapiro, D.** Hysterical style, pp. 108–133. I: Neurotic Styles. New York: Basic Books, **1965.**

An indispensable study of the relatively stable characteristics of the hysterical "character," based on observations from projective testing and from psychodynamic treatment settings.

47. **Sidis, B. and Goodhart, S.P.** Multiple Personality: An Experimental Investigation into the Nature of Human Individuality. New York: Appleton, **1905.**

A reflection of the earlier interest in dissociative phenomena, this monograph contains a fascinating and instructive report of the famous case of the Reverend Mr. Hanna.

48. **Simon, B.** Hysteria and social issues, pp. 238–268. In: Mind and Madness in Ancient Greece: The Classical Roots of Modern Psychiatry. Ithaca: Cornell University Press, **1978.**

A study of the psychological and social setting of hysteria in the culture in which the term was coined, classical Greece. Discusses the relationship among hysteria, male-female role differences, and the social status of the physician. Shows how "theories" in ancient medicine and biology may parallel the unconscious fantasies of modern hysterical patients.

49. **Sutcliffe, J.P. and Jones, J.** Personal identity, multiple personality, and hypnosis. Int. J. Clin. Exp. Hypn. 10: 231–269, **1962.**

An excellent and thorough review of the phenomena of multiple personality, with a discussion of the close relation between the disorder and hypnotizability.

50. **Veith, I.** Hysteria, the History of a Disease. Chicago: University of Chicago Press, **1965.**

Traces the odyssey and vicissitudes of the term "hysteria" through the centuries. This treatise provides an invaluable background for understanding the modern view of the hysterical neurosis.

51.   ***Woodruff, R.A., Clayton, P.J., and Guze, S.B.** Hysterical studies of diagnosis, outcome and prevalence. JAMA 215: 425–428, **1971.**

This is one of the papers characterizing and studying Briquet's syndrome, a syndrome of multiple somatic complaints, part of the spectrum of hysterical disorders. The research has important clinical implications, especially in consultation-liaison settings, as Briquet's syndrome patients typically present in medical, not psychiatric, settings.

52.   ***Zetzel, E.R.** The so-called good hysteric. Int. J. Psychoanal. 49: 256–260, **1968.**

A significant paper that led the way in pointing to the variety of psychodynamic patterns underlying hysterical symptoms, with particular reference to the nature of the hysterical patient's capacity for forming object relationship.

PHOBIC DISORDER

53.   ***Bornstein, B.** The analysis of a phobic child: Some problems of theory and technique in child analysis (4 parts). Psychoanal. Study Child 3/4: (I): 181–195; (II): 196–201; (III): 202–210; (IV): 210–226, **1949.**

The famous "Frankie" case: the first published detailed account of psychoanalysis of a phobic oedipal-aged child. Important information on the determinants of childhood phobia. "Frankie" as an obsessive adult is discussed in the Int. J. of Psychoanal. 47: 130–138, **1966** (S. Ritvo, R.J. van der Leeuw, S. Nacht).

54.   ***Bowlby, J.** Attachment and Loss: Vol. II. Separation, Anxiety and Anger. New York: Basic Books, **1973.**

An important, though controversial, revision of classic analytic theory of anxiety and fear. Chapters 18 and 19 are especially important for understanding phobias in relation to attachment and loss, and for Bowlby's discussion of "Little Hans" (Freud) and "Peter" (Watson).

55.   **Deutsch, H.** (1928) Agoraphobia, pp. 97–116. In: Neuroses and Character Types. Clinical Psychoanalytic Studies. New York: International Universities Press, **1965.**

An extremely useful clinical paper on the oedipal and preoedipal dynamics of agoraphobia. Roles of aggression and attachment are emphasized. This volume includes "Psychoanalysis and the Neuroses," 1932, and contains a number of excellent clinical articles on neurosis.

56.   **Ererra, P. and Coleman, J.V.** A long-term follow-up study on neurotic

phobic patients in a psychiatric clinic. J. Nerv. Ment. Dis. 136: 267–271, **1963.**

In this carefully done clinical investigation, the authors provide cogent evidence for the chronicity of phobic symptoms (especially agoraphobia) over a 23-year period.

57. **Fraiberg, S.H.** A critical neurosis in a two-and-a-half year old girl. Psychoanal. Study Child 7: 195–205, **1952.**

A discussion of the diagnosis, understanding, and psychoanalytic treatment in a 2 1/2-year-old girl where a phobia was prominent among the symptoms. Invaluable for its discussion of symptom formation in relation to precocious ego development.

58. **Frankel, F.H.** Trance capacity and the genesis of phobic behavior. Arch. Gen. Psychiatry 31: 261–263, **1974.**

59. **Frankel, F.H. and Orne, M.T.** Hypnotizability and phobic behavior. Arch. Gen. Psychiatry 33: 1259–1261, **1976.**

As companion pieces, these papers demonstrate the relation of hypnotic dissociation to phobic disorders and its role in the depersonalization phenomena frequently found in phobic patients (cf. Roth, M., "The Phobic Anxiety-Depersonalization Syndrome").

60. ***Freud, S.** (1909) Analysis of a phobia in a five-year-old boy. S.E. 10: 5–149, **1955.**

The classic and endlessly instructive case of "Little Hans," a 4- to 5-year-old boy who became terrified of going out into the street lest he see a horse fall down. Repressed instinctual wishes (oedipal variety) produce the phobia.

61. ***Group for the Advancement of Psychiatry.** Pharmacotherapy and Psychotherapy: Paradoxes, Problems and Progress. GAP 9:(Report no. 93): 260–434, **1975.**

The entire report should be read by anyone concerned with the integration of the biological and psychological elements of mental illness. Of particular interest is Chapter 5, dealing with the nature and treatment of panic anxiety in agoraphobia.

62. **Hall, G.S.** A study of fears. Am. J. Psychol. 8: 147–249, **1897.**

The author presents his findings derived from a national questionnaire survey of a large number of adolescents. Although perhaps overwedded to statistical analysis, he vividly portrays the extent and variety of phobic symptoms and thereby makes a contribution to the phenomenology of phobic disorder.

63.   **Lewin, B.D.** Phobic symptoms and dream interpretation. Psychoanal. Q. 21: 225–322, **1952.**

An elegant, evocative, even if at times fanciful, discussion of manifest and latent content of phobias and the utility of the model of dream interpretation in decoding the meaning of the phobia.

64.   ***Marks, I.M.** Fears and Phobias. New York: Academic Press, **1969.**

By one of the world's foremost authorities on the behavioral treatment of phobic disorders, this volume is now a classic in the field of clinical psychiatry.

65.   **Nemiah, J.C.** A psychoanalytic view of phobias. Am. J. Psychoanal. 41: 115–120, **1981.**

An attempt to integrate the approaches of biology, psychodynamic psychiatry, and learning theory to phobia formation in a conceptual scheme that emphasizes their complementarity.

66.   **Prince, M.** The Unconscious. New York: Macmillan, **1924.**

In "Lecture XIII. Two Types of Phobias," the author presents detailed clinical material clearly documenting the genesis of phobic symptoms from psychological conflict and well illustrating the parts played by displacement, projection, and avoidance in producing them.

67.   ***Roth, M.** The phobic anxiety–depersonalization syndrome. Proc. R. Soc. Med. 52: 587–595, **1959.**

An important clinical paper that calls attention to the frequency with which the experience of depersonalization is associated with the anxiety of the phobic syndrome. (cf. Frankel, "Trance Capacity and the Genesis of Phobic Behavior," and Frankel and Orne, "Hypnotizability and Phobic Behavior.")

68.   **Symonds, A.** Phobias after marriage: Women's declaration of dependence. Am J. Psychoanal. 31: 144–152, **1971.** (Also reprinted in: Psychoanalysis and Women. Ed.: J.B. Miller. Baltimore: Penguin Books, **1973.**)

A brief, but suggestive, article on the interpersonal and social aspects of the formation of phobias in a young woman who had been assertively independent and "counterphobic" before marriage. Important for considering the couples and familial aspects of symptom formation in the individual.

69.   **Watson, J.B. and Rayner, R.** Conditioned emotional reactions. J. Exp. Psychol. 3: 1–14, **1920.**

As an account of the experimental production of a phobia of rats in a nine-month-old baby, this paper is of historical importance and interest and provides the basis for the later behavioral formulations of the genesis of phobic disorders and their treatment.

OBSESSIVE-COMPULSIVE DISORDER

70.   ***Abraham, K.** Contributions to the theory of the anal character (1921), pp. 370–392. In: Selected Papers on Psychoanalysis of Karl Abraham. New York: Basic Books, **1953.**

A fine, concise, and vividly written account of the anal character, including the more ludicrous aspects. A good complement to the paper by Ernest Jones on the anal-erotic character.

71.   **Beech, H.R.,** ed. Obsessional States. London: Methuen, **1974.**

An excellent collection of papers dealing with the clinical, theoretical, and therapeutic aspects of obsessional disorders, this volume is mainly behavioral in its approach.

72.   ***Beech, H.R. and Vaughan, M.** Behavioural Treatment of Obsessional States. New York: Wiley, **1978.**

A recent and thorough systematic exposition of the behavioral approach to obsessive-compulsive disorders.

73.   ***Freud, S.** (1909) Notes upon a case of obsessional neurosis. S.E. 10: 153–318, **1955.**

The first published detailed psychoanalytic study of an obsessional neurosis. Must be read to be believed, for its marvelous description, for its account of symptom formation, and for the wonderful glimpses of Freud's part in the dialogue. The volume includes Freud's daily notes on the case.

74.   **Isberg, R.S.** A comparison of phenelzine and imipramine in an obsessive-compulsive patient. Am. J. Psychiatry 138: 1250–1251, **1981.**

75.   **Jenike, A.** Rapid response of severe obsessive-compulsive disorder to tranylcypromine. Am. J. Psychiatry 138: 1249–1250, **1981.**

These two brief papers may be profitably read together as examples of clinical reports now appearing in the literature that describe the dramatic response of individual patients with obsessive-compulsive disorder to the newer pharmacological agents.

76.   **Jones, E.** Anal-erotic character traits, pp. 413–437. In: E. Jones. Papers on Psychoanalysis. Baltimore: Williams and Wilkins, **1948.** (Also in paperback, Beacon Press, **1961**).

Marvelous descriptions of the anal character, both the anality of everyday life and that of the more seriously disturbed character disorder.

77.   ***Marks, I.M.** Review of behavioral psychotherapy: I. Obsessive-compulsive disorders. Am. J. Psychiatry 138: 584–592, **1981.**

In an up-to-date review of clinical obsessive-compulsive disorder, the author summarizes the evidence for its effectiveness particularly in compulsive rituals as contrasted with obsessional thoughts.

78.   ***Nagera, H.** Obsessional Neurosis. Developmental Psychopathology. New York: Aronson, **1976.**

A thorough and thoughtful review of developmental observation and theory in relation to therapy of adult obsessional patients. Instructive clinical examples.

79.   **Pollitt, J.D.** Natural history studies in mental illness: A discussion based on a pilot study of obsessional states. J. Ment. Sci. 106: 93–113, **1960.**

A model (and all-too-rare) study of the natural history of a neurotic disorder, this paper brings to light many important facts about the onset and course of obsessive-compulsive disorder.

80.   ***Rapaport, J., Elkins, R., Langer, D.H., et al.** Childhood obsessive-compulsive disorder. Am. J. Psychiatry 138: 1545–1554, **1981.**

A ground-breaking prospective study of obsessive-compulsive disorders in young adolescents, the report suggests that, though rare in younger patients, the form of the disorder is similar to that seen in adults.

81.   **Salzman, L. and Thaler, F.H.** Obsessive-compulsive disorders: A review of the literature. Am. J. Psychiatry 138: 286–296, **1981.**

In their review of the recent clinical studies of obsessive-compulsive disorders, the authors include a useful section on the current pharmacological approach to treatament. Still in an early investigative stage, pharmacotherapy of this disorder shows considerable promise.

82.   **Sandler, J. and Joffee, W.G.** Notes on obsessional manifestations in children. Psychoanal. Study Child 2: 425–438, **1965.**

A good overview of the clinical and theoretical issues important in understanding obsessional states in childhood and the relationship to adult neuroses.

83.   ***Shapiro, D.** Obsessive-compulsive style, pp. 23–53. In: Neurotic Styles. New York: Basic Books, **1965.**

An excellent description of the interactional, cognitive, and emotional styles of obsessive people, derived from psychological testing and psychotherapy. Useful for alerting therapists to the more frustrating aspects of working with such patients.

84.   **Zetzel, E.R.** Additional notes upon a case of obsessional neurosis. Freud 1909. Int. J. Psychoanal. 47: 123–129, **1966.**

An important discussion of Freud's "Rat Man" case, emphasizing, among other points, Freud's virtual omission of the role of the mother in the patient's life. Note that pp. 116–217 of this journal volume are devoted to a symposium on obsessional neurosis.

17. PERSONALITY AND CHARACTER DISORDERS: INCLUDING BORDERLINE AND NARCISSISTIC CHARACTER DISORDERS

ROBERT J. WALDINGER, M.D.
JOHN G. GUNDERSON, M.D.

The personality disorders have been the focus of intense interest among mental health professionals in recent decades. Controversies about diagnosis, etiology, and treatment of these disorders abound in the literature, and the revision of the diagnostic criteria for personality disorders in *DSM-III* has prompted further debate and more research than ever before.

There are 11 types of personality disorders listed in *DSM-III,* along with a category for mixed or atypical forms. While the references presented below are organized according to these types, it is important to note some important limitations of our current system of classification.

First, it is a diagnostic system in flux. Several of the personality disorders listed in *DSM-III* are new in the diagnostic nomenclature, and others have been included based on long-standing clinical traditions. Only five of the categories (histrionic, borderline, antisocial, schizoid, and compulsive) have been validated in large-scale empirical studies, while the existence of the others remains the subject of some debate.

Second, many patients with clear-cut personality disorders do not exhibit traits that fit neatly into one diagnostic category, but instead manifest features that are characteristic of more than one personality type (e.g., an individual with histrionic and narcissistic features). Thus it is often easier to diagnose the presence of a personality disorder than to classify it further by particular type.

Finally, the categories in *DSM-III* are used to describe *traits* as well as full-blown personality disorders. Everyone has personality traits that are identifiable among the *DSM-III* categories, and these traits are best conceptualized as existing on a continuum of psychopathology that includes normal psychological functioning at one end of the spectrum and severe personality disorders at the other. Therefore, some references in this chapter familiarize the reader with traits (e.g., obsessive-compulsive traits) without specifying any particular level of psychological impairment.

Also included in this chapter is a set of general references on the personality disorders, designed to provide the reader with an overview of the field. The vignettes and brief clinical descriptions contained in these references may serve as starting points for subsequent reading on individual personality types. Two personality disorders (avoidant and dependent) are not represented by specific references in this chapter because there were no available works of sufficient quality to warrant their inclusion.

The titles listed below are designed to present basic information on clinical presentation, diagnosis, etiology, psychodynamics, and treatment.

PERSONALITY DISORDERS—GENERAL

1.   ***Lion, J.R.** Personality Disorders: Diagnosis and Management (2nd ed.). Baltimore: Williams and Wilkins Company, **1981.**

A basic text that includes chapters on the diagnosis and treatment of the specific personality disorders. The book also contains chapters that provide an overview of the personality disorders with respect to psychodynamics, sociocultural factors, psychological testing, legal issues, and the use of different treatment modalities. Of special note is the chapter by L.J. Siever entitled "Schizoid and Schizotypal Personality Disorder," which presents a useful overview of both the development of these diagnostic categories and the ongoing controversies concerning their use in clinical practice.

2.   ***Millon, T.** Disorders of Personality—DSM-III: Axis II. New York: Wiley, **1981.**

Although he presents a controversial formulation of the personality disorders with the use of three dimensions—active-passive, subject-object, and pleasure-pain—the book is a brilliant and scholarly summary of past and present thinking. An excellent companion to all the other readings in this section.

3.   **Offer, D. and Sabshin, M.** Normality: Theoretical and Clinical Concepts of Mental Health (rev. ed.). New York: Basic Books, **1974.**

Examines concepts of the normal human personality as defined by psychoanalysis, psychology, sociology, and biology.

4. **Reich, W.** On the technique of character analysis, pp. 39–113. In: Character Analysis (3rd ed.). New York: Simon and Schuster, **1949.**

   Provides an excellent introduction to the psychological treatment of the personality disorders, specifically emphasizing the need for persistent and repeated analysis of resistance.

5. **Shapiro, D.** Neurotic Styles. New York: Basic Books, **1965.**

   Contains excellent descriptions of the basic cognitive styles of various personality types. Of particular interest are the chapters on hysterical, paranoid, and obsessive-compulsive styles.

6. **Siever, L.J., Insel, T.R., Uhde, T.W., et al.** Biogenetic factors in personalities. In: Current Perspectives on Personality Disorders. Ed.: J.P. Frosch. Washington, D.C.: Am. Psychiatr. Press, **1983.** (in press)

   An excellent review of empirical research on biologic variables and genetic factors that play a role in the development of human temperament and the pathogenesis of the personality disorders.

7. ***Vaillant, G.E. and Perry, J.C.** Personality disorders. pp. 1562–1590. In CTP III, (Vol. 2), **1980.**

   The authors present a highly useful and comprehensive overview of the clinical features, causes, epidemiology, course and prognosis, differential diagnosis, and treatment of the personality disorders.

PARANOID PERSONALITY DISORDERS

8. **Weintraub, W.** Obsessive-compulsive and paranoid personalities, pp. 85–101. In: Personality Disorders: Diagnosis and Management. Ed.: J.J. Lion. Baltimore: Williams and Wilkins, **1974.**

   A vivid clinical description of the paranoid individual, along with a discussion of diagnosis, etiology, and psychotherapy of this disorder.

SCHIZOID AND SCHIZOTYPAL PERSONALITY DISORDERS

9. **Guntrip, H.J.** The schizoid problem, pp. 145–173. In: Psychoanalytic Theory, Therapy, and the Self. New York: Basic Books, **1971.**

   An eloquent description of the hidden self and the internal life that the author has discovered lie behind the manifest phenomena of schizoid persons. This paper is probably not specific to such patients, but describes an aspect of other severely disturbed personalities as well.

10.   *Meehl, P.E.** Schizotaxia, schizotypy, schizophrenia. Am. Psychologist 17: 827–838, **1962.**

This paper attempted to link certain clinical phenomena associated with schizoid personality to a genetic predisposition to schizophrenia. It provided an impetus for continued studies and remains an area of high interest and controversy.

HISTRIONIC PERSONALITY DISORDER

11.   *Breuer, J. and Freud, S.** Studies on Hysteria (1893–1895). Trans.: J. Strachey. New York: Basic Books, **1957.**

This pioneering work describes Freud and Breuer's early understanding of the mechanism by which hysterical symptoms develop, along with methods of treatment that were the forerunners of psychoanalysis. Of particular importance are Chapter I ("Preliminary Communication," pp. 1–17) and Chapter IV ("The Psychotherapy of Hysteria," pp. 253–305). The case reports are both lively and informative.

12.   **Chodoff, P.** The diagnosis of hysteria: An overview. Am. J. Psychiatry 131: 1073–1078, **1974.**

The author describes three major conditions labeled as "hysterical": Briquet's hysteria, conversion symptoms, and hysterical personality disorder. He differentiates between these uses of the term "hysteria" and points to areas in which greater precision in diagnostic labeling is indicated.

13.   **Zetzel, E.R.** The so-called good hysteric. Int. J. Psychoanal. 49: 256–260, **1968.**

The author describes patients who present with similar hysterical symptoms but whose underlying pathology covers a wide range of severity.

NARCISSISTIC PERSONALITY DISORDERS

14.   **Akhtar, S. and Thomson, J.A.** Overview: Narcissistic personality disorder. Am. J. Psychiatry 139: 12–20, **1982.**

Reviews the major contributions and persisting controversies about narcissistic personality disorder.

15.   *Kohut, H.** The psychoanalytic treatment of narcissistic personality

disorders. Outline of a systematic approach. Psychoanal. Study Child 23: 86–113, **1968.**

This paper outlines a treatment approach that reflects the author's original and seminal ideas about the origins of narcissism and its forms of expression in the transference.

16. **Stolorow, R.D.** Toward a functional definition of narcissism. Inter. J. Psychoanal. 56: 179–185, **1975.**

A scholarly and readable critique of traditional psychoanalytic theories of narcissism.

ANTISOCIAL PERSONALITY DISORDER

17. **Cleckley, H.** The Mask of Sanity (4th ed.). St. Louis: Mosby, **1964.**

Contains the classic description of the "psychopathic personality," along with a pioneering effort to distinguish antisocial personality as a psychiatric diagnosis distinct from criminality.

18. **Glueck, S. and Glueck, E.** Delinquents and Non-Delinquents in Perspective. Cambridge: Harvard University Press, **1968.**

A controlled study of juvenile delinquents, with a comprehensive analysis of the social, psychological, and physical factors contributing to antisocial behavior.

19. ***Robins, L.N.** Deviant Children Grown Up: A Sociological and Psychiatric Study of Sociopathic Personality. Baltimore: Williams and Wilkins, **1966.**

A prospective follow-up study over a period of 30 years. The author analyzes the social and psychological factors that are predictive of adult antisocial behavior and further refines the definition of antisocial personality disorder. Possible implications for treatment are outlined. Chapter 13 ("Summation and Interpretation of Results," pp. 287–289) provides a concise summary of the findings of the study.

20. **Vaillant, G.E.** Sociopathy as a human process. Arch. Gen. Psychiatry 32: 178–183, **1975.**

An important psychodynamic perspective on the apparent intractability of antisocial personality disorder in the community and the possibilities for treatment when acting-out behavior of sociopathic individuals is strictly curtailed in a hospital or prison setting.

BORDERLINE PERSONALITY DISORDER

21. ***Gunderson, J.G. and Singer, M.T.** Defining borderline patients: An overview. Am. J. Psychiatry 132: 1–10, **1975.**

   A scholarly review of the extensive clinical literature that outlines major areas of consensus about the definition of borderline patients. This paper initiated the many attempts to empirically study borderline patients which led to the establishment of this diagnosis in *DSM-III.*

22. **Kernberg, O.** Borderline personality organization. J. Am. Psychoanal. Assoc. 15: 641–685, **1967.**

   A seminal psychoanalytic paper that describes and organizes the intrapsychic characteristics of borderline and other severely disturbed patients.

23. **Mahler, M.S.** A study of the separation-individuation process and its possible application to borderline phenomena in the psychoanalytic situation. Psychoanal. Study Child 26: 403–424, **1971.**

   Identifies specific childhood separation experiences that predispose to the development of adult borderline psychopathology.

24. **Masterson, J.F.** Treatment of the Borderline Adolescent: A Developmental Approach. New York: Wiley, **1972.**

   This book encouraged more enthusiasm for ambitious treatments of borderline patients by illustrating principles of treatment and the potential for adaptive changes in the basic psychopathology of these patients.

COMPULSIVE PERSONALITY DISORDERS

25. **Abraham, K.** Contributions to the theory of the anal character. Inter. J. Psychoanal. 4: 400–418, **1923.**

   In the colorful and broad-ranging style of early psychoanalytic writing, this paper develops Freud's observation of the connection between early anal developmental issues and their role in formation of the adult obsessive-compulsive.

26. ***Freud, A.** Obsessional neurosis: A summary of psychoanalytic views as presented at the Congress (24th Int'l. Congress). Int. J. Psychoanal. 47: 116–122, **1966.**

An effort to synthesize and update the expanding psychoanalytic views of obsessional patients. It draws attention to the enduring characterological forms of obsessionality and attempts to integrate a more ego-centered psychology with earlier theories.

27. **Salzman, L. and Thaler, F.H.** Obsessive-compulsive disorders: A review of the literature. Am. J. Psychiatry 138: 286–296, **1981.**

Reviews the various approaches to diagnosis and treatment of obsessive-compulsive disorders.

PASSIVE-AGGRESSIVE PERSONALITY DISORDER

28. **Small, I.F., Small, J.G., Alig, V.B., et al.** Passive-aggressive personality disorder: A search for a syndrome. Am. J. Psychiatry 126: 973–983, **1970.**

A longitudinal study of 100 patients, this paper attempts to delineate the clinical features that distinguish passive-aggressive personality disorder from other psychiatric disorders. Some comments about treatment are also included.

MASOCHISTIC PERSONALITY DISORDER

29. **Berliner, B.** On some psychodynamics of masochism. Psychoanal. Q. 16: 459–571, **1947.**

This paper discusses masochism from a psychoanalytic perspective, exploring some of the psychodynamic roots of masochistic personality traits. Comments on the differential diagnosis of masochism are included as well.

30. **Shore, M.F., Clifton, A., Zelin, M., et al.** Patterns of masochism: An empirical study. Br. J. Med. Psychology 44: 59–66, **1971.**

An interesting empirical study of patients' masochistic styles. The authors emphasize the diversity of masochistic phenomena and delineate three predominant types of masochism based on their research results.

18. NEUROPSYCHIATRIC SYNDROMES: BRAIN DISORDERS AND TOXIC STATES

RANDOLPH B. SCHIFFER, M.D.
ERIC D. CAINE, M.D.

A neuropsychiatrist treats patients suffering from brain diseases that cause mental and behavioral disorders. One might say that this field represents at once a neurology of the mind and a psychiatry of the brain. The neuropsychiatrist attempts to understand the behavior as partly determined by neuroanatomy, neurophysiology, and neurochemistry, as well as by social, psychological, and genetic factors. We see the brain as the locus of interaction for these forces and behavior as a final common pathway for their expression.

Some of the papers that are discussed in this chapter are old by the usual standards of medical literature reviews. The neuropsychiatric perspective upon behavior is not newly arrived. Earlier workers, even in the nineteenth century, attempted to understand aberrant behavior as potentially produced by various etiologies working through the brain. We strive to elude reductionism, either biological or psychological. We assert that mental and behavioral disorders have unique meanings, which cannot be left solely to biology, and a structure imposed by cerebral pathophysiology, which is often neglected by psychology. Since neuropsychiatry is concerned with the meaning of abnormal behavior, as well as its mechanisms of expression, the dichotomy between "functional" and "organic" pathology is rarely invoked.

In practical terms, the neuropsychiatrist approaches the patient through the sections of the neurological examination, emphasizing the mental status and the behavioral features. Personal history and subjective experience are considered relevant data as well. When the central nervous system is disrupted, it manifests disease symptoms through a limited number of functional systems, including mentation, sensation, and behavior. Behavioral symptoms of disordered CNS function can be grouped into five functional categories, each of which has some neurophysiological and neuroanatomic implications. These categories include: (1) arousal, attention, and concentration; (2) mood and affect; (3) perception (both internal and external, ideational and physical); (4) personality (e.g., "He's changed; he's not the same person he used to be."); and (5) intellectual functioning (e.g., language, memory, etc.).

In this chapter we present a sample of papers and books that are especially relevant to neuropsychiatry. The criterion of maximum clinical utility has guided the selection. Initially, we consider references that broadly address the interface between psychiatry and neurology or provide a useful perspective on disordered behavior. Citations are then arranged according to the functional systems through which we approach our patients in assessment and therapy.

OVERVIEW BOOKS

1. ***Benson, D.F. and Geschwind, N.** Psychiatric conditions associated with focal lesions of the central nervous system, pp. 208–243. In: AHP (2nd ed.), Vol. 4, **1975.**

   This chapter provides a useful overview of neuropsychiatric syndromes associated with focal brain lesions. Memory disorders; aphasias; apraxias; frontal, parietal, and occipital lobe syndromes; and others are briefly described and referenced. This chapter is not a definitive source for any of these syndromes, but it is a road map to the lessons neurology has taught us about the higher functions of the nervous system. It is especially useful as introductory reading for students of neuropsychiatry.

2. ***Lishman, W.A.** Organic Psychiatry: The Psychological Consequences of Cerebral Disorder. Oxford: Blackwell, **1978.** (Distributed in U.S. by Lippincott, Philadelphia)

   This 999-page volume represents the most comprehensive description of the neuropsychiatric syndromes gathered under one cover. Its chapters are organized around physical etiologies of behavioral disorders, with extensive references.

3. ***Strub, R.L. and Black, F.W.** The Mental Status Examination in Neurology. Philadelphia: Davis, **1977.**

   This is a brief and inexpensive description of bedside neuropsychological tests. It is a succinct review of the focal lesion literature that connects abnormalities of mentation with related cerebral anatomy. The limitations are the paucity of psychiatric phenomenology and the little attention given to the nonfocal cognitive syndromes that appear in neuropsychiatric disorders such as Alzheimer's disease or schizophrenia.

4.   **Taylor, M.A.** The Neuropsychiatric Mental Status Examination: A Phenomenologic Program Text. Jamaica, NY: Spectrum, **1982.**

This programmed text for the mental status examination pays better attention to psychiatric phenomenology than the Strub and Black book. Cognitive testing techniques are integrated effectively.

5.   **Trimble, M.R.** Neuropsychiatry. New York: Wiley, **1981.**

The best available attempt to develop an integrated description of neuropsychiatry. This volume describes what is known about connections between brain and behavior across a variety of intellectual and clinical disciplines, including history, neurochemistry, psychological testing, liaison psychiatry, epilepsy, psychopharmacology, and other areas of clinical inquiry. Although readable, and a pioneering work, this book attempts too much in a small space.

6.   **Trimble, M.R.** Post-Traumatic Neurosis. New York: Wiley, **1981.**

A historical perspective upon the debate between "functional" and "organic" explanations of behavior, this book traces psychiatric thinking about traumatic syndromes through the past 150 years and covers issues as diverse as "railway spine," war-related disorders, and forensic considerations. This perspective is enlightening for modern psychiatrists caught up in controversies over etiologies of behavioral disorders.

DISORDERS OF AROUSAL

Intact arousal, attention, and concentration are prerequisites for the adequate performance of the mental status examination. These disorders are warnings that the central nervous system has sustained some physical insult requiring immediate and direct evaluation. The neuroanatomy of this system is perhaps better known than any other section of the mental status.

7.   **Drugs that cause psychiatric symptoms.** Med. Lett. (no. 576)23: 9–12, **1981.**

For those who appreciate brevity and organization, this article will be prize winning. It is a tabulation of 74 drugs commonly used on medical and surgical services along with brief descriptions of the various toxic mental syndromes that have been reported as side effects. The problem of drug interactions is not addressed in this review, but it is documented in other *Medical Letter* publications.

8.   **Engel, G.L. and Romano, J.** Delirium: A syndrome of cerebral insufficiency. J. Chronic Dis. 9: 260–277, **1959**.

A quarter of a century ago this paper placed the challenge of the toxic and metabolic encephalopathies before psychiatry. With an argument that remains cogent today, Romano and Engel distinguish delirium, a potentially reversible syndrome of cerebral insufficiency, from dementia and the major functional psychiatric disorders with which it is often intermingled. The relevance of EEG testing in behavior-disordered patients is well described.

9.   **Goetz, C.G., Klawans, H.L., and Cohen, M.M.** Neurotoxic agents, Chapter 20. In: Clinical Neurology. Eds., A.B. Baker and L.H. Baker. New York: Harper and Row, **1981**.

This chapter is a succinct and useful reference concerning toxic encephalopathies. The slant is somewhat neurological (myotonia and peripheral neuropathy receive attention, along with encephalopathy and dementia), but the reference list runs to 521 citations and is easy to use. This chapter is most relevant to situations where the toxin is known or suspected. It is less helpful in the evaluation of an encephalopathic state of unknown etiology.

10.   ***Plum, F. and Posner, C.** The Diagnosis of Stupor and Coma (3rd ed.). Philadelphia: Davis, **1980**.

The bible for those seeking the truth regarding arousal disorders. This work takes a neuroanatomic perspective for analyzing arousal deficit syndromes. Case examples abound. Bibliographies are thorough and accompany each chapter separately.

DISORDERS OF MOOD AND EMOTION

There is a complex interaction between feeling states and the brain. Mood disturbances can be generated by some neuropathological lesions, and some dementing syndromes can be mimicked by mood disorders. Investigators and clinicians debate the neuroanatomic substrates that subserve emotional expression.

11.   **Caine, E.D. and Shoulson, I.** Psychiatric syndromes in Huntington's disease. Am. J. Psychiatry, 140: 728–733, **1983**.

The authors report a longitudinal follow-up of the psychopathology seen in 30 patients with HD. Among the individuals with this autosomal dominant, reliably defined disease, one encounters a range of symptoms that nearly covers the waterfront of descriptive psychiatric diagnosis, including affective disorders, anxiety states, personality changes, and schizophreniclike psychoses. Some patients remain symptom-free. The implications of this finding for psychiatric diagnostic schemes based on phenomenology, such as *DSM III,* are discussed.

12. **Kiloh, G.** Pseudo-dementia. Acta Psychiatr. Scand. 37: 336–351, **1961.**

Kiloh, drawing upon a series of clinical vignettes, promulgated the concept of pseudodementia, the mimicking of brain disease by emotional disorder. He noted that depression was the most common underlying emotional disorder, but added the caveat (borne out by later research in this area) that a variety of other emotional syndromes can mimic the dementias.

13. ***Papez, J.W.** A proposed mechanism of emotion. Arch. Neurol. Psychiatry 38: 725–743, **1937.**

In this classical paper Papez puts forward the hypothesis that there is a neuroanatomy of the emotions. He describes the limbic system, its neuroanatomic connections, and proposes that emotional tone can be understood in terms of neurophysiologic outflow from this system to the cortex. This hypothesis has stood the test of time and still has no clearer statement than in this original article.

14. **Robinson, R.G. and Szetela, B.** Mood change following left hemispheric brain injury. Ann. Neurol. 9: 447–453, **1981.**

The authors suggest that the language-dominant hemisphere also plays a role in the regulation of emotional states. They describe a series of patients having left anterior frontal damage secondary to stroke, who demonstrate more acute depression than a head trauma control group.

15. **Ross, E.D.** The aprosodias: Functional-anatomic organization of the affective components of language in the right hemisphere. Arch. Neurol. 38: 561–569, **1981.**

Ross sets forth the hypothesis that the affective components of language are regulated by specific regions of the right hemisphere. He presents 10 patients who experienced abnormalities in the emotional modulation of language after vascular lesions in the nondominant hemisphere.

16. **Sackheim, H.A., Greenberg, M.S., Weiman, A.L., et al.** Hemispheric asymmetry in the expression of positive and negative emotions: Neurologic evidence. Arch. Neurol. 39: 210–218, **1982.**

In this retrospective, Sackheim and colleagues review 122 case descriptions of the syndrome of emotional lability in structural brain disease. They discern a functional asymmetry in the regulation of emotional experience by the two sides of the brain. When the lesions are in the dominant hemisphere, pathological weeping is far more common; when in the nondominant hemisphere, pathological laughing occurs more often. The potential relevance of this finding to our understanding of the process of emotional expression in normals is discussed.

17.   **Williams, D.** The structure of emotions reflected in epileptic experiences. Brain 79: 29–67, **1956.**

Williams carefully interviewed 100 persons with epilepsy who felt that emotional changes were included in their ictal experiences. This report did much to further the idea that emotional experience, too, had cerebral representation within the brain.

DISORDERS OF PERCEPTION

We are relatively unenlightened with regard to disturbances of sensory and ideational processing. Much of what is known derives from investigators who have worked with epilepsy or performed surgery for intractable seizures. Others include psychopharmacologists who have been interested in psychoactive drugs.

18.   ***Baldwin, M. and Hofmann, A.** Hallucinations, pp. 327–339. In: The Handbook of Clinical Neurology, Vol. 4. Eds: P.J. Vinken and G.W. Bruyn. Amsterdam: Elsevier North Holland, **1969.**

In this compact and tightly written chapter, Baldwin and Hofmann review the wide range of diseases, metabolic states, and psychoactive drugs that produce illusions and hallucinations. The chapter is particularly graphic in its treatment of psychedelic drugs used in non-Western cultures, and it provides a thorough bibliography of investigations of these drugs as well as LSD derivatives.

19.   ***Davidson, K. and Baggley, C.R.** Schizophrenia-like psychoses associated with organic disorders of the central nervous system: A review of the literature. Br. J. Psychiatry (Special Publication no. 4): 113–184, **1969.**

This is the article to read, for anyone who ever wonders whether a particular physical disease has been reported to mimic schizophrenia. The authors provide an extensive review of the pre-1969 literature organized according to physical etiologies, such as trauma, infection, basal ganglian disorders, demyelinating diseases, and others. This excellent reference article demonstrates the nonspecificity of psychotic states.

20. **Gloor, P., Olivier, A., Quesney, L.F., et al.** The role of the limbic system in experimental phenomena of temporal lobe epilepsy. Ann. Neurol. 12: 129-144, **1982.**

This report of 29 patients with stereotoxically implanted electrodes describes a variety of isolated subjective experiences as ictal phenomena. Illusions, hallucinations, and sudden changes in emotional state are all described in synchrony with limbic system epileptiform discharges. Temporal lobe neocortex is not necessarily involved in these patients' ictal experience, a finding that differs from that of earlier investigators.

21. **Jernigan, T.L., Zatz, L.M., Moses, J.A., et al.** Computed tomography in schizophrenics and normal volunteers.
1. Fluid volume. Arch. Gen. Psychiatry 39: 765-770, **1982.**
2. Cranial asymmetry. Arch. Gen. Psychiatry. 39: 771-773, **1982.**

22. **Nasrallah, H.A., Jacoby, C.G., McCalley-Whitters, M., et al.** Cerebral ventricular enlargement in subtypes of chronic schizophrenia. Arch. Gen. Psychiatry 39: 774-777, **1982.**

23. **Weinberger, D.R., DeLisi, L.E., Perman, G.P., et al.** Computed tomography in schizophreni-form disorder and other acute psychiatric disorders. Arch. Gen. Psychiatry 39: 778-783, **1982.**

A number of studies are accumulating that show abnormalities of brain structure by CT scan in schizophrenia. The most consistent finding has been bilateral ventricular enlargement, though the absence of normal occipital and frontal asymmetries has also been reported. These results have not been found by all investigators. This journal issue presents several empirical reports relevant to this debate, along with editorial discussion. Some of the findings conflict. The publication is an exciting one for those who wish to "judge for themselves."

24. ***Penfield, W. and Jasper, H.** Epilepsy and the Functional Anatomy of the Human Brain. Boston: Little, Brown, **1954.**

This book (especially Chapter 18) contains the neurosurgical observations that marked a major conceptual advance in the neurology of emotions. Penfield and Jasper describe the elicitation of illusions and hallucinations in the waking subject during neurological stimulation. Depending upon the neuroanatomic site of stimulation, they describe the entire range of perceptual distortion, ranging from unformed visual hallucinations to complex hallucinations involving several modalities of sensation. The descriptions are well worth reading.

25. **Slater, E. and Beard, A.W.** The schizophrenic-like psychoses of epilepsy. Br. J. Psychiatry 109: 95-150, **1963.**

The authors rekindle the debate regarding the interictal psychoses associated with epilepsy. They describe their patients in detail, contending that the association between epilepsy and enduring psychotic states is too great for chance alone.

26.   **Stevens, J.R.** An anatomy of schizophrenia? Arch. Gen. Psychiatry 29: 177–189, **1973.**

If schizophrenia can be mimicked by a variety of brain disorders, does schizophrenia itself have its own brain disorder? Dr. Stevens attempts to provide an integration of accumulating evidence for neurochemical, neurophysiologic, and behavioral abnormalities in schizophrenia. Her argument is convincing though speculative.

DISORDERS OF PERSONALITY

The assessment of personality is the least objective section of the mental status examination. Personal or character style is an elusive concept, and considerable clinical experience is required to describe it well. Historical information from other sources must frequently be obtained in order to assess a change in personality. Often a spouse or co-worker will detect a subtle personality alteration that is the first symptom of CNS disease. These alterations are not well localized in terms of brain function and anatomy. Still, some interesting observations have been made concerning connections between certain neural structures and personality.

27.   ***Bear, D.M. and Fedio, P.** Quantitative analysis of interictal behavior in temporal lobe epilepsy. Arch. Neurol. 34: 454–467, **1977.**

Bear and Fedio contend that persons with temporal lobe epilepsy tend to have a certain constellation of character traits that sets them apart from normals, and from other personality disorders. Furthermore, they state that those with right-sided temporal lobe foci are clinically distinguishable from those with left-sided foci.

28.   ***Bigelow, H.J.** Dr. Harlow's case of recovery from the passage of an iron bar through the head. Am. J. Med. Sci. (New Series) 20 (no. 39): 2–22, **1850.**

In 1848, Phinneas Gage, a railroad worker, experienced the passage of an iron bar through the frontal lobe of his brain in a railroad accident. Dr. Harlow's description of the changes in Mr. Gage's character after the accident represent an early report of an organic personality disorder. Although cognition apparently remained normal after the accident (there were no neuropsychologists in 1850), Mr. Gage demonstrated impulsiveness and poor judgment which was attributed to the frontal lobe damage. The day-to-day account of his clinical course after this injury remains captivating.

29.   ***Chapman, L.F. and Wolff, H.G.** The cerebral hemispheres and the highest integrative functions of man. Arch. Neurol. 1: 357–424, **1959.**

This lengthy report of psychological assessments in 60 persons who had undergone focal brain extirpations for lesions such as tumor propounds a non-localizationist point of view. The authors describe a spectrum of behavioral dysfunction, beginning with mild personality change and ending in global dementia. The alterations are related to the number of grams of brain tissue removed, rather than the anatomic site involved. Research since this report has focused almost exclusively on attempts to localize specific anatomic lesions with specific behavioral syndromes. This alternative view should be kept in mind.

30.   **Nauta, W.J.H.** The problem of the frontal lobe: A reinterpretation. J. Psychiatr. Res. 8: 167–187, **1971.**

Written by a prominent neuroanatomist, this thoughtful article covers the whole area with regard to the frontal lobes: human clinical reports, basic animal research, and neuroanatomy. Dr. Nauta puts forth the hypothesis that the frontal lobes are a complex relay and processing network mediating inputs from subcortical structures with those from cortical regions. He describes this region of the brain as the integrating center for information from the internal and external worlds.

31.   **Riggs, H.E. and Rupp, C.** A clinicoanatomic study of personality and mood disturbances associated with gliomas of the cerebrum, J. Neuro-pathol. Exp. Neurol. 17: 338–345, **1958.**

This retrospective study of 86 patients dying of primary supratentorial brain tumors demonstrates a correlation between site of tumor and preterminal changes in personality. Although the authors do not clarify whether their assessment of personality and emotional difficulties was performed without knowledge of brain pathology, they point out a strong association of tumors involving orbital frontal structures with changes in personality or difficulties in emotional control.

DISORDERS OF SPECIFIC INTELLECTUAL FUNCTION

The more we learn of the major psychiatric syndromes, the more we see that intellectual impairments are part of their clinical presentations. The interweaving of intellectual, behavioral, and emotional distress within the dementing disorders represents a great challenge to the physician, both diagnostically and therapeutically. Some syndromes of intellectual impairment are better localized in terms of brain anatomy than others, but there is disagreement regarding the limits of localization theories. Some of the current controversies as well as current knowledge are reflected in the citations below.

32.   **Heilman, K.M. and Valenstein, E.S.** Clinical Neuropsychology. New York: Oxford University Press, **1979.**

This is a comprehensive work on the correspondence between patterns of cognitive deficits and brain lesions. Each chapter covers a specific cognitive dysfunction, ranging from aphasia and alexia through the amnestic disorders. Bibliographies at the end of each chapter are extensive.

33.   **Kuhl, D.E., Phelps, M.E., Markham, C.H., et al.** Cerebral metabolism and atrophy in Huntington's Disease determined by 18-FDG and computed tomography scan. Ann. Neurol. 12: 425–434, **1982.**

Positron emission tomography may provide a functional window upon the brain to complement structural measures such as the CT scan. Kuhl and co-authors present evidence in this paper that measurable metabolic abnormalities in the basal ganglia of patients with Huntington's disease may precede detectable structural changes.

34.   **Luria, A.R.** Higher Coritical Functions in Man (2nd rev. ed.). New York: Basic Books, **1980.**

Perhaps no one has studied individuals with focal lesions of the central nervous system in as great depth as Dr. Luria. He developed his own tools for cognitive assessment and applied them imaginatively to his subjects. Testing procedures are set forth in detail along with his theories of brain function. Speech disorders, disorders of complex sensation, memory disorders, and disorders of conceptual reasoning are among the neuropsychological problems considered. Somes of his theories about the neurological underpinnings of such syndromes run counter to established ideas in the West, making Luria's work valuable as a counterpoint. It is exciting to experience this man's thinking.

35.   **Springer, S.P. and Deutsch, G.** Left Brain, Right Brain. San Francisco: Freeman, **1981.**

It is no longer possible to talk about higher cortical functions in man without some understanding of hemispheric asymmetries and the functions of what is known about the differential functioning of the two hemispheres. Pictures and diagrams abound. Their last chapter includes speculation about the relevance of hemispheric asymmetries for such mysterious mental functions as consciousness and creativity.

36. ***Wells, C.E.** Dementia (2nd. ed.). Philadelphia: Davis, **1977.**

   Dr. Wells has brought together experts who write well; each chapter is an essay unto itself, covering broad areas relevant to cognitive decline. References are incisive, but not profuse. However, the book is somewhat dated and does not include some recent advances in such areas as neuropathology.

37. **Whitty, C.W.M. and Zangwill, O.L.** Amnesia (2nd ed.). London: Butterworths, **1977.**

   This compendium reviews concisely the amnesic disorders, where memory is impaired while other cognitive functions are largely spared. It provides carefully drawn clinical descriptions and serves as an introduction to the assessment of memory dysfunction.

19. AGE-RELATED DEMENTIA

BARRY REISBERG, M.D.

The late life dementias, consisting primarily of senile dementia of the Alzheimer's type (SDAT), multi-infarct dementia (MID), and mixed forms, combining SDAT and MID, are now recognized as a major source of psychiatric morbidity and mortality. The dimensions of these disorders are staggering. There are currently 1.3 million Americans in nursing homes, a total greater than the combined hospital population including acute and chronic care facilities, state mental facilities, and veterans' hospitals. In a recent government survey, 58 percent of the residents of nursing homes were found to have diagnoses compatible with late life dementia, making this by far the most common condition in the nursing home population. Moreover, hundreds of thousands of persons with late life dementia are hospitalized in other institutions, particularly state mental facilities and veterans' hospitals.

Although enormous numbers of persons with late life dementia reside in institutional settings, a majority of persons suffering from these disorders continue to be cared for by family members and friends in private residences. Current estimates indicate that 4–5 percent of the more than 25 million persons in the U.S. over the age of 65 suffer from severe dementia and 11–12 percent suffer from mild-to-moderate age-related dementing illness. Hence, numerically, more than one million Americans have severe dementia and more than two million have mild-to-moderate dementia. Because late life dementia results in a decrease in life expectancy, these disorders are major causes of mortality in developed nations. Alzheimer's disease alone is now thought to be the fourth or fifth leading cause of death in the U.S. and other developed nations.

Despite these dramatic morbidity and mortality statistics, until recently these disorders were virtually ignored by physicians and laymen alike, perhaps because they carried the stigma of being associated with old age and with mental disorder. However, both physicians and laymen have, over the past decade, come to recognize the need for diagnosis, assessment, counseling, and treatment of these disorders. Psychiatrists are frequently called upon to diagnose and treat these disorders for a variety of reasons—because these are diseases that primarily affect mentation; because they are frequently confused with affective disorder; because agitation and psychotic phenomena are frequent manifestations in the severe stages; and because counseling is almost invariably indicated for the caretaker. As public and professional awareness of these disorders increases and as the proportion of the aged in our population continues to increase, the necessity for the psychiatrist to be conversant and knowledgeable with respect to these disorders will increase concomitantly.

COMPREHENSIVE OVERVIEWS OF SENILE DEMENTIA AND ALZHEIMER'S DISEASE

1. ***Corkin, S., Davis, K.L., Growdon, J.H., et al,** eds. Aging. Vol. 19. Alzheimer's Disease: A Report of Progress in Research. New York: Raven Press, **1982.**

    The most comprehensive and up-to-date collection of knowledge in the field available at this time.

2. ***Katzman, R., Terry, R.D. and Bick, K.L.,** eds. Aging. Vol. 7. Alzheimer's Disease: Senile Dementia and Related Disorders. New York: Raven Press, **1978.**

    A comprehensive collection of work in the area of senile dementia. A definitive statement of knowledge in the field at the time of publication.

3. ***Reisberg, B.** Brain Failure: An Introduction to Current Concepts of Senility. Free Press/ Macmillan, **1981.**

    This is the only available comprehensive single-authored, book length overview of the late life dementing disorders. It contains detailed case histories describing the stages in the evolution of the disorder, is easy to read, and is well referenced. It serves a diverse audience of practitioners.

4. ***Schneck, M.K., Reisberg, B., and Ferris, S.H.** An overview of current concepts of Alzheimer's disease. Am. J. Psychiatry 139: 165–173, **1982.**

    An excellent, comprehensive overview of the epidemiology, pathophysiology, clinical presentation, diagnosis, and differential diagnosis of Alzheimer's disease.

5. **Smith, W.L. and Kinsbournes, M.,** eds. Aging and Dementia. New York: SP Books (Spectrum Publications), **1977.**

    Probably the best-edited introductory text in the field. Ideal for medical students and other health professionals with no technical knowledge of the area.

6. *Wells, C. Chronic brain disease: An update on alcoholism, Parkinson's disease, and dementia. Hosp. Community Psychiatry 33: 111–126, 1982.

A superb overview of present knowledge with respect to the dementing disorders of late life.

DIAGNOSIS AND ASSESSMENT OF AGE-RELATED DEMENTIA

7. *Blessed, G., Tomlinson, B.E., and Roth, M. The association between quantitative measures of dementia and of senile changes in the cerebral gray matter of elderly subjects. Br. J. Psychiatry 114: 797–811, 1968.

A classic description of the relationship between clinical and neuropathological findings in late life dementia.

8. de Leon, M.J., Ferris, S.H., Balu, I., et al. Correlations between computerized tomographic changes and behavioural deficits in senile dementia. Lancet 2 (no. 8147): 859–860, 1979.

Provides a capsular summary of the relationship between CT findings and progressive Alzheimer's disease.

9. Farkas, T., Ferris, S.H., Wolf, A.P., et al. ^{18}F-2-deoxy-2-fluoro-D-glucose as a tracer in the positron emission tomographic study of senile dementia. Am. J. Psychiatry 139: 352–353, 1982.

Describes in vivo changes in brain metabolism in Alzheimer's disease, as revealed utilizing the new PET scanning technique.

10. Folstein, M.F., Folstein, S.E., and McHugh, P.R. Mini-Mental State: A practical method for grading the cognitive state of patients for the clinician. J. Psychiatr. Res. 12: 189–198, 1975.

An expanded, more comprehensive version of the Kahn and Goldfarb scale, this instrument is also of broad utility for the assessment of the magnitude of moderate-to-severe dementia.

11. Hachinski, V.C., Iliff, L.D., Zilhka, E., et al. Cerebral blood flow in dementia. Arch. Neurol. 32: 632–637, 1975.

The classic reference for the "Hachinski" risk factor score for multi-infarct dementia.

12. *Kahn, R.L., Goldfarb, A.I., Pollack, M., et al. Brief objective measures for the determination of mental status in the aged. Am J. Psychiatry 117: 326–328, 1960.

The classic reference for this brief, easy-to-utilize assessment of the magnitude of moderate-to-severe dementia.

13. **Merskey, H., Ball, M.J., Blume, W.T., et al.** Relationships between psychological measurements and cerebral organic changes in Alzheimer's disease. Can. J. Neurol. Sci. 7: 45–49, **1980.**

Describes an interesting study of EEG/CT/psychometric interrelationships.

14. **Raksin, A. and Jarvik, L.F.,** eds. Psychiatric Symptoms and Cognitive Loss in the Elderly: Evaluation and Assessment Techniques. New York: Halsted Press, **1979.**

An important introduction to this area.

15. ***Reisberg, B. and Ferris, S.H.** Diagnosis and assessment of the older patient. Hosp. Community Psychiatry 33: 104–110, **1982.**

An excellent and comprehensive overview of the diagnosis and differential diagnosis of late life dementia. Contains descriptions of clinical rating instruments and criteria for differential diagnosis, the adjunctive use of routine laboratory techniques, and the costs of assessment.

16. ***Reisberg, B., Ferris, S.H., de Leon, M.J., et al.** The Global Deterioration Scale for assessment of primary degenerative dementia. Am. J. Psychiatry 139: 1136–1139, **1982.**

Describes a global assessment instrument for the staging of Alzheimer's disease. Also presents in capsular form the clinical evolution of progressive cognitive decline in normal aging and Alzheimer's disease.

17. **Reisberg, B., Schneck, M.K., Ferris, S.H., et al.** The Brief Cognitive Rating Scale (BCRS): Findings in primary degenerative dementia (PDD). Psychopharmacol. Bull. 19: 47–51, **1983.**

Describes a multiaxial scale for the clinical assessment of progressive cognitive decline regardless of etiology. Hierarchical clinical assessments for concentration, recent memory, past memory, orientation, and functioning are described as is the validation of the instrument in patients with Alzheimer's disease.

18. **Shader, R.I., Harmatz, J.S., and Salzman, C.** A new scale for clinical assessment in geriatric populations: Sandoz Clinical Assessment-Geriatric (SCAG). J. Am. Geriatr. Soc. 22: 107–113, **1974.**

The major reference for this widely utilized clinical assessment instrument.

19. ***Tomlinson, B.E., Blessed, G., and Roth, M.** Observations on the brains of demented old people. J. Neurol. Sci. 11: 205–242, **1970.**

A companion article to the 1968 publication (#7 above).

CLINICAL PHENOMENOLOGY OF AGE-RELATED DEMENTIA

20.   **Alzheimer, A.** Über eine eigenartige Erkrankung der Hirnrinde. Centralblatt Nervenheilk. Psychiatr. 18: 177, **1907.**

The classical clinicopathologic description of Alzheimer's disease.

21.   **Esquirol, J.E.D.** Des Maladies Mentales. Paris: Balliere, **1838.**

Provides a clinical definition of senile dementia that remains accurate and current.

22.   **Hachinski, V.C., Lassen, N.A., and Marshall, J.** Multi-infarct dementia. A cause of mental deterioration in the elderly. Lancet 2: 207–209, **1974.**

A classic introduction to this important etiology.

23.   **Kiloh, L.G.** Pseudodementia. Acta. Psychiatr. Scand. 37: 336–351, **1961.**

The classic description of psychiatric symptomatology in the aged due to depression or other disorders that can mimic dementia.

24.   **Kral, V.A.** Senescent forgetfulness: Benign and malignant. Can. Med. Assoc. J. 86: 257–260, **1962.**

The classic description of senescent forgetfulness associated with normal aging, so-called "benign senescent forgetfulness."

25.   **Reisberg, B., Ferris, S.H., and Crook, T.** Signs, symptoms and course of age-associated cognitive decline, pp. 177–181. In: Aging, Vol. 19, Alzheimer's Disease: A Report of Progress in Research. Eds.: S. Corkin, K.L. Davis, J.H. Growdon, et al. New York: Raven Press, **1982.**

The first published description of the seven clinically identifiable stages of age-related cognitive decline and Alzheimer's disease.

TREATMENT AND MANAGEMENT
OF AGE-RELATED DEMENTIA

26.   **Crook, T. and Gershon, S.,** eds. Strategies for the Development of an Effective Treatment for Senile Dementia. New Canaan, CT: Mark Powley, **1981.**

A comprehensive guide to the future of pharmacologic treatment of Alzheimer's disease.

27.   **Folsom, J.C.** Reality orientation for the elderly mental patient. J. Geriatr. Psychiatry 1: 291–307, **1968.**

The classic description of this occasionally useful therapeutic approach.

28. ***Mace, N.L. and Rabins, P.V.** The 36-Hour Day. Baltimore: Johns Hopkins University Press, **1981.**

Subtitled "a family guide to caring for persons with Alzheimer's disease, related dementing illnesses, and memory loss in later life," this excellent guide should be of use to professionals, including physicians, as well as laymen.

29. **Reisberg, B.** Office management and treatment of primary degenerative dementia. Psychiatr. Ann. 12: 631–637, **1982.**

A synopsis of management issues and approaches at each phase of Alzheimer's disease.

30. ***Reisberg, B., Ferris, S.H., and Gershon, S.** Overview of pharmacologic treatment of cognitive decline in the aged. Am. J. Psychiatry 138: 593–600, **1981.**

A comprehensive introduction to the area.

31. **Yesavage, J.A., Tinklenberg, J.R., Hollister, L.E., et al.** Vasodilators in senile dementias: A review of the literature. Arch. Gen. Psychiatry 36: 220–223, **1979.**

An excellent, detailed review of these pharmacotherapeutic agents.

NONDEMENTING PSYCHOPATHOLOGY IN THE AGED

32. **Cutler, N.R. and Post, R.M.** Life course of illness in untreated manic-depressive patients. Compr. Psychiatry 23: 101–115, **1982.**

Probably the best current reference to life course issues in bipolar illness.

33. ***Foster, J.R. and Reisberg, B.** Effects of aging on psychiatric disorders beginning earlier in life. In: Handbook of Studies on Psychiatry and Old Age. Eds.: D.W.K. Lay and G.D. Burrows. Amsterdam: Elsevier Biomedical Press, **in press.**

This paper provides a comprehensive, well-referenced review of age effects on depression, suicide rates, schizophrenia and paranoid states, and obsessional phobic states.

34. ***Gurland, B.J.** The comparative frequency of depression in various old adult age groups. J. Gerontol. 31: 283–292, **1976.**

The classic review of age relationships and depressive illness.

35. **Kay, D.W.K. and Roth, M.** Environmental and hereditary factors in the schizophrenias of old age ("late paraphrenia") and their bearing on the general problem of causation in schizophrenia. J. Ment. Sci. 107: 649–686, **1961.**

The data are not conclusive as to whether paraphrenia is genetically related to, or distinct from, schizophrenia.

36.   **Yolles, S.F. and Kramer, M.** Vital statistics, pp. 66–113. In: The Schizophrenic Syndrome. Eds.: L. Bellak and L. Loeb. New York: Grune and Stratton, **1969.**

Demonstrates that 20 percent of schizophrenics' first admissions are 45 years or older and other interesting age relationships in schizophrenia.

20. PSYCHIATRIC DIMENSIONS OF MENTAL RETARDATION

FRED D. STRIDER, PH.D.
FRANK J. MENOLASCINO, M.D.

This chapter will focus on psychiatric aspects of mental retardation, which are of key importance to the mental health professional. Beyond the basic definition issues are the challenges of the types and frequencies of mental illnesses in the retarded (their nature, treatment, and management considerations). In this annotated bibliography we will initially review the historical aspects of mental retardation with focus on the earlier professional enthusiasm of the past two decades, its re-emergence as an exciting field of applied clinical and psychiatric research activities. The kaleidoscopic nature of the symptoms of mental retardation will be brought together via focus on the issues of its definition, causes, diagnosis, and treatment/management considerations. The education and training, legal, advocacy, and social-political considerations of retardation will be highlighted in the closing section.

OVERVIEW AND HISTORY

1. **Itard, J.** The Wild Boy of Aveyron. Trans.: G. Humphrey and M. Humphrey. New York: Appleton-Century-Crofts, **1962.**

    This publication is the first description of the beneficial effects of a structured, creatively designed, and enriched environment upon the syndrome of mental retardation. Aspects of Itard's work reveal recognition of the variables now designated as motivation, need, and transference. In Itard's work we see the beginnings not only of psychiatric care for the mentally retarded but also the basic approaches currently used in special education.

2. **Kanner, L.** A History of the Care and Study of the Mentally Retarded. Springfield, IL: Thomas, **1964.**

A comprehensive overview of the history of the care and treatment of mental retardation.

3. ***Mercer, J.R.** Labeling the Mentally Retarded: Clinical and Social System Perspectives on Mental Retardation. Berkeley, CA: University of California Press, **1973.**

Mercer's systematic approach to assessment of mental retardation when associated with racial or socioeconomic handicaps has become a basic reference. It is especially useful in legal cases involving misdiagnosis of mental retardation or erroneous education placement.

4. ***Robinson, H.B. and Robinson, N.M.** The Mentally Retarded Child: A Psychological Approach (2nd ed.). New York: McGraw-Hill, **1976.**

A succinct review of basic and advanced aspects of the term mental retardation including the levels and types of mental retardation, basic assessment approaches, and a compilation of treatment-management techniques.

CLINICAL ASPECTS

5. **Balthazar, E.E. and Stevens, H.A.** The Emotionally Disturbed Mentally Retarded: A Historical and Contemporary Perspective. Englewood Cliffs, N.J.: Prentice-Hall, **1975.**

This account presents an excellent composite of both historical and contemporary perspectives on the coexistence of the symptoms of mental retardation and mental illness in the same individual.

6. **Bernstein, N.R. and Menolascino, F.J.** Psychiatric assessment of the mentally retarded child, pp. 201–221. In: Diminished People: Problems in the Care of the Mentally Retarded. Ed.: N.R. Bernstein. Boston: Little, Brown, **1970.**

This chapter extends the basic child psychiatry approach to diagnostic interviewing, collateral family therapy, and basic techniques for treatment intervention to the specific needs of the mentally retarded.

7. **Group for the Advancement of Psychiatry, Committee on Mental Retardation.** Psychiatric consultation in mental retardation, Vol. 10 (Report no. 104). New York: Group for the Advancement of Psychiatry, **1979.**

Clearly presents modes of psychiatric consultation in the field of mental retardation: the application of psychiatric care, secondary consultation to caretakers, and programmatic consultation to human service systems that address themselves to the treatment/management needs of the mentally retarded.

8. **Hardy, R.E. and Cull, J.G.,** eds. Mental Retardation and Physical Disability. Springfield, IL: Thomas, **1974.**

The volume focuses on many of the allied symptoms (e.g., cerebral palsy, convulsive disorders, special sensory handicaps, etc.) that complicate the early education of mentally retarded individuals.

9. **Menolascino, F.J.,** ed. Psychiatric Approaches to Mental Retardation. New York: Basic Books, **1970.**

An edited volume that globally assesses the types of mental illness in the retarded with particular focus on the most frequently occurring diagnostic categories. The book has been viewed as a bridge between the older literature concerning mental illness in the mentally retarded and the newer viewpoints.

10. ***Menolascino, F.J. and Egger, M.** Medical Dimension of Mental Retardation. Lincoln, NE: University of Nebraska Press, **1978.**

Over 350 causes of the symptoms of mental retardation are presented in nontechnical language that can serve as a review for the professional or as a primer for the nonprofessional in the field.

11. **Reiss, S., Levitan, G.W., and McNally, R.J.** Emotionally disturbed mentally retarded people. Am. Psychologist 37: 361–367, **1982.**

An up-to-date review of the mental health needs of the mentally retarded is presented and programs initiated to meet these needs are described. A multidisciplinary professional approach toward understanding mental illness in the mentally retarded is presented.

12. **Solomon, G. and Menolascino, F.** Medical counseling of parents of the retarded. Clin. Pedatr. 7: 11, **1968.**

The key issues in the interpretation interview are succinctly reviewed. This clinically oriented article is a helpful primer for clinicians in developing effective first steps in inaugurating treatment and intervention, which is so often the cornerstone for successful help.

13. ***Szymanski, L. and Tanguay, P.E.,** eds. Emotional Disorders of Mentally Retarded Persons. Baltimore: University Park Press, **1980.**

This edited volume addresses developmental and child psychiatry dimensions of mental retardation. Diagnosis, multiple treatment intervention, social implications, and an excellent section on psychopharmacological adjuncts are included.

SOCIOPOLITICAL ASPECTS: EDUCATION, TRAINING, AND LEGAL ADVOCACY

14. **Bellamy, G.T., Horner, R.H., Dean, P., et al.** Vocational Habilitation of Severely Retarded Adults: A Direct Service Technology. Baltimore: University Park Press, **1979.**

This volume reviews the nature and scope of modern vocational habilitation programs whose major goals are to prepare the adolescent and young adult retarded citizens for the world of work. Rationales and program specifics for a wide variety of vocational training for the retarded are clearly outlined.

15. ***Donaldson, J.Y. and Menolascino, F.J.** Past, current and future roles of child psychiatry in mental retardation. J. Am. Acad. Child Psychiatry 16: 38–52, **1977.**

This article focuses on the past, current, and possible future role of the child psychiatrist in the field of mental retardation, reviews the "roots" of the field of child psychiatry in the institutions for the retarded of the past, and reviews the evolution of the interdisciplinary team approach and the multiple axes of current and future child psychiatry services for the mentally retarded.

16. **Dybwad, G.,** ed. New Neighbors: The Retarded Citizen in Quest of a Home. President's Committee on Mental Retardation, Report to the President MR79. Washington, D.C.: Government Printing Office, **1980.**

The volume outlines the residential alternatives that have mushroomed in the communities throughout our country and provides information about the establishment, operation, and common problems encountered in residential alternatives, especially the challenges of public acceptance of residential facilities within the mainstream of the community.

17. **Menolascino, F.J.** Challenges in Mental Retardation: Progressive Ideology and Services. New York: Human Sciences Press, **1977.**

This account describes the role and impact of the developmental model and parent advocacy in the evolution of modern service programs for the retarded. The developmental model states that the retarded individual, regardless of chronological age, should be viewed as a developing organism whose rate and extent of future development will depend on the nature of the treatment intervention provided. The parent advocacy movement, as noted in this volume, is also an excellent study topic for mental health professionals who wish to effect changes in the provision of mental health services.

18. ***Menolascino, F.J. and Strider, F.D.** Advances in prevention and treatment of mental retardation, pp. 614–645. In: AHP (2nd ed.). Vol. 7. **1981.**

The concept of prevention in mental retardation, from primary through tertiary considerations, is reviewed and summarized via a systems approach wherein the public health model can be effectively utilized to maximize prevention efforts.

19. **Michaelis, C.T.** Home and School Partnerships in Exceptional Education. Rockville, MD: Aspen Systems, **1980.**

Beyond a review of the basic curriculum components of special education approaches to mental retardation, this volume focuses on key national legislation for the mentally retarded (i.e., Public Law 94–142).

20. **Mittler, P.,** ed. Research to Practice in Mental Retardation: International Association for the Scientific Study of Mental Deficiency Proceedings. Baltimore: University Park Press, **1977.** 3 vols.

This three-volume work reviews major research in the field of mental retardation. Each volume presents a synoptic assessment of the biological, psychosocial, and treatment/management approaches present throughout the world concerning the professional understanding of mental retardation.

21. ***President's Comittee on Mental Retardation.** Mental Retardation: The Leading Edge Service Programs that Work. MR78. Washington, D.C.: Government Printing Office, **1979.**

This volume represents a synopsis of model programs for involving mentally retarded citizens in the worlds of education, work, and social/recreational activities.

22. **Wolfensberger, W. and Nirje, B.** The Principles of Normalization in Human Services. Toronto: National Institute on Mental Retardation, **1972.**

The principles of normalization originated in the Scandinavian countries in the late 1960s and have been interpreted in the United States by Wolfensberger. Its major focus is that mentally retarded citizens should be served within the generic programs of his or her community mainstreams.

21. THE CHRONIC MENTALLY ILL

JOHN A. TALBOTT, M.D.

Since deinstitutionalization began in 1955, the number of papers and books on the subject has grown with each year. Earlier, concern focused on the political aspects, e.g., "dumping"; it has now enlarged to include educational, research, and clinical issues.

The problems of the chronic mentally ill can be approached from several different viewpoints: demographic, historical, locus of housing or services, public policy, family burden, public attitudes, treatment modalities, clinical programs, alternatives to hospitals, rehabilitation, finances, and special populations—e.g., young or new chronic patients, the elderly, etc.

It is worth noting that the data are longer standing and more solid regarding statistical and economic areas than clinical aspects—for obvious reasons. However, this is changing, and in the next few years we will see more rigidly controlled studies that will begin to enable us to answer three central questions about this population:

1. What causes, maintains, and prevents chronic mental illness?
2. What treatment, rehabilitation, and care elements work, for which patients, in what settings?
3. How many of each element (halfway house slots, asylum placements, acute beds, etc.) do we need for each 100,000 persons?

These selections are arranged in the following categories: overview and public policy, problems of deinstitutionalization, state hospitals, treatment, community programs, and miscellaneous issues. The readings selected include those that give both a historical perspective on the problems of deinstitutionalization and the chronic mentally ill, as well as landmark contributions that inform the resident about current issues of importance. The selection provided, therefore, should supply the interested reader with the entire spectrum of concern about the clinical, economic, and systems problems posed by and encountered by the chronic mentally ill.

OVERVIEW AND PUBLIC POLICY ISSUES

1. **The Chronic Mental Patient in the Community.** (GAP Report 10:no. 102). New York: Group for the Advancement of Psychiatry, **1978.**

    A brief but thorough exposition of the history, problems, and possible solutions to the problems of deinstitutionalization and community care of the chronic mentally ill. Covers ideology, treatment, education, technology, politics, funding, and research issues.

2. **Report to the President from The President's Commission on Mental Health.** Washington, D.C.: Supt. of Docs., U.S. Government Printing Office, **1978.**

    The second national commission (the first resulted in *Action for Mental Health* and CMHCs), which recommended changes in community supports, services, personnel deployment and training, patient rights, research, prevention, and public understanding of mental illness.

3. **Talbott, J.A.,** ed. The Chronic Mental Patient: Problems, Solutions and Recommendations for a Public Policy. Washington, D.C.: Am. Psychiatr. Assoc., **1978.**

    The APA Committee's state of the art review of chronic mentally ill persons; who, where, and how well they are; what programs work for them; what the obstacles are to implementing such programs; the economic issues; case management; governmental responsibility; and legal issues.

4. **Talbott, J.A.** The Chronic Mental Patient: 5 Years Later. New York: Grune and Stratton, **1983.**

    A review of all the research, political developments, and literature on the chronic mental patient since the major works were published in 1978. Includes public attitudes, treatment modalities, therapeutic programs, and systems issues.

5. **Talbott, J.A.** Towards a public policy on the chronic mentally ill patient. Am. J. Orthopsychiatry 50: 43–53, **1980.**

    Proceeds from the problem of the chronic mentally ill, through critical issues, to proposed solutions. Covers mapping the population, effective treatment programs, and levels of governmental responsibility.

6. **Toward a National Plan for the Chronically Mentally Ill. Report to the Secretary by the Department of Health and Human Services Steering**

Committee on the Chronically Mentally Ill. Washington, D.C.: Public Health Service, **1981.**

The nuts and bolts of legislation and financing that could effect a national policy to care for the chronic mentally ill. Contains a superb discussion of research needs as well as current effective treatment approaches.

PROBLEMS OF DEINSTITUTIONALIZATION

7. **Bachrach, L.L.** Deinstitutionalization: An Analytical Review and Sociological Perspective. Rockville, MD: NIMH, **1976.**

    The definitive analysis of deinstitutionalization's effects on patients, institutions, and government. Successfully attempts to pull together polar positions and answer the critical questions concerning quality of life, the need for asylum and custody, etc.

8. **Bassuk, E.L. and Gerson, S.** Deinstitutionalization and mental health services. Sci. Am. 238: 46–53, **1978.**

    A description of the deinstitutionalization process with attention to the CMHC movement, funding and personnel problems, and directions for research and legislation.

9. **Goldman, H.H., Gattozzi, A.A., and Taube, C.A.** Defining and counting the chronically mentally ill. Hosp. Community Psychiatry 32: 21–27, **1981.**

    A good look at the demographics of the chronic mentally ill—who and where are they. Concludes that there are 1.7–3 million, 40 percent in nursing homes, 40 percent in various community residences, and 20 percent in and out of hospitals.

10. **Pepper, B., Kirshner, M.C., and Ryglewicz, H.** The young adult chronic patient: Overview of a population. Hosp. Community Psychiatry 32: 463–469, **1981.**

    A splendid look at this new, never-institutionalized population of young chronic mentally ill persons.

11. **Returning the Mentally Disabled to the Community. Government Needs to do More.** Washington, D.C.: U.S. General Accounting Office, **1977.**

    The first government look at deinstitutionalization—not from NIMH, but the GAO. Amazingly good analysis of some of the problems such as fragmentation and poor care.

12. **Segal, S.P. and Aviram, U.** The Mentally Ill in Community-Based Sheltered Care. New York: Wiley, **1978.**

A fine report of the experience of 500 deinstitutionalized patients now living in the "community" in California. Arrives at some important but controversial clinical and public policy conclusions.

13. **Talbott, J.A.** Deinstitutionalization: Avoiding the disasters of the past. Hosp. Community Psychiatry 30: 621–624, **1979.**

Analysis of the problems engendered by deinstitutionalization (e.g., poor community care) followed by 10 commandments for future deinstitutionalization efforts (adequate housing, ending conflict of interest between operating and contracting for services, etc.).

STATE HOSPITALS

14. **Morrissey, J.P., Goldman, H.H., Klerman, L.V., and Associates.** The Enduring Asylum: Cycles of Institutional Reform at Worcester State Hospital. New York: Grune and Stratton, **1980.**

Argues convincingly that state hospitals will continue to exist because they perform tasks no one else will. Uses Worcester State Hospital as an example, and uses "Death of the Asylum" as a straw man to post its arguments.

15. **Rothman, D.J.** The Discovery of the Asylum: Social Order and Disorder in the New Republic. Boston: Little, Brown, **1971.**

A social historian looks at the birth of all total institutions in America: mental hospitals, prisons, almshouses, orphanages, etc.

16. **Seitz, P.F., Jacob, E., Koenig, H., et al.** The Manpower Problem in Mental Hospitals: A Consultant Team Approach. New York: International Universities Press, **1976.**

The book itself is OK, but the review of the literature on state hospitals (pp. 155–166) and references (pp. 167–253) are invaluable resources— for scholars, change agents, and administrators of a variety of mental health programs.

17. **Talbott, J.A.** The Death of the Asylum: A Critical Study of State Hospital Management, Services and Care. New York: Grune and Stratton, **1978.**

A contemporary analysis of the problems of state hospitals and possible remedies. Valuable chapter on making changes in such a system, as well as a chapter on *guidelines* for change rather than *solutions*.

18.   **Talbott, J.A.,** ed. The State Mental Hospital. Problems and Potentials. New York: Human Sciences Press, **1980.**

A slice in time concerning problems and potential uses of state hospitals. Its contributors encompass the spectrum from those who think they should be closed to those who argue for retention.

TREATMENT

19.   **Anthony W.A., Cohen, M.R., and Vitalo, R.** The measurement of rehabilitation outcome. Schizophr. Bull. 4: 365–383, **1978.**

Updates their 1972 work on the outcome of rehabilitation and treatment of the mentally ill. Concludes that outcome depends more on the patient's skills and activity than psychopathology (e.g., symptoms).

20.   **Davis, J.M.** Overview: Maintenance therapy in psychiatry: I. Schizophrenia. Am. J. Psychiatry 132: 1237–1245, **1975.**

Review of prophylactic treatment of schizophrenia using maintenance medication: reviews double-blind studies, discusses their methodology, and gives indications for long-term therapy, prevention of side effect, and relationship to social therapies.

21.   **Davis, J.M.** Overview: Maintenance therapy in psychiatry: II. Affective disorders. Am J. Psychiatry 133: 1–13, **1976.**

A similar review of the long-term psychopharmacological treatment of affective disorders, primarily lithium and antidepressants. Covers prevention, drug interactions, rapid cycling, side effects, and maintenance tricyclic use.

22.   **Lamb, H.R. and Associates.** Community Survival for Long-Term Patients. San Francisco: Jossey-Bass, **1976.**

A very good clinical treatise on the care and treatment of the chronic mentally ill. Covers psychotherapy, housing, day centers, and vocational and social rehabilitation.

23.   **Paul, G.L. and Lentz, R.J.** Psychosocial Treatment of Chronic Mental Patients: Milieu versus Social Learning Programs. Cambridge: Harvard University Press, **1977.**

A first-rate scholarly examination of the differences between three treatment approaches with chronic mental patients in a state hospital. Concludes that a social-learning (e.g., behavioral modification) approach is best, followed by milieu therapy, and way behind—traditional state hospital treatment.

24.   **Talbott, J.A.,** ed. The Chronic Mentally Ill: Treatment Programs, Systems. New York: Human Sciences Press, **1981.**

A look at the treatment issues relating to the chronic mentally ill. Describes treatment modalities (medication, psychotherapy, etc.); treatment programs, (in state hospitals, community based, etc.); and systems of care (in California, North Carolina, and Massachusetts).

25.   **Talbott, J.A.** Therapy of the chronic mentally ill. Curr. Psychiatr. Ther. 20: 347–355, **1981.**

A review of current thinking on psychotherapy and psychopharmacology for chronic patients. Also discusses why treatment of chronic patients is different, and different theories of causation, with their derivative treatment implications.

COMMUNITY PROGRAMS

26.   **Bachrach, L.L.** Overview: Model programs for chronic mental patients. Am. J. Psychiatry 137: 1023–1031, **1980.**

Another Bachrach classic, this presenting eight principles for programs serving the chronically ill, including internal evaluation and specially trained staff. Stresses the importance of learning from pilot programs rather than imitating them.

27.   **Braun, P., Kochansky, G., Shapiro, R., et al.** Overview: Deinstitutionalization of psychiatric patients, a critical review of outcome studies. Am. J. Psychiatry 138: 736–749, **1981.**

Reviews all the studies of alternatives to hospitalization including modifications of conventional hospitalization (e.g., short-term vs. long-term and day hospital). Concludes that the alternatives result in the same or better outcomes.

28.   **Budson, R.D.** The Psychiatric Halfway House: A Handbook of Theory and Practice. Pittsburgh: University of Pittsburgh Press, **1978.**

Since there are few works on the various alternative settings for the mentally ill, this excellent book about halfway houses will have to serve as a resource to be translated into other areas. It has a fine conceptual base; covers legal issues, standards and regulations; and goes from the process of planning to the implementation of a program.

29.   **Carpenter, M.D.** Residential placement for the chronic psychiatric patient: A review and evaluation of the literature. Schizophr. Bull. 4: 384–398, **1978.**

A complete review of housing options for the mentally ill: e.g., halfway houses, work camps, satellite housing, and hotels. Concludes that it is the housing element that makes community care slightly less expensive than institutional care and that patients universally prefer such to hospital care.

30.   **Fairweather, G.W., Sanders, D.H., Maynard, H., et al.** Community Life for the Mentally Ill: An Alternative to Institutional Care. Chicago: Aldine, **1969.**

The idea of training chronic mental patients to live together and support themselves and each other is an obvious one, but this explanation of how to do it and its results is unique. The Fairweather experiences are appraised 25 years later in a nice volume in *New Directions for Mental Health Services,* No. 7, **1980.**

31.   **Stein, L.I. and Test, M.A.,** eds. Alternatives to Mental Hospital Treatment. New York: Plenum, **1978.**

This superb book provides the basis for most community-based care for the chronically mentally ill in the 1980s. It describes model programs such as Soteria House; TCL in Madison, Wisconsin; the Southwest Denver Program; and Fountain House, and then extrapolates principles for treatment.

32.   **Stein, L.I. and Test, M.A.** Alternative to mental hospital treatment: I. Conceptual model, treatment program, and clinical evaluation. Arch. Gen. Psychiatry 37: 392–397, **1980.**

Stein and Test's actual implementation of the principles they gleaned from the literature on community-based programs (above). Concludes that they're no worse than "traditional" hospital care and follow-up regarding symptoms, quality of life, and cost, and better in many ways.

MISCELLANEOUS

33.   **Baron, R.C., Rutman, I.D., and Klaczynska, B.** The Community Imperative. Philadelphia: Horizon House Institute, **1980.**

Proceedings of a conference on public attitudes about the mentally ill and their deinstitutionalization and treatment in the community. Discusses dangerousness, deviance, media portrayals, history, community factors, and employees' and union members' attitudes; zoning and legislation; financing, research, and strategies for the future.

34.   **Faloon, I.R.H., Boyd, J.L., McGill, C.W., et al.** Family management

training in the community care of schizophrenia. New Directions for Mental Health Services, No. 12, pp. 61–77, **1981.**

Faloon et al. give a well-reasoned approach to dealing with families of the chronic mentally ill—their outcome results confirm its usefulness. But take a look at the rest of the papers in this issue too—together they bring relations with families of the seriously mentally ill into the contemporary mainstream.

35.   **Talbott, J.A.** Medical education and the chronic mentally ill. J. Natl. Assoc. Priv. Psychiatr. Hosp. 11(5): 58–63, **1980.**

A comprehensive review of what needs to be done to educate medical students, residents, and practicing physicians about the care and treatment of the chronic mentally ill. Divides recommendations into curricular subjects, educational experiences, and attitudinal issues.

36.   **Weisbrod, B.A., Test, M.A., and Stein, L.** I. An alternative to mental hospital treatment: II. Economic benefit-cost analysis. Arch. Gen. Psychiatry 37: 400–405, **1980.**

The economic analysis of Stein and Test's TCL Program in Madison, Wisconsin. Concludes that both community-based care and "traditional" hospital treatment and follow-up are expensive—but shows how community-based care, while costing more, brings more benefits in the long run.

22. SLEEP, SLEEP DISORDERS, AND DREAMING

Marvin D. Wasserman, M.D.

During the 1960s the major emphasis in sleep research was on understanding the basic mechanisms of sleep, and clinical issues remained in the background. Researchers studied the physiology and functions of sleep, describing its stages, ontogenesis, and phylogenesis, and explored the relationship between the physiological changes during Rapid Eye Movement (REM) sleep and dreaming. In the 1970s clinical issues moved to the foreground, and the focus shifted to describing the symptoms, pathogenesis, pathophysiology, and treatment of various sleep disorders.

In keeping with this shift, I have emphasized the literature on sleep disorders. This clinical literature can best be organized into five categories derived from the diagnostic classification of sleep and arousal disorders recently published by the Association of Sleep Disorders Centers: (1) general overview, (2) disorders of initiating and maintaining sleep (insomnias), (3) disorders of excessive somnolence, (4) disorders of the sleep-wake schedule, (5) dysfunctions associated with sleep, sleep stages, or partial arousals (parasomnias). I have attempted to select review articles when possible, but have also included some of the initial or early descriptions of these disorders, as well as books that are required readings for those who want to go beyond the basics. Also included is a selection of classic papers that explored the physiology of sleep and laid the groundwork for the advances in the study and treatment of clinical sleep disorders in the 1970s and 1980s. Finally, there is a group of papers dealing with dreams. In selecting papers from the voluminous dream literature I have attempted to emphasize (1) papers from the classical psychoanalytic literature that raise questions about some of the ideas Freud originally presented in his monumental *Interpretation of Dreams,* and (2) papers from the nonpsychoanalytic literature that discuss the relationship between psychophysiological findings about dreaming and/or findings from other nonpsychoanalytic disciplines and their relationship to psychoanalytic dream theory.

168

Any relatively short bibliography on sleep, sleep disorders, and dreaming must be selective and of necessity leave out many important contributions. Most, if not all, of these omissions will be found in the long bibliographies that accompany many of the articles and books cited.

ACKNOWLEDGMENT

I want to thank Charles P. Pollack, M.D., Arthur J. Spielman, Ph.D., and Elliot D. Weitzman, M.D., for their helpful suggestions in compiling this bibliography.

SLEEP PHYSIOLOGY

1. **Aserinsky, E. and Kleitman, N.** Regularly occurring periods of eye motility, and concomitant phenomena during sleep. Science 118: 273–274, **1953.**

   The original description of rapid eye movement sleep and its association with dreaming.

2. **Berger, R.J.** Physiological characteristics of sleep, pp. 66–79. In: Sleep, Physiology and Pathology. Ed.: A. Kales. Philadelphia: Lippincott, **1969.**

   A concise summary of the physiological changes that occur during REM and NREM sleep. Changes in various systems, e.g., autonomic nervous system, skeletal muscle system, etc., are compared during different sleep stages as well as during waking.

3. **Dement, W.C.** The effect of dream deprivation. Science 131: 1705–1707. **1960.**

   The report of the first systematic REM-sleep deprivation study on human subjects. The occurrence of a "REM-rebound" following REM deprivation in humans is described for the first time.

4. **Jouvet, M.** Neurophysiology of the states of sleep. Physiol. Rev. 47: 117–177, **1967.**

   A classic paper that comprehensively reviews the behavioral and electrophysiological characteristics of, and the mechanisms responsible for, both slow wave and REM sleep. The phylogenics and ontogenesis of these sleep stages are discussed as is the relationship between REM and slow wave sleep.

5. **Jouvet, M.** Biogenic amines and the states of sleep. Science 163: 32–41, **1969.**

A review of neuropharmacological, neurophysiological, histochemical, and lesion studies that attempt to delineate the roles of various neurotransmitters in the induction of both slow wave and REM sleep.

6. **Moruzzi, G.** The sleep-waking cycle. Ergeb. Physiol. 64: 1–165, **1972.**

A lengthy comprehensive review of the neural mechanisms underlying the sleep-waking cycle. It emphasizes studies that attempt to modify or abolish alterations between sleep and wakefulness by lesions or stimulation of the central nervous system.

7. **Rechtschaffen, A., Wolpert, E.A., Dement, W.C., et al.** Nocturnal sleep of narcoleptics. Electroenceph. Clin. Neurophysiol. 15: 599–609, **1963.**

The first report of the occurrence of sleep onset REM periods in narcoleptics. The authors also suggest, for the first time, that the symptoms of narcolepsy can be understood as representing the precocious or inappropriate triggering of some or all of the attributes of REM sleep.

8. **Roffwarg, H.P., Muzio, J.P., and Dement, W.C.** Ontogenetic development of the human sleep-dream cycle. Science 152: 604–619, **1966.**

A classic paper that describes a decrease in REM time from very high levels in infancy to much lower levels in adult life. The authors speculate about the role the high REM time during infancy plays in the maturation and differentiation of the central nervous system.

9. **Wagner, D.R. and Weitzman, E.D.** Neuroendocrine secretion and biological rhythms in man. Psychiatric Clin. of North Am. 3: 223–250, **1980.**

A comprehensive review of the literature on the relation of neuroendocrine rhythms to age and the sleep-wake cycle. Changes in these rhythms with experimental manipulation and disease states, including major psychiatric disorders, are also reviewed.

DREAMS

10. *****Altman, L.L.** The dream in psychoanalysis. New York: International Universities Press, **1969.**

The clinical application of psychoanalytic dream theory is discussed. Rich case material is used to clearly illustrate the concepts with different types of dreams.

11. **Arlow, J.A. and Brenner, C.** Psychoanalytic Concepts and the Structural Theory, pp. 114–143. New York: International Universities Press, **1964.**

This chapter cogently argues that structural theory is superior to topographic theory for understanding dreams. The topographic and structural theories of dreams are reviewed, and specific examples illustrating the superiority of structural theory are discussed.

12. **Erikson, E.H.** The dream specimen of psychoanalysis. J. Am. Psychoanal. Assn. 2: 5–56, **1954.**

A fascinating expansion of Freud's first psychoanalytic interpretation of a dream (the Irma dream). In addition to his psychosocial approach, Erikson utilizes the manifest content much more than Freud did. He emphasizes that, in addition to infantile sexual conflicts, this dream reflects a current crisis in the life of the creative middle-aged dreamer (Freud).

13. **Fisher, C.** Psychoanalytic implications of recent research on sleep and dreaming. J. Am. Psychoanal. Assoc. 13: 197–303, **1965.**

A two-part article that first comprehensively summarizes the empirical physiological findings about sleep available in 1965. In the second part, the implications of these findings for psychoanalytic dream theory are discussed.

14. **Foulkes, D.** A Grammar of Dreams. New York: Basic Books, **1978.**

An extremely important book that attempts to integrate psychoanalytic dream theory, psycholinguistic research, cognitive psychology, and the structuralism of Piaget and Levi-Strauss. It also contains an excellent summary of psychoanalytic dream theory relevant to this attempted synthesis.

15. **Foulkes, D. and Vogel, G.W.** The current status of laboratory dream research. Psychiatric Annals 4(7): 7–27, **1974.**

An excellent review of sleep laboratory findings about dreams and of the literature on the similarities and differences of REM and NREM mentation. Suggestions are made about directions for future dream research in the sleep laboratory.

16. ***Freud, S.** (1900–1901) The Interpretation of Dreams. S.E., Vols. 4 & 5, **1953.**

Freud's monumental two-volume work contains the first psychoanalytic interpretation of a dream and discusses wish fulfillment in dreams, dream distortion, the dream work, and the sources of dreams. The dream literature prior to 1900 is reviewed, and the topographic theory of mental functioning is systematically presented for the first time. A more condensed version by Freud of psychoanalytic dream theory can be found in the "Introductory Lectures on Psychoanalysis," S.E., Vol. 15, pp. 83–129, **1961.**

17.   **Spanjaard, J.** The manifest content and its significance for the interpretation of dreams. Int. J. Psychoanal. 50: 221–235, **1969.**

Suggests using the dreamer's role in the manifest dream as an important element in constructing interpretations about the patient's current conflicts. The psychoanalytic literature on the role of the manifest dream content in psychoanalytic dream interpretation is reviewed.

GENERAL OVERVIEW OF SLEEP DISORDERS

18.   **Diagnostic classification of sleep and arousal disorders** (1st ed.). Sleep Disorders Classification Committee, H.P. Roffwarg, Chmn. Sleep 2: 1–137, **1979.**

A nosology of sleep disorders compiled by the Association of Sleep Disorders Centers based primarily on clinical symptomotology.

19.   ***Weitzman, E.D.** Sleep and its disorders. Annu. Rev. Neurosci. 4: 381–417, **1981.**

A comprehensive review of recent and seminal papers on all of the major, and most of the minor, sleep disorders with an exhaustive bibliography. The paper uses as a framework the nosology of sleep disorders recently proposed by the Association of Sleep Disorders Centers.

20.   **Williams, R.L. and Karacan, I.** Sleep Disorders, Diagnosis and Treatment. New York: Wiley, **1978.**

An excellent overview with chapters covering every major type of sleep disorder. Chapters that are especially noteworthy are: "Sleep Apnea Syndromes and Related Disorders" by C. Guilleminault and W. Dement (pp. 9–28); "EEG Sleep and Depression" by D.J. Kupfer and F.G. Foster (pp. 163–204); "Sleep Disturbances, Alcohol, and Alcoholism" by A.D. Pokorny (pp. 233–260); "Aging and Sleep Disorders" by P.N. Prinz and M. Raskind (pp. 303–321); and "The Role of the Sleep Laboratory in Diagnosis and Treatment of Impotence" by I. Karacan, P.J. Salis, and R.L. Williams (pp. 353–382).

DISORDERS OF INITIATING AND MAINTAINING SLEEP

21. **Coleman, R.M., Pollack, C.P., and Weitzman, E.D.** Periodic nocturnal myoclonus in a wide variety of sleep-wake disorders. Trans. of the Am. Neurolo. Assoc. 103: 230–233, **1978.**

    Briefly reviews the literature on nocturnal myoclonus and presents a large case series suggesting that nocturnal myoclonus is not regularly associated with insomnia as was previously reported.

22. **Gillin, J.C. and Wyatt, R.J.** Schizophrenia: Perchance a dream? Intern. Rev. Neurobiol. 17: 297–342, **1975.**

    Contains an excellent review of the literature on sleep in schizophrenics. Data is presented supporting the hypothesis that most actively ill schizophrenics fail to have a normal REM rebound following deprivation of REM sleep.

23. **Guilleminault, C., Eldridge, F.L., and Dement, W.C.** Insomnia with sleep apnea: A new syndrome. Science 181: 856–858, **1973.**

    The first description of an association between sleep apnea and insomnia. Prior to this report, sleep apnea was believed to be associated only with hypersomnia. Clinical characteristics of these patients are described.

24. ***Sleeping Pills, Insomnia, and Medical Practice.**
    Washington, D.C., National Academy of Sciences, **1979.**

    A comprehensive review of insomnia that discusses the epidemiology of sleep complaints and summarizes research on the diagnosis and treatment of insomnia and the hazards and benefits of hypnotic drugs.

DISORDERS OF EXCESSIVE SOMNOLENCE

25. **Guilleminault, C. and Dement, W.C.** Sleep Apnea Syndromes. New York: Liss, **1978.**

    A book that comprehensively reviews the sleep apnea syndromes. It not only discusses in detail the clinical symptoms and treatment of these symptoms, but also reviews the relevant respiratory physiology and hormonal secretion patterns during sleep in sleep apnea patients.

26. **Guilleminault, C., Dement, W.C., and Passaouant, P., eds.** Narcolepsy. New York: Spectrum Publications, **1976.**

A comprehensive text on the clinical symptoms, differential diagnosis, treatment, pathophysiology, and socioeconomic impact of narcolepsy.

27.   **Kupfer, D.J., Himmelhoch, J.M., Swartzburg, M., et al.** Hypersomnia in Manic-Depressive Disease. Dis. Nerv. System 33: 720–724, **1972.**

The first report of polygraphically documented hypersomnia in manic-depressives and depressives with cyclothymic personalities. The authors speculate that these findings may have important implications for various biochemical hypotheses about depressive syndromes.

DISORDERS OF SLEEP-WAKE SCHEDULE

28.   **Aschoff, J.** Desynchronization and resynchronization of human circadian rhythms. Aerospace Med. 40: 844–849, **1969.**

Reviews the basic concepts relevant to understanding human circadian rhythms including a non–24-hour day, endogenous oscillators, internal desynchronization, Zeitgebers, and entrainment. It then discusses the relevance of these concepts to "Jet lag syndrome."

29.   **Vogel, G.W., Vogel, F., McAbee, R.S., et al.** Improvement of depression by REM-sleep deprivation. Arch. Gen. Psychiatry 37: 247–253, **1980.**

Describes improvement in endogenous depression following REM-sleep deprivation and theorizes that REM-sleep abnormalities in endogenous depression are reflective of a basic circadian rhythm disturbance. The authors suggest that when this disturbance is corrected the depression improves.

30.   **Weitzman, E.D., Czeisler, C.A., Coleman, R.M., et al.** Delayed sleep phase syndrome. Arch. Gen. Psychiatry 38: 737–746, **1981.**

The first description of the clinical characteristics of delayed sleep phase syndrome and a proposed nonpharmacologic treatment. This syndrome, which is often misdiagnosed as sleep onset insomnia, is actually a disorder of the circadian sleep-wake rhythm.

PARASOMNIAS

31.   **Broughton, R.J.** Sleep disorders: Disorders of arousal. Science 159: 1070–1078, **1968.**

An excellent description of the clinical characteristics of nocturnal enuresis, somnambulism, and night terrors. It identifies them as disorders of arousal from slow wave sleep, rather than disturbances of dreaming sleep as was previously believed.

32. **Fisher, C., Byrne, J., Edwards, A., et al.** A psychophysiological study of nightmares. J. Am. Psychoanal. Assoc. 18: 747–782, **1970.**

Discusses the physiological differences between night terrors (a stage 4 phenomenon) and nightmares (a REM phenomenon). Speculations about the psychodynamics operating in these two phenomena are made, and the role of relative desomatization of anxiety in REM nightmares is described.

33. **Kales, A., Soldatos, C., Caldwell, A.B., et al.** Somnambulism. Arch. Gen. Psychiatry 37: 1406–1410, **1980.**

Describes the development, clinical course, and personality patterns of sleepwalking in 50 adults with a current or past complaint of this disorder.

34. **Kales, A. and Tan, T.** Sleep alterations associated with medical illnesses, pp. 143–157. In: Sleep, Physiology and Pathology. Ed.: A. Kales. Philadelphia: Lippincott, **1969.**

A concise description of the relationship between sleep stages and (1) acid secretion in duodenal ulcer patients, (2) angina in patients with coronary artery disease, and (3) asthma attacks in asthmatics. The characteristic sleep pattern in hypothyroid patients is also described.

35. **Wasserman, M.D., Pollack, C.P., Spielman, A.J., et al.** Theoretical and technical problems in the measurement of nocturnal penile tumescence for the differential diagnosis of impotence. Psychosom. Med. 42: 575–585, **1980.**

Reviews the literature on the use of measurement of nocturnal penile tumescence for the differential diagnosis of impotence and discusses the theoretical and technical problems involved in the use of this technique. Criteria for diagnosing psychogenic and organic impotence based on a comprehensive clinical evaluation are proposed.

23.   SEXUAL DISORDERS

PHILIP M. SARREL, M.D.

Sexual disorders have been categorized in different ways, several of which have proved clinically useful. Kaplan, following the model of *DSM III,* divides sex problems into desire phase, excitement phase, and orgasmic phase disorders. Vaginismus, an involuntary muscle spasm that prevents or markedly compromises the capacity for vaginal penetration, is added as an extra disorder. Masters and Johnson present their case material as problems of "sexual inadequacy," dividing the disorders into those of males (premature ejaculation, ejaculatory incompetence, and primary and secondary impotence) and those of females (non-orgasmic response, randomly orgasmic response, dyspareunia, and vaginismus). More recently, Masters and Johnson have added to their initial descriptions reports of less frequently encountered sex response problems and have elaborated on the sexual disorders treated in a homosexual population.

Whelan has proposed a division of sexual disorders into four categories: sex response, sex desire, sex orientation, and sex behavior. This categorization has proved most useful in our clinical experience at Yale and is the framework used for teaching human sexuality to house staff and medical students. The subdivision into these four categories was used as the basis for selection of references for these annotations.

In constructing this section of annotations it seemed to make sense also to include the most important references describing the range of human sexual behavior, for one needs to be educated about nonproblematic sexuality in order to maintain a proper perspective when working with patients/clients who present sexual disorders. Kinsey's work remains the primary reading. By including the works of Ford and Beach, Stoller, Gagnon, Fisher, Bell and Weinberg, Wagner and Green, and Money et al., the scope of understanding is expanded to include observations from such diverse disciplines as anthropology, psychology, psychoanalysis, physiology, and sociology.

Another section of this book focuses on sex therapy. However, this selection does overlap with the other section as so many of the core readings describing disorders use case examples to illustrate the usefulness of these concepts in therapeutic approaches.

BASIC TEXTS

1.   **Bancroft, J.H.J.** Human Sexuality and Its Problems. London: Churchill-Livingstone, **1983.**

   A comprehensive discussion of sex response, behavior, and orientation problems. Useful in both therapy and counseling situations. Drawn from more than a decade's experience treating sex problems at Oxford and at Edinburgh.

2.   **Kaplan, H.S.** Disorders of Sexual Desire and Other New Concepts and Techniques. New York: Brunner/ Mazel, **1979.**

   Loss of interest in sex and development of aversion to sexual behavior are now recognized as two of the more commonly encountered sex problems. Kaplan presents a clear description of these problems, the factors that lead to them, and of a combined behavioral-psychodynamic approach that has proved helpful in treating what have been particularly difficult cases.

3.   **Kolodny, R.C., Masters, W.H., and Johnson, V.E.** Textbook of Sexual Medicine. Boston: Little, Brown, **1979.**

   A comprehensive text covering human sexual response and behavior and summarizing the literature on the impact of disease on sexuality. Chapters cover such areas as cardiovascular disease, urologic and gynecologic disorders, chronic illness, and psychiatric disorders. There is an excellent discussion of therapeutic modalities to be applied in different situations.

4.   ***Sarrel, L.J. and Sarrel, P.M.** Sexual Unfolding: Sexual Development and Sex Therapies in Late Adolescence. Boston: Little, Brown, **1979.**

   A description of interacting social, biological, and psychological factors that influence the development of sexuality in late adolescence, drawn from experience working with Yale students. The second half of the book describes counseling and psychotherapeutic approaches appropriate to this age group.

SEXUAL ORIENTATION

5.   ***Bell, A.P., Weinberg, M.S., and Hammersmith, S.K.** Sexual Preference: Its Development in Men and Women. Bloomington: Indiana University Press, **1981.**

   The findings of a 10-year study by the Institute for Sex Research (Kinsey

Group). Hetero- and homosexual populations were compared to identify those factors that appeared to determine a homosexual orientation. Many myths about homosexuality are dispelled. The factors that are important are carefully documented.

6. **Marmor, J. and Green, R.** Homosexual behavior, pp. 1051–1068. In: Handbook of Sexology. Eds.: J. Money and H. Musaph. New York: Elsevier/North Holland, **1977.**

An excellent review of modern psychiatric thinking about homosexuality.

7. ***Masters, W.H. and Johnson, V.E.** Homosexuality in Perspective. Boston: Little, Brown, **1979.**

The sexual disorders experienced by homosexuals are described, including the issues involved when someone who is primarily homosexual wishes to relate in a heterosexual relationship. Treatment approaches and therapy results are reported.

SEXUAL RESPONSE

8. **Fisher, S.** The Female Orgasm. New York: Basic Books, **1972.**

An early controlled study carefully documenting the social, psychological, and cultural factors that influence female sexual response. An important bridge between the earlier findings of Kinsey and the findings of most recent researchers.

9. **Karacan, I., Goodenough, D.R., Shapiro, A., et al.** Erection cycle during sleep in relation to dream anxiety. Arch. Gen. Psychiatry 15: 183–189, **1966.**

Having pioneered the studies of sex response during the sleep cycle, the Karacan group here documents the impact of anxiety during sleep as a deterrent to normal functioning of sexual physiology.

10. **Karacan, I., Scott, F.B., Salis, P.J., et al.** Nocturnal erections, differential diagnosis of impotence and diabetes. Biol. Psychiatry 12: 373–380, **1977.**

The differentiation of organic and psychologic causes of erectile difficulties is addressed in this paper, which summarizes pioneering work by the authors over the previous decade.

11. **Levine, S.B.** Marital sexual dysfunction: Ejaculation disturbances. Ann. Int. Med. 85: 575–579, **1976.**

An excellent review article and presentation of the problems of ejaculatory incompetence and premature ejaculation.

12. **Marmor, J.** Impotence and ejaculatory disorders. In: The Sexual Experience. Eds.: B.J. Sadock, H.I. Kaplan, and A.M. Freedman. Baltimore: Williams and Wilkins, **1976.**

A presentation of background factors influencing the capacity to relate as a sexual adult. Rooted in a psychoanalytic understanding of behavior, Marmor updates psychoanalytic thought and integrates basic concepts with those of other modern sex researchers. A clinically useful understanding of erectile and ejaculatory disorders.

13. ***Masters, W.H. and Johnson, V.E.** Human Sexual Response. Boston: Little, Brown, **1966.**

Presentation of laboratory findings from 694 men and women whose sex response was normal. These observations of sexual physiology have become the basis for much of today's sex research and sex therapy.

14. ***Masters, W.H. and Johnson, V.E.** Human Sexual Inadequacy. Boston: Little, Brown, **1970.**

Male and female sexual dysfunctions are defined and clarified through numerous case examples. The co-therapy approach to treatment is explained. Approaches to and results of therapy for specific disorders are described. Results of five-year follow-up study are presented.

15. **Munjack, D.J. and Kanno, P.H.** Retarded ejaculation: A review. Arch. Sex. Behav. 8: 139–150, **1979.**

Documents the frequency of ejaculatory inhibitions (found to be far more common than originally believed) and discusses the underlying concepts and dynamics related to it.

16. **Schiavi, R.C. and White, D.** Androgens and male sexual function: A review of human studies. J. Sex Marital Ther. 2: 214–228, **1976.**

A psychobiological point of view bringing together a comprehensive analysis of the important articles about the endocrine aspects of sex behavior, response, and desire.

17. ***Segraves, R.T.** Pharmacologic agents causing sexual dysfunctions. J. Sex. Marital Ther. 3: 157–176, **1977.**

The development of sexual dysfunction as a side effect of drugs that affect blood pressure, muscle tension, nervous discharge, and endocrine function has become a common occurrence. This is an important comprehensive review of the effects reported in the psychiatric and medical literature.

18.   **Stoller, R.J.** Sexual Excitement: Dynamics of Erotic Life. New York: Pantheon, **1979.**

A modern psychoanalytic understanding of the internal tensions that generate the expression of sexuality through the vehicle of a single case description that serves to illuminate more far-reaching issues. An important theoretical discussion for understanding the roots of sexual disorders and of normal sexual function.

19.   **Wagner, G. and Brindley, G.S.** The effect of atropine, anxiety and beta adrenergic blockers upon human penile erection. In: Vasculogenic Impotence. Eds.: A.W. Zorgniotti and G. Rossi. Springfield, IL: Thomas, **1980.**

A pioneering controlled study measuring volume and circumference changes in the penis as affected by different drugs and emotional states.

20.   ***Wagner, G. and Green, R.** Impotence (Erectile Failure): Physiological, Psychological and Surgical Diagnosis and Treatment. New York: Plenum Press, **1981.**

The authors present a comprehensive account of the "state-of-the-art" of physiological investigation and present new concepts for understanding the mechanisms of erection and erectile failure. Psychological theories of erectile failure and an analysis of approaches to therapy are succinctly presented. The bibliographies alone are worth the purchase of this text.

SEXUAL BEHAVIOR

21.   **Ford, C.S. and Beach, F.A.** Patterns of Sexual Behavior. New York: Harper and Row, **1951.** (Also available from Greendwood Press, **1980.**)

A classic text describing cross-cultural aspects of sexual behavior. Findings among primitive peoples throughout the world help to place our definitions of sexual disorders in a different human perspective.

22.   **Gagnon, J.H.** Human Sexualities. New York: Scott, Foresman, **1977.**

A sociologist who worked with the Kinsey group elaborates and emphasizes the role of learning in the development of human sexuality.

23.   **Groth, A.N.** Men Who Rape: The Psychology of the Offender. New York: Plenum Press, **1979.**

An excellent book that explores the personalities of the rapist.

24. **Groth, A.N., Burgess, A.W., and Holmstrom, L.L.** Rape: Power, anger, and sexuality. Am. J. Psychiatry 143: 1239–1243, **1977.**

A thoughtful analysis of sex offenders' psychology, stressing the nonsexual meanings of rape.

25. ***Kernberg, O.F.** Boundaries and structure in love relations. J. Am. Psychoanal. Assoc. 25: 81–114, **1977.**

An important reference for the theory underlying recent approaches to the treatment of couples presenting sexual disorders.

26. ***Kinsey, A.C., Pomeroy, W.B., and Martin, C.E.** Sexual Behavior in the Human Male. Philadelphia: Saunders, **1948.**

Data from the sexual histories of 5,300 males. While Kinsey's observations about sexual behavior, response, and orientation may have been affected by the sex values of society during his time, most of the observations have been confirmed by research of recent years. This book is a basic reading for anyone concerned about understanding human sexuality.

27. **Kinsey, A.C., Pomeroy, W.B., Martin, C.E., et al.** Sexual Behavior in the Human Female. Philadelphia: Saunders, **1953.**

Data from the sexual histories of 5,980 females. While the women's movement has led to almost revolutionary changes in female sex values, attitudes, and behavior, many of the Kinsey observations continue to be a foundation for understanding female sexual behavior.

28. **LoPiccolo, J. and Heiman, J.** Cultural values and the therapeutic definition of sexual function and dysfunction. J. Soc. Issues 33: 166–183, **1977.**

An original contribution focusing on the importance of sociocultural values in the determination of the meaning of sexual behavior. This aspect of sexuality is stressed in assessing the outcome of therapy.

29. ***Money, J.** Paraphilias, pp. 917–928. In: Handbook of Sexology. Eds.: J. Money and H. Musaph. New York: Elsevier/North Holland, **1977.**

The category of sexual disorders previously labeled perversions or deviations or aberrations are described by Money as "paraphilias." As a result of this work most sex researchers have benefited as a formerly diffuse array of disorders are presented in a cohesive way.

30. **Sarrel, P.M. and Masters, W.H.** Sexual molestation of men by women. Arch. of Sex. Behav. 11: 117–131, **1982.**

A description of male sexual assault victims and the sexual consequences brought about by rape.

31. **Stoller, R.J.** Perversion: The Erotic Form of Hatred. New York: Pantheon, **1975.**

Original thinking about a complex and often-puzzling problem. The role of childhood trauma in the development of perverse behavior is illuminated.

24. EATING DISORDERS

Alexander R. Lucas, M.D.

Eating disorders involve deviations from the normal process of meeting the basic biologic need for nourishment. Such deviations take the form of eating too much, eating too little, or other disturbances in eating behavior. They are considered pathological when the eating behavior leads to disease or disability. Whether eating disorders are diseases in and of themselves or reflect underlying conflicts has been an open question. The difficulties in classifying eating disorders have been evident when traditional psychiatric diagnostic categories have been applied to them. The designations "psychosomatic" or "psychophysiologic" perhaps most adequately circumscribe eating disorders, but the *APA Diagnostic and Statistical Manual of Mental Disorders, Third Edition (DSM-III)* avoids theoretical questions and semantic confusion by simply using the term "Eating Disorders" for gross disturbances in eating behavior. This subclass of disorders—usually first evident in infancy, childhood, or adolescence—includes anorexia nervosa, bulimia, pica, rumination disorder of infancy, and atypical eating disorder.

Study and treatment of these disorders has been the province not only of psychiatry, but of internal medicine, pediatrics, and nutrition. Thus it involves the interface among these and other specialties. The writings reflect a multidisciplinary point of view. Understanding the individual with an eating disorder involves knowledge about the family and the larger social and cultural environment.

The list of citations is intended to be a representative sampling reflecting the breadth of writings on eating disorders, giving distinct, often diverse and conflicting, points of view. Works providing a general background and overview of the subject are first noted. Obesity is considered as a major disorder of eating. An historical view is introduced by the classic descriptions of anorexia nervosa in the nineteenth century. Articles viewing eating from the developmental perspective and including special symptoms (rumination and pica) emphasize the psychological meaning of eating behavior. A series of papers focusing on the clinical descriptions and diagnostic features adds breadth and depth to the early descriptions. The essence of the psychological disturbance is the topic of two contrasting studies revealing the evolution of psychoanalytic thinking in recent decades. Another paper relates findings in laboratory animals to the behavior of obese humans. Two papers on the endocrine disturbance in anorexia nervosa epitomize the wealth of investigations now carried out in that area. Articles on treatment were selected that clearly enunciate divergent views focusing variously on medical management, psychotherapy, behavior modification, and family therapy. The appropriateness of particular theoretical and practical orientations in treatment has been a major issue of controversy in the field. Anorexia nervosa is the focus of the majority of citations as the prototypical eating disorder most thoroughly studied by psychiatrists.

Mind-body dualism has been hard to put to rest. Some writers advocate a purely somatic approach to treatment, while others focus on the psyche. By considering the historical trends, however, one senses that treatment has moved toward rational integration of approaches combining biological management, individual psychotherapy, and family work. Outcome is considered by several papers. The syndrome of bulimia, which has lately gained increased recognition, finally is considered.

The citations will give the student a broad overview of the subject and a sense of many of the specific issues and difficulties inherent in eating disorders and their treatment. The student interested in pursuing the topic further can be guided by the bibliographies contained in the cited work.

GENERAL

1. ***Bruch, H.** Eating Disorders: Obesity, Anorexia Nervosa, and the Person Within. New York: Basic Books, **1973.**

    The superb standard volume on eating disorders based on the original ideas and studies of Hilde Bruch. Lucidly and captivatingly written, it probes the meaning beneath the aberrant behaviors and provides penetrating insight into the genesis and treatment of the disorders.

2. **Keys, A., Brovek, J., Henschel, A., et al.** The Biology of Human Starvation. Minneapolis: University of Minnesota Press, **1950.** 2 vols.

    The preeminent reference work on the effects of starvation, physical and psychological, based on experimental studies involving volunteers during World War II. It includes a review of the world literature.

3. ***Stunkard, A.J.,** ed. Obesity. Philadelphia: Saunders, **1980.**

    Standard, up-to-date compendium on obesity, covering basic physiologic mechanisms and treatment by leading authorities in medicine, psychology, and nutrition.

HISTORY

4. **Berkman, J.M.** Anorexia nervosa. Anorexia, inanition, and low basal metabolic rate. Am. J. Med. Sci. 180: 411–424, **1930.**

    The first report of a large number of cases. 117 patients, including 89 females and 28 males, are included. The illness is characterized as a clinical entity—a physiological disorder secondary to a psychic disturbance. Low basal metabolic rate is recognized to be a protective mechanism, the result of inanition. Thyroid extract together with the administration of adequate nourishment is the recommended treatment.

5. **Gull, W.W.** Anorexia nervosa (apepsia hysterica, anorexia hysterica) **(1873)**, pp. 132–138. Lasègue, E.C. On hysterical anorexia (1873), pp. 141–155. In: Evolution of Psychosomatic Concepts: Anorexia Nervosa: A Paradigm. Eds.: M.R. Kaufman and M. Heiman. New York: International Universities Press, **1964.**

    Gull's classic description of anorexia nervosa in which he gives the case histories of three young patients and the essential clinical features of the illness. Concurrent description by the French physician Lasègue who emphasizes the psychological nature of the disorder, and presents the prototypical history describing the development, clinical signs, and progression of the illness.

6. ***Lucas, A.R.** Toward the understanding of anorexia nervosa as a disease entity. Mayo Clinic Proc. 56: 254–264, **1981.**

    An historical overview of medical thought about anorexia nervosa, tracing the models which have evolved for its understanding. An integrated view of its etiology and pathogenesis with multiple factor interaction is proposed based on the biopsychosocial model.

DEVELOPMENTAL ASPECTS

7. **Freud, A.** The psychoanalytic study of infantile feeding disturbances. Psychoanal. Study Child 2: 119–132, **1946.**

    Discussion of eating function in infants and young children as related to instinctual drives and mothering. The development of neurotic feeding disturbances is considered.

8. **Gaddini, R. De B. and Gaddini, E.** Rumination in infancy, pp. 166–185. In: Dynamic Psychopathlogy in Childhood. Eds.: L. Jessner and E. Pavenstedt. New York: Grune and Stratton, **1959.**

Review of rumination in infancy based on direct observational data. The immaturity and inadequacy of the mothers, who demonstrated marked ambivalence toward their babies, is noted. The mother-infant relationship is implicated.

9. ***Lehman, E.** Feeding problems of psychogenic origin, A survey of the literature. Psychoanal. Study Child 3/4: 461–488, **1949.**

A comprehensive review of psychological factors involved in eating problems from the developmental point of view. Considered are the psychic significance of eating, the effects of emotion on appetite, and the effects of parental attitudes. Psychological factors in eating inhibitions as well as in overeating, food idiosyncracies, and the symbolism of food are considered.

10. **Lourie, R.S. and Millican, F.K.** Pica, pp. 455–470. In: Modern Perspectives in International Child Psychiatry. Ed.: J.G. Howells. New York: Brunner/Mazel, **1971.**

A review of the abnormal craving for and eating of inedible substances. The investigation reviews constitutional and environmental factors leading to vulnerability. Parental deprivation, identification with their mothers' pica, and severe ego disturbances are contributing factors in three different groups. The associated hazard of lead poisoning is emphasized.

11. ***Rabinovitch, R.D. and Fischhoff, J.** Feeding children to meet their emotional needs. J. Am. Diet. Assoc. 28: 614–621, **1952.**

A survey of the psychological implications of eating based on developmental psychology. The importance of the emotional climate in infancy is emphasized, as is the relationship between feeding and mothering. Implications for feeding children in hospitals and the special problems of feeding the child with chronic illness and psychiatric disturbance are discussed.

DESCRIPTION AND DIAGNOSIS

12. ***Beumont, P.J.V., Bearwood, C.J., and Russell, G.F.M.** The occurrence of the syndrome of anorexia nervosa in male subjects. Psychol. Med. 2: 216–231, **1972.**

Detailed review of 25 well-documented male cases of anorexia nervosa. This paper reviews the literature comprehensively and establishes beyond any doubt that the syndrome occurs in males and resembles the condition more often seen in females, emphasizing an analagous endocrine disturbance.

13. **Falstein, E.I., Feinstein, S.C., and Judas, I.** Anorexia nervosa in the male child. Am. J. Orthopsychiatry. 26: 751–772, **1956.**

Review of the literature with detailed case reports of four prepubescent boys with anorexia nervosa. The study focuses on psychodynamic issues in their psychopathological attitudes toward food and eating, and psychodynamic formulations regarding treatment and considers bulimia as part of the eating disorder cycle.

14. ***Kay, D.W.K. and Leigh, D.** The natural history, treatment and prognosis of anorexia nervosa, based on a study of 38 patients. J. Ment. Sci. 100: 411–431, **1954.**

One of the earliest psychiatric studies containing a thorough review of clinical features noting precipitating factors, psychiatric symptomatology, family, and social factors. The authors describe diverse psychiatric symptomatology. They provide some long-term follow-up data and conclude that treatment was unsatisfactory.

15. **Lesser, L.I., Ashenden, B.J., Debuskey, M., et al.** Anorexia nervosa in children. Am. J. Orthopsychiatry 30: 572–580, **1960.**

Report of 15 girls with anorexia nervosa focusing on its occurrence in a young population including the prepubertal period. Three distinct personality patterns are delineated, including hysterical, obsessive-compulsive, and schizoid. The difficulties of hospital treatment are discussed. Follow-up information of from 1–17 years suggests better outcome than previously noted, particularly in the group that demonstrated predominantly hysterical personality traits.

16. ***Russell, G.F.M.** Anorexia nervosa: Its identity as an illness and its treatment, pp. 131–164. In: Modern Trends in Psychological Medicine, Vol. 2. Ed.: J.H. Price. New York: Appleton-Century-Crofts, **1970.**

A comprehensive theoretical review that argues for the identity of anorexia nervosa as a distinct illness rather than being symptomatic of various psychiatric conditions. Diagnostic criteria, course, theories of etiology, and treatment in hospital are discussed.

17. ***Russell, G.F.M.** Bulimia nervosa: An ominous variant of anorexia nervosa. Psychol. Med. 9: 429–448, **1979.**

Elucidation of the syndrome of bulimia nervosa, an eating disorder variant related to, but differing in its clinical symptomatology, from anorexia nervosa.

PSYCHOLOGICAL DISTURBANCE

18. ***Bruch, H.** Perceptual and conceptual disturbances in anorexia nervosa. Psychosom. Med. 24: 187–194, **1962.**

The seminal work on body image and concept distortion in anorexia nervosa. A triad of psychological disturbances, including disturbance in body image, disturbance in the perception of hunger and other bodily states including emotions, and a paralyzing sense of ineffectiveness is enunciated.

19. **Schachter, S.J.** Extraordinary facts about obese humans and rats, pp. 15–38. In: The Psychology of Obesity: Dynamics and Treatment. Ed.: N. Kiell. Springfield, IL: Thomas, **1973.**

A thought-provoking and entertaining analysis of the behavior of pathologically obese individuals in comparison to hyperphagic experimentally lesioned rats.

20. **Waller, J.V., Kaufman M.R., and Deutsch, F.** Anorexia nervosa: A psychosomatic entity (1940), pp. 245–273. In: Evolution of Psychosomatic Concepts. Eds.: M.R. Kaufman and M. Heiman. New York: International Universities Press, **1964.**

Psychoanalytic interpretation of the signs and symptoms of anorexia nervosa based on detailed case histories. Specific unconscious meaning of the symptoms is hypothesized to represent fantasies of oral impregnation.

ENDOCRINE DISTURBANCE

21. ***Boyar, R.M., Katz, J.L., Finkelstein, J.W., et al.** Anorexia nervosa: Immaturity of the 24-hour luteinizing hormone secretory pattern. N. Engl. J. Med. 291: 861–865, **1974.**

Demonstration of an immature pattern of luteinizing hormone secretion in women with anorexia nervosa resembling those found in prepubertal and pubertal children.

22. ***Katz, J.L. and Weiner, H.** A functional, anterior hypothalamic defect in primary anorexia nervosa? Psychosom. Med. 37: 103–105, **1975.**

On the basis of their earlier work and that of others, the authors speculate as to the presence of an anterior hypothalamic defect that may initiate or be a consequence of the illness.

TREATMENT AND OUTCOME

23. ***Berkman, J.M.** Anorexia nervosa: The diagnosis and treatment of inanition resulting from functional disorders. Ann. Intern. Med. 22: 679–691, **1945.**

Detailed account of medical treatment, carried out on an outpatient basis, emphasizing gradually increasing caloric intake with the aim of restoring weight. Thyroid hormone is no longer advocated as an adjunct to treatment.

24. ***Cantwell, D.P., Sturzenberger, S., Burroughs, J., et al.** Anorexia nervosa. An affective disorder? Arch. Gen. Psychiatry 34: 1087–1093, **1977.**

A direct interview follow-up study of 26 patients hospitalized during adolescence. A high incidence of psychopathology is found, particularly of affective disorder, in the patients and their families. This suggests a strong relationship between anorexia nervosa and affective disorder.

25. **Dally, P.J. and Sargant, W.** A new treatment of anorexia nervosa. Br. Med. J. 1: 1770–1773, **1960.**

A method of treatment utilizing bed rest, large doses of chlorpromazine, and modified insulin treatment is described as a means of inducing rapid weight gain in anorexia nervosa.

26. ***Eckert, E.D., Goldberg, S.C., Halmi, K.A., et al.** Behavior therapy in anorexia nervosa. Br. J. Psychiatry 134: 55–59, **1979.**

The results of short-term weight gain in hospitals are scrutinized in a controlled, randomized multicenter study comparing operant conditioning treatment with ward milieu therapy containing no behavioral contingencies related to weight gain. No significant difference in weight gain occurs in the two groups.

27. **Garner, D.M. and Bemis, K.M.** A cognitive-behavioral approach to anorexia nervosa. Cogn. Ther. Res. 6: 123–150, **1982.**

A contribution to therapeutic technique that explicitly describes what is to be done. Based upon cognitive therapy, specific techniques for instilling motivation for treatment and altering irrational beliefs and cognitive distortions are given.

28. ***Hsu, L.K.** Outcome of anorexia nervosa: A review of the literature (1954 to 1978). Arch. Gen. Psychiatry 37: 1041–1046, **1980.**

Review of the major follow-up studies on anorexia nervosa summarizing psychiatric, psychosocial, psychosexual, and vocational outcome with information on mortality, nutritional, and menstrual outcome.

29. *Liebman, R., Minuchin, S., and Baker, L.** An integrated treatment program for anorexia nervosa. Am. J. Psychiatry 131: 432–436, **1974.**

Discussion of structural family therapy integrated with initial hospitalization and follow-up outpatient treatment of patients with anorexia nervosa.

30. *Lucas, A.R., Duncan, J.W., and Piens, V.** The treatment of anorexia nervosa. Am. J. Psychiatry 133: 1034–1038, **1976.**

Multifaceted hospital treatment is described with an individualized and flexible approach conceived to meet both the physiologic and psychologic needs of the patients. Treatment of malnutrition aimed to restore eating patterns with the patient assuming increased control and individually planned psychotherapy are emphasized. Concurrent individualized work with the family is advocated.

31. **Maxmen, J.S., Silberfarb, P.M., and Ferrell, R.B.** Anorexia nervosa: Practical initial management in a general hospital. JAMA 229: 801–803, **1974.**

The hospital treatment protocol using high-calorie, liquid food supplements based upon a behavior modification paradigm contingent upon daily weight gain is described.

32. **Mitchell, J.E. and Pyle, R.L.** The bulimic syndrome in normal weight individuals: A review. Int. J. Eating Disorders 1: 61–73, **1982.**

Review of the literature on the bulimic syndrome in normal weight individuals, summarizing findings on epidemiology, clinical characteristics, and the unsatisfactory status of treatment.

33. *Reinhart, J.B., Kenna, M.D., and Succop, R.A.** Anorexia nervosa in children: Outpatient management. J. Am. Acad. Child Psychiatry 11: 114–131, **1972.**

Stresses the outpatient management of children with anorexia nervosa, using psychotherapeutic methods directed to the psychological problems of the child and family.

34. **Stunkard, A.J.** New therapies for the eating disorders. Behavioral modification in obesity and anorexia nervosa, pp. 153–167. In: The Psychology of Obesity: Dynamics and Treatment. Ed.: N. Kiell. Springfield, IL: Thomas, **1973.**

Elaboration of the principles of behavior modification as they apply to the treatment of eating disorders, particularly pathologic obesity.

25. SUBSTANCE ABUSE

WILLIAM A. FROSCH, M.D.

Substance abuse is an artificial cluster of psychiatric diagnoses based on a single similarity: knowing ingestion of an exogenous toxin. The drug groups are pharmacologically distinct, their toxicities individual, and the varying personalities of their users an additional confounding factor. Therefore, this brief list is necessarily a smattering of bits and pieces, an attempt to suggest the breadth of what should be mastered in depth, prolegomena to a proper set of readings.

I have included at least something about each of the major drug groups in common current use. The choice of selections has been guided by the importance of bringing multiple approaches to our study, from basic science to clinical observation, from biologic to psychologic to sociologic views. The readings range from novels (our best, if subjective, accounts of toxicity) to history, from classics to contemporary reports. Despite the current understandable and appropriate brouhaha about endorphins, they do not appear on this list. Although clearly important, the work is new and increasingly complex and confusing, its significance for psychiatry not yet understood. In such a rapidly expanding area, you are best served by reading a recent and hopefully current review of the state of knowledge of endogenous opiates.

Substance abusers, both alcoholic and otherwise, have traditionally been avoided by physicians and mental health workers, dismissed as sociopaths, avoided as difficult and demanding. Present knowledge suggests that they are diagnostically diverse, in need of help, and often accessible to the accurately chosen intervention. These readings are chosen to entice, excite, and inform.

GENERAL

1. **Finnegan, L.P.,** ed. Drug Dependence in Pregnancy: Clinical Management of Mother and Child. NIDA Services Research Monograph. Washington, D.C.: U.S. Government Printing Office, DHEW Publication No. (ADM) 78-678, **1978.**

   Definitive statement of current knowledge of impact of drug abuse on

191

mother and infant and recommendations regarding the factors necessary for advice and appropriate action.

2. **Griffiths, R.R., Bigelow, G.E., and Henningfield, J.E.** Similarities in animal and human drug taking behavior, pp. 1–90. In: Advances in Substance Abuse Behavioral and Biological Research, Vol. 1. Ed.: N.K. Mello. Greenwich, Conn.: JAI Press, **1980.**

An exhaustive (297 references) attempted integration of animal and human data relating to self-administration and abuse of drugs. There is remarkable cross-species and across-drug generality of reports, with, however, evidence that type of drug can determine extent and pattern of use. Underlines the validity of animal models in studying the variables influencing self-administration.

3. **Kandel, D.B.** Convergences in prospective longitudinal surveys of drug use in normal populations, pp. 3–38. In: Longitudinal Research on Drug Abuse: Empirical Findings and Methodological Issues. Ed.: D.B. Kandel. Washington, D.C.: Hemisphere Publishing, **1978.**

A thorough summary of antecedents of drug use—who gets there and why. An impressive bibliography tops off this fine paper.

4. **Lowry, M.** Lunar Caustic. Eds.: E. Birney, and M. Lowry. London: Cape, **1968.**

5. **Waugh, E.** The Ordeal of Gilbert Pinfold. Boston: Little, Brown, **1979.**

A from-the-inside-out view of toxic drug experiences based on the novelist's personal experiences transmuted through his art.

6. **McLellan, A.T., Woody, G.E., and O'Brien, C.P.** Development of psychiatric illness in drug abusers: Possible role of drug preference. N. Engl. J. Med. 301: 1310–1314, **1979.**

A study of "the longitudinal relations between patterns of drug abuse and the development of psychiatric disorders." There are clear drug-specific changes, some drugs are bad for your mental health (psycho-stimulants and psychodepressants), others (opiates) did not produce change over time.

ALCOHOL AND SEDATIVES

7. **Bean, M.,** ed. Alcoholics Anonymous, I, II. Psychiatr. Ann. 5: 2, 3 (February, March), **1975.**

A well-written monograph on a common but rarely studied "treatment."

It is based on both the literature (AA and scientific) and direct observation. Important for all physicians and health practitioners.

8.   **Bohman, M., Sigvardsson, S., and Cloninger, C.R.** Maternal inheritance of alcohol abuse. Arch. Gen. Psychiatry, 38: 965–969, **1981.**

9.   **Cloninger, C.R., Bohman, M., and Siqvardsson, S.** Inheritance of alcohol abuse. Arch. Gen. Psychiatry 38: 861–868, **1981.**

These two studies of cross-fostered men and women suggest heterogeneous etiology among alcoholics. Good list of references.

10.   **Hollister, L.E.** Dependence on benzodiazepines, pp. 70–82. In: Benzodiazepines: A Review of Research Results, 1980. NIDA Research Monograph no. 33, Washington, D.C.: U.S. Government Printing Office, **1980.**

A complete review of the evidence by one of the masters. His cautions and recommendations are generally applicable to all sedatives and hypnotics. The problem, however, is considerably greater with other classes of sedatives-hypnotics: Withdrawal deserves vigorous active treatment.

11.   **Isbell, H., Fraser, H.F., Wikler, R.E., et al.** An experimental study of the etiology of "rum fits" and delirium tremens. Q. J. Stud. Alcohol 16: 1–33, **1955.**

A clinical experiment produced careful observations still true 30 years later. The findings are also applicable to the barbiturates and other sedative drugs. Current treatment would be similar except for the present use of benzodiazapines during controlled withdrawal.

12.   **Lender, M.E. and Martin, J.K.** Drinking in America. New York: Free Press, **1982.**

The *New York Times* describes this as "brilliant social history," and "amazingly free of prejudice or special pleading." Documents the continuing American ambivalence to the delights of drink and the dangers of demon rum. (Reviewed by Anatole Broyard, *The New York Times,* January 8, **1983.**)

13.   **Rosett, H.L., Weiner, L., and Edelin, K.D.** Treatment experience with problem drinking pregnant women. JAMA, **in press.**

Now that the fetal alcohol syndrome has been rediscovered (it had been recognized in London during the gin epidemic in the early 1700s), those at risk should be identified and treatment instituted. The paper outlines an effective treatment approach and presents evidence that outcome is improved.

14. **Vaillant, G.E. and Milosky, E.S.** Natural history of male alcoholism. Arch. Gen. Psychiatry 39: 127–133, **1982.**

A rarity: A long-term longitudinal study. Surprising and important findings: (1) Many alcoholics have relatively good prognosis, (2) Asymptomatic drinking is a common outcome, (3) Anxiety and depression more likely result from rather than lead to alcoholism.

15. **Victor, M. and Hope, J.M.** The phenomenon of auditory hallucinations in chronic alcoholism. A critical evaluation of the status of alcoholic hallucinosis. J. Nerv. Ment. Dis. 126: 451–481, **1958.**

Clinical research at its best—a careful critical analysis of phenomenology and course of a most interesting syndrome. A model for young investigators.

OPIATES

16. **Chein, I., Gerald, D.L., Lee, R.S., et al.** The Road to H: Narcotics, Delinquency, and Social Policy. New York: Basic Books, **1964.**

A trailblazing sociopsychological study of adolescent ghetto addicts, it details both the individual pathology and the adaptive use of heroin. Still important.

17. **Dole, V.P. and Nyswander, M.** A medical treatment for diacetyl-morphine (heroin) addiction. JAMA 192: 646–650, **1965.**

The first report of what is still the most effective intervention for the confirmed addict. Note the emphasis on needed social services and support.

18. **Khantzian, E.K. and Treece, C.J.** Psychodynamics of drug dependence: An overview, pp. 11–15. In: Psychodynamics of Drug Dependence, Eds. J.D. Blaine and D.A. Julius. NIDA Research Monograph no. 12, Washington, D.C.: U.S. Government Printing Office, **1977.**

An excellent complete survey of psychoanalytic thinking about addiction and of the many diagnostic and psychiatric issues still to be resolved.

19. **Kreek, M.J.** Medical management of methadone-maintained patients, pp. 660–673. In: Substance Abuse: Clinical Problems and Perspectives. Eds.: J.H. Lowinson and P. Ruiz. Baltimore: Williams and Wilkins, **1981.**

A thorough, useful review of medically important issues: (1) The medical effects of long-term methadone maintenance and (2) Medical treatment of patients maintained on methadone, e.g., drug-drug interactions, patients with kidney or liver disease, etc.

20.   **Musto, D.F.** The American Disease: Origins of Narcotic Control. New Haven: Yale University Press, **1973.**

The history of social response to opiates in America. An important cautionary tale to guide us in attitudes toward control of all drugs. Good history, good psychiatry.

21.   **Rounsaville, B.J., Weissman, M.M., Cilber, C.H., et al.** The heterogeneity of psychiatric diagnosis in treated opiate addicts. Arch. Gen. Psychiatry 39: 161–166, **1982.**

More addicts are depressed than sociopathic, and those with sociopathy often have additional significant, and treatable (see Woody et al.) psychiatric illnesses. It is important to remember that patients may have more than one problem or disease. Both drugs and alcohol may complicate affective disease, personality disorder, etc.

22.   **Woody, G.E.** Psychiatric aspects of opiate dependence: Diagnostic and therapeutic research issues, pp. 157–178. In: Psychodynamics of Drug Dependence. Eds. J.D. Blaine and D.A. Julius, NIDA Research Monograph no. 12. Washington, D.C.: U.S. Government Printing Office, **1977.**

An excellent complete survey of psychoanalytic thinking about addiction and of the many diagnostic and psychiatric issues still to be resolved.

23.   **Woody, G.E., Luborsky, L., McLellan, A.T., et al.** Psychotherapy for opiate addicts: Does it help? Arch. Gen. Psychiatry 40: 639–645, **1983.**

Answer: Yes, it does, if you do it right with the properly chosen patient. Probably the best psychotherapy outcome study ever done. A model for future investigation.

HALLUCINOGENS, MARIJUANA, PCP, STIMULANTS, AND TOBACCO

24.   **Angrist, B. and Sudilovsky, A.** Central nervous system stimulants: Historical aspects and clinical effects, pp. 99–165. In: Handbook of Psychopharmacology, Vol. 11. Stimulants. Eds.: L.L. Iverson, S.D. Iverson, and S.H. Snyder. New York: Plenum Press, **1978.**

Presents just what the title promises, a thorough review of amphetamines and related compounds.

25. **Becker, H.S.** Becoming a marihuana user. Am. J. Sociology 59: 235–242, **1953.** Also in: The Marihuana Papers. Ed.: D. Solomon. Indianapolis: Bobbs-Merrill Company, **1966.** Also in: Outsiders. New York: Free Press, **1963.**

An early, still-valued study of the social development of the use of marijuana for pleasure.

26. **Frosch, W.A., Robbins, E.S., and Stern, M.** Untoward reactions to lysergic acid diethylamide (LSD) resulting in hospitalization. N. Engl. J. Med. 273: 1235–1239, **1965.**

One of the first reports of "bad trips" of their various sorts. Generally applicable to other hallucinogens and marijuana in high doses.

27. **Gritz, E.** Smoking behavior and tobacco abuse, pp. 91–158. In: Advances in Substance Abuse Behavioral and Biological Research, Vol. 1. Ed.: N.K. Mello. Greenwich, Conn.: JAI Press, **1980.**

A new entity (see *DSM III*) well summarized. Theories of use and of control detailed along with the available data. This is an inadequately studied area important to public health and with many implications for psychiatrists.

28. **Kluver, H.** Mescal and Mechanisms of Hallucinations. Chicago: University of Chicago Press, **1966.**

A classic study by one of the century's greatest psychologists. Describes the drug-induced form constants the user may elaborate into hallucinations. Applicable to all the hallucinogens and marijuana in high doses. First published in 1928, as: Kluver, H. *Mechanisms of Hallucination.* In: McNemar, Q. and Merrill, M.A., Eds., *Studies in Personality.* New York: McGraw-Hill, **1942.**

29. **National Institute on Drug Abuse.** Marijuana and Health: Ninth Report to the U.S. Congress. DHHS Publication Number 82-1216, Washington, D.C., **1982.**

The most recent of a series of reports, it is a timely statement of current facts. Aside from acute toxicity (most commonly its desired effect) and pulmonary changes probably related to the complex smoke, remarkably little of significance is yet proven. Pediatricians, family practitioners, etc., should use this data in answering adolescent and family questions.

30. **Peterson, R.C. and Stillman, R.C.,** eds. Cocaine: 1977. NIDA Research Monograph no. 13. Washington, D.C.: U.S. Government Printing Office, **1977.**

A reasonably up-to-date and thorough summary. An important drug to be familiar with, cocaine use is said to be reaching epidemic proportions.

31. **Petersen, R.C. and Stillman, R.C.** Phencyclidine: An overview, pp. 1–17. In: PCP: Phencyclidine Abuse: An Appraisal. NIDA Research Monograph no. 21, Washington, D.C.: U.S. Government Printing Office, **1978.**

"A brief integrated view of our current knowledge" of angel dust. Often misrepresented as some other drug, supposedly common in ER experience with individual clinical reports of destructive behavior related to its use, the authors provide more questions than answers.

26. TRAUMATIC STRESS DISORDERS

JAMES W. LOMAX II, M.D.

This chapter deals with disturbances related to the experience of traumatic life events that are generally outside the range of usual human experience. The *DSM-III* divides these disorders into acute and chronic or delayed forms. Several references provide overviews of the posttraumatic disorders emphasizing the symptomatology, course, and the importance of early interventions (2, 3, 7, 14, 16, 20, 21). Articles are included that discuss similarities and differences between the major types of events likely to produce posttraumatic syndromes: natural disasters (20), accidental man-made disasters (1, 14, 20, 21), deliberate man-made disasters (8, 22, 23), and combat situations.

Vietnam veterans are currently the largest population at risk for development of posttraumatic syndromes. The high incidence of the delayed form of the disorder in this group led to the modified inclusion of the diagnostic category in *DSM-III*. The largest group of citations included in the chapter are those relating to some aspect of the Vietnam experience (3, 4, 5, 6, 8, 9, 13, 15, 16, 17, 20, 22).

Articles are included that provide different perspectives on the question of the relative importance of predisposing factors (6, 14, 18, 22). Some recent contributions of self-psychology and narcissism have been incorporated into attempts to understand the rage reactions of battle and the refractoriness of treatment of those who have participated in atrocities (5, 18). Other citations describe themes or trends that play a central role in the disorder (1, 12) or survey the spectrum of psychopathology encountered (11, 14). Investigators with a more biological focus have called attention to important parameters of the mechanisms (4) and treatment (17). Similarly, community psychiatrists provide a helpful perspective on the plans for delivery of services to trauma victims (3). Other treatment-oriented references include recommendations about individual psychotherapy (7, 9, 10, 16), group psychotherapy (2, 3, 15, 16), and pharmacotherapy (7, 16, 17).

1. **Adler, A.** Two different types of post-traumatic neuroses. Am. J. Psychiatry 102: 237–240, **1945.**

This article distinguishes between the nature of events that may lead to traumatic neuroses (terrifying events versus head injuries) and differentiates between "fear neurosis" and "conflict neurosis." The different chronology of symptom development (immediate versus delayed) and the development of the neurotic symptoms are also elaborated.

2. **Archibald, H.C., Long, D.M., Miller, C., et al.** Gross stress reaction in combat—a 15 year follow-up. Am. J. Psychiatry 119: 317–322, **1962.**

A follow-up survey of combat versus non-combat veterans that defines the syndrome including startle reactions, sleep difficulties, dizziness, blackouts, avoidance of activities reminiscent of combat experience, and internalization of feelings. Predisposing factors are defined. Group therapeutic activities are suggested to foster previously avoided abreaction.

3. **Borus, J .F.** Re-entry: III. Facilitating healthy readjustment in Vietnam veterans. Psychiatry 36: 428–439, **1973.**

This article is the third of a series of observations about the re-entry problems of Vietnam veterans. It is included because of its specific recommendations about a model program to facilitate optimal readjustment.

4. **Brende, J.O.** Electrodermal responses in post-traumatic syndromes, A pilot study of cerebral hemisphere functioning in Vietnam veterans. J. Nerv. Ment. Dis. 170: 352–361, **1982.**

This pilot study shows evidence of electrodermal responses and, by inference, hemispheric activity during changing emotional states and imagery of prior traumatic experiences. It provides a biological perspective on the psychopathology of stress disorders.

5. ***Fox, R.P.** Narcissistic rage and the problem of combat aggression. Arch. Gen. Psychiatry 31: 807–811, **1974.**

This article raises an important contributing factor in the development of the uncontrolled rage and combat atrocities that are often part of the guilt-ridden ideation of those individuals suffering from the post-traumatic stress syndrome.

6. ***Frye, J.S. and Stockton, R.A.** Discriminant analysis of posttraumatic stress disorder among a group of Vietnam veterans. Am. J. Psychiatry 139: 52–56, **1982.**

This article delineates the differential importance of factors affecting the development of posttraumatic stress disorder in Vietnam veterans. Factors considered are the veteran's perception of his family, level of combat intensity, preservice attitude, and the interval between combat and service discharge.

7. **Grinker, R.R. and Spiegel, J.P.** Men Under Stress. Philadelphia: Blakiston, **1945.**

This classic work summarizes psychoanalytic observations on Air Force personnel during World War II; it addresses disorders appearing during combat as well as delayed onset disorders. Has broad applicability to community mental health treatment and prevention.

8. ***Hillman, R.G.** The psychopathology of being held hostage. Am. J. Psychiatry 138: 1193–1197, **1981.**

Hillman describes the experience of officers held hostage during a prison riot. The hostage experience and the correlated psychopathology are described in detail. Comparisons are made to concentration camps and prisoner-of-war experiences.

9. ***Horowitz, M.** Stress response syndromes: Character style and dynamic psychotherapy. Arch. Gen. Psychiatry 31: 768–781, **1974.**

This article describes the characteristic responses to major psychological stress that occur in various character styles. It provides a strategy for dynamic psychotherapy at different phases of the response to match the character style of the individual patient.

10. ***Horowitz, M.J. and Solomon, G.F.** Delayed stress response syndromes in Vietnam veterans, pp. 268–280. In: Stress Disorders Among Vietnam Veterans: Theory, Research and Treatment. Ed.: C.R. Figley. New York: Brunner/Mazel, **1978.**

This citation provides specific and useful guidance for individual treatment. The entire volume in which this article is found is immensely helpful in understanding and treating the Vietnam veteran.

11. **Kardiner, A.** Traumatic neuroses of war. pp. 245–257. In: AHP (1st ed.), Vol. 1, **1959.**

This chapter is a summary of Kardiner's extensive studies on psychiatric disabilities related to war. It provides a reasonable overview of the situation of the soldier and the symptomatology of traumatic neuroses in both the acute and chronic phases of illness.

12. **Krupnick, J.L. and Horowitz, M.** Stress response syndromes: Recurrent themes. Arch. Gen. Psychiatry 38: 428–435, **1981.**

This article focuses on common conflictual themes in the content of material produced by patients suffering from stress response syndromes. It highlights the differences between those themes associated with the stress of bereavement in contrast to individuals suffering from personal injury.

13.   ***Langer, H.P.** The making of a murderer. Am. J. Psychiatry 127: 950–953, **1971.**

This communication describes some of the most critical subjective factors of the extreme and unneutralized expressions of aggression in the Vietnam War. The article is an excellent starting place for the study of the posttraumatic stress syndrome related to Vietnam experiences.

14.   ***Leopold, R.L. and Dillon, H.** Psychoanatomy of a disaster: A long term study of post-traumatic neuroses in survivors of a marine explosion. Am. J. Psychiatry 119: 913–921, **1963.**

This article describes the immediate evaluation and four-year follow-up of survivors from a maritime disaster. They emphasize that untreated psychopathology worsens over time, that failure of early repression correlates with a poor prognosis. These facts, along with the nature of the accident, are significant determinants of posttraumatic states.

15.   ***Lifton, R.J.** Rap groups. pp. 75–95. In: Home From the War. Vietnam Veterans: Neither Victims nor Executioners. Ed.: R.J. Lifton. New York: Simon and Schuster, **1973.**

The entire book provides a helpful perspective on the Vietnam experience and the psychological casualties following it. The specifically cited chapter describes the development of rap groups. An earlier chapter on "the images of My Lai" (pages 33–73) is a must for anyone involved with Vietnam vetereans who did not personally experience the war.

16.   ***Lipkin, J.O., Blank, A.S., Parson, E.R., et al.** Vietnam veterans and posttraumatic stress disorder. Hosp. Community Psychiatry. 33: 908–912, **1982.**

Part of a special issue on Vietnam veterans, the article describes the syndrome and the malignant effect it has on the life course of its victims, including problems of intimacy in all parameters of social relationships and permanent damage to self-concept. Treatment recommendations are included.

17.   ***Marshall, J.R.** The treatment of night terrors associated with post-traumatic syndrome. Am. J. Psychiatry 132: 293–295, **1975.**

This article describes the successful use of imipramine in the treatment of night terrors occurring as part of a posttraumatic syndrome. The mechanism of action is unknown, but symptom reduction occurs early in the treatment and at lower dosages than for depressive illness.

18. ***Moses, R.** Adult psychic trauma: The question of early predisposition and some detailed mechanisms. Int. J. Psychoanal. 59: 353–363, **1978.**

This article explores narcissistic factors in the predisposition to combat reactions. The author defines six clinical characteristics of the acute traumatic neuroses that he feels must be understood as arising out of a predisposing vulnerability. Poor self-esteem and the lack of feeling of belonging to a primary group predict development of stress disorders.

19. **Rado, S.** Pathodynamics and treatment of traumatic war neurosis (traumatophobia). Psychosom. Med. 4: 362–368, **1942.**

Written early in World War II to address the problem of the large numbers of psychiatric casualties. The article describes the chronological development of war neurosis and a psychological transition from the dread of injury to the dread of recurrence of a particular traumatic experience.

20. ***Rangell, L.** Discussion of the Buffalo Creek disaster: The course of psychic trauma. Am. J. Psychiatry 133: 313–316, **1976.**

This article is part of a special section describing a team study of the Buffalo Creek disaster in 1972 (the entire section is worthwhile). Rangell describes the phases of psychic trauma and notes that the Buffalo Creek disaster include the "human element" that the disaster "could have been prevented."

21. ***Schnaper, N. and Cowley, R.A.** Overview: Psychiatric sequelae to multiple trauma. Am. J. Psychiatry 133: 883–890, **1976.**

This article reviews psychiatric complications of patients in intensive care units after severe trauma. The varied roles of the psychiatric consultant are discussed, and practical recommendations for common situations are offered.

22. ***Terr, L.C.** Children of Chowchilla: A study of psychic trauma. Psychoanal. Study Child 34: 547–623, **1979.**

This is a fine discussion of the effect of a severe trauma on developing personalities that includes an excellent bibliography on traumatic disorders in children.

23. ***Ursano, R.J.** The Vietnam era prisoner of war: Precaptivity personality

and the development of psychiatric illness. Am. J. Psychiatry 138: 315–318, **1981.**

The chief findings are that antecedent psychological disturbances are neither necessary nor sufficient explanations for the development of posttraumatic illness.

27. BEREAVEMENT AND GRIEF

Selby C. Jacobs, M.D.

Bereavement is a source of emotional distress that is experienced inevitably and universally subsequent to a loss. It is a complex emotional response, including components of separation anxiety, despair, depressive symptoms, and avoidance that evolve somewhat independently over time reaching peak intensity 4–5 months, on the average, after a loss. The health consequences of bereavement include a reduced sense of well being; increased help seeking in the minor; nonspecific psychological and psychophysiological ailments; the occurrence of depressive syndromes that do not appear to be psychopathological; and finally an increased morbidity and mortality from cardiovascular diseases, accidents, and injuries, suicide, and perhaps other diseases of middle and later life. When bereavement is unresolved or otherwise pathological in nature, it may cause impairment in its own right.

Bereavement, as a well-defined response to a conspicuous and severe life stressor, provides the opportunity to investigate several questions of psychiatric etiology and psychopathology. It serves as a model for examining the relationship between stress and mental health and the nature of coping or defense that may mediate between. In this regard, general theories of emotional distress and brief treatment interventions such as crisis theory and stress response theory have been developed. Bereavement also serves as a model for investigating depression with the aim of clarifying the difference between "normal" depressive mood, symptoms, or syndromes and "clinical" depressions. Furthermore, in a developmental framework, childhood bereavement serves as a paradigm for elucidating the consequences of crucial, early life experiences for adult personality functioning and mental health.

1. **Bartrop, R.W., Luckhurst, E., Lazarus, L., et al.** Depressed lymphocyte function after bereavement. Lancet I: 834–836, **1977.**

This study is the first report of altered function of one part of the immune system, a depressed response of T-lymphocytes to mitogens during acute bereavement that is apparently not caused by hormonal changes. The immune system is now receiving considerable attention as a key mediator between stressful experiences such as bereavement and diseases that have an immunological basis.

2. ***Bowlby, J.** The making and breaking of affectional bonds. Br. J. Psychiatry 130: 201–210, **1977.**

This article is a brief summary of Bowlby's theoretical position that attachment behavior is a class of behavior distinct from feeding behavior and sexual behavior and of at least equal significance in human life. This proposition is novel and controversial but, nevertheless, important to consider. In Bowlby's *Attachment and Loss,* Volumes I, II, and III. (New York: Basic Books) he provides an expanded account of his theory.

3. **Bowlby, J.** Pathological mourning and childhood mourning. J. Am. Psychoanal. Assoc. 11: 500–541, **1963.**

Bowlby summarizes four variants of pathological grief in dynamic terms. He discusses these processes in relationship to childhood mourning and emphasizes the similarity between pathological and childhood mourning.

4. **Cavenar, J.O., Nash, J.L., and Maltbie, A.A.** Anniversary reactions masquerading as manic-depressive illness. Am. J. Psychiatry 134: 1273–1276, **1977.**

Cavenar and his associates provide an excellent brief review of the literature in this area and give several clinical examples of anniversary reactions masquerading as affective disorder. Severe anniversary reactions are one manifestation of pathological grief.

5. ***Clayton, P.J.** Mortality and morbidity in the first year of widowhood. Arch. Gen. Psychiatry 30: 747–750, **1974.**

Clayton documents that the bereaved experience significantly more psychological and physical symptoms, yet they do not utilize psychiatric services more often than others. She concludes that mortality is not a risk associated with acute bereavement; however, this issue is still controversial, especially for younger persons and for men.

6. ***Clayton, P.J., Halikas, J.A., and Maurice, W.L.** The depression of widowhood. Br. J. Psychiatry 120: 71–77, **1972.**

Clayton documents that a significant proportion of acutely bereaved persons experience a depressive syndrome during the early phases of grief. These syndromes meet the criteria for major depressive disorder, but the vast majority of bereaved persons so afflicted do not seek help.

7.   ***Freud, S.** (1917) Mourning and melancholia. S.E. 14: 243–258, **1957.**

This essay includes seminal thinking about grief and depression. In Freud's view, depression or melancholia is distinguished from mourning by ambivalence and the internalization of conflict when a separation occurs. In addition, the psychoanalytical hypothesis that loss may cause depression is given early expression.

8.   ***Futterman, E.H., Hoffman, I., and Sabshin, M.** Parental anticipatory mourning, pp. 243–272. In: Psychosocial Aspects of Terminal Care. Eds.: B. Schoenberg, et al. New York: Columbia University Press, **1972.**

The best of several reports on anticipatory grief, this chapter reviews the literature on this concept and summarizes data from a large study done by the authors.

9.   ***Hofer, M.A., Wolff, C.T., Friedman, S.B., et al.** A psychoendocrine study of bereavement: Part I and Part II. Psychosom. Med. 4: 481–491, 492–504, **1972.**

This two-part article reports on a study of 17 hydroxycorticosteroid excretion rates and the process of mourning of parents following the death of their children from leukemia. This study during the period of acute mourning is a follow-up of the classical study of the same parents before the death of the child (*Psychosomatic Medicine* 26: 576–591, 1964). The style and effectiveness of ego defenses are important in predicting levels of adrenocortical hormone excretion.

10.   ***Horowitz, M.** Stress response syndromes. Arch. Gen. Psychiatry 31: 768–781, **1974.**

In this article Horowitz characterizes the emotional response to loss and other traumatic experiences as a syndrome of stress response, discusses variation in the syndrome related to personality style, and illustrates the application of such a system of knowledge in the brief, focal, dynamic psychotherapy of persons undergoing a stressful experience. Horowitz offers an expanded account of this approach in his book *Stress Response Syndromes* (New York: Aronson, 1976) for those with an interest in this area.

11.   ***Horowitz, M., Krupnick, J.L., Kaltreider, N., et al.** Initial psychological response to parental death. Arch. Gen. Psychiatry 38: 316–323, **1981.**

Loss may occur at any time in the life cycle. This is a report from the first systematic study of adult persons who have experienced the death of a parent. The article provides a useful, but not yet definitive, discussion of the importance and consequences of this life event for adults.

12. **Horowitz, M., Wilner, N., Marmar, C., et al.** Pathological grief and the activation of latent self-images. Am. J. Psychiatry 137: 1157–1162, **1980.**

Horowitz conceptualizes pathological grief in terms of the re-emergence of self-images and role relationship models associated with depressive ego states that have been held in check by the existence of the deceased person. This is a novel conceptualization of pathological grief that supplements earlier descriptive, motivational, and dynamic views.

13. **Lewis, C.S.** A Grief Observed. New York: Bantam Books, **1976.**

14. **Mooney, E.** Alone: Surviving as a Widow. New York: Putnam, **1981.**

Autobiographical accounts of bereavement are useful in understanding the subjective experience of the acutely bereaved. Lewis's book is a modern classic that has a strong religious-philosophical tone rather than a psychological one. Mooney's work is written from the perspective of a widow.

15. ***Lindemann, E.** Symptomatology and management of acute grief. Am. J. Psychiatry 101: 141–148, **1944.**

Lindemann's observations of the survivors of the Coconut Grove Fire are a classical description of the manifestations of grief. He noted essential features of grief and described several manifestations and syndromes associated with severe or unresolved grief, the first descriptive characterization of pathological grief.

16. ***Miller, J.B.M.** Children's reactions to the death of a parent: A review of the psychoanalytic literature. J. Am. Psychoanal. Assoc. 19: 697–719, **1971.**

The article delineates a controversy that centers on the question of whether children mourn in the same way as do adults in the sense of gradually and painfully detaching from the inner representation of the lost parental figure. Most observers agree that they do, but not without active clinical efforts with the child or, alternatively, facilitative efforts on the part of a surviving parent or other significant adult.

17. **Parkes, C.M.** The first year of bereavement. Psychiatry 33: 444–467, **1970.**

This article summarizes the findings in a longitudinal study of 22 acutely bereaved widows in London. It is the first such study and documents the evolving manifestations of grief over time.

18. **Parkes, C.M.** The psychosomatic effects of bereavement, pp. 71–80. In: Modern Trends in Psychosomatic Medicine. Ed.: O. Hill. London: Butterworth, **1970.**

Many clinical studies have investigated the etiological role of loss in the occurrence of several "psychomatic" disorders, and many claims have been made about the importance of loss in such illnesses as cancer, reticulosis, ulcerative colitis, and asthma. This article reviews that literature critically in a broad framework that discusses several basic methodological issues.

19.   ***Parkes, C.M.** Bereavement: Studies of Grief in Adult Life. New York: International Universities Press, **1972.**

In this book, Parkes, the most thorough and creative empirical investigator of grief in the past 20 years, summarizes the findings of his studies.

20.   **Raphael, B.** Preventive intervention with the recently bereaved. Arch. Gen. Psychiatry 34: 1950–1954, **1977.**

Raphael's well-designed prospective study of a "preventive" intervention for one group of recent bereaved versus none in another group showed a significant lowering of morbidity in the intervention group 13 months after the intervention. The bibliography is a good introduction to treatment literature.

21.   **Siggens, L.D.** Mourning: A critical survey of the literature. Int. J. Psychoanal. 47: 14–25, **1966.**

This article is a good, fairly modern review of the psychoanalytical literature on bereavement. It incorporates Freud's ideas into the broader framework of subsequent psychoanalytic thought and clarifies that many of Freud's conclusions, such as the idea that ambivalence distinguishes melancholia from mourning, have not stood the test of time.

22.   **Tennant, C., Bebbington, P., and Hurry, J.** Parental death in childhood and risk of adult depressive disorders: A review. Psychol. Med. 10: 289–299, **1980**.

This article reviews the literature on the long-term risks of depressive disorder for children who suffer the tragedy of parental death and carefully addresses methodological issues and conceptual distinction (i.e., the difference between help-seeking behavior and illness occurrence). They conclude that long-term consequences must be small.

28. PSYCHOPHYSIOLOGIC DISORDERS

Milton Viederman, M.D.

The systematic scientific study of the causes of disease began in the nineteenth century with the development of a new scientific methodology. A reductionistic causal model of disease (a biomedical model) was elaborated and was a useful structure for research and advancement of understanding. Important contributions were made by the physiologist Helmholtz, the pathologist Virchow, and by Koch and Pasteur whose infectious theory of disease was a perfect prototype of the view that a healthy organism became disordered when invaded by noxious external elements. It is only in the last 50 years that this model has given way to another more complex model that conceptualizes disease as resulting from multiple influences both physical and psychosocial and sees it in part as a failure in adaptation (Wolff). Alexander, one of the pioneers in this development, elaborated the concept of specificity, i.e., specific unconscious conflicts lead to specific diseases. He recognized, however, that genetic factors and life experience also played a role and consequently developed a multicausal model. Coincident with the work of Alexander was the work of Wolff who established psychophysiological correlations emphasizing bodily changes that were specific to the nature of aroused affect. All of this work had been strongly influenced by Cannon's contributions, in particular his elaboration of physiologic fight-flight mechanisms and the development of the concept of bodily homeostasis.

However, the matter proved more complicated, and new models had to be developed. Two basic, though not contradictory, models are most currently used by workers in the field. The first, the biopsychosocial model elaborated by Engel, is based upon systems theory and recognizes a hierarchy of structures of increasing complexity starting with the biologic—molecules, organelles, cells, organs, organ systems, etc.—but including the critical transition from organism to person as psychosocial being. Input into any system can affect systems above and below, and disease occurs when response to input is not adequate to preserve healthy homeostatic balance. The second model, the stress model, hypothesizes that environmental input may disturb homeostasis and lead to permanent (physiological change) particularly if adequate coping does not occur. Hence, the environment input is seen as a "potential activator" and activation of physiological responses is dependent upon mediating psychological and physiological variables that will determine response (temporary disequilibrium) or consequences (permanent alterations). With this model, whether or not physiological change or disease occurs will depend upon many factors including genetic predisposition, early life experience, the state of the organism at the time potential activation occurs, psychological coping mechanisms, which are related to perception of threat, and the resultant degree of emotional arousal.

The wide, encompassing nature of these models offers the possibility for research in many discrete areas and by scientists in many different fields. Mason points out that there have been two important strategies in this research: (1) the attempt to study discrete and atomic elements in the stress process (analysis) and (2) an attempt to determine how the component parts work together (integration).

It is with these models in mind that the following bibliography is offered. The articles have been selected and ordered by their methodologic approach to the solution of the problems described above. They have been selected because they represent either classical attempts to deal with some of the problems, particularly lucid descriptions of such experiments, or useful review articles. Each of them is to represent a strategy for dealing with the question of how biology, psychology, and environment contribute to the development of disease in man.

ANIMAL MODELS OF DISEASE

1. *Hofer, M.A. Animals models in the understanding of human disease. Psychiatr. Clin. of North Am. 2: 211–226, **1979.**

    A very thoughtful discussion of the application of animal models of disease to human beings.

2. Hofer, M.A. Some thoughts on the "Transduction of Experience" from a developmental perspective. Psychosom. Med. 44: 19–28, **1982.**

    An interesting example of the problems in research methodology and the intricate relationship between experimental design and theorizing.

BODY IMAGE

3. Druss, R.G. Changes in body image following breast augmentation. Int. J. Psychoanal. Psychother. 2: 248–256, **1973.**

An interesting paper that runs counter to the view that low self-esteem related to dissatisfaction with body form is necessarily resistant to change with surgery.

4.   **Kolb, L.C.** Disturbances of the body-image, pp. 810–837. In: AHP (2nd ed.), Vol. 4, **1975.**

A broad perspective on body image as it pertains to physical abnormalities and manifest changes in the body among other things. Scholarly discussion of the literature.

BRONCHIAL ASTHMA

5.   **Knapp, P.H.S.** Psychosomatic aspects of bronchial asthma, pp. 693–708. In: AHP (2nd ed.), Vol. 4, **1975.**

An excellent review article on the data pertinent to psychosocial factors in bronchial asthma by one of the pioneering researchers in this area.

CARDIOVASCULAR DISEASE

6.   **Hackett, T.P., Cassem, N.H., and Wishnie, H.A.** The coronary care unit: An appraisal of its psychologic hazards. N. Engl. J. Med. 279: 1365–1370, **1968.**

A classical article in which denial of anxiety correlated with a decrease of morbidity and mortality of patients with acute myocardial infarction.

7.   **Kimball, C.P.** Psychological aspects of cardiovascular disease, pp. 608–617. In: AHP (2nd ed.), Vol 4, **1975.**

Summarizes the literature on coronary artery disease with special reference to Friedman and Rosenman's Type "A" and Type "B" behavior patterns as they relate to coronary disease.

8.   **Lown, B., Desilva, R.A., Reich, P., et al.** Psychophysiological factors in sudden cardiac death. Am. J. Psychiatry 137: 1325–1335, **1980.**

An excellent study of the impact of stress on ventricular excitability. Describes an animal model and a series of 117 patients who had experienced cardiac arrest. Over 21 percent had a severe and major stress either in the preceding 24 hours or immediately preceding the cardiac arrest.

9.   **Reiser, M.F. and Bakst, H.** Psychophysiological and psychodynamic problems of the patient with structural heart disease, pp. 618–652. In: AHP (2nd ed.), Vol. 4, **1975.**

Offers a comprehensive picture of the research that has been done in this area, including psychological and physiological data about stress and heart function as well as hypertension and cardiovascular surgery.

DEVELOPMENTAL MODEL OF DISEASE

10.   **Dowling, S.** Seven infants with esophageal atresia: A developmental study. Psychoanal. Study Child 32: 215–256, **1977.**

An elegant study of the critical important aspects of early care on later ego development in children with esophageal atresia.

11.   **Engel, G. and Schmale, A.** Conservation withdrawal: a primary regulatory process for organismic homeostasis, pp. 57–75. In: Physiology, Emotion and Psychosomatic Illness. New York: Elsevier, **1972.**

A careful theoretical discussion of the concept of conservation withdrawal with description of the historical origin of the concept in the first observations of Engel's famous patient, Monica.

DIABETES MELLITUS

12.   ***Hinkle, L.E. and Wolf, S.** A summary of experimental evidence relating life stress to diabetes mellitus. J. Mt. Sinai Hosp. 19: 537–570, **1952.**

An excellent general study and theoretical discussion of the issue of stress and carbohydrate metabolism across the lifespan of individuals with diabetes.

DISEASE AND HOMEOSTASIS

13.   **Cannon, W.B.** Stresses and strains of homeostasis. Am. J. Med. Sci. 189: 1–14, **1935.**

A classical and extremely well-written article describing bodily homeostasis as an adaptive process. Though focused entirely on physiology, it reveals a brilliant and imaginative mind attempting to understand bodily processes.

DUODENAL ULCER

14.   ***Weiner, H.M., Thaler, M., Reiser, M.F., et al.** Etiology of duodenal ulcer: I. Relation of specific psychological characteristics to rate of gastric secretion. (serum pepsinogen). Psychosom. Med. 19: 1–10, **1957.**

An aspect of the classical study on army inductees undergoing basic training in which significant correlations are established between serum pepsinogen and unconscious conflicts.

GASTROINTESTINAL DISEASE—ULCERATIVE COLITIS AND PEPTIC ULCER

15. **Engel, G.L.** Psychological aspects of gastrointestinal disorders, pp. 653–692. In: AHP (2nd ed.), Vol. 4, **1975.**

   Excellent summary chapter on the wide array of gastrointestinal diseases viewed from both physiological and psychosocial points of view. Written by one of the figures who has been in the forefront of research on ulcerative colitis. Interesting case ancedotes enrich the text.

HUMAN DISEASE

16. **Weiner, H.** Psychobiology and Human Disease. New York: Elsevier North-Holland, **1977.**

   An encyclopedic textbook that has accumulated all of the data pertinent to the "psychosomatic diseases" of Alexander but now including systematically—epidemiology, genetics, social factors, psychological factors, early environmental factors, etc. Focuses on the heterogeneity of all of these diseases, the multiple influences that go to create them and the special problems of methodology in attempting to elucidate causes. A reference text.

MODELS OF DISEASE

17. **Alexander, F., French, T.M., and Pollock, G.H.** Psychosomatic Specificity. Chicago: University of Chicago Press, **1968.**

   This book is a definitive statement of the classical psychoanalytic viewpoint as expounded by Alexander that focuses on specificity, i.e., the role of specific unconscious conflicts in the genesis of specific "psychosomatic diseases."

18. **Cannon, W.B.** Voodoo death, pp. 80–94. In: Stress and Coping. An Anthology. Ed.: A. Monat and R.S. Lazarus. New York: Columbia University Press, **1977.**

   A classic article reprinted from the *American Anthropologist,* which describes Cannon's thinking about mechanisms of sudden death due to magic. An imaginative and witty article in the grand clinical tradition.

19.   *Engel, G.L. The need for a new medical model: A challenge for biomedicine. Science 196: 129–136, **1977.**

Discussion of the reductionistic and unicausal thinking in the establishment of the biomedical model. Presents an integrated systems theory model of human behavior and disease.

20.   *Engel, G.L. A reconsideration of the role of conversion in somatic disease. Compr. Psychiatry 9: 316–326, **1968.**

Discards the classic idea of conversion as related to the voluntary nervous system and emphasizes that any bodily experience that can achieve psychic represention may become the focus of a conversion symptom—if underlying physiological changes occur, disease may result.

21.   *Engel, G.L. and Schmale, A. Psychoanalytic theory of somatic disorder. J. An. Psychoanal. Assoc. 15: 344–365, **1967.**

A thoughtful discussion of the relationship between conversion reactions and physiological changes. Discusses the issue of specificity, conceptualizes somatopsychic-psychosomatic interaction emphasizing a multiplicity of reciprocal interactions that include the predisposing biological factors present at birth. Discusses the significance of the disease onset situation and the "giving up–given-up" complex as a nonspecific onset condition.

22.   Holmes, T.H. Development and application of a quantitative measure of magnitude of life change. Psychiatr. Clin. North Am. 2: 289–306, **1979.**

An exposition by one of the founders of the life-stress methodology (with Rahe). The Social Readjustment Rating Scale is described as are ancillary scales such as Seriousness of Illness Rating Scale.

23.   Nemiah, J.C. Alexithymia and psychosomatic illness. J. Cont. Educ. Psychiatry 38: 25–39, **1978.**

This highly controversial concept in psychosomatic medicine is described clearly in this paper.

24.   Reiser, M.F. Changing theoretical concepts in psychosomatic medicine, pp. 477–500. In: AHP (2nd ed.), Vol. 4, **1975.**

Excellent overall discussion of the current status of psychosomatic medicine. Includes the historical antecedents of current thinking, the types of data and methodological approaches to validating hypotheses in this area and ends with a proposed model for understanding disease.

OBESITY

25.   **Hirsch, J.** The psychobiology of obesity, pp. 183–192. In: Critical Issues in Behavioral Medicine. Eds.: L.J. West and M. Stein. Philadelphia: Lippincott, **1982.**

A short but excellent up-to-date summary of the work on obesity by a leading researcher.

26.   **Stunkard, A.J.** Obesity, pp. 767–786. In: AHP (2nd ed.), Vol. 4, **1975.**

An excellent general summary of what is known about obesity by one of the leading researchers in the field.

PEPTIC ULCER

27.   ***Mirksy, I.A.** Physiologic, psychologic and social determinants in the etiology of duodenal ulcer. Am. J. Dig. Dis. 3: 285–314, **1958.**

The classic paper on the relationship between high pepsinogen levels and psychological traits.

PSYCHOENDOCRINOLOGY

28.   **Carruthers, M.** 'Field Studies': Emotion and beta blockage, pp. 223–241. In: Foundations of Psychosomatics. Eds.: M.J. Christie and P.G. Mellett. New York: Wiley, **1981.**

A very interesting discussion of catecholamine metabolism in various situations of stress.

29.   **Katz, J.L., Ackman, P., Rotwax, Y., et al.** Psychoendocrine aspects of cancer of the breast. Psychosom. Med. 32: 1–18, **1970.**

A classic psychoendocrine study in which correlations were established between failing defenses and adrenocortical reactions.

30.   **Mason, J.W.** Clinical psychophysiology-psychoendocrine mechanisms, pp. 553–582. In: AHP (2nd ed.), Vol. 4, **1975.**

A general discussion of psychoendocrinology by the outstanding worker in this field discusses various experiments and how they demonstrate the relationship between stress and endocrine response.

31.   **Tennes, K.** The role of hormones in mother-infant transactions, pp.

75–80. In: The Development of Attachment and Affiliative Systems. Eds.: R.N. Emde and R.J. Harn. New York: Plenum, **1982.**

An elegant study of the impact of 2 hours of separation from their mothers on 1-year-olds in terms of emotional arousal and cortisol excretion rates.

32.   **Wolff, C.T., Friedman, S.B., Hofer, M.A., et al.** Relationship between psychological defenses and mean urinary 17-hydroxycorticosteroid excretion rates. (I) Psychosom. Med. 26: 576–591, **1964;** (II) Psychosom. Med. 26: 592–609, **1964.**

The classical study of the parents of leukemic children in which correlations are established between 17 OHCS and characteristic defenses leading to high or low arousal.

PSYCHOIMMUNOLOGY

33.   **Locke, S.E.** Stress, adaptation and immunity: Studies in humans. Gen. Hosp. Psychiatry 4: 49–58, **1982.**

A good general article describing the current literature on the relationship between stress, adaptation, and immunity with an excellent bibliography that is up-to-date. Discusses methodologic issues.

34.   *****Riley, V.S.** Psychoendocrine influences on immunocompetence and neoplasia. Science 212: 1100–1109, **1981.**

An elegant study, demonstrating that stress in animals leads to adrenocortical hyperplasia and thymic involution, making the animals more susceptible to takes of transplanted neoplastic tissue.

35.   **Rogers, M., Dubey, D., and Reich, P.** The influence of the psyche and the brain on immunity and disease susceptibility: A critical review. Psychosom. Med. 41: 147–164, **1979.**

A detailed discussion of the impact of emotional events on the immune system.

STRESS

36.   *****Conceptual issues in stress research,** pp. 11–24. In: Stress and Human Health. Analysis and Implications of Research. Eds.: G.R. Elliott and C. Eisdorfer. New York: Springer, **1982.**

An excellent general article that presents the conceptual issues and difficulties in formulating a definition of stress. Emphasizes that part of the difficulty relates to the fact that research in this area is done by workers in many separate disciplines. Presents a framework to integrate data.

37. ***Monat, A. and Lazarus, R.S.** Stress and Coping: An Anthology. New York: Columbia University Press, **1977.**

An excellent anthology of previously published articles covering a wide array of topics including a discussion of the impact of psychological stress on the development of disease, the role of cognition and coping processes in emotion, modes of adaptation and defense as they affect behavior, etc. An excellent source book for those interested in stress.

STRESS AND HUMAN DISEASE

38. **Dohrenwend, B.P., Pearlin, L., Clayton, P.J., et al.** Report on stress and life events, pp. 55–80. In: Stress and Human Health. Analysis and Implications of Research. Eds.: G.R. Elliott and C. Eisdorfer. New York: Springer, **1982.**

Excellent article elucidating the many factors that must be considered in determining the effect of stress on the human being. Important research in the various areas is presented. Excellent bibliography.

ULCERATIVE COLITIS

39. **Karush, A., Daniels, G.E., Flood, C., et al.** Psychotherapy in Chronic Ulcerative Colitis. Philadelphia: Saunders, **1977.**

Places ulcerative colitis patients in different categories based upon psychopathology and psychodynamic constellations with different recommendations for psychotherapy.

29. SUICIDE

JAMES W. LOMAX II, M.D.

Suicide, a complex behavior occurring predominantly in mentally ill individuals, represents the most compelling psychiatric emergency. Important contributions to the field of suicide care are made by individuals with backgrounds ranging from sociology to neurophysiology. The psychiatry resident facing a potentially suicidal patient must rapidly integrate sometimes subtle material from the interview with knowledge of the many risk factors from the patient's past history, sociocultural background, and interpersonal field.

Articles in this chapter are divided into four sections: general considerations, psychiatric assessment, treatment, and suicide and the psychiatrist. Of course there is overlap among these sections (e.g., Comstock's article is included in the treatment section but certainly contains valuable information about assessment). The articles in the general section emphasize epidemiology (1, 2, 3, 7, 9) myths (5), suicide rates in psychiatric disorders (6), and topic overviews (7, 8). The assessment section includes information about biological factors (10, 14, 20, 22), psychological assessment and psychological testing (11, 12, 13, 18, 21), the sociocultural field (15, 17, 19), and interpersonal mechanisms (16, 17). The treatment section includes overall management and specific interventions in both inpatient and outpatient settings. The section on suicide and the psychiatrist is included because of special problems in the education of psychiatrists in suicide care (29–31).

GENERAL CONSIDERATIONS

1. **Barraclough, B., Bunch, J., Nelson, B., et al.** A hundred cases of suicide: Clinical aspects. Br. J. Psychiatry 125: 355–373, **1974.**

   Parameters studied included the presence or absence of mental illness, personality factors of successful suicides, the tendency to communicate suicidal intent, and the interaction with medical personnel prior to suicide.

2. **Fredrick, C.J.** Current trends in suicidal behavior in the United States. Am. J. Psychother. 32: 172–200, **1978.**

This is a rather detailed article that has current demographic data and provides substantial information about the state of the art of suicide assessment. There are some practical suggestions about the nature and process of psychotherapy strategies for suicidal individuals.

3. **Guze, S.B. and Robins, E.** Suicide and primary affective disorders. Br. J. Psychiatry 117: 437–438, **1970.**

This is a succinct article summarizing findings from a review of the course and outcome of affective disorders. The most important features are the definition of the statistical risk for suicide in affective disorders and the observation of the greater risk early in the course of the illness.

4. **Motto, J.A.** Suicidal patients in clinical practice. Weekly Psychiatric Update Series 1: no. 18, **1977.**

A concise but rich summary article by an experienced psychiatrist. The article makes several points of particular cogency in the diagnosis and treatment of suicidal patients: (1) No diagnostic category is free of risk; (2) dealing with suicidal patients involves losing patients to suicide; (3) the decision-making process regarding hospitalization; and (4) advice on managing the predictable obstacles to care of suicidal patients.

5. **Pokorny, A.D.** Myths about suicide, pp. 57–72. In: Suicidal Behaviors: Diagnosis and Management. Ed.: H.L.P. Resnik. Boston: Little, Brown, **1968.**

This article breaks down myths or incorrect beliefs about suicide into general beliefs, causes, and management. Each myth is exposed by succinctly presented data and references to appropriate research. Many of these myths are part of the common "knowledge" residents bring into professional training.

6. ***Pokorny, A.D.** Suicide rates in various psychiatric disorders. J. Nerv. Ment. Dis. 139: 499–506, **1964.**

This article reports a study of suicide among patients followed by a large Veterans Administration hospital over a 15-year period. The article compares the rates for suicide in eight broad psychiatric diagnostic categories.

7. ***Robins, E., Murphy, G.E., Wilkinson, R.H., et al.** Some clinical considerations in the prevention of suicide based on a study of 134 successful suicides. Am. J. Public Health 49: 888–899, **1959.**

The authors studied all suicides occurring in metropolitan St. Louis in a one-year period. In the majority of instances, suicide was a premeditated act for which the person gave ample warning. Furthermore, the great majority of suicide victims are clinically ill (98 percent) and most (68 percent) suffer from a major affective disorder or chronic alcoholism.

8. ***Shneidman, E.S.** Suicide, pp. 1774–1785. In: CIP II, Vol. 2, **1975.**

An appropriate reference to begin a study of suicide or serve as a review article. The author reviews the major parameters of suicide ranging from historical and philosophical views to statistics and management considerations.

9. **World Health Organization.** Prevention of Suicide. (Public Health Paper no. 35) Geneva: WHO, **1968.**

This monograph gives an extensive survey of the epidemiological features of suicide rather than how to prevent it (in spite of its title). It includes summaries of 73 epidemiological studies and has extensive references.

ASSESSMENT

10. **Hankoff, L.D.** Physiochemical correlates, pp. 105–110. In: Suicide, Theory, and Clinical Aspects. Eds.: L.D. Hankoff and B. Einsidler. Littleton, MA: P.S.G. Publishing, **1979.**

This chapter in a very comprehensive book provides a brief overview of such diverse areas as neurochemistry, pharmacology, electroencephalography, genetics, and meteorology.

11. ***Havens, L.L.** The recognition of suicidal risk through the psychologic examination. N. Engl. J. Med. 276: 210–215, **1967.**

This article examines the "here and now" of interviewing suicidal individuals. The article elaborates the principal elements of the psychologic examination that should be considered in the assessment of suicidal risk. It encourages the interviewer to confront the question of suicide and provides useful instructions about how to address the question and how to assess the response of the patient.

12. **Kiev, A.** Prognostic factors in attempted suicide. Am. J. Psychiatry 131: 987–990, **1974.**

This article is a one-year follow-up study of 300 suicide attempters. It focuses on the prognostic significance of three factors of the population: interpersonal conflict, symptom distress, and social setting.

13.   *Kirstein, L., Prusoff, B.A., Weissman, M.M., et al.** Utilization review
      of treatment of suicide attempters. Am. J. Psychiatry 132: 22–27, **1975.**

      Written with an orientation toward utilization review, it is included
      because it provides seven clinical criteria for hospitalizing suicidal
      patients. The operational definition of each criterion is also specified,
      which makes the article of special merit.

14.   **Krieger, G.** Biochemical predictors of suicide. Dis. Nerv. System 31:
      478–482, **1970.**

      This study reports on 205 male patients who were at risk for suicide. The
      study focuses on the ratio of 17-OHCS to creatinine as a predictor of
      violent suicide. Krieger mentions similar work by Bunney and advances
      a hypothesis concerning underlying biological factors in suicidal
      behavior.

15.   **Lester, D.** Sociological theories of suicide, pp. 75–114. In: Why People
      Kill Themselves. Springfield, IL: Thomas, **1972.**

      This chapter in a generally rather interesting book provides a succinct
      summary of the major sociological theories of suicide. While far from a
      complete treatment of the individuals mentioned, it has the advantage of
      covering a large amount of material in a succinct manner.

16.   **Maddison, D. and Mackey, K.H.** Suicide: The clinical problem. Br. J.
      Psychiatry 112: 693–703, **1966.**

      This article describes both the assessment and understanding of suicidal
      risk as well as the vicissitudes of responding to a patient who has made a
      suicidal attempt. Of particular note is the interpersonal focus in the
      article, which the author feels has major consequences in clinical
      practice.

17.   **Menninger, K.A.** Part II: Suicide, pp. 11–83. In: Man Against Himself.
      New York: Harcourt, Brace, **1938.**

      While this entire book is worthy, the three chapters on suicide address
      the specific topic at hand most directly. The first chapter discusses the
      taboo quality of suicide and places it in a cross-cultural perspective. A
      longer chapter addresses motives in suicide. Menninger elaborates the
      complex nature of suicidal acts noting the ambiguities of intent and aim
      of the murderous wish implicit in suicide. A final chapter addresses
      several points from a more theoretical level.

18.   *Minkoff, K., Bergman, E., Beck, A.T., et al.** Hopelessness, depression,
      and attempted suicide. Am. J. Psychiatry 130: 455–459, **1973.**

      The authors demonstrate that hopelessness has a closer relationship to suicidal intent than does depression in their population of suicide attempters. The importance of hopelessness is particularly noted in the nonschizophrenic diagnostic group.

19. **Paykel, E.S., Prusoff, B.A., and Myers, J.K.** Suicide attempts and recent life events: A controlled comparison. Arch. Gen. Psychiatry 32: 327–333, **1975.**

This article reviews the relationship between life events and uncompleted suicide attempts. Suicide attempts have a strong relationship to life events, particularly exits from the social field. The crisis nature of the suicidal state is emphasized.

20. **Snyder, S.H.** Biology, pp. 113–129. In: A Handbook for the Study of Suicide. Ed.: S. Perlin. New York: Oxford University Press, **1975.**

This chapter reviews the psychobiology of depression with an emphasis on catecholamine metabolism and the reward centers of the brain. These hypotheses are the theoretical basis to intervene in suicidal states with psychotropic agents.

21. **Solomon, P.** The burden of responsibility in suicide and homicide. JAMA 199: 321–324, **1967.**

Although a little dated with respect to confidentiality and right to refuse treatment, this paper has a clear and reasonable outline for assessment of suicide and homicide risk and the corollary responsibilities of the physician.

22. **Traskman, L., Asberg, M., Bertilsson, L., et al.** Monoamine metabolites in CSF and suicidal behavior. Arch. Gen. Psychiatry 38: 631–636, **1981.**

This article is one of the more recent reports from this group of Swedish investigators who are correlating the dopamine metabolism in the brain with violent suicide attempts.

MANAGEMENT

23. ***Comstock, B.S.** Suicide: Emergency issues. In: Phenomenology and Treatment of Psychiatric Emergencies. Eds.: R.L. Williams, W.E. Fann, A.D. Pokorny, et al. New York: Spectrum Publications, **1983** (in press).

One of the most comprehensive and clinically relevant surveys available. It provides an excellent overview of the considerations most important to emergency assessment of suicidal patients. Practical management recommendations for crisis intervention, crisis hospitalization, and referral phases will be welcomed by emergency room personnel.

24. **Farberow, N.L.** The suicidal crisis in psychotherapy, pp. 119–130. In: Clues to Suicide. Eds.: E. Shneidman and N.L. Farberow. New York: McGraw-Hill, **1957.**

This chapter in a generally rather good and nearly "classic" book has the particular advantage of including a considerable amount of therapeutic dialogue. The case material and discussion point out the need for increasing activity and flexibility on the part of the therapist.

25. **Krieger, G.** Common errors in the treatment of suicidal patients. J. Clin. Psychiatry 3: 649–651, **1978.**

This article describes five groups of common errors in the management of suicidal patients. The data comes from psychological autopsies of over 150 suicides that took place in northern California. Each common error is illustrated with a clinical example and an explanation of both the error and a preferred response.

26. **Litman, R.E. and Wold, C.I.** Beyond crisis intervention, pp. 528–546. In: Suicidology: Contemporary Developments. Ed.: E.S. Shneidman. New York: Grune and Stratton, **1976.**

This article from the Los Angeles Suicide Prevention Center defines a population of individuals at an unusually high risk for suicide. The population under consideration has relatively less acute stress and a greater unwillingness to accept help and is therefore, less appropriately served by a crisis intervention model.

27. ***Mintz, R.S.** Some practical procedures in the management of suicidal persons. Am. J. Orthopsychiatry 36: 896–903, **1966.**

This article follows its title precisely. Background epidemiological data is followed by specific suggestions for managing suicidal persons. Each suggestion is followed by an explanation along with some very practical advice.

28. ***Paykel, E.S., Hallowell, C., Dressler, D.M., et al.** Treatment of suicide attempters: A descriptive study. Arch. Gen. Psychiatry 31: 487–491, **1974.**

This paper examines treatment patterns and determinants of suicide attempts seen in an emergency room. The study attempts to clarify the determinants for inpatient versus outpatient referral and the factors that are likely to increase the success of outpatient referral.

PSYCHIATRIST AND SUICIDE

29. **Kelly, W.A.** Suicide and psychiatric education. Am. J. Psychiatry 130: 463–468, **1973.**

While the topic of suicide among physicians, psychiatrists, and psychiatry residents is taken up in several good articles, this author defines the epidemiological problem and reviews a number of key articles on the emotional health of the psychiatric resident.

30.   *Kolodny, S., Binder, R.L., Bronstein, A.A., et al. The working through of patients' suicides by four therapists. Suicide Life Threat. Behav. 9: 33–46, 1979.

Describes the experiences of four trainee therapists at a single institution, each of whom experienced suicide in a patient. The frequency and importance of suicide amongst the patients of trainee psychotherapists is emphasized and an example of one approach to dealing with the postvention phase of suicide is offered.

31.   *Shein, H.M. Suicide care: Obstacles in the education of psychiatric residents. Omega 7: 75–81, 1976.

This article describes obstacles to the education of psychiatric residents and offers some practical suggestions about managing the obstacles. Dr. Shein contends that the most common and difficult obstacles in suicide care arise from misinformation and from personal/professional anxieties.

30. VIOLENCE

KENNETH TARDIFF, M.D., M.P.H.

We have focused on violence defined as assaultive behavior or physical aggression directed toward others; particularly, the focus is on the pathological aspects of physical aggression by humans of interest to the clinician, although some of the texts present research in animal aggression and discuss instrumental forms of human aggression such as organized crime, riots, and wars. The violent behaviors included in these references represent a wide variety of different types of violence including assault and homicide directed toward family members such as children, spouses, siblings, and parents as well as violence directed toward nonfamily members and also rape. Epidemiological and multiple etiological perspectives are presented, as are approaches to the evaluation and treatment of violent individuals, and the impact of violence on staff, patients, and society.

The most recent references have been selected; however, some older references have been included if they represent classic readings or especially useful clinical approaches to the evaluation and management of violent patients.

GENERAL

1. ***Graham, H.D. and Gurr, T.R.** Violence in America: Historical and Comparative Perspectives. Beverly Hills: Sage Publications, **1979.**

   This is a revision of the original report of 10 years ago of the National Commission on the Causes and Prevention of Violence. The aspects of violence in this report are beyond clinical ones and include the subjects of the history of violence in America, criminal violence, firearms control, the role of the mass media, political assassinations, terrorism, and protest groups.

2. ***Lion, J.R. and Reid, W.** Assaults within Psychiatric Facilities. New York: Grune and Stratton, **in press.**

225

An extensive collection of papers written by clinicians who manage problems with violence in a variety of treatment settings including emergency rooms and inpatient units of general hospitals, psychiatric hospitals, and state hospitals. It contains guidelines for clinical management as well as epidemiological information about violence within facilities.

3.   **Madden, D.J. and Lion, J.R.** Rage, Hate, Assault and Other Forms of Violence. New York: Halstead Press, **1976.**

A short text describing patterns of violence and intervention. It covers a wide range of violence including violence in the family, criminals, national and international data, suicide, and some nonhuman aggressive behavior.

4.   ***Monahan, J.** The Clinical Prediction of Violent Behavior. Rockville, MD: National Institute of Mental Health, **1981.**

A scholarly and clinically relevant review of the literature on the prediction of individual violent behavior.

5.   **Mulvihill, D. and Tumin, M.** Crimes of Violence: A Staff Report to the National Commission on the Causes and Prevention of Violence, Vol. 13. Washington, D.C.: U.S. Government Printing Office, **1969.**

A comprehensive collection of papers from scholars in a wide range of disciplines covering violence in terms of statistics, etiology, evaluation of individuals drug abuse, the correctional system, cross-cultural perspectives, and treatment. It has withstood the test of time in terms of providing this broad perspective.

6.   **Savitz, L.D. and Johnston, N.** Crime in Society. New York: Wiley, **1978.**

This is a basic textbook of criminology that provides a perspective of how the clinical aspects of violence fit into this discipline. It presents papers on the psychological, biological, sociological, and economic causes of crime and covers violent crimes including sex offenses, gang violence, and organized crime.

7.   **Steinmetz, S.K.** Violence prone families. Ann. N.Y. Acad. Sci. 347: 251–265, **1980.**

An excellent review of the research literature on frequency and characteristics of spouse abuse, child abuse, and sibling violence. Characteristics discussed include psychiatric disorders, income, education, occupation, length of marriage, race, sex, pregnancy, and alcohol use.

8.   ***Thorman, G.** Family Violence. Springfield, IL: Thomas, **1980.**

A text about battered children and spouses that reviews some research literature and presents social service and psychotherapeutic interventions in a clear, easily read manner.

ETIOLOGY

9. **Anderson, A.C.** Environmental factors and aggressive behavior. J. Clin. Psychiatry 43: 280–283, **1982.**

   A brief but well-referenced review of the research literature, some controversial, on the effects of the physical environment on aggressive behavior. Environmental characteristics included are lunar influences, month of birth, climate, crowding, and exposure to certain chemicals.

10. **Braucht, G.N., Loya, F., and Jamieson, K.J.** Victims of violent death: A critical review. Psychol. Bull. 87: 309–333, **1980.**

    An extensive review of the research on the victims of homicide, suicide, and accidents. Although it is primarily a critique of research models, the references are complete and include the classic studies of the epidemiology of violence.

11. **Friedrich, W.N. and Wheeler, K.K.** The abusing parent revisited: A decade of psychological research. J. Nerv. Ment. Dis. 170: 577–587, **1982.**

    This extensive review of the research in child abuse follows up a major review of the literature by Spinetta and Rigler in 1972. This paper critically analyzes whether their conclusions have been supported by research. The paper is not concerned with clinical issues in terms of intervention.

12. ***Hamburg, D.A. and Trudeau, M.B.** Biobehavioral Aspects of Aggression. New York: Liss, **1981.**

    A collection of papers on aggression with the preponderance of the best papers being those on the psychobiology of aggression including biochemical, genetic, endocrinological and, especially, pharmacological aspects of violence and aggression.

13. **Moyer, K.E. and Crabtree, M.** Bibliography of Aggressive Behavior: A Reader's Guide to the Research Literature, Vol. II. New York: Liss, **1981.**

    A listing of 3,600 references in alphabetical order by the first authors' surnames. A very wide range of topics are covered including animal studies, human clinical studies, sociological and criminological studies, and more. Although recently published, the most recent references are from the late 1970s.

14. **Parens, H.** Development of Aggression in Early Childhood. New York: Aronson, **1979.**

A text that reviews the psychoanalytic literature of the development of aggression in early childhood. It is a complex, detailed, and well-referenced review of the reformulation of psychoanalytic theories of aggression from early Freudian theory to the present time.

15. **Saul, L.J.** The Childhood Emotional Pattern and Human Hostility. New York: Van Nostrand Reinhold, **1980.**

An easy-to-read text that explores human development in regard to hostility and aggression from a psychodynamic perspective. It encompasses social, legal, political, and even physiological aspects of hostility as it relates to psychodynamics.

16. **Valzelli, L.** Psychobiology of Aggression and Violence. New York: Raven Press, **1981.**

An extensive and scholarly review of the literature on the biological basis of human and animal aggression. It begins with the origin of life, goes on to discuss the brain in regard to anatomy and physiology of aggression and ends with control of human violence not only from a biological perspective but also considering the family and society.

17. **Wolfgang, M.E. and Ferracuti, F.** The Subculture of Violence: Towards an Integrated Theory in Criminology. London: Tavistock Publications, **1967.**

A classic text on the theory synonomous with the name of the first author. It maintains that there are subcultures or systems of values and beliefs in certain populations, usually of the lower socioeconomic classes, that foster the use of violence as the major form of human interaction.

MANAGEMENT

18. **Cornfield, R.B. and Fielding, S.D.** Impact of the threatening patient on ward communications. Am. J. Psychiatry 137: 616–619, **1980.**

Based on clinical observations, the authors describe ways that the potentially violent patient provokes strained communication patterns among staff and patients on an inpatient unit. These patterns include apathy and emotional detachment, displaced affect, and mutual criticism. Staff intervention strategies are presented.

19. **Helfer, R.E.** Child Abuse and Neglect: The Diagnostic Process and Treatment Programs. Washington, D.C.: Government Printing Office, **1976.**

A very brief manual intended to provide all physicians and nurses with the necessary background for the diagnosis of child abuse or neglect and for the planning of treatment for these children and their families. It covers a spectrum of physical, psychological, and social issues.

20. **Levy, P. and Hartocollis, P.** Nursing aides and patient violence. Am. J. Psychiatry 133: 429–431, **1976.**

A report of a study that decreased the incidence of violence in a psychiatric unit organized as a therapeutic community whose nursing staff was composed entirely of women. The use of nonconfrontational approaches on this special treatment unit is discussed.

21. ***Lion, J.R.** Evaluation and Management of the Violent Patient: Guidelines in the Hospital and Institution. Springfield, IL: Thomas, **1972.**

A very useful, concise, and brief book that outlines the emergency management of the violent patient as well as the evaluation process including the anamnesis, mental status examination, and organic evaluation. He specifically describes techniques of treatment in a variety of settings.

22. **Lion, J.R. and Monroe, R.R., eds.** Special section: Drugs in the treatment of aggression. J. Nerv. Ment. Dis. 160: 75–155, **1975.**

A series of articles presenting original research and review of the literature on the effectiveness of a variety of drugs for the treatment of violence including neuroleptics, minor tranquilizers, lithium, anti-convulsants, hormones and psychostimulants.

23. **Lion, J.R. and Pasternak, S.A.** Countertransference reactions to violent patients. Am. J. Psychiatry 130: 207–210, **1973.**

A short, practical paper that presents with clinical case examples a number of reactions to violent patients that can interfere with treatment as well as the safety of staff. These include anger, denial, identification with the aggressor, prejudice, and reinforcement of violence by staff.

24. **Rada, R.T.** The violent patient: Rapid assessment and management. Psychosomatics 22: 101–105, 109, **1981.**

A practical guide to the evaluation and management of violent patients in emergency situations.

25. **Reid, W., ed.** The Treatment of Antisocial Syndromes. New York: Van Nostrand Reinhold, **1981.**

A comprehensive series of papers reviewing the literature on the treatment of antisocial syndromes, which are broadly defined and often are accompanied by violent behavior. These individuals range from the asocial child to criminal offenders. Treatment modalities range from psychotherapy to medication to community-based programs for offenders.

26. **Richmond, J.S. and Ruparel, M.K.** Management of violent patients in a psychiatry walk-in clinic. J. Clin. Psychiatry 41: 370–373, **1980.**

A description of how to manage violent outpatients using the concepts of emergency psychiatry and institutional transference. Case vignettes are excellent.

27. ***Roth, L.H.** Clinical Treatment and Management of the Violent Person. Rockville, MD.: National Institute of Mental Health, **in press.**

A useful series of papers discussing broad topics in the management of violent individuals including legal and ethical issues, evaluation of individuals, and treatment.

28. **Stuart, R.B.** Violent Behavior: Social Learning Approaches to Prediction, Management and Treatment. New York: Brunner/Mazel, **1981.**

A collection of articles predominantly with a behavioral approach to the control of violence, although medication is discussed in one chapter. It covers various types of violence including that in families, streets and residential treatment facilities as well as rape and child molestation.

OTHER RESEARCH

29. **Hatti, S., Dubin, W.R., and Weiss, K.J.** A study of circumstances surrounding patient assaults on psychiatrists. Hosp. Community Psychiatry 33: 660–661, **1982.**

Brief report of the results of a mail survey of 650 psychiatrists in the Philadelphia area. It presents the rate of assault on psychiatrists and the characteristics of patients and situations more likely to be associated with assault.

30.   **Kermani, E.J.** Violent psychiatric patients: A study. Am. J. Psycho-
      therapy 35: 215–225, **1981.**

      The results of a study of 53 violent patients in a psychiatric hospital. It
      delineates two types of patients: those with a long history of assaultive,
      suicidal and antisocial behaviors and those who were acutely assaultive
      only during the course of the psychiatric illness. The characteristics of
      each group and their management are discussed.

31.   **Madden, D.J., Lion, J.R., and Penna, M.W.** Assault on psychiatrists by
      patients. Am. J. Psychiatry 133: 422–425, **1976.**

      A report from a survey of psychiatrists regarding assaults by patients. In
      addition to reporting a 40 percent rate of psychiatrists having been
      assaulted, the authors discuss the characteristics of the patients and
      therapists involved in the assaults as well as the attitudes of the therapists
      toward assault. Case vignettes are presented.

32.   **Petrie, W.M., Lawson, E.C., and Hollender, M.H.** Violence in geriatric
      patients. JAMA 248: 443–444, **1982.**

      Describes a number of geriatric patients who committed acts dangerous
      to others as well as the nature of the acts, which often involved guns or
      knives.

33.   **Rabkin, J.G.** Criminal behavior of discharged mental patients: A critical
      appraisal of the research. Psychol. Bull. 86: 1–27, **1979.**

      A complete, objective, and detailed review of the conflicting research
      literature on whether mental patients are at greater risk of violence and
      other criminal behavior than is the general population.

34.   **Tardiff, K.** Emergency control measures for psychiatric inpatients. J.
      Nerv. Ment. Dis. 169: 614–618, **1981.**

      A survey of a large number of patients in psychiatric hospitals that
      assessed the use of emergency medication, seclusion, or restraint and
      one-to-one supervision to manage behavior dangerous to self or others.
      The discussion cites other useful references addressing the use of these
      emergency control measures.

35.   **Tardiff, K. and Maurice, W.L.** The care of violent patients by
      psychiatrists: A tale of two cities. Can. Psychiatr. Assoc. J. 22: 83–86,
      1977.

      A comparison of the results of two surveys, one in the U.S. and the other
      in Canada, of the number of psychiatrists who evaluate or treat violent
      patients. Data also includes the types of treatments preferred as well as
      sources of referral and whether they have been injured by patients.

36. ***Tardiff, K. and Sweillam, A.** Assaultive behavior among chronic
     inpatients. Am. J. Psychiatry 139: 212–215, **1982.**

     A survey of thousands of patients residing in state hospitals that assessed
     the rate and patterns of assault by patients. The characteristics of
     patients more likely to be assaultive are presented and contrasted with
     another large survey by the authors that assessed assaultive behavior just
     before admission to hospitals.

PART III
ASSESSMENT

31. PSYCHIATRIC INTERVIEWING

Harriet L. Wolfe, M.D.

The interview is the central assessment tool in psychiatry. It is the primary source of data for diagnosis and treatment planning. The nature and outcome of an assessment interview is molded by a number of factors. These include the setting in which the interview takes place, the purpose of the interview, the type of patient being interviewed, and the technical expertise of the interviewer.

While these factors are generically applicable to clinical interviewing, the psychiatric interviewer is especially alert to additional important aspects of the clinical interview: the existence of a relationship between the interviewer and the patient; the concept of historical facts as including the patient's symbolic perception of signs, symptoms, and events; the concept of clinical data as including the interviewer's emotional experience of the patient; and the necessity of integrating a wide range of theoretical frameworks in order to accomplish a thorough biopsychosocial assessment and to generate meaningful hypotheses for task completion.

The existence of a relationship between interviewer and patient has major implications for data-gathering and healing. In the context of a relationship the patient demonstrates patterns of interpersonal interaction that permit the interviewer to draw inferences about the patient's longitudinal history despite access limited to a cross-sectional view. The quality of the interaction sets the stage for a therapeutic alliance and has implications for compliance with treatment.

The patient's perceptions of himself and his difficulties constitute his view of reality. The evaluator may consult with family members, previous treators, and other relevant sources in order to attain a balanced view of what may be a highly symbolic presentation of events. Nevertheless, the patient's perceptions of his experience are the focus of treatment.

The psychiatric evaluator remains alert to feelings as a compelling aspect of medical problems and medical care. Not only are the patient's feelings acknowledged and explored but also the interviewer's. The interviewer's ability to differentiate between his objective and subjective emotional response to the patient yields data about the patient's effect on others and, at times, data about the patient's feelings of which he himself is unaware.

The references that follow address: general principles of interviewing and the influence of the setting, the type of patient, and the goals and technical expertise of the interviewer; special situations and techniques; the teaching of interviewing; and educational and process research. Citations range from classical presentations of principles to review articles that provide further bibliographies in special areas.

GENERAL PRINCIPLES

1. **Balint, M.** The Doctor, His Patient and the Illness. New York: International Universities Press, **1957** (available 2nd ed., **1963**).

    Based on seminar discussion of work by British general practitioners, this is a classic study of the doctor-patient relationship. The subtleties of a patient's "offers" to discuss psychological distress, the effect of a doctor's personal response to a patient and his illness, and the impact of the setting in which an interview occurs are discussed in rich detail.

2. ***Edelson, M.** Language and medicine. pp. 177–204. In: Applied Psycholinguistics and Mental Health. Ed.: R.W. Rieber. New York: Plenum Press, **1980.**

    The study of language and keen attention to linguistic phenomena are seen as essential activities of the physician who talks with patients and seeks to understand human behavior and competence. Rules of language, properties of utterances, the problem of signs, and the difference between fact and inference are addressed in elegant and clinically relevant fashion.

3. **Garrett, A.** Interviewing: Its Principles and Methods. New York: Family Service Association of America, **1942.** (Also available in 2nd ed., **1972**).

    A very practical and concise introduction to principles of interviewing written by an experienced, psychoanalytically-oriented social worker. Basic attitudinal and technical considerations are well described. A series of interviews drawn from fiction or casework reports and discussed by the author provide practice in thinking actively about the problems and techniques of interviewing.

4. ***Gill, M.M., Newman, R., and Redlich, F.C.** The Initial Interview in Psychiatric Practice. New York: International Universities Press, **1954.**

    This classic work focuses on evaluation for psychotherapy. It provides a good review of the early literature on first interviews, discusses the issues related to audio-recording for both interviewer and patient, and makes an argument for appraising motivation and capacity for therapy rather than past history in a first interview. Full transcripts of three different patient interviews are provided with dynamic and technical comments by the authors.

5. ***Kleinman, A., Eisenberg, L., and Good, B.** Culture, illness, and care: Clinical lessons from anthropologic and cross-cultural research. Ann. Int. Med. 88: 251–258, **1978.**

An excellent introduction to the concept of clinical reality as a cultural construction. Case material illustrates the potential for discrepant explanatory models between doctors and patients and their families. Social science concepts lead to strategies for managing doctor-patient transactions realistically.

6. ***MacKinnon, R.A. and Michels, R.** The Psychiatric Interview in Clinical Practice. Philadelphia: Saunders, **1971.**

An extremely useful introduction to general principles of interviewing and psychodynamics. Its special contribution is a focus on common clinical syndromes and their influence on the course of an interview. The book also considers clinical situations in which the setting determines the course of the interview.

7. **Platt, F.W. and McMath, J.C.** Clinical hypocompetence: The interview. Ann. Intern. Med. 91: 898–902, **1979.**

Five syndromes of defective interviewing are defined based on analysis of over 300 medical interviews: failure to alleviate emotional distress, inadequate collection of data about the patient as a person, failure to formulate and explore hypotheses, acceptance of secondary and tertiary data rather than primary data about symptoms, and tendency to control rather than facilitate the interview. Specific suggestions for correcting deficits are offered.

8. ***Stevenson, I. and Sheppe, W.M., Jr.** The psychiatric examination, pp. 1157–1180. In: AHP (2nd ed.), Vol. I., **1974.**

This introduction to the psychiatric mental status examination considers broadly the impact of biologic, psychologic, and social forces on a patient's mental state. An outline of the psychiatric exam is presented and elaborated with helpful guidelines for the assessment of nonverbal behavior, emotions, destructive potential, defensive repertoire, cognitive functions, and perceptual experiences.

9. ***Sullivan, H.S.** The Psychiatric Interview. New York: Norton, **1954.**

A classic description of the psychiatric interview as an interpersonal event in which the interviewer acts as participant-observer and the patient experiences the onset of therapy.

10.   **Whitehorn, J.C.** Guide to interviewing and clinical personality study. Arch. Neurol. Psychiatry 52: 197–216, **1944.**

This classic treatment of the interview focuses on assessment of the patient's attitudes. Common personality patterns and stages of emotional growth are described in terms of their effect on interpersonal interactions.

SPECIAL SITUATIONS AND TECHNIQUES

11.   **Adatto, C.P.** Transference phenomena in initial interviews. Int. J. Psychoanal. Psychother. 6: 3–13, **1977.**

Although written for psychoanalysts, this article is generally useful to interviewers through its review of pertinent literature and its use of case material to illustrate and discuss technical management of transference phenomena.

12.   ***Gunderson, J.G., Kolb, J.E., and Austin, V.** The diagnostic interview for borderline patients. Am. J. Psychiatry 138: 896–903, **1981.**

This semistructured diagnostic interview demonstrates the principle of combining the current state of psychiatric knowledge with interviewing skills to elicit relevant data. This important syndrome is not included in MacKinnon and Michels.

13.   **Gurland, B.J., Copeland, L., Sharpe, J., et al.** The geriatric mental status interview (GMS). Int. J. Aging Hum. Dev. 7: 303–311, **1976.**

The construction of this exam reflects technical considerations with the aging patient: fatigability, hypersensitivity to tests of intellectual function, difficulty with complex psychological questions. The entire GMS is not reproduced.

14.   ***Grumet, G.W.** Telephone therapy: A review and case report. Am. J. Orthopsychiatry 449: 574–584, **1979.**

Telephone contacts are an important aspect of clinical work and often constitute the only form of contact when an assessment must be done. The author focuses on the use of the telephone for intensive, long-term supportive psychotherapy. An extensive bibliography indicates the broad range of reported uses.

15.   ***Lazare, A.** The psychiatric examination in the walk-in clinic:

Hypothesis generation and hypothesis testing. Arch. Gen Psychiatry 33: 96–102, **1976.**

The systematic use of 16 key hypotheses drawn from psychologic, social, biologic, and behavioral models is suggested as a means of accomplishing thorough, efficient assessment.

16. **Lucas, R.W., Mullin, P.J., Luna, C.B.X., et al.** Psychiatrists and a computer as interrogators of patients with alcohol-related illnesses: A comparison. Br. J. Psychiatry 131: 160–167, **1977.**

A study supporting the prevalent notion that substance abusers report more accurately in interview situations that are structured, directive, and/or minimize interpersonal contact. Extent of alcohol consumption reported to the computer was higher than that reported to doctors. Assessment of attitudes showed 50 percent of patients preferred medical interviews with a computer to those with a doctor.

17. **Perry, J.C. and Jacobs, D.** Overview: Clinical applications of the amytal interview in psychiatric emergency settings. Am. J. Psychiatry 139: 552–559, **1982.**

The use of sodium amytal to aid clinical assessment of mute and stuporous patients is discussed in terms of its diagnostic and therapeutic applications. A protocol for administration of the drug is provided.

18. **Price, J.** Foreign language interpreting in psychiatric practice. Aust. N.Z. J. Psychiatry 9: 263–267, **1975.**

Special problems of using a translator are described. Errors in interpreting from psychiatrist to patient and vice versa are defined. An interpreter's tendency to omit material from psychotic patients appears to delay rather than obstruct accurate diagnosis.

19. **Schwartz, D.A., Waldron, R. and Tidd, C.W.** Use of home visits for psychiatric evaluation, clinical and teaching aspects. Arch. Gen. Psychiatry 3: 57–65, **1960.**

The teaching value of home assessments as described by the authors remains relevant to modern psychiatry. The effect of decreased anxiety in patients on their report of symptoms and the effect of a visual experience of a patient's social and physical environment on trainees are described.

20. ***Shwed, H.** Teaching emergency room psychiatry. Hosp. Community Psychiatry 31: 558–562, **1980.**

The author proposes that special interviewing and management skills are required in the emergency room: a crisp interviewing style and facility with the mental status exam, sharp observational skills, an ability to consult broadly and effectively with outside sources, up-to-date medical knowledge, and disposition skills. Assessment of the violent patient, the drifter, and the drug addict are addressed.

21.   **Sletten, I.W. and Barton, J.L.** Suicidal patients in the emergency room: A guide for evaluation and disposition. Hosp. Community Psychiatry 30: 407–411, **1979.**

In addition to reviewing pertinent rating scales of risk factors, the authors describe the clinical approach to the potentially suicidal patient. The use of indirect questioning and the attitude of the interviewer are emphasized.

INTERVIEW TEACHING

22.   **Gibbon, M., McDonald-Scott, P., and Endicott, J.** Mastering the art of research interviewing: A model training procedure for diagnostic evaluation. Arch. Gen. Psychiatry 38: 1259–1262, **1981.**

A model for training interviewers in standard assessment procedures that require clinical judgment is presented. Its four phases (case vignettes, videotapes, live interviews, continued monitoring of raters) represent key methods of teaching and reinforcing interviewing skills.

23.   ***Jason, H., Kagan, N., Werner, A., et al.** New approaches to teaching basic interviewing skills to medical students. Am. J. Psychiatry 127: 1404–1407, **1971.**

Multimedia methods of teaching interviewing are now commonly used. This report provides important details about training simulators and faculty instructors and about a special videotape and observation setting that facilitates the making and review of taped practice interviews.

24.   ***Leon, R.L.** Psychiatric Interviewing: A Primer. New York: Elsevier North Holland, **1982.**

This text is intended for medical students and is a useful tool for clinical teachers. It surpasses the goal of being an elementary how-to-do-it book through skillful use of clinical material to illustrate the potency and subtleties of the doctor-patient relationship as well as special problems like "the patient who won't talk" and "crying," and common pitfalls like "asking more than one question."

25.   **Junek, W., Burra, P., and Leichner, P.** Teaching interviewing skills by encountering patients. J. Med. Educ. 54: 402–407, **1979.**

A course is described in which first-year psychiatric residents improved in areas called empathy, congruence, and level of regard through intensive attention to interview process. Relatively simple methods of evaluation were used: self-report and expert ratings of videotaped interviews before and after the course.

26.   ***Reiser, D.E. and Schroder, A.K.** Patient Interviewing: The Human Dimension. Baltimore: Williams and Wilkins, **1980.**

Although written for medical students, the text seems better suited for medical educators. Its use of autobiographical and fictional descriptions of student-patient interactions is inspired and sophisticated. Principles of interviewing like listening on several levels simultaneously are presented in innovative terms.

27.   ***Stein, S.P., Karasu, T.B., Charles, E.S., et al.** Supervision of the initial interview: A study of two methods. Arch Gen. Psychiatry 32: 265–268, **1975.**

This study suggests that a supervisor's assessment of a patient's psychopathology, prognosis, and level of insight and motivation are negatively skewed when he/she does not observe the patient. Dynamic aspects of the supervisory relationship and contradictory views regarding the direction of bias are discussed.

EDUCATION AND PROCESS RESEARCH

28.   ***Carroll, J.G. and Monroe, J.** Teaching clinical interviewing in the health professions: A review of empirical research. Evaluation Health Professions 3: 21–45, **1980.**

This review summarizes the major difficulties present in the research on interview teaching including the lack of equivalent control groups. The 36 studies reviewed acquaint one with the broad spectrum of attempts to combine methods of presentation, practice, and feedback.

29.   **Nurcombe, B. and Fitzhenry-Coor, I.** How do psychiatrists think? Clinical reasoning in the psychiatric interview: A research and education project. Aust. N.Z. J. Psychiatry 16: 13–24, **1982.**

Teachers of interviewing will appreciate this paper's review of research into medical reasoning and description of a current project at the University of Vermont that uses narrative case problems, videotaped case problems, and stimulated recall to explore the process of psychiatric decision making.

30. ***Rutter, M. and Cox, A.** Psychiatric interviewing techniques: I. Methods and measures. Br. J. Psychiatry 138: 273–282, **1981.**

This paper reports the first segment of a rigorous three-stage project designed to develop measures of interview performance, to assess effects of different interviewing styles and to determine the techniques most effective in achieving specific goals.

31. **Rutter, M., Cox, A., Egert, S., et al.** Psychiatric interviewing techniques: IV. Experimental study: Four contrasting styles. Br. J. Psychiatry 138: 456–465, **1981.**

A study that tests the hypothesis that certain clusters of techniques cause different responses. The description of styles (sounding board, active psychotherapy, structured and systematic exploratory), of experimental design, of interviewer training, and of data analysis provides rich food for thought.

32. **Samph, T. and Templeton, B.** The interpersonal skills project, pp. 331–516. In: Strategies for the Evaluation of Competence of Physicians Who Assume Responsibilities for Patient Care in Graduate Medical Education. Washington, D.C.: Health Resources Administration Contract Report, Contract no. HRA-231-76-067, 7/1/76–12/31/79.

Experts at the National Board of Medical Examiners report their development and testing of measures of interviewing competence. The investigators conclude that each methodology assess a different aspect of the multidimensional skill of interviewing.

33. **Sandifer, M.G., Jr., Hordern, A., and Green, L.M.** The psychiatric interview: The impact of the first three minutes. Am. J. Psychiatry 126: 968–973, **1970.**

This study of a group of experienced psychiatrists demonstrates their tendency to arrive at a diagnostic impression quite early in an interview. It raises the question of what and how much interview information is actually used in making a diagnosis.

34. **Siegman, A.W.** Review of interview research, pp. 481–530. In: The Behavioral and Social Sciences and The Practice of Medicine, The Psychiatric Foundations, Vol. 2. Eds.: G.U. Balis, L. Wurmser, E. McDaniel, et al. Boston: Butterworth, **1978.**

The author describes studies of message and relationship ambiguity, the meaning of status in the interview situation, the effect of nonverbal cues, the role of task variables, and the effect of contingent versus noncontingent reinforcements. Controlled conditions clearly provide rigor, but the jump from laboratory investigation to clinical experience is difficult.

32. PSYCHOLOGICAL TESTS

ARTHUR C. CARR, PH.D.

Psychological tests can make a significant contribution to the understanding of a psychiatric patient and clarify issues related to the patient's classification, psychodynamics, management, and prognosis through providing an objective means for comparing a controlled sample of the patient's behavior with available normative data representative of a larger reference group.

Proper administration and interpretation of most psychological tests require extensive training and experience, with the most valid evaluation of the patient's functioning requiring the use of a battery of carefully chosen tests. Although such evaluations usually are done by experienced psychologists, psychiatrists and all psychotherapists should have familiarity with tests if they are to make proper referrals of their patients for testing and if they are to integrate test evaluations with other clinical data. Knowledge about available tests is also useful in planning research, an increasingly common responsibility and experience of all mental health workers.

In this presentation, two general categories of psychological tests are highlighted: the projective and the nonprojective.

Projective tests are so classified on the basis of their presenting stimuli, whose meaning is not immediately obvious—that is, where some degree of ambiguity forces the subject to project his own mental organization into or onto an amorphous, somewhat unstructured situation. Since usually they involve tasks that offer no necessarily right or wrong answer, they might better be referred to as projective *techniques* (or *methods*) than as *tests,* although the latter designation persists. Typical projective tests included in the test battery are the Rorschach test (the most widely used projective technique in clinical practice), the Thematic Apperception Test (TAT), a sentence completion test (SCT), and various graphomotor techniques (often the Draw-a-Person and the Bender-Gestalt tests).

Nonprojective tests are typically based on items and questions having obvious meaning and limited response categories that offer the advantage of yielding numerical scores and profiles easily subject to mathematical or statistical analysis. Interpretation of these tests usually requires less training and experience on the part of the examiner than are required with projective techniques, since the level of inference is usually less. Typical nonprojective tests include the intelligence tests as well as such personality tests as the frequently used Minnesota Multiphasic Personality Inventory (MMPI), or the Catell Sixteen Personality Factor Questionnaire.

Comprehensive evaluations of a patient's functioning usually necessitates tests (techniques) that are both projective and nonprojective, providing information on how the patient functions in both unstructured and structured situations. The suggested readings that follow are organized so as to reflect both their content and their length. *General References* pertain to the nature of the psychological testing in general and offer briefer presentations on various single tests or techniques.

Fuller background on and rules for administering and interpreting each test will be found in relevant references listed under the test's name.

PSYCHOLOGICAL TESTS—GENERAL

1.   *Anderson, H.H. and Anderson, G.L.,** eds. Introduction to Projective Techniques. New York: Prentice-Hall, **1951.**

Although not a recent contribution, this reference provides excellent chapters on the widest range of projective techniques, even such exotic approaches as finger painting, graphology, and the Szondi test. An extra bonus is provided by chapters on the two major intelligence tests, illustrating their use for personality appraisal, thus narrowing the distinction between projective and nonprojective or objective tests.

2.   **Appelbaum, S.A.** The Anatomy of Change: A Menninger Foundation Report on Testing the Effects of Psychotherapy. New York: Plenum, **1977.**

This volume illustrates the use of the test battery for evaluating change in patients who were part of a 20-year study of the effects of psychoanalytic psychotherapy conducted at the Menninger Foundation in Topeka. While the results of the overall study are deemed meager by most professionals (healthy patients appear to profit most—"the rich get richer"), the report demonstrates that test results may be more valid than ratings based on nontest clinical information.

3.   **Buros, O.K.** The Mental Measurements Yearbooks. Highland Park, NJ: Gryphon, **1938–1978.**

The 8th edition (1978) of this invaluable series continues its high tradition in offering the best source of information about any test published in English. For each test, it generally provides factual information, a comprehensive bibliography, and original test reviews written by measurement specialists who often are more critical of a given test than are the clinicians who find it valuable.

4.   ***Carr, A.C.** Psychological testing of personality. pp. 940–966. CT III, Vol. 1, **1980.**

This chapter was designed specifically for psychiatrists preparing for their board examinations and offers a succinct review of the major psychological tests with emphasis on their integration in the test battery. An earlier version in the 2nd edition of the *Textbook* (1975) covered both intelligence and personality testing, while this later version relates only to personality tests but offers expanded clinical examples, particularly around the "borderline" patient.

5.   ***Holt, R.R.** Methods in Clinical Psychology, Vols. I and II. New York: Plenum, **1978.**

Two volumes dealing with (1) projective assessment, and (2) prediction and research, together deal with issues related to personality assessment, particularly through the use of the TAT and the Rorschach test. Especially valuable for the clinician are the normative guide for the use of the TAT cards and the system of gauging primary and secondary processes in Rorschach responses.

6.   **Rabin, A.I.,** ed. Assessment with Projective Techniques: A Concise Introduction, 2nd ed. New York: Springer, **1981.**

As indicated in its full title, this book presents an introduction to the major projective techniques, although also including material on WAIS interpretation. With a chapter illustrating case study integration, the volume is a useful, concise survey for newcomers to the area of assessment.

7.   ***Rapaport, D., Gill, M.M., and Schafer, R.** Diagnostic Psychological Testing, rev. ed. Ed.: R.R. Holt. New York: International Universities Press, **1968.**

In a single volume, this is a summary and updating of a classic two-volume edition originally presented in 1945–46 and now out of print. Acknowledging the limitations of the earlier work (and the seemingly naive assumptions underlying such decisions as to use the Kansas Highway Patrol for a control group), Holt has sifted grain from chaff in what now constitutes a classic in its own right and perpetuates the Menninger Clinic (and David Rapaport) tradition in the use of psychological tests.

8.   ***Schafer, R.** The Clinical Application of Psychological Tests. New York: International Universities Press, **1948.**

This presentation offers a series of diagnostic case summaries illustrating utilization of tests that comprise the usual test battery. While not dealing with the distinctions that now perplex us (manic-depression vs. schizophrenia; organic vs. functional), it is a brilliant exposition of the distinctions that were thought to be represented at the Menninger Clinic at that time and is particularly helpful in the area of the neurotic disorders that some professionals today might claim are hard to find.

PSYCHOLOGICAL TESTING—INTELLIGENCE TESTS

9.   **Kaufman, A.S.** Intelligent Testing with the WISC-R. New York: Wiley, **1979.**

Kaufman brings special understanding to the Wechsler Intelligence Scales for Children, having played a significant role in its present revision. The text illuminates the observations that can be made on the bases of the test profile, quite apart from the determination of an intelligence quotient (IQ) and justifies its title—not a misprint.

10.   ***Matarazzo, J.D.** Wechsler's Measurement and Appraisal of Adult Intelligence (5th and enlarged ed.). Baltimore: Williams and Wilkens, **1972.**

Matarazzo presents an excellent discussion of the concept of intelligence as well as of the Wechsler Adult Intelligence Scale (WAIS), the most widely used individual intelligence test in clinical practice. While there may be nothing sacred about the IQ as a number, Matarazzo reviews the evidence to show that it correlates well with variables considered important in our culture: academic success, occupational attainment, socioeconomic status, etc.

11.   **Raven, J.C.** Guide to the Standard Progressive Matrices. London: H.K. Lewis, **1960.** (Distributed in the U.S. by The Psychological Corp., New York City.)

This guide and its accompanying updated manuals cover the Raven Progressive Matrices, a nonverbal test series used widely in Great Britain to assess mental ability by means of problems related to abstract figures. Although there is probably no such thing as a totally culture-free test, these tasks comprise a relatively culture-free test yielding percentile scores that correlate well with other measures of general intelligence.

12. **Terman, L.M. and Merrill, M.A.** Stanford-Binet Intelligence Scale: Manual for the Third Revision, Form L-M. Boston: Houghton-Mifflin, **1972.**

This volume presents a description (with revised 1972 norms) of the individual intelligence test derived from the Binet-Simon scales developed shortly after the turn of the century. While applicable for adult use, the test is nevertheless used primarily with children, where its reliance on graded, age-related tasks makes it particularly useful.

13. **Wechsler, D.** Wechsler Intelligence Scale for Children–Revised. New York: Psychological Corporation, **1974.**

Like the adult form of the Wechsler test (WAIS-R), the WISC-R provides deviation IQs rather than relying on the concept of mental age. With similarities extending also to the inclusion of both verbal and performance subtests, Wechsler's tests cover all age levels although many clinicians prefer the Stanford-Binet scales for children because of their reliance on age-graded tasks.

PSYCHOLOGICAL TESTS—RORSCHACH TEST

14. **Ames, L.B., Metraux, R.W., Rodell, J.L., et al.** Rorschach Responses in Old Age (2nd ed.). New York: Brunner/Mazel, **1973.**

The senior author of this volume has been responsible for a series of publications dealing with the Rorschach test and specific developmental levels (children, adolescents, old age). Typical of such emphasis, this book covers a period we all must confront increasingly, either in our clinical activities or our mirrors.

15. **Beck, S.J.** Rorschach's Test, Vols. 1, 2, and 3. New York: Grune and Stratton, **1944–1952.**

These volumes are the work of one of the earliest Rorschach teachers and leaders in America, who always strove to make Rorschach interpretation a science rather than a process relying on qualitative and subjective judgment. Since Beck was reluctant to accept any Rorschach change, his approach fails to include worthwhile developments, although his own contribution to what is now called the "Comprehensive System" (see Exner) is substantial.

16. ***Exner, J.** The Rorschach: A Comprehensive System. Vols. I–III. New York: Wiley, **1974–1982.**

The "comprehensive" system derives from an attempt to integrate the best from all the various systems of administration and scoring that have accumulated since Rorschach's original publication, in an attempt to arrive at consistency in approach throughout the field. The volumes offer a significant contribution, constituting a full course on the test and representing an ideal introductory and advanced course for those not already committed to some earlier idealized Rorschach "authority."

17.   **Klopfer, B., et al.** Developments in the Rorschach Technique, Vols. 1–3. New York: World Book Co., **1954–1970.**

In the early history of the test, the training seminars given by Bruno Klopfer and the seminal volume *The Rorschach Technique* (Klopfer & Kelly) did much to popularize the Rorschach in this country. These later contributions continue the influence of Klopfer, a Jungian who relied on intuition and clinical judgment in his approach while also making a major contribution to objectification of Rorschach interpretation.

18.   **Kwawer, J.S., Lerner, H.D., Lerner, P.M., et al.,** eds. Borderline Phenomena and the Rorschach Test. New York: International Universities Press, **1980.**

Presumably the first book dedicated solely to the relatively new concept of borderline disorders and the Rorschach test, this volume unites a series of papers that illuminate aspects of borderline disorders quite apart from how they may be reflected in the Rorschach test itself. Views of the latter should best be accepted as interesting hypotheses yet to be validated.

19.   **Piotrowski, Z.A.** Perceptanalysis: A Fundamentally Reworked, Expanded, and Systemized Rorschach Method. New York: Macmillan, **1957.**

One of the basic references on the Rorschach, this volume presents the approach through percept analysis of an outstanding clinician and Rorschach enthusiast. Presenting unique contributions to Rorschachiana, it should perhaps nevertheless be complemented by other references, if it were to be used as a course textbook.

20.   **Rorschach, H.** Psychodiagnostics: A Diagnostic Test Based on Perception (2nd ed.). New York: Grune and Stratton, **1942.** (available in 8th ed., **1978.**)

This translation of Herman Rorschach's classic monograph (1921) on his inkblot experiments testifies to the genius whose untimely death at the age of 37 was a great loss to his field (psychiatry) and to all the social sciences. Although not the first person to experiment with ambiguous forms as a way of stimulating the imagination. Rorschach presents herein a formal method for relating response characteristics to personality factors that constitutes the basis for all scoring systems presently used with his test.

21. ***Schafer, R.** Psychoanalytic Interpretation in Rorschach Testing. New York: Grune and Stratton, **1954.**

This volume is an excellent review of the psychoanalytically conceived defenses (repression, denial, etc.), from the standpoint of both their clinical and their Rorschach test manifestations. When initially presented, it represented a giant step (and a giant's step), for all psychologists who aspired to be more "psychoanalytical" in their interpretations.

PSYCHOLOGICAL TESTS—MINNESOTA MULTIPHASIC PERSONALITY INVENTORY (MMPI)

22. **Dahlstrom, W.G., Welsh, G.S., and Dahlstrom, L.E.** An MMPI Handbook, Vol. 1. Clinical Interpretation (rev. ed.). Minneapolis: University of Minnesota Press, **1972.**

This and its companion volume, *Research Applications,* present what probably constitute the major references on the MMPI (Minnesota Multiphasic Personality Inventory), the prototype of an "objective" personality test. Based empirically on what various diagnostic groups actually reported about themselves in terms of 550 true-false questions, the test has become a major research and clinical tool.

23. **Lachar, D.** The MMPI: Clinical Assessment and Automated Interpretation. Los Angeles: Western Psychological Services, **1974.**

This paperback provides a useful supplement to other interpretative guides for the MMPI. The "cookbook" (i.e., automated) interpretations to 2- and 3-point common code types nevertheless do not eliminate the necessity for the best guide of all: sound clinical judgment.

24. **Marks, P.A., Seeman, W., and Haller, D.L.** The Actuarial Use of the MMPI with Adolescents and Adults. New York: Oxford University Press, **1974.**

An ideal companion and addition to the Dahlstrom, Welsh, and Dahlstrom volumes, this book includes newly developed code types and descriptors for adolescent subjects. The discussion of actuarial versus clinical procedures is excellent, with relevance to the general issue of predicting behavior by whatever technique.

PSYCHOLOGICAL TESTS—THEMATIC
APPERCEPTION TEST (TAT)

25.   **Bellak, L.** The Thematic Apperception Test. The Children's Apperception Test and The Senior Apperception Test in Clinical Use (2nd ed.). New York: Grune and Stratton, **1971.** (Also available in 3rd ed., **1975.**)

This revision of an original seminal contribution offers a system of interpretation applicable to all thematic material, with particular emphasis on the TAT and CAT. Illustrative protocols include TAT stories of two Nazi war criminals and short stories by Somerset Maugham.

26.   *****Murray, H.A.** Explorations in Personality. New York: Oxford University Press, **1938.**

This classic reports a monumental study conducted at the Harvard Psychological Clinic in the 1930s. Its seminal features include (1) presentation of the then newly created TAT, a test designed "to stimulate literary creativity and thereby evoke fantasies that reveal covert and unconscious complexes"; (2) Murray's need-press theory of personality; (3) a single case presentation ("The Case of Earnest") illustrating numerous approaches to the study of personality.

27.   *****Shneidman, E.S., Joel, W., and Little, K.B.,** eds. Thematic Test Analysis. New York: Grune and Stratton, **1951.**

Several (15) experts' interpretation of a patient's picture-thematic data are presented for both the Thematic Apperception Test (TAT) and the Make-a-Picture Story Test (MAPS). Combined with one expert's interpretation of the patient's Rorschach, Wechsler, MMPI, Draw-a-Person, and Bender-Gestalt tests, the volume constitutes a rich source book illustrating how clinical experts approach the influential process of interpretation.

PSYCHOLOGICAL TESTS—SENTENCE COMPLETION TEST (SCT)

28.   **Forer, B.R.** The Forer Structured Sentence Completion Test Manual. Beverly Hills: Western Psychological Services, **1957.**

Seemingly a contradiction in terms, this "structured" sentence completion test is systematically organized to tap attitudes to specific interpersonal figures: mother, father, females, males, people, and authority figures. Specified sentence stems also tap predominant wishes, causes of one's major affects, and reactions to motivations of others.

29.   **Goldberg, P.A.** A review of sentence completion methods in personality assessment. J. Proj. Tech. Pers. Assess. 29: 12–45, **1965.**

This summary review acquaints the reader with the nature of the sentence completion method and introduces him to various published forms of the test. Since the method can be adapted easily to suit the examiner's purpose, it is worthy of consideration as an approach for assaying relatively conscious, overt attitudes, feelings, and interests.

PSYCHOLOGICAL TESTS—GRAPHOMOTOR TECHNIQUES

30.   ***Bender, L.** A Visual Motor Gestalt Test and its Clinical Use. New York: American Orthopsychiatric Assoc., **1938.**

This is the original monograph on what has become known as the Bender-Gestalt test. Conceived as a test of maturation by its developer (a psychiatrist) and based on nine of Wertheimer's patterns, the test has many clinical uses, including detection of organicity and use as a projective technique.

31.   **Goodenough, F.L.** Measurement of Intelligence by Drawings. New York: World Book Company, **1926.** (Also available in reprint edition, Darby, PA: Darby Books, **1981.**)

Presently used as an assessment method that is assumed to elicit projections of significant personality attributes, the Draw-a-Person test was originally used as a means for measuring the intelligence of children. This source reference continues to have its value, particularly for those who work with children and who seek an approach to children's non-verbal expressive capacities.

32.   **Hutt, M.L. and Briskin, G.J.** The Clinical Use of the Revised Bender-Gestalt Test. New York: Grune and Stratton, **1960.** (Also available in 3rd ed., **1977.**)

On the basis of extensive clinical experience with the Bender-Gestalt test during the Second World War, Hutt developed the procedures for using the test as a projective technique, far extending the purpose of the test from what Bender conceived it to be: a test of maturation. This manual presents the rules and principles of interpretation with a variety of case illustrations.

33.   **Machover, K.** Personality Projection in the Drawing of the Human Figure. Springfield, IL: Thomas, **1949.**

This brief book represents the work of a pioneer on the use of human figure drawings for diagnosis and therapy. While few clinicians today would depend solely upon drawings for these purposes, the volume illustrates the work of a master who has the reputation for being able to make valid predictions on the basis of what appear to be insignificant aspects of a drawing.

33. THE CLINICAL NEUROPSYCHOLOGICAL EXAMINATION: METHODS AND CONCEPTS

Robert A. Novelly, Ph.D.

Systematic appraisal of patients with disorders of higher cortical function has led to the development of an array of standardized neuropsychological tests for many behavioral functions. Concomitantly, the concept of brain damage as a unitary state differing only in severity and embodied in the older term "organicity" has been replaced by the demonstration that lesions, occurring in different areas of brain tissue at different stages of development produce discreet alterations in specific areas of praxis, perception in the three major modalities, memory, language, intelligence and personality. The older antithesis between models of cerebral organization of mass action versus localization is being replaced by dynamic models of cortical function based on information processing theory, systems and hierarchically arranged cerebral strategies that guide behaviors with varying degrees of efficiency towards substitutable goals. Quantification of function, while still present, is simply an intermediate and organizing process, and specific values may take on quite different interpretations in the context of interpreting the pathological process in a given individual.

The bibliography covers the application of particular neuropsychological test instruments and both classical and contemporary views on the pathological manifestations of specific areas of higher cortical function. The emphasis is on clinical relevance and clinical application.

CONCEPTUAL MODELS OF DISORDERED BEHAVIOR FOLLOWING BRAIN INJURY

1. *Filskov, S.B., Grimm, B.H., and Lewis, J.A. Brain-behavior relationships, pp. 39–73. In: Handbook of Clinical Neuropsychology. Eds.: S.B. Filskov and T.J. Boll. New York: Wiley, 1981.

This chapter is an excellent current overview of the primary theoretical, clinical, and methodological issues and findings of clinical neuropsychology. Specific behavioral test instruments, their relationship to physical diagnostic findings, and the differentiation in psychiatric disorders is discussed.

2. *Gardner, H.* The Shattered Mind: The Person After Brain Damage. New York: Knopf, **1975.**

   In this highly readable and informative narrative, the author reviews some of the classical models of higher cortical dysfunction following brain injury and integrates this with specific patient examples. The author teaches neuroanatomy and diagnostic neuropsychology while never losing sight of his relationship to the patient.

3. **Luria, A.R.** The Working Brain: An Introduction to Neuropsychology. New York: Basic Books, **1973.**

   Of Luria's several texts that have been translated from Russian to English, this is by far the most readable. His highly dynamic, insightful, and creative approach to the examination of the patient and the diagnosis of higher cortical deficit at the bedside of the patient is presented.

4. ***Newcombe, F. and Ratcliff, G.** Long-term psychological consequences of cerebral lesions, pp. 495–542. In: Handbook of Behavioral Neurobiology: Neuropsychology, Vol. 2. Ed.: M.S. Gazzaniga. New York: Plenum, **1979.**

   These excellent British authors review a wide vareity of specific behavioral deficits that occur in both focal and diffuse brain injury. Importantly, they integrate the findings of numerous studies in the literature with current models of cerebral organization.

5. **Reitan, R.M.** Assessment of brain-behavior relationships, pp. 186–242. In: Advances in Psychological Assessment, Vol. 3. Ed.: P. McReynolds. San Francisco: Jossey-Bass, **1974.**

   The influential Ralph Reitan summarizes the history of prior attempts to appraise and quantify higher cortical dysfunction and illustrates his approach to the clinical neuropsychological examination.

6. ***Smith, A.** Principles underlying human brain functions in neuropsychological sequelae of different neuropathological processes, pp. 175–226. In: Handbook of Clinical Neuropsychology. Eds.: S.B. Filskov and T.J. Boll. New York: Wiley, **1981.**

   This is a current treatise on brain-behavior relationships by a distinguished neuropsychiatrist that already has the status of a contemporary classic.

7. **Teuber, H.L.** Some alterations in behavior after cerebral lesions in man, pp. 157–194. In: Evolution of Nervous Control from Primitive Organisms to Man. Ed.: A.D. Bass. Washington, D.C.: American Association for the Advancement of Science, **1959.**

The author critically reviews his monumental study of the behavioral manifestations of focal brain injury. Many of the ideas presage current theories and models.

MENTAL STATUS EXAMINATION

8. **Delaney, R.C.** Screening for organicity: The problem of subtle neuropsychological deficit and diagnosis. J. Clin. Psychol. 38: 843–846, **1982.**

With specific reference to the disorder of complex-partial epilepsy, the author discusses a new adaptation of the Bender-Gestalt test and results of its use in this population. The broader issue of what constitutes an appropriate screening method for brain disorders is discussed.

9. **Hayman, M.** Two minute clinical test for measurement of intellectual impairment in psychiatric disorders. Arch. Neurol. Psychiatry 47: 454–464, **1942.**

This is the classic article that developed the use of the serial sevens substraction test as part of the mental status examination. The thorough and perceptive clinical analysis by the author is an example of the early tradition of astute clinical observation and careful analysis of the findings.

10. **Reisberg, B., Ferris, S.H., DeLeon, M.J., et al.** The global deterioration scale for assessment of primary degenerative dementia. Am. J. Psychiatry 139: 1136–1139, **1982.**

The authors present a systematic and highly useful series of indices for staging the degree of cognitive impairment associated with a progressive dementia. The characteristic features of each of the progressive stages is presented and discussed.

11. ***Strub, R.L. and Black, F.W.** The Mental Status Examination in Neurology. Philadelphia: Davis, **1977.**

A highly readable and practical book on conducting a systematic mental status examination.

12. ***Taylor, M.A., Abrams, R., Faber, R., et al.** Cognitive tasks in the mental status examination. J. Nerv. Ment. Dis. 168: 167–170, **1980.**

The authors provide a variety of measures of higher cortical function and their reliability in assessing a series of psychiatric inpatients. A variety of useful examination maneuvers easily employed by the clinician are presented.

STANDARDIZED NEUROPSYCHOLOGICAL TEST INSTRUMENTS

13. **Anastasi, A.** Psychological Testing (5th ed.). New York: Macmillan, **1982.**

The author is considered the dean of American psychological testing theory. The book discusses a number of neuropsychiatry instruments with regard to their construction, standardization, validity, and reliability, as well as other measures not applicable to neuropsychology.

14. **Benton, A.L.** Psychological testing. In: Clinical Neurology, Vol. 1, Chap. 6, pp. 1–18. Eds: A.B. Baker and L.H. Baker. New York: Harper and Row, **1976.**

The author, a major contributor to the field of clinical neuropsychology, surveys a range of neuropsychological diagnostic instruments and their relative validity in various types of brain lesions. The functional deficits associated with certain brain lesions are discussed in the context of the test instruments.

15. **Boll, T.J.** The Halstead-Reitan neuropsychological battery, pp. 577–607. In: Handbook of Clinical Neuropsychology. Eds.: S.B. Filskov and T.J. Boll. New York: Wiley, **1981.**

The standardized Halstead-Reitan battery of neuropsychological test instruments is presented and explained in this very readable text. The author discusses the basis, administration, scoring, and interpretation of these well-known test procedures.

16. **Lezak, M.D.** Neuropsychological Assessment. New York: Oxford University Press, **1976.**

This is the single best compendium of neuropsychological test instruments available. It deals primarily with instrumentation rather than conceptual issues or interpretation. A highly valuable resource.

17. **Smith, A.** Neuropsychological testing in neurological disorders. Adv. Neurol. 7: 49–110, **1975.**

The author reviews a variety of neuropsychological test instruments and their composition to form a particular battery. Specific results in varying types of lesion processes are presented and discussed.

INTELLIGENCE AND IQ

18. ***Bornstein, R.A. and Matarazzo, J.D.** Wechsler VIQ versus PIQ differences in cerebral dysfunction: A literature review with emphasis on sex differences. J. Clin. Neuropsychol. 4: 319–334, **1982.**

    The authors review the published literature with regard to the verbal and performance IQ indices in lateralized brain lesions. Importantly, they find an important sex difference in the degree to which the disparity in verbal and performance IQ is manifest in the presence of a lateralized lesion.

19. ***Filskov, S.B. and Leli, D.A.** Assessment of the individual in neuro-psychological practice, pp. 545–576. In: Handbook of Clinical Neuro-psychology. Eds.: S.B. Filskov and T.J. Boll. New York: Wiley, **1981.**

    The meaning of the IQ index and its role in the appraisal of functional capacity in the patient with a brain lesion is presented, as well as other neuropsychological test instruments.

20. **Matarazzo, J.D.** Wechsler's Measurement and Appraisal of Adult Intelligence (5th ed.). Baltimore: Williams and Wilkins, **1972.**

    This important text reviews the current research findings on the Wechsler Adult Intelligence Scale. Numerous areas are discussed including a separated chapter on brain-behavior relationships and the IQ index.

21. **Zangwill, O.L.** Intellectual status in aphasia, pp. 105–111. In: Handbook of Clinical Neurology: Disorders of Speech, Perception and Symbolic Behavior, Vol. 4. Eds.: P.J. Vinken and G.W. Bruyn. New York: Wiley, **1969.**

    The very important relationship between intellectual ability and aphasia is discussed with a review of the relevant literature and specific case findings.

DISORDERS OF MEMORY

22. ***Hecaen, H. and Albert, M.L.** Disorders of memory. pp. 331–353. In: Human Neuropsychology. Eds.: H. Hecaen and M.L. Albert. New York: Wiley, **1978.**

This is a thorough and up-to-date discussion of the numerous clinical syndromes associated with memory disorder. Specific and general disorders are discussed and their relationship to current models of memory processes is presented.

23. *Milner, B. Psychological defects produced by temporal lobe excision. Res. Publ. Assoc. Res. Nerv. Ment. Dis. 36: 244–257, 1958.

This article is one of Milner's early reports on systematic evaluation of patients with right or left temporal lobectomy for control of epileptic seizures. The specific types of memory deficits unique to excision of either the left or right temporal lobe are presented and discussed.

24. Russell, W.R. and Nathan, P.W. Traumatic amnesia. Brain 69: 280–300, 1946.

In this classic article the relationship between posttraumatic amnesia and numerous variables attendant on traumatic head injury are presented and discussed. Particular attention is paid to the different aspects of memory that recover at differential rates.

25. Talland, G.A. and Waugh, N.C. The Pathology of Memory. New York: Academic Press, 1969.

This is an extremely valuable book covering an extensive range of clinically relevant issues in the area of memory disorders. These include memory disorders related to senility, epilepsy, focal lesions, post-ECT, and head trauma.

LANGUAGE DISORDERS

26. *Albert, M.L., Goodglass, H., Helm, N.A., et al. Clinical Aspects of Dysphasia. New York: Springer Verlag, 1981.

For the clinician searching for a systematic presentation of the language examination for the bedside examination of the patients, this small book is particularly useful. Each of the major aphasia syndromes together with a variety of direct and practical clinical tests are presented.

27. *Geschwind, N. Language and the brain. Sci. Am. 226(4): 76–83, 1972.

The author is well known for his development of disconnection models of aphasia. In this well-written article, the basic tenets of a variety of aphasic syndromes and their nueroanatomical disconnections are elucidated.

28. **Searleman, A.** A review of right hemisphere linguistic capabilities. Psychol. Bull. 84: 503–528, **1977.**

The author critically appraises that the right hemisphere also possesses linguistic skills.

29. **Smith, A.** Lenneberg Locke, Zangwill, and the neuropsychology of language and language disorders. In: Psychology and Biology of Language and Thought: Essays in Honor of Eric H. Lenneberg. Eds.: G.A. Miller and E. Lenneberg. New York: Academic Press, **1978.**

This is a highly thoughtful comparison of the contributions of several major theorists to the understanding of language disorders by an author who has extensively studied language acquisition in individuals undergoing early left hemispherectomy.

PSYCHIATRY AND NEUROPSYCHOLOGY INTERFACES

30. ***Benson, D.F. and Blumer, D.** Psychiatric Aspects of Neurologic Disease. New York: Grune and Stratton, **1975.** (Vol. 2, **1982.**)

This is a rather unusual and highly valuable text for its interface between specific neurological disorders and their psychiatric concomitants. These disorders include temporal lobe epilepsy, frontal lobe lesions, hydrocephalus, Huntington's Chorea, and a variety of other topics.

31. ***Galin, D.** Implications for psychiatry of left and right cerebral specialization. A neurophysiological context for unconscious processes. Arch. Gen. Psychiatry 31: 572–583, **1974.**

In this provocative article, the author reviews evidence for hemispheric specialization based on numerous neuropsychological studies. He then proposes a relationship between this specialization of cognitive function in each hemisphere and the mechanisms of repression and unconscious motivation.

32. ***Heaton, R.K. and Crowley, T.J.** Effects of psychiatric disorders and their somatic treatments on the neuropsychological test results, pp. 481–525. In: Handbook of Clinical Neuropsychology. Eds.: S.B. Filskov and T.J. Boll. New York: Wiley, **1981.**

These authors review the extensive literature using neuropsychological tests to distinguish between organic and the functional psychiatric patients. In addition, they review studies on the effects of neuroleptic drug dosage as well as ECT effects on neuropsychological test results.

This is a most unusual and extensive review of an important area of the clinical research literature.

SPECIAL TOPICS

33. **Bogen, J.E.** The callosal syndrome, pp. 308–359. In: Clinical Neuropsychology. Eds.: K.M. Heilman and E. Valenstein. New York: Oxford University Press, **1979.**

The author, a neurosurgeon, provided the first recent series of surgical section of the human corpus callosum for control of epileptic seizures. In this thorough and well-written article he presents an analysis of the clinical examination of the patient suspected of having a lesion of the corpus callosum.

34. **Hecaen, H. and Albert, M.L.** Disorders of gestural behavior—the apraxias, pp. 90–127. In: Human Neuropsychology. Eds.: H. Hecaen and M.L. Albert. New York: Wiley, **1978.**

Disorders of learned movement patterns, apraxis, are probably more common in psychiatric and neurological populations than appreciated. The authors describe the clinical methods necessary to reveal the various disorders of praxis and their proposed pathological substrates.

35. ***Joynt, R.J. and Goldstein, M.N.** Minor cerebral hemisphere, pp. 147–183. In: Current Reviews of Higher Nervous System Dysfunction: Advances in Neurology, Vol. 7. Ed.: W.J. Friedlander. New York: Raven Press, **1975.**

The numerous behavioral features of lesions of the minor cerebral hemisphere and the clinical techniques necessary to elucidate them are presented and reviewed.

34. NEUROLOGY FOR PSYCHIATRISTS

JOEL YAGER, M.D.
F. DAVID RUDNICK, M.D.

A neurological consciousness and point of view in the assessment and management of patients is important to the psychiatrist for several reasons, least of which is the continuing marriage of the specialties in the American Board of Psychiatry and Neurology and the certainty that the board examinations will contain questions about neurology. Far more important is the fact that subtle neurological problems are highly prevalent in the most central of psychiatric disorders. Neurological assessments and CT scans reveal abnormalities in many psychiatric patients never treated with drugs. Neuropsychological assessments reveal abnormalities of cognitive function not previously considered. Increasing knowledge about hemispheric specialization and about brain areas that mediate affect, cognition, memory and drive have clear implications for psychiatric theory and treatment.

Furthermore, there is a high prevalence of psychiatric disturbance in patients with neurological disease. Not only are the psychiatric problems of the many patients with epilepsy, brain damage and other neurological disorders in need of attention and treatment, but these clinical syndromes provide important observations that must be woven into a comprehensive understanding of the etiology and pathogenesis of psychiatric disorders.

The references in this section emphasize the assessment of higher cortical functions and syndromes of central concern to psychiatrists. Although references are provided that describe the overall neurological exam in detail, except for a small number of standard neurological textbooks we have attended primarily to neurological diseases that are on the "borderland" between traditionally neurological and psychiatric disorders. We have focused on clinical problems that are as likely to present initially to the psychiatrist as to the neurologist, those problems ordinarily seen first by neurologists that commonly lead to (or should lead to) requests for psychiatric consultation, and some disorders traditionally seen by psychiatrists about which an exceptionally high index of suspicion with respect to neurological thinking is merited. The recent textbooks can guide the interested reader to journal articles about other specific neurological diseases.

GENERAL REFERENCES FOR NEUROLOGY AS A WHOLE

1.   ***Adams, R.D. and Victor, M.** Principles of Neurology (2nd ed.). New York: McGraw-Hill, **1981.**

     A definitive textbook of neurology. Contains sections on the major signs and symptoms of neurological disease, as well as major disease entities.

2.   **Baker, A.B. and Baker, L.H.,** eds. Clinical Neurology. New York: Harper and Row, **1976.**

     Another excellent textbook of neurology.

3.   **Gilman, S. and Winans, S.S.** Manter and Gatz's Essentials of Clinical Neuroanatomy and Neurophysiology (6th ed.). Philadelphia: Davis, **1982.**

     Latest edition of this classic, brief review that lucidly explains nervous system organization and function. Clinical correlations provided.

4.   **Samuels, M.A.** Manual of Neurologic Therapeutics: With Essentials of Diagnosis. Boston: Little, Brown, **1978.**

     An excellent, concise book in the Little, Brown spiral-bound series. Part I is arranged by neurological symptoms including intellectual dysfunction, dizziness, backache, epilepsy, and brain death. Part II is devoted to neurological diseases. Discussions of work up and treatment are specific. Pharmacological management is outlined precisely.

5.   **Vinken, P.J. and Bruyn, G.W.,** eds. Handbook of Clinical Neurology. New York: Elsevier North Holland, **1969.**

     Multivolumed handbook published in 1960s and 1970s. An encyclopedia of neurology with detailed articles on all aspects of basic and clinical neurology. If you can't find a discussion elsewhere, the odds are you can find it in this series.

GENERAL NEUROBEHAVIOR REFERENCES

6.   ***Benson, D.F. and Blumer, D.,** eds. Psychiatric Aspects of Neurological Disease. New York: Grune and Stratton. (Vol. 1: **1975,** Vol. 2: **1982.**)

Highly readable, clinically useful books with chapters by recognized authorities covering many pertinent areas for psychiatrists including organic brain syndromes, mental concomitants of physical disease, hydrocephalic dementias, dementia and pseudodementia with depression, disorders of verbal expression, frontal and temporal lobe pathology and associated mental and personality changes, temporal lobe epilepsy and its psychiatric significance, neurological aspects of sexual behavior, movement disorders, Huntington's Chorea, etc.

7. **Benson, D.F.** Aphasia, Alexia and Agraphia. New York: Churchill Livingstone, **1979.**

A text that discusses higher cortical processes of language from all aspects including clinical presentation, neuroanatomical location, examination, and behavioral correlates. It is easily readable and provides a practical grounding in the clinical approach to language disorders.

8. ***Critchley, M.** The Parietal Lobes. London: Edward Arnold, **1953.** (Also available from Hafner, **1966.**)

Based on extensive clinical material this classic book describes in detail the specific syndromes of parietal lobe dysfunction.

9. ***Heilman, K.M. and Valenstein, E.S.,** eds. Clinical Neuropsychology. New York: Oxford University Press, **1979.**

Eighteen excellent chapters include discussions of aphasias, alexias, agraphias, acalculias, body schema disturbances, apraxias, agnosias, callosal syndromes, and commissurotomy syndromes—emotional disorders resulting from lesions of the CNS, amnesias, dementias. There is a good chapter on recovery and treatment.

10. ***Penfield, W.** The Mystery of the Mind: A Critical Study of Consciousness and the Human Brain. Princeton: Princeton University Press, **1975.**

The neurosurgeon who pioneered investigation of the temporal lobes reflects on the organization and integration of higher cortical functions. An engaging narrative.

11. ***Pincus, J.H. and Tucker, G.J.** Behavioral Neurology (2nd ed.). New York: Oxford University Press, **1978.**

A concise, clearly written text for students. Coauthored by a neurologist and a psychiatrist, it has chapters on seizure disorders, the limbic system, schizophrenia, disorders of intellectual functioning, movement disorders, depression, psychosis, and sleep. A concluding section on distinguishing neurological from psychiatric disorders considers headache, hyperventilation, and conversion syndromes.

12. **Strub, R.L. and Black, F.W.** Organic Brain Syndromes: An Introduction to Neurobehavioral Disorders. Philadelphia: Davis, **1981.**

An authoritative discussion of common neurobehavioral problems designed for students and beginning residents. Includes sections on anatomy, clinical evaluations, major clinical organic brain syndromes, neurobehavioral syndromes of specific etiologies including epilepsies and other major brain diseases, and "borderland" organic brain syndromes. Well referenced.

13. **Trimble, M.R.** Neuropsychiatry. New York: Wiley, **1981.**

An extensively referenced neurobehavior text by one of the major contributors in the area.

AMNESIA

14. **Benson, D.F.** Amnesia. South. Med. J. 71: 1221–1227, 1231, **1978.**

This article provides a clear definition of amnesia as a distinct mental disorder and describes the main clinical settings in which it is observed. Bedside clinical testing of memory function is also outlined.

15. **Whitty, C.W.M. and Zangwill, O.L.,** eds. Amnesia (2nd ed.). London: Butterworth, **1977.**

A scholarly volume on the clinical syndromes of amnesia, from Wernicke-Korsakoff to transient global amnesia.

AGGRESSION AND VIOLENCE

16. **Bach-Y-Rita, G., Lion, J.R., Climent, C.E., et al.** Episodic dyscontrol: A study of 130 violent patients. Am. J. Psychiatry 127: 4, 1473–1478, **1971.**

An important clinical study of patients with violent behavior in whom a high prevalence of brain dysfunction was found. Discusses the comprehensive evaluation and treatment of these patients.

17. ***Goldstein, M.** Brain research and violent behavior: A summary and evaluation of the status of biomedical research on brain and aggressive violent behavior. Arch. Neurol. 30: 1–35, **1974.**

Summary report of four NINDS workshops on neuroanatomical and neurophysiologic studies; neuroendocrine pharmacological and genetic studies; behavioral studies; and clinical studies. Heavily referenced.

18. ***Mark, V.H. and Ervin, F.R.** Violence and the Brain. New York: Harper and Row, **1970.**

A controversial book describing cases of violent persons with subtle brain disorders, the implication being that certain abnormalities of limbic structures may predispose to violence.

BRAIN DAMAGE/TRAUMA

19. **Goldstein, K.** Functional disturbances in brain damage, pp. 182–207. In: AHP (2nd ed.), Vol. 4, **1975.**

Classic paper describing the manner in which brain-damaged patients adapt to their deficits. Discusses how some observed behaviors result directly from injury whereas others reflect adaptive reactions and psychological defenses of varying effectiveness. The behaviors of brain-damaged people are formulated from an integrative biopsychosocial point of view.

20. ***Lishman, W.A.** The psychiatric sequelae of head injury: A review. Psychol. Med. 3: 304–318, **1973.**

This review focuses on chronic psychiatric sequelae of head injury, considering organic, psychological, and social factors that lead to disability. Types of resulting psychiatric disability are discussed, including intellectual impairment, personality change, psychosis and neurotic disturbances.

21. **Ross, E.D. and Rush, J.** Diagnosis and neuroanatomical correlates of depression in brain-damaged patients: Implications for a neurology of depression. Arch. Gen. Psychiatry 38: 1344–1354, **1981.**

Excellent discussion of the differentiation of aphasias and aprosodias (disorders of affective language and behavior resulting from right hemisphere lesions). Detailed case studies with clinical-pathological correlations based on CAT scans are presented. From this material there are derived an extensive list of clues for diagnosing depression in neurologically impaired patients and a neuroanatomical model for endogenous depression.

22. **Rutter, M.** Psychological sequelae of brain damage in children. Am. J. Psychiatry 138: 1533–1544, **1981.**

This careful review concludes that brain injury causes a markedly increased risk in intellectual and psychiatric impairment. Various features in the nature of the injury and the child's preinjury situation that contribute to the impairments are discussed.

CEREBRAL LATERALITY

23. **Gazzaniga, M.S. and Volpe, B.I.** Split-brain studies: Implications for psychiatry, pp. 25–45. In: AHP (2nd ed.), Vol. 7, **1981.**

An account of research in humans who had commissurotomies by one of Sperry's close collaborators. Illustrations of the experiments contribute to this highly readable chapter.

24. **Gruzelier, J.H.** Cerebral laterality and psychopathology: Fact and fiction. Psychol. Med. 11: 219–227, **1981.**

Critical review of recent studies relating schizphrenialike and affective disorders to lateralized functions. Neurotic and character problems are also considered.

CLINICAL EXAMINATION

25. ***Mayo Clinic and Mayo Foundation for Medical Education and Research.** Clinical Examinations in Neurology (5th ed.). Philadelphia: Saunders, **1982.**

This well-regarded book on the neurological examination has been periodically updated and is now in its 5th edition.

26. **Strub, R.L. and Black, F.W.** The Mental Status Examination in Neurology. Philadelphia: Davis, **1977.**

A highly readable, thorough review of the mental status examination. Particular attention is given to those higher cortical functions of most interest to neurobehaviorists.

DEMENTIA

27. **Schneck, M.K., Reisberg, B., and Ferris, S.H.** An overview of current concepts of Alzheimer's disease. Am. J. Psychiatry 139: 165–173, **1982.**

A comprehensive review of clinical features, differential diagnosis and neurobiology. Good discussion of "phases" of the disorder and suggested workup to rule out reversible dementias.

28. **Wells, C.E.** Dementia (2nd ed.). Philadelphia: Davis, **1977.**

Classic volume on the pathogenesis and differential diagnosis of dementia. Wells's chapters on definition, workup, and treatment are particularly useful for the clinician.

EPILEPSY

29. ***Bear, D.M. and Fedio, P.** Quantitative analysis of interictal behavior in temporal lobe epilepsy. Arch. Neurol. 34: 454–467, **1977.**

A report of 48 patients assessed by means of detailed questionnaires that assessed 18 separate behavioral traits. A profile emerged that included dependence, obsessionalism, and humorless sobriety. Psychological differences in left- and right-sided lesions are discussed. Previous studies in this field are nicely summarized.

30. **Pincus, J.H.** Can violence be a manifestation of epilepsy? Neurology 30: 304–307, **1980.**

This is a review of human studies that suggests a connection between violent behavior and epilepsy, particularly psychomotor epilepsy. The author takes an affirmative view of the correlation that in turn has potent psychosocial and legal implications in assessing violent crime.

31. **Scott, D.F.** Psychiatric aspects of epilepsy. Br. J. Psychiatry 132: 417–430, **1978.**

Review article by a long-term student of this field. Includes good discussions of classification, intellectual functioning, and causes of deterioration, psychiatric morbidity, personality, automatisms, crime, aggression, association with specific psychiatric syndromes and symptoms, differential of true epilepsy and "hysterical" seizures, and schizophreniform psychoses.

32. **Slater, E. and Beard, A.W.** The schizophrenia-like psychoses of epilepsy. (5 parts). Br. J. Psychiatry 109: 95–150, **1963.**

A classic paper that delineates the phenomenology of psychotic symptoms and various thought disturbances in epilepsy. Clinically rich with many detailed case descriptions.

33. **Waxman, S.G. and Geschwind, N.** The interictal behavior syndrome of temporal lobe epilepsy. Arch. Gen. Psychiatry 32: 1580–1586, **1975.**

A clinically detailed account of the changes in sexual behavior, religiosity, and compulsive writing and drawing found in some temporal lobe epilepsy patients during interictal periods.

34.   **Williams, D.T., Spiegel, H., and Mostofsky, D.I.** Neurogenic and hysterical seizures in children and adolescents: Differential diagnostic and therapeutic considerations. Am. J. Psychiatry 135: 82–86, **1978.**

The murky problem of separating true seizures from pseudoseizures in patients with known epilepsy is discussed. Six cases are considered in detail to illustrate the differential diagnostic process. Treatment plans are described.

HEADACHE

35.   ***Diamond, S. and Dalessio, D.J.** The Practicing Physician's Approach to Headache (3rd ed.). Baltimore: Williams and Wilkins, **1982.**

This thin book details the differential diagnosis of all major recognized categories of headache and offers excellent discussions of their treatment.

36.   **Saper, J.R.** Migraine: I. Classification and pathogenesis. II. Treatment. JAMA 239: 2380–2383; 239: 2480–2484, **1978.**

A complete review of signs, symptoms, pathogenesis, and treatment. Includes consideration of psychological and environmental triggers and treatment approaches in addition to a full pharmacological treatment review.

MOVEMENT DISORDERS

37.   **Duvoisin, R.** Clinical diagnosis of the dyskinesias. Med. Clin. North Am. 56: 6: 1321–1341, **1972.**

A concise description of the major phenomenological categories of the movement disorders and the principal disease entities in each category. Included are chorea, athetosis, dystonia, drug-induced dyskinesias, Wilson's disease, and tremor. The photographic illustrations are excellent.

38.   ***Granacher, R.P., Jr.** Differential diagnosis of tardive dyskinesia: An overview. Am. J. Psychiatry 138: 1288–1297, **1981.**

Since many neurological disorders may resemble tardive dyskinesia, the psychiatrist needs to be able to distinguish them from one another. This paper clearly describes the differentiation of many types of abnormal involuntary movements including parkinsonism; the dystonias, choreas and choreoathetosis; tremors; tics; stereotypes and mannerisms; and others. There are two useful appendices to assist in diagnosis.

39. **Klawans, H.L., Goetz, C.G., and Perlik, S.** Tardive dyskinesia: Review and update. Am. J. Psychiatry 137: 900–908, **1980.**

This review article describes the clinical syndrome, theories of pathogenesis and neuropathology, attempts at pharmacotherapy and recommendations for prevention. An exhaustive bibliography is provided.

40. **Owens, D.G.C., Johnstone, E.C., and Frith, C.D.** Spontaneous involuntary disorders of movement. Their prevalence, severity, and distribution in chronic schizophrenics with and without treatment with neuroleptics. Arch. Gen. Psychiatry 39: 452–461, **1982.**

Using standardized recording techniques, the authors assessed 411 hospitalized patients with chronic schizophrenia including 47 never treated with neuroleptics. The prevalence, severity, and distribution of abnormal movements were similar in both groups and high overall. The article includes a detailed enumeration of the various types of abnormal movements one may encounter.

NEUROPSYCHOLOGICAL ASSESSMENT

41. **Diamant, J.J.** Similarities and differences in the approach of R.M. Reitan and A.R. Luria. Acta Psychiatr. Scand. 63: 431–443, **1981.**

A critical analysis and attempt at integration of models of the two major independent pioneer investigators in neuropsychology. A pilot study comparing the results of the two approaches is described.

42. **Grant, I., Mohns, L., Miller, M., et al.** A neuropsychological study of polydrug users. Arch. Gen. Psychiatry 33: 973–978, **1976.**

A methodologically sophisticated study that found impaired neuropsychological function in 41–64 percent of polydrug users who were drug free for an average of two months prior to testing.

43. ***Luria, A.R.** The Working Brain: An Introduction to Neuropsychology. New York: Basic Books, **1973.**

A classic book by one of the most distinguished Russian psychologists of our time. Notable for his ideas on the subsystems of the brain in relation to higher cortical activity. Bedside methods for the assessment of Luria's "functional units" of the brain are described.

PHARMACOTHERAPY

44. **Shader, R.I., Weinberger, D.R., and Greenblatt, D.J.** Problems with drug interactions in treating brain disorders. Psychiatr. Clin. North Am. 1(1): 51–69, **1978.**

Thorough review of pharmacokinetics of major classes of anticonvulsants and their interactions with phenothiazines, tricylic antidepressants, benzodiazepines, lithium carbonate, and other common psychiatric drugs. Both theoretical and practical clinical issues are addressed.

SPECIFIC DISEASES AND SYNDROMES

45.   **Cartwright, G.E.** Diagnosis of treatable Wilson's disease. N. Engl. J. Med. 298: 1347–1350, **1978.**

Review of an often-overlooked metabolic disorder that may present with psychiatric symptoms resembling schizophrenia and related neurological and hepatic problems.

46.   **Cohen, D.J., Young, J.G., Nathanson, J.A., et al.** Clonidine in Tourette's syndrome. Lancet II: 551–553, **1979.**

This article suggests an alternative to haloperidol in the treatment of Tourette's syndrome. It also presents eight brief case reports that provide a view of the spectrum of psychopathology that may be part of the syndrome.

47.   ***Plum, F. and Posner, J.B.,** eds. The Diagnosis of Stupor and Coma (3rd ed.). Philadelphia: Davis, **1980.**

This fine volume deals with pathophysiology, signs and symptoms, supra and subtentorial causes, metabolic brain diseases, psychogenic unresponsiveness, and prognosis. It does not consider treatment in any detail.

48.   **Shapiro, A.K., Shapiro, E., Bruun, R.D., et al.** Gilles de La Tourette Syndrome. New York: Raven Press, **1978.**

Volume that fully discusses this disorder estimated to occur in 2.6 percent of the general population that is frequently mistaken for a psychological disorder. Diagnosis, theories of pathogenesis, and pharmacological and psychosocial treatment aspects are included.

TECHNIQUES FOR INVESTIGATION

49.   **Naidich, T.P., Solomon, S., and Leeds, N.E.** Computerized tomography in neurological evaluations, JAMA 240: 565–568, **1978.**

Excellent review of the utility and limitations of CT scans in the identification of CNS lesions. Particularly good at discussing indications for scans, false positives, and false negatives.

50. **Nierdermeyer, E. and Lopas da Silva, F.** Electroencephalography: Basic Principles, Clinical Applications and Related Fields. Baltimore: Uran and Schwarzenberg, **1982.**

A unique monumental single volume that is encyclopedic in coverage. Chapters deal with basic and clinical electroencephalography pertinent to neurology, psychiatry, and neurosurgery; research aspects of newer diagnostic approaches, evoked potentials. Destined to become a classic.

PSYCHODYNAMIC PERSPECTIVES ON NEUROPSYCHIATRY

51. **Betlheim, S. and Hartmann, H.** On parapraxes in the Korsakoff psychosis, pp. 288–307. In: Organization and Pathology of Thought. Ed.: D. Rapoport. New York: Columbia University Press, **1951.**

This is a translation of the original 1924 article. The authors study from a psychoanalytic perspective the symbolic representations in the distortions and confabulations of Korsakoff psychosis.

52. **Rapaport, D. and Gill, M.M.** A case of amnesia and its bearing on the theory of memory, pp. 113–119. In: The Collected Papers of David Rapaport. Ed.: M.M. Gill. New York: Basic Books, **1967.**

In this 1942 paper, two distinguished psychoanalysts consider memory alterations in a patient with fugue. Several other papers in this fine collection discuss psychoanalytic theories of memory in detail.

53. **Schilder, P.** Studies concerning the psychology and symptomatology of general paresis, pp. 519–580. In: Organization and Pathology of Thought. Ed.: D. Rapaport. New York: Columbia University Press, **1951.**

This classic article was translated from the original German paper published in 1930. In it Schilder, who made numerous important contributions to our understanding of mind-body relationships, describes at length object relations, sensations, speech, thinking, judgment, and action in general paresis. His discussion of the thought disorders is superb. Rapaport's scholarly notes on the paper are edifying.

PART IV
TREATMENT

35. PSYCHOPHARMACOLOGY

David E. Sternberg, M.D.

The field of psychopharmacology is growing rapidly, not only in quantity, but also in quality; developments during the past quarter-century have led to revolutionary changes in both the treatment and scientific investigation of psychiatric disorders. The development of drugs with proven efficacy in schizophrenia, mania, depression, anxiety, and other clinical states has dramatically changed psychiatric practice, and the number of patients in state mental hospitals has sharply declined. The importance of matching the patient's clinical disorder with a specific drug treatment has led to the development of more reliable criteria and methods for diagnosing psychiatric illness. Perhaps most important, these psychoactive drugs, which were largely discovered through a combination of serendipity and astute clinical observation, have provided an important arena for research interchange between clinical psychiatry and neurobiology—an arena that has generated new hypotheses concerning brain function in normal and abnormal states and that offers promise for understanding the pathophysiologies of the major psychiatric disorders. At the present time, we are beginning to see clinical discoveries made less from serendipitous findings and more from a basic neuroscientific understanding of brain function.

The references cited are classified into general texts, antipsychotics, antidepressants, lithium, antianxiety drugs, and miscellaneous pharmacologic issues (i.e., overdosage, geriatrics, pregnancy, psychopharmacology in the context of psychotherapy, and drug interactions). The selection of the references reflects a number of issues. General articles are comprehensive yet concise summaries that include the essential references allowing for more detailed study. The more specific articles address an important clinical issue or break new ground. Whenever possible, well-designed studies using double-blind placebo-controlled methodology in a sufficiently large group were chosen.

The literature of psychopharmacology is a vast and often confusing maze. These references should provide a beginning entry into that literature and a practical guide to help clinicians make informed decisions in the use of pharmacology.

GENERAL TEXT

1. ***Appleton, W.S.** Fourth psychoactive drug usage guide. J. Clin. Psychiatry 43: 12–27, **1982.**

    An unusually concise yet comprehensive guide for the rational prescription of psychotropic drugs. Most of the data derives from well-designed, carefully controlled, double-blind studies. An excellent source for the beginning psychiatric resident.

2. ***Barchas, J.D., Berger, P.A., Ciaranello, R.D., et al.,** eds. Psychopharmacology: From Theory to Practice. New York: Oxford University Press, **1977.**

    The authors have successfully endeavored to explain the scientific principles behind psychopharmacology and then to demonstrate their relevance to the use of psychopharmacological agents in clinical care.

3. ***Cooper, J.R., Bloom, F.E., and Roth, R.H.** The Biochemical Basis of Neuropharmacology (3rd ed.). New York: Oxford University Press, **1977.**

    A brief, scholarly introduction and guide to the complex area of neurotransmitters and the mechanisms of action of psychopharmacological agents.

4. ***Lipton, M.A., DiMascio, A., and Killam, K.F.,** eds. Psychopharmacology: A Generation of Progress. New York: Raven Press, **1978.**

    A magnificent in-depth review of the field. Subjects covered are up-to-date and range from basic science to practical psychopharmacotherapy.

ANTIPSYCHOTICS

5. ***Ayd, F.J.** The depot fluphenazines: A reappraisal after ten years clinical experience. Am. J. Psychiatry 132: 491–500, **1975.**

    The types of patients most likely to benefit from therapy with injectible drugs, the techniques of this therapy, the therapeutic efficacy and side effects of the drugs, and how they interact with other medications are reviewed.

6. **Baldessarini, R.J. and Davis, J.M.** What is the best maintenance dose of neuroleptics in schizophrenia? Psychiatry Res. 3: 115–122, **1980.**

    Data from controlled studies are gathered to evaluate the doses of neuroleptics required to significantly prevent relapse during maintenance treatment with the finding that effective maintenance doses can probably be lower than those used in acute phases of treatment.

7. ***Davis, J.M., Erickson, S., and Dekirmenjian, H.** Plasma levels of antipsychotic drugs and clinical response, pp. 905–915. In: Psychopharmacology: A Generation of Progress. Eds.: M.A. Lipton, A. DiMascio, and K.F. Killam. New York: Raven Press, **1978.**

A review of a topic which will become increasingly important in neuroleptic treatment over the next years.

8. ***Davis, J.M., Schaffer, C.B., Killian, G.A., et al.** Important issues in the drug treatment of schizophrenia. Schizophr. Bull. 6: 70–87, **1980.**

An excellent summary of the data concerning neuroleptics includes: indications for selective treatment, characteristics of drug responders and nonresponders, indications for high dosage treatment, indications for maintenance therapy, and risks and benefits of antipsychotic drugs.

9. ***Kane, J.M. and Smith, J.M.** Tardive dyskinesia: Prevalence and risk factors, 1959–1979. Arch. Gen. Psychiatry 39: 473–481, **1982.**

An excellent survey of tardive dyskinesia in neuroleptic-treated patients, addressing the prevalence and risk factors. They challenge the assumptions that the risk of TD increases with increasing neuroleptic exposure, CNS dysfunction, or exposure to antiparkinsonian medication.

10. **Linden, R., Davis, J.M., and Rubinstein, J.** High vs. low dose treatment with antipsychotic agents. Psychiatr. Ann. 12: 769–781, **1982.**

This summary of dose-response studies finds neither any short-term or longer-term benefit of high doses of antipsychotics. For the vast majority of patients there was no evidence of additional therapeutic benefit to the use of doses in excess of the 600–1000 mg range of chlorpromazine equivalents.

11. ***Neborsky, R., Janowsky, D.S., Munson, E., et al.** Rapid treatment of acute psychotic symptom with high and low dose haloperidol: Behavioral considerations. Arch. Gen. Psychiatry 38: 195–199, **1981.**

A careful investigation of the "rapid neuroleptization technique." Acutely psychotic inpatients were treated with two different haloperidol dose schedules. Both groups improved and did not differ as to degree or rapidity of symptom alleviation.

12. ***Snyder, S.H., Greenberg, D., and Yamamura, H.** Antischizophrenic drugs and brain cholinergic receptors: Affinity for muscarinic sites predicts extrapyramidal effects. Arch. Gen. Psychiatry 31: 58–61, **1974.**

The anticholinergic side effects (e.g., dry mouth, blurred vision, constipation, urinary difficulties) are positively correlated with, and the extrapyramidal side effects are negatively correlated with, the affinity of various neuroleptic drugs for muscarinic cholinergic receptor sites.

13.   ***Sovner, R. and DiMascio, A.** Extrapyramidal syndromes and other neurological side effects of psychotropic drugs, pp. 1021–1032. In: Psychopharmacology: A Generation of Progress. Eds.: H.A. Lipton, A. DiMascio, and K.F. Killam. New York: Raven Press, **1978.**

An excellent overview of the neurological side effects of neuroleptic and other drugs. Time course, treatment, and possible pathophysiologies are discussed.

ANTIDEPRESSANTS

14.   **Ananth, J. and Luchins, D.** A review of combined tricyclic and MAOI therapy. Compr. Psychiatry 18: 221–230, **1977.**

The assumption that combined treatment with tricyclic and MAO inhibitor antidepressants is always dangerous is shown to be erroneous; however, the therapeutic advantages remain questionable. Methods to combine these drugs safely are described.

15.   ***Davis, J.M.** Overview: Maintenance therapy in psychiatry: II. Affective Disorders. Am. J. Psychiatry 133: 1–13, **1976.**

In this review of the maintenance therapy of affective disorders with lithium or tricyclic antidepressants, the author concludes that maintenance treatment is necessary to prevent recurrences of both mania and depression in bipolar disease and depression in unipolar disease and may provide the basis for a preventive approach.

16.   ***DeMontigny, C. de, Grunberg, F., Mayer, A. et al.** Lithium induces rapid relief of depression in tricyclic antidepressant drug nonresponders. Br. J. Psychiatry 138: 252–256, **1981.**

This nonblind study found a rapid (i.e., one–three day) improvement in depression in patients nonresponsive to chronic tricyclic treatment, when lithium was added. A clinically useful finding that derives from basic neuroscience research.

17.   **Everett, H.C.** The use of bethanechol chloride with tricyclic antidepressants. Am. J. Psychiatry 132: 1202–1204, **1975.**

The author describes the use of bethanechol chloride to relieve the anticholinergic side effects, such as urinary retention from treatment with tricyclic antidepressants that may allow for their use in patients who find such side effects very troublesome. However, some of the newer antidepressants, with fewer anticholinergic effects, may be especially useful for such patients.

18. *Glassman, A.H. and Bigger, J.T. Cardiovascular effects of therapeutic doses of tricyclic antidepressants: A review. Arch. Gen. Psychiatry 38: 815–820, 1981.

Clinicians have been hesitant to treat patients with overt heart disease using tricyclic drugs. The authors report that the tricyclics are essentially free of adverse effects in patients without cardiovascular disease. Only in patients with bundle-branch disease is there a risk of heart block. Patients with ventricular arrythmias are likely to improve. The authors conclude that these drugs can often be used to benefit patients with overt heart disease.

19. *Goodwin, F.K., Prange, A.J., Post, R.M., et al. Potentiation of antidepressant effects by L-triiodothyronine in tricyclic non-responders. Am. J. Psychiatry 139: 34–38, 1982.

Out of 12 patients with major depressive illness who did not respond to treatment with tricyclic antidepressants, 9 of these patients showed improvement in depression when T3 was added to their antidepressant regimen. Previous uncontrolled studies showed that the rates of response after T3 administration was in the range of 64–90 percent. Side effects of this addition were minimal.

20. Holinger, P.C. and Klawans, H.L. Reversal of tricyclic overdosage-induced central anticholinergic syndrome by physostigmine. Am. J. Psychiatry 133: 1018–1023, 1976.

Since such symptoms as delirium, stupor, coma, and seizure seen following overdosage with tricyclic antidepressants and antiparkinsonian drugs are due to the central anticholinergic activity of these agents, the authors find the intravenous use of the centrally acting cholinergic agent, physostigmine useful in treatment.

21. *Kuhn, R. The treatment of depressive states with G#22355 (imipramine hydrochloride). Am. J. Psychiatry 115: 459–464, 1958.

The discovery of the first tricyclic antidepressant. An outstanding example of astute clinical observation. Kuhn in a quest for new antipsychotic drugs found that imipramine improved mood.

22. McCabe, B. and Tsuang, M.T. Dietary consideration in MAO inhibitor regimens. J. Clin. Psychiatry 43: 178–181, 1982.

The authors suggest that exaggerated fears of adverse interactions between MAO inhibitors and foods have resulted in these useful drugs being withheld from patients. They propose a reasonable MAO inhibitor diet, provide principles for dietary counseling, and make suggestions for achieving dietary adherence.

23. **Nelson, J.C. and Bowers, M.B.** Delusional unipolar depression: Description and drug response. Arch. Gen. Psychiatry 35: 1321–1328, **1978.**

The authors describe the successful response of delusional unipolar depressives to combined neuroleptic and tricyclic antidepressant drug therapy and contrast this to the poor response when such patients are treated with antidepressants alone. Characteristics of this group of patients are described. Other studies suggest that ECT is the treatment of choice for this subgroup.

24. *****Quitkin, F., Rifkin, A., and Klein, D.F.** Monoamine oxidase inhibitors: A review of anti-depressant effectiveness. Arch. Gen. Psychiatry 36: 749–760, **1979.**

Review of carefully controlled trials of MAO inhibitors reveal the effectiveness of these drugs in depression. Implications of fast acetylation, types of MAO, selective MAO inhibitor drugs, and measures of platelet MAO inhibition are discussed. These drugs have been underutilized, yet they may be the drugs of choice in depressed patients with atypical features such as lethargy, hypersomnolence, rejection sensitivity, and reactivity of mood.

25. **Richelson, E.** Tricyclic antidepressants and neurotransmitter receptors. Psychiatr. Ann. 9: 16–32, **1979.**

The author summarizes the data that relate the side effects of tricyclic antidepressants to the blockade of various adrenergic, histaminergic, and cholinergic receptors providing for a rational choice of side effects.

26. *****Risch, S.C., Huey, L.Y., and Janowsky, D.S.** Plasma levels of tricyclic antidepressants and clinical efficacy: Review of the literature—I, II. J. Clin. Psychiatry 40: 4–16; 58–69, **1979.**

This is a comprehensive and critical review of the literature concerning the relationship of plasma levels of the tricyclic antidepressants and clinical efficacy. Some of the tricyclic antidepressants may have critical ranges of plasma levels that must be achieved for maximal therapeutic efficacy. For other antidepressants this is less clear. Data on the specific drugs are reviewed.

27. **Stern, S.L. and Mendels, J.** Drug combinations in the treatment of refractory depression: A review. J. Clin. Psychiatry 42: 368–373, **1981.**

The authors survey the literature on the use of drug combinations in the management of depressed patients not responsive to treatment with a single drug. Such combinations include tricyclic and MAO inhibitor antidepressants, plus thyroid, methylphenidate, lithium, tryptophan, reserpine, and neuroleptics.

28. ***Stern, S.L., Rush, A.J., and Mendels, J.** Toward a rational pharmaco-therapy of depression. Am. J. Psychiatry 137: 545–552, **1980.**

The authors review approaches to the choice of antidepressant medication that include clinical and historical characteristics, psychological testing, biochemical and EEG, variables, and response to amphetamine.

29. **Wehr, T.A. and Goodwin, F.K.** Rapid cycling in manic-depressives induced by tricyclic antidepressants. Arch. Gen. Psychiatry 36: 555–559, **1979.**

The authors report that when tricyclic antidepressants were given to bipolar patients, rapid cycling between mania and depression was induced, which was not prevented by lithium treatment. Thus the possibily of tricyclic-induced rapid cycles should be considered when patients who have been treated with tricyclics have stormy courses.

LITHIUM

30. ***Ballenger, J.C. and Post, R.M.** Carbamazepine in manic-depressive illness: A new treatment. Am. J. Psychiatry 137: 782–790, **1980.**

Carbamazepine, a drug useful in the treatment of temporal lobe epilepsy, was found to be useful in the treatment of mania and possibly depression in patients with manic-depressive illness. It may also have prophylactic and acute efficacy in patients who may not respond to lithium.

31. ***Biederman, J., Lerner, Y., and Belmaker, R.H.** Combination of lithium carbonate and haloperidol in schizo-affective disorder: A controlled study. Arch. Gen. Psychiatry 36: 327–333, **1979.**

In this study of haloperidol plus lithium vs. haloperidol plus placebo treatment of excited schizo-affective patients, significant clinical benefits of lithium plus haloperidol were found. The benefit of lithium was not restricted to affective symptoms. This report suggests a clinical synergism between lithium and neuroleptics in the treatment of psychotic disorders.

32. ***Cade, J.F.J.** Lithium salts in the treatment of psychotic excitements. Med. J. Aust. 36: 349–352, **1949.**

The original paper that showed that lithium can abort an acute manic attack went relatively unnoticed.

33. **Cohen, W.J. and Cohen, N.H.** Lithium carbonate, haloperidol and irreversible brain damage. JAMA 230: 1283–1287, **1974.**

This article brought attention to the potential of neurotoxicity when lithium is combined with neuroleptics. Although lithium and neuroleptics have been administered together to thousands of patients, with few showing such symptoms, the potential of such symptomatology ought to be borne in mind.

34. **Flemenbaum, A., Weddige, R., and Miller, J.** Lithium erythrocyte/plasma ratio as a predictor of response. Am. J. Psychiatry 135: 336–338, **1978.**

The patients who had significant improvement with lithium were found to have high intracellular lithium ratios. Intracellular lithium levels should prove increasingly important over the next few years with regard to clinical response and side effects.

35. **Himmelhoch, J.M., Detre, T.P., Kupfer, D.J., et al.** Treatment of previously intractable depressions with tranylcypromine and lithium. J. Nerv. Ment. Dis. 155: 216–220, **1972.**

The authors describe a significant subpopulation within the bipolar depressive group, characterized by hypersomnia and a lack of therapeutic response to tricyclic antidepressants or lithium alone, who appear to respond favorably to the combination of lithium with the MAO inhibitor antidepressant tranylcypromine.

36. **Himmelhoch, J.M., Forrest, J., Neil, J.F., et al.** Thiazide-lithium synergy in refractory mood swings. Am. J. Psychiatry 134: 149–152, **1977.**

The authors show that thiazide diuretics may be safely used in the treatment of the severe polyuria associated with lithium-induced nephrogenic diabetes insipidus. They further suggest that thiazides may actually synergize with lithium in some lithium-refractory manic-depressive patients.

37. ***Jefferson, J.W. and Griest, J.M.** Primer of Lithium Therapy. Baltimore: Williams and Williams, **1977.**

Effectively covers all the practical clinical issues in the use of lithium.

38. ***Kane, J.M., Quitkin, F.M., Rifkin, A., et al.** Lithium carbonate and imipramine in the prophylaxis of unipolar and bipolar II illness: A prospective placebo-controlled comparison. Arch. Gen. Psychiatry 39: 1065–1069, **1982.**

In this careful double-blind study, lithium was found to prevent depressive relapse among both unipolar and bipolar depressives. No prophylactic effect of imipramine was found. The data lends strong support to the value of prophylaxis with lithium in unipolar depression.

39. **Mendels, J.** Lithium in the treatment of depression. Am. J. Psychiatry 133: 373–378, **1976.**

The author reviews the evidence for lithium's antidepressant action and evaluates whether there might be a specific subgroup of patients for whom it is effective. The observation that acute antidepressant responses are significantly more frequent in bipolar compared to unipolar patients is an especially strong one. However, some patients with apparent unipolar depressive illness do respond to lithium.

40. ***Ramsey, T.A. and Cox, M.** Lithium and the kidney: A review. Am. J. Psychiatry 139: 443–449, **1982.**

The authors review the effects of lithium on renal tubular transport, examine the reports of lithium-induced renal disease and recommend careful assessment of patients' renal function before the initiation of lithium therapy, including urinalysis, BUN, and/or serum creatinine concentrations, serum electrolytes, and creatinine clearance. Patients with marked polyuria should be monitored with particular care.

41. ***Reisberg, B. and Gershon, S.** Side effects associated with lithium therapy. Arch. Gen. Psychiatry 36: 879–887, **1979.**

This comprehensive review focuses on the toxic and side effects of lithium. Effects on the central nervous system, neuromuscular, renal, hematologic, cardiac, gastrointestinal, endocrinologic, dermatologic, and bone are noted.

42. **Schou, M.** Lithium in the treatment of other psychiatric and non-psychiatric disorders. Arch. Gen. Psychiatry 36: 856–859, **1979.**

Reports have claimed therapeutic efficacy of lithium in premenstrual tension, anorexia nervosa, movement disorders, to migraine and cluster headaches. This short review lists all studies and points out the need for placebo-controlled investigations.

43. ***Sheard, M.H., Marini, J.L., Bridges, C.I., et al.** The effect of lithium on impulsive aggressive behavior in man. Am. J. Psychiatry 133: 1409–1413, **1976.**

In a double-blind placebo-controlled study, the authors found that prisoners with histories of chronic impulsive behavior showed a significant reduction in aggressive behavior during lithium treatment.

ANTIANXIETY DRUGS

44. ***Braestrup, C. and Squires, R.F.** Brain specific benzodiazepine receptors. Br. J. Psychiatry 133: 249–269, **1978.**

    Braestrup and his colleagues discovered a brain-specific binding site for pharmacologically and clinically active benzodiazepines with a good correlation between the pharmacological effects of benzodiazepines and the affinity for this receptor. The search is on for the endogenous ligand.

45. ***Greenblatt, D.J. and Shader, R.I.** Pharmacotherapy of anxiety with benzodiazepines and beta-adrenergic blockers, pp. 1381–1390. In: Psychopharmacology: A Generation of Progress. Eds.: M.A. Lipton, A. DiMascio, and K.F. Killam. New York: Raven Press, **1978.**

    Greenblatt and Shader have pointed out differences between the benzodiazepines in their rate and route of elimination. The presence or absence of pharmacologically active metabolites have important clinical implications in terms of dosage schedules, chronic treatment, treatment in the elderly, and drug interactions. They also review the antianxiety effects of beta-adrenergic blocking agents.

46. ***Grunhaus, L., Gloger, S., and Weisstub, E.** Panic attacks: A review of treatments and pathogenesis. J. Nerv. Ment. Dis. 169: 608–613, **1981.**

    The authors review the relationships between panic attacks, panic disorder, and agoraphobia and present the results of controlled pharmacological trials on patients complaining of panic attacks. The clear distinction between panic disorder as a distinct nosological entity separate from chronic anxiety is stressed.

MISCELLANEOUS

47. ***Ewing, J.A. and Bakewell, W.E.** Diagnosis and management of depressant drug dependence. Am. J. Psychiatry 123: 909–917, **1967.**

    The authors emphasize differentiating between the toxic effects of overdosage and the withdrawal syndrome from depressant drugs and describe the use of a test dose of pentobarbital to ascertain degree of dependence, which is especially helpful in patients presenting with multidepressant drug dependence.

48. ***Gaultieri, C.T. and Powell, S.F.** Psychoactive drug interactions. J. Clin. Psychiatry 39: 720–729, **1978.**

    The authors describe the methods by which interactions can occur between drugs and concisely review drug interactions of clinical interest to psychiatry. The drugs reviewed include stimulants, neuroleptics, tricyclic antidepressants, MAO inhibitors, lithium, anticonvulsants, and sedative-hypnotic drugs. The outline format of this review is especially useful in pressing clinical situations.

49. *Goldberg, H.L. and DiMascio, A. Psychotropic drugs in pregnancy, pp. 1047–1055. In: Psychopharmacology: A Generation of Progress. Eds.: M.A. Lipton, A. DiMascio, and K.F. Killam. New York: Raven Press, 1978.

The authors review the literature on the use of psychotropic drugs during pregnancy as well as during nursing. The clear teratogenic effects of lithium in the first trimester of pregnancy are stressed. In addition they point out that all psychotropic drugs are secreted in mothers' milk.

36. ELECTROCONVULSIVE THERAPY AND PSYCHOSURGERY

JAMES H. KOCSIS, M.D.

Limited efficacy and troublesome toxicities of psychotropic medications have spurred renewed interest in ECT in recent years. Studies of effectiveness, mechanisms of action, and side effects have been further stimulated by legal and ethical controversy surrounding this treatment modality. In response to these issues the American Psychiatric Association and Royal College of Psychiatrists both formed task forces in the mid-1970s to survey psychiatric practitioners, experts in the area of ECT, and the existing literature for purposes of writing comprehensive reviews and making recommendations about current practice and future research. These activities resulted in a monograph on *Electroconvulsive Therapy* (APA Task Force Report no. 14, 1978) and a review in the *British Journal of Psychiatry* (1977). In addition, these deliberations prompted a resurgence of research on ECT, many of the results of which are included in this bibliography. Much of the newer work has been recently reviewed and summarized by Kendell (*British Journal of Psychiatry,* 1981).

While still poorly understood, representative citations are included referring to use of ECT for psychiatric conditions other than depression. Other major areas of interest include studies comparing unilateral electrode placement and studies of memory impairment secondary to ECT. Some references cited also discuss the important issues of physiological effects of ECT and potential mechanisms of antidepressant action.

Psychosurgery in contrast to ECT remains a controversial, marginally acceptable, modality of therapy at best. A small number of references are included to enable the readers to review observations that have been made in human patients receiving this form of treatment, as well as to gain information about some of the ethical and scientific controversies involved.

GENERAL REVIEWS AND MONOGRAPHS

1. ***American Psychiatric Association.** Electroconvulsive Therapy. Task Force Report no. 14. Washington, D.C.: APA, **1978.**

   Complete and authoritative outline of indications, adverse effects; methods of administration; physiological, social, ethical, and legal aspects of ECT. Excellent bibliography, although now five years old. Summarizes research data on topic and proposed research areas.

2. **Kalinowsky, L.B., Hippins, H., and Klein, H.E.** Biological Treatments in Psychiatry. New York: Grune and Stratton, **1982.**

   Encyclopedic treatment of drug therapies, ECT, psychosurgery and other somatic forms of therapy. Excellent review of historical aspects of development and/or discarding of many somatic treatments. Section on psychosurgery is a good complement to M. Greenblatt et al. Written by clinicians of vast experience.

3. ***Kendall, R.E.** The present status of electroconvulsive therapy. Br. J. Psychiatry 139: 265–283, **1981.**

   This is the most up-to-date review of ECT. It incorporates findings from recent research studies and is very well written. It covers efficacy, mode of action, adverse effects, techniques, and ethical considerations.

4. **The Royal College of Psychiatrists memorandum on the use of electroconvulsive therapy.** Br. J. Psychiatry 131: 261–272, **1977.**

   Excellent brief review of effectiveness for various indications, proposed mechanisms of action, morbidity, and mortality associated with ECT. Also addresses legal aspects and practical procedures for ECT administration.

EFFICACY IN DEPRESSION AND OTHER DISORDERS

5. **Folstein, M.F., Folstein, S.E., and McHugh, P.R.** Clinical predictors of improvement after electroconvulsive therapy of patients with schizophrenia, neurotic reactions, and affective disorders. Biol. Psychiatry 7: 147–152, **1973.**

   A study of predictors of response to ECT in 110 consecutive patients given ECT having various hospital diagnoses. Of note was the result that schizophrenic patients who responded tended to have affective symptoms and to respond to a short course of treatment.

6. **Greenblatt, M.** Efficacy of ECT in affective and schizophrenic illness. Am. J. Psychiatry 134: 1001–1005, **1977.**

Good brief review of studies that have compared efficacy of ECT and drugs for treatment of both affective illness and schizophrenia. Paper concludes with recommendations about indications for ECT and combinations of drugs and ECT.

7. **McCabe, M.S.** ECT in the treatment of mania: A controlled study. Am. J. Psychiatry 133: 688–691, **1976.**

One of a small number of controlled studies examining effectiveness of ECT for mania. Methodologically flawed in that it is a retrospective chart review study and no formal behavioral ratings were done. However it does provide valuable data in a generally neglected area.

8. **May, P.R.A.** Treatment of Schizophrenia: A Comparative Study of Five Treatment Methods. New York: Science House, **1968.**

Now classic study of comparing antipsychotic drugs, psychotherapy, ECT, milieu therapy and psychotherapy plus drugs for treatment of acute or relapsed schizophrenics. It is one of the few prospective methodologically well-designed studies comparing drugs with ECT for treatment of schizophrenia.

9. **May, P.R.A., Tuma, A.H., Yale, C., et al.** Schizophrenia—a follow-up study of results of treatment. II: Hospital stay over two to five years. Arch. Gen. Psychiatry 33: 481–486, **1976.**

This report addresses the relative efficacy of drugs and ECT and the possible existence of a drug resistant, ECT responsive population.

TECHNIQUES OF ADMINISTRATION

10. **Barton, J.L.,. Mehta, S., and Snaith, R.P.** The prophylactic value of extra ECT in depressive illness. Acta Psychiatr. Scand. 49: 386–392, **1973.**

Paper reports an investigation of the effect on relapse rates of giving additional ECT after full symptomatic relief has been attained. It addresses the important practical issue of how many ECTs to administer for depressive illness.

11. **d'Elia, G. and Raotmo, H.** Is unilateral ECT less effective than bilateral ECT? Br. J. Psychiatry 126: 83–89, **1975.**

Thorough review of 29 studies comparing these two treatments. Studies are grouped according to methodology. Suggestions are made for the technique of administration of unilateral treatment.

12. **Strain, J.J., Brunschwig, L., Duffy, J.P., et al.** Comparison of therapeutic effects and memory changes with bilateral and unilateral ECT. Am. J. Psychiatry 125: 294–304, **1968.**

   One of the most methodologically sound comparisons of efficacy and side effects of these two treatments.

COMPLICATIONS AND SIDE EFFECTS

13. **Gerring, J.P. and Shields, H.M.** The identification and management of patients with a high risk for cardiac arrhythmias during modified ECT. J. Clin. Psychiatry 43: 140–143, **1982.**

   This report addresses the important issues of identification and management of high-risk cardiac patients during general anesthesia and electroshock therapy.

14. ***Squire, L.R. and Chase, P.M.** Memory functions six to nine months after electroconvulsive therapy. Arch. Gen. Psychiatry 32: 1557–1564, **1975.**

   Memory functions were tested six to nine months after either unilateral or bilateral ECT. Results were compared to those of a control group treated without ECT. Although no significant differences were found, patients receiving bilateral ECT were found to have more subjective memory complaints.

15. **Squire, L.R. and Slater, P.C.** Bilateral and unilateral ECT: Effects on verbal and nonverbal memory. Am. J. Psychiatry 135: 1316–1320, **1978.**

   Memory loss associated with bilateral and nondominant unilateral ECT was compared using memory tests differentially sensitive to left and right hemisphere dysfunction. Findings are discussed with recommendations for use of the two treatments.

PHYSIOLOGY AND MECHANISMS OF ACTION

16. **Abrams, R. and Taylor, M.A.** Diencenphalic stimulation and the effects of ECT in endogenous depression. Br. J. Psychiatry 129: 482–485, **1976.**

   An interesting study from a theoretical point of view. It compares standard bilateral ECT vs. simultaneous unilateral dominant and nondominant ECT. Results are discussed in terms of likely mechanisms of antidepressant action.

17.   ***Fink, M., Kety, S.S., McGaugh, J., et al., eds.** Psychobiology of Convulsive Therapy. Washington, D.C.: Winston, **1974.**

An excellent compendium of information on basic physiological and psychological aspects of effects of ECT in animals and man. Includes chapters on clinical behavioral and biochemical aspects of ECT.

18.   **Posner, J.B., Plum, F., and Van Poznak, A.** Cerebral metabolism during electrically induced seizures in man. Arch. Neurol. 20: 388–395, **1969.**

Older studies reporting brain damage in ECT patients usually were based on autopsy material from patients treated without hyperoxygenation and muscle relaxants. This study examined *in vivo* metabolic effects of ECT in humans treated according to modern standards.

PSYCHOSURGERY

See: Kalinowsky under "General Reviews and Monographs."

19.   **Greenblatt, M., Arnot, R., and Solomon, H.C.** Studies in Lobotomy. New York: Grune and Stratton, **1950.**

Careful psychological and sociological follow-up of 205 cases 1–4 years after surgery are presented.

20.   **Valenstein, E.S., ed.** The Psychosurgery Debate: Scientific, Legal and Ethical Perspectives. San Francisco: Freeman, **1980.**

Brings together a wide range of views written by medical, legal, and lay experts and critics with interests in psychosurgery. Includes medical aspects such as indications and outcome studies and ethical and legal questions pertaining to psychosurgical procedures. This volume is relatively balanced and moderate in tone in comparison to other more polemical monographs on the topic.

37. PSYCHOANALYTIC PSYCHOTHERAPY

Howard B. Levine, M.D.

The readings below have been chosen to address the pragmatic needs of the student therapist. They emphasize clinical theory rather than metapsychology and are organized around key concepts related to the process of therapy, the doctor-patient relationship, and psychotherapeutic technique. They cover such topics as resistance, transference, countertransference, therapeutic and working alliance, interventions, curative factors, the dynamics of the opening and termination phases, and the analysis of resistance, transference, and dreams. I have attempted to include articles that are classics, whose ideas travel well from psychoanalysis to psychotherapy, and in which the case material presented can serve as a model for psychotherapeutic technique. In addition, since there is often a preponderance of more disturbed patients in the caseloads of student therapists, I have cited a number of references that are specifically relevant to the understanding and treatment of psychotic, narcissistic, and borderline personalities. Above all, I have tried to select material that will bear rereading over time and that can serve not only as points of reference, but as points of departure for further discussion and exploration.

THEORETICAL PERSPECTIVES AND OVERVIEWS

1. ***Freud, A.** The Ego and the Mechanisms of Defense. New York: International Universities Press, **1936.** (Also, Vol. 2, The Writings of Anna Freud)

   A landmark contribution to ego psychology that remains as fresh, clear, and relevant to current psychotherapeutic practice as when it first appeared.

2. ***Schafer, R.** On becoming a psychoanalyst of one persuasion or another. Contemp. Psychoanal. 15: 345–360, **1979.** (Also, Chapter 17,

pp. 281–296, in Schafer, R., The Analytic Attitude. New York, Basic Books, **1983.**)

Although not strictly a paper on psychotherapy per se, no student should graduate from a training program without the benefit of reading this. Originally intended for a graduating class of psychoanalytic candidates, this article considers issues of orthodoxy and sectarianism in so thoughtful a way that the reader cannot help but come away from it feeling more open-minded, humble, and intellectually curious about the competing claims of the various schools and orientation of psychoanalysis and psychotherapy.

3.   ***Winnicott, D.W.** The Maturational Processes and the Facilitating Environment: Studies in the Theory of Emotional Development. New York: International Universities Press, **1965.**

A broad-ranging collection of papers that deals with issues of dependence, object relations theory, personality formation, and their implications for psychotherapy. Includes many thought-provoking, classic contributions that are particularly relevant to the treatment of primitive personality disorders. A must reading is "Hate in the Countertransference."

4.   ***Zetzel, E.R.** The Capacity for Emotional Growth. New York: International Universities Press, **1970.**

A major developmental and ego psychological contribution to a number of clinical and theoretical problems that lie at the heart of the therapeutic encounter. The essays on anxiety, depression, and doctor-patient relationship, transference, therapeutic alliance and the so-called good hysteric are classics in the field.

THE UNCONSCIOUS AND THE CONCEPT OF CONFLICT

5.   **Arlow, J.A.** Unconscious fantasy and disturbance of conscious experience. Psychoanal. Q. 38: 1–27, **1969.**

Discusses the structure, formation, and defensive function of unconscious fantasy as well as its relationship to metaphor, déja vu, depersonalization experiences, identity maintenance, self-representation, and the self. An excellent, experientially oriented, advanced paper on the unconscious.

6.   ***Deutsch, H.** (1930) The part of the actual conflict in the formation of neurosis, pp. 3–13. In: Neuroses and Character Types. Ed.: H. Deutsch. New York: International Universities Press, **1965.**

Examines the relationship between the actual (conscious, manifest) conflict in the patient's current reality and the underlying (unconscious, latent) conflicts from the patient's past. A very useful article for introducing the dynamic unconscious and the classical view of neurosis and for strengthening a beginning therapist's appreciation of the intrapsychic, subjective reality of their patients' experience.

7.   **Freud, S.** (1901) The forgetting of proper names and the forgetting of foreign words. Chapters 1 and 2 in The Psychopathology of Everyday Life. In: S.E. 6: 1–14, **1960.**

These two chapters illustrate the relationship between unconscious motivations, conflict, and repression ("forgetting"). They serve as a valuable introductory demonstration of unconscious mental processes, as well as an opportunity to introduce the concepts of associative links between chains of thought and psychic determination.

8.   **Freud, S.** (1909) Analysis of a phobia in a five-year-old boy. S.E. 10: 3–149, **1955.**

A delightful and engaging case history that acquaints students with the psychodynamics of neurosis, including sexual and aggressive wishes, the oedipus and castration complexes, mechanisms of defense, primary and secondary process modes of thought, and the relationship between conflict and symptom formation. It also illustrates an early use of child observation data to support inferences about unconscious mental processes derived from the clinical setting.

THE THERAPEUTIC RELATIONSHIP: TRANSFERENCE AND ALLIANCE

9.   ***Bird, B.** Notes on transference: Universal phenomenon and hardest part of analysis. J. Am. Psychoanal. Assoc. 20: 267–301, **1972.**

A profound essay on transference and transference neurosis, which considers the relationship of transference to ego functioning, reality, negative therapeutic reactions, and the psychoanalytic process.

10.   **Brenner, C.** Working alliance, therapeutic alliance, and transference. J. Am. Psychoanal. Assoc. 27 (Suppl.): 137–157, **1979.**

An exceptionally clear, well-reasoned paper that re-examines the original descriptions of the therapeutic and working alliance and attempts to demonstrate that they are not discrete entities, but simply aspects of the transference.

11.   **Corwin, H.A.** The narcissistic alliance and progressive transference neurosis in serious regressive states. Int. J. Psychoanal. Psychother. 3: 299–316, **1974.**

Explores the nature of the attachment that exists between nonclassically analyzable (borderline, narcissistic, and psychotic) patients and their therapists and how that attachment can be used to foster a workable treatment situation.

12.   ***Friedman, L.** The therapeutic alliance. Int. J. Psychoanal. 50: 139–153, **1969.**

A profound essay on the problems and sources of the patient's motivations for treatment. Includes a historical evaluation of the concept of the therapeutic alliance and its relationship to the transference.

13.   ***Gill, M.M.** Analysis of Transference, Vol. 1. Theory and Technique. New York: International Universities Press, **1982.**

Examines the evolution of the concept of the transference and critically reviews the literature on the relation of transference analysis to the theory of technique and therapeutic change.

14.   **Greenacre, P.** Certain technical problems in the transference relationship. J. Am. Psychoanal. Assoc. 7: 484–502, **1959.**

A classic essay concerning therapist activity, patient autonomy, and the impact of the reality situation on the balance between therapeutic alliance and transference.

15.   **Loewald, H.W.** The transference neurosis: Comments on the concept and the phenomenon. J. Am. Psychoanal. Assoc. 19: 54–66, **1971.** Also Chapter 17, pp. 302–314, in Loewald, H.W., Papers on Psychoanalysis. New Haven: Yale University Press, **1980.**

Re-examines the transference neurosis in the light of recent advances in ego psychology and the understanding of preoedipal development and character neuroses, emphasizing the creative, adaptive dimension to this phenomenon.

16.   **Oremland, J.D.** Transference cure and flight into health. Int. J. Psychoanal. Psychother. 1: 61–75, **1972.**

"Transference cure" and "flight into health" are defined, differentiated, and discussed in terms of their underlying dynamic motivations.

THE THERAPEUTIC RELATIONSHIP: COUNTERTRANSFERENCE

17.   **Adler, G.** Helplessness in the helpers. Br. J. Med. Psychol. 45: 315–326, **1972.**

Examines the vicissitudes of intense feelings of helplessness and hopelessness that are inevitably stirred up in therapists who work with patients with borderline, narcissistic, and other primitive personality disorders. Negative countertransference reactions stimulated by oral ambivalence and rage, defenses against such reactions, and their sources in the patient-therapist relationship are discussed.

18.   ***Maltsberger, J.J. and Buie, D.H.** Countertransference hate in the treatment of suicidal patients. Arch. Gen. Psychiatry 30: 625–633, **1974.**

An excellent clinical discussion of the various types of overt and defensively disguised angry and rejecting responses likely to be elicited in therapists by suicidal, sadomasochistic, borderline, and other hard-to-treat character-disordered patients.

19.   **Tower, L.E.** Countertransference. J. Am. Psychoanal. Assoc. 4: 224–255, **1956.**

A lucid discussion of countertransference and other affective responses of therapists, which the author believes are ubiquitous in treatment situations.

20.   **Wile, D.B.** Negative countertransference and therapist discouragement. Int. J. Psychoanal. Psychother. 1: 36–67, **1972.**

A clear and well-illustrated study of the relationship between negative countertransference reactions and discouragement in the therapist.

PSYCHOTHERAPEUTIC TECHNIQUE

21.   ***Bibring, E.** Psychoanalysis and the dynamic psychotherapies. J. Am. Psychoanal. Assoc. 2: 745–770, **1954.**

The classic description of the basic psychotherapeutic techniques—(1) suggestion, (2) abreaction, (3) manipulation, (4) clarification, and (5) interpretation—and their relation to the curative factors in psychoanalysis and psycyhotherapy.

22.   **Blanck, G. and Blanck, R.** Descriptive developmental diagnosis, pp. 91–118. In: Ego Psychology: Theory and Practice. Eds.: G. Blanck and R. Blanck. New York: Columbia University Press, **1974.**

This chapter attempts to address the problem of the relationship between traditional psychiatric classification and treatment by proposing a diagnostic scheme based on personality development. It is clinically illustrated, usefully addresses some therapeutic problems of the evaluation phase, and is especially helpful for introducing the concepts of "lines of development," "intact vs. modified ego," "ego distortion," "ego deviation," "ego defect," and "ego regression."

23.   **Fleming, J.** Early object deprivation and transference phenomena: The working alliance. Psychoanal. Q. 41: 23–49, **1972.**

Through a study of the therapeutic process in adults who experienced developmental disruptions due to object loss in childhood or adolescence, the author examines the persistence of immature ego organization into adult life and its implications for treatment.

24.   **Fleming, J.** Some observations on object constancy in the psychoanalysis of adults. J. Am. Psychoanal. Assoc. 23: 743–759, **1975.**

A masterful case presentation illustrating the application of Mahler's work on separation—individuation to psychotherapeutic technique.

25.   ***Freud, S.** (1911–1915) Papers on technique. S.E. 12: 85–173, **1958.**

This group of papers encompasses a wealth of clinical wisdom about many issues, including the interpretation of dreams, the beginning phase of treatment, transference, acting out, and the repetition compulsion.

26.   ***Greenson, R.R.** The Technique and Practice of Psychoanalysis. New York: International Universities Press, **1967.**

This is a marvelous source book on clinical technique that applies equally well to psychoanalytic psychotherapy as it does to psycho-analysis. The sections on the analysis of resistance, the working alliance, and the transference are clear, pragmatic, and abundantly illustrated.

27.   **Lichtenberg, J.D.** The empathic mode of perception and alternative vantage points for psychoanalytic work. Psychoanal. Inquiry 1: 329–355, **1981.**

An excellent, clinically illustrated account of empathy and its use as a tool for listening and understanding patients in psychotherapy.

28.   ***Myerson, P.G.** Issues of technique where patients relate with difficulty. Int. Rev. Psychoanal. 6: 363–375, **1979.**

A major contribution to the understanding of the therapeutic process in the treatment of patients with impaired capacities for object relations. Problems of the patient's unrelatedness to the analyst, unrealistic expectations of the analyst, and incapacity to understand interpretations and adopt a reflective stance are discussed in terms of technique and pathogenesis.

29.   **Wolf, E.** Ambience and abstinence. Annu. Psychoanal. 4: 101–115, **1976.**

Examines the consequences of misapplying Freud's "rule of abstinence" on the evolving ambience of the therapeutic situation, particularly in the treatment of neurotic patients with narcissistic defenses or patients with narcissistic personality disorders.

DREAMS AND DREAM ANALYSIS

30. **Blum, H.P.** The changing use of dreams in psychoanalytic practice: Dreams and free association. Int. J. Psychoanal. 57: 315–324, **1976.**

    Re-evaluates the clinical and technical importance of dream analysis in the light of contemporary ego psychology.

31. **Erikson, E.H.** The dream specimen of psychoanalysis. J. Am. Psychoanal. Assoc. 2: 5–56, **1954.**

    Erikson draws on biographical, cultural, and historical data relevant to Freud's life to brilliantly expand on the analysis of the famous Irma dream. The intimate connections between manifest dream content and the dreamer's creativity, conscience, stage of adult development, and identity maintenance are discussed.

32. **Freud, S.** (1900) The method of interpreting dreams: An analysis of a specimen dream. Chapter II, The Interpretation of Dreams, In: S.E. 4: 96–121, **1958.**

    Freud's *Interpretation of Dreams* remains one of his most profound and major contributions to psychological understanding. This section, which contains his analysis of the famous Irma dream also includes his analogy between the structure of the dream and the structure of the neurotic symptom and his famous pronouncement that the dream is a fulfillment of a wish.

33. ***Greenson, R.R.** The exceptional position of the dream in psychoanalytic practice. Psychoanal. Q. 39: 519–549, **1970.**

    Following Freud, Greenson argues that dreams possess a special proximity to childhood memories and affects in the unconscious. As such, their analysis offers both patient and therapist a unique, convincing, and immediate experience of access to the dreamer's unconscious mind and conflicts.

MASOCHISM AND NEGATIVE THERAPEUTIC REACTION

34. **Asch, S.S.** Varieties of negative therapeutic reaction and problems of technique. J. Am. Psychoanal. Assoc. 24: 383–407, **1976.**

Expands Freud's original descriptions of the negative therapeutic reaction to include contributions from difficulties in separation-individuation and offers recommendations for treatment.

35.   **Valenstein, A.F.** On attachment to painful feelings and the negative therapeutic reaction. Psychoanal. Study Child 28: 365–392, **1973.**

Explores issues of masochism and the negative therapeutic reaction in the light of early development and the persistence of residues of archaic ego states in adult patients.

PRIMITIVE PERSONALITY DISORDERS, SELF-PSYCHOLOGY, AND DISORDERS OF NARCISSISM

36.   **Bernstein, S.B.** Some psychoanalytic contributions to the understanding and treatment of patients with primitive personalities, pp. 74–117. In: Psychoanalysis: Critical Explorations in Contemporary Theory and Practice. Eds.: A. Jacobson and D. Parmelee. New York: Brunner/Mazel, **1982.**

A concise, thorough, and clinically illustrated review of contemporary psychoanalytic approaches to the understanding and treatment of borderline and narcissistic personality disorders, with particular emphasis on the contributions of Kernberg and Kohut.

37.   ***Buie, D.H. and Adler, G.** The uses of confrontation with borderline patients. Int. J. Psychoanal. Psychother. 1: 90–108, **1972.**

A succinct and lucid description of the subjective experiences of the borderline patient and the drives, defenses, and object needs that underlie these phenomena. Includes a useful description of the place of confrontation as a therapeutic technique.

38.   ***Kernberg, O.** Borderline Conditions and Pathological Narcissism. New York: Aronson, **1975.**

Several papers in this collection are classics that helped establish a standard in psychoanalytic thinking about the psychopathology and treatment of primitive personality disorders. In particular, the chapters on the borderline syndrome, its treatment and prognosis, and the treatment and clinical problems of the narcissistic personality disorder, which Kernberg views as a variant of the borderline personality, are of special relevance and value.

39.   ***Kohut, H.** The psychoanalytic treatment of narcissistic personality disorders: Outline of a systematic approach. Psychoanal. Study Child 23: 86–113, **1968.**

Introduces the concepts of the idealizing and mirror transferences, central to the clinical contribution of Kohut and the self-psychologists, and examines issues of technique, transference, and countertransference in the treatment of narcissism personality disorders.

40. **Kohut, H.** Thoughts on narcissism and narcissistic rage. Psychoanal. Study Child 27: 360–400, **1972.**

Examines manifestations of narcissistic rage in relation to problems in the vulnerability of underlying personality structures to narcissistic injury.

41. **Kohut, H.** The two analyses of Mr. Z. Int. J. Psychoanal. 60: 3–27, **1979.**

A landmark contribution illustrating Kohut's clinical position regarding the treatment of narcissistic personality disorders. It is very useful in helping to conceptualize the differences in formulation and technique that arise from a self-psychological, as opposed to a classical ego psychological, approach to patients.

42. **Levine, H.B.** Some implications of self psychology. Contemp. Psychoanal. 19: 153–171, **1983.**

Discusses clinical concepts embodied in Kohut's self-psychology that are generalizable to the practice of psychotherapy, including empathy, the self-object concept, the narcissistic (self-object) transferences, and the application of self-psychology to supportive psychotherapy.

43. **Masterson, J.F.** Psychotherapy of the Borderline Adult: A Developmental Approach. New York: Brunner/Mazel, **1976.**

A major contribution to the understanding and treatment of borderline patients that views the syndrome as originating in disturbed mother-child interactions during separation-individuation. Includes detailed treatment histories of reconstructive and supportive psychotherapies.

44. ***Modell, A.H.** A narcissistic defense against affects and the illusion of self-sufficiency. Int. J. Psychoanal. 56: 275–282, **1975.**

Conceptualizes the central problem in narcissistic personality disorders as a pseudoindependent defensive stance vis-à-vis later relationships, which stems from various forms of early object disturbance and gives rise to a pathognomonic transference relationship, "the cocoon transference," based on the defense of affect blocking.

45. **Modell, A.H.** "The holding environment" and the therapeutic action of psychoanalysis. J. Am. Psychoanal. Assoc. 24: 285–307, **1976.**

The function of the analytic situation as "holding environment" is contrasted in the treatment of neurotic and narcissistic personality disorders.

46.   **Reich, A.** Pathologic forms of self-esteem regulation. Psychoanal. Study Child 15: 215–232, **1960.**

A classic, ego psychoanalytic contribution to problems of self-esteem regulation. Raises crucial questions concerning the places of aggression, pregenital trauma, and concerns about annihilation and bodily intactness in the pathogenesis of narcissistic imbalances.

47.   **Stolorow, R.D. and Lachmann, F.M.** Psychoanalysis of Developmental Arrests: Theory and Treatment. New York: International Universities Press, **1980.**

An innovative book that explores and contrasts preoedipal pathologic formations that arise from conflict with those that arise from developmental arrest.

48.   **Tolpin, M.** Self-objects and oedipal objects. A crucial developmental distinction. Psychoanal. Study Child 33: 167–184, **1978.**

Draws the distinction between self-objects and oedipal objects that is so crucial to an understanding of self-psychology and examines various manifestations of self-object phenomena in the clinical setting.

49.   **Volkan, V.D.** Primitive Internalized Object Relations: A Clinical Study of Schizophrenic, Borderline and Narcissistic Patients. New York: International Universities Press, **1976.**

An excellent clinical contribution to the psychoanalytic psychotherapy of schizophrenic, borderline, and narcissistic patients. Of particular merit are the chapters illustrating transitional objects, the use of real relationships as substitutes for internal psychic structure, and the mechanism of structural change in psychotherapy. Also provides useful discussions and illustrations of the work of Kernberg, Winnicott, and Strachey.

THE PSYCHOTHERAPEUTIC PROCESS (INCLUDING OPENING PHASE AND TERMINATION)

50.   **Dewald, P.A.** The therapeutic process: Termination, pp. 273–292. In: Psychotherapy: A Dynamic Approach (2nd ed.). New York: Basic Books, **1971.**

A valuable introduction to the termination phase in both insight-oriented and supportive psychotherapies. Includes discussions of the termination of unsuccessful, as well as successful, treatments and the appropriate tactics and strategies to be employed in various situations.

51. **Firestein, S.K.** Termination of psychoanalysis of adults: A review of the literature. J. Am. Psychoanal. Assoc. 22: 873–894, **1974.**

Summarizes indications for termination, issues of technique, and the justification for designating termination as a separate and distinct phase of treatment.

52. **Langs, R.** The framework for understanding the communications from patients in psychotherapy, pp. 279–326. In: The Technique of Psychoanalytic Psychotherapy, Vol. 1. New York: Aronson, **1973.**

An elegant conceptual framework for listening to and understanding the structure of a psychotherapy session, in terms of manifest and latent content and its important roots in the adaptive stresses presented by the patients' current life experiences, especially the therapeutic relationship.

53. ***Loewald, H.W.** The waning of the oedipus complex. J. Am. Psychoanal. Assoc. 27: 751–775, **1979.** Also Chapter 23, pp. 384–404 in Loewald, H.W., Papers on Psychoanalysis, op. cit.

A masterful essay on the place of the oedipus complex in contemporary psychoanalytic practice and theory.

54. **Stone, L.** The Psychoanalytic Situation. An Examination of its Developmental and Essential Nature. New York: International Universities Press, **1961.**

Explores the affective essence of the psychoanalytic relationship by examining the tensions inherent in the basic emotional ties existing between patient and analyst and the psychobiological developmental structures that underlie them.

CURATIVE FACTORS IN PSYCHOTHERAPY AND PSYCHOANALYSIS

55. **Alexander, F.** The principle of flexibility and the principle of corrective emotional experience, pp. 25–70. In: Psychoanalytic Therapy: Principles and Application. Eds.: F. Alexander and T. French. New York: Ronald Press, **1946.**

Alexander's attempts to shorten analytic treatment through the use of active role playing techniques designed to counterbalance patients' early pathogenic object relations remains the *bête noir* of contemporary psychoanalytic clinical theory and should be read as an important point of contrast and departure for understanding the theory of how analysis produces change.

56.   **Dewald, P.A.** The process of change in psychoanalytic psychotherapy. Arch. Gen. Psychiatry 35: 535–542, **1978.**

Describes the emotional responses of patients in psychoanalytic psychotherapy and their relation to the changes that occur. Concepts of "core" and "derivative" psychic conflicts and functions are discussed and used to contrast psychoanalysis and psychotherapy.

57.   ***Loewald, H.W.** On the therapeutic action of psychoanalysis. Int. J. Psychoanal. 41: 16–33, **1960.** Also chapter 14, pp. 221–254 in Loewald, H.W. Papers on Psychoanalysis, op. cit.

A classic formulation of the therapeutic action of psychoanalysis as arising from the integrative impact of the therapeutic relationship. Draws a parallel between the treatment process and the early mother-child relationship.

58.   ***Strachey, J.** The nature of the therapeutic action of psychoanalysis. Int. J. Psychoanal. 15: 127–159, **1934.**

The classic statement of how psychoanalytic treatment produces change. Strachey's description of the dynamics of the mutative transference interpretation remains the benchmark of the theories of technique and therapeutic factors in psychoanalysis.

38. CLIENT-CENTERED EXPERIENTIAL PSYCHOTHERAPY

PHILIPPA MATHIEU-COUGHLAN, PH.D.

Carl Rogers's contributions to the disciplines of psychology, psychiatry, and education have been extensive and significant. For example, he was the first to use tape recordings to study systematically the process of psychotherapy; he was the first to study comparatively the process of psychotherapy with normals, neurotics, and schizophrenics; he was the only psychotherapy theorist-researcher to have developed a theory of the normal personality that could serve as a therapy outcome criterion; he initiated basic encounter groups; and he founded the so-called human potential movement. It is not so surprising, therefore, that in a career that has spanned 50 years and has in-depth involvement in so many areas, Rogers would have a publication and presentation roster in excess of 1,000 titles. It has been through these writings and his personal accessibility that he has influenced thousands of clinicians, researchers, and theorists.

The following selections provide the reader with a grasp of Rogers's basic model of client-centered therapy and of the developments that have taken place within the theory. The approach to therapy is known as client-centered, and this accurately reflects Rogers's belief that the term "client," rather than "patient," more accurately describes the reciprocal interaction of good psychotherapy, where it is the client who determines the focus for therapeutic exploration. These citations will also introduce the evolving existential focus that has been theoretically developed with Rogers's endorsement by Dr. Eugene Gendlin, a colleague of Rogers. Landmark research studies and research instruments based in the theory are also included.

1. *Gendlin, E.T. Therapeutic procedures in dealing with schizophrenics, pp. 369–400. In: The Therapeutic Relationship and Its Impact. Ed.: Carl R. Rogers. Madison, WI: University of Wisconsin Press, 1967. (Reprint available, Greenwood, 1976.)

303

This chapter describes effective methods of working with particularly difficult patients. A rich array of therapist options is presented in the context of the "experiential" method, which is central to client-centered therapy. Close attention is paid to the therapist as a person, to his/her responsibilities, perceptions, and self-monitoring.

2. **Gendlin, E.T.** Values and the process of experiencing, pp. 180–205. In: The Goals of Psychotherapy. Ed.: R. Mahrer. New York: Appleton-Century-Crofts, **1967.**

This is a key theoretical and clinical statement. Gendlin provides a basis for the specific ways that a therapist should "be" in order to enhance the client's experiential focus. The interactional process is viewed as much from the therapist's role as from the client's; specific examples are given.

3. **Gendlin, E.T.** The role of knowledge in practice, pp. 266–294. In: The Counselor's Handbook. Eds.: G.F. Farwell, N.R. Gamsky, and P. Mathieu-Coughlan. New York: Intext Educational Publishers, **1974.**

In this chapter Gendlin stresses that theoretical conceptions, formulations, and external information should be subordinated to the primary task of listening and attending to what the client is saying.

4. ***Gendlin, E.T.** Experiential psychotherapy, pp. 317–352. In: Current Psychotherapies (2nd ed.). Ed.: R. Corsini. Itasca, IL: Peacock, **1979.**

This current statement of the experiential/client-centered paradigm is particularly valuable for the conceptualization and practice of therapy within this model. The role of the therapist is discussed as the teacher of experiential focusing and the one who draws the client forward in this process forward a "felt shift" and then resolution. A clear and precise article.

5. **Klein, M.H., Mathieu-Coughlan, P., Gendlin, E.T., et al.** The Experiencing Scale: A Research and Training Manual. Madison, WI: University of Wisconsin Extension Bureau of Audiovisual Instruction. Published, **1969** (Copyright, **1970**).

This seven-stage scale, developed from both Rogers and Gendlin's theoretical work on the experiential component, measures the quality of a person's participation in therapy, that is, the extent to which inner referents become the felt datum of attention, and the presence of efforts to focus on, expand and probe that datum. The scale has been used as a research tool and also as a teaching method for increasing therapists' sensitivity.

6. ***Mathieu-Coughlan, P. and Klein, M.H.** Experiential psychotherapy: Key events in client-therapist interaction. In: Patterns of Change:

Intensive Analysis of Psychotherapy Process. Eds.: L.S. Greenberg and L.N. Rice. New York: Guilford Press, **1983** (in press).

This article draws heavily on research findings and theory to provide an understanding of the key events in experiential/client-centered psychotherapy. The exact process stages and transitions for the patient and the therapist are discussed and illustrated. The Therapist Experiencing Scale is presented for the first time.

7.   **Meador, B. and Rogers, C.R.** Client centered therapy, pp. 119–165. In: Current psychotherapies (2nd ed.). Ed.: R. Corsini. Itasca, IL: Peacock, **1979.**

The most recent and comprehensive integration of the clinical and theoretical status of the client-centered model. Valuable case study material and comments are presented.

8.   **Rogers, C.R. and Dymond, R.F.** Psychotherapy and personality change. Chicago, IL: University of Chicago Press, **1954.**

This is a landmark psychotherapy study in that it was the first research to make use of adequate methodology, instrumentation, and controls. It represents a decade of research and the culmination of critical thinking in the client-centered school at the time.

9.   ***Rogers, C.R.** A theory of therapy, personality, and interpersonal relationships, as developed by the client-centered framework, pp. 184–256. In: Psychology: A Study of a Science: Formulations of the Person and the Social Context, Vol. 3. Ed.: S. Koch. New York: McGraw-Hill, **1959.**

This is the classic exposition of Rogers's theory of therapy and of personality. The concepts of the therapist's conditions and of the fully functioning normal personality are explained. The therapeutic relationship is viewed as a possible model for more broadly defined interpersonal relationships.

39. JUNGIAN PSYCHOTHERAPY

JEFFREY SATINOVER, M.D.

It has been 70 years since Jung broke from Freud and set out to establish his own approach to psychoanalysis. In that time, and until only very recently, the development of Jungian psychotherapy has proceeded exclusively along lines laid down by Jung, in isolation from the great controversies that have altered the psychiatric, psychotherapeutic, and psychoanalytic communities. That isolation has been precious—in both senses of the word. On the one hand, in the Jungian literature here annotated, the reader will find addressed few of the important questions that currently divide psychiatric thinking. On the other hand, the Jungian literature provides an approach to the psyche so strikingly original that it will appear for the most part both alien and hauntingly familiar, in the way that sometimes we suddenly better grasp our own self by seeing it mirrored in the actions of another, or another culture.

Of late, there has been an upsurge of interest in Jung. There are probably many reasons for this, but one in particular is the growing interest in, and perhaps number of, narcissistic personalities. Jung's approach to the psyche may be thought of as an early, highly intuitive investigation of narcissism (though he didn't call it that), somewhat narcissistic in character itself.

Jung's genius was thus not that of the careful, systematic investigator. He was rather a visionary whose view of the psychic world is as if from the peak of a mountain: broad patterns of existence not seen from the valley of quotidian life are revealed to his eye, but the details that compose the pattern are sometimes lost.

The careful student of Jung and of his followers will therefore be aided in acquiring two important skills:

1. an understanding of narcissism; specifically, a view of so-called "healthy narcissism," of how the process of self-development, and its distortion, is reflected in symbolic imagery from the individual and the culture.
2. more generally, the capacity to intuitively grasp psychodynamic *Gestalten* on the basis of the usually fragmentary symbolic productions of patients.

What the reader will not find is a careful, step-by-step description of the conduct of Jungian analysis. Such a description does not really exist; in practice there are myriad approaches.

The ideal reader of Jung is therefore someone who has, or will have, acquired a familiarity with the practice of psychotherapy, but who is sensitive to and still puzzled about how disruptions in a sense of larger meaning and personal wholeness contribute to mental illness.

1. ***Frey-Rohn, L.** From Freud to Jung: A Comparative Study of the Unconscious. New York: Putnam (for the C.G. Jung Foundation), **1974.**

2. **Glover, E.** Freud or Jung? London: George Allen and Unwin, **1950.**

    There exist few comparisons of Jungian and classical psychoanalytic theory. Edward Glover's polemic against Jung could be read profitably alongside Frey's oppositely partisan, but more scholarly, appraisal.

3. ***Focus on Narcissism. Schwartz, N.** Narcissism and narcissistic character disorders: A Jungian view, pp. 4–45; **Kalsched, D.** Narcissism and the search for interiority. pp. 46–74; **Satinover, J.** Puer Aeternus: The narcissistic relation to the self. pp. 77–108. In: Quadrant 13: 2, **1980.**

    Three of the four articles in this issue of the most widely read American Jungian journal address the nature and treatment of the narcissistic disturbances. They are each from rather different perspectives and are a good cross-section of Jungian thought since Jung.

4. **Jung, C.G.** The Archetypes of the Collective Unconscious. (2nd ed.), Vol. 9. The Collected Works of C.G. Jung. Princeton: Bollingen Series/Princeton University Press, **1969.**

    Jung is most well known for his hypothesis of the "archetype." Essays written prior to these propose and defend the notion; this volume presumes it and proceeds to elucidate the phenomenology of a small number of important archetypes. The volume sketches in the characteristics and dynamics of the personality traits to which each of these archetypes gives rise.

5. ***Jung, C.G.** Man and His Symbols. With contributions by M.L. von Franz, J. Henderson, J. Jacobi and A. Jaffe. New York: Doubleday, **1964.**

    This collection of essays by Jung and a number of his students is the clearest and most concise English-language survey of the domain of Jungian psychology. Perhaps because it was one of the few pieces he wrote exclusively for a lay readership, Jung's own contribution is a particularly lucid account of his notion of the "archetype."

6. ***Jung, C.G.** Memories, Dreams and Reflection. New York: Pantheon, **1963.**

Written a few years before his death at 86, Jung's autobiography is a fascinating glimpse into the inner workings of an astonishingly complex and original mind. To his followers, it is a prime instance of the "individuation process." Jung uses his autobiography to discuss many of his key concepts, perhaps because, to an unusual degree, these concepts played a role in the stabilizing and development of his personality.

7. **Jung, C.G.** Psychology and religion. pp. 3–106. In: Psychology and Religion. Vol. 11. The Collected Works of C.G. Jung. Princeton: Bollingen Series/Princeton University Press, **1958.**

In these Terry Lectures at Yale in 1937, Jung uses the carefully noted dreams of a Nobel laureate in physics to demonstrate the spontaneous emergence of symbols analogous to archaic religious thought and to discuss the relevance of this kind of symbolism to the maturation of personality.

8. **Jung, C.G.** Two Essays in Analytical Psychology (2nd ed.), Vol. 7. The Collected Works of C.G. Jung. Princeton: Bollingen Series/Princeton University Press, **1966.**

These two essays were written by Jung after his break from Freud, but prior to the expansion of his interests into more esoteric realms. They summarize Jung's alternate approach to a psychology of the unconscious.

9. ***Neumann, E.** The Origins and History of Consciousness. Princeton: Bollingen Series/Princeton University Press, **1970.**

By Jung's most brilliant pupil, *Origins* is an ambitious attempt to collate the major themes of world mythology into a unified, stadial schema. Neumann then uses this schema to analyze both the development of the ego and the evolution of culture. As a psychosocial version of "ontogeny recapitulates phylogeny," the attempt is only partially successful; as a demonstration of how cultural myth and individual self-representation reflect each other, it is a *tour de force.*

40. COGNITIVE PSYCHOTHERAPY

Aaron T. Beck, M.D.

The readings provide a comprehensive introduction to the therapy and practice of cognitive therapy. Cognitive psychotherapy is an active, time-limited, structured approach used to treat a variety of psychiatric problems (e.g., depression, anxiety, phobias, etc.). It is based on the assumption that an individual's affect and behavior are largely determined by the way in which he structures the world. The thesis of this therapy is that emotional disorders are related to cognitive distortions or systematic errors in thinking. For example, the depressed patient's thinking is dominated by a negative view of himself, his experiences, and his future that is maintained by errors in the way he infers, recollects, and generalizes information.

A variety of cognitive and behavioral strategies are utilized in cognitive therapy. The cognitive techniques are aimed at delineating and testing the individual's specific misconceptions and maladaptive assumptions. This approach consists of highly specific learning experiences designed to teach the patient the following operations: (1) to monitor his negative or distorted thoughts; (2) to recognize the connection between cognition, affect, and behavior; (3) to examine the evidence for and against his distorted thoughts; (4) to substitute more reality-oriented interpretations for these biased cognitions; and (5) to learn to identify and alter the dysfunctional beliefs that predispose him to distort his experiences. The therapy focuses on specific "target symptoms" (for example, suicidal impulses). The cognitions supporting these symptoms are identified (for example, "My life is worthless and I can't change it.") and then subjected to logical and empirical investigation.

In addition to texts that provide a clear account of the above outlined cognitive theory and treatment procedures, the bibliography includes readings on the application of cognitive therapy to suicide, depression, anxiety, loneliness, and stress as well as readings comparing cognitive psychotherapy to pharmacotherapy and behavior therapy.

1. **Beck, A.T.** Cognitive approaches to stress. In: Clinical Guide to Stress Management. Eds.: C. Lehrer and R.L. Woolfolk. New York Guilford Press, **1984** (in press).

An excellent, comprehensive chapter for theoretical understanding and practical management of stress. Beck conceptualizes a clinical case in terms of the outlined principles and uses it to illustrate specific therapeutic strategies and techniques.

2. *Beck, A.T. Cognitive Therapy and the Emotional Disorders. New York: International Universities Press, 1976.

This clear, comprehensive text presents a broad extension of the cognitive model to each of the neuroses (i.e., depression, anxiety, phobia, obsession, and psychosomatic disorders). It outlines the specific cognitive aberrations in each of the neuroses and specific procedures for treatment.

3. Beck, A.T. Cognitive therapy: Nature and relation to behavior therapy. Behav. Ther. 1: 184–200, 1970.

Describes basic techniques of cognitive therapy and compares and contrasts it with behavior therapy. Beck suggests that the cognitive model not only provides a greater range of concepts for explaining psychopathology and therapeutic processes, but also provides a framework for developing new intervention strategies.

4. Beck, A.T. Depression: Clinical, Experimental, and Theoretical Aspects. New York: Hoeber, 1967. (Republished as Depression: Causes and Treatment. Philadelphia: University of Pennsylvania Press, 1972.)

Widely acknowledged as a major contribution to the psychiatric literature, this volume summarizes the early evolution of the cognitive model and cognitive therapy of depression and other neuroses. It provides both a theoretical and practical understanding of depression.

5. Beck, A.T., Kovacs, M., and Weissman, A. Assessment of suicidal intention: The scale for suicide ideation. J. Consult. Clin. Psychol. 47: 343–352, 1979.

This important article describes the rationale, development, and validation of the Scale for Suicide Ideation, a 19-item clinical research instrument designed to quantify and assess suicidal intention. Additionally, the scale is a valuable tool in the investigation of the correlates of suicide ideation and as a measure of treatment outcome.

6. Beck, A.T. and Rush, A.J. A cognitive model of anxiety formation and anxiety resolution, pp. 69–80. In: Stress and Anxiety, Vol. 2. Eds.: I.G. Sarason and C.D. Spielberger. Washington: Hemisphere Publishing, 1975.

A concise chapter examining the role of cognitions and imagery in individuals with anxiety and phobic neuroses. It compares and contrasts the cognitions of patients with anxiety and phobias and accounts for the greater functional impairment of the anxiety patient in terms of these cognitive differences. A course of treatment outline is then presented.

7. ***Beck, A.T., Rush, A.J., Shaw, B.F., et al.** Cognitive Therapy of Depression. New York: Guilford, **1979.**

An excellent practical guide to the cognitive-behavioral treatment of depression. The text provides a clear account of cognitive procedures and is filled with protocols that illustrate specific techniques.

8. **Harrison, R. and Beck, A.T.** Cognitive therapy of depression. In: Innovations in Clinical Practice. Ed.: P. Keller. Sarasota, FL: Professional Resource Exchange, **1982.**

Provides concise overview of the history, rationale, techniques, and latest conceptualizations of the cognitive therapy of depression.

9. **Kovacs, M., Rush, A.J., Beck, A.T., et al.** Depressed outpatients treated with cognitive therapy or pharmacotherapy: A one-year follow-up. Arch. Gen. Psychiatry 38: 33–39, **1981.**

A one-year naturalistic follow-up of the patients who participated in the Rush et al., study. It reveals that although both treatment groups remained generally well, self-rated depressive symptomology was significantly lower for the cognitive therapy than for the drug treatment group. The results are especially important in light of depressed patients who cannot be treated with or will not accept tricyclic antidepressant medication.

10. **Rush, A.J., Beck, A.T., Kovacs, M., et al.** Comparative efficacy of cognitive therapy and pharmacotherapy in the treatment of depressed outpatients. Cog. Ther. Res. 1: 17–37, **1977.**

One of the first studies to confirm that a nonsomatic intervention is efficacious in the symptomatic relief of depression. Using a controlled clinical trial format, 41 unipolar depressed outpatients were randomly assigned to treatment with cognitive therapy or imipramine over a 12-week period. Although both groups improved, the cognitive therapy patients showed greater symptomatic improvement and a lower relapse rate.

11. **Rush, A.J., Hollon, S.D., Beck, A.T., et al.** Depression: Must pharmacotherapy fail for cognitive therapy to succeed? Cog. Ther. Res. 2: 199–206, **1978.**

In this article a reply is made to criticism voiced by Becker and Schuckit

("Cognitive Therapy and Research," 2: 193–197, 1978) about the comparison of cognitive therapy with imipramine in the treatment of outpatients with unipolar depression. Becker and Schuckit contend that the study was biased against the pharmacotherapy treatment group. Using evidence from past research and further analysis of their data, Rush et al., convincingly reply to this concern.

12.   **Sacco, W.P.** Cognitive therapy in vivo, pp. 271–287. In: New Directions in Cognitive Therapy. Eds.: G. Emery, S.D. Hollon and R.C. Bedrosian. New York: Guilford Press, **1981.**

Sacco describes how cognitive therapy *in vivo* may be used to aid patients in transferring learned concepts and skills to their everyday environment and outlines strategies for dealing with potential problems in applying cognitive therapy *in vivo.*

13.   **Young, J.E.** Cognitive therapy and loneliness, pp. 139–159. In: New Directions in Cognitive Therapy. Eds.: G. Emery, S.D. Hollon and R.C. Bedrosian. New York: Guilford Press, **1981.**

Young outlines a comprehensive psychotherapy for the treatment of loneliness. He describes seven stages of treatment and for each stage elaborates specific dysfunctional cognitions and behaviors that hamper the attainment of the stated goals. He presents a case for illustration.

41. BRIEF PSYCHOTHERAPY

William H. Sledge, M.D.

Although born in part out of impatience with the duration and costs of conventional psychoanalysis and the administrative attempts to solve the problems of oversubscription of psychotherapeutic services in public institutions, the brief psychotherapies have become established because of their proven effectiveness, their cost-benefit advantages, public interest, and research advantages. Brief therapy is an area of active development and evolution, and it would be premature to give an exact definition. For our purposes, brief treatment is psychological treatment in which therapist and patient agree at the onset that treatment will have a limited duration, usually less than 40 sessions. Brief treatment here is distinguished from crisis intervention in that crisis intervention usually has the focus on a specific stressor(s) and the orientation toward support and adaptation. Brief treatment usually deals with more subacute problems and has the orientation toward personality integration and development. Emergency and crisis treatment are addressed elsewhere in this volume (see Chapter 42).

Brief treatment forms characteristically address indications for the selection of patients and technical procedures for the conduct of the therapy. Usually, technically there is an early narrowing of a content focus and a more active and earlier deployment of the therapist's executive function. Individual brief treatment can be divided into "dynamic" forms that rely heavily on psychoanalytic theory and practice. The work of Balint, Davanloo, Malan, Mann, and Sifneos are psychoanalytically derived forms of brief treatment that, while differing from one another along the structures of selection of patients and techniques, resemble one another in their use of interpretation and the centrality of the therapist-patient relationship. Other forms of individual brief treatment include cognitive psychotherapy and behavioral therapy.

For the purposes of this bibliography, I have divided the annotations into overview; dynamic individual; other individual; group and marital; and miscellaneous. The *overview* section includes references that examine broad topics (such as the choice of particular forms of brief treatment) or are of historical interest. The *dynamic individual* section introduces the major

313

schools as developed by Balint, Davanloo, Malan, Mann, and Sifneos. The *other individual* section contains references to cognitive therapy and behavior therapy, which are addressed in more depth in other sections of this book. The brief *group and marital therapy* literature is much less rich and well defined than the literature addressing the individual dynamic therapy, but some representative work in this areas is included. The *miscellaneous* section addresses some research findings, teaching of brief treatment, and ultrabrief treatment.

OVERVIEW

1. **Alexander, F. and French, T.M.** Psychoanalytic Therapy: Principles and Applications. New York: Ronald Press, **1946.**

   Included primarily for its historical place, this work nevertheless has some interesting modern "pearls." They advocate flexibility, planning (setting a contract), an active therapist with a focal orientation, and the controversial idea of "corrective emotional reaction." This work still has much to tell us.

2. **Clarkin, J.F. and Frances, A.** Selection criteria for the brief psychotherapies. Am. J. Psychother. 36: 166–180, **1982.**

   A practical, clinically oriented guide to indications, patient-enabling factors, and contraindications for crisis intervention, long-term versus brief psychotherapy, and forms of brief psychotherapy (dynamic, problem-solving, marital/family, and behavioral).

3. **Eisenstein, S.** The contributions of Franz Alexander, pp. 25–41. In: Short-Term Dynamic Psychotherapy. Ed.: H. Davanloo. New York: Aronson, **1980.**

   An overview of the work of Alexander as it relates to present efforts to formulate and establish brief treatment.

4. **Freud, S.** (1937). Analysis terminable and interminable. S.E. 23: 216–253, **1964.**

   Included here for its emphasis and warning about factors that limit the effect of psychoanalysis and by extension other forms of psychological treatment. Although he inveighs against attempts to limit the duration of treatment, he also gives provocative indications for considering shortened treatment as the more desirable choice and suggests by implication what kinds of factors effective brief treatment must consider.

5. **Marmor, J.** Short-term dynamic psychotherapy. Am. J. Psychiatry 136: 149–155, **1970.**

An overview, it gives a historical background that emphasizes the contribution of Ferenzci and Rank, and Alexander and French as well as an account of modern short-term treatments and the substructures of selection and technique. Marmor explores the features common to modern schools of short-term treatment.

6. **Pardes, H. and Pincus, H.A.** Brief therapy in the context of national mental health issues, p. 7–22. In: Forms of Brief Therapy. Ed.: S.H. Budman. New York: Guilford Press, **1981.**

A summary of some of the historical and present social forces that contribute to the recent increased interest in brief treatment. Also presented is a rationale for brief treatment.

7. **Strupp, H.H.** Toward the refinement of time-limited dynamic psychotherapy, pp. 219–242. In: Forms of Brief Therapy. Ed.: S.H. Budman. New York: Guilford Press, **1981.**

An overview of the critical elements of a successful brief treatment, this paper addresses the selection of patients and technical aspects as well as the influence of the personality of the therapist and the integration of technique with the therapist's personality.

8. ***White, H.S., Burke, J.D. Jr., and Havens, L.L.*** Choosing a method of short-term therapy: A developmental approach, pp. 243–267. In: Forms of Brief Therapy. Ed.: S.H. Budman. New York: Guilford Press, **1981.**

9. **Burke, J.D., White, H.S., and Havens, L.L.** Which short-term therapy? Matching patient and method. Arch. Gen. Psychiatry 36: 177–186, **1979.**

These two very similar papers (the White et al., enjoys the advantage of being more recent) explore the hypothesis that different schools of individual brief therapy are more suitable for different developmental issues. They advocate that patients and treatments should be matched accordingly.

DYNAMIC INDIVIDUAL BRIEF PSYCHOTHERAPY

10. ***Balint, M., Ornstein, P.H., and Balint, E.*** Focal Psychotherapy: An Example of Applied Psychoanalysis. London: Tavistock Publications, **1972.**

A brilliant account of Michael Balint's successful "focal psychotherapy" of a severely disturbed individual. This is an excellent, phenomeno-logically oriented study that stays close to the clinical material.

11. **Bellak, L. and Small, L.** Emergency Psychotherapy and Brief Psycho-therapy (2nd ed.). New York: Grune and Stratton, **1978.**

A "how-to-do-it" book that gives a five-session version of brief treatment related closely to Bellak's ego-function assessment scale; it also explores the relationship with emergency psychotherapy and gives useful hints for a variety of specific situations, including depression, panic, depersonalization, incipient and acute psychotic states, acting out, severe somatic disorders, sex therapies, old age, critical life situations, and extrinsic traumata.

12. ***Davanloo, H.** A method of short-term dynamic psychotherapy, pp. 43–71. In: Short-term Dynamic Psychotherapy. Ed.: H. Davanloo. New York: Aronson, **1980.**

13. **Davanloo, H.** Techniques of short-term dynamic psychotherapy. Psychiatr. Clinics N.A. 2: (1) 11–22, **1979.**

Overviews of the author's method of broad-focused, short-term dynamic psychotherapy with a general account of the organizing conception, selection of patients, and techniques (with some examples). In the Davanloo-edited book there are more chapters expanding his account of his method.

14. ***Gustafson, J.P.** The complex secret of brief psychotherapy in the works of Malan and Balint, pp. 83–128. In: Forms of Brief Therapy. Ed.: S.H. Budman. New York: Guilford Press, **1981.**

A review of Malan and Balint's different contributions to the "science of brief treatment" with an original contribution of its own in the form of a hypothesis about the nature of interventions, particularly in reference to the control-mastery theory of Sampson and Weiss.

15. **Malan, D.H.** A Study of Brief Psychotherapy. Springfield, IL: Thomas, **1963.**

A retrospective study that demonstrated stable and enduring change could be effected with brief therapy even with moderately disturbed patients.

16. **Malan, D.H.** Individual Psychotherapy and the Science of Psycho-dynamics. London: Butterworth, **1979.**

An account of psychotherapy that advocates the centrality of brief therapy in demonstrating the basic principles of psychodynamic knowledge.

17. ***Mann, J.** Time-Limited Psychotherapy. Cambridge: Harvard University Press, **1973.**

18. **Mann, J.** The core of time-limited psychotherapy: Time and the central issue, pp. 25–43. In: Forms of Brief Therapy. Ed.: S.H. Budman. New York: Guilford Press, **1981.**

Mann's book gives a full account of his method with an articulate and elegant exposition of the role of time and the predetermined termination date. It also includes session-by-session transcripts of a case treated in this fashion. The paper is an up-to-date overview with a further elaboration of the role of time and setting the central focus that enjoys the benefit of almost a decade more of experience for the author.

19. **Schafer, R.** The termination of brief psychoanalytic psychotherapy. Int. J. Psychoanal. Psychother. 2: 135–148, **1973.**

An account of the psychotherapeutic process and its relationship to termination, particularly in brief therapy. Schafer highlights the role of reduction of discontinuities; the development of self-knowledge, and his view of psychotherapy as a "historical" process.

20. **Sifneos, P.E.** Short-term Psychotherapy and Emotional Crisis. Cambridge: Harvard University Press, **1972.**

21. **Sifneos, P.E.** Short-term Dynamic Psychotherapy. New York: Plenum Press, **1979.**

His initial statement (1972), which goes into more depth about short-term anxiety-provoking psychotherapy, and a follow-up account (1979).

22. ***Sifneos, P.E.** Short-term anxiety provoking psychotherapy: Its history, techniques, outcome and instruction, pp. 45–81. In: Forms of Brief Therapy. Ed.: S.H. Budman. New York: Guilford Press, **1981.**

An interesting demonstration of the techniques of short-term anxiety-provoking psychotherapy through presentation of transcripts of two sessions. A good introduction.

OTHER FORMS OF INDIVIDUAL BRIEF PSYCHOTHERAPY

23. **Beck, A.T. and Greenberg, R.L.** Brief cognitive therapies. Psychiatr. Clinics N.A. 2: (1) 23–27, **1979.**

A summary overview of cognitive therapy as brief therapy.

24. **Wilson, G.T.** Behavior therapy as a short-term therapeutic approach,

pp. 131–166. In: Forms of Brief Therapy. Ed.: S.H. Budman. New York: Guilford Press, **1981.**

A review of the literature that also comprehensively reviews the conditions treated with behavior therapy, the treatment formats, and the evaluations of outcome.

GROUP AND MARITAL BRIEF THERAPY

25. **Brown, S.L.** Dynamic family therapy, pp. 193–206. In: Short-term Dynamic Psychotherapy. Ed.: H. Davanloo. New York: Aronson, **1980.**

An account of a brief family treatment with some generalized applied principles of brief family therapy.

26. **Budman, S.H., Bennett, M.J., and Wisneski, M.J.** An adult developmental model of short-term group psychotherapy, pp. 305–342. In: Forms of Brief Therapy. Ed.: S.H. Budman. New York: Guilford Press, **1981.**

A comprehensive account of several types of brief group psychotherapy based on an adult developmental model. Good review of the literature.

27. **Gurman, A.S.** Integrative marital therapy: Toward the development of an interpersonal approach, pp. 415–457. In: Forms of Brief Therapy. Ed.: S.H. Budman. New York: Guilford Press, **1981.**

A fine paper that argues that for marital therapy to be brief it must simultaneously address multiple levels and issues in the marital relationship. These levels are described along with theoretical and practical considerations.

28. ***Kinston, W. and Bentovim, A.** Creating a focus for brief marital or family therapy, pp. 361–386. In: Forms of Brief Therapy. Ed.: S.H. Budman. New York: Guilford Press, **1981.**

An account of some of the elements to be considered in creating a focus in brief marital and family therapy that also has relevance for creating a focus in individual work. A sensitive and interesting paper. Provides a bibliography for more study of brief family therapy.

29. **Sabin, J.E.** Short-term group psychotherapy: Historical antecedents, pp. 271–282. In: Forms of Brief Therapy. Ed.: S.H. Budman. New York: Guilford Press, **1981.**

An introduction to the idea of short-term group psychotherapy. Provocative and interesting.

MISCELLANEOUS

30.   ***Bloom, B.L.** Focused single-session therapy: Initial development and evaluation, pp. 167–216. In: Forms of Brief Therapy. Ed.: S.H. Budman. New York: Guilford Press, **1981**.

A review of the literature, some general principles, and presentation of an interesting one-session case. A thoughtful piece on the subject.

31.   **Butcher, J.H. and Kolotkin, R.L.** Evaluation of outcome in brief psychotherapy. Psychiatr. Clinics N.A. 2: (1) 157–169, **1979**.

A partial review of the literature and a brief discussion of some of the issues involved in systematic, empirical outcome research in brief individual psychotherapy.

32.   **Clare, A.W.** Brief psychotherapy: New approaches. Psychiatr. Clinics N.A. 2: (1) 93–109, **1979**.

An overview of "alternative" therapies that also tend to be brief (Gestalt therapy, transactional analysis, structural interaction, bioenergetics, primal therapy, psychodrama, emotive therapy, and Erhard seminar training). The author concludes there is no evidence that these treatments have much to offer psychiatric patients. A good bibliography.

33.   **Frances, A. and Clarkin, J.F.** No treatment as the prescription of choice. Arch. Gen. Psychiatry 38: 542–545, **1981**.

Although not specifically about brief treatment, this paper gives a useful perspective in considering the selection of patients for any form of therapy. They present some of the risk/reward and cost/benefit considerations in thinking of patients who may have a negative response, nonresponse, or spontaneous remission. They propose rough guidelines for considering these in evaluating patients.

34.   **Malan, D.H., Bacal, H.A., Heath, E.S., et al.** A study of psychodynamic changes in untreated neurotic patients: I. Improvements that are questionable on dynamic criteria. Br. J. Psychiatry 114: 525–551, **1968**.

35.   **Malan, D.H., Heath, E.S., Bacal, H.A., et al.** Psychodynamic changes in untreated neurotic patients: II. Apparently genuine improvements. Arch. Gen. Psychiatry 32: 110–126, **1976**.

Fascinating attempts to determine the "natural course" of patients who present requesting psychotherapy; demonstrates therapeutic aspects of single interviews.

36.   **Strupp, H.H.** Problems of research, pp. 379–392. In: Short-term Dynamic Psychotherapy. Ed.: H. Davanloo. New York: Aronson, **1980**.

A sober, thoughtful review and account of some research questions and the difficulties in answering them in psychotherapy in general, but particularly in brief treatment.

37. **Winokur, M. and Dasberg, H.** Teaching and learning short-term dynamic psychotherapy. Bull. Menninger Clin. 47: 36–42, **1983.**

An interesting paradigm for teching brief treatment that focuses on identifying and dealing with resistance to learning and doing brief treatment.

[The author wishes to acknowledge the help and advice rendered by Ann Back, R.N. and Michael Sacks, M.D.—both of whom read earlier versions of this contribution.]

42. EMERGENCY PSYCHIATRY AND CRISIS INTERVENTION

JONATHAN SCHWARTZ, M.D.
ARTHUR T. MEYERSON, M.D.

The practice of emergency psychiatry and crisis intervention represents a significant area for almost all psychiatrists and certainly constitutes a crucial aspect of the training of all residents in psychiatry. The evaluation of patients in acute distress and the multitude of diagnostic, management, and dispositional decisions that must be made as a consequence of that assessment is clearly a central issue for the training of mental health care providers. The reading list suggested constitutes an attempt to garner the leading literature on the subject of emergency psychiatry and crisis intervention. In particular, we have attempted to provide references in the following areas: textbooks that serve as good general introductions to the fields of emergency psychiatry and crisis theory and therapy; articles that describe the typical presentations of patients in an emergency setting; differential diagnosis of emergencies; the management and assessment of patients who have suffered from traumas, such as disasters, rape, etc.; indications for hospitalization; the historical and theoretical background of crisis intervention theory and therapy; and specific interventions, psychopharmacological and psychotherapeutic, appropriate to emergency or acute care situations.

Other chapters in this text cover particular areas that clearly overlap with emergency psychiatry, such as suicide, substance abuse, stress, and situational disorders, bereavement and grief, violence, brief therapies, and psychopharmacology (see Chapters 29, 25, 26, 27, 30, 41, 35). These should be used in conjunction with the list in this chapter. We view this annotated reading list as a minimal core for those who will be exposed to clinical work in the area of emergency psychiatry and crisis intervention. Genuine expertise requires a greater degree of exposure to the literature.

OVERVIEW

1. **Bellak, L. and Small, L.** Emergency Psychotherapy and Brief Psychotherapy (2nd ed.). pp. 107–221. New York: Grune and Stratton, **1978.**

The authors describe modalities useful in treatment planning and present therapeutic procedures useful for one-time or several visit treatments.

2. **Donion, P.T., Hopkin, J., and Tupin, J.P.** Overview: Efficacy and safety of the rapid neuroleptization method with injectable haloperidol. Am. J. Psychiatry 136: 273–278, **1979.**

The authors review the literature and conclude that rapid neuroleptization with injectable haloperidol produces a favorable result in reducing and controlling excitement and agitation in psychotic patients.

3. **Farley, G.K., Eckardt, L.O., and Herbert, E.B.** Handbook of Child and Adolescent Psychiatric Emergencies. Garden City, N.Y.: Medical Examination Publishing, **1979.**

Using a phenomenologic approach, the authors present general principles and then specific child psychiatric emergencies. There is also a section of pediatric psychopharmacology.

4. ***Glick, R.A., Meyerson, A.T., Robbins, E., et al.** Psychiatric Emergencies. New York: Grune and Stratton, **1976.**

A general overview of those conditions most frequently requiring emergency intervention. Chapters include assessment of psychiatric emergencies and the organization of psychiatric emergency services. In addition to the management of particular emergencies, a series of chapters on life-cycle–related crises in children, adolescents, students, married adults, and the aged offer an approach to these areas. Another excellent beginning text.

5. **MacKinnon, R.A. and Michels, R.** The Psychiatric Interview in Clinical Practice, pp. 401–427. Philadelphia: Saunders, **1971.**

The authors focus on the phenomenologic and psychodynamic aspect of patients' presentation in the emergency room.

6. ***Slaby, A.E., Lieb, J., and Tancredi, L.R.** Handbook of Psychiatric Emergencies: A Guide for Emergencies in Psychiatry. Garden City, N.Y.: Medical Examination Publishing, **1981.**

This text provides a basic introduction to many areas of emergency room psychiatry, including assessment, management, psychopharmacology, and legal and ethical issues. It also includes brief descriptive segments dealing with various psychiatric emergencies. An excellent beginning text.

CRISIS: THEORY AND PRACTICE

7. **Burgess, A.W. and Holmstrom, L.L.** Rape trauma syndrome. Am. J. Psychiatry 131: 981–986, **1974.**

   The authors identify a specific post-traumatic stress syndrome and its symptomatology. This article is of both historical significance and clinical utility in the assessment and treatment of rape victims.

8. ***Caplan, G.** Principles of Preventive Psychiatry, pp. 26–55. New York: Basic Books, **1964.**

   In this chapter, Caplan develops a crisis theory including characteristics of crisis, sociocultural influences, family influences, community influences, and finally a model for professional involvement and intervention. This chapter and indeed the book is of both historical and pragmatic value in defining the principles by which crisis theory and therapy have developed.

9. **Glick, R.A. and Meyerson, A.T.** The use of psychoanalytic concepts in crisis intervention. Int. J. Psychoanal. Psychother. 8: 171–188, **1980– 1981.**

   This article provides the beginning resident with an extensive bibliography of psychoanalytic contributions to the dynamic theory of crisis structure and intervention. Management strategies and transference and countertransference responses within the emergency and crisis situation are discussed.

10. **Langsley, D.G. and Kaplan, D.M.** The Treatment of Families in Crisis, pp. 1–66. New York: Grune and Stratton, **1968.**

    This is a seminal contribution to crisis work and theory that provides a rational approach to the entire family or social structure of an individual presenting in an emergency or crisis situation. The initial chapters are devoted to a general description of crisis models and technique as well as selected topics in family crisis therapy. The remainder of the book is recommended for those who wish to look more deeply at specific cases.

11. ***Langsley, D.G., Machotka, P., and Flomenhaft, K.** Avoiding mental hospital admission: A follow-up study. Am. J. Psychiatry 127: 1391– 1394, **1971.**

    Using the family crisis techniques described in Langsley's book, the authors randomly divided 300 patients requiring immediate hospitalization into an outpatient treatment group and a group admitted to the hospital. Follow-up showed that those treated in crisis therapy were less likely to be hospitalized after treatment, and subsequent hospitalizations, if needed, were shorter.

12.   ***Lindemann, E.** Symptomatology and management of acute grief. Am. J. Psychiatry 101: 141–148, **1944.**

This is a classic article and essential reading for any resident. It represents the prototype of rapid intervention following acute physical and psychological trauma, as produced by the Coconut Grove fire. Lindemann points to the differentiation of normal and abnormal grieving responses and the benefits of specific early interventions in the prevention of a prolonged depression.

13.   **Raphael, B.** Preventive intervention with the recently bereaved. Arch. Gen. Psychiatry 34: 1450–1454, **1977.**

Widows who received three months of specific support and encouragement of mourning were found to have lower morbidity at 13 months as compared to a control group.

14.   **Special Section: Disaster at Buffalo Creek.** Am. J. Psychiatry 133: 295–316, **1976.**

This section contains article by Titchener, J.L., et al.; Stern, G.; Erikson, K.T.; Newman, C.J.; and Rangell, L. The articles cover the range of responses to the Buffalo Creek disaster from a variety of perspectives. Given the change in psychiatric diagnostic and theoretical perspectives since the earlier work of Lindemann and Tyhurst, these later contributions are essential reading.

15.   **Tyhurst, J.S.** The role of transition states—including disasters in mental illness, pp. 149–172. Symposium on Preventive and Social Psychiatry. Washington: U.S. Government Printing Office, **1957.**

This important article focuses on psychiatric responses to specific events, including civilian disaster, forced migration, and industrial retirement. The events are viewed as states of transition, and through study of populations suffering such events or transitional states, Tyhurst defines characteristic patterns of response and appropriate models of intervention.

MEDICAL ISSUES IN EMERGENCY PSYCHIATRY

16.   ***Fauman, M.A. and Fauman, B.J.** The differential diagnosis of organic based psychiatric disturbances in the emergency department. J. Am. Coll. Emerg. Physicians 6: 315–323, **1977.**

An excellent discussion of the guidelines for diagnosis of organic brain disorders in the emergency room is presented.

17. ***Hall, R.C.W., Beresford, T.P., Gardner, E.R., et al.** The medical care of psychiatric patients. Hosp. Community Psychiatry 33: 25–34, **1982.**

A review of studies showing the high incidence of undiagnosed medical disorders in psychiatric patients is presented. A large percentage of these were causative of the psychiatric condition.

18. **Hall, R.C.W., Popkin, M.K., Devaul, R.A., et al.** Physical illness presenting as psychiatric disease. Arch. Gen. Psychiatry 35: 1315–1320, **1978.**

This outpatient study replicates prior work on inpatients that has shown high incidences of medical illnesses that were either coincident with, exacerbated, or actually caused what was a presumed functional psychiatric disorder. The need for physical examination and laboratory tests on all emergency room patients is underscored.

19. **Rappolt, R.T., Sr., Gay, G.R., and Farris, R.D.** Emergency management of acute phencyclidine intoxication. J. Am. Coll. Emer. Physicians 8: 68–76, **1979.**

Treatment for the various levels of phencyclidine intoxication, a very prevalent problem in emergency rooms is presented.

SPECIFIC CLINICAL PROBLEMS AND PRESENTATIONS

20. ***Bassuk, E. and Gerson, S.** Chronic crisis patients: A discrete clinical group. Am. J. Psychiatry 137: 1513–1517, **1980.**

The characteristics of, and possible emergency room approaches to, "repeaters," frequent visitors, and difficult-to-manage patients is discussed.

21. **Lion, J.R., Bach-Y-Rita, G., and Ervin, F.R.** Violent patients in the emergency room. Am. J. Psychiatry 125: 1706–1711, **1969.**

This study reviewed 45 patients who presented to the emergency room with violence-related thoughts or behaviors. Strategies for intervention and disposition are discussed.

22. **Mattsson, A., Hawkins, J.W., and Seese, L.R.** Child psychiatric emergencies: Clinical characteristics and follow-up results. Arch. Gen. Psychiatry 17: 584–592, **1967.**

A study of 170 child psychiatric emergencies and a comparison to a similar number of walk-in visits is presented. Significant demographic differences were found and a history of past emotional disorder known to community agencies was present in the emergencies. The lack of coordination between agencies is stressed and the emergency room's role in aiding this process is clear.

23. **Skodol, A.E. and Karasu, T.B.** Emergency psychiatry and tha assaultive patient. Am. J. Psychiatry 135: 202–205, **1978.**

These authors describe the successful management of the majority of emergency room patients with violent ideation or action.

24. **Skodol, A.E., Kass, F., and Charles, E.** Crisis in psychotherapy: Principles of emergency consultation and intervention. Am. J. Orthopsychiatry 49: 585–597, **1979.**

A study of an emergency room group of patients who were in ongoing psychotherapy.

RESEARCH APPROACHES TO EMERGENCY PSYCHIATRIC ISSUES

25. **Baxter, S., Chodorkoff, B., and Underhill, R.** Psychiatric emergencies: Dispositional determinants and the validity of the decision to admit. Am. J. Psychiatry 124: 1542–1546, **1968.**

26. **Krystal, H.** Discussion. Am. J. Psychiatry 124: 1546–1548, **1968.**

Factors affecting the decision to admit were studied, including diagnosis, dangerousness, and prognosis, and comparisons made to similar factors evaluated for the same patients by inpatient staff. There was a lack of agreement between groups about all factors except decision to admit. Krystal emphasizes that a psychodynamic approach to the patient allows the therapist to provide much greater help.

27. ***Gerson, S. and Bassuk, E.** Psychiatric emergencies: An overview. Am. J. Psychiatry 137: 1–11, **1980.**

An overview of various emergency room topics with implications for improving therapist-patient interactions and making better dispositional judgments.

28. **Meyerson, A.T., Moss, J.Z., Belville, R., et al.** Influence of experience on major clinical decisions: Training implications. Arch. Gen. Psychiatry 36: 423–427, **1979.**

In this study, two groups of approximately 775 psychiatric patients in a general hospital emergency room were treated by either first- or second-year residents or by more advanced clinicians. The more advanced group admitted one-half as many patients as the lesser-trained group. The authors were able to demonstrate that the difference could be eliminated by changing the training process.

43. GROUP THERAPY

HOWARD D. KIBEL, M.D.

Group therapy has been used to treat almost every kind of psycho-pathology in virtually every clinical setting, with a large number of techniques and theoretical orientations. As a core reading list, this bibliography's focus is on psychodynamic approaches, since most practitioners in the field agree that a grounding in psychodynamic group processes and group dynamics must precede any venture into more select areas.

The reading list begins with some general references and then progres-sively proceeds to the detailed aspects of treatment. It culminates with several references for treatment of common special patient populations. The list includes a number of classic articles, but also many recent ones that synthesize the development of thinking in the field.

A confusing problem in the group literature is that different practitioners emphasize different aspects of group life. Parloff has devised a very useful classification based upon the therapists' focus of intervention in the group: (1) the intrapersonalists, who transpose the theories and practice of individual psychoanalytic treatment directly into the group; (2) the transactionalists or interpersonalists, who focus on the therapeutic potential of the relationships among members; and (3) the integralists (a coined term), who examine group-as-a-whole phenomena and each member's participation in these dynamics. In using this chapter, his classification will enable the student to appreciate the perspective of each of the authors. Wolf belongs to the first group; Durkin and Glatzer, Yalom, and Stein to the second; Heath and Bacal, Foulkes, Stock, and Horwitz to the third.

The remainder of this reading list is more self-evident. The articles on selection and preparation of patients for treatment refer to adult outpatient groups. Those on transference, resistance, working through, and termination are basic to any curriculum. The articles on co-therapy and the concurrent use of individual psychotherapy are included because these practices are wide-spread. The references on groups for patients with severe psychopathology span the prominent trends in treatment. Those on adolescents and children serve as introductions to these subspecialties.

GENERAL REFERENCES

1. ***Stein, A., Kibel, H.D., Fidler, J.W., et al.** Chapter 2. The group therapies, pp. 45–85. In: Treatment Planning in Psychiatry. Eds.: J.M. Lewis and G. Usdin. Washington, D.C.: American Psychiatric Press, **1982.**

   This chapter highlights notable group phenomena and dynamics, surveys the variety of groups in use and discusses group composition, selection and preparation of patients for referral. It reflects a consensus in the field and is designed to acquaint the generalist with the appropriate use of groups for treatment planning.

2. **Yalom, I.D.** The Theory and Practice of Group Psychotherapy (2nd ed.). New York: Basic Books, **1975.**

   This widely used, basic source book covers most of the practical aspects of treatment. Of particular interest are the chapters on the curative factors in treatment, since the author's work here has stimulated research by many others.

THEORY AND ITS PRACTICAL APPLICATIONS

3. ***Foulkes, S.H.** Group analytic dynamics with special reference to psychoanalytic concepts. Int. J. Group Psychother. 7: 40–52, **1957.** Also: (title slightly modified) pp. 108–119. In: Therapeutic Group Analysis. New York: International Universities Press, **1965;** and pp. 147–162. In: Psychoanalytic Group Dynamics. Ed.: S. Scheidlinger. New York: International Universities Press, **1980.**

   Major group phenomena are described, such as mirror reactions, resonance, and the group matrix. The therapeutic emphasis here on communication within the group emanates from the view that neuroses have a social origin.

4. **Kaplan, S.R.** Therapy groups and training groups: Similarities and differences. Int. J. Group Psychother. 17: 473–504, **1967.**

   Rich clinical material illustrates parallel phases of development in therapy and training groups around common themes of dependency, power, and intimacy. Yet, the distinct structure and goals of each produces differences in the emergence of transference and regressive group emotions.

5. ***Kaplan, S.R. and Roman, M.** Phases of development in an adult
    therapy group. Int. J. Group Psychother. 13: 10–26, **1963.**

    This is a vivid clinical account of the progress of a psychotherapy group
    from a relatively loosely organized state into a dynamic system.
    Understanding this process of group development can help the clinician
    identify phase specific behavior of the members.

6. **Kissen, M.** General systems theory: Practical and theoretical implica-
    tions for group intervention. Group 4: 29–39, **1980.**

    This paper succinctly defines general systems theory (GST) concepts and
    describes their relevance to the practice of group psychotherapy. The
    author considers object relations theory to be a useful complement.

7. **Redl, F.** Group emotion and leadership. Psychiatry 5: 573–596, **1942.**
    Also in: Psychoanalytic Group Dynamics. pp. 15–68. Ed.: S. Scheid-
    linger. New York: International Universities Press, **1980.**

    An understanding of groups can be gained by examining the formative
    group processes that crystallize around a central person. The article
    describes a variety of relationships to this central person and derivative
    emotions that develop among group members.

8. **Rioch, M.J.** The work of Wilfred Bion on groups. Psychiatry 33: 56–66,
    1970. Also in: Progressin Group and Family Therapy. pp. 18–32. Eds.:
    C.J. Sager and H.S. Kaplan. New York: Brunner/Mazel, **1972.**

    This article succinctly describes a theory that has had a major impact on
    group dynamic approaches to treatment. In groups, simultaneously
    there exist two levels of functioning: one is task-oriented, while the other
    is concerned with security, aggression, or intimacy.

9. ***Scheidlinger, S.** On the concept of the "mother-group." Int. J. Group
    Psychother. 24: 427–428, **1974.**

    This paper presents an important theoretical discussion on therapeutic
    regression. Identification by group members with the group as an entity
    promotes the therapeutic alliance and the development of cohesion and
    provides support.

10. **Stock, D.** Interpersonal concerns during early sessions of therapy
    groups. Int. J. Group Psychother. 12: 14–26, **1962.**

    A method called "group focal conflict" analysis is used to identify
    conflictual concerns among the members and their compromise solu-
    tions. This approach, derived from Thomas French's work, translates
    the familiar analytic triad of wish, anxiety, and defense to the level of the
    group-as-a-whole.

METHODS OF TREATMENT

11. ***Durkin, H.E. and Glatzer, H.T.** Transference neurosis in group psychotherapy: The concept and the reality, pp. 129–144. In: Group Therapy: **1973.** Eds.: L.R. Wolberg and E.K. Schwartz. New York: Intercontinental Medical Book Corp., **1973.**

This article applies psychoanalytic ego psychology to group psychotherapy. Structural change is achieved through systematic interpretation in the here-and-now of a myriad of intragroup transferences, along with attendant character defenses and their translation in terms of genetic origin.

12. ***Heath, E.S. and Bacal, H.A.** A method of group psychotherapy at the Tavistock Clinic. Int. J. Group Psychother. 18: 21–30, **1968.** Also in: Progress in Group and Family Therapy, pp. 33–42. Eds.: C.J. Sager and H.S. Kaplan. New York: Brunner/Mazel, **1972.**

This is an excellent summary of a method that has influenced many practitioners. The technique is highly stylized in that the therapist uses transference interpretation exclusively. The unique contribution of this method is its focus on the collective unconscious process within the group, which is designated as the "common group tension."

13. **Horwitz, L.** A group-centered approach to group psychotherapy. Int. J. Group Psychother. 27: 423–439, **1977.**

The author persuasively argues for viewing discrete events in a group session as part of the collective reactions of the total membership. This group-centered hypothesis offers unique advantages for treatment, which can be integrated with a clinical focus on individuals and peer interactions.

14. ***Parloff, M.B.** Analytic group psychotherapy, pp. 492–531. In: Modern Psychoanalysis. Ed.: J. Marmor. New York: Basic Books, **1968.**

The author classifies the multiplicity of group psychotherapy methods according to whether the focus is on the individual in the group, subgroups, or member dyads, or on the group as a unit. While his title refers to analytic groups, this classic work provides a basic typology for the field in general.

15. ***Stein, A.** The nature and significance of interaction in group psychotherapy. Int. J. Group Psychother. 20: 153–162, **1970.**

Freud's treatise on group psychology is translated here to explain why in group psychotherapy there are specific alterations of the transference to the therapist and a rapid exposure of members' character pathology.

This thesis is adopted by most American therapists who view these as unique advantages to group treatment and, thus, focus on member dyads and subgroups as the core of therapy.

16. ***Wolf, A.** Psychoanalysis in groups, pp. 321–335. In: Group Psychotherapy and Group Function (rev. ed.). Eds.: M. Rosenbaum and M.M. Berger. New York: Basic Books, **1975.**

This author, a pioneer in the field, translates the principles of individual psychoanalysis to the group setting, using transference, free association, dream analysis, and historical development. He views the group as a re-creation of the original family wherein the patient works through unresolved problems, but he eschews the application of group dynamics to treatment.

SELECTION AND PREPARATION OF PATIENTS

17. ***Freedman, M.B. and Sweet, B.S.** Some specific features of group psychotherapy and their implications for selection of patients. Int. J. Group Psychother. 4: 355–368, **1954.**

The authors provide a rich analysis of several features of groups that are relevant to treatment planning. Their bias is toward a view that group is the preferred mode of psychotherapy for many difficult-to-treat outpatients.

18. ***Grunebaum, H. and Kates, W.** Whom to refer for group psychotherapy. Am. J. Psychiatry 134: 130–133, **1977.**

The authors present fundamental and practical indications for group therapy. Referral is advised for treatment of various characterological problems and for those individuals in whom there is a potential or existing transference that impedes individual therapy.

19. **Rabin, H.M.** Preparing patients for group psychotherapy. Int. J. Group Psychother. 20: 135–145, **1970.**

Adequate preparation of patients for entry into group psychotherapy is vital, since there is generally a period of weeks to months of inculcation into the group culture. Several preparatory practices are described here, and practical suggestions for induction are given.

PROCESS AND STRUCTURE OF TREATMENT

20. **Glatzer, H.T.** Working through in analytic group psychotherapy. Int. J. Group Psychother. 19: 292–306, **1969.**

Analytic group psychotherapy facilitates the working through process in several ways. Old hurts and traumas are vividly revived in group. Because fellow members suffer from similar character problems and transference distortions, they are mutually accepting and are more receptive to peer interpretations than those that emanate from the therapist.

21. **Kauff, P.F.** The termination process: Its relationship to the separation-individuation phase of development. Int. J. Group Psychother. 27: 3-18, **1977.**

Termination of any one group member, therapist, or patient has a profound impact on that individual and an appreciable effect on everyone else in the group. Using the paradigm of the separation-individuation process, clinical vignettes illustrate the reactivation of primitive defense mechanisms in the face of loss.

22. ***Kibel, H.D.** A schema for understanding resistances in groups. Group Process 7: 221-235, **1977.**

Resistances are described and categorized. Using a group-centered approach, suggestions are given, with illustrations, to enable the therapist to prioritize interpretations and appreciate the relationship of individual pathology to groupwide resistances.

23. ***McGee, T.F. and Schuman, B.N.** The nature of co-therapy relationship. Int. J. Group Psychother. 20: 25-36, **1970.**

These authors provide practical advice and guidance for the use of co-leaders. A group conducted by co-therapists tends to replicate the original family constellation and alters the transference accordingly. The co-therapy relationship influences the group's operation and vice versa.

24. **Scheidlinger, S. and Porter, K.** Group therapy combined with individual psychotherapy, pp. 426-440. In: Specialized Techniques in Individual Psychotherapy. Eds.: T.B. Karasu and L. Bellak. New York: Brunner/Mazel, **1980.**

The authors discuss the use of simultaneous treatment, conducted by different therapists (conjoint therapy) and by the same therapist (combined therapy). They review the literature, discuss indications and contraindications, structuring of this approach, and special issues such as confidentiality.

25. ***Sugar, M.** Multitransferences and divarications in group therapy. Int. J. Group Psychother. 21: 444-445, **1971.**

Transference reactions in group psychotherapy are described, as are certain complementary pairing reactions between members that serve as transference stimuli. Transference itself is distinguished from other group phenomena that it resembles (i.e., narcissistic ties, ego-ideal reactions, dependency ties, role suction, displaced transference, and a contagion-of-affects reaction.)

SPECIAL PATIENT POPULATIONS

26.   **Gootnick, I.** Transference in psychotherapy with schizophrenic patients. Int. J. Group Psychother. 25: 379–388, **1975.**

Group therapy for these patients has special value because peer interactions can overcome a potentially frightening, infantile, therapist transference, improve patients' reality testing, and strengthen object ties. The author describes techniques for shifting the members' focus of attention away from the therapist and toward each other.

27.   ***Horwitz, L.** Group psychotherapy of the borderline patient, pp. 399–422. In: Borderline Personality Disorders. Ed.: P. Hartocollis. New York: International Universities Press, **1977.**

This article provides an excellent review of the literature and discusses the special features of groups that are suited to the treatment of these patients. These include dilution of transference, a reality orientation, emotional support through belonging, unique means for the expression of hostility, the unfolding of character armor, peer confrontation, and the development of sustained identifications.

28.   **Hurst, A.G. and Gladieux, J.D.** Guidelines for leading an adolescent therapy group, pp. 151–164. In: Group and Family Therapy: **1980.** Eds.: L.R. Wolberg and M.L. Aronson. New York: Brunner/Mazel, **1980.**

This paper outlines several practical strategies for forming and conducting these outpatient groups. Developmental issues of adolescence are related to modifications in technique. The therapist is advised to conduct the group as an authority who actively guides the members in mutual exploration of their lives.

29.   **Kibel, H.D.** A conceptual model for short-term inpatient group psychotherapy. Am. J. Psychiatry 138: 74–80, **1981.**

The author first reviews the history of the literature on this subject and then presents his own treatment model, using general systems and object relations theory. Techniques are presented that clarify the members' experience in the small therapy group and its relevance to the entire experience on the psychiatric unit.

30.   **Lothstein, L.M.** The group psychotherapy dropout phenomenon revisited. Am. J. Psychiatry 135: 1492–1495, **1978.**

Despite an elaborate program to minimize dropouts during the early phase of group formation, this study reported a rate consistent with the average of 30 percent found by most workers. These results suggest that some premature termination is inevitable and inherent for the development of cohesion. The character of dropouts and the group's reactions are described.

31.   **Maxmen, J.S.** An educative model for inpatient group therapy. Int. J. Psychother. 28: 321–338, **1978.**

A method is described here that has a limited but specific goal, namely, to teach patients to think clinically and respond effectively to the consequences of their illness. The leader focuses on behaviors in the here-and-now as these relate to accepting help and to target symptoms.

32.   **Schamess, G.** Group treatment modalities for latency age children. Int. J. Group Psychother. 26: 455–473, **1976.**

This excellent review of the literature categorizes the plethora of outpatient methods according to the specific patient population for which they were designed. The author notes that children's groups must be homogeneously composed. For each type, the literature prescribes distinct approaches to treatment, including specifics for the therapist's role, the structure of the group, and the equipment employed.

33.   ***Stone, W.M. and Gustafson, J.P.** Technique in group psychotherapy of narcissistic and borderline patients. Int. J. Group Psychother. 32: 29–47, **1982.**

Concepts from self-psychology are explained and translated to group treatment. Modifications in usual technique are advised. Suggestions are given and illustrated for the use of group interpretations and noninterpretative therapist activity, including empathy and benign confrontation.

44. FAMILY AND MARITAL THERAPY

JOHN F. CLARKIN, PH.D.

It is premature to select "classic" articles or books that have "stood the test of time" in a field such as family and marital therapy, which is barely 30 years of age. Hence, one is charting a somewhat presumptuous course in selecting out those publications that will prove of most benefit to students of family and marital therapy, students who in the next decade will shape the field in a way that is probably unforeseen at the moment. However, the field is budding with enthusiasm about its new-found insights and orientation. The current bibliography, then, is most likely an intermingling of publications that will stand the test of time with those that will eventually be regarded as inconsequential.

Since this bibliography is intended for students and their teachers, the aim is to provide adequate coverage of salient aspects of family and marital therapy rather than a listing of the 25 "best" and/or "classic" articles. Areas chosen for review include the assessment of the family and marital unit, theoretical concepts, therapeutic techniques, and texts and handbooks.

There is, of course, overlap between the various sections. A handbook such as that of Gurman's and Kniskern's, while listed under the section of texts and handbooks, also has relevance to the areas of theory and therapeutic techniques. Likewise, articles and books listed under techniques often have sections that are quite important in terms of theory and vice versa.

ASSESSMENT AND TREATMENT PLANNING

1. ***Clarkin, J.F., Frances, A., and Glick, I.D.** The decision to treat a family: Selection criteria and enabling factors, pp. 149–167. In: Group and Family Therapy: 1981. Eds.: L.R. Wolberg and M.L. Aronson. New York: Brunner/Mazel, **1981.**

   This is the most recent summary of criteria for marital and family intervention.

2. **Reiss, D.** The Family's Construction of Reality. Cambridge: Harvard University Press, **1981.**

   A fascinating and extraordinary mixture of sound reasoning and experimental investigation is presented on how the family fashions its assumptions about the world. The book is the fruit of many years of experimental labor and is an example of one of the best approaches to deriving meaningful classifications of families.

3. **Walsh, F.** Normal Family Processes. New York: Guilford Press, **1982.**

This edited work is the best review to date. Noteworthy are the chapters on research contrasting normal and abnormal families (Beavers), the McMaster model of assessment (Epstein), families at risk (Wynne and colleagues) and a view of the family life cycle (McGoldrick and Carter).

4. **Wynne, L.C.** Some indications and contraindications for exploratory family therapy, pp. 289–322. In: Intensive Family Therapy. Eds.: I. Boszomenyi-Nagy and J.L. Framo. New York: Harper and Row, **1965.**

Somewhat limited because of its focus on only one type of family therapy (i.e., exploratory), nevertheless, this is a classic article on indications for family intervention. The article is outstanding in its perception of the family as a pathological unit and target of intervention.

5. ***Wynne, L.C. with Gurman, A.S., Ravich, R., et al.** The family and marital therapies, pp. 227–285. In: Treatment Planning in Psychiatry. Eds.: J.M. Lewis and G. Usdin. Washington, D.C.: American Psychiatric Association, **1982.**

The authors provide an excellent guideline to the data needed for family therapy treatment planning and practical aspects of obtaining such information in interaction with the family. A detailed clinical vignette is provided for illustration.

THEORY

6. ***Ackerman, N.W.** The Psychodynamics of Family Life: Diagnosis and Treatment of Family Relationships. New York: Basic Books, **1958.**

This early work bridged the gap between psychodynamic thinking about the individual and the family context within which the individual develops and is shaped. More than just historically interesting, its dynamic concepts are still relevant.

7. **Boszormenyi-Nagy, I. and Spark, G.M.** Invisible Loyalties: Reciprocity in Intergenerational Family Therapy. New York: Harper and Row, **1973.**

In the dynamic tradition, this volume explores the multigenerational family "justice" system in a convincing way.

8. **Bowen, M.** Family Therapy in Clinical Practice. New York: Aronson, **1978.**

This volume contains most of the seminal papers written by Murray

Bowen, whose ideas on structure of family relations under stress have done much to shape the field.

9.   **Brown, G.W., Birley, J.L.T., and Wing, J.K.** Influence of family life on the course of schizophrenic disorders: A replication. Br. J. Psychiatry 121: 241–258, **1972.**

This clinical study showed a significant association between relapse of a schizophrenic, and the expressed emotion in the family environment, and promises to be a major area of investigation for the future.

10.   ***Dicks, H.V.** Marital Tensions. New York: Basic Books, **1967.**

This relatively unknown work is a gem. Dicks illustrates that internalized representations of significant relationships from childhood shape the choice of marital partner and form the backdrop for interlocking patterns of marital and family pathology.

11.   **Framo, J.L.** Symptoms from a family transactional viewpoint, pp. 125–171. In: Family Therapy in Transition. Ed.: M.W. Ackerman. New York: Little, Brown, **1970.**

This is an early but seminal paper making a crucial theoretical link between family interaction patterns and the emergence of psychiatric symptoms.

12.   ***Hoffman, L.** Foundation of Family Therapy: A Conceptual Framework for Systems Change. New York: Basic Books, **1981.**

Besides providing historical insight into the developments of systems thinking, this book is a *tour de force* on general systems theory and the cybernetic paradigm as applied to the family. It places such therapists as Minuchin, Bon, Whitaker, Haley, Erikson, and Palazzoli in theoretical perspective.

13.   **Watzlawick, P., Beavin, J.H., and Jackson, D.D.** Pragnatics of Human Communications: A Study of Interactional Patterns, Pathologies, and Paradoxes. New York: Norton, **1967.**

Delightful and provocative view of human relationships seen with the concepts of homeostasis, positive and negative feedback, and paradoxical qualities of communication. These concepts are cleverly illustrated—e.g., an analysis of Albee's *Who's Afraid of Virginia Woolf.*

TREATMENT STRATEGIES AND TECHNIQUES

14.   ***Goldstein, M.J.** New developments in interventions with families of schizophrenics. New Directions for Mental Health Services, 12, **1981.**

This entire issue is a brief introduction to new developments in intervention with families containing a schizophrenic member that derives from the work of Brown et al. on expressed emotion.

15. **Gurman, A.S.** Integrative marital therapy: Toward the development of an interpersonal approach, pp. 415–457. In: Forms of Brief Therapy. Ed.: S.H. Budman. New York: Guilford Press, **1981.**

The authors cogently argues for an integration of dynamic, behavioral, and structural strategies.

16. **Haley, J.** Problem-Solving Therapy. San Francisco: Jossey-Bass, **1976.**

Any review of techniques must include the seminal ideas of Jay Haley. His earlier books, *Strategies of Psychotherapy* (1963) and *Uncommon Therapy* (1973), explored family and marital techniques as influenced by the ideas of hypnotherapist Milton Erickson. This latest book on strategic technique is lucid, provocative, and practical on topics such as conducting the first family interview, delivering therapy directives to families, and the stages in family therapy.

17. **Haley, J. and Hoffman, L.** Techniques of Family Therapy. New York: Basic Books, **1967.**

One way to learn the techniques of family therapy is to observe the experts at work through studying actual sessions. This book provides transcripts of such leading family therapists as Charles Fulweiler, Virginia Satir, D.D. Jackson, Carl Whitaker, and Frank Pittman. The authors provide questions and expert commentary.

18. **Jacobson, N.S. and Margolin, G.** Marital Therapy: Strategies Based on Social Learning and Behavioral Exchange Principles. New York: Brunner/Mazel, **1979.**

This is a scholarly look at marriage from a behavioral orientation. Initial interview, assessment and behavioral techniques for encouraging positive exchanges, improving communication, and developing contingency contracts are explored.

19. ***Minuchin, S. and Fishman, H.C.** Family Therapy Techniques. Cambridge: Harvard University Press, **1981.**

This book provides an excellent description in concrete and succinct language of such basic family therapy techniques as reframing, restructuring, balancing, marking boundaries, and making paradoxical statements.

20. **Napier, A.Y. and Whitaker, C.A.** The Family Crucible. New York: Harper and Row, **1978.**

The authors provide one of the few readable accounts in the literature of a family therapy case through the progression of the whole treatment. Interestingly, patients in family therapy find this book enjoyable reading and informative about the therapeutic goals and process.

21. ***Paolino, T.J. and McCrady, B.S.** Marriage and Marital Therapy: Psychoanalytic, Behavioral, and System Theory Perspectives. New York: Brunner/Mazel, **1978.**

Chapters contrast marital theory and therapeutic strategies from the psychoanalytic, behavioral, and systems perspectives. This book is a marvelous pedagogical tool, scholarly and extremely well written.

22. ***Selvini-Palazzoli, M., Oscolo, L., Cecchin, G.F., et al.** Paradox and Counter-Paradox: A New Model in the Therapy of the Family in Schizophrenic Transaction. New York: Aronson, **1978.**

Taking seriously the cybernetic hypothesis that families are self-regulating systems that control themselves through a set of rules, Palazzoli and colleagues set out to strategically change families with a psychotic or schizophrenic child by changing a crucial family rule. With clinical detail, this book illustrates strategic intervention—paradoxical or otherwise—at its best.

BASIC TEXTS AND HANDBOOKS

23. ***Glick, I.D. and Kessler, D.R.** Marital and Family Therapy (2nd ed.). New York: Grune and Stratton, **1980.**

This book would be a most useful beginning text in orienting students familiar with the medical model (medical students and psychiatric students) to the field of marital and family therapy. It has sections on the assessment of the family, treatment in hospital settings, and diagnoses of the identified patient and related family pathology.

24. ***Glick, I.D., Weber, D.H., Rubenstein, D., et al.** Family Therapy and Research: An Annotated Bibliography of Articles, Books, Videotapes and Films Published 1950–1979 (2nd ed.). New York: Grune and Stratton, **1982.**

This is an indispensable guide to family literature from 1950 to 1979 for the student and teacher of family therapy. Books, articles, videotapes, and films are covered.

25. ***Gurman, A.S. and Kniskern, D.P.** Handbook of Family Therapy. New York: Brunner/Mazel, **1981.**
This is the best summary under one bookcover of the major orientations to family/marital treatment, including the psychoanalytic, intergenerational, systems, and behavioral. Editor's footnotes are informative, comparative, provocative, and delightful.

45. INPATIENT PSYCHIATRY AND MILIEU

JOHN M. OLDHAM, M.D.

Within the last 30 years, hospital psychiatry in the United States has been greatly altered by advances in treatment methods, as well as by the changing sociocultural climate in this country. The average length of hospital stay dropped from a few years to a few weeks, largely as a result of developments in psychopharmacotherapy. At the same time, the civil rights movement and the community mental health movement promoted a view of the hospitalized mental patient as an inmate robbed of his rights. Advocates of the newly articulated therapeutic community principles criticized the traditional medical model as dehumanizing and infantilizing, and studies on brief hospitalization and day hospitalization added impetus to the trend against extended inpatient care. State hospitals throughout the nation began to reduce their populations, and "deinstitutionalization" became a crusade. Yet no adequate alternative care was available for these "liberated" patients, who still needed extensive treatment; increasing recidivism (the "revolving door syndrome") was too often the result.

There is now greater awareness of the importance of carefully planned continuity of care, to include comprehensive community support as well as some inevitable and appropriate periods of inpatient care to maximize patients' time out of the hospital. When hospitalization is indicated, careful structuring of the milieu may prove helpful. Some therapeutic community principles have proven inappropriate for certain hospitalized patients, leading to increased recognition of the need for a diversity of types of inpatient care. Controlled research studies of milieu therapy and hospital treatment programs are becoming more frequent, and it is gradually becoming feasible to intelligently and knowledgeably prescribe hospitalization of specific type and duration to meet each patient's specific needs.

The readings summarized here are selected from among many more in the literature, and the focus is on references other than standard, well-known comprehensive textbooks. Two major categories are represented: hospital psychiatry and milieu therapy with its subcategory, the therapeutic community. An effort has been made to include selected works of historical importance, works that define guiding principles and theory, practical clinical guides, and representative reviews of research on hospital psychiatry and milieu.

HISTORY AND DEFINING PRINCIPLES

1. **Abroms, G.M.** Defining milieu therapy. Arch. Gen. Psychiatry, 21: 553–560, **1969.**

    The author argues that milieu therapy is a "meta-treatment," i.e., a treatment context within which multiple types of specific treatment can be carried out, such as psychotherapy, somatic therapy, activities therapy, and the like.

2. **Almond, R.** Issues in milieu treatment. Schizophr. Bull. 13: 12–26, **1975.**

    Geared primarily toward the treatment of the schizophrenic patient, this paper gives careful attention to inevitable problems of balance in structuring an inpatient service: management vs. therapy, delabeling vs. relabeling, medication vs. milieu, authority vs. nurture, etc. Clear differences in approach are outlined, for acute treatment settings, intermediate-stay settings, and long-term residential treatment settings.

3. ***Cumming, J. and Cumming, E.** Ego and Milieu: Theory and Practice of Environmental Therapy. New York: Atherton, **1962.**

    One of the few attempts to analyze milieu therapy of chronic schizophrenics in a state hospital system from a psychoanalytic perspective. Central assumptions of milieu therapy are explicated.

4. ***Goffman, E.** Asylums: Essays on the Social Situation of Mental Patients and Other Inmates. Garden City, N.Y.: Doubleday, **1961.**

    A sociologist's study of the life of chronic institutionalized mental patients, based on a one-year period of study at St. Elizabeth's Hospital in Washington, D.C. He characterizes the hospital as a "total institution," comparable in some ways to jails and boarding schools, and he concludes that persons confined to such institutions sacrifice much of their uniqueness and individuality in adjusting to a routine imposed on them.

5. **Gunderson, J.G.** Defining the therapeutic processes in psychiatric milieus. Psychiatry 41: 327–335, **1978.**

    A clear model is provided by which to conceptualize the therapeutic functions provided by an inpatient mileu. Five therapeutic processes are suggested and discussed: support, involvement, validation, containment, and structure.

6.   ***Jones, M., Baker, A., Freeman, T., et al.** The Therapeutic Community: A New Treatment Method in Psychiatry. New York: Basic Books, **1953.**

The initial report of the work of Jones and his colleagues in which the newly conceptualized principles of the therapeutic community were presented as a method for treating patients with severe character disorders, chronic neuroses, and substance abuse. Subsequent publications by Jones provide updated information, but this volume has the freshness and enthusiasm of early innovation.

7.   ***Main, T.F.** The hospital as a therapeutic institution. Bull. Menninger Clin. 10: 66–70, **1946.**

The paper in which the term "therapeutic community" was first introduced, referring to the "Northfield Experiment" in England (work carried out at Northfield Military Hospital in Birmingham). A short, readable paper, taking issue with the medical model, and something of a historical landmark.

8.   ***Rapoport, R.N.** Community as Doctor: New Perspectives on a Therapeutic Community. Springfield, IL: Thomas, **1960.**

A follow-up study of the continued work at Belmont Hospital, originated by Maxwell Jones. Principles of the therapeutic community are clarified effectively, and the initial zeal of the early years of the project is tempered by a more critical look at the advantages and disadvantages of the therapeutic community.

9.   ***Stanton, A.H. and Schwartz, M.S.** The Mental Hospital: A Study of Institutional Participation in Psychiatric Illness and Treatment. New York: Basic Books, **1954.**

A classic work, written by a psychiatrist and a social psychologist who spent three years studying the sociology of a mental hospital, Chestnut Lodge. Their reports of noncommunication between staff members resulting in greatly increased stress on patients have become well known (Chapter 15).

THEORY

10.   **Edelson, M.** Sociotherapy and Psychotherapy. Chicago: University of Chicago Press, **1970.**

A scholarly, eloquent, and well-known volume that addresses the complex systems and large group issues relevant to hospital psychiatry. How these group processes can be harnessed in the interest of sociotherapy is then discussed in terms of the actual operation of an inpatient service that provides individually focused psychotherapy.

11.   ***Kernberg, O.** The individual in groups, pp. 211–273. In: Internal World and External Reality: Object Relations Theory Applied. New York: Aronson, **1980.**

A highly sophisticated object relations analysis of aspects of large group processes, containing chapters on regression in groups, organizational regression, and regression in leaders. Amply illustrated with clinical examples from inpatient psychiatry.

12.   ***Kreeger, L.** The Large Group: Dynamics and Therapy. Itasca, IL: Peacock, **1975.**

One of the few publications with an extended focus on large group processes. An initial section examines the theory of large groups from a variety of perspectives. A second section of the book is devoted to practical applications of the theory, including views about sociotherapy in hospital-based milieu programs.

RESEARCH

13.   ***Carpenter, W.T., McGlashan, T.H., and Strauss, J.S.** The treatment of acute schizophrenia without drugs: An investigation of some current assumptions. Am. J. Psychiatry 134: 14–20, **1977.**

One of the few carefully detailed studies of the results of inpatient treatment of acute schizophrenics using mainly psychosocial methods contrasted to usual medication-centered treatment methods that revealed a superior outcome for the patients treated by psychosocial methods.

14.   ***Glick, I.D. and Hargreaves, W.A.** Psychiatric Hospital Treatment for the 1980s: A Controlled Study of Short Versus Long Hospitalization. Lexington, MA: Heath, **1979.**

A summary of the authors' detailed research comparing the effectiveness of hospitalization lasting three to four weeks with that lasting from two to four months. An important set of studies, leading to suggestions regarding how long to recommend hospitalization for selected groups of patients.

15.   **Gunderson, J.G., Will, O.A., and Mosher, L.R.,** eds. Principles and
      Practice of Milieu Therapy. New York: Aronson, **1983.**

      An information-packed, thought-provoking book organized into three
      major sections: clinical practice, research, and theory relating to milieu
      therapy. Contributors include Gunderson, Tucker, Wendt, Ellsworth,
      Almond, Jones, and others. The book's strength lies in its first two
      sections, particularly the extensive review and evaluation of the research
      literature in this area. In addition, the book provides a provocative
      challenge, suggesting that for selected schizophrenics milieu therapy
      may be equally effective, if not preferable, to other forms of therapy,
      including pharmacotherapy.

16.   ***Moos, R.H.** Evaluating Treatment Environments: A Social Ecological
      Approach. New York: Wiley, **1974.**

      An amibitious and innovative monograph, presenting newly developed
      scales for evaluating treatment programs: Ward Atmosphere Scale
      (WAS) and Community-Oriented Programs Environment Scale
      (COPES). Emphasis on both subjective and objective measures of the
      effectiveness of treatment programs is combined with a sophisticated
      discussion of the many variables affecting such programs.

17.   ***Paul, G.L. and Lentz, R.J.** Psychosocial Treatment of Chronic Mental
      Patients: Milieu Versus Social-Learning Programs. Cambridge: Harvard
      University Press, **1977.**

      A carefully designed and presented study comparing milieu thcrapy with
      a token economy type of social learning, hospital-based treatment
      program for chronic schizophrenics. Strong conclusion that the social
      learning program is far superior to milieu programs for chronic
      schizophrenics.

18.   **Spadoni, A.J. and Smith, J.A.** Milieu therapy in schizophrenia: A
      negative result. Arch. Gen Psychiatry 20: 547–551, **1969.**

      A remarkable report of the use of milieu therapy on a small inpatient
      unit, where a dedicated staff remained persistently enthusiastic and
      convinced of the efficacy of their approach in spite of demonstrably poor
      results.

19.   ***Van Putten, T. and May, P.R.A.** Milieu therapy of the schizophrenics,
      pp. 217–243. In: Treatment of Schizophrenia: Progress and Prospects.
      Eds.: W. West and D.E. Flinn. New York: Grune and Stratton, **1976.**

      The authors strongly conclude that milieu therapy may add to the
      therapeutic effects of antipsychotic medications for schizophrenics, but
      that it does not represent an adequate substitute.

PRACTICAL CLINICAL GUIDES

20. **Bettelheim, B.** The love that is enough: Countertransference and the ego processes of staff members in a therapeutic milieu, pp. 251–278. In: Tactics and Techniques in Psychoanalytic Therapy, Vol. II. Ed.: P.L. Giovacchini. New York: Aronson, **1975.**

    Focusing on long-term therapy with severely disturbed children, this paper is an eloquent and compassionate look at the countertransference processes experienced by staff working in an intensive therapeutic milieu.

21. **Bjork, D., Steinberg, M., Lindenmayer, J.P., et al.** Mania and milieu: Treatment of manics in a therapeutic community. Hosp. Community Psychiatry 28: 431–436, **1977.**

    A report outlining treatment principles for hospitalized manic patients, clearly written and practical.

22. **Henisz, J.E.** Psychotherapeutic Management on the Short-Term Unit: Glimpses at Inpatient Psychiatry. Springfield, IL: Thomas, **1981.**

    One of the few recent volumes to focus on practical issues of short-term inpatient psychiatry. The organization of the unit is described, as well as the clinical approach to the treatment of specialized patient populations: the paranoid patient, the suicidal patient, the violent patient, and the borderline patient. Readable and useful particularly for those working on acute services for the first time.

23. *****Maxmen, J.S., Tucker, G.J., and LeBow, M.** Rational Hospital Psychiatry: The Reactive Environment. New York: Brunner/Mazel, **1974.**

    The most well-known single text on hospital psychiatry, which continues to be relevant and practical.

24. *****Moline, R.A.** Hospital psychiatry in transition: From the therapeutic community toward a rational eclecticism. Arch. Gen. Psychiatry 33: 1234–1238, **1976.**

    A thoughtful review of recent developments in hospital psychiatry. The author advocates a problem-solving approach and careful selectivity in applying therapeutic community principles.

25. **Oldham, J.M. and Russakoff, L.M.** The medical-therapeutic community. J. Psychiatr. Treat. and Eval. 4: 347–353, **1982.**

    The authors contend that a unified and flexible medical-therapeutic community model is an effective organization for an acute inpatient service.

26. **Russakoff, L.M. and Oldham, J.M.** The structure and technique of community meetings: The short-term unit. Psychiatry 45: 38–44, **1982.**

A particular model for community meetings on a short-term service is presented in detail, complemented by a clinical description of a typical meeting.

27. ***Sacks, M.H. and Carpenter, W.T.** The pseudotherapeutic community: An examination of anti-therapeutic forces on psychiatric units. Hosp. Community Psychiatry 25: 315–318, **1974.**

Defining psychiatric units that operate as pseudo-therapeutic communities as units that subscribe to a particular treatment philosophy but covertly function in a contradictory fashion, the authors present five situations that make such a development more likely.

28. **Sacks, M.H., Carpenter, W.T., and Scott, W.H.** Crisis and emergency on the psychiatric ward. Compr. Psychiatry 15: 79–85, **1974.**

The authors define a ward crisis as persistent group behavior that prevents the ward from accomplishing its therapeutic task. A useful set of guidelines is outlined to aid staff in recognizing and preventing such group-induced crises.

29. **Schlesinger, H.J. and Holzman, P.S.** The therapeutic aspects of the hospital milieu. Bull. Menninger Clin. 34: 1–11, **1970.**

A set of recommendations about prescribing activities programs for hospitalized patients, based on the work of William and Karl Menninger. An unusual paper, linking psychodynamic theory to milieu therapy.

30. **Sederer, L.I.,** ed. Inpatient Psychiatry: Diagnosis and Treatment. Baltimore: Williams and Williams, **1983.**

A *DSM-III*-based diagnostic and treatment guide, ideal for the resident on inpatient rotation. Well written, well referenced, and biopsychosocially comprehensive.

31. **Van Putten, T.** Milieu therapy: Contraindications? Arch. Gen. Psychiatry 29: 640–643, **1973.**

Focusing particularly on the hospital treatment of schizophrenic patients, the author suggests that forced participation and open communication inherent in the principles of milieu therapy may be "toxic" for certain patients.

46. CONSULTATION-LIAISON

Samuel W. Perry, M.D.

The selected articles address the problems a psychiatrist confronts when consulting in a general hospital. Although some papers are included to provide a theoretical and historical perspective, the selection emphasizes the more clinical aspects—the specific difficulties a psychiatrist can anticipate in working with physically-ill patients and nonpsychiatric colleagues.

Along with emphasizing the practical, the selection was based on three other considerations: first, most articles have an excellent bibliography of their own and thereby provide a link toward pursuing the given area in more detail and depth; second, the articles were chosen in collaboration with Dr. Viederman whose selection for Chapter 25 on psychophysiological disorders addresses the more theoretical and investigative aspects of the field; third (and perhaps most important), the selection was based on the response of psychiatry residents who found the following articles to be the most helpful and stimulating during their consultation-liaison rotation at The New York Hospital.

GENERAL TEXTBOOKS

1. **Benson, D.F. and Blumer, D.** Psychiatric Aspects of Neurologic Disease. New York: Grune and Stratton, Vol. 1, **1975**; Vol. 2, **1982.**

   In a relevant, concise and readable manner, the articles in these books deal with the very kinds of neurologic problems confronting the C-L psychiatrist. Especially effective on organic brain syndromes, personality changes with frontal and temporal lobe lesions, temporal lobe epilepsy, and amnesia.

2. ***Hackett, T.D. and Cassem, N.H.,** eds.: Massachusetts General Hospital Handbook of General Hospital Psychiatry. St. Louis: Mosby, **1978.**

   This superb book emphasizes the crucial clinical considerations regarding delirium, pain, hysteria, dialysis, surgery, burns, intensive care, dying, etc. It also provides sufficient background, depth and references to be far more than a "cookbook" list of instructions.

3. **Sherman, M.,** ed. Pediatric consultation-liaison. Psychiatr. Clin. of North Am. 5: 2, **1982.**

This book not only places under one cover many relevant issues for the C-L pediatric psychiatrist (child abuse, asthma, behavioral aspects of childhood diabetes, young leukemics, neonatal intensive care, etc.), but also discusses liaison issues (promoting the alliance between pediatrics and child psychiatry, setting up a pediatric C-L service, communicating with pediatricians, etc.).

GENERAL ARTICLES

4. ***Engel, G.L.** The need for a new medical model: A challenge for biomedicine. Science 196: 129–136, **1977.**

After presenting the limitations of the biomedical model, Dr. Engel introduces the biopsychosocial model as a "systems approach" to the physically ill patient. The article provides a conceptual scheme that is useful to consider and discuss with nonpsychiatric colleagues.

5. ***Kahana, R.J. and Bibring, G.L.** Personality types in medical management, pp. 108–123. In: Psychiatry and Medical Practice in a General Hospital. Ed.: N. Zinberg. New York: International Universities Press, **1964.**

This article demonstrates how therapeutic interventions can be tailored to the personality types of those who are physically ill. The examples given are specific, colorful, and easily recognizable.

6. ***Perry, S. and Viederman, M.** Adaptation of residents to consultation-liaison psychiatry. Part I: Working with the physically ill. Part II: Working with the non-psychiatric staff. Gen. Hosp. Psychiatry 3: 141–147, 149–156, **1981.**

Part I describes the special requirements for working with physically ill patients; Part II describes the defensive reactions psychiatrists may assume when confronted with the skepticism about the value of psychiatry. The two articles are particularly helpful for introducing psychiatry residents to C-L.

7. **Perry, S. and Viederman, M.** Management of emotional reactions to acute medical illness. Med. Clin. North Am. 65: 3–14, **1981.**

In a very pragmatic way—suitable for the internist or medical student—the authors describe the specific tasks of physically ill patients and how problems arise when patients fail in these tasks. The article presents a framework and feasible solutions for a psychiatrist starting C-L work.

8. ***Viederman, M. and Perry, S.** Use of psychodynamic life narrative in the treatment of depression in the physically ill. Gen. Hosp. Psychiatry 2: 177–185, **1980.**

The authors discuss with clinical illustrations how a succinct, supportive summary can be used therapeutically to explain to the patient the meaning of his depression.

C-L CHART NOTE

9. **Garrick, T.R. and Stotland, N.L.** How to write a psychiatric consultation. Am. J. Psychiatry 139: 849–855, **1982.**

The article presents a conceptual and practical scheme for making decisions about the content, style, and wording of the consultation note.

CANCER

10. **Dunphy, J.E.** Annual discourse—on caring for the patient with cancer. N. Engl. J. Med. 295: 313–319, **1976.**

Along with outlining what can be done, the author discusses the physician's helplessness when seemingly nothing can be done at all.

11. **Holland, J.** Psychological aspects of oncology. Med. Clin. North Am. 61: 737–748, **1977.**

Dr. Holland describes concisely the kinds of emotional reactions and management problems that occur with cancer patients.

CARDIAC ILLNESS

12. **Heller, S.S., Frank, K.A., Malm, J.R., et al.** Psychiatric complications of open-heart surgery: A reexamination. N. Engl. J. Med. 283: 1015–1020, **1970.**

The authors summarize the reports of delirium and other emotional responses to open-heart surgery. They re-examine these earlier conclusions in view of changes in the procedure and in psychiatric management.

CHILDHOOD ILLNESS

13. **Freud, A.** The role of bodily illness in the mental life of children. Psychoanal. Study Child 7: 69–81, **1952.**

    In a readable and poignant style, Dr. Freud describes the consequences of bodily illness intercepting, and at times impeding, different phases of childhood development.

CHRONIC ILLNESS

14. **Bernstein, N.R.** Chronic illness and impairment. Psychiatr. Clin. of North Am. 2: 331–346, **1979.**

    Dr. Bernstein explains the kinds of difficulties that can develop in both patients and doctors when a patient cannot ("refuses to get") completely well.

CONSULTATION-LIAISON ORGANIZATION

15. **Lipowski, Z.J.** Consultation-liaison psychiatry: An overview. Am. J. Psychiatry 131: 623–630, **1974.**

    The author summarizes how consultation-liaison psychiatry must adjust to two systems: the structure of the general hospital and the departmental and theoretical organization of psychiatry.

CONVERSION REACTIONS

16. **Merskey, M. and Trimble, M.** Personality, sexual adjustment, and brain lesions in patients with conversion symptoms. Am. J. Psychiatry 136: 179–182, **1979.**

    This systematic review makes clear that "conversion" and "hysteria" are not the same, although they are traditionally confused.

COPING

17. **Hamburg, D.A., Hamburg B., and DeGoza, S.** Adaptive problems and mechanisms in severely burned patients. Psychiatry 16: 1–20, **1953.**

    This article, now over 30 years old, has withstood the test of time because of its cogent clinical illustrations and method of studying individual coping styles.

18. **Janis, I.L.** Adaptive personality changes, pp. 272–284. In: Stress and Coping—An Anthology. Ed.: A. Monat and R. Lazarus. New York: Columbia University Press, **1977.**

Included in this excellent anthology on stress and coping, this article shows how too much or too little anxiety may prevent the necessary worrying and trial action before surgery.

DEATH AND DYING

19. **Kübler-Ross, E., Wessler, S., and Arioli, L.V.** On death and dying. JAMA 221: 174–179, **1972.**

The authors summarize their vast experience working with dying patients. The different stages of dying, though admittedly too simplified, provide a structure for discussing with staff this broad and difficult topic.

20. **Norton, J.** Treatment of a dying patient. Psychoanal. Study Child 18: 541–560, **1963.**

The author gives her own personal account of an intense therapeutic involvement with a depressed, dying woman. An excellent account of the psychology and phenomenology of dying.

DEPRESSION

21. **Schmale, A. and Engel, G.L.** The giving up–given up complex. Illustrated on film. Arch. Gen. Psychiatry 17: 135–145, **1967.**

The authors vividly describe the apathy and withdrawal that accompanies physical illness and distinguish this phenomenon from typical depression. The article's strength is the way it describes the interplay between the patient's reaction to his illness and the staff's reaction to the patient.

22. **Spitz, R.A.** Hospitalism. Psychoanal. Study Child 1: 53–74, **1945.**

Almost 40 years ago, Dr. Spitz described the typical responses in a child when hospitalized: protest, despair, and detachment. The model is still useful today—for adults as well.

DIFFICULT PATIENT

23. **Gillum, R.F. and Barsky, A.J.** Diagnosis and management of patient noncompliance. JAMA 228: 1563–1567, **1974.**

This well-referenced article reminds us that noncompliance is the rule rather than the exception. The authors suggest how noncompliance can be predicted and possibly avoided.

24. **Groves, J.E.** Taking care of the hateful patient. N. Engl. J. Med. 298: 883–887, **1978.**

Dr. Groves discusses the difficulties of defining and dealing with "crocks" and the negative reactions they elicit in physicians.

25. **Main, T.F.** The ailment. Br. J. Med. Psychol. 30: 129–145, **1957.**

Although this article is concerned primarily with the effects of "special patients" on their psychiatric caretakers, physicians, and nurses, it offers an interesting perspective for conceptualizing the social disruption that some medically ill patients can cause on nonpsychiatric units.

26. **Perry, S. and Gilmore, M.M.** The disruptive patient or visitor. JAMA 245: 755–757, **1981.**

The article succinctly outlines how to approach, restrain, medicate, and evaluate a patient or visitor who becomes disruptive on a medical ward. The legal considerations are also discussed.

27. **Wise, T.N.** Psychiatric management of patients who threaten to sign out against medical advice. Int. J. Psychiatry Med. 5: 153–160, **1974.**

By understanding what factors contribute to signing out against medical advice, the psychiatrist may be able to intercept potentially destructive behavior.

ETHICS

28. **Imbus, S.H. and Zawacki, B.E.** Autonomy for burn patients when survival is unprecedented. N. Engl. J. Med. 297: 308–311, **1977.**

The authors suggest that some severely burned patients be given a choice about whether they wish to undergo stressful, painful procedures with little hope of survival. The paper stimulates a discussion of relevant ethical, moral, and legal concerns.

FACTITIOUS ILLNESS

29.   **Asher, R.** Munchausen's syndrome. Lancet 1: 339–341, **1951.**

The author provides a colorful, historical perspective of a problem that has intrigued and baffled physicians through the ages.

30.   **Hyler, S.E. and Sussman, N.** Chronic factitious disorders with physical symptoms. (The Munchausen syndrome) Psychiatr. Clin. of North Am. 4: 365–377, **1981.**

The authors review this challenging subject and offer suggestions about interviewing and managing a "deceitful" patient.

31.   **Spiro, H.R.** Chronic factitious illness: Munchausen's syndrome. Arch. Gen. Psychiatry 18: 569–579, **1968.**

Offering vivid illustrations, the author discusses the dynamics and difficulties of patients who are compelled to make themselves ill.

HISTORICAL BACKGROUND

32.   **Lipowski, Z.L.** Review of consultation psychiatry and psychosomatic medicine.
     I: General principles. Psychosom. Med. 29: 153–171, **1967.**
     II: Clinical aspects. Psychosom. Med. 29: 201–224, **1967.**
     III: Theoretical issues. Psychosom. Med. 30: 395–422, **1968.**

These three articles, though now somewhat dated, provide a scholarly historical account of liaison psychiatry.

HYPOCHONDRIASIS

33.   **Barsky, A.J. and Kerman, G.L.** Overview: Hypochondriasis, bodily complaints and somatic styles. Am. J. Psychiatry 140: 273–283, **1983.**

In an excellent literature review, the authors summarize the confusing ways hypochondriasis has been conceptualized phenomenologically, psychodynamically, perceptually, and socially. They suggest the term "amplifying somatic style" be used for further systematic investigation.

34.   **Richards, A.D.** Self theory, conflict theory, and the problem of hypochondriasis. Psychoanal. Study Child 36: 319–337, **1981.**

In addition to discussing the management problems of hypochondriacal patients, the author explores the dynamics and fragility in this distressed population.

INTENSIVE CARE

35. **Holland, J., Sgroi, S.M., Marwit, S.J., et al.** The ICU syndrome: Fact or fancy? Int. J. Psychiatry Med. 4: 241–249, **1973.**

On the basis of a systematic study, the authors conclude that the phrase "intensive care psychosis" too often implies no further evaluation is necessary even though an underlying treatable medical problem may be present.

PAIN

36. **Engel, G.L.** "Psychogenic" pain and the pain prone patient. Am. J. Med. 26: 899–918, **1959.**

Despite many advances in the past 25 years regarding the mechanisms of pain, Dr. Engel's article remains a classic in describing how the meaning of pain can influence its expression, severity, and management.

37. ***Marks, R.M. and Sachar, E.J.** Undertreatment of medical inpatients with narcotic analgesics. Ann. Intern. Med. 78: 173–181, **1973.**

A survey of two teaching hospitals indicated that physicians were generally ignorant about narcotic analgesics, overconcerned about iatrogenic addiction, and unwilling to provide adequate analgesia.

PLASTIC SURGERY

38. **Druss, R.G.** Changes in body image following breast augmentation. Int. J. Psychoanal. Psychother. 2: 248–256, **1973.**

On the basis of semistructured interviews with women who underwent breast augmentation, the author describes their motivation and emotional reactions. The article provides a model for applying a psychodynamic understanding to a specific clinical problem.

PSYCHOTROPIC DRUGS

39. **Greenblatt, D.J. and Shader, R.I.**
1. Psychotropic drugs in a general hospital, pp. 1–26.
2. Drug interactions in psychopharmacology, pp. 269–279.
Both in: Manual of Psychiatric Therapeutics. Ed.: R.I. Shader. Boston: Little Brown, **1975.**

Although newer drugs have become available since this article was first published, the authors provide a model for conceptualizing the problem of using psychotropic drugs with physically ill patients who are often on other medications.

RENAL ILLNESS

40. **Reichsman, F. and Levy, N.B.** A four year study of 25 patients. Problems in adaptation to maintenance hemodialysis. Arch. Intern. Med. 130: 859–865, **1972.**

    This paper describes how "the honeymoon period" is followed by depression and ultimately an adaptive adjustment.

41. ***Viederman, M.** Adaptive and maladaptive regression in hemodialysis. Psychiatry 37: 68–77, **1974.**

42. **Viederman, M.** The search for meaning in renal transplantation. Psychiatry 37: 283–290, **1974.**

    The author describes how regression, fantasy, transference, and partial identifications influence the response to hemodialysis and renal transplantation.

SURGERY

43. **Egbert, L.D., Battit, G.E., Welch, C.D., et al.** Reduction of postoperative pain by encouragement and instruction of patients. N. Engl. J. Med. 270: 825–827, **1964.**

    A generation ago the authors documented the value of psychological intervention with "normal" surgical patients.

SYSTEMS

44. **Karasu, T.B., Plutchnik, R., Conte, H., et al.** What do physicians want from a psychiatric consultation service? Compr. Psychiatry 18: 73–81, **1977.**

    The authors examine the basis of tensions and devaluations that commonly arise between psychiatrists and their medical colleagues: what "we" are and what "they" want are not always the same.

47. BEHAVIOR THERAPY

GORDON G. BALL, PH.D.

Behavior therapy is best defined as a set of treatment procedures based on experimental results from psychology and the social sciences. The focus is on maladaptive behavior, and the assumption is that the behavior is not simply a symptom of disordered intrapsychic processes, but is an integral part of those events. Consequently, modification of the behavior should result in a modification of the internal state. Behavior therapy focuses on current rather than historical events. It prescribes treatment in operational terms and specifies target behaviors for measuring outcome. Treatment derives from a behavioral diagnosis and assessment and is directed at the problem behavior itself.

With new information from research, behavior therapy procedures are constantly being modified. This makes it difficult to produce a list of core references that will not be obsolete several years hence. If the momentum of the past 30 years is maintained, one would predict more powerful behavior therapy procedures in the near future.

The references cover methods of behavioral assessment and outcome evaluation, descriptions and critiques of a variety of behavioral procedures, and the behavioral treatment of specific diagnostic categories. In addition to a knowledge of these techniques, one is advised to consult the behavior therapy journals for current modification of these procedures.

GENERAL TEXTS

1. ***Bellack, A.S., Hersen, M., and Kazdin, A.E.** International Handbook of Behavior Modification and Therapy. New York: Plenum Press, **1982.**

   This book offers the best overview of behavior therapy to date. It covers the foundations of behavior therapy, assessment and methodology, ethical issues, treatment of anxiety, depression, schizophrenia, substance abuse, sexual problems, obsessive-compulsive disorders, mental conflicts, and childhood disorders.

2. **Davidson, P.O. and Davidson, S.M.,** eds. Behavioral Medicine: Changing Health Lifestyles. New York: Brunner/Mazel, **1980.**

   The integration of behavior therapy with medicine is subsumed under the heading of "Behavioral Medicine." This book offers an overview of a variety of medical illnesses where the two disciplines have been combined effectively.

3. **Kazdin, A.E.** History of Behavior Modification: Experimental Foundations of Contemporary Research. Baltimore: University Park Press, **1978.**

   This book traces the development of behavior therapy from its early beginnings through to the present day.

4. **Kazdin, A.E. and Wilson, G.T.** Evaluation of Behavior Therapy: Issues, Evidence and Research Strategies. Cambridge, MA: Ballinger, **1978.**

   This book, written by two of the most prominent people in the field, offers a critical examination of the present status of behavior therapy.

5. ***Wolpe, J.** The Practice of Behavior Therapy (2nd ed.). New York: Pergamon Press, **1973.**

   This book describes in detail the basic procedures involved in systematic desensitization made famous by Wolpe and also discusses the alternate behavioral strategies for handling the various forms of anxiety.

BEHAVIORAL ASSESSMENT

6. ***Barlow, D.H.,** ed. Behavioral Assessment of Adult Disorders. New York: Guilford Press, **1981.**

   This book covers the underlying assumptions associated with behavioral assessment, and offers an approach for classifying clinical problems within a behavioral framework.

7. **Hersen, M.** Historical perspectives in behavioral assessment. In: Behavioral Assessment: A Practical Handbook. Eds.: M. Hersen and A.S. Bellack. Oxford: Pergamon Press, **1976.**

   This chapter criticizes the reliability and validity of the disease model of mental disorders in the areas of diagnosis, assessment, and treatment. Recommendations are made for more stringent criteria for psychiatric evaluation and procedural outcome.

BEHAVIORAL PROCEDURES

8.   **Ayllon, T. and Azrin, N.H.** The Token Economy: A Motivational System for Therapy and Rehabilitation. New York: Appleton-Century-Crofts, **1968.**

The two authors describe an extensive and extremely useful reinforcement system for shaping behaviors in an institutional setting.

9.   **Azrin, N.H., Schaeffer, R.M., and Wesolowski, M.D.** A rapid method for teaching profoundly retarded persons to dress by a reinforcement-guidance method. Ment. Retard. 14: 29–33, **1976.**

Considerable progress has been made in recent years in helping the retarded individual to master such basic skills as toilet training, feeding, and dressing by the application of a variety of behavioral procedures. This article illustrates how one of these procedures is typically applied by leading researchers in this area.

10.   ***Hersen, M. and Barlow, D.H.** Single Case Experimental Designs: Strategies for Studying Behavior Change. Oxford: Pergamon Press, **1976.**

Accurate behavioral observation is the first crucial step leading to behavioral assessment and treatment. This book describes observational procedures and behavioral analysis useful for evaluating single case studies in the clinical setting.

11.   **Lange, A.S. and Jakubowski, P.** Responsible Assertive Behavior. Champaign, IL: Research Press, **1976.**

The general approach to problems of interpersonal dysfunction involve a combination of assertiveness skills training to improve social functioning, and cognitive coping strategies to reduce anxiety. This is an excellent book on assertiveness training.

12.   **Leiblum, S.R. and Pervin, L.A.,** eds. Principles and Practice of Sex Therapy. New York: Guilford Press, **1980.**

This book evaluates the current behavioral approaches to sexual dysfunction, focusing on actual clinical cases and identifying the factors leading to varying degrees of success with the different problems.

13.   **Marks, I.M.** Drugs combined with behavioral psychotherapy, pp. 319–345. In: International Handbook of Behavior Modification. Eds.: A.S. Bellack, M. Hersen, and A.E. Kazdin. New York: Plenum Press, **1982.**

The use of pharmacological agents in conjunction with behavior therapy has occurred mainly in the area of anxiety and depression. This article presents some of the more significant findings in this controversial area as well as indicating where further research is needed.

14. **Patterson, G.R., Cobb, J.A., and Ray, R.S.** A social engineering technology for retraining the families of aggressive boys. In: Issues and Trends in Behavior Therapy. Eds.: H.E. Adams and I.P. Unikel. Springfield, IL: Thomas, **1973.**

Modification of children's behavior by training parents to modify their own behavior around the child is well illustrated in this book which concentrates on diminishing aggressive behavior in boys.

15. **Paul, G.L. and Lentz, R.J.** Psychosocial Treatment of Chronic Mental Patients: Milieu vs. Social Learning Programs. Cambridge: Harvard University Press, **1977.**

A variety of behavioral procedures have been used with limited success with the chronic schizophrenic population, usually in hospital settings. One of the most effective procedures has incorporated the token economy, which is well illustrated in this research study.

16. **Schreibman, L. and Koegel, R.L.** A guideline for planning behavior modification programs for autistic children. In: Handbook of Clinical Behavior Therapy. Eds.: S.M. Turner, K.S. Calhoun, and H.E. Adams. New York: Wiley, **1981.**

The results to date on the behavioral treatment of autism are extremely encouraging. This chapter outlines the basic strategy.

17. **Stuart, R.B.** Behavioral remedies for marital ills: A guide to the use of operant-interpersonal techniques, pp. 241–257. In: Couples in Conflict: New Directions in Marital Therapy. Eds.: A.S. Gurman and D.G. Rice. New York: Aronson, **1975.**

Behavioral marital therapy has grown rapidly since its inception in the late 1960s. This chapter demonstrates how several theoretical approaches can be combined to produce an integrated system for handling marital discord.

18. **Watson, J.B. and Rayner, R.** Conditioned emotional reactions. J. Exp. Psychol. 3: 1–14, **1920.**

The conditioning of Albert, an 11-month-old-boy, to be afraid of a white rat. This classic article describes the most famous case in the history of behavior therapy. It also presents the first rudimentary approaches toward the development of behavior therapy in this country.

BEHAVIOR THERAPY FOR SPECIFIC DISORDERS

19. **Azrin, N.H. and Nunn, R.G.** Habit reversal: A method of eliminating nervous habits and tics. Behav. Res. Ther. 11: 619–628, **1973**.

    Habit disorders, such as stuttering, enuresis, encopresis, vomiting, thumbsucking, nail biting, and motor tics have met with mixed but generally favorable success using behavior therapy procedures. This article outlines the basic procedure employed and researched by Azrin and his co-workers.

20. **Foa, E.B. and Steketee, G.** Obsessive-compulsives. In: Progress in Behavior Modification. Eds.: M. Hersen, R.M. Eisler and P. Miller. Vol. 8. New York: Academic Press, **1979**.

    This critical review offers an excellent summary of the types of behavioral procedures that can be used for treating obsessive-compulsive disorders.

21. **Lichtenstein, E. and Brown, R.A.** Smoking cessation methods: Review and recommendations. In: The Addictive Behaviors: Treatment of Alcoholism, Drug Abuse, Smoking and Obesity. Ed.: W.R. Miller. Oxford: Pergamon Press, **1980**.

    Major strategies are discussed in this article along with outcome data.

22. **Matthews, A.M., Gelder, M.G., and Johnston, D.W.** Agoraphobia. New York: Guilford Press, **1981**.

    Theoretical issues, assessment procedures, supportive drug therapy, and behavioral intervention strategies for effectively alleviating agoraphobia are described in detail in this book.

23. **Mavissakalian, M. and Barlow, D.H.** Phobia: Psychological and Pharmacological Treatment. New York: Guilford Press, **1981**.

    The ability to successfully treat fears and phobias has been the hallmark of behavior therapy. This book evaluates the present behavioral and pharmacological interventions and offers a critical analysis of the state of the art.

24. **Vogler, R.E., Compton, J.V., and Weissbach, T.A.** Integrated behavior change techniques for alcoholics. J. Consult. Clin. Psychol. 43: 233–243, **1975**.

    Alcoholism has been treated by a variety of behavior methods with only moderate success. To date, the multimodal approaches have produced the highest positive results, with this study being a fine example of how the procedure is used.

25. **Wilson, G.T.** Behavior modification and the treatment of obesity, pp. 325–344. In: Obesity. Ed.: A.J. Skunkard. Philadelphia: Saunders, **1980.**

The author reviews different behavioral procedures for controlling obesity and their efficacy in a book that emphasizes the complexity of the variables surrounding eating behavior.

48. HYPNOSIS

JOHN T. PATTEN, M.D.

Franz Anton Mesmer (1734–1815) is regarded as the father of modern hypnosis. He steadfastly denied mystical powers and repeatedly offered to present his theory and performance to the scientific community. A commission appointed to investigate him declared that he indeed effected remarkable cures *but* merely as a result of "suggestion." His colleagues who practiced the acceptable arts of bleeding and blistering ignored his cures because Mesmer used "only suggestion."

Medical hypnosis subsequently was used only sporadically until Charcot and Bernheim spurred new interest. Freud, as a student of Charcot, was initially fascinated and used simple hypnotic inductions, direct suggestion, and abreaction. According to Freud's biographer, Jones, Freud thought himself to be a poor hypnotist and found free association to give better access to unconscious processes. Hypnosis again fell into disrepute.

It was not until after World War II that hypnosis again regained respectability. Perhaps the most diligent and brilliant clinician in this renaissance was Milton Erickson. He contributed a vast body of techniques and research findings that has stimulated scientific interest in a field traditionally enveloped in superstition and magic. His work has been studied by Haley, Rossi, Bandler and Grindler, Zieg, Langton, Gordon, and others. Suddenly hypnosis became accepted as an alternative treatment for symptom-oriented problem-solving therapy.

Hypnosis employed with psychoanalytic technique, labeled *hypnoanalysis,* utilizing regression, revivification, and posthypnotic suggestion has not received an enthusiastic reception.

Much scientific and experimental research on hypnosis has been done by Erica Fromm, Martin Orne, Herbert Spiegel, Ernest Hilgard, and Lewis Wolberg. They perhaps still regard Milton Erickson, like Mesmer, as "unscientific," but they do not diminish his contribution to the field.

OVERVIEWS OF HYPNOSIS

1. ***Haley, J.** Uncommon Therapy: The Psychiatric Techniques of Milton H. Erickson, M.D. New York: Norton, **1973.**

The author describes Erickson's hypnotic techniques with children, adolescents, and adults as well as with couples and families. The focus is on content and storytelling. It's a good book for an introductory overview, but one needs to read Rossi, Grinder, and Bandler to understand the microdynamics of Ericksonian techniques.

2. ***Schilder, P.** The Nature of Hypnosis, Chaps. 3–7. New York: International Universities Press, **1956.**

A theoretical overview of hypnosis from a variety of perspectives, including biological, neurological, biochemical, and psychoanalytic. Although 25-years-old, still the most thoughtful and interesting overview on the subject.

3. **Van der Walde, P.H.** Interpretation of hypnosis in terms of ego psychology. Arch. Gen. Psychiatry 12: 438–447, **1965.**

An explanation of the hypnotic process that allows a person to study hypnotic states using the language of ego psychology.

4. **Wolberg, L.R.** The technique of hypnosis, pp. 98–169. In: The Principles of Hypnotherapy: Medical Hypnosis. Vol. I. New York: Grune and Stratton, **1948.**

Wolberg outlines traditional methods of trance inductions, eye fixation, hand levitation, hypnotic suggestion, relaxation techniques, and post-hypnotic suggestions. This book is important as a whole in outlining the "state-of-the-art" of medical hypnosis in the United States.

HISTORY

5. **Breuer, J. and Freud, S.** (1893–1895) Studies on Hysteria. S.E. 2: **1955.**

Theoretical discussions about hysterical phenomena, hysterical conversion, hypnoid states, innate predisposition to hysteria, splitting of the mind, direct access to the unconscious mind. Viewed from the present from a "hypnotic" point of view, one can see that Freud and Breuer understood hypnotic phenomena well.

6. **Ellenberger, H.F.** The Discovery of the Unconscious, pp. 57–83. New York: Basic Books, **1970.**

Ellenberger, in a scholarly text on the discovery of the unconscious, gives Franz Anton Mesmer a major position, comparing him to Columbus: both "discovered a new world, both remained in error for the remainder of their lives about the real nature of their discoveries, and both died bitterly disappointed men." Ellenberger documents the diffusion of mesmerism and its increasing connection with the extraordinary, occult, and quackery after Mesmer's death. Fascinating reading.

HYPNOSIS AND RESEARCH

7. **Erickson, M.H.** Basic psychological problems in hypnotic research. In: Collected Papers of Milton H. Erickson on Hypnosis, Vol. II. Ed.: E. Rossi. New York: Irvington, **1980.**

Erickson addresses the issues of outcome research, statistical reliability, and many other problems of hypnosis research.

8. **Erickson, M.H.** Hypnotic techniques for the therapy of acute psychiatric disturbances in war. In: Collected Papers of Milton H. Erickson on Hypnosis, Vol. IV. Ed.: E. Rossi. New York: Irvington, **1980.**

Using case histories, involving suicide, catatonia, violence, paranoia, and more, Erickson describes some ingenious trance inductions and goes on to imply their usefulness in an acute psychiatric setting.

9. **Kline, M.V.** The production of antisocial behavior through hypnosis: New clinical data. Int. J. Clin. Exp. Hypn. 20: 80–94, **1972.**

Examines the power of suggestion in destructively influencing human behavior. Also describes antisocial behaviors an inexperienced hypnotist may inadvertently induce.

10. **Kubie, L.S.** Illusions and reality in the study of sleep, hypnosis, psychosis and arousal. Int. J. Clin. Exp. Hypn. 20: 205–223, **1972.**

Discussion of the various states of human arousal and the reticular activating system. Kubie specifically addresses the false beliefs surrounding the relationship between sleep and hypnosis as well as between hypnosis, hysteria, hysterical psychosis, and other psychotic processes.

11. **Levitt, E.E. and Chapman, R.** Hypnosis as a research method, pp. 185–215. In: Hypnosis: Developments in Research and New Perspectives. Eds.: E. Fromm and R.E. Shor. New York: Aldine, **1979.**

The least-known use of hypnosis is as a research tool. Rarely has it been used in the investigation of psychological and physiological phenomena. This literature is reviewed, and some possible experimental models for using hypnosis in this sort of research are discussed.

12. **Naruse, G.** Hypnosis as a meditative concentration and its relationship to the perceptual process. In: The Nature of Hypnosis. Ed.: M.V. Kline. Baltimore: Waverly Press, **1962.** Also in: Transactions of International

Congress on Hypnosis. **1961.** New York: New York Institute for Research in Hypnosis. **1962.**

The relationship between hypnosis and meditation is explored. Perceptual changes that occur in altered states of consciousness are discussed. Time distortion, hypnotic hallucinations, concentration association are also examined.

13. **Orne, M.T.** The nature of hypnosis: Artifact and essence. J. Abnorm. Soc. Psychol. 58: 277–299, **1959.**

The author tests rigorously how his subject's knowledge regarding hypnotic behavior influence his hypnotizability and trance behavior. He concludes that the effectiveness of trance appears to lie in the subjective experience rather than prior knowledge or experience.

MEASUREMENT OF HYPNOSIS

14. **Orne, M.T.** Hypnosis, motivation and compliance. Am. J. Psychiatry, 122: 721–726, **1966.**

Discussion of definition of hypnosis, the relationship between hypnotist and patient motivation resistance and posthypnotic phenomena. Paper is based partially on valuable outcome research.

15. **Spiegel, H. and Spiegel, D.** Trance and Treatment, pp. 35–108. New York: Basic Books, **1978.**

The hypnotic induction profile provides an empirical way of measuring hypnotizability. It also may provide some indicators of personality style. Different strategies for hypnosis treatment are based on the induction profile.

16. **Weitzenhoffer, A.M. and Hilgard, E.R.** Stanford Hypnotic Susceptibility Scale—Forms A and B, Forms I and II. Palo Alto: Consulting Psychology Press, **1963.**

A test for hypnotizability with a good track record on statistical validity.

PSYCHOPHYSIOLOGICAL CORRELATES

17. **Sarbin, T.R. and Slagle, R.W.** Hypnosis and psychophysiological outcomes, pp. 273–303. In: Hypnosis: Developments in Research and New Perspectives. Eds.: E. Fromm and R.E. Shor. New York: Aldine, **1979.**

The authors review what is known about altered physiological process brought about by hypnotic induction. Respiratory, cardiovascular, endocrine, and cutaneous changes are discussed as well as CNS and ocular movement changes.

18. **Sternbach, R.A.** On strategies for identifying neurochemical correlates of hypnotic analgesia. Int. J. Clin. Exp. Hypn. 30: 251–256, **1982.**

A test was made of the general hypothesis that central cholinergic mechanisms underlie hypnotic analgesia. There was some evidence found. Strategies for identifying neurotransmitters in a trance state are discussed.

CLINICAL TREATMENT ISSUES

19. **Gardner, G.G.** Hypnosis with children. Int. J. Clin. Exp. Hypn. 22: 20–38, **1974.**

Presents clinical and research findings and issues in use of hypnosis with children. Implications, patient selection, induction techniques, and creative approaches are discussed.

20. **Grinder, J., Delozier, J., and Bandler, R.** Patterns of hypnotic techniques of Milton H. Erickson, M.D., Vol. II, pp. 1–115. Cupertino, CA: Meta Publications, **1977.**

The authors provide a model, later called *neurolinguistic programming*, for understanding, making operational, and teaching many of the nonverbal, unconscious, and indirect techniques used by Erickson and other good hypnotists. Coming from a linguistic background, the authors also provide a superficial/deep structure analysis of the language of hypnosis.

21. **Hilgard, E.R. and Hilgard, J.R.** Hypnosis in the Relief of Pain, Chaps. 8–10. Los Altos, CA: Kaufman, **1975.**

A comprehensive look at the scientific and clinical aspects of hypnosis and pain. Specific hypnotic techniques are discussed and their differing applications in a wide variety of types of pain.

22. **Lankton, S.R.** The occurrence and use of trance phenomena in non-hypnotic therapies. In: Ericksonian Approaches to Hypnosis and Psychotherapy. Ed.: J.K. Zeig. New York: Brunner/Mazel, **1982.**

The author discusses the implications for nonhypnotic therapies of the spontaneous occurrence of trance phenomena like catalepsy, amnesia, age regressions, and hallucinations.

23.   **Spiegel, H.** A single treatment method to stop smoking using ancillary self-hypnosis. Int. J. Clin. Exp. Hypn. 18: 235–250, **1970.**

Technique of treatment, including rationale of approach, induction procedure, assessment of hypnotizability, and training instructions to stop smoking. A six-month follow-up study is also described.

49. SEX THERAPY

PHILIP M. SARREL, M.D.

During the past decade an explosion of interest in the treatment of sex response disorders (premature ejaculation, ejaculatory incompetence, erectile failure, female anorgasmia, and vaginismus) has led to the development of numerous treatment modalities. Individual, couples, and group therapy approaches have been described. Psychoanalytic, psychodynamic, and behavioral therapy and combinations of these disciplines are represented by many contributions, including a significant number of control studies. Most recently, there has been a growing appreciation for the incidence of biological causes of sexual dysfunction and the need for careful medical screening as part of the assessment of sexually dysfunctional couples.

Several worthwhile textbooks have been published for the field of sex therapy. Those that have proved most useful are annotated below. In addition, there are many references in this section to individual articles that were the first to present new therapy approaches or that summarize the literature relevant to a particular set of therapy principles, e.g., psychoanalytic concepts and sex therapy.

Sexual disorders also include problems of lack of desire, deviant behavior, and issues related to homosexuality. While not as extensive as that for the treatment of sex problems, the literature dealing with these other aspects of sexuality is significant and probably represents an area in which there will be more intense focus in coming years.

BASIC TEXTS

1. ***Kolodny, R.C., Masters, W.H., and Johnson, V.E.** Sexual aversion and inhibited desire, pp. 557–574. In: Textbook of Sexual Medicine. Eds.: R. Kolodny, W.H. Masters, and V.E. Johnson. Boston: Little, Brown, **1979.**

The problem of sexual aversion and inhibited sexual desire are presented clearly, and an effective approach to treatment is well described.

2. **Leiblum, S.R. and Pervin, L.A.** Principles and Practice of Sex Therapy. New York: Guilford Press, **1980.**

    Several excellent contributions (e.g., Lazarus's behavioral approaches and McWhiter's on homosexual issues) combine to make this a useful guide to recent approaches to sex therapy.

3. ***LoPiccolo, J. and LoPiccolo, L.** Handbook of Sex Therapy. New York: Plenum Press, **1978.**

    A compendium of articles by leading sex therapists. Recommended as a basic reading for the trainees to become familiar with the range of approaches in current use.

SEXUAL ORIENTATION

4. **Bieber, I.** The psychoanalytic treatment of sexual disorders. J. Sex Marital Ther. 1: 5–15, **1974.**

    Psychoanalytic understandings of sexual dysfunction should be understood for working with sexual issues that arise during the course of analysis, but also for their relevance in cases being treated through other approaches. This paper presents and updates psychoanalytic concepts regarding sex.

SEXUAL RESPONSE

5. ***Annon, J.S.** Behavioral Treatment of Sexual Problems: Brief Therapy. New York: Harper and Row, **1976.**

    A therapeutic manual describing four levels of intensity of therapist involvement. The model has been widely used for counseling and educational approaches and is an excellent one for teaching trainees an introduction to sex therapy.

6. ***Barbach, L.G.** Women Discover Orgasm: A Therapist's Guide to a New Treatment Approach. New York: Free Press, **1980.**

    Barbach pioneered the women's group approach to the problem of female nonorgasmic response. The approach is highly effective and is now used by therapists throughout the world. This book is a therapist's guide detailing the issues raised at each stage of the therapy.

7. **Caird, W. and Wincze, J.P.** Sex Therapy: A Behavioral Approach. New York: Harper and Row, **1977.**

A comprehensive presentation of the various behavioral approaches and the results of treatment.

8. *Green, R. Psychotherapy of erectile failure, pp. 131–141. In: Impotence: (Erectile Failure) Physiological, Psychological and Surgical Diagnosis and Treatment. Eds.: G. Wagner and R. Green. New York: Plenum Press, 1981.

A concise review article summarizing the important psychotherapy concepts of the past century as they relate to understanding male erectile dysfunction.

9. *Kaplan, H.S. The New Sex Therapy: Active Treatment of Sexual Dysfunctions. New York: Brunner/Mazel, 1974.

One of the formative books in the field of sex therapy, it is an extensive description of an approach that integrates psychodynamic, behavioral, and couples' therapy procedures.

10. *Kaplan, H.S., Kohl, R.N., Pomeroy, W.B., et al. Group treatment of premature ejaculation. Arch. Sex Behav. 3: 443–452, 1974.

An important first paper describing the group treatment of sexual dysfunction, particularly effective for the treatment of premature ejaculation, the approach is now widely used by other therapists.

11. Levay, A. and Kagle, A. A study of treatment needs following sex therapy. Am. J. Psychiatry 134: 970–973, 1977.

A study that looks at treatment failure in sex therapy and clarifies the situations in which psychotherapy or psychoanalytic work are needed.

12. Lobitz, C. and LoPiccola, J. New methods in the behavioral treatment of sexual dysfunction. J. Behav. Ther. Exp. Psychiatry 3: 265–271, 1972.

Couples were treated once a week for 15 weeks in a modification of the Masters-Johnson approach. The practices incorporated in this early work have now become routine in many programs and have continued to prove effective in the ongoing therapy program at State University of New York, Stony Brook.

13. *Masters, W.H. and Johnson, V.E. Principles of the new sex therapy. Am. J. Psychiatry 133: 548–554, 1976.

This is a brief and clearly written article that describes the brief concepts determining the co-therapy approach originally described by Masters and Johnson. It is listed to provide an alternative reading for the therapist who wishes to gain an understanding of the approach as an introduction to further reading.

14. *Mathews, A., Bancroft, J., Whitehead, A., et al. The behavioral treatment of sexual inadequacy: A comparative study. Behav. Res. Ther. 14: 427–436, 1976.

A study comparing brief psychotherapeutic intervention, medication, and combinations of approaches to treating couples with sexual dysfunctions. An excellent model for research design.

15. Maurice, W.L. and Guze, S.B. Sexual dysfunction and associated psychiatric disorders. Compr. Psychiatry 11: 539–543, 1970.

One of the rare papers dealing with the sexual problems of psychiatric patients.

16. *Munjack, D., Cristol, A., Goldstein, A., et al. Behavioural treatment of orgasmic dysfunction: A controlled study. Br. J. Psychiatry 129: 497–502, 1976.

The need for controlled studies are as great in sex therapy as in any other field. This study indicates the effectiveness of a behavioral approach and also defines its limitations.

17. *O'Connor, J.F. and Stern, L.O. Results of treatment in functional sexual disorders. N.Y. State J. Med. 72: 1927–1934, 1972.

An evaluation of psychoanalytic versus other brief psychotherapies for sexual dysfunctions. A retrospective study spanning some 17 years, the presence of concurrent psychopathology proved to be the most important prognostic indicator.

SEXUAL BEHAVIOR

18. Bancroft, J. Deviant Sexual Behavior: Modification and Assessment. New York: Oxford, 1974.

A researcher's book describing the problems of sexually deviant behavior and the approaches and results of different forms of therapy.

19. *Kaplan, H.S., Fyel, A.J., and Novick, A. The treatment of sexual phobias: The combined use of antipanic medication and sex therapy. J. Sex Marital Ther. 8: 3–28, 1982.

Sexual phobias are described along with a differential diagnosis. An approach to treatment is illustrated through several extensive case descriptions.

20. Money, J., Wiedeking, C., Walker, P.A., et al. Combined antiandrogenia and counseling program for treatment of 46, xy and 47, xyx sex

offenders, pp. 105–120. In: Hormones, Behavior, and Psychopathology. Ed.: E. Sachar. New York: Raven Press, **1976.**

Antiandrogens have proved effective in treating sex offenders. Albeit a very specialized area of sexual dysfunction, the problems of sexual molestation affect many people. Psychotherapists should be aware of treatment modalities for this problem.

21. **Rosen, R.C. and Kapel, S.A.** Penile plethysmography and biofeedback in the treatment of a transvestite-exhibitionist. J. Consult. Clin. Psychol. 45: 908–916, **1977.**

An approach that proved effective in treating a problem ordinarily very resistant to therapy. The approach described has been used as a model for treatment of other sexually deviant behaviors.

22. ***Sagar, C.J.** The role of sex therapy in marital therapy. Am. J. Psychiatry 133: 555–558, **1976.**

Sexual problems play a major role in fostering and maintaining marital conflict. This paper indicates ways to integrate sex therapy into a more generalized marital therapy.

PART V

NORMALITY AND DEVELOPMENT

50. INFANT AND CHILD DEVELOPMENT

PETER B. HENDERSON, M.D.
MINA K. DULCAN, M.D.

The following chapter represents our selection of the most significant references in the areas of infant and child psychiatry. In a relatively small number of citations, we have attempted to cover classical and contemporary writing on normal and abnormal development from birth to puberty and techniques of assessment and treatment especially relevant to this age group. We have also selected readings that integrate etiology, assessment, and treatment of many of the common and/or severe syndromes and symptoms found in infants and children. In addition, we have included references that address those parental problems that significantly affect children, such as child abuse and divorce.

Throughout this section we have kept in mind the needs and interests of trainees and educators in general psychiatry. This listing is therefore not as extensive as would be recommended for child psychiatrists. We have given preference to those readings that provide practical guidance in understanding infants, children, and their families, and in the basic techniques of evaluation and treatment. We have also sought the literature referring to infants and children that is most relevant to the practice of general psychiatry, with consideration of the continuities of child and adult development and psychopathology and the interactions of children and adults within the family system.

The fields of infant and child psychiatry are in a state of rapid development and change. Research findings have not supported all of the theories proposed in the "classical" articles we have selected. We have included them, nonetheless, because of our belief in the importance of a general knowledge of the development of the field. We would not be surprised if new research findings call into question even some of the most current selections. Our approach is an attempt to be comprehensive in that we include works from empirical perspectives as well as the "traditional" approaches of psychoanalysis and Piaget. It is our goal to give the psychiatrist in training the basic information from which to proceed in a continual process of critical evaluation of knowledge and methods. For those who wish to explore further the literature in infant and child psychiatry, we recommend the bibliographies compiled by Berlin (1) and Henderson (2).

The readings are organized into the following subheadings: general reference, normal infant and child development, abnormal infant and child development, diagnosis and assessment in infancy and childhood, psychiatric treatment of infants and children, and special topics.

GENERAL REFERENCE

1. ***Chess, S. and Hassibi, M.** Principles and Practice of Child Psychiatry. New York: Plenum Press, **1978.**

    This book represents a fundamental organization of information in a textbook format. The factors involved in the etiology and treatment of child psychiatric disorders are reviewed. Individual chapters cover major areas related to disordered behavior, syndromes, and methods of child psychiatric intervention.

2. ***Noshpitz, J.D.,** sr. ed. Basic Handbook of Child Psychiatry. New York: Basic Books, **1979.**
    Vol. I: Development (J.D. Call, J.D. Noshpitz, R.L. Cohen and I.N. Berlin, eds.)
    Vol. II: Disturbances of development (J.D. Noshpitz, ed.)
    Vol. III: Therapeutic interventions (S.J. Harrison, ed.)
    Vol. IV: Prevention and current issues (I.N. Berlin and L.A. Stone, eds.)

    This is an encylcopedic reference collection covering a multiauthored contribution to the child and adolescent psychiatric literature. Each of the four volumes' titles relate directly to their contents, which are the most comprehensive collection of papers regarding normal and abnormal development, assessment, treatment, special syndromes, research, etc., presently available.

NORMAL INFANT AND CHILD DEVELOPMENT

3. **Anders, T.F.** The development of sleep patterns and sleep disturbances from infancy through adolescence. Advances Behav. Ped. 2: 171–190, **1981.**

    A detailed account of the clinical and polygraphic characteristics of normal and abnormal sleep patterns at each developmental stage from the premature infant to the adolescent. Syndromes described include disturbances of sleep onset or continuity, night terrors, sleepwalking, enuresis, narcolepsy, sleep apnea, and disturbance of sleep-wake phase shifts.

4.   **Bornstein, B.** On latency. Psychoanal. Study Child 6: 279–285, **1951.**

This reference underscores the prevailing belief that all children in the school age, or latency period of development (not just those manifesting disturbance) use uninvested libidinal energy in evolving character development. During latency, environmental trauma should be reduced as much as possible in order not to interfere with healthy ego development.

5.   **Brinich, P.M.** Some potential effects of adoption on self and object representations. Psychoanal. Study Child 35: 107–134, **1980.**

This work addresses some of the special hazards of adoption in normal child development and is useful in considering aspects of the mental life of children and adults who were adopted.

6.   ***Chess, S.** Temperament and children at risk, pp. 121–130. In: The Child in His Family, Vol. 1. New York: Wiley-Interscience, **1970.**

Beyond the usual concepts of vulnerability to psychiatric disorder, traits of temperament have been added as a category of risk. The term "temperament" relates to the behavioral style of an individual, the manner of behavior rather than the content and motivation. Patterns of temperament are likely to make a child vulnerable to a damaging interaction with his environment. This parameter is assessed in terms of nine categories of reactivity and/or risk.

7.   **Chess, S. and Thomas, A.** Infant bonding: Mystique and reality. Am. J. Orthopsychiatry 52: 213–222, **1982.**

A major "counterpoint" made by two highly distinguished clinical investigators in personality development. The article offers several alternate views of the critical nature of infant-mother bonding, as this occurrence is viewed by several recent clinical researchers in infant development as the primary cornerstone of healthy or abnormal personality formation.

8.   **Dibble, E.D. and Cohen, D.J.** Personality development in identical twins: The first decade of life. Psychoanal. Study Child 36: 45–70, **1981.**

This is one of the very few rigorous and systematic studies of personality development in twins, built upon an important prospective longitudinal twin study using a reliable sampling process. This reference could be used as a "best example" of twin studies.

9. ***Erikson, E.H.** Childhood and Society (2nd ed.). New York: Norton. **1963.**

The book is a classic. Psychoanalytic developmental theory is extended through the full life cycle, with focus on "epigenesis." This approach stresses social context while broadening psychoanalytic theory to a psychosocial theory of sequential developmental stages, each based on the integration of earlier stage(s).

10. ***Fraiberg, S.H.** The Magic Years: Understanding and Handling the Problems of Early Childhood. New York: Scribner, **1959.**

This book is a historical marker. It represents one of the earliest efforts to translate major psychoanalytic concepts in child development into a successful and widely read handbook on development, enjoyable to read as well as understandable to parents without advanced knowledge of development. Suggestions for common problems in child rearing are a highlight of this book. Any psychiatrist should know about this work and would find it useful early reading before seeing any child for intervention.

11. ***Freud, A.** The concept of developmental lines, pp. 62–92. In: Normality and Pathology in Childhood: Assessments of Development. New York: International Universities Press, **1965.**

A major contributor in the field of child development. Miss Freud recommends that adults attune themselves to the child's own interpretation of his world. The latter depends upon the development of mental organization through the integrative concept of historical lines of development. The reference is a landmark in developmental theory.

12. ***Ginsburg, H. and Opper, S.** Piaget's Theory of Intellectual Development: An Introduction. Englewood Cliffs, N.J.: Prentice-Hall, **1969.** (Also available in 2nd ed., **1979.**)

An understandable account of the basic features of Piaget's developmental theories, including descriptions of Piaget's methods, helpful examples, and the characteristics of each stage.

13. ***Lewis, M.** Clinical Aspects of Child Development: An Introductory Synthesis of Developmental Concepts and Clinical Experience (2nd ed.). Philadelphia: Lea and Febiger, **1982.**

Lewis includes updated, well-balanced cross-sectional descriptions of developmental stages, as well as a section on longitudinal perspectives.

describing 10 different developmental schemes. The section on introduction to clinical psychiatric diagnosis provides the basics for the evaluation of psychopathology in children and adolescents. Should be required reading for all psychiatric residents.

14. **Lidz, T.** Family studies and changing concepts of personality development. Can. J. Psychiatry 24: 621–632, **1979.**

The author states that the failure to recognize the importance of the family has interfered with the formation of an integrated developmental theory, both in training and in practice. The conditions the family must provide to assure integrated development of its children are discussed in detail. Parental nurturant functions that change with each phase of child development are listed and also make this a valuable reference article.

15. ***Mahler, M.S.** Symbiosis and individuation: The psychological birth of the human infant, pp. 149–165. In: The Selected Papers of Margaret S. Mahler, Vol. II. New York: Aronson, **1979.**

A major contribution in early childhood developmental theory, the separation-individuation process is reviewed by its originator and principal author. Important to the resident in psychiatry for didactic knowledge and clinical application, as it refers to the "psychology of the self." The reference details major libidinal concepts in preverbal development of young children.

16. **Osofsky, J.D.,** ed. The Handbook of Infant Development. New York: Wiley-Interscience, **1979.**

This book presents an encyclopedic review of current theoretical ideas, data, and issues in the research on infancy from birth to two years. It brings together in a single source the latest thinking about infant assessment and interventions, combined new views of theories of development, clinical issues, and could be a major foundation reference in personality developmental theory as well as clinical applications.

17. **Rutter, M.** Social-emotional consequences of day care for preschool children. Am. J. Orthopsychiatry. 51: 4–28, **1981.**

Rutter reviews the research evidence on the social and emotional sequelae of day care for young children. He avoids the highly polarized positions taken by many authors and concludes that the effects vary according to the quality of the day care and the characteristics of the child and family.

18. **Winnicott, D.W.** Transitional objects and transitional phenomena: A study of the first not-me possession. Int. J. Psychoanal. 34: 89–97, **1953.**

A historically pertinent reference, this is the original description of the earliest stages of infant personality development to include both external objects (the transitional objects) and the internal and interpersonal experiences (the transitional phenomena) in negotiating this early developmental set of sequences. Prototype similarity to later, more complex, transformations in internal and interpersonal development can be identified from these first successful (or unsuccessful) developmental accomplishments.

ABNORMAL INFANT AND CHILD DEVELOPMENT

19.   ***Bender, L.** The nature of childhood psychosis, pp. 649–684. In: Modern Perspectives in International Child Psychiatry. Ed.: J.G. Howells. New York: Brunner/Mazel, **1971.**

A strongly recommended reference on the perspectives, both in the United States and other countries, of seminal clinicians and researchers in the field of psychoses that have onsets before puberty. Connections between these aspects of severe early psychopathology and later adult mental functioning make this historical view applicable to understanding varied theories of later life maladjustment. Richly referenced (210 bibliographic citations).

20.   ***Bowlby, J.** The Adolf Meyer lecture: Childhood mourning and its implications for psychiatry. Am. J. Psychiatry 118: 481–498, **1961.**

A strong predictor of difficulties in normal childhood development relates to a child's response to early object loss. Stages of protest, despair, and object detachment are examined in this article and shown to be analogous to those in adult mourning. A helpful reference in early childhood developmental theory from this historical viewpoint.

21.   **Earle, E.M.** Psychological effects of mutilating surgery in children and adolescents. Psychoanal. Study Child 34: 527–546, **1979.**

Clinical observations made during crisis work with children and adolescents undergoing amputation of a limb and long-term cancer chemotherapy are presented. A literature review on the effects of hospitalization, loss of limb and grief reactions, body image and phantom limbs, and major coping mechanisms are well examined in this article. This is relevant to clinical work with younger to older age child patients.

22.   **El-Guebaly, N. and Offord, D.R.** The offspring of alcoholics: A critical review. Am. J. Psychiatry 134: 357–365, **1977.**

A critical review of research on the effects of parental alcoholism on children, organized according to the age group of the subject offspring.

23.   **Kornberg, M.S. and Caplan, G.** Risk factors and preventive intervention in child psychopathology: A review. J. Prevention 1: 71–133, **1980.**

A critical and exhaustive review of 650 papers on biopsychosocial risk factors and on primary prevention of childhood psychological disorders. Useful for psychiatrists treating adults who happen to be parents, as well as for those psychiatrists seeing children and consulting to schools, hospitals, or agencies serving children and families.

24.   **Kotelchuck, M.** Nonorganic failure to thrive: The status of interactional and environmental etiologic theories. Advances Behav. Ped. 1: 29–51, **1980.**

The author begins with a discussion of the history and differential diagnosis of organic and nonorganic failure to thrive. He questions many of the widely held clinical assumptions concerning etiology and associated features of failure to thrive, using a critical review of the research literature, and ends with a summary of what has been objectively demonstrated concerning this syndrome.

25.   **Mattison, R.E., Cantwell, D.P., and Baker, L.** Behavior problems in children with speech and language retardation. Child Psychiatry Hum. Dev. 10: 246–257, **1980.**

A report of a systematic survey of behavioral problems and psychiatric disorders in 100 children age 2 to 13 years seen in a community speech and hearing clinic.

26.   **Nagera, H.** Children's reactions to hospitalization and illness. Child Psychiatry Hum. Dev. 9: 3–19, **1978.**

This reference is important both in training for consultation-liaison practice, as well as the importance of this data in anamestic histories taken from older age individuals regarding earlier hospitalizations. Children's reactions to illness and hospitalization are described from a developmental point of view, illuminating the nature of potential damage, as well as resources for the prevention of chronic sequelae.

27.   **Orvaschel, H., Weissman, M.M., and Kidd, K.K.** Children and depression: The children of depressed parents; the childhood of depressed patients; depression and children. J. Affective Disord. 2: 1–16, **1980.**

Relevant particularly for psychiatrists' understanding of the development of depression in children, drawn from three types of studies: of the children of depressed adults; the childhood histories of depressed adults; and depression in childhood. The data support an increased frequency of depression and other psychopathology in the children of depressed adults. This study's methodology has clinical applications that will help sort out the relative influences of genetic and environmental factors in patient populations.

28.   ***Pfeffer, C.R.** Suicidal behavior of children: A review with implications for research and practice. Am. J. Psychiatry 138: 154–159, **1981.**

Pfeffer reviews the definition and incidence of suicidal behaviors in children and factors that lead to an increased risk of this behavior. She makes recommendations for the evaluation of suicidal potential in children and for further study.

29.   **Philips, I. and Williams, N.** Psychopathology and mental retardation: A study of one hundred mentally retarded children: I. Psychopathology. Am. J. Psychiatry 132: 1265–1271, **1975.**

This article emphasizes the effects of organicity on otherwise typical presentations of clinical psychopathology in a childhood population. The children's symptoms did not differ in kind from those found in a group of nonretarded children. Implications for studies in childhood and adult psychopathology, with and without mental retardation, are emphasized.

30.   ***Rohrlich, J.A., Ranier, R., Beig-Cross, L., et al.** The effects of divorce: A research review with a developmental perspective. J. Clin. Child Psychol. 6: 15–20, **1977.**

A thorough review of the effects of divorce on children. Well-organized description of the different emotional and behavioral responses manifested by children at each developmental stage, with recommendations for management.

31.   ***Rutter, M.** Maternal deprivation, 1972–1978: New findings, new concepts, new approaches. Child Dev. 50: 283–305, **1979.**

Rutter critically reviews the literature on syndromes related to maternal deprivation and re-examines earlier formulations. Such controversial issues as social relationships, attachment behaviors, bonding, critical periods in intellecutal and social development, and infants at high risk who do not develop psychopathology are examined. The bibliography is extensive.

32.   **Rutter, M.** Emotional disorder and educational underachievement. Arch. Dis. Child. 49: 249–256, **1974.**

A critical review, in which the reader is taken step by step from the definition and classification of several categories of educational under-achievement to the variety of proposed relationships with emotional disorders. Rutter evaluates the available data and distinguishes carefully between fact and theory.

33.   **Rutter, M.** Psychologic sequelae of brain damage in children. Am. J. Psychiatry 138: 1533–1544, **1981.**

An outstanding review of the empirical evidence on the psychological sequelae of brain damage in childhood (including Rutter's own prospec-tive study). The influences of severity and locus of brain injury, type of neurologic pathology, age at injury, temperamental and behavioral features, psychological adversity, and cognitive factors on the incidence and type of psychiatric disturbance are summarized.

34.   ***Solnit, A.J. and Stark, M.H.** Mourning and the birth of a defective child. Psychoanal. Study Child 16: 523–537, **1961.**

This article illustrates the psychological effects of the birth of a congenitally defective child, discussed from the point of view of direct impact on adult and sibling family members, as well as medical personnel dealing with the family (the mother, in particular).

35.   ***Spitz, R.A.** Hospitalism: An inquiry into the genesis of psychiatric conditions in early childhood. Psychoanal. Study Child 1: 53–74, **1945.**

This paper presents one of the most potentially serious and severe psychopathologic developments in infancy. The study, concerned with the effects of continuous institutional care of infants age one year and under placed in hospitals for reasons other than sickness, i.e., generally death of or abandonment by one or both parents, has major implications. The outcome in the most severe cases is fatal, and for the less severe marked emotional and cognitive scarring in future development.

36.   ***Spitz, R.A. and Wolf, K.M.** Anaclitic depression: An inquiry into the genesis of psychiatric conditions in early childhood: Part II. Psychoanal. Study Child 2: 313–342, **1946.**

This important early literature contribution has continuing implications in developmental outcome for later life personality functioning. It provides a clear discussion of anaclitic depression in infants in their first year of life, including diagnosis, dynamic and structural considerations in evolving ego functions and in general personality development.

37.   ***Tarjan, G., Wright, S.W., Eyman, R.K., et al.** Natural history of mental retardation: Some aspects of epidemiology. Am. J. Ment. Defic. 77: 369–379, **1973.**

This article summarizes information presented on the prevalence and incidence of mental retardation in the general population, on the processes of institutionalization patterns, and on recent changing trends in the care of retarded children. Data are also included providing demonstration of the highly transitional and changing nature of the present scene in the care of mentally retarded individuals.

DIAGNOSIS AND ASSESSMENT IN INFANCY AND CHILDHOOD

38. **Cantwell, D.P., Russell, A.T., Mattison, R., et al.** A comparison of DSM-II and DSM-III in the diagnosis of childhood psychiatric disorders. Arch. Gen. Psychiatry 36: 1208–1228, **1979.**

This four-part reference is important for general psychiatrists in their use of the *DSM-III* classification of childhood psychopathology. The average rater error agreement for 24 actual child case histories, computed for each case, was less than 50 percent. It was highest in cases of mental retardation, psychosis, hyperactivity, and conduct disorder. The use of collaboration with specialists in child psychiatry for diagnostically complex cases is examined in this article.

39. **Grunebaum, H. and Chasin, R.** Relabeling and reframing reconsidered: The beneficial effects of a pathological label. Fam. Process 17: 449–455, **1978.**

This article confronts the controversy that pathological labels contribute to entrenching childhood psychopathology, while the converse, i.e., benign labels, help alleviate adjustment difficulties. It is suggested that the etiological role of labeling has been overstated and overgeneralized. Reframing and relabeling in childhood conditions are well illustrated in this article.

40. **Hayden, T.L.** Classification of elective mutism. J. Am. Acad. Child Psychiatry 19: 118–133, **1980.**

From a study of 68 cases of elective mutism, the author has distinguished four types of this disorder: symbiotic, speech phobic, reactive, and passive-aggressive mutism. The presumed etiology, associated features, and prognosis of each type are described.

41. **Rothstein, A.** Hallucinatory phenomena in childhood: A critique of the literature. J. Am. Acad. Child Psychiatry 20: 623–635, **1981.**

A critical review of the literature on hallucinations in children who are not in states of altered brain function or experimentally induced states. The diagnostic implications and psychodynamic functions of childhood hallucinations are discussed in the context of normal and abnormal development.

42. **Rudel, R.C.** Learning disability: Diagnosis by exclusion and discrepancy. J. Am. Acad. Child Psychiatry 19: 547–659, **1980.**

A discussion of the diagnosis of learning disability and associated neurologic findings. A detailed description of the variety of skill deficits found in learning-disabled children is preceded by a brief review of intelligence testing. The author also describes the characteristics of dyslexic and nondyslexic learning-disabled children.

43. ***Simmons, J.E.** Psychiatric examination of children. (3rd ed.). Philadelphia: Lea and Febiger, **1981.**

A new edition of an essential practical handbook for medical students and psychiatric residents who are learning to evaluate children and their families. It is designed to be used in conjunction with the *DSM-III* manual and includes an introduction to the rationale for diagnosis in general, and *DSM-III* in particular. Simmons addresses the clinical and attitudinal questions asked by beginners.

44. **Tseng, W.S., Arsendorf, A.M., McDermott, J.F., et al.** Family diagnosis and classification. J. Am. Acad. Child Psychiatry 15: 15–35, **1976.**

One of the significant early and major attempts to include adults and children in a family diagnostic and assessment schema. Six major classifications systems of family pathology are identified, discussed, and illustrated with case histories. A continuum of pathological interactions operating within a family system, utilizing innovative diagnostic concepts, is also illustrated.

45. **Zucker, K.J.** Childhood gender disturbance: Diagnostic issues. J. Am. Acad. Child Psychiatry 21: 274–280, **1982.**

A critical evaluation of three diagnostic models developed for use with children suffering from gender-related syndromes. The clinical usefulness, reliability, and validity of each is examined, with recommendations for further study.

PSYCHIATRIC TREATMENT OF INFANTS AND CHILDREN

46. ***Adams, P.L.** A Primer of Child Psychotherapy (2nd ed.). Boston: Little, Brown, **1982.**

This second edition (1982) offers updated references in several chapters, but not a major change of view or format of the earlier 1974 edition. It gives inexperienced trainees an optimistic view of practical ways to help disturbed children. It has little in technical theories of change to offer, but focuses regularly on "how-to" approaches to handle strategies and techniques in beginning clinical work with young patients.

47.   ***Arnold, L.E.** Strategies and tactics of parent guidance, pp. 3–21. In: Helping Parents Help their Children. Ed.: L.E. Arnold. New York: Brunner/Mazel, **1978.**

A practical introduction to understanding and working with parents of child psychiatric patients. Addresses all of the common questions and errors of the novice therapist. Also useful in the treatment of adult patients who happen to be parents.

48.   **Barkley, R.A.** A review of stimulant drug research with hyperactive children. J. Child Psychol. Psychiatry 18: 137–165, **1977.**

A critical and comprehensive review of the research literature on stimulant drug treatment of hyperactivity in children. Barkley specifically addresses the topics of clinical effectiveness; biochemical, psychophysiologic, behavioral, and test performance measures of change; and side effects.

49.   **Dimascio, L., Steinfels, M., Brown, L., et al.** MBD, drug research and the schools: A conference on medical responsibility and community control. pp. 1–23. In: The Hastings Center Report (Special Suppl.), June, **1976.**

Stimulus for the conference reported in this article was a 1972 controversy in Boston over a research project testing the effects of three psychotropic drugs on learning difficulties and behavior disorders. Discussion participants, including the disciplines of medicine, law, education, and philosophy examine the ethics of use of drugs for children with minimal brain dysfunction (MBD), the validity of this term as a diagnostic category, and the appropriateness of labeling children with this term.

50.   **Geist, R.A.** Onset of chronic illness in children and adolescents: Psychotherapeutic and consultative intervention. Am. J. Orthopsychiatry 49: 4–23, **1979.**

The author draws on his extensive clinical experience with children and adolescents in the early stages of a variety of chronic mental illnesses to describe their psychological reactions and to recommend consultative and psychotherapeutic interventions. They also discuss the emotional reactions in professionals who care for these patients.

51. **Harley, J.P.** Dietary treatment of behavioral disorders. Advances Behav. Ped. 1: 129–151, **1980.**

The dietary treatment of PKU (phenylketonuria) is used as a model for dietary treatment of behavioral disorders. The author then critically evaluates the evidence regarding megavitamins, refined sugar, caffeine, food allergies, and food additives in the etiology and treatment of behavior disorders in children. This review is particularly useful in answering questions asked by parents regarding these unconventional treatments.

52. ***Jefferson, J.W.** The use of lithium in childhood and adolescence: An overview. J. Clin. Psychiatry 43: 174–177, **1982.**

A review of the history of lithium therapy for children and adolescents, with a discussion of diagnostic issues in manic-depressive disorder in youth. Included are guidelines for the use of lithium in this age group, with special attention to side effects.

53. ***Jorgensen, O.S.** Psychopharmacological treatment of psychotic children: A survey. Acta Psychiatr. Scand. 59: 229–238, **1979.**

Controlled investigations on the psychopharmacological treatment of infantile autism, schizophrenia, and manic-depressive psychoses are reviewed in order to discuss the developmental, environmental, and ethical problems associated with the treatment of psychotic children. Important considerations include factors related to facilitated learning in children when psychoactive medication is used to inhibit psychotic symptoms. This article confronts the idea that schizophrenia and major affective psychosis in childhood are treated differently than in adults; developmental considerations are emphasized in this article.

54. ***Masten, A.S.** Family therapy as a treatment for children: A critical review of outcome research. Fam. Process 18: 323–335, **1979.**

The outcome research literature on the value of family therapy as a treatment for childhood psychopathology is reviewed. Some of the empirical evidence demonstrates that family therapy is an effective treatment for children; the data from studies of adolescents seem even more encouraging. A helpful reference in the "individual vs. family therapy" argument.

55. **Minde, K.K. and Minde, R.** Psychiatric intervention in infancy: A review. J. Am. Acad. Child Psychiatry 20: 217–238, **1981.**

A historic account of the field of infant psychiatry, including a critical evaluation of treatment methods, including psychoanalysis, behavioral approaches, and indirect treatment via parents or other primary caretakers. The data on the effectiveness of early intervention and stimulation programs are reviewed.

56.   ***Minuchin, S. and Montalvo, B.** Techniques for working with disorganized low socioeconomic families. Am. J. Orthopsychiatry 37: 880–887, **1967.**

This adaptation of traditional family therapy takes into account specific characteristics of communication style, cognition, and ways children in these families might experience affect. It is proposed that similar adaptations of traditional family therapy may apply to disorganized families, regardless of their socioeconomic position, and have greater general applicability in psychiatry.

57.   **Minuchin, S., Baker, L., Rosman, B.L., et al.** A conceptual model of psychosomatic illness in children: Family organization and family therapy. Arch. Gen. Psychiatry 32: 1031–1038, **1975.**

An innovative approach to children's predisposition for psychosomatic illness, "symptom choice," and maintenance of psychopathology are discussed in this article within the conceptual framework of structural family therapy. A provocative and important method for the psychiatrist to conceptualize onset and maintenance of childhood symptomatology (involving linear and systems models), as well as an important intervention modality.

58.   **Ollendick, T.H.** Fear reduction techniques with children. Prog. Behav. Modification 8: 127–168, **1979.**

An extensive discussion of the incidence, classification, etiology, and prognosis of childhood fears and phobias, followed by a description of the methods and outcome data of three types of behavioral treatments. Ollendick also includes recommendations for an integrated treatment approach and an exhaustive bibliography.

59.   ***Phillips, J.S. and Ray, R.S.** Behavioral approaches to childhood disorders. Behav. Modification 4: 3–34, **1980.**

A critical review, with extensive bibliography, of behavioral treatment methods including parent training, classroom interventions, and self-regulation and self-control techniques. The authors present outcome data for the behavioral treatment of hyperactivity, social isolation and social skills deficits, fears, phobias, avoidance, habit disorders, as well as autism and childhood psychosis.

60.   **Proskauer, S.** Focused time-limited psychotherapy with children. J. Am. Acad. Child Psychiatry 10: 619–639, **1971.**

A description of a psychodynamic model of brief individual psychotherapy with children and adolescents. Key features are a focus on a specific dynamic issue and a termination date that is set during the first treatment session. The stages of therapy are delineated, using clinical examples. The author also discusses selection criteria and issues in training and supervision.

61.   **Schulman, J.L., delaFuente, M.E., and Suran, B.G.** An indication for brief psychotherapy. The fork in the road phenomenon. Bull. Menninger Clin. 41: 553–562, **1977.**

A clinically oriented paper, including two case reports, which proposes mechanisms for the development of certain psychopathology in children that responds well to brief psychotherapy with the child and family. Selection criteria and principles of brief psychotherapy are described.

62.   **Smith, H.F., Bemporad, J.R., and Hanson, G.** Aspects of the treatment of borderline children. Am. J. Psychother. 36: 181–197, **1982.**

The authors begin with a history of the concept of borderline children followed by a description of diagnostic criteria for the syndrome. They then describe in detail the treatment of these children, using individual and family therapy, pharmacotherapy, and environmental support.

63.   **Strelnick, A.H.** Multiple family group therapy: A review of the literature. Fam. Process 16: 307–325, **1977.**

A careful analysis of this therapeutic intervention modality for parents and children that would be of practical utility for both practicing general and child psychiatrists. A review of the literature on multiple family group therapy is presented that examines its use in a variety of settings (inpatient and outpatient), specific techniques, and group dynamics. Common themes include parenting, dependency, individuation, emotional environments, and mental health of families of young children.

64.   **Urbain, E.S. and Kendall, P.C.** Review of social-cognitive problem-solving interventions with children. Psychol. Bull. 88: 109–143, **1980.**

A critical review of studies of training in interpersonal problem solving, self-control, and social perspective taking with children. The authors describe treatment procedures, evaluate outcome data, and discuss clinical and research questions that remain unanswered. An introduction to these relatively new treatment methods, with an extensive bibliography.

65.   **Vincent, J.P.** The empirical-clinical study of families: Social learning theory as a point of departure. Advances Fam. Intervention, Assessment Theory 1: 1–28, **1980.**

A readable and clear account of major family intervention models, written by a sophisticated clinical methodologist. Target populations studied range from the families of children exhibiting behavior problems from hyperactivity to aggressive conduct disorders. Summaries of the best examples of methodologically sound family therapy outcome research are presented.

66.   ***Weiner, J.M.** Psychopharmacology in Childhood and Adolescence. New York: Basic Books, **1977.**

This textbook presents an overview of childhood and adolescent psychopharmacology, examining the pharmacologic treatment of children, and particularly raising important questions to be considered by psychiatrists-in-training of the largely unknown interactions between psychoactive drugs and the developing organism. Potential advantages and disadvantages of psychoactive medication in childhood are well covered, acknowledging limitations and absence of adequate clinical trials with childhood patients, where that status is available.

67.   **Werry, J.S.** An overview of pediatric psychopharmacology. J. Am. Acad. Child Psychiatry 21: 3–9, **1982.**

For the practicing psychiatrist, as well as in training, this represents a good (and brief) current overview that illuminates many of the areas in which pharmacoactive drugs in wide use in adult psychiatry have been used both correctly, and more often incorrectly, with child patients. The article also reviews the history and current knowledge-in-the-field of pediatric psychopharmacology and its differences from adult psycho-pharmacology.

SYNDROMES IN INFANCY AND CHILDHOOD

68.   ***Bemporad, J.R.** Encopresis, pp. 161–178. In: Handbook of Treatment of Mental Disorders in Childhood and Adolescence. Eds.: B.B. Wolman, J. Egan, and A.O. Ross. Englewood Cliffs, N.J.: Prentice-Hall, **1978.**

A comprehensive account of the psychological factors in the etiology and psychotherapeutic treatment of this common and distressing symptom. Different types of fecal soiling are described, using case examples.

69.   **Dykman, R.A. and Ackerman, P.** Long-term follow-up studies of hyperactive children. Advances Behav. Ped. 1: 97–128, **1980.**

An excellent, detailed review of clinical, retrospective, and prospective studies of the long-term outcome of hyperactive children (*DSM-III* equivalent: attention deficit disorder with hyperactivity). The authors also comment on research design issues in longitudinal studies of childhood disorders.

70. **Eggers, C.** Course and prognosis of childhood schizophrenia. J. Aut. Childhood Schizophr. 8: 21–36, **1978.**

A useful reference for understanding work with schizophrenic populations. A 15-year follow-up of 57 schizophrenic patients, between ages 7 and 13, is reported to clarify the course and prognosis of childhood schizophrenia. Premorbid childhood personality development was found to be a strong prognostic factor in later chronic psychopathology or favorable outcomes.

71. ***Eisenberg, L.** School phobia: Diagnosis, genesis and clinical management, pp. 424–436. In: Sourcebook in Abnormal Psychology. Boston: Houghton-Mifflin, **1967.**

All psychiatrists should be clearly aware that school phobia is distinct from truancy, as pointed out in this early original contribution to the literature. Quite often, the mother is as involved as the child in school nonattendance. Suggestions for intervention are included in this article, many of which are pertinent for current practice.

72. **Elkins, R., Rapoport, J.L., and Lipsky, A.** Obsessive-compulsive disorder of childhood and adolescence: A neurobiological viewpoint. J. Am. Child Psychiatry 19: 511–524, **1980.**

A description of the syndrome of obsessive-compulsive disorder as manifested in children and adolescents. The authors critically examine data from genetic, epidemiologic, neurologic, and psychopharmacologic research, which suggests a neurobiological hypothesis concerning etiology.

73. **English, O.S. and Pearson, G.H.J.** Irrational fears and phobias, pp. 375–381. In: Childhood Psychopathology. Eds.: S.I. Harrison and J.F. McDermott. New York: International Universities Press, **1972.**

The authors distinguish between ordinary childhood fears and irrational phobias and then give a brief account of the psychodynamic theory of the development of phobias in children, using a case example.

74. **Gerard, M.W.** Enuresis: A study in etiology, pp. 418–430. In: Childhood Psychopathology: An Anthology of Basic Readings. Eds.: S.I. Harrison and J.F. McDermott. New York: International Universities Press, **1972.** (Repr. Am. J. Orthopsychiatry 9: 48–58, **1939.**)

A classic paper, which is still valid, reporting on the histories and treatment of 72 children referred for enuresis. Most noteworthy is the discussion of the variety of etiologic and psychodynamic factors.

75.   ***Green, A.H.** Psychopathology of abused children. J. Am. Acad. Child Psychiatry 17: 92–103, **1978.**

A report on the clinical findings, psychopathology, psychodynamics, and family circumstances of 20 abused children seen in a psychotherapeutic treatment program. Although there is no comparison group of nonabused children from similar families, the data is useful to mental health professionals working with abused children and their families.

76.   **Hollingsworth, C.E., Tanguay, P.E., Grossman, L., et al.** Long-term outcome of obsessive compulsive disorder in childhood. J. Am. Acad. Child Psychiatry 19: 134–144, **1980.**

A longitudinal study covering 16 years of child outpatient treatment of diagnosed obsessive-compulsive disorder revealed in structured interviews with young adults (17 cases total within the study) that nearly 70 percent still reported serious problems with social life and peer relations, even though major treatment interventions had been rendered during the childhood and adolescent courses of the disorder. It assists in reasonable prognosis planning.

77.   ***Kanner, L.** Early infantile autism revisited. Psychiatry Digest 29: 17–28, **1968.**

As a historical document, this reference covers developments in the field of infantile autism from the first reported cases in 1943 up to 1968. Even when this article was published little was known concerning the etiology and therapy of this condition. Recognition that autism is not primarily an acquired disease is valuable for contemporary training. Theories advanced concerning etiology and therapeutic techniques remain speculative, but a rigorous review and "state-of-the-art" circa 1968 provides lasting value to this reference.

78.   ***Ornitz, E.M. and Ritvo, E.R.** The syndrome of autism: A critical review. Am. J. Psychiatry 133: 609–621, **1976.**

A summary of the clinical features, differential diagnosis, and treatment of autism. Research on etiology, prevalence, prognosis, and neurophysiologic and biochemical abnormalities is briefly reviewed.

79.   ***Pine, F.** On the concept of "borderline" in children: A clinical essay. Psychoanal. Study Child 29: 341–368, **1974.**

As psychiatry increasingly considers the "borderline" conditions in adults, this article gives an important developmental perspective to these individuals when they would have been younger, i.e., children and adolescents. It is suggested that what unites the children exhibiting these phenomena is the presence of severe developmental failure in the realm of ego functions and object relationships, as is prevalently believed in the adult conditions.

80. **Poznanski, E.** Childhood depression: The outcome. Acta Paedopsychiatr. 46: 297–304, **1980/81.**

An overview of diagnosis and outcome of affective disorder in children and adolescents.

81. ***Puig-Antich, J.** Affective disorders in childhood: A review and perspective. Psychiatr. Clin. North Am. 3: 403–424, **1980.**

A review of the data on prevalence, diagnosis, and treatment of manic disorder and major depressive disorder in school-age children and adolescents. The author describes clinical and research methods of assessment of depression in youth.

82. **Robins, L.N.** Epidemiological approaches to natural history research: Antisocial disorders in children. J. Am. Acad. Child Psychiatry 20: 566–580, **1981.**

A summary of epidemiological studies of antisocial disorders in children and adolescents, with an emphasis on the implications of these studies for etiology and treatment. A bonus is the understandable, jargon-free introduction to methods used in psychiatric epidemiology and the usefulness of the data obtained.

83. **Rutter, M.** The development of infantile autism. Psychol. Med. 4: 147–163, **1974.**

This article gives the most comprehensive account of research over the last 30 years that has led to progress in the delineation of the mechanisms involved in the etiology and genesis of the behavior covered by the term "infantile autism." The validity, nature, and basis of the syndrome are discussed with reference to treatment possibilities.

84. ***Rutter, M.** Syndromes attributed to "minimal brain dysfunction" in childhood. Am. J. Psychiatry 139: 21–33, **1982.**

A detailed, critical review of the literature on "minimal brain dysfunction" in childhood. Rutter examines the evidence for various definitions of this disorder.

85. **Serrano, A.C., Zuelzer, M.B., Hume, D.D., et al.** Ecology of abusive and non-abusive families: Implications for intervention. J. Am. Acad. Child Psychiatry 18: 67–75, **1979.**

A report of the findings of a study comparing 70 families under supervision for verified child abuse and/or neglect with 70 nonabusive families from a guidance clinic matched for age, sex, and diagnosis of child. Parameters evaluated include family interactions, resources, income, situational stress, and contributing factors in parent and/or child. The findings are used to make recommendations for treatment of abusive families.

86.   **Wender, P.H.** Minimal Brain Dysfunction in Children. New York: Wiley-Interscience, **1971.**

A historical reference text that provides readers with theoretical and clinical aspects of minimal brain dysfunction in children with an extensive review of literature of the time as well as a section on management. Much of the information in this book is anecdotal and based on the author's experiences in treating several hundred children with this disorder (as it was diagnosed during the 1960s).

87.   **Wolff, S. and Chick, J.** Schizoid personality in childhood: A controlled follow-up study. Psychol. Med. 10: 85–100, **1980.**

A description of a 10-year follow-up study of 22 boys initially diagnosed as having schizoid personality disorder and clinic controls that demonstrated the predictive validity of this diagnostic category. The authors also review the history of the concept of schizoid personality in children and adults.

SPECIAL TOPICS

88.   **Benedek, E.P. and Benedek, R.S.** Joint custody: Solution or illusion. Am. J. Psychiatry 36: 1540–1544, **1979.**

General psychiatrists are often involved in divorce proceedings that include custody decisions. It is asserted that parents who express interest in joint custody have widely differing objectives, expectations, and motivations. The risks and benefits of joint custody are examined in this article and recommendations for practical application are salient to all clinical psychiatrists.

89.   ***Cohen, D.J. and Young, J.G.** Neurochemistry and child psychiatry. J. Am. Acad. Child Psychiatry 16: 353–411, **1977.**

A clear, understandable summary of neurobiology, including excellent diagrams. The authors distinguish between fact and theory in biochemistry, physiology, and neuroanatomy and apply this information to research and treatment strategies. The major portion of the article is equally applicable to adults and children, but the final section specifically addresses childhood psychopathology.

90. ***Derdeyn, A.P.** A consideration of legal issues in child custody contests. Arch. Gen. Psychiatry 33: 165–171, **1976.**

An account of current and proposed law, and the usual criteria used by courts in cases of contested child custody. A useful guide for psychiatrists treating any member of a divorcing family that includes children.

91. **Goldstein, J., Freud, A., and Solnit, A.J.** Beyond the Best Interests of the Child. New York: Free Press, **1974.**

This book is a sensitive review and covers a variety of opinions regarding some of the inherent problems of foster family care. They recommend that the child in a contested settlement be represented by legal counsel, and that specific legal guidelines be set up emphasizing the least detrimental alternative for safeguarding a child's growth and development. The role of the psychiatrist as a consultant in these proceedings is strongly highlighted.

92. ***Heller, J.R. and Derdeyn, A.P.** Child custody consultation in abuse and neglect: A practical guide. Child Psychiatry Hum. Dev. 9: 171–179, **1979.**

A practical guide for the mental health professional consultant regarding custody in cases of suspected child abuse and neglect. The authors describe the knowledge of local law and child development required and make specific suggestions for structuring the evaluation, defining the questions being asked by the court, dealing with family resistance, and writing the report. The advice given on testifying in court is particularly valuable for the novice.

93. **Rutter, M., Tizzard, J., Yule, W., et al.** Research report: Isle of Wight studies, 1964–1974. Psychol. Med. 6: 313–332, **1976.**

A paper based on the final research report on a decade of epidemiologic studies conducted on the Isle of Wight and in inner London. A valuable summary of the significant findings concerning the assessment, etiology, prevalence, and prognosis of psychiatric symptoms in childhood.

94. **Turnbull, A.O., Strickland, B., and Hammer, S.E.** The individualized education program: Part II. Translating law into practice. J. Learning Disabilities 11: 67–72, **1978.**

The impact of Public Law 94-142 (the Education for All Handicapped Children Act) enacted in 1977 at the federal level, will be felt by psychiatrists and child psychiatrists in their professional work over years to come. This article identifies and lists the components of the "Individualized Education Program"(IEP). The most important one for psychiatrists relates to the psychiatric evaluation of all children to be placed in the so-called "least restrictive educational environment." This Act applies to child and general psychiatrists alike.

95.   **Wallerstein, J.S. and Kelly, J.B.** Children and divorce: A review. Social Work 24: 468–475, **1979.**

A thorough description of the effects of divorce on children and adolescents, based on a review of the literature and the authors' five-year longitudinal study. Also included are recommendations for clinical practice, research, and public policy.

51. ADOLESCENT AND YOUNG ADULT

AARON H. ESMAN, M.D.

The references on adolescence and young adulthood cover both "classical" and more recent contributions so as to provide the reader with a broad survey of critical development issues as they have evolved over the century. Though the list is primarily psychoanalytic in orientation, other approaches have been included when it seemed helpful—particularly with regard to cognitive and biological development.

Beginning, then, with Freud, the readings move from the work of his students and followers (Aichhorn, A. Freud, Blos) to more "revisionist" views (Erikson, Masterson, Offer) of normal development. Stress on sexual issues (Tanner, Laufer, Borowitz) is balanced by consideration of intergenerational conflicts (Blos, Anthony) and other phase-related concerns (Esman). The papers on psychopathology tend to emphasize contemporary writings in order to benefit from newer ideas on diagnosis, ego psychology, and object relations theory. Since adolescents are on the front line of social and cultural change, such current issues as drug abuse, adolescent pregnancy, cultism, suicide, and revisions of feminine psychology are considered, as is the (by now essentially resolved) controversy about the "normality" of adolescent turmoil.

Finally, there is consideration of the recent efforts to conceptualize "youth" as a definable phase, distinct from adolescence on the one hand and adulthood on the other. Here again, social and technological changes are revealed as crucial determinants of our ways of seeing the evolution of personality.

GENERAL CONSIDERATIONS

1. *Adolescent Psychiatry, Vol. 1 . . . , Eds.: S.C. Feinstein et al. Chicago: University of Chicago Press, 1971.

   An annual collection of papers on all aspects of adolescence.

2.   **Caplan, G. and Lebovici, S.,** Eds. Adolescence: Psychosocial Perspectives. New York: Basic Books, **1969.**

A collection of papers on various aspects of adolescent development, psychopathology, and therapy. Emphasis is placed on sociocultural issues and their influence on development.

3.   ***Esman, A.,** ed. The Psychology of Adolescence: Essential Readings. New York: International Universities Press, **1975.**

Contains a selection of classical and more recent papers on adolescent development and psychopathology, primarily from a psychoanalytic perspective. Historical and cross-cultural studies are also included.

4.   ***Greenspan, S.I. and Pollock, G.H.,** eds. The Course of Life, Vol. II. Latency, Adolescence and Youth. Bethesda: NIMH, **1980.**

A collection of original papers by major figures in child and adolescent psychiatry presenting current psychoanalytic views of normal and pathological personality formation.

5.   **Spiegel, L.** Comments on the psychoanalytic psychology of adolescence. Psychoanal. Study Child 13: 296–308, **1958.**

Concise summary of psychoanalytic formulations regarding the psychology of adolescence, using an ego-psychological frame of reference. Emphasis on language and cognitive factors makes it particularly valuable.

NORMAL DEVELOPMENT I: PHYSICAL AND SEXUAL

6.   **Borowitz, G.** The capacity to masturbate alone in adolescence. Adolesc. Psychiatry 2: 130–143, **1973.**

The author regards the ability to engage in (relatively) guilt-free solitary masturbation as a crucial developmental achievement in the adolescent's sexual and characterological development.

7.   **Chilman, C.** Adolescent Sexuality in a Changing American Society: Social and Psychological Perspectives. Washington: DHEW, **1979.**

A thoroughgoing survey of current patterns of adolescent sexuality, based on a systematic review of basic and recent research. It includes an annotated bibliography, suggestions for further research, and implications for social policy.

8.   ***Freud, S.** (1905) The transformations of puberty. S.E. 7: 207–230, **1953.**

Freud discusses here his basic ideas about the primacy of genital sexuality, patterns of object choice, and the psychological differences between the sexes as they are consolidated during and after puberty.

9. **Laufer, M.** The central masturbation fantasy, the final sexual organization, and adolescence. Psychoanal. Study Child 31: 297–316, **1976.**

Laufer regards the "central masturbation fantasy," conscious or unconscious, as the paradigm for personality organization, which is consolidated in adolescence.

10. ***Tanner, J.M.** Sequence, tempo and individual variation in the growth and development of boys and girls aged 12 to 16. Daedalus 100: 907–930, **1971.** Also in: New Directions in Childhood Psychopathology, Vol. 1. Developmental Considerations. Eds.: S. Harrison and J. McDermott, pp. 182–205. New York: International Universities Press, **1980.**

An illustrated review of the normal variations in pubertal development, with some reflections on the psychosocial consequences of deviations from the norm. An essential reference for the assessment of biological development and its emotional impact.

NORMAL DEVELOPMENT II: COGNITIVE AND PSYCHOSOCIAL

11. **Anthony, E.J.** Normal adolescent development from a cognitive viewpoint. J. Am. Acad. Psychiatry 21: 318–327, **1982.**

This paper imaginatively integrates Piagetian with other approaches to cognitive development and demonstrates its central contribution to normal adolescent psychology.

12. **Anthony, E.J.** The reactions of adults to adolescents and their behavior, pp. 54–78. In: Adolescence: Psycho-social Perspectives. Eds.: G. Kaplan and S. Lebovici. New York: Basic Books, **1969.** Also in: The Psychology of Adolescence. Ed.: A. Esman, pp. 467–493. New York: International Universities Press, **1975.**

The author considers here some of the factors that generate adult antagonism to adolescents. He demonstrates how adults stereotype adolescents in order to defend themselves against incompletely resolved impulses and conflicts.

13. **Blos, P.** The Adolescent Passage. Developmental Issues. New York: International Universities Press, **1979.**

A collection of Blos's major papers on adolescent psychological development. It includes some recent articles that propose revisions of classical psychoanalytic ideas on the basis of newer clinical and sociocultural findings.

14. ***Blos, P.** The second individuation process of adolescence. Psychoanal. Study Child 22: 162–186, **1967.**

Blos considers here the phenomenon of disengagement from the parents during the adolescent process, analogizing it to Mahler's "separation-individuation" process in the young child. He emphasizes, too, what he sees as the central role of aggression in promoting normal adolescence.

15. ***Erikson, E.** The problem of ego identity. J. Am. Psychoanal. Assoc. 4: 56–121, **1966.**

In this essay Erikson formulates his now familiar concept of identity formation as the normative developmental crisis of adolescence, placing it in his epigenetic sequence. He further presents a number of pathological variants of the syndrome he calls *identity diffusion.*

16. ***Freud, A.** Adolescence. Psychoanal. Study Child 13: 255–278, **1958.** Also in: The Psychology of Adolescence: Essential Readings. Ed.: A. Esman, pp. 122–140. New York: International Universities Press, **1975.**

The classic statement of the psychoanalytic view of the ubiquity—even the necessity—of "adolescent turmoil" for normal development.

17. ***Group for the Advancement of Psychiatry.** Normal Adolescence: Its Dynamics and Impact. Vol. 6. GAP Report No. 68, **1968.**

An excellent, concise summary of the biology, psychology, and sociology of adolescence in American society. It includes a comprehensive bibliography (as of the date of publication).

18. **Kaplan, E.H.** Adolescents, age fifteen to eighteen: A psychoanalytic developmental view, pp. 373–396. In: The Course of Life, Vol. II. Eds.: S. Greenspan and G. Pollock. Bethesda: NIMH, **1980.**

A comprehensive scholarly survey of midadolescent development within a modern psychoanalytic framework. It incorporates cognitive, biological, and psychosocial perspectives. The "extensive intra-psychic reorganization" of this subphase is detailed.

19. ***Keniston, K.** Postadolescence (youth) and historical change, pp. 34–50. In: The Psychopathology of Adolescence. Eds.: J. Zubin and A. Freedman. New York: Grune and Stratton, **1970.**

Sets forth the rationale for defining the 18–24-year-old period as a separate developmental phase with its own characteristic tasks and conflicts.

20. ***Lewis, M.** The phase of young adulthood, age eighteen–twenty-three years, pp. 523–527. In: The Course of Life, Vol. II. Eds.: S. Greenspan and G. Pollock. Bethesda: NIMH, **1980.**

A concise survey of the developmental issues in the transition between late adolescent and mature adult status.

21. ***Offer, D. and Offer, J.** From Teenage to Young Manhood: A Psychological Study. New York: Basic Books, **1975.**

This work continues the authors' normative study of adolescent males into their young adult years, demonstrating the paths of personality consolidation and adaptive progress of the three groups defined in their earlier work.

22. ***Offer, D.** Adolescent development: A normative perspective. pp. 357–372. In: The Course of Life, Vol. II. Eds.: S. Greenspan and G. Pollock. Bethesda: NIMH, **1980.**

A report of the author's longitudinal study of adolescent development in "normal" populations, which effectively challenges the classical concept of normative "adolescent turmoil." It describes three modes of passage through this process, only one of which can be considered to show significant signs of turmoil.

23. **Piaget, J.** Intellectual development of the adolescent, pp. 22–26. In: Adolescence: Psychosocial Perspectives. Ed.: G. Kaplan and S. Lebovici. New York: Basic Books, **1969.** Also in: The Psychology of Adolescence, pp. 104–108. Ed.: A. Esman. New York: International Universities Press, **1975.**

This brief paper presents a succinct statement of Piaget's views on cognitive development in adolescence—specifically the development of formal operational thought. It also raises important questions regarding the universality of this development and its possible effects under varying cultural conditions.

24. **Ritvo, S.** Late adolescence: Developmental and clinical considerations. Psychoanal. Study Child 26: 241–263, **1971.**

This paper details the psychoanalytic view of the transformations of late adolescent males in terms of object relations, ego ideal formation, psychopathology, and consequent treatment implications.

25. **Spruiell, V.** Narcissistic transformations in adolescence. Int. J. Psychoanal. Psychother. 4: 518–536, **1975.**

Traces the shifts in 3 "strands" of narcissistic development—self-love, sense of omnipotence, and self-esteem regulation—during adolescence, correlating them with parallel developments in object relations.

26.   **Weissman, S. and Barglow, P.** Recent contributions to the theory of female adolescent psychological development. Adolesc. Psychiatry 8: 214–230, **1980.**

A comprehensive review of classical and recent ideas about the psychological development of female adolescents. Emphasis is placed on contemporary research on aspects of the adolescent's cerebral and cortical functioning and its implications.

PSYCHOPATHOLOGY

27.   ***Aichhorn, A.** Wayward Youth. New York: Viking Press, **1948.**

This pioneering discussion of the psychopathology and psychoanalytic treatment of delinquency was originally published in 1917, and it continues to form the basis for much of the current work in this field. It provides impressive examples of virtuoso interview technique.

28.   ***Anthony, E.J.** Two contrasting types of adolescent depression and their treatment. J. Am. Psychoanal. Assoc. 18: 841–859, **1970.** Also in: The Psychology of Adolescence, pp. 285–300. Ed.: A. Esman. New York: International Universities Press, **1975.**

The distinction is made between a more phase-appropriate oedipal "neurotic" type of depression and a more pervasive preoedipally based depression, which may show a cyclical pattern.

29.   **Bruch, H.** The Golden Cage: The Enigma of Anorexia Nervosa. Cambridge: Harvard University Press, **1978.**

A concise presentation of the author's views on the syndrome of anorexia nervosa, derived from a lifetime of clinical study. She emphasizes the ego-psychological and family relations aspects of the disorder.

30.   ***Esman, A.** Mid-adolescence—foundations for later psychopathology, pp. 419–430. In: The Course of Life, Vol. II. Eds.: S. Greenspan and G. Pollock. Bethesda: NIMH, **1980.**

Delineates a group of psychopathological reactions of older adolescents and young adults and demonstrates their roots in specific aspects of midadolescent development and/or failure to resolve earlier conflicts during this subphase.

31. ***Feinstein, S.C. and Miller, D.** Psychoses of adolescence, pp. 708–722. In: Basic Handbook of Child Psychiatry, Vol. 2. Ed.: J. Noshpitz. New York: Basic Books, **1979.**

Reviews the phenomenology, dynamics, phase-specific characteristics, and treatment of psychotic disorders in adolescence.

32. **Fisher, S. and Scharf, K.** Teenage pregnancy: An anthropological, sociological, and psychological overview. Adolesc. Psychiatry 8: 393–403, **1980.**

A review of the recent literature and a report of two programs that offer service to pregnant adolescents.

33. **Holzman, P. and Grinker, R.R., Sr.** Schizophrenia in adolescence. Adolesc. Psychiatry 5: 276–290, **1977.**

Describes current thinking on schizophrenia and schizophrenialike psychoses in adolescents.

34. **Johnson, A.B.** Drifting on the God circuit, pp. 524–534. In: The Psychology of Adolescence. Ed.: A. Esman. New York: International Universities Press, **1975.**

An early but still valid contribution to the understanding of the "cult" phenomenon and its appeal to adolescents and young adults. Psychodynamic and sociocultural factors are concisely spelled out.

35. ***Johnson, A.M.** Sanctions for superego lacunae of adolescents, pp. 225–245. In: Searchlights on Delinquency. Ed.: K. Eissler. New York: International Universities Press, **1949.** Also in: The Psychology of Adolescence, pp. 245–266. Ed.: A. Esman. New York: International Universities Press, **1975.**

This is a classic description of the ways in which unresolved parental conflicts are unconsciously communicated to children, resulting in antisocial behavior.

36. ***Kernberg, O.** The diagnosis of borderline conditions in adolescence. Adolesc. Psychiatry 6: 298–319, **1978.**

This paper applies Kernberg's concepts of borderline personality disorder and its differential diagnosis to the specific conditions of adolescence.

37. **Masterson, J.F.** The borderline adolescent: An object relations view. Adolesc. Psychiatry 6: 294–359, **1978.**

A distilled statement of Masterson's ideas about the borderline syndrome in adolescence within the context of separation-individuation theory and the English school of object relations theory. Special emphasis is placed on anorexia nervosa and its relationship to the borderline syndrome.

38. ***Masterson, J.F.** The psychiatric significance of adolescent turmoil. Am. J. Psychiatry 124: 1549–1554, **1968.**

One of the first papers to challenge the classical psychoanalytic view of the normality of "adolescent turmoil."

39. **Miller, D.** Adolescent suicide: Etiology and treatment. Adolesc. Psychiatry 9: 327–342, **1981.**

A discussion of the psychodynamics, family dynamics, and sociodynamics of adolescent suicide, with a typology of suidical behavior. Biological factors and treatment considerations are also presented.

40. **Petzel, S. and Riddle, M.** Adolescent suicide: Psychosocial and cognitive aspects. Adolesc. Psychiatry 9: 343–398, **1981.**

Formulates a profile of the suicidal adolescent, based on an extensive review of the literature of family and sociocultural factors and individual characteristics. A valuable reference source.

41. ***Sours, J.** Anorexia nervosa: Nosology, diagnosis, developmental patterns and power-control dynamics, pp. 185–212. In: Adolescence: Psychosocial Perspectives. Eds.: G. Kaplan and S. Lebovici. New York: Basic Books, **1969.**

A comprehensive review of the syndrome formulating its dynamics within an object-relational and ego-psychological framework.

42. **Wallerstein, J.B. and Kelly, J.** The effects of parental divorce: The adolescent experience, pp. 386–407. In: New Directions in Childhood Psychopathology, Vol. 1. Developmental Considerations. Eds.: S. Harrison and J. McDermott. New York: International Universities Press, **1980.**

A product of the "Children of Divorce" study: this paper focuses on the range of responses of adolescents to family breakup.

43. ***Weider, H. and Kaplan, E.H.** Drug use in adolescents: Psychodynamic meaning and pharmacogenic effect. Psychoanal. Study Child 24: 399–431, **1969.** Also in: The Psychology of Adolescence, pp. 348–375. Ed.: A. Esman. New York: International Universities Press, **1975.**

Adolescent drug use is not a random matter, but is determined by specific conflictual and developmental considerations. The adolescent's preference for a particular drug is a consequence of the correlation between his specific psychological needs and the pharmacological property of the particular drug.

CULTURAL ISSUES

44.   **Arlow, J.A.** A psychoanalytic study of a religious initiation rite: Bar Mitzvah. Psychoanal. Study Child 6: 353–374, **1951.**

This paper illuminates the role of rites of passage in their relation to character and symptom formation in puberty and early adolescence. It emphasizes the changing relationship between father and son as the latter begins the process of detachment and individuation.

45.   **Muensterberger, W.** The adolescent in society, pp. 346–368. In: Adolescents: Psychoanalytic Approach to Problems and Therapy. Eds.: S. Lorand and H. Schneer. New York: Hoeber, **1961.** Also in: The Psychology of Adolescence, pp. 12–31. Ed.: A. Esman. New York: International Universities Press, **1975.**

The author, an anthropologist, provides a cross-cultural panorama of adolescent roles in non-Western societies and the rites of passage and other social institutions that promote them.

52. ADULT DEVELOPMENT

STEFAN P. STEIN, M.D.

Although observations about stages of adult development have been made since ancient times, relatively few clinicians have utilized this perspective in modern psychology or psychiatry. In the early part of the twentieth century, child psychiatrists and psychologists demonstrated the usefulness of the developmental framework as an approach allowing the intertwining strands of psychology, biology, and sociology to be combined. But it is only recently that this viewpoint has been adopted by adult psychologists and psychiatrists, providing a vehicle for the modern biopsychosocial approach to the study of both health and illness in the adult years.

Longitudinal studies (Vaillant) as well as cross-sectional studies (Gould, Levenson) have now provided preliminary data that allow theoretical models of normal development (Erikson, Jung, Colarusso, and Nemiroff) to be evaluated.

The focus on middle age has revealed it as a period of active biological and psychological change. When they reach the forties and fifties, for example, women may undertake second careers; men must frequently deal with the achievement of an asymptote in relation to their own career aspirations. The necessity of adaptation to changing biology, and increasing awareness of one's vulnerability to a variety of major illnesses also enters into the complex developmental challenges of the fourth, fifth, and sixth decades.

The editor has selected references in order to acquaint the reader with: (1) The "classical" modern theoreticians of the adult life cycle, with an acknowledged bias in the direction of psychoanalytic thinkers; (2) Clinical studies that have examined midlife; (3) Collections of essays that present either specialized resources or interesting theoretical points of view; (4) Major resources in the study of the biology and psychology of the geriatric age group; and (5) Articles that focus on special aspects of death and dying in relation to aging. Finally, the editor has added a few articles on the basis of his personal interests.

408

MIDLIFE DEVELOPMENT—NORMAL AND ABNORMAL

1. **Anthony, E.J., et al.** The life cycle, Chaps. 11–17, pp. 224–425. In: Depression and Human Existence. Eds.: E.J. Anthony and T. Benedek. Boston: Little, Brown, **1975.**

   A primarily psychoanalytical view informs the comments on affective disease in relation to phases of the life cycle. Particularly of interest is Anthony's article on the influence of a manic-depressive environment on the developing child.

2. **Brim, O.G., Jr. and Kagan, J.,** eds. Constancy and Change in Human Development. Cambridge: Harvard University Press, **1980.**

   Studies presented here re-examine the question of the permanence of early childhood psychological structures as they may effect later developmental events. It is interdisciplinary and contains scholarly considerations of biological, social, and particularly, cognitive aspects of development. It is not easy reading, but contains interesting approaches to both cognitive and personality development in the midlife period.

3. ***Colarusso, C.A. and Nemiroff, R.A.** Adult Development. New York: Plenum Press, **1981.**

   A well-written book, which opens with a review of the current psychodynamic theories of adult development and presents an integrated developmental diagnostic scheme. It is particularly useful in discussing transformations of narcissism. This scholarly work stands out from the majority of collections of essays in that it is well researched and presents an original conceptualization.

4. **Cytrynbaum, S., Blum, L., Patrick, R., et al.** Midlife development: A personality and social systems perspective. In: Aging in the 1980s: Psychological Issues. Ed.: L.W. Poon. Washington, D.C.: American Psychological Association, **1980.**

   The social systems perspective here integrates a wide variety of studies (many of which are cited on this list) in a coherent and useful manner. This article is particularly interesting in that it presents its arguments in the form of assumptions that are presented and then challenged. There is an extensive bibliography.

5. **Erikson, E.H.,** ed. Adulthood. New York: Norton, **1978.**

   Chapters in this collection of essays contrast features of adulthood in a variety of cultures, including America, Russia, Japan, India, and China.

in the search for distinctions between that which may be viewed as primarily cultural, and that which appears universal.

6. ***Erikson, E.H.** Childhood and Society (2nd ed.). New York: Norton, **1963.**

Erik Erikson may be considered among the first major modern students of the adult life cycle. Chapter 7, "Eight Ages of Man," is the basic text of the ego-psychological approach to adult development. Here Erikson emphasizes issues stressed by Freud, particularly in the *Three Essays on Sexuality,* and adds, importantly, the stages of young adulthood and middle adulthood, as well as those of the later years.

7. **Frankel, S.A. and Wise, M.J.** A view of delayed parenting: Some implications of a new trend. Psychiatry 45: 220–225, **1982.**

This small study of women who chose to delay the beginning of the parenting phase to midlife is interesting in that it shows the relationship of broad social change to individual psychological developmental issues in adulthood.

8. **Freud, A.** Psychopathology seen against a background of normal development. Br. J. Psychiatry 129: 401–406, **1976.**

Miss Freud's emphasis here is on the relationship of childhood psychopathology to adult development and psychopathology; she also emphasizes the importance of the developmental perspective as a major theme in the study of psychopathology.

9. **Giele, J.Z.** Women in the Middle Years. New York: Wiley, **1982.**

Authored by members of a study group at Brandeis University, this volume includes essays on nonpatient issues for adult women, including health, work, and marriage. A new resource in the sparsely studied area of the adult woman's life cycle.

10. **Gould, R.** Transformations: Growth and Change in Adult Life. New York: Simon and Schuster, **1978.**

Gould, using a cross-sectional questionnaire approach, compared patients with nonpatients to identify common themes of concern in adult development. While his work may be criticized as somewhat facile and lacking in the complexity and depth of other contemporary adult developmentalists, Gould's studies, carried out in the 1960s, were important in identifying a sequence of patterns through the adult years.

11. ***Greenspan, S.I. and Pollock, G.H.,** eds. The Course of Life, Vol. 3. Adulthood and the Aging Process. Adelphi, Md.: Mental Health Study Center, **1981.**

The editors have gathered major psychoanalytic thinkers, who consider both normal and pathological conditions in adulthood. Pathological states are related to adult development. Of particular note is Elliott Jaques's essay on the "Midlife Crisis," and E. James Anthony's article on "Psychoanalysis and Development." While there is no continuity from one to another, the quality of these essays is extremely high.

12. **Howells, J.G.,** ed. Modern Perspectives in the Psychiatry of Middle Age. New York: Brunner/Mazel, **1981.**

This edited collection of essays is of uneven quality but offers a number of interesting articles on the midlife aspects of divorce, work, homosexuality, parenting one's own parents, and grandparenting.

13. **Jung, C.G.** Modern Man in Search of a Soul. New York: Harcourt-Brace, **1933.**

Carl Jung, another important early student of the life cycle, argues that the sense of self undergoes major changes in adulthood and that one can relate clinical phenomena, such as incidence of illnesses, to phases of adulthood. While largely personal speculation, his comments are of interest.

14. **Lamb, M.E. and Sutton-Smith, B.** Sibling Relationships: Their Nature and Significance Across the Life Span. Hillsdale, N.J.: Erlbaum, **1982.**

This book specifically addresses the issue of sibling influence throughout the life span, and in Chapter 11 presents a review of social and developmental psychologists' studies of sibling relationships as they effect development in the adult years. Of particular interest is the focus on the fate of sibling relationships in adulthood.

15. **Levinson, D.J., Darrow, C.N., Klein, E.B., et al.** Seasons of a Man's Life. New York: Knopf, **1978.**

Levinson's group studied men from three vocational groups and attempted to identify themes in common, related to adult development. His views, centering on the importance of transitional periods and their relationship to fixed chronological points, are discussed in the context of presentation of detailed data about these men's lives.

16. **Nadelson, C.C. and Notman, M.,** eds. The Woman Patient, Vol. 2. Concepts of Femininity and the Life Cycle. New York: Plenum Press, **1982.**

While the overall focus of this work is on the woman patient, Vol. 2 addresses normal developmental concerns for women and life cycle considerations in both social and biological spheres. This book specifically addresses adult developmental issues for women, an area largely unexamined in the literature.

17.   ***Neugarten, B.L.,** ed. Personality in Middle and Late Life. New York: Arno Press, **1980.**

Neugarten, whose important writings on personality development in the second half of life have contributed to a conceptualization integrating psychoanalytic, cognitive, and social perspectives, is the major author of this work which reports a series of studies carried out using a "normal" population drawn from the subjects of the Kansas City Study of Adult Life. The summary chapter by Dr. Neugarten is useful not only as a review of the results of the studies, but as a statement of the problems of social-psychological research related to adult development.

18.   **Norman, W.H. and Scaramella, T.J.,** eds. Midlife Developmental and Clinical Issues. New York: Brunner/ Mazel, **1980.**

A collection of interesting and varied essays about midlife ranging from normal developmental phenomena to psychotic illness and suicide in the middle years.

19.   ***Schaie, K.W.** Psychological changes from midlife to early old age: Implications for the maintenance of mental health. Am. J. Orthopsychiatry 51: 199–218, **1981.**

An inviting essay that integrates biological, cognitive, and personality views in a careful manner. Of particular interest is the final section of the essay, which attempts to relate the findings of the adult life cycle theorists to mental health maintenance.

20.   **Schwab, J.J.** Affective disorders and the life cycle. In: Affective Disorders: Psychopathology and Treatment. Eds.: E.R. Val, F.M. Gaviria, and J.A. Flaherty. Chicago, IL: Yearbook Medical Publishers, **1982.**

A primarily epidemiological view of depression and the life cycle, useful in identifying the particular features of phases of the adult years when there is special disposition to affective illness. In addition, the author reviews specific diagnostic problems in the late years.

21.   **Sze, W.C.,** ed. Human Life Cycle. New York: Aronson, **1975.**

A collection of source writings, prepared primarily for social work trainees, that includes excellent contributions from the intra-, interpersonal and cultural perspectives. In addition, useful comments on social class roles are presented for both middle and old age.

22.   ***Vaillant, G.E.** Adaptation to Life. Boston, MA: Little, Brown, **1977.**

Vaillant presents data from a major longitudinal study of the male adult life cycle from an ego psychological point of view. Drawing on the work of Erikson, Freud, Ann Freud, and others, Vaillant re-examined, with a 40-year follow-up, the men of the Grant study. The book is well written and presents an important perspective on adult psychopathology, long-term adult adaptation, "health," and maturity.

ELDERLY—DEVELOPMENT, NORMAL, AND ABNORMAL

23. *Binstock, R.H. and Shanas, E., eds. Handbook of Aging and the Social Sciences. New York: Van Nostrand, Reinhold, **1976.**

24. *Birren, J.E. and Schaie, K.W., eds. Handbook for the Psychology of Aging. New York: Van Nostrand, Reinhold, **1977.**

25. *Finch, C.E. and Hayflick, L., eds. Handbook for the Psychology of Aging. New York: Brunner/Mazel, **1980.**

These three volumes are the major resource for technical, comprehensive state-of-the-art information about normal aging. Ranging from technical considerations of cellular aging to large social science studies regarding aging populations, they are authored by respected experts who provide detailed and thorough information. An encyclopedia.

26. *Busse, E. and Blazer, D., eds. Handbook of Geriatric Psychiatry. New York: Van Nostrand, Reinhold, **1980.**

The title of this volume is deceiving; the first half of the book is largely about developmental processes in the older person. It is broad ranging and eclectic, with a good chapter on the epidemiology of mental illness in late life.

27. Butler, R.N. Why Survive? Being Old in America. New York: Harper and Row, **1975.**

Butler has a broad perspective overlooking the late years. His book identifies social and psychological problems common amongst older individuals and is useful in providing an overview of the developmental issues in late years.

28. Eissler, K.R. On possible effects of aging on the practice of psycho-analysis: An essay. J. Phila. Assoc. Psychoanal. 2: 138–152, **1975.**

Reflections of an aging analyst on the vicissitudes of the therapist's aging process as it affects his work. A complex and inconclusive paper, but one that is interesting for the focus on this aspect of aging.

29. Glick, P.C. Updating the life cycle of the family. J. Marriage Fam. 39: 5–13, **1977.**

An overview of the cycle of parenting and family life, this article presents an organizing scheme for a view of the family's late years developmentally.

30. **Howard, J.H., Marshall, J., Rechnitzer, P.A., et al.** Adapting to retirement. J. Am. Geriatr. Soc. 30: 488–500, **1982.**

A thoughtful review of the general health and psychosocial adaptational issues facing the retired person. Well written and researched, this is a single article that serves as a good general resource in the area of retirement.

31. **Lieberman, M.A.** Adaptive processes in late life, pp. 135–159. In: Lifespan Developmental Psychology. Eds.: N. Daton and L. Ginsberg. New York: Academic Press, **1975.**

Studies using measures of personality highlight the study of adaptive capacities, coping, and development in the old undergoing the stress of placement. Of particular interest is Lieberman's view of what may constitute health in old age.

32. **Neugarten, B. and Weinstein, K.** The changing American grandparent. J. Marriage Fam. 26: 199–204, **1964.**

Of interest because it specifically addresses the developmental task of grandparenting, this paper also focuses on generational issues in aging.

33. **Poon, L.W.,** ed. Aging in the 1980s. Washington, D.C.: American Psychological Association, **1980.**

An edited book of academic, psychological, focused reports of cognitive, adaptational, interpersonal, and biological phenomena of aging. This volume summarizes available data and is an excellent resource with comprehensive reference lists following each article.

34. **Usdin, G. and Hofling, C.K.,** eds. Aging: The Process and the People. New York: Brunner/Mazel, **1978.**

A selection of readings primarily by psychiatrists including chapters on death and dying, aging and depression, and the doctor's relationship to the aging patient. The chapters are well written and provide good overview of major areas, in a fairly compact manner.

35. **Vallery-Masson, J., Poltrenaud, J., Burnat, G., et al.** Retirement and morbidity: A three year longitudinal study of a French managerial population. Age Ageing, 10: 271–276, **1981.**

A study of retirement that challenges the popular belief that retirement, per se, is associated with an increase in medical illness and morbidity in general.

DEATH AND DYING

36. **Agate, J.** Ethical considerations: Death and dying, pp. 489–510. In: The Practice of Geriatrics (2nd ed.). Springfield, IL: Thomas, **1970.**

   The physician's responsibility to the dying elderly patient is discussed carefully along with practical suggestions for dealing with related problems: consultation to a dying patient, how much to tell, etc. A practical and sensitive general medical guide.

37. ***Carr, A. C.,** ed. Grief—Selected Readings. New York: Health Sciences Publishing, **1975.**

   Particularly useful for its selection of papers on grief in childhood, this volume is a good general resource for theories of grieving and distinctions between normal and pathological grief.

38. **Eissler, K.R.** The Psychiatrist and the Dying Patient. New York: International Universities Press, **1955.**

   A psychoanalyst views death using myth, culture, and history as reference points. Three case histories of dying patients are presented in detail with psychodynamic issues centrally considered.

39. **Feifel, H.** The Meaning of Death. Part 2. Developmental Orientation Toward Death. New York: McGraw-Hill, **1959.**

   These essays on attitudes toward death of children, adolescents, and mentally ill adults use writings by children, and questionnaire responses by adolescents to provide some narrative information on death and dying in young people.

40. **Jaques, E.** Death and the midlife crisis. Int. J. Psychoanal. 46: 502–514, **1965.**

   Jaques views the midlife crisis (his term) as a period in which death and its meanings are critically important and become central in working through the crisis to a renewed awareness and coming to terms with the presence of death.

41. **Karasu, T.B. and Waltzman, S.A.** Death and dying in the aged, pp. 247–278. In: Geriatric Psychiatry: A Handbook for Psychiatrists and Primary Care Physicians. Eds.: L. Bellak and T.B. Karasu. New York: Grune and Stratton, **1976.**

   An overview of death from social, caretaker, patient, and institutional perspectives, this chapter discusses clinical management for the psychiatrist working with the dying patient and his/her family. It is useful in its attention to issues for the caretaker in dealing with the dying patient.

42.   ***Kübler-Ross, E.** On Death and Dying. New York: MacMillan, **1969.**

Although it lacks a careful scientific base, Dr. Kübler-Ross's conceptualization of stages of dealing with death is useful in providing an approach to psychological work with the dying patient and his/her family. A good resource for the psychiatrist working on a consultation-liaison service in general, but on an oncology service in particular.

43.   ***Norton, J.** Treatment of a dying patient. Psychoanal. Study Child 18: 541–560, **1963.**

Janice Norton reports a detailed case summary of the final three and a half months of a cancer-ridden 32-year-old woman's life. While this eloquent document does not ordinarily come into a bibliography of the mid or late adult life cycle, it is a compelling document describing important biological phenomena related to anticipating death.

44.   **Pollock, G.H.** Mourning and adaptation. Int. J. Psychoanal. 42: 341–361, **1961.**

This paper does not specifically address issues of adult development; it is, however, concerned with grieving and focuses on both normal and pathological grieving in relationship to adaptation. It relates psychoanalytic conceptualizations of mourning as a developmental process to those of ethology and social psychology.

45.   **Ruitenbeck, H.M.,** ed. Death: Interpretations. New York: Dell, **1969.**

Well-selected essays primarily by psychoanalysts on the psychology of dying and the treatment of the dying patient. A separate section on mourning collects essays on grief and the mourning process.

53. PSYCHOLOGY OF SEXUAL DIFFERENCES

CAROL C. NADELSON, M.D.
MALKAH T. NOTMAN, M.D.

Social change in the past decade has substantially altered concepts of the roles and relationships between men and women. In order to be therapeutically effective, psychiatrists must be aware of new data and evolving theory in the psychology of sex differences and related areas. This bibliography is intended to provide a guideline for reference to relevant current literature. It includes a number of outstanding compendia with substantial reviews of the field, and, in addition, selected individual articles that either have historical importance or provide major direction for our field are also included.

This curriculum is by no means exhaustive; it is intended to be a guide to the study of men's and women's lives and the factors that shape them. It includes material from psychiatry, psychoanalysis, psychology, sociology, medicine, biology, endocrinology, and anthropology. It attends to our current understanding of the differences between men and women, the various proposed ideologies for these differences, and the diagnostic and therapeutic implications of emerging data and clinical experience.

This bibliography is intended to guide the clinician who is familiar with traditional clinical and theoretical works, e.g., Freud, Deutsch, Horney, etc. The contributions of these authors are therefore not specifically included, but important papers by them appear in several of the edited books that are suggested. This bibliography is designed for those who need to keep abreast of the field in order to be effective and for the resident who will find that it adds to the core of classical teaching and supplements the literature generally available and recommended.

OVERVIEW: PSYCHOLOGY OF WOMEN

1. **Rohrbaugh, J.B.,** ed. Women: Psychology's Puzzle. New York: Basic Books, **1979.**

An extensive review of the biological aspects of female behavior, theories of female personality, women's place in society, women and their bodies, and women and mental health.

2.   **Seiden, A.** Overview: Research on the psychology of women I; Gender differences and sexual and reproductive life. Am. J. Psychiatry 133: 995–1007, **1976.**

The author discusses the social and intellectual context of research in this area, reviewing recent literature on gender differences and behavior and on women's sexual and reproductive lives including aspects of the menstrual cycle, menopause, diseases of reproductive organs, coitus, rape, childbirth, lactation, and fertility control.

3.   **Seiden, A.** Overview: Research on the psychology of women II; Women in families, work and psychotherapy. Am. J. Psychiatry 133: 1111–1123, **1976.**

The author of this paper reviews recent research and selected aspects of the social psychology of women's lives especially around families, childbearing, work, and achievement motivation. She includes implications for psychiatric treatment of women that can be drawn from the psychotherapy research literature.

4.   **Williams, J.** Psychology of Women. New York: Norton, **1979.**

A comprehensive and current overview of the psychology of women, including myths and stereotypes, psychoanalytic views, biological perspectives and developmental aspects of sex differences, sexuality and reproductive issues, lifestyle changes, societal concerns, and women in the aging process.

OVERVIEW: PSYCHOLOGY OF MEN

5.   **Cath, S., Gurwitt, A., and Ross, J.,** eds. Father and Child: Developmental and Clinical Perspectives. Boston: Little, Brown, **1982.**

A comprehensive review of the history of fatherhood, developmental perspectives through the phases of childhood and adolescence, cross-cultural and historical variations, and clinical problems and applications including divorce, abuse, incest, and loss.

6.   **Pleck, J. and Sawyer, J.,** eds. Men and Masculinity. New Jersey: Prentice-Hall, **1974.**

A range of articles about the developmental experiences of men, relationships between men and women, men and children, and men with each other. Also included are sections on work and men's roles in society and current changes in men's concepts of themselves.

7. ***Solomon, K. and Levy, N.B.**, eds. Men in Transition: Theory and Therapy. New York: Plenum, **1982.**

This volume contains chapters on gender role conflict and the masculine gender role, psychoanalytic theory, androgyny, male inexpressiveness, the effect of changing sex roles on male homosexuals, sexual functioning in relation to the changing roles of men, dual careers and fatherhood and relationships, and a large section on therapeutic issues and techniques.

THEORETICAL PERSPECTIVES

8. ***Blum, H.P.**, ed. Female Psychology. New York: International Universities Press, **1977.**

A series of contemporary psychoanalytic papers by major theoretical and clinical authors. These writings bring new perspective and thinking to psychoanalytic views on the psychology of women. Included in this volume is R. Schafer's article, "Problems in Freud's Psychology of Women," which is an incisive and critical review of Freud's major points and his conceptualization of the psychology of women with discussion, revision, and refutation.

9. **Chodorow, N.**, ed. The Reproduction of Mothering: Psychoanalysis and the Sociology of Gender. Berkeley: University of California, **1978.**

An elegant and illuminating discourse on the relationship between daughters and mothers reviewing and rethinking psychoanalytic theory from a sociological perspective.

10. **Gilligan, C.**, ed. In a Different Voice. Cambridge: Harvard University Press, **1982.**

A thoughtful and penetrating discussion of male/female differences. The author hypothesizes that females are viewed theoretically as variants of the male model rather than understanding a separate developmental and psychological theory.

11. **Horner, M.** Toward an understanding of achievement related conflicts in women. J. of Soc. Issues 28: 157–175, **1972.**

The original paper defining fear of success and conceptualizing it as a psychological motive.

12. **Kaplan, A.**, ed. Psychological androgyny: Further considerations. Psychology of Women Quarterly 3: 3, **1979.**

A series of papers that present the concept of androgyny and its implications, theoretically and clinically.

13.   ***Miller, J.B.** Psychoanalysis and Women. New York: Brunner/Mazel, **1973.**

Selected writings by those who have influenced psychoanalysis focusing on contemporary views, many of which refute traditional positions and add new perspective. The book is divided into three parts and begins with papers by Horney, Adler, Thompson, Fromm-Reichman, and Zilborg. In the second part, entitled "The Emergence of New Evidence," the work of Sherfey, Cohen, Chodoff, Salzman, Marmor, Moulton, and Stoller is presented. An important article reprinted is R. Stoller's "The Bedrock of Masculinity and Femininity: Bisexuality," which is an excellent analysis of theories of sexual development and critique of psychoanalytic theory with particular emphasis on masculinity and femininity. The final section of the book deals with current problems and future directions.

14.   **Miller, J.B.** Toward a New Psychology of Women. Boston: Beacon Press, **1976.**

An important new perspective on some key aspects of women's psychology focusing on the self-image and self-esteem of women.

15.   **Person, E.S.** Sexuality as the mainstay of identity: Psychoanalytic perspectives. Signs 5: 605–630, **1980.**

The author evaluates psychoanalytic paradigms and develops a theory of female sexuality, relating it to identity formation. It differentiates female and male sexuality emphasizing the dependence of gender identity on sexuality in the male but not the female.

PSYCHOTHERAPY

16.   ***Brodsky, A. and Hare-Mustin, R.,** eds. Women in Psychotherapy. New York: Guilford Press, **1980.**

A comprehensive assessment of research and practice, this multiauthored book includes chapters on the relationship between gender and psychotherapeutic outcome for specific disorders such as depression, anxiety, eating disorders, and marital conflicts; on the traditional and alternative therapeutic approaches; and on the crises including reproductive crises and physical and sexual abuse. Priorities for further research and investigation are also included.

17. **Mogul, K.** Overview: The sex of the therapist. Am. J. Psychiatry 139: 1–11, **1982.**

    The author reviews research about the relevance of therapist gender to assessment, duration of treatment, and satisfaction with treatment as well as outcome. She also considers clinical writing in this area and reviews considerations of values, transference, and countertransference issues, and the reasons for choices. She emphasizes the large number of variables that make definitive conclusions impossible and stresses the need for further research as well as careful clinical attention to special issues and needs.

18. **Notman, M., Nadelson, C.C., and Bennet, M.** Achievement conflict in women: Psychotherapeutic considerations. Psychother. Psychosom. 29: 203–213, **1978.**

    This paper considers the conflicts that continue for women despite success and takes up therapeutic implications.

PSYCHIATRIC EDUCATION AND TRAINING

19. **Alonso, A. and Rutan, J.S.** Cross-sex supervision for cross-sex therapy. Am. J. Psychiatry 135: 928–931, **1978.**

    The authors review complex issues in supervision, including the transference and countertransference aspects of the supervisory process, particularly as it affects men and women.

20. **Nadelson, C.C. and Notman, M.** Psychotherapy supervision: The problem of conflicting values. Am. J. Psychiatry 31: 275–283, **1977.**

    Psychotherapy supervision offers an opportunity for examination of value differences between therapist and patient and therapist and supervisors. This paper discusses the effects of the availability of female supervisors and the value differences between male and female psychiatrists that may affect referrals, therapeutic goals, assessment of psychopathology, and the process of supervision and therapy.

21. **Robinowitz, C., Nadelson, C.C., and Notman, M.** Women in academic psychiatry: Politics and progress. Am. J. Psychiatry 138: 1357–1361. **1981.**

    The authors of this paper discuss the progress of women in academic psychology over the past several decades and present some issues that account for the success or failure of women to achieve in academia.

22. **Scher, M.** Gender issues in psychiatric supervision. Compr. Psychiatry 22: 179–183, **1981.**

This paper considers the influence of gender on psychiatric supervision and the impact of cross- and same-gender supervisors.

SEX DIFFERENCES, SEX ROLES, LIFE CYCLE

23. **Block, J.H.** Another look at sex differentiation in the socialization behaviors of mothers and fathers, pp. 29–88. In: Psychology of Women: Future Directions of Research. Eds.: F.L. Denmark and J. Herman. New York: Psychological Dimensions, **1978.**

This paper reanalyzes the data and critiques the methodology of Maccoby and Jacklin in "The Psychology of Sex Differences," and suggests that sex-differentiated parental socialization occurs in many areas and increases from early childhood to adolescence.

24. ***Frieze, E., Parson, J., Johnson, P., et al.,** eds. Women and Sex Roles. New York: Norton, **1978.**

A comprehensive and informative volume that provides an overview of aspects of women's sex role including research issues, sex differences in personality, biological factors, class theory, the roles of women, women's development, sexuality, achievement, women in power, and women's lives in contemporary society.

25. **Kirkpatrick, M.** Women's Sexual Development. New York: Plenum, **1980.**

This volume presents developmental aspects of sexuality for women including some discussion of father-daughter relationships and the role of the father; the history, physiology, and psychology of female sexuality; masturbation; homosexuality; sex education; self-help for sexual problems; and the impact of the sexual revolution on young women.

26. **Kirkpatrick, M.** Women's Sexual Experience. New York: Plenum, **1982.**

A companion piece to *Women's Sexual Development,* this is a collection of essays on women's sexuality, including its many manifestations and implications. Special aspects of sexuality; pregnancy, including teenage motherhood; childlessness; incest; wife battering; extramarital sex; and sex and aging are considered. There is also attention to cultural issues involving sexuality.

27. **Kopp, C.B.,** ed. Becoming Female. New York: Plenum, **1979.**

An edited volume encompassing identity development including the relationships between parents and their daughters, sex differences and behavioral symptoms, female achievement and biological considerations. The authors primarily come from backgrounds in the social sciences and review the extensive research literature in their fields.

28. **Lee, P. and Stewart, R.**, eds. Sex Differences. New York: Urizen, **1976.**

A collection of articles by some of this century's most influential writers, divided into sections including psychoanalytic, anthropological, sociological, bio-ethological, and psychological perspectives. The work is scholarly, historically important, and well chosen. Authors include Freud, Deutsch, Erikson, Horney, Malinowski, Mead, Parens, Lorenz, Tinbergen, Kohlberg, Maccoby, etc.

29. **Nadelson, T. and Eisenberg, J.** The successful professional woman: On being married to one. Am. J. Psychiatry 134: 1071–1076, **1977.**

A light and uplifting view of dual career couples who have "made it."

30. **Neugarten, B.L.** Time, age and the life cycle. Am. J. Psychiatry 136: 887–894, **1979.**

This paper considers the stages of the life cycle, particularly as they relate to adulthood for both men and women, and emphasizes the continued process of development throughout life.

31. **Parsons, J.,** ed. The Psychobiology of Sex Differences and Sex Roles. New York: McGraw-Hill, **1980.**

An integration of material on sexual differences, sexuality, reproduction, and the life cycle.

32. **Pepitone-Rockwell, F.,** ed. Dual Career Couples. Beverly Hills: Sage, **1980.**

A consideration of dual career couples including marital and family as well as career issues. The authors include Rhona and Robert Rapaport, who report on the long-term research in this area as well as chapters on the costs and benefits of dual career marriages, spouses' contributions to each other's roles, parenthood, marriage and careers, and time management and the dual career couple.

33. **Rossi, A.** Life span theories and women's lives. Signs 6: 4–32, **1980.**

This paper reviews theories of life cycle and its particular relevance to the lives of women. The author notes the lack of theory related to women's lives, especially older women.

34. **Sugar, M.,** ed. Female Adolescent Development. New York: Brunner/ Mazel, **1979.**

This edited volume considers research and biological and societal aspects of adolescent development in the female including some cross-cultural material. In the section on "Psychodynamics" there is material on the body image of the adolescent, ego and superego development, consideration of adolescent motherhood, and femininity.

THE FEMALE PATIENT INCLUDING
SEXUAL AND REPRODUCTIVE ASPECTS

35. **Lennane, K. and Lennane, R.** Alleged psychogenic disorders in women: A possible manifestation of sexual prejudice. N. Engl. J. Med. 288: 288–292, **1973.**

The authors of this important paper point to the psychogenic ideology often attributed to problems that appear to have major biological-etiologic factors, e.g., symptoms during pregnancy, and the depreciation attached to psychogenic diagnoses.

36. **Nadelson, C.C. and Notman, M.** Diseases and illnesses specific to women, pp. 475–497. In: Psychiatry in General Medical Practice. Eds.: G. Usdin and J. Lewis. New York: McGraw-Hill, **1979.**

A review of major issues in Ob/Gyn Liaison Psychiatry, including the doctor/patient relationship and the psychiatric consultant, and specific issues involving pregnancy, including teenage pregnancy, menstrual cycle and premenstrual syndome, menopause, and surgical procedures including hysterectomy, sterilization, mastectomy, as well as discussion of amniocentesis, rape and life stage considerations, and counseling and therapeutic implications.

37. ***Nadelson, C.C. and Notman, M.,** eds. The Woman Patient: Vol. II. Concepts of Femininity and Life Cycle. New York: Plenum, **1982.**

Provides an overview of theoretical issues involved in understanding the psychology of women including psychoanalytic theory and changing views about reproduction and sexuality. In addition, there is a section on life cycle considerations including mother-child relationships, developmental issues for the Black woman, decisions to marry, the impact of maternal work on children, and issues of aging.

38. ***Notman, M. and Nadelson, C.C.,** eds. The Woman Patient: Vol. I. Sexual and Reproductive Aspects of Women's Health Care. New York: Plenum, **1978.**

This volume focuses primarily on reproduction and sexuality, with chapters including genetic counseling, contraception, pregnancy, sexuality, fertility and infertility, surgical and medical gynecology, hysterectomy, abortion, breast disease, and sexual abuse.

39.   *Notman, M. and Nadelson, C.C., eds. The Woman Patient: Vol. III. Aggression, Adaptation and Psychotherapy. New York: Plenum, 1982.

Theoretical and clinical aspects of aggression and violence including violent women, battered women, and delinquency are presented, followed by a section on symptom formation that includes a general overview with special attention to specific problems for women, including miscarriage and alcohol abuse. The final section on therapy presents issues involving gender and therapy.

40.   Parlee, M.B. Psychological aspects of menstruation, childbirth and menopause: An overview with suggestions for further research, pp. 179–238. In: The Psychology of Women: Future Directions and Research. Eds.: J. Sherman and F. Denmark. New York: Psychological Dimensions, 1978.

A review of research on the biological and psychosocial aspects of menstruation, childbirth, and menopause with specific critique of research and suggestions for future direction.

41.   *Youngs, D. and Ehrhardt, A., eds. Psychosomatic Obstetrics and Gynecology. New York: Appleton-Century-Croft, 1980.

An important volume containing sections on critical biological, social, and cultural influences during the female life cycle, psychological needs in the doctor/patient relationship, new obstetric techniques and their implications for the patient, the adolescent patient, and some common gynecologic disorders from a psychologic perspective.

MENTAL HEALTH AND MENTAL ILLNESS

42.   Al-Issa, I., ed. The Psychopathology of Women. New Jersey: Prentice-Hall, 1980.

This book considers female psychopathology including women in therapy and specific disorders including schizophrenia, depression, phobias, and hysteria. It also contains discussions of sexuality, alcoholism, drug abuse, criminality, and psychophysiologic disorders.

43.   Carmen, E.H., Felipe-Russo, N., and Miller, J.B. Inequality of women's mental health: An overview. Am. J. Psychiatry 138: 1319–1330, 1981.

This paper considers the complex problem of sex bias and sex role stereotyping, which the authors believe continue to detract from the quality of mental health services provided to both sexes, but particularly to women. The authors also suggest means of ameliorating these problems.

44. **Dohrenwend, B.P. and Dohrenwend, B.S.** Sex differences and psychiatric disorders. Am. J. Sociol. 81: 1447–1454, **1976.**

A careful epidemiologic explication of sex differences in mental illness with hypotheses to explain these differences.

45. ***Gomberg, E. and Franks, V.,** eds. Gender and Disorder Behavior. New York: Brunner/Mazel, **1979.**

A comprehensive, well-edited collection of current papers on mental health issues encompassing behavior and sex differences in mental disorders, life cycle crises, problem behaviors including alcohol and sexual abuse, and disorders including schizophrenia and hysteria. It includes M. Weissman and G. Klerman's article, "Sex Differences and the Epidemiology of Depression," which reviews the evidence for different rates of depression between the sexes and analyzes the various explanations offered, concluding that the complexity of interacting variables suggests no single explanation.

46. **Howell, E. and Bayes, M.,** eds. Women and Mental Health. New York: Basic Books, **1981.**

An edited volume by authors from several disciplines with reprinted papers that have had major impact over the last several decades. The book examines theories of female development, gender role stereotypes, socialization, gender bias in treatment, diagnosis and psychopathology in women, and particular treatment needs arising from developmental issues or trauma, which includes treatment of rape victims, battered wives, and incest. There is also an exploration of the differences between traditional and feminist therapies and an overview of recent changes in psychotherapy.

SEXUAL AND PHYSICAL ABUSE

47. **Goodwin, J.,** ed. Sexual Abuse: Incest Victims and their Families. Boston: John Wright, **1982.**

A clinical appraisal of sexual abuse victims, including their evaluation, treatment, and the sequelae. There are references to literature and history that serve to emphasize the roots and pervasiveness of the problem.

48. **Herman, J. and Hirshman, L.** Families at risk for father-daughter incest. Am. J. Psychiatry 138: 967–970, **1981.**

This paper considers the impact on women of having had incestuous relationships with their fathers, including the repercussions for subsequent behavior and adaptation.

49. **Hilberman, E.** Overview: The "wife beater's wife" reconsidered. Am. J. Psychiatry 137: 1336–1347, **1980.**

The author of this review article describes the physical abuse of wives and connects her discussion to a theoretical understanding of masochism and psychological adaptation. She discusses societal attitudes toward violence, especially as they relate to sex roles.

50. ***Hilberman, E.** The Rape Victim. New York: Basic Books, **1976.**

This volume addresses sociocultural, legal, and medical aspects of rape as well as acute treatment and the role of the psychiatrist. It also includes a section on the child rape victim.

51. **Nadelson, C.C., Notman, M., Zackson, H., et al.** A follow-up study of rape victims. Am. J. Psychiatry 139: 1266–1270, **1982.**

The authors emphasize the clinical repercussions of rape, particularly in symptoms like depression and sexual dysfunction, which persist beyond the acute phases and may impair life functioning.

52. **Notman, M. and Nadelson, C.C.** The rape victim: Psychodynamic considerations. Am. J. Psychiatry 133: 408–413, **1976.**

This paper discusses the rape response in terms of its psychodynamic implications as a stress response syndrome and emphasizes life stage considerations.

54. SOCIALLY DISADVANTAGED AND CROSS-CULTURAL POPULATIONS

Ezra E.H. Griffith, M.D.

Psychiatric care of disadvantaged and minority populations has recently become a pressing area of importance. This has been due at least partially to an increasing sociopolitical interest of our society in problems that concern the underprivileged. Similarly, American psychiatrists have been forced to confront cross-cultural issues raised by the impact of heightened immigration to our shores of Cubans, Haitians, Puerto Ricans, Mexicans, Vietnamese, West Indians, and other groups. In addition, black Asians and native Americans continue to emphasize their need for a type of psychiatric care that is appreciative of and founded on their unique sociocultural context. Similar arguments have been made about the special needs of women, the deaf, and others in our society. Thus the understanding of principles that must inform the psychiatric care of these groups of Americans is now a serious and specialized enterprise.

Nevertheless, it remains a major task to structure core readings in these aspects of psychiatry because of the multiplicity of problems and subgroups that exist. For example, there is ample literature that is specific to the needs of Mexican-Americans and also to Puerto Ricans. Yet space does not allow the treatment of these groups separately. Neither will these readings address the psychiatric problems of native Americans or of Asians. Rather, emphasis has been placed on appreciating issues relevant to one or two groups in such a way that a model can be developed for thinking clinically about others. A similar style has been utilized in approaching the psychiatric care of the many unique groups in the disadvantaged category. The readings have been grouped into topics that conceptualize major issues in this area of psychiatry, and, where possible, material has been chosen that simultaneously addresses problems encountered in clinical care of the disadvantaged and of the culturally distinct group.

DEFINITIONS OF THE UNDERPRIVILEGED
AND DISADVANTAGED: CONSIDERATION OF THE
CATEGORIZATION OF PEOPLE: A SOCIOCULTURAL,
SEXUAL, RACIAL, AND ECONOMIC PHENOMENON.
GENERAL PROBLEMS IN THE PSYCHIATRIC
APPROACHES TO THESE GROUPS

1.   **Ablon, J.** Stigmatized health conditions. Soc. Sci. Med. (Med. Anthropol.) 15B: 5–9, **1981.**

   The mechanism is explored whereby groups are categorized negatively, thereby producing stigma. The consequences of stigma are explained, with emphasis on the ultimate development of a handicap that impacts on identity. Special burdens are inherently borne by the stigmatized who are ultimately disadvantaged.

2.   **Carmen, E.H., Russo, N.F., and Miller, J.B.** Inequality and women's health: An overview. Am. J. Psychiatry 138: 1319–1330, **1981.**

   Consideration of gender inequality as a means of producing disadvantaged status. Article reviews how the subordinate social status of women decreases their access to quality mental health services and negatively affects their psychological development.

3.   ***Peck, H.B.** Psychiatric approaches to the impoverished and underprivileged, pp. 524–534. In: AHP (2nd ed.), Vol. 2, **1974.**

   Discusses the underprivileged as defined by their lack of money and the implications of that status in regards to limiting access to psychiatric care. The complications of being poor as well as a minority group member are reviewed. An attempt is made to understand the psychological consequences of powerlessness.

CONCEPT OF EQUITY IN PSYCHIATRIC CARE:
PATIENT CHARACTERISTICS AND TREATMENT PATTERNS;
DEMOGRAPHIC CHARACTERISTICS VERSUS NEED;
ISSUE OF PROFESSIONAL BIAS IN THE TREATMENT CONTEXT

4.   ***Mollica, R.F. and Redlich, F.C.** Equity and changing patient characteristics—1950–1975. Arch. Gen. Psychiatry 37: 1257–1263, **1980.**

   A follow-up of Hollingshead and Redlich's *Social Class and Mental Illness.* This study focuses on treatment settings for the disadvantaged population; it confirms the continued importance of the state hospital as a primary source of inpatient care for these low-status patients and a community-categorized treatment unit as the primary outpatient unit for this group. The authors confront the crucial issue of whether such treatment patterns for the disadvantaged reflect inequity.

5.   **Umbenhauer, S.L. and DeWitte, L.L.** Patient race and social class: Attitudes and decisions among three groups of mental health professionals. Compr. Psychiatry 19: 509–515, **1978.**

Studies the effect of a patient's race and social class on his or her diagnosis, prognosis, and subsequent fate in the hands of mental health professionals. Authors suggest that it may indeed be easier to sensitize professionals to racial bias than to social class discrimination.

OPPRESSION THROUGH STIGMA

Childism is the basic form of oppression in our society. A wide range of stigmatization and oppression is demonstrated by the models of dwarfism and deafness. This section deals with the applicability of this knowledge to our understanding of dominant group reactions to nondominant subgroups.

6.   **Ablon, J.** Dwarfism and social identity: Self-help group participation. Soc. Sci. Med. (Med. Anthropol.) 15B: 25–30, **1981.**

Authors examine different aspects of the dwarfism experience and its impact on social identity and lifestyle. The reconstruction of the stigmatized identity is described, particularly within the context of self-help group membership.

7.   **Becker, G.** Coping with stigma: Lifelong adaptation of deaf people. Soc. Sci. Med. (Med. Anthropol.) 15B: 21–24, **1981.**

Societies develop negative attitudes toward people who have certain blemishes or behaviors. Deafness as an example. Deafness and its impact on the development of identity. Review of some of the mechanisms used to cope with the stigmatization.

8.   ***Pierce, C.M. and Allen, G.B.** Childism. Psychiatric Ann. 5: 266–270, **1975.**

Makes the basic point that the child is discriminated against simply because he is a child; and all of us engage in such practices. Childism is carried out through microaggressions, not gross brutalization. Authors consider the consequences of childism for the child and the adult and emphasize that sexism and racism are derivatives thereof.

CROSS-CULTURAL FACTORS IN THE ASSESSMENT OF PSYCHOPATHOLOGY: CONCEPT OF THE CLINICIAN'S FRAME OF REFERENCE

9. **Adebimpe, V.R.** Overview: White norms and psychiatric diagnosis of black patients. Am. J. Psychiatry 138: 279–285, **1981.**

Extensive consideration of the allegation that there is constant psychiatric misdiagnosis of black patients and that there are differences in diagnostic error between white and black clinicians. Contribution of cultural, social, and ethnic elements to the establishment of a diagnosis. The sociocultural distance between diagnostician and patient can create fundamental problems.

10. **Marcos, L.R., Alpert, M., Urcuyo, L., et al.** The effect of interview language on the evaluation of psychopathology in Spanish-American schizophrenic patients. Am. J. Psychiatry 130: 549–553, **1973.**

Assessment of the influence of interview language on the psychiatric evaluation of schizophrenic patients whose native tongue is Spanish. Psychiatric ratings reflected greater psychopathology when the patients were interviewed in English. Possible impact of these findings on clinical care is discussed.

PSYCHOLOGICAL TESTING OF AMERICAN MINORITIES: PROBLEMS AND PITFALLS

11. ***Adebimpe, V.R., Gigandet, J., and Harris, E.** MMPI diagnosis of black psychiatric patients. Am. J. Psychiatry 136: 85–87, **1979.**

The fact is emphasized here that psychological testing may be influenced by ethnicity, culture, and nationality. Specifically, then, the MMPI produces different results for whites and blacks. These differences can lead to misdiagnosis. Clinicians must guard against such errors.

12. **Samuda, R.J.** Psychological Testing of American Minorities: Issues and Consequences. New York: Harper and Row, **1975.**

This book lends itself to use in its entirety or by chapters. It alerts us all to the social, economic, educational, and psychological implications of testing. It examines in a useful way the traditional assertion that tests systematically lead to the assigning of improper labels on minority children. It also explores how factors such as nutrition, language, and self-concept affect test performance.

THE BLACK FAMILY.
MYTHS AND REALITY OF BLACK FAMILY STRUCTURE

This section deals with the historical development of the notion of the maternal family; legacy of white-dominated research; and observations on family therapy with black families.

13.   **Foley, V.D.** Family therapy with black, disadvantaged families: Some observations on roles, communication and technique. J. Marriage Fam. Counseling 1: 29–38, **1975.**

An article that emphasizes the differences between the ways in which black and white families operate. The therapist must then understand that the point is not to change the way the black family operates, but to help it to function more smoothly. The authors point out that there is an important cultural dimension to roles, tasks, and communication within the family.

14.   ***TenHouten, W.D.** The black family: Myth and reality. Psychiatry 33: 145–173, **1970.**

The significance of this paper lies in its power to force you to reconsider the rampant stereotypes about black family structure. Naturally, it evokes serious thought about the precision and accuracy of the Foley citation above. It should also make us think seriously about what we think is the traditional family structure of other ethnic groups.

THE HISPANIC FAMILY: REVIEW OF THE
PREMISES ON WHICH NOTIONS OF THE HISPANIC
FAMILY ARE BASED; COMPARISONS OF CHICANO
AND PUERTO RICAN FAMILY STRUCTURE;
SOME TREATMENT CONSIDERATIONS

15.   ***Canino, I.A. and Canino, G.** Impact of stress on the Puerto Rican family: Treatment considerations. Am. J. Orthopsychiatry 50: 535–541, **1980.**

Emphasis here is on the urban, low-income Puerto Rican family in the United States. Reviews the characteristics of such families and the impact of stress on their structure and function. Explores effective treatment considerations.

16.   **Montiel, M.** The Chicano family: A review of research. Soc. Work 18: 22–31, **1973.**

An excellent piece that reviews the literature about Chicano family structure and raises the question of whether the traditional descriptions center on the Chicano family or on individuals living in the culture of poverty. The author also wonders why so many scholars perceive the Chicano family as a nonviable institution. Is it simply another example of labeling?

GENERAL CONSIDERATIONS OF THE LOWER-CLASS FAMILY: POSSIBLE EXISTENCE OF A COHERENT SYNDROME

17.   ***Minuchin, S.** The disorganized and disadvantaged family: Structure and process, pp. 192–243. In: Families of the Slums. Ed.: S. Minuchin, B. Montalvo, B.G. Guerney, et al. New York: Basic Books, **1967.**

A significant review of families who share the culture of the slum. The crucial thesis here is that whether black, Puerto Rican, or other, these families of the urban ghettoes share a style of thinking, coping, communicating, and behaving.

RACIAL DIFFERENCES BETWEEN CLIENT AND THERAPIST: CRITICAL REVIEW OF RESEARCH SOCIAL CLASS AND PSYCHOTHERAPY OUTCOME

18.   ***Griffith, M.S.** The influences of race on the psychotherapeutic relationship. Psychiatry 40: 27–40, **1977.**

Asserts that psychotherapy is not a culture-free activity and raises questions about the effect of the race variable. Emphasizes the need for therapists to develop solid knowledge about the culture of the patient, particularly when the therapist and patient are from different races. Reviews the research in the area.

19.   **Jones, E.** Social class and psychotherapy: A critical review of research. Psychiatry 37: 307–320, **1974.**

Author traces development from when Freud expressed a feeling that patients lacking a certain education and a reliable character should be refused psychoanalysis. Article reviews the characteristics that render anyone amenable to psychotherapy and explores whether these elements are class bound.

SPECIAL PROBLEMS IN PSYCHOTHERAPY WITH THE
DISADVANTAGED—NECESSARY ADJUSTMENT OF
APPROACHES AND TECHNIQUES; SHOULD THE THERAPIST
AND PATIENT BE OF THE SAME ETHNIC BACKGROUND?

20.   *Schachter, J.S. and Butts, H.F. Transference and countertransference
in interracial analyses. J. Am. Psychoanal. Assoc. 16: 792–808, 1968.

The authors present two cases: a white man's being analyzed by a black
male analyst; a black man's analysis by a white female analyst. They
discuss both cases and conclude that the obscuring or overestimation of
racial stereotypes by either analyst or patient can retard the analysis;
racial differences may quicken the analysis.

21.   *Shapiro, E.T. and Pinsker, H. Shared ethnic scotoma. Am. J.
Psychiatry 130: 1338–1341, 1973.

This article squarely confronts the assertion that efficacy is assured in
psychotherapy when the patient and therapist share the same ethnic
background. With use of a case report, the authors point out that the
therapist's own scotoma may be maintained when therapist and patient
(because of similar experiences and background) collude too quickly to
agree that certain issues have an objective importance. In so doing, the
therapist may fail to recognize a common form of resistance.

22.   Shen, J. and Murray, J. Psychotherapy with the disadvantaged. Am. J.
Psychother. 35: 268–275, 1981.

Psychotherapists must first examine their personal attitudes toward
offering psychotherapy to the working class and the poor. The authors
alert therapists to the traditional tendency to sabotage a treatment
alliance with the poor so that premature termination is the result. They
also discuss other elements that operate to produce impediments to
maintenance of the disadvantaged in therapy. A useful case example is
offered.

CULTURE-BOUND ADAPTATIONS TO STRESS:
CULTURAL VALUES AND EGO FUNCTIONING;
FOLK HEALING AS A SYSTEM OF MEDICAL CARE;
RITUAL AS AN IMPORTANT THERAPEUTIC
ELEMENT IN EVERY CULTURE

23.   Griffith, E.E.H., English, T., and Mayfield, V. Possession, prayer, and
testimony: Therapeutic aspects of the Wednesday night meeting in a
black church. Psychiatry 43: 120–128, 1980.

The use of the church service as a ritual that provides a therapeutic experience is highlighted. The authors utilize participant-observation and case examples to argue that such a church service is a culture-bound resource for meeting the mental health needs of a special group.

24.   **Jilek, W.G.** "Brainwashing" as therapeutic technique in contemporary Canadian Indian spirit dancing: A case of theory building, pp. 201–213. In: Anthropology and Mental Health. Ed.: J. Westermeyer. The Hague: Mouton, **1976.**

This incisive report describes how Salish Indians use spirit singing and dancing to restore and preserve physical, mental, and social well being. In addition, the author examines the therapeutic aspects of this phenomenon in the light of established Western treatment principles.

25.   **Ness, R.C. and Wintrob, R.M.** Folk healing: A description and synthesis. Am. J. Psychiatry 138: 1477–1481, **1981.**

Systems of folk healing are explored in the indigenous evolution of specific cultural settings. Faith healing, rootwork, curanderismo and espiritismo are conceptualized as useful purveyors of health care within the relevant culture.

26.   ***Weidman, H.H. and Susses, J.N.** Cultural values and ego functioning in relation to the atypical culture-bound reactive syndromes. Int. J. Sci. Psychiatry 17: 83–100, **1971.**

The authors here underline the notion that cultural values and one's world view determine the type of cosmic experiences to which people must adapt and the kinds of stress that must be handled. Methods of coping are explained, particularly in the context of the culture that gives birth to them.

USE OF THE AUTOBIOGRAPHY TO FACILITATE THE STUDY OF IMPORTANT ISSUES IN THE CLINICAL CARE OF THE DISADVANTAGED OR ETHNIC MINORITY

27.   ***Thomas, P.** Down These Mean Streets. New York: Vintage, **1967.**

This work assures an excellent longitudinal study of the interplay of psychological, social, cultural, and racial forces and of the ways in which they affect the development of a Hispanic growing up in the U.S. The notions of machismo and of the search for racial identity are portrayed. The reader can explore and consider whether black and Hispanic self-hatred are mythical or real concepts. The utility of paranoid and other coping stances for minorities can be examined.

PART VI
SPECIAL TOPICS

55. SOCIAL AND COMMUNITY PSYCHIATRY

JONATHAN F. BORUS, M.D.
DAVID R. GASTFRIEND, M.D.

Social and community psychiatry are controversial areas of our field that deal not only with the individual but also with external social forces and systems that impinge on or support his functioning and mental health. *Social psychiatry* is a research and theoretical area that studies man and his multiple interrelationships with social systems. It includes the content areas of psychiatric epidemiology; culture, class and ethnicity, and mental health; and coping behaviors under ordinary and extraordinary stress. Only a few core social psychiatry readings are suggested here, as these areas are covered elsewhere in this book. *Community psychiatry* is a public health–related clinical field in which psychiatrists apply social psychiatric theory and knowledge to the delivery of mental health services to defined populations. Our cited readings are mainly drawn from the literature on *community mental health*, the multidisciplinary delivery system of public mental health services to geographically defined populations that was set up in the U.S. in the early 1960s. Community psychiatrists have been major forces in the development of this public delivery system, and we have focused the readings on topics relevant to psychiatrists interested in this practice area.

Community psychiatry differs from other areas of psychiatric practice in being concerned with "the denominator"—that is, all the persons in a defined population at risk of illness. Although in some places community mental health programs have become constricted to the care of chronically ill, indigent patients without other treatment resources, community psychiatry has a broader focus that includes exploration of opportunities for primary prevention of mental disorders through changes in a person's internal and external environments; early case findings and effective treatment (secondary prevention) of a variety of mental disorders for patients with or without the financial means necessary for private therapy; and rehabilitative services to limit disability from persistent mental illness (tertiary prevention).

439

The following reading list combines historical and theoretical papers, program examples to provide the "flavor" of community-based practice, and reports highlighting the critical research questions in the field.

BASIC CONCEPTS AND CRITICAL ISSUES

1. **Borus, J.F.** Issues critical to the survival of community mental health. Am. J. Psychiatry 135: 1029–1035, **1978.**

   Delineation of the critical issues facing community mental health delivery systems in the age of deinstitutionalization.

2. **Caplan, G.** Principles of Preventive Psychiatry. New York: Basic Books, **1964.**

   The "Bible" of the community mental health movement, which lays out the basic premises of the field's conceptual founders (Caplan and Lindemann) concerning psychiatry's ability to provide both illness-preventing and illness-ameliorating services under a public health rubric for a defined community.

ANTECEDENTS OF COMMUNITY MENTAL HEALTH

3. **Caplan, G. and Caplan, R.** Development of community psychiatry concepts, pp. 1499–1516. In: CTP I, **1967.**

   A review article detailing some of the historical antecedents of community mental health and defining some of its key concepts.

4. **Kennedy, J.F.** Message from the President of the United States Relative to Mental Illness and Mental Retardation. Document 58, 86th Congress, Feb. 5, **1963.**

   President Kennedy's message is the only presidential statement on mental illness, and it set the tone for the federal community mental health centers program. It is noteworthy in demonstrating the optimism of that era in which a country determined to be the first on the moon could similarly concentrate its resources to launch an "attack" on mental illness and mental retardation.

5. **Querido, A.** The shaping of community mental health care. Br. J. Psychiatry 114: 293–302, **1968.**

   Details the origins of community mental health, deinstitutionalization, and social psychiatry in Amsterdam in the 1930s. Its charming anecdotal quality is as interesting as its relevance to events forty years later.

6. **Rubin, B.** Community psychiatry: An evolutionary change in medical psychology in the United States. Arch. Gen. Psychiatry 20: 497–507, **1969.**

   Details the overdetermined nature of community psychiatry and traces some of its historical, professional, social, and political antecedents. It is especially helpful in demonstrating the importance of the 60s political trend for distributive social justice to the emergence of community psychiatry.

PSYCHIATRIC EPIDEMIOLOGY

7. **Schwab, J.J. and Schwab, M.E.** Epidemiologic terms, concepts, and levels of investigation, pp. 39–51. In: Sociocultural Roots of Mental Illness: An Epidemiologic Survey. New York: Plenum, **1978.**

   A review of basic concepts in psychiatric epidemiology (epidemiologic hypothesis, case, risk, population at risk, prevalence, and incidence) with good examples. A starting point for the psychiatrist entering the field of psychiatric epidemiology.

8. **Weissman, M.M. and Klerman, G.L.** Epidemiology of mental disorders. Arch. Gen. Psychiatry 35: 705–712, **1978.**

   Updates the recent change in psychiatric epidemiology that in the last decade has increasingly shifted its focus to studies of discreetly defined mental disorders using data elicited from structured interviews and more disease-specific diagnostic criteria.

DEFINING, ENTERING, AND WORKING WITH THE COMMUNITY

9. **Fiedler, F.E., Fiedler, J., and Campf, S.** Who speaks for the community. J. Appl. Soc. Psychol. 1: 324–333, **1971.**

   A fascinating study contrasting the views of self-designated "community leaders" with those of a random telephone sample of the community-at-large concerning the important issues for the community.

10. **Panzetta, A.F.** The concept of community. Arch. Gen. Psychiatry 25: 291–297, **1971.**

    A gem that contrasts the cohesive community with significant relationships between its members, common goals and values, and natural support systems posited in community mental health theory with the reality of the federally defined "catchmented communities" of 75,000 to 200,000 people.

11.   **Tischler, G.L., Aries, E., Cytrynbaum, S., et al.** The catchment area concept, pp. 59–83. In: Progress in Community Mental Health, Vol. 3. Ed.: L. Bellak. New York: Brunner/Mazel, **1975.**

A logical, concise overview of theoretical and practical implications of the catchment area concept for community mental health delivery. It considers the impact of this model on patient care, consultation, and community involvement.

INFLUENCE OF CULTURE ON THE EXPRESSION OF SYMPTOMS, HELP SEEKING, AND PSYCHOTHERAPY OF MENTAL ILLNESS

12.   **Favazza, A.R. and Oman, M.** Overview: Foundations of cultural psychiatry. Am. J. Psychiatry 135: 293–303, **1978.**

A densely referenced, broad overview of cultural studies that justify the inclusion of this field as a cornerstone of social psychiatry.

13.   **Griffith, M.S.** The influences of race on the psychotherapeutic relationship. Psychiatry 40: 27–40, **1977.**

A provocative survey of research on the influence of race in the psychotherapeutic relationship.

14.   **LeVine, R.A.** Group differences in individual behavior patterns, pp. 15–39. In: Culture, Behavior and Personality. Chicago: Aldine, **1973.**

The article provides a conceptual frame for understanding cultural aspects of personality and different ways that cultural groups are characterized and differentiated from each other. It makes the reader question how generalizable certain stereotypes of an ethnic group are to the behaviors of an individual member of that group.

15.   **Spiegel, J.** Cultural aspects of transference, pp. 324–336. In: Transactions. New York: Science House, **1971.**

This chapter demonstrates the implicit reliance of dynamic psychotherapy on the predominant values of our society and how they may contribute to therapeutic stalemate with patients from ethnic groups with different value orientations.

DELIVERING DIRECT AND CONSULTATIVE SERVICE TO LARGE POPULATIONS

16.   **Borus, J.F., Anastasi, M.A., Casoni, R., et al.** Psychotherapy in the goldfish bowl: The role of the indigenous therapist. Arch. Gen. Psychiatry 36: 187–190, **1979.**

An account of the advantages and disadvantages of indigenous therapists who have grown up and live in the community in which they provide therapeutic services. It concludes that simply being indigenous to a neighborhood or being culturally or racially similar to one's patients in and of itself is insufficient without acquiring the necessary therapeutic skills.

17. **Caplan, G.** The Theory and Practice of Mental Health Consultation. New York: Basic Books, **1970.**

The classic text on consulting to community agencies with a focus on consultee-centered case consultation. The book is most helpful in defining types of mental health consultation and the difficult initial steps in contracting for consultation.

18. **Stein, L.I. and Test, M.A.** Alternative to mental hospital treatment: I. Conceptual model, treatment program and clinical evaluation. Arch. Gen. Psychiatry 37: 392–397, **1980.**

19. **Weisbrod, B.A., Test, M.A., and Stein, L.I.** II. Economic benefit—cost analysis. Arch. Gen. Psychiatry 37: 400–405, **1980.**

20. **Test, M.A. and Stein, L.L.** III. Social cost. Arch. Gen. Psychiatry 37: 409–412, **1980.**

The best-controlled study to date that examines clinical, social, and economic cost outcome measures of a community-based alternative program to mental hospital treatment for patients with schizophrenia.

COORDINATING MENTAL HEALTH WITH PRIMARY HEALTH CARE DELIVERY

21. **Borus, J.F., Burns, B.J., Jacobson, A.M., et al.** Coordinated Mental Health Care in Neighborhood Health Centers. Institute of Medicine Series on Mental Health Services in General Health Care, Vol. 2. Washington, D.C.: National Academy of Sciences, **1979.**

A review of the advantages in accessibility, acceptability and utilization of care; case finding and coordination of care; efficacy of care; interaction with the community; and training of providing community-based mental health services as a coordinated part of a primary care delivery system. Also reviews the literature on the interaction of primary care and mental health and makes policy recommendations for closer coordination.

22. **Jones, K.R. and Vischi, T.R.** Impact of alcohol, drug abuse and mental

health treatment on medical care utilization. Suppl. Med. Care 17, No.12, **1979.**

A detailed review of studies of the so-called "offset effect," which measures the effectiveness of providing specialist alcohol, drug abuse, and mental health treatment in decreasing medical care utilization. The paper also sets a framework for future studies of this important phenomenon.

THE ROLES OF THE COMMUNITY PSYCHIATRIST

23. **Levinson, D.J. and Klerman, G.L.** The clinician-executive. Psychiatry 30: 3–15, **1967.**

The authors describe the difficulties psychiatrists have in undertaking the executive-administrative responsibilities frequently required of them in community mental health systems. Some of the specific problematic role tasks for psychiatrists in achieving a synthesis of their clinician and executive roles are described.

24. **Stern, R. and Minkoff, K.** Paradoxes in programming for chronic patients in a community clinic. Hosp. Community Psychiatry 30: 613–617, **1979.**

This paper reviews six fundamental paradoxes in professional values that give psychiatrists in community mental health settings difficulty dealing with chronic patients and suggests that training and practice modes are responsible for these problems.

NORMALITY AND COPING

25. **Hamburg, D.A. and Adams, J.E.** A perspective on coping behavior. Arch. Gen. Psychiatry 17: 277–284, **1967.**

A review of studies of the coping behaviors used by a variety of populations ranging from students entering college to those coping with severe physical and medical insults.

26. **Kinston, W., and Rosser, R.** Disaster: Effects on mental and physical state. J. Psychosom. Res. 18: 437–456, **1974.**

A review article of the stages and psychiatric consequences of disasters.

27. **Offer, D., and Sabshin, M.** Normality, pp. 459–464. In: CTP II, Vol. 2, **1975.**

A conceptual review of differing concepts of normality (as health, statistical average, utopia, or process).

28.   **Parkes, C.M.** Psychosocial transitions: A field for study. Soc. Sci. and Med. 5: 101–115, **1971.**

Theoretical discussions defining psychosocial transitions and the role of the assumptive world using grief reactions as a model for illustration.

PREVENTIVE INTERVENTIONS

29.   **Adler, D.A., Levinson, D.J., and Astrachan, B.M.** The concept of prevention in psychiatry: A re-examination. Arch. Gen. Psychiatry 35: 786–789, **1978.**

A review of the application of the public health concepts of primary, secondary, and tertiary prevention to psychiatry's medical, rehabilitative, social control, and humanistic tasks. The authors emphasize the limited capability psychiatry has in primary prevention and its legitimate role in secondary (treatment) and tertiary (rehabilitative) preventive efforts for patients with defined mental disorders.

30.   **Borus, J.F. and Anastasi, M.A.** Mental health prevention groups in primary care settings. Int. J. Ment. Health 8(2): 58–73, **1979.**

A description of attempts within a primary care-based mental health program to provide group programs as preventive interventions for people who are experiencing similar life stresses and are at high risk of developing disabling emotional disorders.

EVALUATION OF COMMUNITY MENTAL HEALTH PROGRAMS

31.   **Weiss, C.H.** Introduction. Chapter 1, pp. 1–23. In: Evaluation Research. Englewood Cliffs: Prentice-Hall, **1972.**

A brief primer on methodologies for evaluating any human service program. The initial two chapters outline reasons why evaluation research is and is not conducted, and the complexity of evaluations of ongoing service programs.

32.   **Wing, J.K.** Principles of evaluation, pp. 11–39. In: Evaluating a Community Psychiatric Service. Eds.: J.K. Wing and A.M. Hailey. Oxford: Oxford University Press, **1972.**

Suggests the logical priority of first evaluating a program's effects in decreasing morbidity and mortality due to mental disorder; next evaluating its effectiveness in increasing accessibility to care; and last evaluating which effective, accessible programatic efforts are most cost effective.

DEINSTITUTIONALIZATION AND COMMUNITY TREATMENT OF THE CHRONICALLY ILL

33.   **Bachrach, L.L.** Deinstitutionalization: An Analytical Review and Sociological Perspective. DHEW publication No. (ADM)76-351. Washington, D.C.: U.S. Government Printing Office, **1976.**

A comprehensive review and sociologic theoretical synthesis of the issues of deinstitutionalization by one of the most lucid writers on this topic.

34.   **Borus, J.F.** Deinstitutionalization of the chronically mentally ill. N. Engl. J. Med. 305: 339–342, **1981.**

A review of the policy of deinstitutionalization as an oversimplified political "solution" to the complex issues of improving public sector treatment of the chronically mentally ill. It discusses five often conflicting wishful assumptions or "fantasies" about deinstitutionalization and predicts that reinstitutionalization may well be the next "new" political solution.

35.   **Borus, J.F. and Hatow, E.E.** The patient and the community, pp. 171–196. In: Schizophrenia: Science and Practice. Ed.: J. Shershow. Cambridge: Harvard University Press, **1978.**

This chapter provides a comprehensive review of the range of social and therapeutic services needed by the schizophrenic patient before he leaves the hospital and once in the community to actively sustain him outside of an institutional setting.

36.   **Creer, C. and Wing, J.K.** Living with a schizophrenic patient. Br. J. Hosp. Med. 14: 73–82, **1975.**

A report of the reactions of relatives who have had a schizophrenic patient return to live in their home. It describes both the patient's and the relatives' coping and makes a plea for closer coordination between professionals and families who together provide care for patients living in the community.

37.   **Hansell, N. and Willis, G.L.** Outpatient treatment of schizophrenia. Am. J. Psychiatry 134: 1082–1086, **1977.**

A clinical report of a population of chronic schizophrenics followed by a mental health center that describes long-term management, resource utilization, and rehospitalization rates (including the effects of deinstitutionalization). Especially notable for its emphasis on patient education about medication side effects and self-regulation.

38. **Hogarty, G.E., Goldberg, S.C., Schooler, N.R., et al.** The collaborative study group: Drug and sociotherapy in the aftercare of schizophrenic patients: II. Two year relapse rates. Arch. Gen. Psychiatry 31: 603–608, **1974.**

Prospective, controlled, double-blind study at three clinics of hospitalization relapse rates for schizophrenic patients treated with placebo, chlorpromazine maintenance, and major role therapy. Emphasizes the interactive effects of neuroleptics and sociotherapy in the treatment of the schizophrenic in the community.

39. **Lamb, H.R. and Goertzel, V.** The long term patient in the era of community treatment. Arch. Gen. Psychiatry 34: 679–683, **1977.**

A study of all persons in a California county with psychosis who were psychiatrically disabled. Provides a useful discussion of outcome, benefits, costs, and limitations of deinstitutionalization.

40. **Mosher, L.R. and Keith, S.J.** Research on the psychosocial treatment of schizophrenia: A summary report. Am. J. Psychiatry 136: 623–631, **1979.**

An overview of research on psychosocial treatments for schizophrenia in both inpatient and community-based settings. Definitions, outcome measures, and clinical utility are critically assessed.

41. **Pasamanick, B., Scarpitti, F.R., and Dinitz, S.** Schizophrenics in the Community. New York: Appleton-Century-Crofts, **1967.**

42. **Davis, A., Dinitz, S., and Pasamanick, B.** Schizophrenics in the New Custodial Community. Columbus: Ohio State University Press, **1974.**

The first of these books describes the award-winning experimental study that demonstrated significant advantages to home care with active drug treatment of schizophrenics over other treatments on a variety of outcome measures. The second book details a five-year follow-up study that found that without aggressive home care the different treatment groups were no longer differentiated, and all had deteriorated. It demonstrates the need for continued, aggressive outreach to schizophrenics in the community over an extended, perhaps indefinite, period.

43. **Sharfstein, S.S., Turner, J.E.C., and Clark, H.W.** Financing issues in the delivery of services to the chronically mentally ill and disabled, pp.

137–150. In: The Chronic Mental Patient. Ed.: J.A. Talbott. Washington, D.C.: American Psychiatric Association, **1978.**

A discussion of some of the costs, cost benefits, and policy problems in financing mental health care and community support systems. Notes the problems of lack of adequate funding and the fragmentation of funding resources.

44.   **Vaughn, C.C. and Leff, J.P.** The influence of family and social factors on the course of psychiatric illness: Comparison of schizophrenic and depressed neurotic patients. Br. J. Psychiatry 129: 125–137, **1976.**

Detailed report of a study that finds that those schizophrenics whose key relatives expressed emotions of significant criticism, hostility, or overinvolvement had higher relapse rates during the next nine months. The data also suggest that maintenance phenothiazines and reduction of face-to-face contact with the relative reduces relapses in the high-expressed-emotion families.

45.   **Wing, J.K.** The social context of schizophrenia. Am. J. Psychiatry 135: 1333–1339, **1978.**

An upbeat review of issues in the biopsychosocial treatment of schizophrenia. Advances in diagnostic reliability, social causes of disability, the relationship between social and pharmacologic managements and a historical perspective on institutionalism and community care are discussed.

56. ADMINISTRATIVE PSYCHIATRY

John A. Talbott, M.D.

Until very recently, there was only one book in administrative psychiatry, Walter Barton's estimable *Administration in Psychiatry*. Faculty and trainees interested in the topic were forced to adapt what was essentially a state-hospital administrative model to their setting. Now, however, things are very different. We have three major texts and one journal, *Administration in Mental Health,* devoted to the area.

It is interesting to speculate on why the area of administration has been so underplayed over the years since so much of our lives is dependent upon administrative factors. Perhaps it is because in training we spend so much time on clinical problems relating to individual patients; perhaps because administration is devalued and seen as an obstacle to psychiatric practice; or perhaps because one must have a thorough grounding in clinical psychiatry before moving on to administrative and systems issues. In any case, it is clear now that the field of psychiatry has made sufficient progress in clinical, research, and teaching areas and is now much more concerned with the administrative factors that enable those clinical, research, and training programs to be carried out in the most efficient and effective manner. Administration, after all, is the ability to do best what one wants to do.

The subject areas, today as yesterday, remain the same: administrative theory, community psychiatry, budget and finance, ethics, law, accreditation and evaluation, personnel, and the change process itself. The selection of the contributions below was based both on what areas were important within the field of administrative psychiatry, as well as on which books and articles represented the essential components of administrative psychiatric practice. While most of the areas of interest will not be of immediate concern to the resident in training, many will become so in the years to come, during psychiatric practice.

GENERAL TEXTS

1. **Barton, W.E. and Barton, G.M.** Mental Health Administration: Principles and Practices. 2 Vols. New York: Human Sciences Press, **1982.**

An update of Walter Barton's classic and pioneering work. This two-volume edition covers everything from institutional management to community services. To be dipped into on entering jobs, confronting problems, or when desiring to gain information about issues, systems, or diverse administrative subjects.

2. **Drucker, P.** Management: Tasks, Practices, Responsibilities. New York: Harper and Row, **1974.**

America's dean of management tells us all. A marvelous mixture of anecdotes, case examples, and scientific findings from the U.S., Scandinavia, Japan, etc.: must reading, and it goes fast.

3. **Feldman, S.** The administration of Mental Health Services, 2nd ed. Springfield, IL: Thomas, **1980.**

A panorama of administrative issues: from planning to budgeting to management information and program evaluation; covers personnel, finances, and law; as well as intraorganizational change, interorganizational behavior, and governmental and community relations.

4. **Feldman, S., Goldstein, C., and Offutt, J.** Mental Health Administration: An Annotated Bibliography. Rockville, MD: NIMH, **1978.**

1,085 references in administration of mental health services broken down by topic area. Where to go if you're looking something up or doing the first cut in a research project or paper.

5. Massie, J.L. and Douglas, J. Managing: A Contemporary Introduction, 3rd ed. Englewood Cliffs, N.J.: Prentice-Hall, **1981.**

When I was "giving" the "Administrative Boards," this was the most widely used text. It covers the classic elements of management (e.g., planning, controling, leading); the process of motivation and change; and teaches organization and systems issues in a sensible and painless way.

6. **Talbott, J.A. and Kaplan, R.,** eds. Psychiatric Administration: A Comprehensive Text for the Clinician-Executive. New York: Grune and Stratton, **1983.**

A comprehensive text in administrative psychiatry that explores theory and practice in governmental, private, and voluntary settings. Includes history, training, politics, staff relationships, organizational development, planning, quality assurance, program evaluation, accreditation, data systems, budget and finance, and civil and criminal law.

ADMINISTRATIVE THEORY

7. **Dennis, W.G.** A new role for the behavioral sciences: Effecting organizational change. Adm. Sci. Q. 8: 125–164, **1963.**

    This article will not tell you how to change an organization, but will spell out the types of models used in changing them: i.e., Tavistock, T-groups, Team Management, and Argyris's developmental models. A classic, critical, theoretical piece.

8. **Grusky, O. and Miller, G.** The Sociology of Organizations: Basic Studies. New York: Free Press, **1970.**

    A terrific selection of readings about administrative theory—from classical theories to systems theory. Includes Max Weber, Robert Michels, Frederick Taylor, Chester Bernard, Talcott Parsons, Herbert Simon, Peter Blau, Katz and Kahn, etc., etc.

9. **Herzberg, F.** One more time: How do you motivate employees? Harvard Bus. Rev. 46: 53–62, **1968.**

    The by now classic piece explaining that people are satisfied and dissatisfied by different factors on the job. Suggests that after asking, telling, giving money, and showing, one try a "kick in the...."

10. **Lawrence, P. and Lorsch, J.W.** Traditional organizational theories, pp. 159–184. In: Organization and Environment. Homewood, IL: Irwin, **1969.**

    Just one chapter (7) makes the book exceptional. Lawrence and Lorsch describe organizational theories and practices and how to tighten or loosen an organization so it changes in the optimal direction.

11. **Levinson, D.J. and Klerman, G.L.** The clinician-executive: Some problematic issues for the psychiatrist in mental health organizations. Psychiatry 30: 3–15, **1967.**

    Describes in exquisite and believable detail the shift necessary to go from clinical work to administration. Provides a framework for conceptualization of administrative tasks in psychiatry as well as providing someone contemplating this shift a roadmap of what to expect and anticipate.

12. **Maslow, A.** Motivation and Personality, 2nd ed. New York: Harper and Row, **1970.**

    One of the earliest managerial theorists who understood that man's need to understand his work and grow falls on the heels of his satisfying his basic needs (food, shelter, etc.).

13. **McGregor, D.** The Human Side of Enterprise. New York: McGraw-Hill, **1960.**

The presentations of theories X and Y of management: X being the old-line autocrat and Y being the humanistic encourager of productivity. In this work McGregor foresees the current theory Z of Japanese management.

14. **National Industrial Conference Board.** Behavior Science, Concepts and Management Applications. New York: N.I.C.B., **1969.**

Presents succinct descriptions of current behavioral science management theories and their applications: e.g., MacGregor's theories X and Y; Maslow's hierarchy, Herzberg's motivation; Argyris's mix model; Likert's linking pin and leadership ideals; sensitivity training; Blake and Monton's managerial grid; and the Menninger seminars. Only available from the Nat. Conf. Bd., but worth the effort.

15. **Simon, H.A.** Administrative Behavior: A Study of Decision-Making Processes in Administrative Organization, 3rd ed. New York: Macmillan, **1976.**

This is what really won Herbert Simon the Nobel Prize. Tough sledding at times, but worth it to understand the process of decision making from available facts and values.

COMMUNITY PSYCHIATRY

16. **Joint Information Service of the American Psychiatric Association and National Association Mental Health.** The Community Mental Health Center: An Interim Appraisal. Washington, D.C.: Jt. Info. Service— APA and NAMH, **1969.**

Recaps the first five years' experience with federally funded CMHCs. While the earlier (1964) JIS book gave some models of CMHCs, this presents a discouraging picture of bureaucratic implementation, but a well-done look at CMHC functions, at least early on.

17. **Kaplan, S.R. and Roman, M.** The Organization and Delivery of Mental Health Services in the Ghetto—The Lincoln Hospital Experience. New York: Praeger, **1973.**

What went wrong at Lincoln Hospital with the goal to have the workers control the mental health program. Lovely figures explaining complex interorganizational relationships.

18. **Langsley, D.G.** Community psychiatry, pp. 2836–2854. In: CTP III, Vol. 3, **1980.**

Langsley gives a nice, brief, but complete, review of community psychiatry—including history, concepts, activities, and problems. Subsequent chapters cover definitions (Bert Brown), prevention (Herz Spiro), and consultation, community workers, and volunteers (Milton Greenblatt).

19. **Whittington, H.G.** Psychiatry in the American Community. New York: International Universities Press, **1966.**

Written in the heyday of community psychiatry, Whittington's book presents the essentials of community services. Covers teamwork, primary prevention, consultation, and administration.

BUDGET AND FINANCE

20. **American Hospital Association.** Budgeting Procedures for Hospitals. Chicago, IL: Financial Management Series, **1971.**

If looking at balance sheets bewilders you, this is a brief, albeit pithy, description of all varieties of budgets in hospitals—i.e., statistical, expense, revenue, capital, and cash. It also puts the budgetary process into the perspective of planning, implementing, and monitoring programs.

21. **American Hospital Association.** Capital Financing for Hospitals. Chicago, IL: Financial Management Series, **1974.**

If you don't understand debt financing, sinking funds, and negative pledges, this won't explain them to you. But if you do some preliminary reading and then want a crisp but somewhat dry view of capital financing for hospitals—try this.

22. **Berman, H.J. and Weeks, L.E.** The Financial Management of Hospitals, 4th ed. Ann Arbor, Mi.: Health Administration Press, **1979.**

Not the least of this book's assets are a 12-page glossary and 134-page annotated bibliography. Add to it meaty discussions of accounting, financial organization, cost analysis, Blue Cross, Medicaid and Medicare, charges and rate-setting, capital management, budget, and control, and you have quite a tome.

23. **Cleverley, W.O.,** ed. Financial Management of Health Care Facilities. Rockville, MD: Aspen, **1976.**

A multiauthored work covering all aspects of hospital budgeting and finance culled from journals like *Hospital* and *Hospital Financial Management*. From revenue to reimbursement, forecasting to auditing, incentives to income, capital investment to long-term financing, as well as failure in health organizations and cooperative ventures.

24.   **Cleverley, W.O.** Essentials of Hospital Finance. Germantown, MD: Aspen Systems Corp, **1978.**

A general but detailed review of hospital finance: with charts, balance sheets, and equations. Covers decision making, accounting, financial statements, cost measurement, management control, budgeting, and capital issues.

ETHICS AND LAW

25.   **American Psychiatric Association.** The principles of medical ethics with annotations especially applicable to psychiatry. Washington, D.C.: APA, **1981.**

Everything about ethical issues you need to know, including sex, money, relationships with other professionals, treatment of law breakers, confidentiality, racism, consultations, records, and media contacts.

26.   **Bayer, R., Feldman, S., and Reich, W.** A Selected Annotated Bibliography on Ethics and Mental Health in Ethical Issues in Mental Health Policy and Administration, pp. 22–48. Rockville, MD: NIMH, **1981.**

Limited by the few publications in this area, this annotated bibliography is nonetheless quite useful. Covers ethical issues related to hospitals, computers, forensic psychiatry, management, etc.

27.   **Brooks, A.D.** Law, Psychiatry and the Mental Health System. Boston: Little, Brown, **1973.** Also, **1980** supplement.

An exhaustive (1150 pages) tome on forensic psychiatry that is best used as an encyclopedia or reference work. Covers civil and criminal law, competence, and the doctor-patient relationship.

28.   **Slovenko, R.** Psychiatry and Law. Boston: Little, Brown, **1973.**

Another comprehensive text on forensic psychiatry. Covers civil and criminal law: the psychiatrist-expert witness, and competency issues; privileged communication and hospitalization; wills and family law; and specific conditions such as substance abuse, traumatic neurosis and sexual offenses.

29.   **Stone, A.A.** Mental Health and Law: A System in Transition. Washington, D.C.: National Institute of Mental Health, **1975.** Also, New York: Aronson, **1976.**

A superb review of the major issues in forensic psychiatry: commitment, dangerousness, right to treatment and right to refuse treatment, institutional peonage, competency, and the insanity defense. Also discusses lawyers in the mental health system and special populations such as children, the aged, and the mentally retarded.

CHANGE, QUALITY ASSURANCE AND PERSONNEL

30.   **Consolidated Standards Manual for Child, Adolescent, and Adult Psychiatric Alcoholism, and Drug Abuse Facilities. 1981 ed.** Chicago, IL: Joint Commissions on Accreditation of Hospitals, **1981.**

This manual gives the exact standards by which all psychiatric programs, except CMHCs, are accredited by the JCAH. It will soon be supplanted by the Hospital Accreditation Process, but in the meantime has what's necessary.

31.   **Durbin, R. and Springall, H.** Organization and administration of Health Care. St. Louis: Mosby, **1969.**

One of the few books available that addresses innovative ways of reorganizing hospital tasks and delivery of care more efficiently. Gives the change-oriented person a good example of how to see the hospital in systems terms.

32.   **Flippo, E.B.** The Principles of Personnel Management. New York: McGraw-Hill, **1976.**

The classic text on personnel. Covers hiring and firing, training and promotion, compensation and collective bargaining, in a complete, detailed, illustrative way.

33.   **Greenblatt, M.** Dynamics of Institutional Change: The Hospital in Transition. Pittsburgh, PA: University of Pittsburgh Press, **1971.**

A marvelous inside report of changing a public institution through successive projects at Boston State Hospital in the post-Barton years. Each move is described and analyzed and conclusions drawn about the change process in mental institutions.

34.   **Woy, J.R., Lund, D.A., and Attkisson, C.C.** Quality assurance in human service program evaluation, pp. 411–444. In: Evaluation of Human Service Programs. Eds.: C.C. Attkisson, W.A. Hargreaves, M.J. Horowitz, et al. New York: Academic Press, **1978.**

A complete review of quality assurance: its history, goals, concepts, activities, trends, and critical issues. It covers relevant legislation, regulation and accreditation, as well as inpatient and outpatient quality assurance efforts.

57. ETHICS

ROGER C. SIDER, M.D.

Ethics, the inquiry into the nature of morality, of human conduct where values are concerned, and of vice and virtue, is a subject of central concern to mental health professionals. Although it overlaps with questions of law and of professional codes of conduct, ethics should be distinguished from each of these. For beyond the rationale for any professional act, its legality or consistency with present codes of practice, one looks for deeper and firmer evidence that it is ethically justified. Moreover, far from being an esoteric topic, ethical considerations continuously shape our decisions and those of our patients and thus are grist in the mill of our daily clinical work. But until recently there has been little interest in the formal study of ethical issues in psychiatry. Now, however, biomedical ethics has become a growth industry and psychiatric ethics is beginning to take its place within that domain. Ethical issues receiving special attention in the mental health field include the nature of the physician-patient relationship, therapeutic modality choice, involuntary hospitalization and treatment, informed consent, values in psychotherapy, confidentiality, suicide, double agency, behavior control, sexuality and sex therapy, psychiatric diagnosis, and research with human subjects.

This literature is not as helpful as one would hope, however, for two reasons. First, ethics is essentially a disputatious subject, allowing for deep differences of opinion. Clinicians, quite comfortable with theoretical controversy, are less sanguine when what one ought ethically to do in professional work is itself the subject of unresolved argument. Moreover, in contrast to scientific disputes, the methodology is not clear for the resolution of ethical differences. The second source of disappointment in the literature is that medical ethics, psychiatric aspects included, has not yet developed as a genuine interdiscipline. Rather, the tendency has been for medicine to supply the ethical problems and philosophy to provide the conceptual categories and methodologic tools for analysis of these problems. Consequently the present preoccupation with a rights-autonomy model in medical ethics, imported from philosophy, continues to frame ethical debate in spite of repeated cautions from physicians questioning its appropriateness in the clinical context. Psychiatrists would do well, however, to acknowledge the present status of psychiatric ethics and begin contributing more actively to the dialogue. My own view is that over time a truly clinical psychiatric ethics can be developed, integrating what we know of the psychobiology of human nature and the therapeutic relationship, thereby enabling us to make ethical choices that are more adequately informed than those based only upon the rationalist abstraction of the autonomous moral agent.

The readings identified in this section of the bibliography are best considered, then, as representative of work now in progress in psychiatric ethics. The extent to which they ask the right questions or provide clinically helpful answers is left for the reader to decide.

1.   ***Bloch, S. and Chodoff, P.,** eds. Psychiatric Ethics. New York: Oxford University Press, **1981.**

This valuable, recent, edited volume comprising 18 chapters by as many contributors covers a wide range of topics of special interest to psychiatrists. Among them are chapters dealing with ethical aspects of psychotherapy, forensics, psychiatric diagnosis, suicide, sex therapy, and psychiatric research. Although no uniform ethical framework is provided within which to discuss specific issues, the book is strengthened by contributions from well-known psychiatrists thoroughly grounded in the real ethical problems of their field.

2.   **Breggin, P.R.** Psychotherapy as applied ethics. Psychiatry 34: 59–74, **1971.**

The author, who has become a controversial polemicist regarding the ethics of psychiatric treatment, nonetheless provides in this paper a valuable exposition of the inseparability of psychotherapy and ethics.

3.   ***Brody, H.** Ethical Decisions in Medicine, 2nd ed. Boston: Little, Brown, **1981.**

A well-written basic text in medical ethics in a programmed-text format featuring the extensive use of case histories. Of particular interest to mental health professionals will be five chapters on ethical reasoning, the doctor-patient relationship, behavior control, defining health and disease, and the foundations of values.

4.   **Culver, C., Ferrell, R.B., and Green, R.M.** ECT and special problems of informed consent. Am. J. Psychiatry 137: 586–591, **1980.**

A clear statement with illustrative case histories of ethical dilemmas with ECT and informed consent from the perspective of autonomy ethics.

5.   ***Culver, C. and Gert, B.** Philosophy in Medicine: Conceptual and Ethical Issues in Medicine and Psychiatry. New York: Oxford University Press, **1982.**

This is a thorough exposition of the rights-autonomy approach in ethics. Co-authored by a psychiatrist and a philosopher, it deals with issues currently identified as central to psychiatric practice. Beginning with a conceptual analysis of "rationality" and "irrationality," they go on to discuss competence, valid consent, mental maladies, volitional disabilities, and paternalism.

6. ***Edwards, R.,** ed. Psychiatry and Ethics: Insanity, Rational Autonomy, and Mental Health Care. Buffalo: Prometheus Books, **1982.**

This new volume of previously published articles is organized into 10 sections and includes an excellent selection of papers on most of the current issues being debated in psychiatric ethics. Although a range of views is represented, the editor clearly favors an ethic based upon rational autonomy. The book is considerably strengthened by an extensive list of references for further reading at the end of each section.

7. **Havens, L.L.** Approaches to the Mind: Movement of the Psychiatric Schools from Sects toward Science. Boston: Little, Brown, **1973.**

Not usually considered a volume on psychiatric ethics, this book provides ample documentation for the insight that all psychiatric schools are value laden. Hence our theoretical affiliations shape our concepts of what is normal or ideal. These in turn shape our views of what is ethically justified in treatment.

8. **Holt, R.R.** Freud's impact on modern morality. Hastings Cent. Rep. 10(2): 38–45, **1980.**

This article is a brief but thoughtful analysis of the effects of Freud's thought on contemporary moral consciousness. Although of limited immediate relevance in the ethics of psychiatric treatment, it clearly shows that major psychiatric theories, like psychoanalysis, play a profound role in shaping social views of morality as well as in contributing to current moral dilemmas.

9. **Macklin, R.** Values in psychoanalysis and psychotherapy: A survey and analysis. Am. J. Psychoanal. 33: 133–150, **1973.**

This helpful article documents the inextricable ethical content of psychoanalytic theory and psychotherapeutic practice. By providing a framework for considering the nature and sources of these values, the author assists psychiatrists in thinking through the ethical nature of their work.

10. **Masters, W.H., Johnson, V.E., Kolodny, R.C., et al.,** eds. Ethical Issues in Sex Therapy and Research, Vols. 1 and 2. Boston: Little, Brown, **1977** and **1980.**

These two volumes, the results of conferences sponsored by the Masters and Johnson Institute in 1976 and 1978 respectively, exhaustively discuss their topic and culminate in a 16-page statement of ethics guidelines for sex therapists, sex counselors, and sex researchers, found in Chapter 18 of Vol. 2.

11. ***May, W.F.** Code, covenant, contract, or philanthropy. Hastings Cent. Rep. 5(6): 29–38, **1975.**

This seminal article, already widely quoted in the ethics literature, probes deeply into the ethical basis of the physician-patient relationship. Although not oriented toward psychiatry in particular, it has fundamental implications for mental health professionals.

12. **Michels, R.** Professional ethics and social values. Int. Rev. Psychoanal. 3: 377–384, **1976.**

This paper examines the social context in which professionals formulate ethical codes of professional practice and clarifies the moral legitimacy of professional expertise.

13. **Moore, R.A.** Ethics in the practice of psychiatry-origins, functions, models, and enforcement. Am. J. Psychiatry 135: 157–163, **1978.**

This paper, by a senior psychiatrist and former chairman of the Ethics Committee of the APA, provides a balanced overview of contemporary issues in psychiatric ethics together with an analysis of empirical data from the work of the committee 1973 to 1976.

14. ***The Principles of Medical Ethics.** Washington, D.C.: American Psychiatric Association, **1981,** and **Opinions of the Ethics Committee on the Principles of Medical Ethics: with Annotations Especially Applicable to Psychiatry.** Washington, D.C.: American Psychiatric Association, **1979.**

These two booklets, official publications of the American Psychiatric Association, deserve careful scrutiny. The first is a statement of the principles of medical ethics of the AMA, with detailed annotations for psychiatrists. The second is in question-and-answer format with over 50 actual questions submitted to the APA Ethics Committee between 1973 and 1979 with the committee's responses.

15. **Redlich, F.C. and Mollica, R.F.** Overview: Ethical issues in contemporary psychiatry. Am. J. Psychiatry. 133: 125–136, **1976.**

This overview article considers a range of ethical issues in practice, from rights to treatment and to nontreatment, to behavior control, conflict of interest, confidentiality, and human experimentation. Its fundamental orientation stated early in the paper reads, "We believe that informed consent is the basis of all psychiatric intervention and that without it no psychiatric intervention can be morally justified."

16.   ***Reich, W.,** ed. Encyclopedia of Bioethics, 4 Vols. New York: Macmillan, **1978.**

This excellent four-volume work, the only encyclopedia of its kind, is an authoritative, comprehensive, and carefully edited reference work. Of special interest to psychiatrists are 28 articles on specific mental health and behavioral issues (indexed in Vol. 4, "Systematic Classification of Articles," p. 1830).

17.   **Sider, R.C. and Clements, C.** Family or individual therapy: The ethics of modality choice. Am. J. Psychiatry 139: 1455–1459, **1982.**

This paper examines the ethical conflict inherent in the choice between individual and social unit therapies, analyzing this conflict in terms of a general systems perspective.

18.   **Special Section: Life, liberty and the pursuit of madness—The right to refuse treatment.** Am. J. Psychiatry 137: 329–358, **1980.**

This collection of five papers focuses mainly upon the clinical and ethical issues arising from patients' refusal of psychotropic medications. Taken together, they admirably convey the complexities of these problems and document how principles that sound good in theory may work poorly in clinical practice.

19.   ***Szasz, T.S.** The Myth of Mental Illness: Foundations of a Theory of Personal Conduct, Rev. ed. New York: Harper and Row, **1974.**

Szasz is a literate, prolific, and controversial author whose writings are of profound ethical importance. He is the clearest and most consistent exponent of a strict autonomy ethics for the mental health professions, and this volume, although first published over 20 years ago, admirably states his case.

58. FORENSIC PSYCHIATRY

Seymour L. Halleck, M.D.

Forensic psychiatry has two major dimensions. First, it deals with the manner in which psychiatric practice is regulated by statutes, administrative agencies, and the courts. In working with patients who will often be incompetent or nonconsenting, psychiatrists assume certain legal obligations and must practice within certain constraints. Psychiatrists must also be aware of the regulatory aspects of malpractice litigation and learn to provide the most beneficial treatment to their patients while at the same time avoiding the painful consequences of a lawsuit. The second aspect of forensic psychiatry deals with the manner in which psychiatry can assist the society in resolving complex legal problems. The law is often concerned with the state of mind of various participants in the litigation process. Psychiatrists assist the criminal courts by testifying or consulting on issues such as competency to stand trial, legal insanity, sentencing, and release. They assist the civil courts in assessing psychological damages, in determining various aspects of competency and in resolving child custody disputes.

There are thousands of articles and books on forensic psychiatry, many of which are complicated theoretical inquiries into the relation of law and psychology. The emphasis here is on up-to-date sources that are accurate, readable, and comprehensive. This is material the practicing psychiatrist needs to know. A few classical articles have been included to provide some sense of the scope of the field and to allow the reader the option of delving into some of the more complex and fascinating issues.

1. **American Psychiatric Association.** Model law on confidentiality of health and social service records. Am. J. Psychiatry 136: 137–144, **1979.**

   A description of current problems of confidentiality and recommendations for maximum protection of the patient's disclosures.

2. **American Psychiatric Association.** Professional Liability Insurance and Psychiatric Malpractice, Task Force Report No. 13. Washington, D.C.: American Psychiatric Association, **1978.**

   The emphasis here is more on insurance than on the practical issue of

461

malpractice. The appendices illustrating variation in insurance coverage and the glossary are excellent.

3.   ***American Psychiatric Association.** Psychiatry 1982 Annual Review, Part IV: Law and Psychiatry. Washington, D.C.: American Psychiatric Association, **1982.**

Eight prominent psychiatrists and attorneys present an update on recent developments in psychiatry and law. The most current compendium available.

4.   **Annas, G.** The Rights of Hospital Patients: The Basic American Civil Liberties Union Guide to Hospital Patients' Rights. New York: Avon Books, **1975.**

This book is directed toward patients, but it provides the physician with a clear picture of medical responsibility and the limits of intervention. The question-and-answer form make for easy readability.

5.   **Appelbaum, P.S. and Roth, L.H.** Clinical issues in the assessment of competency. Am. J. Psychiatry 138: 1462–1467, **1981.**

A detailed analysis of an increasingly important issue. Emphasis is placed on the situations which require competency determination and the conceptual framework for thinking about the problem is provided.

6.   **Davidson, H.A.** Forensic Psychiatry, 2nd ed. New York: Ronald Press, **1965.**

This is the classic textbook in forensic psychiatry. Noteworthy for its comprehensive discussion of civil as well as criminal issues. Must reading for any psychiatrist planning to be a witness.

7.   **Ennis, B.J. and Emery, R.D.** The Rights of Mental Patients. New York: Avon Books, **1972.**

A manual for patients that articulates the classical civil libertarian attack upon institutional psychiatry. There are many inaccuracies here, and much of this material will trouble the psychiatrist. Reading this book, however, provides insights into the thinking of the antipsychiatry movement.

8.   ***Fishalow, S.E.** The tort liability of the psychiatrist. Bull. Am. Acad. Psychiatry Law 3: 191–230, **1975.**

A brief outline of malpractice risks in psychiatry. Malpractice is explained in just a few pages and all possible categories of lawsuits are considered.

9.   ***Goldstein, A.S.** The Insanity Defense. New Haven: Yale University Press, **1967.** (Also available from Greenwood, **1980.**)

Primarily a legal treatise on the difficult issue of criminal responsibility. This book is for psychiatrists who need to understand the historical, moral, and legal meaning of the insanity defense in depth.

10.   ***Goldzband, M.G.** Child custody: The ugliest litigation: A guarded word of welcome. Bull. Am. Acad. Psychiatry Law 4(2), **1976.**

This issue of the *Bulletin* is devoted to the issue of child custody litigation. There are many practical guidelines here for the practicing psychiatrist that will assist the clinician in providing more useful testimony and in minimizing the painfulness of this litigation for all participants.

11.   ***Halleck, S.L.** Law in the Practice of Psychiatry: A Handbook for Clinicians. New York: Plenum, **1980.**

A comprehensive survey of forensic psychiatry. The section on malpractice is more detailed. Question-and-answer format makes this book a convenient reference.

12.   ***Halpern, A.** Use and misuse of psychiatry in competency examination of criminal defendants. Psychiatr. Ann. 5: 8–73, **1975.**

A detailed description of the incompetency plea, emphasizing its legal justification and its abuses in practice. The author makes an eloquent plea for abolition, but gives practical advice for psychiatrists who participate in this process.

13.   **MacDonald, J.M.** The Murderer and His Victim. Springfield, IL: Thomas, **1961.**

Easy reading covering issues related to homicide. The case illustrations are excellent and the style is lively. A comfortable way to learn about legal systems.

14.   **Menninger, K.A.** The Crime of Punishment. New York: Viking Press, **1968.**

The classical argument for a rehabilitative rather than a punitive approach to criminal behavior. A powerful reminder of the moral responsibilities of the psychiatrist.

15.   ***Modlin, H.** Psychiatry and the civil law, pp. 721–738. In: Modern Legal Medicine, Psychiatry and Forensic Science. Eds.: W. Curran, L. McGarry, and C. Petty. Philadelphia: Davis, **1980.**

Special emphasis here is on litigation involving personal injury. Patient responses to injury and to the process of litigation are considered.

16.   ***Monahan, J.** The Clinical Prediction of Violent Behavior: Crime and Delinquency Issues. Rockville, MD: NIMH, **1981.**

The most up-to-date analysis of the problem of predicting violence. Clear definitions are provided and the current state of the art reviewed. Clinicians are provided with a detailed outline of factors to be considered in predicting violence.

17.   ***Rennie, Y.F.** The Search for Criminal Man. Lexington, MA: Heath, **1978.**

A comprehensive study of theoretical criminology. The historical role of psychiatry in the study and treatment of the criminal is presented in useful perspective and with remarkable clarity.

18.   ***Roth, L.H.** Correctional psychiatry, pp. 677–719. In: Modern Legal Medicine, Psychiatry and Forensic Science. Eds.: W. Curran, L. McGarry, and C. Petty. Philadelphia: Davis, **1980.**

A comprehensive and up-to-date description of mental health service in jails and prisons. Describes the limits of treatment in a custodial setting but also emphasizes the possibility of useful intervention.

19.   **Roth, L.H.** Involuntary civil commitment: The right to treatment and the right to refuse treatment. Psychiatr. Ann. 7(5): 50–76, **1977.**

A succinct overview of the emerging legal problems involved in hospitalizing and treating the involuntary mental patient in the 1970s. A good general introduction to the legal problems in this area.

20.   **Sadoff, R.L.** Forensic Psychiatry: A Practical Guide for Lawyers and Psychiatrists. Springfield, IL: Thomas, **1975.**

As the title states, this is a practical book. Theoretical issues are gone over lightly, but the book has many valuable suggestions for the practicing psychiatrist.

21.   **Sadoff, R.L.** New malpractice concerns for the psychiatrist. Legal Aspects Med. Practice 6: 31–35, **1978.**

Special emphasis is placed on issues of dangerousness, informed consent, and civil commitment. There is an excellent description of the psychiatrist's ambiguous role in the process of dealing with involuntary patients, which is characterized by increasing responsibility and diminishing power.

22.   **Shah, S.** Dangerousness and mental illness: Some concerns, prediction, and policy dilemmas, pp. 153–191. In: Dangerous Behavior: A Problem in Law and Mental Health. Crime and Delinquency Issues. Rockville, MD: NIMH, **1978.**

Reviews the many situations in which the psychiatrist is asked to predict dangerousness. The obscure nature of the concept of dangerousness and problems of prediction are considered in detail.

23.   ***Stone, A.A.** Mental Health and Law: A System in Transition. Washington, D.C.: GPO, DHEW no. (ADM) 75-176, **1975.** (Also available from New York: Aronson, **1976.**)

The first book to document the impact of the civil libertarian approach to patient's rights on patient care. This is a textbook of forensic psychiatry as well as a position statement on the scope and limits of the rights of the mentally ill.

24.   **Szasz, T.S.** Law, Liberty, and Psychiatry: An Inquiry into the Social Uses of Mental Health Practices. New York: MacMillan, **1963.**

This book was the first exposé of psychiatric practices that allegedly compromise the rights of the mentally ill. It became the rallying point for a generation of civil liberties attorneys who radically changed commitment practices and treatment of the mentally ill.

25.   **Usdin, G.** Psychiatric participation in court. Psychiatr. Ann. 7(6): 42–51, **1977.**

A brief article that offers practical advice on being an expert witness.

59. MILITARY PSYCHIATRY

David R. Jones, M.D., M.P.H.

Military psychiatric practice is qualitatively different from its traditional civilian counterpart. These writings focus on these differences. The military psychiatrist is concerned with a person's ability to function in worldwide settings, some with very little medical support. Some military people must work in chronically severely stressful situations, and extremes of personal and group danger may be involved. Overt psychotic and severe anxiety-based mental diseases disqualify a person for such duty; our focus is thus on stress tolerance, healthy psychological defenses, the ability to handle fear, and the affirmation of mental health. Frequently the military psychiatrist must predict the degree of incapacity for productive work resulting from personality disorders of varying severity. Medical care occurs in an authoritarian and judgmental subsegment of society that maintains an active third-party role in the patient-therapist relationship. The military psychiatrist must also deal with two unique manifestations of stress, combat reactions and fear of flying, which are almost never seen in the civilian world. On the more positive side, the needs of military psychiatrists have produced some concepts of community mental health programs, group support systems, rapid and goal-directed therapeutic techniques, and preventive mental health programs that have been integrated into the mainstream of American psychiatry. These writings provide a reasonably broad introduction to military psychiatry, and their references will carry the interested reader into the mainstream of this literature.

GENERAL MILITARY PSYCHIATRY

1. **Bey, D.R.** Change of command in combat: A locus of stress. Am. J. Psychiatry 129: 698–701, **1972.**

   The administrative style of the departing commander contributes to the stress his unit feels at his departure. Grief and anger of the troops at his departure must be worked through; preventive psychiatric techniques may help clarify these dynamics and ease the process, thus sparing the unit from traumatic acting out. A clear case history illustrates the author's theme.

2. ***Bey, D.R. and Chapman, R.E.** Psychiatry—the right way, the wrong way, and the military way. Bull. Menninger Clin. 38: 343–354, **1974. 1974.**

The authors present an even-handed comparison of the differences in focus, goals, and methods of military and civilian psychiatric practice. Some of the military approaches may be useful in civilian organizational or industrial applications, especially in considering the needs of society.

3. ***Blaustein, M., and Proctor, W.C.** The active duty conscientious objector: A psychiatric-psychological evaluation. Milit. Med. 142: 619–621, **1977.**

This article reviews the life stories, clinical presentations, and psychological assessments of a group of conscientious objectors, as well as the administrative procedures necessary to establish CO status.

4. **Boydstun, J.A. and Perry, C.J.G.** Military psychiatry, pp. 2888–2901. In: CTP III, Vol. 3, **1980.**

5. **Sledge, W.H.** Aerospace psychiatry, pp. 2902–2914. In: CTP III, Vol. 3, **1980.**

These two chapters furnish an introduction to military and aerospace psychiatry, providing sufficient information for anyone seeking a brief, broad overview. The references, which cover the field through 1977, furnish greater depth on specific subjects.

6. **Goldman, N.L. and Segal, D.R.** The Social Psychology of Military Service. (Sage Research Progress Series on War, Revolution and Peacekeeping, Vol. VI) Beverly Hills, Cal.: Sage, **1976.**

This series of excellent presentations covers areas of military stress: basic training, combat, the organizational environment, family pressures, reentry into the civilian community, and civil-military relations. The extensive bibliography will allow the interested reader to follow up any of these topics in depth.

7. ***In the service of the state: The psychiatrist as double agent.** (Special supplement) The Hastings Cent. Rep. 8(2): 1–24, **1978.**

This paper reports a conference sponsored by the APA and by the Institute of Society, Ethics, and the Life Sciences in 1977. It is a responsible and articulate look at the dilemma of the psychiatrist who must serve not only the interests of the patient, but also the interests of an institution or organization. It addresses issues of loyalty, confidentiality, societal interests, and individual rights. It offers no specific answers, but certainly clarifies the questions.

8. ***Jones, D.R.** Aeromedical transportation of psychiatric patients: Historical review and present management. Aviat. Space Environ. Med. 51: 709–716, **1980.**

The author traces the history of aeromedical transportation. Present indications and cautions are considered from the aeromedical and from the psychiatric points of view.

9. ***Rosen, H. and Corcoran, J.F.** The attitudes of USAF officers toward mental illness: A comparison with mental health professionals. Milit. Med. 143: 570–574, **1978.**

This questionnaire-based study of the attitudes of 455 officers and 40 military mental health professionals demonstrates a rather liberal attitude by the former group toward mental illness, although it was more authoritarian and less benevolent than the second group. The authors question the assumptions of some articles written by psychiatrists with limited military experience.

10. **Shanfield, S.B.** The military psychiatrist: Themes of separation and dislocation. Psychiatr. Ann. 8: 255–260, **1978.**

The author discusses his experiences (and those of some of his peers) in his two years as a "Berry Plan" military psychiatrist. This is a thoughtful paper about the dynamics of adjustment to military psychiatry for psychiatrists trained in civilian institutions.

11. ***Steyn, R.W.** Retrospections: A sketch of nautical psychiatry through World War II. Milit. Med. 145: 407–412, **1980.**

This article reviews psychiatric factors unique to naval practice, with special emphasis on the historical perspective. The comments on early attempts to associate somatic habitus with emotional instability is of interest in this regard.

12. **Tiffany, W.J., Jr. and Allerton, W.S.** Army psychiatry in the mid-60's. Am. J. Psychiatry 123: 810–821, **1967.**

This article summarizes preventive psychiatry in the Army at this time. It presents a clear statistical picture of changes and trends during the preceding 15 years, and speaks of the anticipated effectiveness of these approaches to Vietnam.

13. ***Watson, P.** War on the Mind: The Military Uses and Abuses of Psychology. New York: Basic Books, **1978.**

A very readable and complete review of psychological factors in military endeavors, covering combat factors, stress research, loyalty (and its dark side, treason), and counterinsurgency with specific attention to psychological warfare, combat psychiatry (preventive and therapeutic measures), and issues of leadership. The author is far from being a military apologist, and sees his viewpoint as a moderate attitude. If you can read only one book on the interface between emotional factors and military life, this is the book to read.

COMBAT PSYCHIATRY

14. **Bloch, H.S.** Army clinical psychiatry in the combat zone—1967–1968. Am. J. Psychiatry 126: 289–298, **1969.**

    The author reviews the principles of treatment of psychiatric casualties, and presents six case histories. He also describes the facilities, resources, and specialty teams available to him during his tour in Vietnam. This is a good working-level paper.

15. **Fox, R.P.** Narcissistic rage and the problem of combat aggression. Arch. Gen. Psychiatry 31: 807–811, **1974.**

    The author distinguishes between individual aggression as a response to combat dangers and as a quest for personal revenge for a significant loss. This dynamic distinction may be of use in working with issues of guilt and grief in combat veterans.

16. *****Grinker, R.R., Sr. and Spiegel, J.P.** Men Under Stress. New York: McGraw-Hill, **1945.**

    This book is mainly concerned with the reactions of U.S. troops to the campaign in North Africa in WWII, and is one of the classics of combat psychiatry. Its discussion of the dynamics of the individual case histories is particularly valuable.

17. *****Hausman, W. and Rioch, D. McK.** Military psychiatry—A prototype of social and preventive psychiatry in the United States. Arch. Gen. Psychiatry 16: 727–739, **1967.**

    This superb historical review summarizes the evaluation of Army doctrine on the care of men with combat neurosis. Some of these principles were applied to community psychiatry after WWI and are still used in primary, secondary, and tertiary preventive settings, and in evaluating some aspects of the relationship between the individual and the environment.

18. *****Ingraham, L.H. and Manning, F.J.** Psychiatric battle casualties. Milit. Rev. 60: 19–29, **1980.**

    This up-to-date summary reviews the roles of the commander and of the mental health professional in preventing or at least minimizing losses from combat exhaustion in a fluid battle situation such as anticipated in a major conventional war.

19.   **Kalinowsky, L.B.** Problems of war neuroses in the light of experiences in other countries. Am. J. Psychiatry 107: 340–346, **1950.**

This unique paper compares and contrasts some of the English, American, German, and Japanese experiences with the psychological effects of combat on civilian and military populations in WWI and WWII. Such an epidemiological approach allows for an assessment of the role of secondary gain and compensation factors in judging the long-term effects of "war neuroses" with concomitant implications for treatment.

20.   **Levav, I., Greenfield, H., and Baruch, E.** Psychiatric combat reactions during the Yom Kippur War. Am. J. Psychiatry 136: 637–641, **1979.**

The authors report selected epidemiologic factors involved in these reactions, including an 18-month follow-up, which is rare in the literature on this subject. They develop a composite profile of the man at risk on a day of intense fire.

21.   ***Moses, R., Bargal, D., Calev, J., et al.** A rear unit for the treatment of combat reactions in the wake of the Yom Kippur War. Psychiatry 39: 153–162, **1976.**

This describes a behind-the-lines, therapeutic community approach to chronic combat exhaustion. The description of the logistical support and the interplay of group and individual dynamics is particularly practical.

22.   **Richardson, F.M.** Fighting Spirit: A Study of Psychological Factors in War. New York: Crane, Russak, **1978.**

Written by a British Army physician with extensive combat experience and a thorough grounding in medical and military history, this is an articulate and convincing presentation of the author's views on the causes, treatment, and (most important) the prevention of combat fatigue. This book is a basic text for any military physician who may face combat.

23.   ***Salmon, T.W.** War neuroses ("shell shock"). Milit. Surg. 41: 674–693, **1917.**

This is truly a classical reference. The author had visited the psychiatric hospitals of several allied nations and distilled their experiences with "war neurosis" and its treatment into a formulation that has consistently been successful in rapidly returning to duty about 75 percent of soldiers thus affected. His epidemiologic point of view was remarkably advanced and accurate.

24.   **Steiner, M. and Neumann, M.** Traumatic neurosis and social support in the Yom Kippur War returnees. Milit. Med. 143: 866–868, **1978.**

The authors conclude that lack of social support, poor unit identification, lack of trust in leadership, displacement, and rotation all contribute to the condition of late onset post-traumatic combat reactions. In contrast, positive social support helps prevent "traumatic neurosis of war," even in conditions of severe stress.

AEROSPACE PSYCHIATRY

25.   **Bond, D.C.** The Love and Fear of Flying. New York: International Universities Press, **1952.**

An often-cited classic, this book summarizes the World War II experience with combat stress disorders and fear of flying in the fliers of that day. Of particular note is the psychoanalytical perspective on the emotional components of flying, the development of fear of flying and aspects of treatment. This volume is the starting-point for any knowledgeable discussion of aviation psychiatry.

26.   **Fine, P.M. and Hartman, B.O.** Psychiatric strength and weaknesses of typical Air Force pilots. Report No. SAM-TR-68-121, Brooks AFB TX 78235, Nov. **1968.**

This is an extensive report of psychodynamic and psychometric studies of Air Force pilots, comparing them with the "super pilots" chosen as astronaut candidates in the early 1960s. These characterizations are of particular value to anyone who routinely deals with professional fliers.

27.   ***Perry, C.J.G.,** ed. Psychiatry in Aerospace Medicine. Int. Psychiatr. Clin. 4(1): 1–238, **1967.**

The editor has brought together a highly qualified panel of authors who cover this complex and little-known field in depth. Among the subjects covered are the emotional considerations in selecting a flying career, the psychophysiology of aerospace medicine, normative psychological data, fear of flying, emotional factors in aircraft accidents, psychiatric aspects of man in space, and clinical aspects of psychiatric illness in flying. It is a solid background text for those who must deal with the emotional aspects of flying.

28.   ***Reinhardt, R.E.** The outstanding jet pilot. Am. J. Psychiatry 127: 732–736, **1970.**

This study of 105 Navy pilots, selected by their peers as the best, showed most to be firstborn, with unusually good father-son relationships. They were self-confident, not introspective, and tended toward interpersonal distance. It is a fine study of a mentally healthy and successful population.

VETERANS

29.   ***Figley, C.R.,** ed. Stress Disorders among Vietnam Veterans: Theory, Research, and Treatment. New York: Brunner/Mazel, **1978.**

This is a collection of essays and scientific publications that reflects the continuing ambiguous reaction of our society toward this war and its veterans. Some of the authors are explicit in their political attitudes, others write from a less passionate and more objective stance. Both viewpoints are of value in working with such patients.

30.   **Helzer, J.E., Robins, L.N., Wish, E., et al.** Depression in Vietnam veterans and civilian controls. Am. J. Psychiatry 136: 526–529, **1979.**

The value of this article lies in its epidemiologic approach, comparing the incidence of depressive symptoms in Vietnam veterans with a civilian control group. It demonstrated more symptoms in the veteran group one year after return, but not three years after return.

PRISONERS OF WAR

31.   **Beebe, G.W.** Follow up studies of World War II and Korean war prisoners. Am. J. Epidemiol. 101: 400–422, **1975.**

This is a large and rather carefully controlled follow-up study of the morbidity, disability, and maladjustments of three groups of U.S. prisoners of war: those captured by the Germans and the Japanese in WWII, and by the Koreans in the Korean War. Data are given on both somatic and psychiatric conditions. The role of malnutrition is especially emphasized.

32.   **Segal, J., Hunter, E.J., and Segal, F.** Universal consequences of captivity: Stress reactions among divergent populations of prisoners of war and their families. Int. Soc. Sci. J. 28: 593–609, **1976.**

This study compares data on individual and family reactions to wartime captivity, drawing on data from WWII, Korea, and Vietnam. Children suffer too, not only as prisoners, but in the families where the father has been absent because of captivity. This is an excellent review article.

33.   **Ursano, R.J.** The Viet Nam era prisoner of war: Precaptivity personality and the development of psychiatric illness. Am. J. Psychiatry 138: 315–318, **1981.**

This unique study of six fliers with extensive precaptivity psychiatric and psychologic evaluations indicates that the presence of precaptivity psychiatric symptoms is neither necessary nor sufficient for the development of psychiatric illness after repatriation.

34. **Ursano, R.J., Boydstun, J.A., and Wheatley, R.D.** Psychiatric illness in U.S. Air Force Viet Nam prisoners of war: A five-year follow-up. Am. J. Psychiatry 138: 310–314, **1981.**

The incidence of psychiatric disorders rose between repatriation and five-year follow-up in the group shot down before 1969 (long-term prisoners) and fell in the group shot down after 1969 (short-term prisoners).

MILITARY FAMILIES

35. **Beckman, K., Marsella, A.J., and Finney, R.** Depression in the wives of nuclear submarine personnel. Am. J. Psychiatry 136: 524–526, **1979.**

Nuclear submarine crews live in a continuing cycle of three months at sea and three at home. Their wives, studied in a crossover research design, showed evidence of increased depressive symptoms during the cruise months. Anecdotal data (including use of medical facilities) supports this report.

36. **Bey, D.R. and Lange, J.** Waiting wives: Women under stress. Am. J. Psychiatry 131: 283–286, **1974.**

This is an excellent report of a seldom-mentioned subject: the stresses and conflicts of wives whose husbands are away in combat (or on other prolonged absences, such as remote overseas tours). The author suggests some specific support structures that might lessen the personal and marital stress.

37. **Lagrone, D.M.** Letter: More on the military family syndrome. Am. J. Psychiatry 139: 133–134, **1982.**

This letter, and Dr. Morrison's reply (same page), continue the dialogue begun in their articles in 1978 and 1981, respectively. The questions raised are applicable to much that has been published about military families and highlight the epidemiologic problems inherent in comparing spouses or children of military members with their civilian counterparts.

38. **Lagrone, D.M.** The military family syndrome. Am. J. Psychiatry 135: 1040–1043, **1978.**

This study compares 792 juvenile military family members with a comparable civilian group and concludes that the former group has a predominance of behavioral disorders. The author cites several possible causes, although these are admittedly theoretical, and suggests several possible alleviating programs.

39. **Morrison, J.** Rethinking the military family syndrome. Am. J. Psychiatry 138: 354–357, **1981.**

   Written in reply to Dr. Lagrone's 1978 paper, this report cites data on children of military and nonmilitary families seen in the author's practice. No denominator data is given for the population base from which these patients are drawn. The author is skeptical about any "military family syndrome" and raises some significant questions.

SUBSTANCE ABUSE

40. **Brownell, S.M.** The Navy alcoholism prevention program. Worldwide. Alcoholism. (N.Y.) 2: 362–365, **1978.**

   The U.S. Navy now keeps 70 percent of its alcoholic members on active duty. This article presents the demographics of the military members involved and discusses the setup and administration of their remarkable program.

41. **Manning, J.F.** Cohesion and Readiness. Air Univ. Rev. 32(2): 66–70, **1981.**

   Although this is not a medical journal article, it is one of the best descriptions of life in the barracks and the reasons for drug abuse in military troops overseas. Army enlisted men are thrown together with little group identity and few resources; the drug culture furnishes both. Dr. Manning's ideas on prevention warrant close attention.

42. **Pursch, J.A.** Alcohol in aviation: A problem of attitudes. Aerospace Med. (now: Avia. Space Environ. Med.) 45: 318–321, **1974.**

   The author discusses the social settings for drinking in the military and cites case histories of fliers to show the extent to which the problem has been ignored. Alcoholic aviators can recover and be returned to flying duties.

43. **Pursch, J.A.** Physicians' attitudinal changes in alcoholism. Alcoholism (N.Y.) 2: 358–361, **1978.**

   Of 475 physicians who took the author's short course in treating alcoholism 44(9.2 percent) volunteered to undergo rehabilitation. A total of 202 recovering alcoholic medical departmental officers were in the Navy in 1978. The author discusses the philosophy of his remarkable program and the Navy's support of his methods.

60. OCCUPATIONAL PSYCHIATRY

ALAN A. McLEAN, M.D.

Perhaps the most familiar role for the psychiatric consultant in an occupational setting is clinical contact with individual patients. But other important roles include evaluation of prospective employees during pre-placement medical examinations to determine the applicant's ability to adapt to a specific assignment, evaluation of employees who have been disabled because of psychiatric disorder and the education of their managers, and, finally, perhaps the most important clinical role, consultation to those both in occupational health and personnel or management. Other issues of interest to the occupational psychiatrist include knowledge of the organizational setting, concern with morale, job satisfaction, the utilization of psychiatric benefits, work stress, and issues of worker compensation for psychiatric disability.

In attempting to delineate a field of occupational psychiatry, one must presume a primary concern with the mental health or psychiatric disorder of people at work. Effects of mental disorder in an occupational setting and factors deriving from work that influence the mental health status of people on the job form the primary focus of concern of any such unified system of knowledge.

Accordingly, items included in this list meet one or more of the following criteria:

1. Are concerned with the role of the psychiatrist in the work setting.
2. Are concerned with the mentally ill employee.
3. Are concerned with factors in the work environment that may have an etiological relationship to mental illness.
4. Are concerned with factors in the work environment that stimulate mentally healthy behavior.
5. Are concerned with morale, job satisfaction, and specific occupational roles that may also be related to mental health in the work setting.

Publications were included if:

1. The author was a recognized authority on some phase of occupational psychiatry and his/her subject field was within the scope of the general criteria.
2. The subject was specifically concerned with occupational psychiatry in a memorable way.
3. The publication was regarded as being of historic significance and therefore eligible for consideration as a "classic."

OVERVIEW

1. **Felton, J.S.** Psychiatric orientation in the education of occupational physicians. In: Occupational psychiatry. Ed.: R.T. Collins. Int. Psychiatr. Clin. 6(4): 123–139, **1969.**

    A key responsibility of the occupational psychiatrist is training those in other occupational health disciplines.

2. **International Labour Organization.** Encyclopedia of Occupational Health. New York: McGraw-Hill, **1972.**

    This 1,600-page two-volume reference book is a useful source, principally for information about the physical aspects of health and potential hazards in the working environment.

3. ***McLean, A.A.** Occupational Psychiatry, Chapter 47, pp. 2915–2925. In: CTP III, Vol. 3, **1980.**

    This is a comprehensive review of the role of the psychiatrist in work organizations.

4. **National Clearinghouse for Mental Health Information.** A selected bibliography on occupational mental health. (Public Health Service Publication no. 1338). Bethesda: National Institute of Mental Health, **1965.**

    A bibliographic definition of occupational mental health with 803 clinical entries and 1,976 related entries from the behavioral sciences. Partially annotated. An excellent overview of the pre–mid-sixties literature.

5. ***Weiner, H.J., Akabas, S.H., and Sommer, J.J.** Mental Health Care in the World of Work. New York: Association Press, **1973.**

    The first report on the introduction of mental health services to union organizations and members.

ROLE OF THE PSYCHIATRIST IN THE WORK SETTING

6. **Burling, T. and Longaker, W.** Training for industrial psychiatry. Am. J. Psychiatry 111: 493–496, **1955.**

   A description of formal training in industrial psychiatry at the New York State School of Industrial and Labor Relations at Cornell University, which includes both didactic work and supervised clinical experiences in industry.

7. **Rohrlich, J.B.** Work and Love: The Crucial Balance. New York: Summit Books, **1980.**

   From the perspective of a sophisticated psychiatrist practicing on New York's Wall Street, this volume explores the experiences of working and loving and defines them as unique and contrasting states of mind.

8. ***Ross, W.D.** Practical Psychiatry for Industrial Physicians. Springfield, IL: Thomas, **1956.**

   This was the first textbook for occupational physicians and covers a wide range of occupational psychiatric practice.

9. **Southard, E.E.** The modern specialist in unrest: A place for the psychiatrist in industry. Ment. Hygiene 4: 550–563, **1920.**

   From a historical viewpoint, this is one of the first comments on industry by a psychiatrist. This paper makes a strong plea for the psychiatrist "not to hide his light under a bushel but to step forth to new community duties (in industry)...."

STRESS AND MENTAL ILLNESS IN WORK ORGANIZATIONS

10. **American Medical Association Committee on Rating of Mental and Physical Impairment.** Mental Illness, Chapter 8. In: Guides to the Evaluation of Permanent Impairment. Chicago: AMA, **1978.**

    The standard reference for classification of psychiatric impairment, including that which obtains in occupational disability.

11. **American Psychiatric Association Committee on Occupational Psychiatry.** The Mentally Ill Employee: His Treatment and Rehabilitation. New York: Harper and Row, **1965.**

    Provides a useful guide for work organizations which desire to improve the health services for employees by including psychiatric services.

12.   **Elliott, G.R. and Eisdorfer, C.** Stress and Human Health: Analysis and Implications of Research. New York: Springer, **1982.**

This reports the conclusions of a study by the Institute of Medicine of the National Academy of Sciences. It is an excellent overview of all facets of stress including those in organizational settings. It comments on work stress psychosocial aspects and modifiers of stress as well as stress and life events.

13.   **Farmer, E. and Chambers, E.G.** A psychological study of individual differences in accident rates. (Medical Research Council, Industrial Health Research Board, Report No. 38) London: HM Stationery Office, **1926.**

This publication discusses psychological factors in industrial accidents. Also covered were studies of prevalence and incidence of psychiatric disorders in the world of work.

14.   **Kahn, R.L. et al.** Report on stress in organizational settings, Chapter 5. In: Stress and Human Health. Eds.: G.R. Elliott and C. Eisdorfer. New York: Springer, **1982.**

Part of a study by the Institute of Medicine/National Academy of Sciences, this chapter presents an overview largely from the perspective of the behavioral sciences.

15.   **Kahn, R.L., Wolfe, D.M., Quinn, R.P., et al.** Organizational Stress: Studies in Role Conflict and Ambiguity. New York: Wiley, 1964 (Also available from Krieger, **1981**).

This is a classic study of a work organization. The perspective is that of role theory in social psychology. In addition to presenting the results of a careful interview and questionnaire study of one organization, it discusses the consequences of role stress, organizational process, and interpersonal relationships in role stress.

16.   ***Moss, L.** Management Stress. Reading, MA: Addison-Wesley, **1981.**

From the perspective of a psychiatric consultant to a major corporation, this book explores the stresses and crises that characterize careers of managers and executives.

17.   **Shostak, A.B.** Blue Collar Stress. Reading, MA: Addison-Wesley, **1979.**

From the perspective of a sociologist, this volume explores the current impact of major stressors on the working lives of American white male blue collarites. Discussed in some detail is labor's role both as a source of and as a critical antidote to stress.

MORALE AND JOB SATISFACTION

18. **Jaques, E.** Changing Culture of a Factory. New York: Dryden, **1952.**

This volume reports a classic and original research study of a British factory from a psychoanalytic viewpoint. It is a well-documented and detailed volume and regarded as a milestone in occupational psychiatry.

19. **Levinson, H., Price, C.R., Munden, K.J., et al.** Men, Management and Mental Health. Cambridge: Harvard University Press, **1962.**

This book is based on the results of a study of the gratifications people seek in their work and the processes they use to obtain them. A part of the book centers on the psychological contract between the employee and the employer.

20. **Rose, R.M., Jenkins, C.D., and Hurst, M.W.** Air Traffic Controller Health Change Study. Boston: Boston University School of Medicine, **1978.**

The definitive research report on air traffic controllers that lays to rest the myth that such work is unusually stressful. Chapter 1 (p. 1–16) is a summary of the report.

21. **Tredgold, R.F.** Human Relations in Modern Industry. New York: International Universities Press, **1950.** (2nd rev. ed., **1963**)

This volume is included to cite a British leader in occupational psychiatry who was extraordinarily active in the Western European occupational mental health movement from the Second World War until his death in 1975.

22. ***Tredgold, R.F.** The role of the psychiatrist in industry. In: Occupational Psychiatry. Ed.: R.T. Collins. Int. Psychiatr. Clin. 6: (4) 49–60, **1969.**

As seen by a thoroughly experienced British occupational psychiatrist who outlines a fairly broad role.

61. CLINICAL RESEARCH

JOHN P. DOCHERTY, M.D.

This bibliography is intended to provide a review of the essential issues involved in designing, conducting, and interpreting clinical research in psychiatry. There are three sections of the bibliography devoted to generic areas relevant to clinical research and one section devoted to useful reference books for clinical psychiatric research. The sections are: "Basic Principles and Design," "Psychotherapy," "Psychopharmacology," "Epidemiology," "Ethical Issues," and "Data Analysis." Finally, there is one additional section devoted to some useful reference books for clinical psychiatric research.

Clearly, there are many specialized and specific issues in clinical research. However, this bibliography gives a broad background of reading that will provide an educated overview of this area.

BASIC PRINCIPLES AND DESIGN

1. ***Chassan, J.B.** Research Design in Clinical Psychology and Psychiatry (2nd ed.), New York: Irvington, **1979.**

   A fairly comprehensive textbook on methodology and design in clinical psychology and psychiatry. It is supposed to be designed for consumers as well as a reference for researchers; it is more appropriate for researchers but obviously has value for the consumer as well.

2. **Davidson, P.O. and Costello, C.G.,** eds. N=1: Experimental Studies of Single Cases, An Enduring Problem for Psychology. New York: Van Nostrand Reinhold, **1969.**

   This little book is full of accounts of using single-case methods to study simple as well as complex problems. A good demonstration piece of the method.

3. **Glaser, E. and Taylor, S.** Factors Influencing the Success of Applied Research: A Study of Ten NIMH-Funded Projects. Los Angeles: Human Interaction Research Institute, **1969.**

   This very interesting monograph is a case study of social and organizational variables associated with very successful clinical research ($N=5$)

and those associated with less successful research (*N*=5). A very valuable "how-to-do-it" book for organizing and administering a research project.

4.   **Hersen, M. and Barlow, D.H.** Single Case Experimental Designs: Strategies for Studying Behavior Change. New York: Pergamon, **1976.**

A comprehensive account of single-case methods. An excellent book.

5.   ***Holt, R.R.** Methods in Clinical Psychology, Vol. 2: Prediction and Research. New York: Plenum, **1978.**

This book is a very rigorous introduction to the "fuzziness" of clinical research. The author has identified and dealt with major conceptual problems of applying quantitative methods to human experience. The novice clinical researcher will have his or her view of the meaning and significance of research decisions profoundly transformed.

6.   **Maser, J. and Seligman, M.E.P.,** eds. Psychopathology: Experimental Models. San Francisco: Freeman, **1977.**

This interesting book presents 12 models developed to permit the application of the experimental method to a diverse group of clinical phenomena. The first chapter, particularly, by Abramson and Seligman presents an instructive historical overview of the use of animal models for human psychopathology.

7.   **Megargee, E.,** ed. Research in Clinical Assessment. New York: Harper and Row, **1966.**

This now somewhat old book still retains much usefulness. Particularly impressive is Section I, "Problems in Validating Clinical Methods," which deals with issues still basic to clinical assessment such as the criterion problem, the concept of construct validity, and others.

8.   **Office of Technology Assessment.** Assessing the Efficacy and Safety of Medical Technologies. Washington, D.C.: Government Printing Office, **1978.**

This monograph provides a detailed review, discussion, and case example illustration of the complex issues involved in determining the safety, efficacy, and effectiveness of medical technology.

9.   ***Platt, J.R.** Strong inference. Science 146: 347–352, **1964.**

This is a clear and important statement of the essential conceptual characteristics of modern science. It should not be missed.

10.   ***Scott, W. and Wertheimer, M.** Introduction to Psychological Research. New York: Wiley, **1962.**

This book is an excellent introduction to clinical psychological research. It is a still timely discussion of basic elements that should be considered in developing a research plan.

11. **Surwillo, W.W.** Experimental Design in Psychiatry: Research Methods for Clinical Practice. New York: Grune and Stratton, **1980.**

A very readable overview of basic design considerations, hypothesis testing, and the use and selection of statistical tests with an account of the basic statistical tests. Psychiatric residents are the intended audience.

PSYCHOTHERAPY

12. ***APA Commission on Psychotherapies.** Psychotherapy Research: Methodological and Efficacy Issues. Washington, D.C.: American Psychiatric Association, **1982.**

This extremely well-done book provides a succinct, accurate, and understandable overview of the correct status of psychotherapy research. It makes an excellent core text for a basic course on psychotherapy research.

13. ***Fiske, D.W., Hunt, H.F., Luborsky, L., et al.** Planning of research on effectiveness of psychotherapy. Arch. Gen. Psychiatry 22: 22–32, **1970.**

This paper has for the last decade been the classic in the field. It is a "must read" for someone interested in psychotherapy outcome research.

14. ***Waskow, I.E. and Parloff, M.B.,** eds. Psychotherapy Change Measures. DHEW no.(ADM) 74-120. Washington, D.C.: Government Printing Office, **1975.**

This book is a "must read" in the area of psychotherapy research. It provides a fairly comprehensive review of the major approaches to assessment of outcome of adult individual psychotherapy and the last chapter by Waskow, "Fantasied Dialogue with a Researcher," is essential reading for the new clinical investigator.

PSYCHOPHARMACOLOGY

15. **Bunney, W.E.** Neuronal receptor function in psychiatry, pp. 241–255. In: Neuroreceptors: Basic and Clinical Aspects. Eds.: E. Usdin, W.E. Bunney, and J. Davis. New York: Wiley, **1981.**

This is an elegant article that is an example of the design of a clinical research strategy formulated to test hypotheses derived from the more basic biological research.

16. ***Guy, W.** ECDEU Assessment Manual for Psychopharmacology. DHEW no. (ADM) 76-338. Washington, D.C.: Government Printing Office, **1976.**

The book is a compilation of the scales employed in the Early Clinical Drug Evaluation Program. It provides the reader with access to the most commonly used scales in adult and pediatric clinical psychopharmacological research such as the Brief Psychiatric Rating Scale, the American Depression Scale, and so on.

17. **Journal of Clinical Psychopharmacology** Vol. 1(4), July **1981.**

This entire edition consists of eight articles, all of which address the issue of the use of "challenge" strategies in psychobiological research.

18. ***Levine, J., Schiele, B., and Bouthilet, L.** Principles and Problems in Establishing the Efficacy of Psychotropic Agents. USPHS no. 2138. Washington, D.C.: Government Printing Office, **1971.**

This book is or should be the fundamental text for the clinical trials investigator in psychopharmacology. It covers the development and selection of drugs for study issues in special populations, designs, documentation, data analysis, and interpretation issues.

19. **Levine, J.** Coordinating Clinical Trials in Psychopharmacology. DHEW no.(ADM) 79-803. Washington, D.C.: Government Printing Office, **1979.**

This book may be read as a companion volume to *Principles and Problems in Establishing the Efficacy of Psychotropic Agents.* It is an outstanding review of methods for summarizing and synthesizing data from multiple clinical trials.

EPIDEMIOLOGY

20. ***Kleinbaum, D.G., Kupper, L.L., and Morgenstern, A.** Epidemiologic Research: Principles and Quantitative Methods. Belmont, Cal.: Lifetime Learning Publications, **1982.**

Most modern and thorough review of the principles of epidemiologic research.

ETHICAL ISSUES

21. ***Howard-Jones, N.** Human experimentation in historical and ethical perspectives. Soc. Sci. Med. 16: 1429–1448, **1982.**

This is an extremely interesting article that reviews the history of biomedical research with human subjects and the evolution of formal ethical codes governing such activity.

22. **Levine, R.** Ethics and Regulation of Clinical Research. Baltimore: Urban and Schwarzenberg, **1981.**

This is a finely done, well-written book that reviews "human subjects," the major issue in clinical research.

DATA ANALYSIS

23. **Bartko, J.J. and Carpenter, W.T.** On the methods and theory of reliability. J. Nerv. Ment. Dis. 163: 307–317, **1976.**

This article gives a good summary of the different statistical methods for the assessment of interrater reliability and the appropriate use of each.

24. **Bentler, P.M., Lettieri, D., and Austin, G.** Data Analysis Strategies and Designs for Substance Abuse Research. Washington, D.C.: Government Printing Office, **1976.**

This book presents lucid reviews of eight relatively advanced but frequently used data analysis strategies, discussing rationale, procedures, assumptions, advantages, and disadvantages of each method. It additionally includes a very good paper on longitudinal designs and on single N studies.

25. **Buros, O.K.,** ed. The Mental Measurements Yearbook (8th ed.). Highland Park, N.J.: Gryphon Press, **1978.**

This is an encyclopedic survey, which is published every several years. It covers commercially published tests and scales of various kinds and includes reviews and bibliographies.

26. ***Feinstein, A.** Clinical Biostatistics. St. Louis: Mosby, **1977.**

A compendium of selected topics in research design and data analysis. Very readable and clear summary of complex and too often obscure issues.

27. ***Linton, M. and Gallo, P., Jr.** The Practical Statistician: Simplified Handbook of Statistics. Monterey, CA: Brooks/Cole, **1975.**

This is an extraordinarily well-organized and intelligent book that is most helpful for any level of sophistication but particularly useful for someone who knows the basics but is not a trained statistician. It is indeed a practical handbook that helps people use statistics well.

28. **Lyerly, S.** Handbook of Psychiatric Rating Scales (2nd ed.). DHEW no. (ADM) 78-775. Washington, D.C.: Government Printing Office, **1978.**

   This is a valuable source book for the clinical researcher. It is a collection, with brief explanation and commentary (including the original source), of the most widely used and useful clinical rating scales.

REFERENCE BOOKS

29. **Burdock, E.I., Sudilovsky, A., and Gershon, S.** Behavior of Psychiatric Patients: Quantitative Techniques for Evaluation. New York: Marcel Dekker, **1982.**

   A good book that reviews different methods for quantifying clinical phenomena.

30. **Lowman, R., Holt, V., and O'Bryant, C.** American Psychological Association's Guide to Research Support. Washington, D.C.: American Psychological Association, **1981.**

   This book addresses an extremely important aspect of clinical research—where and how to obtain federal funding.

62. PSYCHIATRIC EDUCATION AND SUPERVISION

James S. Eaton, Jr., M.D.

For psychiatry there is no activity more important than education, since it is through the education of young psychiatrists and the continuing education of experienced psychiatrists that the specialty determines its future. The goals of psychiatric education are complex. Psychiatry's broad *knowledge* base and the large repertoire of *skills* required to practice effectively are easily identified as concerns in residency and postresidency training.

Attitudes, however, are less easily identified, notwithstanding the fact that they are more long lived and set the tone for professional behaviors during the remainder of the psychiatrist's career. Important attitudes for the psychiatrist are:

1. A sense of comfort with ambiguity and uncertainty.
2. An intellectual and emotional tolerance for social deviance.
3. A capacity for productive introspection and for emotional resiliency.
4. An appreciation of oneself as a therapeutic instrument.
5. A cognitive style that is comfortable with both deductive and inductive processes.
6. An ability to be a continuing self-educator.

Because most of these attitudes are personality characteristics, many psychiatric educators believe that personal psychotherapy or analysis for the fledgling psychiatrist is a worthwhile educational endeavor, aside from possible therapeutic benefits. But these attitudes can also be developed, nurtured, and fine tuned during the processes of carefully supervised clinical experience.

Although not unique to psychiatry, the supervisory relationship in which a more experienced psychiatrist teaches and interacts with another, usually junior colleague, is a central feature of psychiatric education and is an important means by which these attitudes can be taught by both precept and example. It also sets a model for peer supervision that will remain throughout the trainee's professional career. Role modeling, while an important aspect of supervision, can go only so far in terms of its educational benefits for the beginning psychiatrist. The good supervisor helps the resident develop his own mode of expression, his own unique style of dealing with patients, and his own best method of learning.

The formative years of one's professional life, i.e., one's years in a formal training program, can be thought of much like a period of adolescence. It has been said that if the psychologic work of adolescence is done...it is never done. Just as the healthy individual should emerge from adolescence with an increased capacity for adaptation and change, so the student of psychiatry should emerge from a formal training program with a cognitive and psychological matrix that is capable of processing new knowledge and accommodating new relationships. In other words, one's cognitive and emotional "epiphyses" need to remain open.

The references listed in this chapter have been selected with this in mind. Little effort has been made to see that the list is "complete" in any sense. Rather, the reader is expected to be an active participant in his own learning process, and it is hoped that he will use these works only as guides for continued study, stimulation, and growth.

Special efforts have been made to give ample reference to the psychiatrist's own feelings, including his reactions to patients and to the specialty of psychiatry itself. In particular, attention is focused on the patient-therapist and therapist-supervisor dynamics, since it is in these relationships that psychologic "blind spots" often occur.

The well-educated psychiatrist is one who continually uses peers, colleagues, the literature, and patients for self-education. The beginning resident is welcomed to this lifelong process of stimulation and engagement.

PHILOSOPHY OF LEARNING

1. **Adler, M.J.** How to Mark a Book, pp. 188–192. In: The Saturday Review Treasury. J. Haverstick, ed. New York: Simon and Schuster, **1957.**

   A delightful essay about the proper way to read a book—or anything, for that matter. A fun five minutes to read, but the message is for a lifetime.

2. **Bruner, J.D.** On Knowing: Essays for the Left Hand. Cambridge: Belknap/Harvard University Press, **1962.**

   These brilliantly subtle essays by a noted educational psychologist deftly discuss issues such as creativity, man's search for identity, the use of myth and symbol, the nature of aesthetics, and the nature of control and freedom in human behavior. This slim volume is a powerful aid for helping the young psychiatrist to become a more sensitive and apperceptive educator of students, patients, peers—and of self.

GENERAL ISSUES OF PSYCHIATRIC EDUCATION

3. **Eaton, J.S., Jr.** The psychiatrist and psychiatric education, pp. 2926–2946. In: CTP III, Vol. 3, **1980.**

    An overview of the psychiatrist as a person, psychiatry as a discipline and psychiatric education. Contains an extensive bibliography.

4. ***Lewin, B.D. and Ross, H.** Psychoanalytic Education in the United States. New York: Norton, **1960.**

    This volume reports the condition and future needs of psychoanalytic education as it was seen in the 1950s. Although too detailed and a bit self-congratulatory, this time-capsuled view of American psychoanalysis at its zenith makes it a classic in the literature of psychiatric education.

5. **Grinker, R.R., Sr.** The future educational needs of psychiatrists. Am. J. Psychiatry 132: 259–262, **1975.**

    A distinguished psychiatric educator, researcher, and clinician discusses the personal and professional qualities the young psychiatrist should cultivate. Although written almost a decade ago, the author's advice is still very much on the mark, and his wisdom is timeless.

6. ***Langsley, D.G. and Hollender, M.H.** The definition of a psychiatrist. Am. J. Psychiatry 139: 81–85, **1982.**

    Both of these distinguished and experienced psychiatrists report the findings of a large survey of current practice patterns and educational ideals in psychiatry.

7. **Nemiah, J.C.** The idea of a psychiatric education. J. Psychiatr. Educ. 5: 183–194, **1981.**

    A wise and experienced educator accepts the inherent tension between biologic and psychologic modes of thinking and calls for a psychiatric educational experience that will weave them together.

8. **Rubinton, P., Sacks, M.H., and Frosch, W.A.** In searching the literature: An annotated bibliography of selected psychiatric sources. J. Psychiatr. Educ. 4: 57–75, **1980.**

    An oft-neglected "basic science" or skill for the psychiatrist is the ability to make intelligent use of the library and other sources of recorded information. This useful article contains an annotated bibliography of psychiatric reference sources as well as a brief example of how to research a subject.

9.   ***Yager, J.,** ed. Teaching Psychiatry and Behavioral Science. New York: Grune and Stratton, **1982.**

An up-to-date collection of various topics in psychiatric education, including the teaching of medical students, residents, and primary care physicians; aspects of clinical supervision; problems in teaching psychiatric theory and technique; assessment; teaching the treatment of specific populations; and a discussion of certain institutional aspects of psychiatry. Well indexed and richly referenced. A "must" for all psychiatric educators.

PSYCHIATRIC TRAINING AND CURRICULUM ISSUES

10.   **Berger, M.M.,** ed. Videotape Techniques in Psychiatric Training and Treatment. New York: Brunner/ Mazel, **1978.**

A dated but nevertheless useful guide to videotaping in psychiatry. Many examples are given for its use in both therapy and training. Legal considerations and issues of privacy and privileged communication are discussed, and a useful glossary of technical and production terms, as well as a reasonably good index and bibliography are included.

11.   **Bowden, C.L., Humphrey, F.J., and Thompson, M.G.C.** Priorities in psychiatric residency training. Am. J. Psychiatry, 137: 1243–1246, **1980.**

Based on a survey of psychiatric educators, this article lists in priority order the residency training objectives thought to be essential. Helpful in curriculum planning.

12.   **Cohen-Cole, S., Haggerty, J., and Raft, D.** Objectives for residents in consultation psychiatry: Recommendations of a task force. Psychosomatics 23: 699–703, **1981.**

The article contains a brief and useful discussion about the objectives, responsibilities, and limitations of the psychiatric consultant; about the characteristics of the consultation relationship; and about the knowledge and skills expected of the finishing resident.

13.   **Eaton, J.S., Jr., Daniels, R.D., and Pardes, H.,** eds. American psychiatric education: A review. Am. J. Psychiatry, 134(Supp.): 1–29, **1977.**

This supplement about the state of American psychiatric education in the mid-1970s contains data derived from a review of over 500 programs. Strengths and weaknesses of various educational approaches are discussed, as well as directions for future growth.

14.   ***Marmor, J.** Psychoanalytic training: Problems and perspectives. Arch. Gen. Psychiatry 6: 486–489, **1979.**

The author argues that if psychoanalysis is to remain vital, it must be open to growth and change and must not foster rigidity and dogmatism among either trainees or faculty.

15.   **Semrad, E.V. and Van Buskink, D.,** eds. Teaching Psychotherapy of Psychiatric Patients. New York: Grune and Stratton, **1969.**

An exploration of the problems encountered by psychiatric residents as they learn to deal with psychotic patients.

16.   **Shore, J.H., Kinzie, J.D., and Bloom, J.D.** Required educational objectives in community psychiatry. Am. J. Psychiatry 136: 193–195, **1979.**

This article describes briefly a model community psychiatry training program for all psychiatric residents—one which stresses the psychiatrist's unique role as a physician in the interdisciplinary community setting.

SUPERVISION IN PSYCHIATRY

17.   **American Psychiatric Association.** Improving Psychiatric Supervision: Videotaped Vignettes for Discussion. Washington: APA, **1981.**

Thirty-three brief vignettes of issues and problems commonly encountered by supervisors in a variety of settings. Professional actors and expert psychiatric consultation helped to make this instructional package (videotape plus a printed guide for discussion leaders) a uniquely helpful production.

18.   **Borus, J.F. and Graves, J.E.** Training supervision as a separate faculty role. Am. J. Psychiatry 139: 1339–1342, **1982.**

Describes the benefits of psychiatric residents having not only a "clinical supervisor," but also a "training supervisor," a senior faculty member who orients and advises the residents and systematically reviews training progress and problems. The training supervisor offers a major source of nonjudgmental support to the resident.

19.   **Buckley, P., Karasu, T.B., and Charles, E.** Common mistakes in psychotherapy. Am. J. Psychiatry 136: 1578–1580, **1979.**

A survey of resident therapists' most frequent mistakes (as indicated by their supervisors) including: wanting to be liked by patients, premature interpretations, intellectualization, intolerance of patients' aggressiveness, and avoidance of fee setting.

20.   **Cavenar, J.O., Rhoads, E.J., and Sullivan, J.L.** Ethical and legal aspects of supervision. Bull. Menninger Clin. 44: 15–22, **1980.**

A discussion of confidentiality, legal responsibility, and supervisee resistance in the supervisory setting. Oft-neglected but very important topics.

21.   **Ekstein, R. and Wallerstein, R.S.** The Teaching and Learning of Psychotherapy. New York: Basic Books, **1958.**

This book is difficult reading because of its convoluted style. Nevertheless, it is one of the classic works about the theory and technique of the supervisory process.

22.   ***Fleming, J. and Benedek, T.** Psychoanalytic Supervision. New York: Grune and Stratton, **1966.**

A thorough exploration of psychoanalytic supervision, including many verbatim transcripts and discussions of 28 supervisory sessions covering most problems that would arise in supervision. A bit turgid, but the book's detail and its organization, index, and bibliography make it a classic in the supervisory literature.

23.   ***Gediman, H.K. and Wolkenfeld, F.** The parallelism phenomenon in psychoanalysis and supervision: Its reconsideration as a triadic system. Psychoanal. Q. 49: 234–255, **1980.**

This paper discusses the multiple identification processes occurring during psychoanalytic supervision, i.e., the frequently observed phenomena of parallel processes between supervisor and supervisee, and between supervisee and patient.

24.   **Granet, R.B., Kalman, T.P., and Sacks, M.H.** From supervisee to supervisor: An unexplored aspect to the psychiatrist's education. Am. J. Psychiatry 137: 1443–1446, **1980.**

This article discusses the special difficulties encountered by neophyte supervisors and offers suggestions for dealing with these problems.

25.   **Kline, F., Goin, M., and Zimmerman, W.** You can be a better supervisor! J. Psychiatr. Educ. 1: 174–179, **1977.**

This article reports data showing that the better supervisor is active; focuses on the case being presented; and gives opinions about the patient, the therapist, and the transference.

26. ***Schuster, D.B., Sandt, J.J., and Thaler, O.F.** Clinical Supervision and the Psychiatric Resident. New York: Brunner/ Mazel, **1972.**

This book focuses upon a broader field than just psychotherapy; it is concerned with supervision of the resident's contacts with patients from the first to the last days of formal graduate education. Its greatest value is the series of verbatim transcripts of "supervisory conferences" in which the three authors discuss the problems of the supervisory process and cite examples from their own work with residents in supervision.

27. **Solomon, S., Saravay, S.M., and Steinberg, H.** Supervision in liaison and consultation psychiatry. Gen. Hospital Psychiatry 2: 294–299, **1980.**

Psychiatric consultation/ liaison activities are assuming more importance in the general psychiatric residency program. This paper reports special problems and techniques of teaching liaison and consultation psychiatry to psychiatric residents.

28. **Winstead, D.K., Benowitz, J.S., Gayle, M.S., et al.** Resident peer supervision of psychotherapy. Am. J. Psychiatry 131: 318–321, **1974.**

Describes four residents' experiences in setting up a peer supervisory group. The authors discuss five stages in the development of the group and comment about the advantages (increased comfort in discussing countertransference issues) and disadvantages (excessive empathy with the presenter) of such an activity.

PERSONALITY CHARACTERISTICS/EMOTIONAL PROBLEMS OF PSYCHIATRY RESIDENTS

29. **Campbell, H.D.** The prevalence and ramifications of psychotherapy in psychopathology in psychiatric residents: An overview. Am. J. Psychiatry 138: 1405–1411, **1982.**

A well-referenced overview article.

30. ***Garetz, F.K., Raths, O.N., and Morse, R.H.** The disturbed and disturbing psychiatric resident. Arch. Gen. Psychiatry 33: 446–450, **1976.**

A large retrospective study of residents in one training program yields two important findings: (1) personal psychotherapy is an important positive factor in the eventual lives and careers of disturbed residents; (2) "disturbing" residents are not all "disturbed," and many make outstanding psychiatrists.

31.   **Halleck, S.L. and Woods, S.M.** Emotional problems of psychiatric residents. Psychiatry 25: 339–346, **1962.**

The authors discuss the many stresses on psychiatric residents, including the pressures of an interdisciplinary setting, the anxieties generated by severely disturbed patients, the residents' need to develop psychological-mindedness, and the stressfulness of psychotherapy supervision. A classic article.

32.   **Holt, R.R. and Luborsky, L.B.** Personality Patterns of Psychiatrists, Vol. 1. New York: Basic Books, **1958;** and Vol. 2. Topeka: Menninger Foundation, **1958.**

These two volumes are based on the classic study at Menninger School of Psychiatry in which the selection processes for psychiatric residents and psychoanalytic candidates were carefully examined. Especially interesting are the changes that were found to take place as residents matured and began to develop their professional identities.

33.   **Oken, D.** The doctor's job—An update. Psychosom. Med. 40: 449–461, **1978.**

The author discusses personality assets and liabilities that the doctor brings to his "job": looks at the expectations, if not needs, of patients; and talks about the crucial but fragile doctor-patient relationship.

34.   **Russell, A.T., Pasnau, R.O., and Taintor, Z.C.** Emotional problems of residents in psychiatry. Am. J. Psychiatry 132: 263–267, **1975.**

A large study of psychiatric residents in training revealed that many residents who prematurely terminated their programs had an emotional disturbance. The authors emphasize the importance of screening procedures for residency candidates and the ready availability of psychotherapy for residents in training.

ISSUES OF PROFESSIONAL SOCIALIZATION

35.   **Knight, J.A.** Medical Student: Doctor in the Making. New York: Appleton-Century-Crofts, **1973.**

This book deals with the psychologic and sociologic issues of becoming a physician, including the difficult task of learning to tolerate uncertainty and ambiguity.

36.   **Sharaf, M.R. and Levinson, D.J.** The quest for omnipotence in

professional training—the case of the psychiatric resident. Psychiatry 27: 135–149, **1964.**

The authors take a sociopsychologic approach in describing the efforts of all psychiatry residents to achieve the impossible—total mastery of knowledge and of self.

37.   **Yager, J.** A survival guide for psychiatric residents. Arch. Gen. Psychiatry 30: 494–499, **1974.**

An experienced educator and witty author discusses the psychiatric resident's difficult task of developing a professional identity in an environment where contradictions and confusion seem the rule.

MANPOWER AND PROFESSIONAL RECRUITMENT

38.   **Pardes, H. and Pincus, H.A.** Report of GEMENAC and Health Manpower Development—Implications for Psychiatry. Arch. Gen. Psychiatry 40: 97–102, **1983.**

Federal efforts at health manpower planning have been problematic, yet GEMENAC's projected shortfall of psychiatrists by 1990 already seems to be having a positive impact on psychiatric recruitment. This article discusses the study's methods, conclusions, and recommendations in terms of the challenges and opportunities facing psychiatry.

39.   **Regier, D.A., Goldberg, I.D., and Taube, C.A.** The de facto U.S. Mental Health Services System: A public health perspective. Arch. Gen. Psychiatry 35: 685–693, **1978.**

Documents the fact that most mental illness in the U.S. is treated by non–mental health professionals and non-professionals. Important in its implications for psychiatry's role in the general health care system, and especially the role of the consultation-liaison psychiatrist.

40.   **Taintor, Z.C. and Robinowitz, C.** The career choice of psychiatry: Report to the National Institute of Mental Health on a National Conference of Recruitment into Psychiatry. J. Psychiatr. Educ. 5: 151–178, **1981.**

A concise summary of 101 recommendations deriving from a 1980 national conference on the topic of career choice of psychiatry. The recommendations represent the best judgment of almost 200 distin- guished medical educators and consultants and cover topics as varied as premedical education, medical school admissions requirements, and psychiatry's relationship with primary care.

AUTHOR INDEX

SUBJECT INDEX